MACMILLAN WORK OUT SERIES

SOCIOLOGY

The titles in this series

For GCSE examinations

- Accounting
- Biology
- Business Studies
- Chemistry
- Computer Studies
- Economics
- English
- French
- Geography
- German
- Graphic Communication
- Human Biology
- Maths
- Modern World History
- Numeracy
- Physics
- Social and Economic History
- Sociology
- Spanish
- Statistics

For A-level examinations

- Accounting
- Applied Maths
- Business Studies
- Chemistry
- Economics
- English
- French
- Pure Maths
- Sociology
- Statistics

Macmillan College Work Outs for degree and professional students

- Dynamics
- Electric Circuits
- Electromagnetic Fields
- Electronics
- Elements of Banking
- Engineering Materials
- Engineering Thermodynamics
- Fluid Mechanics
- Genetics
- Mathematics for Economists
- Molecular Genetics
- Operational Research
- Organic Chemistry
- Physical Chemistry
- Structural Mechanics
- Waves and Optics

MACMILLAN WORK OUT SERIES

WORK OUT SOCIOLOGY

Paul Selfe

Revise with the Experts with Past A-Level Questions

Shipley College

150th YEAR
M
MACMILLAN

First published 1987 by Pan Books Ltd
Reprinted six times

This edition published 1993 by
THE MACMILLAN PRESS LTD
Houndmills, Basingstoke, Hampshire RG21 2XS
and London
Companies and representatives
throughout the world

ISBN 0–333–58688–3

Typeset by Florencetype Ltd, Kewstoke, Avon
Printed in Great Britain by Unwin Brothers Ltd,
The Gresham Press, Old Woking, Surrey.
A member of Martins Printing Group

10 9 8 7 6 5 4 3 2 1
02 01 00 99 98 97 96 95 94 93

This book is dedicated to Jessica and Amy

Contents

ACKNOWLEDGEMENTS

The author and publishers wish to thank the following for permission to use copyright material:

The Economist for 'Sisters Marching', *The Economist*, 5.9.92.

The Controller of Her Majesty's Stationery Office for Crown copyright material sourced to the Department of Employment, Inland Revenue, Employment Gazette, Central Statistical Office and the Office of Population, Censuses and Surveys.

Gallup for data included in *The Guardian*, 14.4.92.

Guardian News Service Ltd for extracts from various issues of *The Guardian*. Ewan MacNaughton Associates on behalf of The Telegraph plc, for extract from an article by Clare Hargreaves, *Daily Telegraph*, 6.11.87. Copyright © The Telegraph plc, 1987.

Newspapers Publishing plc for extracts from various issues of *The Independent* and *The Independent on Sunday*.

The Observer Ltd for extracts from various issues of *The Observer* and *New Statesman and Society*.

The author and publishers would also like to thank the Examination Boards (WJEC, UCLES, ULSEB, UODLE, JMB, AEB) for permission to use the questions from their past papers.

The author is grateful to Alec Gill for permission to use his photographs and to his editor and colleagues for their helpful guidance and advice.

Every effort has been made to trace all the copyright-holders, but if any have been inadvertently overlooked the publishers will be pleased to make the necessary arrangement at the first opportunity.

INTRODUCTION

The aim of this book is to provide a comprehensive revision aid which covers the areas examined by the six Examining Boards. The past papers from recent years have been used as the basis of the revision material presented in it. Representative examples have been taken from each topic area to illustrate how the student could approach particular types of question.

It is important to remember that there are no 'correct' answers to questions: of course, you may be incorrect in your reference to an authority, your use of statistical detail or your definitions of terms, but assuming this is not the case, it would be possible for two students using similar accurate data to reach different conclusions. In sociology, you are being asked to discuss or debate an issue. This means that you must be able to approach the question from different perspectives and to decide whether one produces a more valid conclusion than another.

Each of the chapters in the book contains a section in which the theoretical perspectives are considered. However, you should be aware that there is always a danger in categorising material in a way that oversimplifies its complexities. Although it is useful from the point of view of revision to examine issues from the functionalist, Marxist and interactionist perspectives you must remember that in the course of research a variety of methods and approaches may be adopted.

You should also be aware that examination questions often ask you to produce an answer by drawing on material from a range of topic areas; for example the family and religion or the mass media and politics. You must, therefore, learn to become flexible in your thinking when revising for exams.

To assist you in your revision programme, each of the chapters in this book begins by noting the question areas which appear to be tested most frequently in the exam, so that you can decide which specific issue you intend to work on. Generally, however, you are advised to look at a range of issues within the topic to see how they interrelate.

The book is oriented around typical examination questions, but there are no 'model answers' provided. This is because examiners are looking for your ability to debate an issue and not for some 'correct' explanation. The student must be active in revision and use the relevant material presented to tackle alternative questions.

All the Boards assess the ability of the candidate to write a structured essay. Suggested structures are presented in summary form to indicate the approach which a student could adopt. However, the candidate should endeavour to think through the issues relevant to the question, then develop, clarify and evaluate the material selected for an effective answer. Some Boards also include questions based on stimulus-response passages to test the ability to draw conclusions from data and to present a critical analysis of issues raised. Examples of these are presented in the self-test section at the end of each chapter. It is most important to be very familiar with the structure of the examination paper that you are going to face and to be aware of the precise requirements specified in the rubric of the paper. The general assumption of this book is that you will require a certain amount of detailed sociological knowledge in order to do well in the exam. The skill you must practise is that of applying it in relevant ways.

Table A Examining Boards

Board		Number of papers	Time allowed	Any optional studies	Number of questions to answer	Number of questions on the paper (choice)	Number of compulsory questions	Structured data response Does the paper contain any SDR questions?	Maximum number of full essays to write
Ox	9848	1	3 hours	No	4	14	0	YES (few)	4
Ox	9848	2	3 hours	No	4	14	0	YES (few)	4
AEB	639	1	3 hours	No	3	5	1	YES (all)	0
AEB	639	2	3 hours	No	4	9	0	No	4
AEB	664	1	3 hours 50%	Yes	3	5	1	YES (all)	0
AEB	664	2	1½ hours 25%	Yes	2	16	0	NO	2
AEB	664	3	12 months 25%	Coursework					
JMB	54	1	3 hours	No	5	10	4	YES (most)	1
JMB	55	2	3 hours	No	5	10	4	YES (most)	1
Cam	9060	1	3 hours	No	4	14	0	NO	4
Cam	9060	2	3 hours	No	4	21	0	NO	4
Lon	585	1	3 hours	No	4	14	1	YES (few)	2
Lon	585	2	3 hours	No	4	21	0	NO	4
Lon	585	3	3 hours	No	4	15	0	NO	4
Wel		1	3 hours	No	4	14	0	YES (few)	3
Wel		2	3 hours	No	4	24	0	NO	4

See page 3 for full names and addresses of Examining Boards.

Table B Specific skills tested

Skill being tested	Paper 1		Paper 2		Both papers	
	Mark	%	Mark	%	Mark	%
Knowledge	20	10	32	16	52	26
Interpretation	40	20	34	17	74	37
Evaluation	40	20	34	17	74	37
Total	100	50	100	50	200	100

Preparing for the Examination

There are six boards which examine A-level sociology.

You should become familiar with the syllabus that you are studying, since there are some variations between boards (see Table A).

You should also be familiar with the structure of the examination paper. Past papers are available at a small cost from the boards.

It is often helpful to check the syllabus booklet of the board you are using to see if the assessment objectives are specified.

For example, AEB 639 (1993) gives the following information:

'The examination will assess the candidate's ability to:

1. demonstrate a knowledge and understanding of sociological material.
2. interpret sociological material.
3. use such material to analyse social issues and personal experience.
4. evaluate sociological theories and methods.
5. evaluate sociological and non sociological evidence.
6. present explanations in a logical way.'

Also listed are the specific skills which examiners are testing and the weighting they give to each in their marking (see Table B).

It is important to realise that you may lose up to 37 per cent of your marks if you fail to evaluate the material being used. Equally, it is interesting to know that you can only get a maximum of 26 per cent for displaying detailed knowledge. Therefore, it is a waste of time to seek to impress by unloading a mass of facts (however accurate) into an answer at the expense of interpreting and evaluating their relevance.

Similar details are provided for candidates taking the Coursework option (Paper 664).

Although other Boards may not be quite so forthcoming in their syllabus documents, it seems safe to assume that they are using similar marking schemes. You should therefore seek to develop your skills of evaluation and interpretation from an early point in your studies. Do not work under the misapprehension that you can sail through the exam by learning a detailed list of authors, studies and statistics. You must always show why the facts you supply help to support or refute an argument in relation to the question you are seeking to answer. Do not assume that the facts automatically speak for themselves and do not frequently require justification or to have their validity questioned.

It is important to remember that success normally comes to those who prepare carefully for the exam and who work consistently throughout the course of study.

You are therefore advised to keep an orderly file; read widely around the subject matter; debate the issues you are studying from time to time with someone; start revision programmes early and ask questions when in doubt.

The Examination Boards

The addresses below are those from which copies of syllabuses and past examination papers may be ordered. The abbreviations (AEB, etc.) are those used in the text to identify actual questions.

Associated Examining
Board (AEB),
Stag Hill House, Guildford,
Surrey GU2 5WX

University of Cambridge Local
Examinations Syndicate (UCLES),
Syndicate Buildings,
1 Hills Road,
Cambridge CB1 2EU

Joint Matriculation Board (JMB),
Manchester M15 6EU

University of London School
Examinations Department
(ULSEB),
52 Gordon Square,
London WC1H 0PJ

Oxford Delegacy of Local
Examinations (UODLE),
Ewert Place, Summertown,
Oxford OX2 7BZ

Welsh Joint Education
Committee (WJEC),
245 Western Avenue,
Cardiff CF5 2YX

Writing an Essay in Sociology

1. Read the questions carefully.

   To test your understanding rewrite the question in your own words.
   Example: Do the mass media have an influence on the attitudes of the audience?
   Meaning:

   ■ **Do you agree that the media (TV, radio, press) cause people to modify, change or reinforce their beliefs and behaviour?**

2. Do you know a possible answer to the question?

   ■ **'Yes, I do agree'; 'No, I do not agree'; 'Perhaps, in special circumstances'.**

3. Decide on the answer you intend to pursue. This is important since it will determine the shape your essay will take and the conclusion you will reach. If you do not know an answer at the start, you would be unwise to embark on the question.
4. Organise your material according to a simple plan: Introduction, discussion, development and conclusion.
   Start by explaining what the question is asking and indicate how you will answer it. For example:

   'There is much debate among the sociologists of the media as to whether or not they do cause people to modify, change or reinforce their attitudes and patterns of behaviour. Some have argued that they do have a direct effect, citing evidence that indicates that aggression, racial hostility, etc. are shaped by media messages. Others argue that this is not necessarily the case and they point to other influences such as the family, school, etc. A third view is that in some cases they may shape attitudes, although this is unusual, and depends on particular circumstances in which the information is received. . . .'

   Notice how an opening such as this sets up a structure for your essay. It should go on to take up these three positions. If you can only think of two main arguments then these will form the two halves of the essay.
5. The conclusion is very important. You have been asked a question and you must endeavour to answer it. Do not merely summarise your essay, but try to show how your arguments and evidence lead to a justifiable conclusion. This may be 'we do not know whether or not the mass media affect attitudes because there is so much conflicting evidence arising from research studies'. This is an acceptable point on which to end, provided it follows from the main body of your answer.
6. A moderator for the AEB Board has made it clear that the first ten marks in the exam are easy to get. It is possible to pass the exam on the first page of each of your answers. The mistake that many candidates make is to try to get the last five marks before they have the first ten.
   To get ten marks:

   (a) Explain what the question is asking.
   (b) Explain why it is a problem worth considering.
   (c) Specify some authorities who have thrown light on the question.
   (d) Specify some answers to the questions.

   To obtain the next ten marks go on to elaborate and debate the points made in the introduction in finer detail. Argue logically, step by step, using references, statistics and other supporting evidence. It is possible for an outstanding answer to get twenty-five marks.
7. You are advised to write simply. Use sociological language which you understand. Use your own language but not slang or ambiguous terms. Do not try to memorise or quote large sections of text books.
8. Avoid using value judgements (for example, 'think that the functionalist perspective is a bad one because all it does is support the status quo').
9. The better answers will contain perceptive criticisms and evaluation of studies, articles or books (where relevant to a question). Students are not expected to introduce any original theories in their answers. Criticisms must be based on ideas worked out before entering the exam room. Don't attempt criticisms of studies if you have not first studied them to ensure your points are justified.
10. It is useful to be able to quote studies and examples to

illustrate points; knowledge of particular authors and their work may also help the student to recall detail. However, it is possible to write adequate answers with few references. Do not be afraid to use well-known examples if necessary so long as they are relevant and provide weight to the answer.

11. It is also wise to raise what may seem to be simple and obvious points in an answer. For example, when discussing methods of sociological research explain why a particular method was used in preference to another; explain how a particular method arises from a perspective or theory; explain the problems and constraints that face researchers.
12. Although examiners may try to ignore spelling mistakes, errors of punctuation and poor handwriting, where there is a combination of these the answer is unlikely to impress. Some Boards (for example, JMB) clearly state that 'candidates are reminded of the need for good English and clear presentation'.

Interpreting questions

You must read the wording of the question carefully and answer it in the terms specified:

1. *Discuss* Present a thorough analysis of the question by examining all sides of the arguments.
2. *Compare* Present the similarities and differences between the features mentioned.
3. *Evaluate* Present a judgement as to the relative value of the features mentioned.
4. *To what extent* Weigh up the arguments and state the relative importance of the feature mentioned.
5. *Interpret* Present an explanation of the facts.
6. *Critically examine* State clearly the pros and cons of the issue raised. Your final decision must be supported by evidence and the reasons why you have rejected alternatives explained.
7. *Distinguish between* Draw clear distinctions between the features mentioned.
8. *Assess* Establish the strengths and weaknesses of the feature mentioned.

Remember that examiners are looking for an answer to their questions which follows logical arguments. Relevant facts, statistics and other authorities to support your line of analysis are always useful, but reference to authors and their books may not be essential to your success. It is crucial to show an understanding of the question and a possible answer to it, using sociological ideas.

Stimulus Response and Structured Data Response Questions

Several Boards (especially AEB, JMB, ULSEB) include many questions of this type. To do well in answering them you must read the passage carefully and note how many marks are available for each section. You should try to write as fully as possible on each section and consider that you will gain marks for each point you make; it would therefore be unwise to write too expansively on a single issue when there may be several different points to make. Remember, too, that you may be able to spend as many as forty minutes on the question; a thorough discussion is therefore expected, especially on those parts of the question which may carry eight to ten marks.

For example, consider the following question and the suggested marking scheme:

■ **Sociologists use a variety of methods in their research. Much use is made of questionnaires and interviews. There are some examples of small-scale experiments, usually conducted in the field to discover more about behaviour in its social context. But important information has been obtained by correlating statistical details obtained from court records, divorce proceedings, etc. and the social backgrounds of those involved. Some researchers have used observational techniques alone to great effect, especially in the understanding of group behaviour. In some cases sociologists have had to make use of secondary sources such as diaries, letters and biographical details in order to add depth to their knowledge. The reliability of such results has been questioned by some critics; the question has been raised as to whether it is only by traditional scientific methods that valid results can be obained.**

(a) Which is the most reliable method of obtaining data, and why? (8)
(b) Discuss the advantages of recorded statistics over diaries and letters. (8)
(c) Why would a researcher choose one method at the expense of another? (9)

Marking scheme

Remember: there is no 'correct' answer.

	Possible marks
(a) Which is the most reliable method of obtaining data, and why?	
Discuss problems of 'reliability'	2
Choose **one** method – show why/how it is reliable	2
Show the source of its reliability	2
Explain how **every** method has limitations and success levels; whether or not a method is reliable depends to a great extent on the care and skill of the researcher. The collection of statistics may not be reliable if the researcher is careless (expand briefly/illustrate).	2

A social survey, using structured interviews, in which a large random sample has been carefully selected according to the principles of selection, ought to be reliable in its results. (Explain *random; sampling frame; representative sample.*)

The source of the reliability is in the scientific procedures that are followed (briefly expand).

However, it must be said that every method has its limitations, as well as its chances of success.

Observational techniques may be criticised for the element of subjectivity that enters the account. But, if well trained, the researcher may produce extremely reliable results.

(b) Advantages of recorded statistics over diaries and letters

1. Explain secondary sources (and primary sources) **2**
2. State a range of advantages of statistics and records; list the disadvantages of diaries and letters: **6**

Advantages of statistics/records	*Disadvantages of diaries/letters*

3. Can you suggest an example of a study in which it was an advantage to use recorded statistics rather than other secondary sources? For example *The World We Have Lost*, page 81.)

(c) Reasons for choosing a particular method

1. Suggest a wide selection of factors which affect the decision to use a particular research method (think of about six) **6**
2. Try to relate these suggestions to particular theories or perspectives: i.e. a positivist chooses a method in terms of the perspective from which s/he starts, as does an interactionist **3**

Total **25**

Remember that this represents a marking scheme: you must always write a coherent answer in normal 'essay' style – and not as a series of points; but it is worth making the points first and then linking them into a series of paragraphs.

Study Skills

1. When revising, establish a set of goals. Make sure that you achieve them. For example, analyse one question; or read five pages of a text book during a specific revision period.
2. Make a timetable which specifies the time available for revision and the tasks to be achieved. Keep to it.
3. Work in comfortable, silent conditions.
4. Establish your concentration span and work within it. Take a break before continuing. There is no point in revising when very tired.
5. Before each period of revision spend ten minutes recalling the material on which you had been working previously. It is important to recall recently learned material frequently.
6. Use a range of revision and learning techniques: for example, write detailed notes; make notes of notes; make skeleton essay plans for lengthy essays, from which it would be possible to rebuild the essay to its original length; write timed essays; analyse questions; establish their meanings and possible answers to them; debate and discuss ideas with someone so that you verbalise the arguments. This will help later recall.
7. If problems arise in your understanding of questions or issues, be sure to make a note of them and ask for clarification as soon as possible, or seek the answer in a textbook.
8. Use coloured pens for making notes, each colour representing a different aspect of a question; use coloured highlighting pens for marking articles, cuttings, etc. (so long as they belong to you!). Make additional notes from these to supplement or update your own existing information.
9. There are many useful books on the market* which may assist you in your study techniques. For example, Maddox, *How to Study*, Pan; Buzan, *Use Your Head*, BBC Publications; Open University, *Preparing to Study*; Freeman, *Mastering Study Skills*, Macmillan; Rowntree, *Learning How to Study*, Macdonald; Salimbene, *Strengthening Your Study Skills*, Newby House.

Coursework and Projects

It is possible to submit coursework for two syllabuses: AEB (A-level) 25 per cent and ULSEB (AS level) 50 per cent. It is marked internally by a teacher and then moderated by the Board.

Candidates are required to submit a sociological study undertaken in the twelve months prior to the exam. It is an opportunity for candidates to carry out an analysis using primary or secondary data to investigate a subject of sociological interest. It is the responsibility of the teacher to ensure that candidates select an appropriate subject.

Points to remember

(i) This option is not available for external candidates.
(ii) The study must address theoretical issues.
(iii) It may be based on one or more areas of the syllabus.
(iv) It should not exceed 5000 words.
(v) It should contain the following sections clearly labelled and indexed:

(a) *Rationale* a reason for choosing the subject; a clear hypothesis.
(b) *Context* an outline of the theoretical context of the study.
(c) *Methodology* a statement of the methods used; reasons for their use; a recognition of associated problems.
(d) *Content* clear presentation of the evidence.
(e) *Evaluation* an assessment of the project; its strengths and weaknesses.
(f) *Sources* a list of the sources and references used.

The marking scheme (AEB)

1. Knowledge and understanding: context; methodology; content – maximum 16 marks.
2. Interpretation and application: rationale; aplication; presentation – maximum 17 marks.
3. Evaluation: methodological justification; assessment and conclusion – maximum 17 marks.

* The section on suggested reading at the end of each chapter gives you full publication details of the key books and other studies discussed in the chapter, followed by a further brief section of additional suggested reading.

Planning a research project

1. Do some reading. Look at the different types of study that have been conducted (see page 7).
2. Make a careful plan before starting to gather data. Be sure to have a clear aim in mind. Keep this as simple as possible. State a question to which an answer is required (**Why do some children hate school**? for example). While this may be your starting point it may change, become more sharply focused or broaden as you proceed.
3. Specify a hypothesis which could be tested (for example, **They display strong characteristics of alienation**).
4. Select a range of possible methods which could be used to gather data. Are some more appropriate than others?
5. Research programmes can arise out of several possibilities:
   (a) To suggest the causes or extent of a problem; to establish its characteristics; to suggest solutions.
   (b) To establish social policy or to see if the policy is working.
   (c) To examine social changes over time.
   (d) To find out about existing attitudes or changes in attitudes.
   (e) To gather facts about an issue or to gain insights into behaviour.
   (f) To make comparisons between social institutions.

   It may be helpful for you to decide in which category your question falls.
6. Your plan should establish:
   (a) A clear aim.
   (b) The population from whom you want the information.
   (c) The number you will sample or observe.
   (d) The type of sample that will be drawn and from what source.
   (e) What questions will you ask or what themes will you follow?
   (f) Whether you can enlist help from others in your college. (A statistician may help frame your questions for ease of analysis; a computer teacher may help you prepare your material on disk.)
   (g) Whether or not you will require a tape recorder; funds for postage, etc? Beware of undertaking a costly study or one that requires much time transcribing interviews from tape.
   (h) Whether the project is within your competence to complete competently and in good time.
   (i) Whether you will require permission from people to gain your data (to visit a school).
7. You must keep in close contact with your teacher and seek advice if necessary.
8. It is sensible to conduct a small pilot study before you embark on the major project, to make sure your questions are well framed and easily understood.
9. If you are satisfied that you can cope with your proposed study, then proceed.

Warning

M. D. Shipman, in his book *The Limitations of Social Research*, points out some of the dangers which face 'students and enthusiastic amateurs' who are keen to practise the research methods of the social scientist. He describes some of the consequences of the work of 98 anthropology students in California, reported in an article entitled 'Unleashing the Untrained':

> "The students investigated relentlessly with blatant disregard for the rights of others. They gave away confidences, acted as Peeping Toms, reported illegal practices, violated promised anonymity and obtained information by fraud. They obtained and used tests that required long training for proper administration. One stirred up an industrial dispute . . . ."

Shipman describes this as an example of a Gresham's Law of Research: 'The bad drives out the good'. His advice in this respect is excellent and must be remembered by all those who wish to undertake projects of social research:

> "The essence of reliable research is the extent of control exercised, not only over extraneous variables that could interfere in the relation being examined, but over the researcher himself."

It is important to bear the warning in mind. There are dangers in acting in unethical ways and in causing the public to become suspicious and wary because of researchers who have not been well briefed in the techniques they are endeavouring to use. Too frequently, perhaps, they have been pestered by children armed with ill-thought-out questionnaires which are too time-consuming or too difficult to answer. The suggestions made in the following pages are intended to avoid such pitfalls. But the onus is on researchers, and those who direct and advise them, to ensure that sensible areas of study are selected, as well as the most appropriate methods and procedures.

Suggestions for studies

You should try to read some studies that have been conducted by professional sociologists. Examine the questions they are seeking to answer and note the methods they use. You may decide to try to replicate some aspect of the research (on a smaller scale). You should keep a note of the studies you come across. Table C shows some examples to which you could add your own reading.

Points to note

There are many methods available. You must select those which are most appropriate to the question you wish to answer. It is important to go beyond mere description of the feature studied; you must place your work in a theoretical perspective and draw out some sociological significance from your results.

The use of scientific methods

(i) *Questionnaires* and *closed interviews* (precise answers to brief questions) are most frequently used bcause they provide a means of measuring responses.

(ii) *Open-ended interviews* which allow respondents to expand fully on their answers. Often a tape recorder is required, but it is time-consuming to transcribe answers and they may be hard to quantify. But they are useful in gaining a clearer picture of a person's

Table B Examples of research studies

Authors	Title	Methods used	Aims
Newson	*Patterns of Infant Care*	Questionnaire	To see if child-rearing patterns vary between classes
Young and Willmott	*Family and Class in a London Suburb*	Questionnaire Sampling method	To see if family structures vary between classes
Bell	'Reflections on the Banbury Restudy'	Questionnaire Documents Interviews (Participant Observation)	To assess the significance of social change in Banbury 1950–60
Rex and Moore	*Race, Community and Conflict*	Interviews Documents Observation	To find out how and why different groups come to inhabit different areas of a city; what community ties they have
Parkin	*Middle Class Radicalism: The Social Bases of the British Campaign for Nuclear Disarmament*	Questionnaires	To see whether the typical CND supporter was predominantly middle-class
Laslett and Wrigley	*The World We Have Lost* *Population and History*	Documents Parish registers	To assess the impact of industrialisation on family structures
Hargreaves *et al.*	*Deviance in Classrooms*	Observation	To discover the processes by which labels are attached to some children
Myerson	'Experiments Without Rats'	Observation	To discover how people use space in public places and to create and protect territory
Homans	*The Human Group*	Observation	To see how groups create social norms and to assess their significance in shaping behaviour
Turner	'Role Taking'	Observation	To see the ways in which a person's social role shapes their behaviour
Roth	'The Treatment of TB as a Bargaining Process'	Observation	To examine the negotiating processes that occur between hospital patients and staff
Marsh	*Rules of Disorder*	Observation	To see the world of the football terraces through the eyes of fans; to understand the rules of disruption
Becker	*Outsiders*	Observation	To see how acts come to be defined as deviant by some observers but not by others
Morse	*The Unattached*	Observation	To discover why a group of young people would not join youth clubs
Newby	'In the Field: Reflections on the Study of Suffolk Farm Workers'	Case studies	To examine the extent of deference between farm owner and tenant; also the comparative nature of deference
Lane and Roberts	*Strike at Pilkingtons*	Case study	To examine the causes and the developments of a strike
Blythe	*Akenfield*	Case study	A detailed analysis of a Suffolk village
Philo (Glasgow Media Group)	*Bad News,* *More Bad News,* *Really Bad News*	Content analysis	To examine the content of TV news broadcasts for evidence of political bias in reporting

views. (They can be used effectively in observational studies to add detail and depth.)

(iii) *Recorded statistics*. Useful studies can be undertaken by gathering data on issues from local council offices, police reports, courts, schools, colleges, universities and so on. The use of parish registers has provided fruitful information about changes in family structures over time. But be aware of the problems of interpretation and examine the data critically.

(iv) *Experiments* are seldom used in sociology but some limited field experiments are possible. Studies can be conducted, for example, into the ways that people defend space in crowded environments (cafés, libraries, trains, etc.). What happens when space is invaded? Beware of placing people in embarrassing or unethical situations.

(v) *Case study*. This is a closely-focused analysis of a single group, institution, classroom, etc. in which all behaviour is examined using a range of methods.

Some measurement is likely to be required (for example, frequency with which males wash up in a household).

(vi) *Content analysis*. This requires careful measurement of the feature being examined (newspaper, TV, radio programme, etc.). There are often problems in defining terms (for example, violence; political bias, etc.). Be sure to establish your working definitions.

Observational methods (ethnography)

(i) *Participant observation* usually requires complete secrecy and the observer must adopt a normal role. In observing the structure of a classroom and interaction patterns, you would maintain your role as a student. Changes in role can occur, depending on the nature of the research. The complete participant gains inside information and hopes to see the world though the eyes of those being studied. But note the dangers of losing objectivity and bias in interpretation. You must remain marginal.

(ii) *Non-participant observation*: the observer is detached from the group under observation, who may or may not know they are being studied. You must put yourself in the position of the 'acceptable incompetent'. M. Hammersley and P. Atkinson say 'it is only through watching, listening, asking questions, formulating hypotheses, and making blunders that the ethnographer can acquire some sense of the social structure of the setting and begin to understand the culture of the participants'.

These methods are not necessarily alternatives: they can be used in conjunction with each other. It depends on what you wish to discover. One method may be more appropriate than another for different aspects of the same study. A survey, for example, may also require observational detail to supplement it.

Some suggestions

Research using documents

J. Scott (*Social Studies Review*) notes that most of the work done by the most eminent sociologists has made use of documentary sources. These include: government reports, medical records, statistical publications, biographical reference books, letters, diaries, newspapers, parish registers. Also household ephemera, such as shopping lists and address books; pictorial documents such as photographs, paintings and maps.

He suggests that such sources can be assessed through four criteria:

(a) *Authenticity*: is the evidence genuine and of unquestionable origin?
(b) *Credibility*: is the evidence free from error and distortion?
(c) *Representativeness*: is the evidence typical of its kind, and if not, is the extent of its untypicality known?
(d) *Meaning*: is the evidence clear and comprehensible?

An example: *the use of parish registers* In 1964 Laslett and Wrigley founded the Cambridge Group for the History of Population and Social Structure. They wished to:

(i) study the impact of industrialisation on the family structure; and
(ii) find facts relating to the family in pre-industrial times.

Parish registers were first established in 1538 for the purpose of recording births, marriages and deaths in English parishes. They continued in use until 1837, when the state took over the responsibility for the collection of the statistics.

The authors suggest it is possible to reconstitute families (to rebuild them) by examining the relationships of those listed in the registers. The birth record states when and where a child was born as well as the surname and occupation of the father and perhaps the maiden name of the mother. The marriage record gives the ages of the husband and wife and possibly the names of their parents. The death records give details of age, occupation and cause of death.

Much information can be gained where the records are full: the size of family, the birth and death rates over time, even whether or not forms of family limitation were practised, depending on whether there is a marked lengthening of birth intervals.

Areas of investigation

(i) Laslett suggests that the nuclear family was in evidence in pre-industrial times. Can you verify this?
(ii) How do average family sizes vary over time? How can these be explained?
(iii) How do death rates vary over time? How can these be explained?
(iv) How do illegitimacy rates vary over time? How can these be explained?

Research based on observation

Hammersley and Atkinson issue a warning: they note that the conduct of ethnography is deceptively simple, apparently 'anyone can do it'; there is the assumption that it is unproblematic, requires little preparation and no special expertise. However, they do point out that with careful thought useful data can be obtained:

(i) The initial field work is important: where to observe, when, who to talk to, what to ask, what to record and how. It is important to know what you wish to examine, but be flexible in your approach.
(ii) Be aware of problem issues: it may be hard to establish credibility; personal appearance may be important to establish good relations.
(iii) You must be non-directive in your questioning; avoid leading questions.
(iv) Seek out helpful documentary evidence (eg: school reports may throw light on teacher expectations).
(v) Practise the recording and organising of data: don't rely on memory; keep field notes; use a tape if it is convenient.
(vi) Your analysis of events is ongoing; relate analysis to theoretical issues.
(vii) Writing up: allow plenty of time for writing up and then double it. You are engaged in telling a story; you need to develop a good literary style. Allow the text to unfold as your discoveries proceed.

Questions

1. Examine photograph 1
Suggest ways of conducting a research project which would examine:
- (i) The attitudes and values of the leaders of a demonstration.
- (ii) The social class of a cross-section of the demonstrators.
- (iii) What it is like to be a demonstrator.
- (iv) The perceptions of the police.
- (v) The perceptions of spectators.
- (vi) The ways it is reported in the local or national press.
- (vii) The success or failure of the demonstration.

Consider and justify some of the methods you would recommend.
Outline some of the possible problems you might anticipate.

2. Examine photograph 2
Many interesting research projects fail because they are too ambitious and under-resourced; and some because the information is too difficult to obtain.
- (i) Suggest some of the problems which might arise in:
  - (a) Using questionnaires and interviews to investigate political or religious attitudes in the area shown in this photograph.
  - (b) Using observational techniques to investigate children's street games.
- (ii) Can you suggest a study that might be feasible?

3. Examine photograph 3
Social action theorists argue that human beings define situations and act in terms of the meanings they attribute to their observations; phenomenologists examine the way that people interpret events in order to understand the meanings they have established.

Discuss some of the questions they may raise about events in this picture, which was taken in a city in Northern Ireland.
- (i) Consider how positive or negative labels might be attached to the various actors based on their perceptions by:
  - (a) the boy;
  - (b) the soldiers; and
  - (c) the other spectators (including yourself).
- (ii) Consider the possibility of an observational study in a city centre; in an institution such as a church, court, welfare centre or job centre, so that you try to see the world through the eyes of a stranger. All the behaviour you watch must be problematic and require explanation.

1

Source: Alec Gill

2

Source: Alec Gill

3

Source: Alec Gill

Examples *of possible studies*

(i) Hargreaves *et al.* asked such questions as:
What are the rules in schools and a classrooms?
Which rules are allegedly broken in acts of deviance?
Who made the rules?
Are the rules ever negotiated? If so, how?
What justifications are given for the rules? By whom? When?
Do teachers and students/pupils view the rules in the same ways?
How do students know when rules are in operation?
Do rules vary much in importance?
What is the process of interpretation that different teachers use to define acts as deviant?
How does the label 'deviant' come to be attached to some children?
How does the labelled child respond to the process of labelling?

(ii) Measor noted that girls tend to do less well than boys in science exams. She wished to know why and looked at them in class as well as interviewing them.

(iii) Hammersley and Atkinson asked whether employers operate with stigmatising stereotypes (that is, do they have preconceived ideas about types of young people based on their appearance?)

(iv) Myerson asked, 'Have you ever walked into a cafe and noticed where people sit when they come in? Have you ever tried to see what happens when you attempt to share a table when there are other ones free?' What happens when a person's space is violated? How do you learn the location of invisible boundaries?

(v) Homans defines a norm as those unwritten rules which develop in a group and which shape and control aspects of behaviour. What norms exist in your friendship groups? What happens if a norm is broken? Which norms are particularly important?

(vi) Roth was a patient in a hospital and observed the way that patients and medical staff develop a negotiating process in the course of their treatment. Patients learn how to manipulate the restrictive system to maximise their freedoms and choices. Nurses bargain with patients in order to impose their power. Do people who have spent lengthy periods in hospital confirm this view? Do such bargaining processes go on in other institutions such as schools and colleges? Can illustrations be found of such processes in everyday arenas of social life?

(vii) Godwin suggests that many recently founded public schools deliberately introduced new rituals into everyday life in the school to act as a bridge between past and present. They also help establish hierarchical divisions of power. What kinds of ritual are evident in everyday life? What functions do they serve? What happens when people fail to perform the expected ritual?

Social surveys

You must read a reliable book on the subject. For example, Gardner (*Social Surveys for Social Planners*) notes that social surveys have become part of our way of life: hardly a week passes without one being mentioned in the newspapers. But he warns that the methods used can be more journalistic than scientific unless the researcher is well prepared:

(i) The purpose is to gain accurate information from a large number of people as quickly as possible.

(ii) You must establish what it is you wish to know and from whom. Ideally you should draw a random sample. But this is more time-consuming than using a less scientific quota sample.

(iii) You must plan carefully. Remember to phrase your questions in ways that will make analysis as easy as possible and that will make it easy for respondents to answer them.

(iv) The range of investigations based on the survey is obviously immense. Try to be inventive and either use some originality in your research (for example, Why have people dropped out of your college from the first day of the new term to the present?) or seek to critically retest some question already examined by a professional sociologist (for example, Are CND campaigners or those in the Peace Movement in the main well-educated middle-class people?).

Picture research

You may decide to carry out a project in which you make use of photographs, both your own and others', obtained from the archives of local newspapers, old postcards, etc. these could be used to examine concepts – like class stereotyping; as aids in prompting memories in interviews; to illustrate changes in neighbourhoods overtime, as well as changes in dress, customs, work and leisure activities. Examples of the power of photographs to raise issues and capture significant images can be examined throughout this book.

Should you do a coursework project?

This may depend on your teacher's advice or policy. Where you have a choice you need to be aware of the following:

(a) You must be a conscientious student who can work steadily without constant guidance.
(b) You must show initiative and perseverance.
(c) Once under way try to stick to your plan. You are not expected to produce startlingly original work. Where problems occur use them to your advantage in your evaluation section.
(d) A group can collect and pool data but coursework must be written up independently. It need not be typed.

Comments from an examiner

Clynch (*'Questions and Answers'*) discusses good and weak projects in terms of the three areas in which marks are awarded:

Knowledge and understanding

Good projects

(a) Locate their study in the correct theoretical context and do not merely rewrite chapters from books.
(b) They use a variety of sources and references to pertinent research.
(c) The advantages of the chosen method is made clear.

Weak projects
(a) There is an inability to identify and review relevant material.
(b) The project is treated like an essay.
(c) There is no discrimination shown with regard to possible methods.

Interpretation and application

Good projects
(a) There is a clear statement of reasons for choosing the topic.
(b) There is constant reference back to their rationale throughout their study.
(c) Main issues are clearly identified and defined.

Weak projects
(a) There is little if any reference to the reasons for their study.
(b) No attempt is made to link such statement to their research.
(c) There is no identifiable hypothesis being investigated.
(d) Findings are seldom interpreted with any sociological insight.

Evaluation

Good projects
(a) The rationale is carried through to the end.
(b) There is cross reference of findings to research addressed in the context section.
(c) There is a sophisticated understanding of issues addressed throughout the project.
(d) Strategies are offered for improvement whilst addressing the sociological implications of their findings.
(e) The overall hallmark is that of coherence.

Weak projects
(a) Run out of steam in this section.
(b) There is minimal evaluation.
(c) There is no distinction between evaluation and a conclusion (which is merely a summary).
(d) There is a failure to make any useful critical comments either of their own work or that of a professional researcher who has done some similar work.

Final points

1. Keep copies of your work.
2. Keep a record of your sources and references, including a work-log or diary of your progress, ideas, problems, etc. (useful for evaluation).
3. Be familiar with the marking scheme.
4. Number your pages. Start each section on a new page.
5. Use treasury tags not a file.
6. Provide a title page with your name, centre name, candidate number, centre number.
7. Ensure that all labels, graphs, data are clearly presented.

Suggested Reading

Works noted in this chapter

H. Becker (1963) *Outsiders*, Free Press
C. Bell (1977) 'Reflections on the Banbury Restudy', in C. Bell and H. Newby (eds), (1977) *Doing Sociological Research*, Allen & Unwin
R. Blythe (1982) *Akenfield*, Penguin
T. Buzan (1975) *Use Your Head*, BBC Publications
A. Clynch (1991) 'Question and Answer', *Sociology Review* (November) pp. 15–17 Vol. 1, No 2
Freeman (1985) *Mastering Study Skills*, Macmillan
G. Gardner (1978) *Social Surveys for Social Planners*, Open University Publications
T. Godwin (1975) *Ritual in 19th Century Education*, Open University Press
M. Hammersley and P. Atkinson (1983) *Ethnography Principles in Practice*, Tavistock
D. Hargreaves *et al.* (1975) *Deviance in Classrooms*, Routledge & Kegan Paul
G. Homans (1962) *The Human Group*,
P. Laslett (1983) *The World We Have Lost*, Methuen
T. Lane and K. Roberts (1971) *Strike at Pilkingtons*, Fontana
P. McNeill (1985) *Research Methods*, Tavistock
H. Maddox (1963) *How to Study*, Pan
P. Marsh *et al.* (1980) *Rules of Disorder*
M. Morse (1965) *The Unattached*, Penguin
J. Myerson (1979) 'Experiments Without Rats', in R. Meighan *et al.*, *Perspectives on Society*, Nelson
H. Newby (1971) 'In the Field: Reflections on the Study of Suffolk Farm Workers', in C. Bell and H. Newby (eds), *Doing Sociological Research*, Allen & Unwin
J. and E. Newson (1965) *Patterns of Infant Care*, Penguin
Open University (1980) *Preparing to Study*, Open University Publications
F. Parkin (1968) *Middle Class Radicalism: The Social Bases of the British Campaign for Nuclear Disarmament*, Manchester UP
G. Philo, Glasgow Media Group (1976) *Bad News*, Routledge & Kegan Paul
—— (1980) *More Bad News*, Routledge & Kegan Paul
—— (1982) *Really Bad News*, Writers and Readers
J. Rex and J. Moore (1974) *Race, Community and Conflict*, Oxford University Press
J. Roth (1972) 'The Treatment of TB as a Bargaining Process', in A. Rose (ed.), *Human Behaviour and Social Processes*, Routledge & Kegan Paul
D. Rowntree (1970) *Learning How to Study*, Macdonald
M. Salimbene (1983) *Strengthening Your Study Skills*, Newby House
M.D. Shipman (1981) *The Limitations of Social Research*, Longman
S. Taylor (1990) 'Beyond Durkhein: Sociology and Suicide', *Social Studies Review,* Vol 6, No. 2
R. Turner (1972) 'Role Taking', in A Rose (ed.), *Human Behaviour and Social Processes*, Routledge & Kegan Paul
M. Young and P. Willmott (1971) *Family and Class in a London Suburb*, New English Library
E. Wrigley (1973) *Population and History*, World University Library

Works for further reading

R. Burgess. (ed) (1982) *Field Research. A Source Book and Field Manual*, Allen & Unwin

A Clynch (1991) 'Sociology A Level Course Work', *Sociology Review* (November) No. 2

P. Jones (1985) *Theory and Method in Sociology*, UTP

M. Morison (1986) *Methods in Sociology*, Longman

J. Scott (1990) 'Documents in Social Research', *Social Studies Review* (September) Vol. 6, No. 1

Self-test Questions

Study the following material and answer the questions below.

Item A

'Getting a taste of participant observation is not particularly easy because it is not just a matter of joining in with some suitable group. The skill is to "join in" but to maintain a degree of detachment and to analyse the experience systematically from a sociological point of view. Nevertheless the following exercise should be of value.

Choose a "new experience" – some social situation or activity that you have never undertaken before. The experience should be one where there are not serious problems of "entry", "gatekeepers' or 'acquiring a native costume". As far as possible try to find out about the situation before you participate in it. Go into the observation with some broad issue that you wish to focus on; it is not enough to "just experience". Observe with care. Write up a detailed description as soon as possible afterwards, noting any aspect that seemed relevant and also the ways that other participants interpreted or "made sense" of their world.'

Source: Adapted from M. Morison, *Methods in Sociology*, Longman.

Item B

'We are all familiar with the image of the scientist as the uncommitted searcher after truth. He is the explorer of nature – the man who rejects prejudice at the threshold of his laboratory, who collects and examines the bare and objective facts, and whose loyalty is to such facts and to them alone. These are the characteristics which make the testimony of scientists so valuable when advertising products. To be scientific is, among other things, to be objective and openminded.'

Source: Adapted from T. S. Kuhn, *The Function of Dogma in Scientific Research*, Penguin.

1. With reference to one or more examples, explain why 'acquiring a native costume' might cause problems for the researcher using participant observation (Item A, lines 8–9). *(4 marks)*

2. To what extent can participant observation be regarded as scientific in the sense described in Item B? *(12 marks)*

3. How far is the image of scientists presented in Item B an accurate portrayal of how natural scientists actually work? *(9 marks)*

Source: ARB (June 1991) (AS Level).

1

THEORIES AND METHODS IN SOCIOLOGY

All the Examining Boards include numerous questions to test your knowledge and understanding of these areas. Questions are wide-ranging. Some boards provide stimulus-response questions and others have compulsory sections on either or both areas. It is important therefore to be familiar with the following:

1. The origins of sociology.
2. Positivism and phenomenology.
3. Factors affecting choice of method in research.
4. Methods of data collection:
   (a) Social surveys.
   (b) Sampling techniques.
   (c) Interviewing.
5. The reliability of data.
6. Secondary sources of data.
7. Sociology and ideology: can sociology be value-free?
8. Theories in sociology.
9. The relationship between theory and method: Types of study and relevant methods.
10. The sociological perspectives:
    (a) Functionalism.
    (b) Marxism.
    (c) Phenomenology.
    (d) Ethnomethodology.
11. Observational methods.
12. Sociology: art or science?
13. The comparative and the experimental methods.
14. Social problems and social policy.

The Origins of Sociology

■ **To what extent is it correct to suggest that sociology emerged out of the aftermath of the industrial and political revolutions of the eighteenth and nineteenth centuries and is still obsessed with their consequences?**

In this period there developed a greater awareness of the need to understand the causes and consequences of changes in society following the major upheavals in social life.

Political revolutions

1789, the French Revolution; 1832, the Great Reform Bill; 1848, revolutionary movements throughout Europe (publication of the *Communist Manifesto*); 1848, Chartist demands in Britain.

Industrial revolution

This began in the eighteenth century in Britain. It helped develop the factory system and greater division of labour. There was also the growth of *urbanisation*, with the movement of population from rural to urban areas and the development of *secularisation*, the decline in the significance of religious values, especially following the publication of Charles Darwin's *Origin of Species* (1857).

The Enlightenment

This was a philosophical movement which encouraged a more scientific analysis of the social world and opposed the more traditional metaphysical speculations based on religious principles. Beliefs in individual liberty and equality were promoted. New disciplines emerged, including sociology, psychology, economics and anthropology.

The development of sociology

1. The word was first used by Auguste Comte (1834). He wished to establish a science of society that would help to reveal the social laws which he believed controlled development and change.
2. The application of scientific rationalism to an analysis of society was an attempt to find the source of order in a time of rapid change.
3. The origin of sociology is within a strong conservative tradition. The aim was to conserve the best of the past and to find ways of controlling the dangerous forces of change.
4. As the discipline became more established new perspectives emerged:

Functionalism maintained an interest in order and stability.

Marxism focused on areas of conflict and disorder.

Interactionism provided an analysis of how people's behaviour is shaped by their interactions in social situations.

Ethnomethodology has more recently returned to the problem of how people establish and maintain order and meaning in their everyday lives.

Positivism and Interpretivism

It is convenient (although an oversimplification) to divide sociological theories into two main descriptive perspectives. These are Positivism (the traditional scientific approach) and Phenomenology, which can be described as 'less scientific' in that some researchers reject the idea of building theories by the application of the scientific method, preferring to use more interpretive methods.

Questions appear on all the Examination Boards' papers to test your knowledge of these approaches. It is important to know the fundamental differences between them and also to know some details from the theories they subsume.

You will notice from an examination of the questions that the underlying issue generally is 'Is sociology a science?' You should notice, too, that some are phrased to imply that it is:

- **Examine the claim that it is possible to apply the methods of natural science to the study of man. (AEB)**
- **Sociological data, like the data examined by physicists, must be examined objectively. Discuss. (UODLE)**

Other questions imply that it is not:

- **The logic and method of science are inappropriate for sociology. Discuss. (AEB)**
- **It is not possible to make use of the experimental method in the study of the social world. Do you agree? What are the implications of your conclusions for the conduct of sociological research? (UCLES)**

These questions imply that more interpretive methods should be adopted by sociologists. Although you may recognise the central area of debate, you must approach the question according to its phraseology. Do not prepare a general answer to a hoped-for question in the exam; you must use your material to answer the question set and not the one you hoped would be asked!

Perspectives in sociology

Within the Positivist school of sociology there are two dominant theoretical perspectives: these are functionalism and Marxism. Both tend to produce their findings from scientific techniques. Interactionists belong to the Interpretivist Phenomenological school, although they may also use some scientific observational methods.

Questions may be asked specifically about Marxism, functionalism or interactionism, or about the underlying philosophies which direct the methods of Positivism and phenomenology that are associated with them.

Frequently questions can be answered from either point of view.

Functionalism

- **Using a range of examples, explain and illustrate the main features of functional analysis. What are the main strengths and weaknesses of this form of analysis? (JMB)**

Functionalism provides a perspective from which to base an analysis of a society. The central concern is with the source of order and stability in society. The focus is on:

(a) the way social institutions help maintain order in social life; and
(b) the way structural arrangements in society influence behaviour.

Main concepts used by functionalists are:

Social system An organised structure made up of interrelated parts: social culture, family, school, etc.

Social structure The interrelated parts of a society which form a framework for social organisation.

Institutions Approved customs or organisations which help establish relevant behaviour (for example, family, religion).

Some criticisms of functionalism

1. Functionalist views emphasise the significance of the social structure of behaviour. They do not take account of an individual's motives in acting.
2. It is difficult to know what all the functions of a social institution are and which are the most essential.
3. It cannot be assumed that something functional for one group is functional for everyone else.
4. It may be difficult to see how all institutions are related: for example marriage and political system.

Some strengths of functionalism

1. It is a perspective that is concerned with order and directs attention to agencies which help to promote it.
2. It is preoccupied with discovering the positive functions of institutions which will support the smooth running of society.
3. The argument that certain arrangements in society are functional and beneficial leads to arguments against radical change. It focuses on institutions which need protection when under threat (for example, marriage, family, etc.).

Culture The values and beliefs which are transmitted from one generation to the next.

Socialisation The process by which values and beliefs are transmitted and absorbed by people through such agencies as family, school or work place.

Value consensus Values and beliefs shared by members of a group or in society as a whole, which promote order.

Manifest functions Those which are clearly intended.

Latent functions Those functions which are less obvious or hidden below the surface (a latent function of education may be to promote punctuality and obedience).

Dysfunction This explains those features of a social system which are not functional in a positive way (for example, the imposition of new school rules may be dysfunctional if they result in more conflict and hostility).

Example of functional analysis

1. Shils and Young, *The Meaning of the Coronation*. They note how particular ceremonies and rituals serve a positive function to promote social integration. The series of rituals involving monarch, church leaders, government leaders, etc., involves public promises. As a result the monarch 'symbolically proclaims her community with her subjects'.
2. Functionalists argue that the continued existence of the family as a social institution can be accounted for in terms of the functions it performs for society and the individual. Parsons argues that industrial society requires a stable family system to maintain the balanced personalities of those subject to its demands. It also functions to promote the successful socialisation of the young into the values of industrial society.

■ 'Emile Durkheim's theory of suicide is based on a functionalist perspective.' Discuss

Durkheim endeavoured to ground his work in empirical fact. He studied suicide rates in different societies and produced a theory that it was the result of factors relating directly to the structure and functioning of groups in society. He tied his explanation to sources of stability and social order. In particular he looked at levels of integration and regulation, and on the basis of statistical analysis he identified three types of suicide.

Egoistic This resulted from the individual's lack of integration and desire to escape the excessive pressures of the group; once ties are weakened risk increases. This is seen as a state of excessive individualism. Intellectuals and sceptics were said to be especially susceptible.

Altruistic This results from over-integration in the values of the group, causing the individual to submit to its claims (the captain going down with the ship).

Anomic This results from inadequate regulation of the individual's moral and ethical life by group norms. It occurs especially at times of social change (of both prosperity and depression). As normally accepted ethical values disintegrate the individual is left in a state of normlessness and confusion. There is an increasing gap between what a person may aspire to and what they can achieve. The immigrant, the disillusioned businessman, the successful pop star, may be susceptible to this type.

His analysis of levels of integration led him to say that:

(a) married people have lower rates than single, with parents even lower;
(b) Catholics have lower rates than Protestants, and Jews even lower; and
(c) in periods of crisis when there is more group solidarity, rates fall. When this decreases, in times of sudden prosperity or depression, rates increase.

As a functionalist, Durkheim wished to show that the causes of suicide were to be found in the social structure and not necessarily in the individual. This is why he emphasised the importance of social solidarity and community, and he pointed out the need for social institutions which promoted these ends (for example in religion, work or education).

Points of criticism

1. Taylor (*Beyond Durkheim: Sociology and Suicide*) argues that many of Durkheim's concepts are not testable; he seems to posit invisible moral forces that shape behaviour (egoism, altruism). Therefore, he is not being scientific and so cannot be described as a traditional positivist.
2. He also notes that Durkheim's theory does not explain why some people commit suicide rather than become mentally ill.
3. It has been argued that the statistics may be full of serious inaccuracies and subject to cultural bias.

4. Atkinson (*Discovering Suicide*) presents a phenomenological critique. He argues that statistics are open to interpretation; it is necessary to discover how the label 'suicide' is attached to an act. He examines the ways coroners make their judgements, and concludes that they are not a valid way of measuring the amount of suicide that occurs. Coroners were found to be using subjective interpretations to make sense of acts. These may also vary from one society to another.

■ **Outline and assess the usefulness of the analogy between society and a biological organism. (UODLE)**

This question is asking you to explain why some sociologists compare society to a living organism, and to state the strengths and weaknesses of this view.

Functionalism first developed among the earliest sociologists in the nineteenth century, especially Comte and Spencer (and later Durkheim.) They had been influenced by the work of biologists, (for example, Darwin, *Origin of Species*). They made use of such concepts as:

(a) evolutionary changes, from simple to complex over long periods of time;
(b) hierarchy of function in the human body which suggested that some organs were more functional for survival than others (for example, heart, brain, lungs, etc.); and
(c) living organisms developed self-regulating mechanisms to promote health.

The early sociologists made use of such assumptions in their image of society as a dynamic system made up of interconnected parts. The analogy enabled them to say:

(a) society is a whole, functioning system;
(b) it is constructed of people and institutions, both of which have needs which must be met for survival;
(c) some people and some institutions are functionally more important than others;
(d) a healthy society is one in which there is order and stability; and
(e) a society, like any living thing, is open to careful scientific analysis.

The advantages of the analogy

By imitating the biological model, the functionalist can:

1. Justify a scientific approach to the study of society.
2. Place a strong emphasis on locating sources of order.
3. Adopt a holistic approach, looking for the interconnection between events and features in a society which might otherwise be overlooked (for example, suicide rate and religious affiliation).
4. Show how changes in one part of the system have an effect elsewhere (for example, just as poor circulation can damage the brain, so poverty can cause underachievement in school).

Some criticisms of the use of the analogy

(i) The model assumes that all social change is evolutionary, whereas much occurs in revolutionary ways.
(ii) Whilst causes of ill-health can generally be identified in living organisms, causes of social disorder and instability often cannot.
(iii) The structure of living organisms is fixed; those of societies are not. They can be changed in dramatic ways (for example, capitalistic/communistic)
(iv) The approach does not take much account of micro-analysis and sees little value in it.
(v) Equilibrium in a biological organism is beyond normal human control but in a society humans must intervene to achieve order.
(vi) It presents a deterministic image of humans, being manipulated by the structure and social organisation of their society.
(vii) The functionalist is led to the view that everything that exists must serve a function; but a hierarchy of such functions is impossible to establish.
(viii) The functionalist view is shown to be as ideological as that of a Marxist since it promotes a conservative perspective (that is, the value of slow evolutionary change, hierarchy and strong agencies of control to maintain the system.)

Conclusion

The analogy has some limited value and merit in drawing attention to the importance of certain social structures, but there are major criticisms which undermine its value.

Marxism

Marxists who operate with a conflict perspective would interpret the same events in a different way. For example, the Coronation, seen by functionalists as a source of social integration, would be seen by a Marxist as a means of deluding the public. The conflict structuralist would explain such events as evidence of the power of the ruling class to exploit and dupe people and to reinforce their domination, and that the failure to realise this is an indication of the power of the ruling élite to control thought and consciousness.

Criticisms of Marxism

1. Marxism sees a conspiracy at every level of organisation in a capitalist society so that exploitation can continue.
2. It is hard to prove that people are necessarily duped in the process of watching the Coronation.
3. Excessive reference to ideology may make arguments presented less acceptable and encourage a belief in the bias of the researchers.

Some possible strengths

1. It forces us to look critically at structures and institutions which may otherwise be taken for granted.
2. It is a perspective that concentrates on sources of conflict and may encourage social change to remedy major inequalities.
3. It provides an alternative view to the functionalist justification for the 'status quo'.

Questions

1. Examine photographs 4, 5 and 6. Functionalists see society as a system of inter-related cultural and institutional parts which fit to produce social order and stability. These photographs were taken of a street party to celebrate the Queen's Jubilee.
   (i) Suggest how functionalists would interpret the events.
   (ii) How do children know the rules of a party?
   (iii) What functions are served by decorating the street?
   (iv) At what point might such celebrations become dysfunctional?
   (v) What criticisms might a Marxist make of such events?

2. Marxists focus their analysis more on the causes of social inequalities. They see clear evidence of class divisions based on the control of wealth and political power.
   (i) Suggest some points that such an analysis might focus on in the photograph of these workers (photograph 8).
   (ii) Why might those living in this section of the city (photograph 7) be said to be marginalised?
   (iii) In what ways and by whom might such people be exploited?
   (iv) How might Marxists explain any failure of such people to act in effective political ways?
   (v) What criticisms might functionalists make of the implications of exploitation?

4

Source: Alec Gill

5

Source: Alec Gill

6

Source: Alec Gill

7

Source: Alec Gill

8

Source: Alec Gill

Some key differences between the two perspectives

Positivism

The traditional method of sociology. It is based on the attempt to emulate the methods of natural science:

(a) Identification of a problem.
(b) Collection of data.
(c) Explanatory hypothesis.
(d) Method to test hypothesis.
(e) Analysis of results.
(f) Re-test if necessary.
(g) Interpreting results: report.

Implications

1. There is an objective world which is capable of being understood in objective, scientific terms.
2. The whole of society is subject to investigation to see how behaviour is influenced by the structure and function of institutions.
3. Scientific analysis using interviews, surveys, statistical data, etc. shows the extent to which people are shaped and controlled by agencies of socialisation.
4. Behaviour is fairly predictable since the actors are 'trained' to keep to their 'scripts'. Order is thereby maintained and conflict managed.

Major theories include

(a) Functionalism: (structural/organic).
(b) Marxism: conflict structuralism.
(c) Non-Marxist sociology (emphasing conflict).

Interpretive Perspectives (Phenomenology)

There provides a different way of viewing social phenomena. Less emphasis is placed on the need to develop objective methods of study and more on the value of seeing the world through the eyes of those being studied.

Implications

1. There is not necessarily a social world capable of objective study. More interpretive methods are required.
2. If people constantly construct their reality in every situation of interaction then methods of interview, questionnaire, etc. are generally inappropriate. People may not know or be able to explain their actions.
3. People act according to the meanings they derive from situations of interaction, not just as a result of environmental pressures.
4. Behaviour is less predictable because the actors can 'improvise' as situations and knowledge change.

Major theories include

(a) Action theory.
(b) Symbolic interactionism.
(c) Ethnomethodology.

Method	Underlying philosophy	Perspective
1. Comparative	This stresses the need to use historical and cross-cultural data to understand social structures and institutions	Positivism and phenomenology
2. Survey/statistical	These stress the need for neutrality and objectivity in research.	Positivism
3. Ethnography observational	These stress the need to understand the subjective interpretations of actors.	Interpretivist (Phenomenology)

Choice of Research Method

■ **Different methods of sociological research are appropriate for different types of research problem. Discuss with reference to examples from empirical sociological studies with which you are familiar. (UODLE)**

Ackroyd and Hughes (*Data Collection in Context*) say that 'to put it very simply, social science is concerned with the explanation of human behaviour. Data of some kind will play an important role in such explanations, and to this end social scientists have devised methods for the systematic collection of data.'

Empirical evidence That which derives from scientific analysis. Knowledge is obtained from experiences of the world. There is some debate as to whether this is strictly the province of the positivist who adopts 'scientific' methods in research, since the interpretivist accepts subjective, data as part of his or her explanations. However, if science is taken to mean a method rather than a body of knowledge then so long as this is rational, logical and methodical and produces insights about the social world and why people behave as they do, then both perspectives may be said to produce empirical evidence.

Data Ackroyd and Hughes also make the point that what counts as data will be determined by the theory involved in the formulation of the research project. They say 'the world only exists as data through the interpretations that are placed upon it'. Marxists and functionalists, adopting a scientific perspective, may agree on the evidence but reach different conclusions about its significance.

Types of research problems A sociologist undertakes research to achieve an answer to a question. The research may:

(a) Add to the knowledge we have of the world and society.
(b) Explain a phenomenon which has been observed.
(c) Examine social problems.
(d) Justify a social policy.
(e) Explain both normal and abnormal behaviour.
(f) Monitor the effects of a particular policy.

The choice of topic This may arise out of the specific interests of the researcher or following a directive from a university department; a company; a government department; a charity and so on.

Methods of Data Collection

There are frequently questions which ask you to discuss, evaluate or examine critically, particular methods of data collection.

- **What are the limitations of the social survey as a method in sociology?**
- **Outline a method of gaining sociological data and discuss the advantages and disadvantages associated with it.**

General points

1. Data is collected by a method (or methods) related to the research design.
2. Problems should be revealed in a pilot study, when a small sample is taken and the method is tested on them. Revisions can be made if it is necessary.
3. The collected data must be analysed, tabulated and processed with greater care.
4. Conclusions must be drawn on the basis of the interpretations arising from the analysis. The original hypothesis may be accepted or rejected according to the findings.

Social surveys

Gardner (*Social Surveys for Social Planners*) says that the purpose of a survey is to provide information. The more accurate and comprehensive the information the better can be the planning. The hopes of the community can then be achieved more fully.

The classification of surveys

1. Descriptive: to describe what exists and to identify need.
2. Explanatory: to identify changes and their causes.
3. Predictive: to predict future changes and possible effects of new policies.
4. Evaluative: to evaluate the results of past policies.

Preparing the survey

1. It must be clear what the objectives are. A careful plan must be made.
2. The researchers must remain unbiased. They must be familiar with the problem area.
3. A pilot study must be undertaken to test the methods to be used.
4. The researchers must decide whether to use a random or a quota sample. This may depend on whether or not they have an adequate sampling frame from which to draw a random sample, and whether statistical tests are to be used.
5. Interviewers must be recruited and trained.

Sampling

Researchers normally obtain a sample of the large population in whom they are interested. It is not necessary to ask everyone so long as the sample drawn is representative of the whole. The quality of the data is more important than the quantity.

Random (probability) sampling Each unit in the population has an equal chance of being included. This is the only way of obtaining a sample which is representative (see page 20).

Non-random sampling (quota samples) These are easy to obtain but while they may be representative in some known respects (for example age, sex, class), they are not in terms of others. There may be interviewer bias, preference for particular faces, dealing with the more articulate, and so on (see page 21).

Sampling frame The lists, registers or records from which the random sample is drawn must be accurate, contain the relevant information, be up to date and be easily accessible.

Sample size Accuracy is increased by obtaining a large sample, but it is possible to obtain accuracy by using a sampling ratio of as low as eleven out of every 100 000 voters. Gardner suggests that samples of less than thirty or forty from a relatively large population are usually inadequate for statistical analysis.

Non-response The efforts of the researcher will be wasted if response rates are very low. Respondents selected at random may have to be visited several times. This may increase the costs of the survey but it is necessary. This can be a major problem with a postal survey.

The questionnaire This must be carefully prepared and tested to check its value. Words and phrases must be familiar and simple; questions must not be ambiguous; it should demand short and easy-to-analyse answers; it should be value-free and it should provide the data from which the hypothesis can be tested.

The researchers must decide whether to use it in a face-to-face interview or to send it through the post.

Interviews

The structured, formal interview follows a set pattern. All the questions are decided beforehand and the exact wording remains the same in each one. It is standardised and controlled.

The advantages of interviews

(a) They are more personal than questionnaires.
(b) The interviewer can clarify problems of meaning
(c) Answers can be probed if necessary.
(d) The respondent may be better motivated to reply;
(e) There is a better chance of a full response.
(f) The interviewer has better control over the situation in which responses are made. (Consultations can be prevented.)
(g) Problems can be more easily located and remedied.

The disadvantages of interviews

(a) The interviewer may cause antagonism in the respondent.
(b) The interviewer may be biased in selecting respondents.
(c) Errors may be made in recording answers.
(d) It may add greatly to the cost to recruit and train interviewers.
(e) Failure to train the interviewer may result in incomplete answers, mistakes, etc.

The informal, unstructured interview allows the respondent to expand and develop answers. A tape recorder is essential. The interviewer must be skilled and able to direct the respondent in order to obtain information relevant to the study.

Gardner describes the continuum:

Informal ◄——————————————► **Formal**

Unsystematic questioning	Casual conversation	Unguided non-directive	Gently guided	Firmly guided, systematic

The choice of the interview method depends on the aim of the study, the time and funds available and the skill of the researcher. The more standardised answers may help to provide a more specific picture of attitudes and opinions since comparisons can be made between answers. The more open-ended answers help to provide a more detailed picture which is particularly useful in a case study.

Conclusions

1. It may be argued that one limitation of the survey is that it makes use of fixed-choice questions. These are selected by the researcher and imposed on the respondent, and it is assumed that they have the same understanding of terms and concepts as the researcher.
2. Marxists might argue that opinion surveys reveal nothing more than the false ideologies of the ruling class which have been absorbed by working-class respondents.
3. Ethnomethodologists might argue that the only valid means of understanding people's behaviour is to observe it in naturalistic settings. Formal interviewing is an inadequate method.
4. Phenomenologists might argue that structured questionnaires do not allow people to define their own meanings and interpretations, so that answers to such questionnaires are largely valueless.
5. Other critics may argue that social surveys can help create attitudes which previously did not exist. This is sometimes used to explain the failure of polls to predict election results accurately.
6. It may also be argued that the limitations of the social survey are similar to the limitations of any method of data collection. They are all subject to the problems of reliability, validity and representativeness. Where these can be controlled the social survey should be a useful tool of research; if not its value is seriously limited.

The Reliability of Data

Consider the following more specific question.

■ **A major problem of sociological research concerns the validity and reliability of data. Discuss with reference to questionnaires and interviews. (Cam)**

Main points

McNeill (*Research Methods*) emphasises three key concepts:

Reliability This means that it ought to be possible to repeat interviews at a later time with the same respondents and the same interviewers and achieve the same results; it ought to be possible, too, for others to repeat the study under similar conditions and confirm the results.

Validity This means that the researcher should be confident that the picture which has emerged is one that really describes what is being studied and is not contaminated by bias, mistakes, or any kind of deliberate deception on the part of the respondents.

Representativeness This means that those questioned must be typical of everyone in the population affected by the event (for example, the election) with which the survey is concerned. If they are not, then the results will be misleading. (In the 1930s a researcher obtained a large sample from a telephone directory and failed to predict the result of a presidential election because it was an unrepresentative sample.)

Social surveys are used to obtain data quickly from a large number of people, using questionnaires and interviews. Their use is advocated particularly in positivist research projects. This approach is based on the following principles:

1. It should be possible to establish a hypothesis which can be tested.
2. It must be possible to obtain a sample which is representative and of sufficient size to test the hypothesis.
   (a) *Random sample*: each person in the population from which sample is drawn has an equal chance of selection. Everyone who can be sampled is listed and every *n*th name is drawn until the sample is filled. This allows complicated statistical tests to be undertaken on results.
   (b) *Stratified samples* may be drawn if the study requires division by age, sex, class, etc.; multi-phased samples allow detailed comparisons of results from a smaller sub-sample.

(c) *Quota samples* may be used where results are required more quickly and with less statistical precision (for example, street-corner sampling; 150 people in the quota: 75 men and 75 women all aged 30–50).

3. A schedule of questions must be drawn up. Concepts may have to be operationalised (defined for research purposes; for example, leisure will mean 'free from the constraints of paid work'). These should be tested in a provisional pilot study to clarify difficulties.
4. If the study is on a large scale interviewers may have to be trained.
5. The results must be carefully analysed and written up in a final report. This must be done in a thorough and honest way. All material must be open to inspection so that others may criticise or repeat the study and compare results.

Researchers may fail to produce valid and reliable results if:

(a) They have not followed the rules of the scientific method.
(b) In the course of interviewing they have antagonised respondents and received dubious answers.
(c) There has been low response rate, making it impossible to draw conclusions or apply statistical tests.
(d) There have been careless mistakes in coding and analysing results.
(e) There has been deliberate bias in the interpretation of results.
(f) Results are inadvertently drawn which are not supported by the evidence.

Sources of Data

■ **Discuss the advantages and disadvantages for the sociologist of using secondary sources of data in research.**

Sociologists make use of both *primary* and *secondary data* in research. Primary data is that which they collect themselves by means of interviews, questionnaires, observation and so on directly from respondents.

Secondary data is that which they collect from other sources and which has already been recorded (although not necessarily for public consumption) for other purposes.

It is important to remember that much research makes use of both types.

Secondary data can be considered in terms of level of reliability.

Low reliability (expressive documents)

(i) biography;
(ii) autobiography;
(iii) letters;
(iv) diaries; and
(v) novels.

Advantages

(a) Useful where the sociologist is conducting a case study or community study and wishes to gain a rich picture of the social life of a period, or particular people and their perceptions.
(b) Novelists and so on may have particular skills in portraying the life and culture of a period and reveal the impact of social change. (For example, Alan Sillitoe; *Saturday Night and Sunday Morning*, for alienation; Albert Camus; *The Outsider*, for anomie).

Disadvantages

(a) Such sources have a high level of subjective interpretation on the part of the authors.
(b) Such documents were not necessarily produced for publication (for example diaries) and may not be reliable.
(c) They must be handled with care to be sure they are dealt with in a systematic way – from most to least reliable.

Greater reliability

(i) journals;
(ii) quality newspapers;
(iii) radio broadcasts; and
(iv) TV programmes.

Advantages

(a) Media reports, especially in specialist sections, are likely to be accurate and well researched.
(b) They may be presented and compiled by people trained in the field. They can be subjected to content analysis.
(c) The data obtained may be useful in supporting evidence obtained from primary sources.

Disadvantages

(a) Reports in the popular press may distort issues and extract elements of sensation at the expense of accuracy.
(b) There is the danger of bias in the construction of press reports to suit the political position of the publication.

High reliability

(i) census data from the office of the Registrar General;
(ii) records from business firms;
(iii) registration data: births, deaths, etc.;
(iv) court records; social service departments, etc.;
(v) government records, relating to economy, etc.;
(vi) data from charities; pressure groups, etc.

Advantages

(a) The data is likely to be carefully recorded.
(b) It is published frequently and easily obtained.

Disadvantages

The key question for critics of such data is always: Who has collected it? For what purpose? What are the interpretations produced by those who make use of it? (For example, is more policing of an area justified by reference to an 'increasing crime rate' based on statistics which the police themselves have collected?)

Areas of Debate in Sociology

- **Is sociology inevitably ideological? (UODLE) Examine the view that sociology should be value-free. (AEB)**

Concept An idea of the attributes of the thing being analysed: its main characteristics.

Model An abstract construction in which various features to be analysed are organised into their related parts. For example, a functionalist model of society shows the relationships between parts of society.

Arguments for the view that it is not inevitably ideological and can be value-free.

1. Positivism is based on the principles of scientific objectivity.
2. To be objective means to study some social feature without allowing one's own values, moral beliefs or ideological preferences to influence the work in any way.
3. All conclusions reached will be true facts. The sociologist may disapprove of them but if so this is evidence of lack of bias in the study. Therefore, it is quite possible for the entire project, from choice of subject to final conclusions, to be value-free.
4. The interactionist, although using interpretive methods, could argue that seeing the world through the eyes of those studied avoids the danger of introducing one's own values. Behaviour is understood in terms of the interpretations of the other person. This kind of study also remains value-free

Arguments for the view that it is inevitably ideological and that it cannot be value-free.

1. An ideology is a set of beliefs and values which provide a person with a way of interpreting the world. Sociologists must have theirs, like anyone else. This is bound to influence them.
2. Their own values will influence:
   (a) the choice of subject for research; and
   (b) ways of interpreting data.
3. *Marxists* start from a radical and utopian view of society. They see a constant conspiracy by the ruling class. *Functionalists* hold a more conservative ideology which justifies the *status quo*, including major inequalities in a society since they are functionally necessary.
   Interactionists introduce value into their studies by defining a situation as 'a problem' worthy of investigation. Becker says 'it is impossible to conduct research uncontaminated by personal sympathies'.
4. Sociologists cannot escape their own past experiences or their intellectual analysis of 'problems' and their causes and consequences. Therefore, values and ideology enter at every point.

You should now consider a conclusion to the question; for example: Although sociologists must have values and their own ideological preferences, it would be possible to imagine a situation in which a study was conducted by a functionalist, Marxist and Weberian using agreed methods, which uncovered inequality in the distribution of housing in a city. They may all agree on the data, but each would interpret the material in a different way according to their values.

Theories in Sociology

- **To what extent and why should sociologists concentrate on developing theory? (UODLE)**
- **'No real observation of any kind of phenomena is possible, except in so far as it is first directed and then finally interpreted by some theory' (Comte). Discuss.**

Whatever school of sociology the researchers work in, the aim is to make clear sense of some aspect of social behaviour or social organisation.

In making their analysis they may make use of the following:

Hypotheses Assumptions or guesses about particular events to try to establish their causes. A very early stage in the research process.

Theories A network of ideas which state the existence of a relationship between a number of features which normally vary. The linked ideas help to explain the observed events. A theory explains by showing the relations between a number of variables.

Types of theory

Cohen (*Sociological Theory*) describes four main types:

Analytic

Like those of mathematics which are true by definition but which state nothing about the social world.

Normative

Specify ethical values.

Metaphysical

Not testable in a scientific way.

Scientific

Open to scientific test.

A strong theory	A weak theory
1. It is a scientific theory which can be tested and re-tested. Each time it produces similar results.	1. It is not scientific.
2. There may be some competing theories but they are less effective as explanations.	2. It is difficult to re-test (too time consuming, costly).
3. It helps to focus on new areas for research and raises new questions.	3. It leaves much unexplained, e.g.: how are middle-class failures or deviants explained if the theory predicts that the key factor is low class membership?
	4. The theory is too general or wide-ranging as an explanation.

Main points

1. Sociologists are concerned with the scientific type. Positivists in particular make propositions which at their simplest level link two or more variables. They state that whenever A occurs, then B follows. Such statements must be open to empirical test: it must be possible to observe results and see whether they confirm or refute the hypothesis.
2. A theory that linked social class, parental occupation, attitude towards school and academic success of the child should enable the sociologist to make predictions about the conditions under which particular patterns of behaviour occur; for example, the social class background of a child (in terms of parental occupation) has a strong effect on the child's academic performance and attitude towards school. The higher the social class the more likely is the child to achieve high academic success.
3. Karl Popper (a philosopher) says that it is never possible to prove any theory conclusively, because although the same results have been achieved a hundred times we cannot be sure that on the one hundred and first test they will not be different. This is true in both natural and social science.

You may be asked to assess or evaluate a theory. To answer such a question you must be able to explain what theories are and why they are used and then show why some theories are more useful than others.

The Relationship between Theory and Method

- **Different types of research problem require different research methods. (UODLE)**
- **'It is increasingly clear to sociologists that theoretical and methodological issues are well nigh inseparable' (Cuff and Payne). Examine this statement with reference to one perspective. (AEB)**

Every sociologist who conducts research sets out to find possible answers to a series of questions. To obtain these answers will require the use of an appropriate method or possibly a variety of methods.

To answer the question adequately you must be familiar with:

(a) The main sociological perspectives: positivism and interpretivism.
(b) The schools of thought associated with each (see pages 18 and 25).
(c) The methods associated with each (see pages 19 and 26).

Research methods will be selected according to:

(a) The school of thought in which the sociologist has been trained. The pure positivist will tend to rely on methods which will result in quantifiable facts. The pure phenomenologist will tend to prefer interpretive methods which may rely much more on observation and recall.
(b) The type of question being asked may make one method more suitable than another. It may not be possible to interview football fans on the rampage with a questionnaire in order to discover the factors that motivate their behaviour.

Note the examples below and on page 24

Type of study	Brief details	Methods	Examples
1. Case study	Usually small scale; a single group or event is studied in great depth. May help to reveal details of the processes by which changes occur over time.	Observation; interviews; questionnaire; press reports; letters; diaries; participation.	Lane and Roberts (*Strike at Pilkington*); see page 315.
2. Comparative	Information is collected about the institution or structure being examined in different societies so that similarities and differences can be established (e.g. families; political organisation).	Use of statistics; interviews; observation;	Durkheim (*Suicide*); see page 15.

Type of study	Brief details	Methods	Examples
3. Content analysis	A means of studying an event by examining the frequency with which it appears in the media; it is a means of supporting evidence obtained from other sources.	Books, papers, advertisements, etc. may be examined for bias (gender; race; political, etc.). Statistical data can be obtained.	Philo, Glasgow Media Group (*Bad News; More Bad News*); see page 120.
4. Experimental	(a) Researcher conducts a small-scale study in which subjects can be manipulated, observed and tested in a controlled environment.	Laboratory conditions are required; frequently statistical data is obtained.	Daniel (*Racial Discrimination in England*); see page 274.
	(b) Ethnomethodologists often make use of experiments where they seek to disrupt patterns of taken-for-granted behaviour (e.g. 'candid camera'-type situations).	Statistical results are not considered important. Researchers break social rules to see what happens.	Garfinkel (*Studies in Ethnomethodology*).
5. Life history	An unusual method; the aim is to provide an account of what it was like to live in a specific area or time by studying an individual who is representative of it.	Use of letters; diaries; interviews.	Blythe (*Akenfield*); Thomas and Znanieki (*The Polish Peasant in Europe and America*).
6. Longitudinal	A study is conducted and the sample re-interviewed at different periods of time to see what changes have occured in the group.	Questionnaires; interviews (observation less likely since sample is large).	Davie, Butler and Goldstein (*From Birth to Seven*); Douglas (*The Home and the School*); Newson (*Patterns of Infant Care*).
7. Observational Ethnographic	(a) The researcher is involved in the lives of those being studied, either openly or covertly.	Participant observation.	Whyte (*Street Corner Society*); Patrick (*A Glasgow Street Gang Observed*).
	(b) The observer is in the group but detached from it emotionally. In both cases the aim is to see behaviour in the context in which it occurs.	Non-participant observation ('complete observer'); e.g. classroom observation.	Hargreaves (*Deviance in the Classrooms*).
8. Questionnaires	(a) A researcher wishes to obtain data from a scattered population.	Questionnaires are sent by post.	The Census.
	(b) A researcher wishes to obtain detailed answers to a complex questionnaire; respondents can give elaborate answers.	Face-to-face interview. NB these may be used in addition to observation, etc. Opinion polls.	Willmott and Young (*Family and Kinship in East London*).
9. Statistical studies: Contemporary	(a) The researcher wishes to correlate variables by reference to statistical data (e.g. class and rates of delinquency).	Statistics are collected from such sources as court records; doctors' files; school records, etc.	West (*The Young Offender*); Willet (*Criminal on the Road*).
Demographic historical	(b) The researcher wishes to study the changes in population, family structure, etc., over time.	Use of parish registers; historical records; novels.	Laslett (*The World We Have Lost*); Wrigley (*Population and History*).
10. Community research	A large team of sociologists spend time in an area. Each member has a specific task. The aim is to provide a rich description of a place and its inhabitants, and processes of development and change.	Observation; use of public records; press reports; attending meetings; informal visits; formal interviews; diaries; biographical data.	Stacey (*Tradition and Change*); Frankenberg (*Village on the Border*); Lynd (*Middletown*); Gans (*The Urban Villagers*).

Examples

Questions asked	Method used
How many divorces occur each year? Are some categories of people more likely to divorce than others? Do children from homes where there has been divorce do less well in school?	*Positivist*: would use recorded statistics; use statistical techniques to establish correlations between occupation and frequency of divorce. *Phenomenologist*: might spend time observing children in social situations to see whether they had lower self-esteem than those from other homes.

(c) The sociologist's own preference for a particular technique may cause one method to be favoured at the expense of another.

Concluding points

1. It must be remembered that Positivism and Phenomenology are not necessarily alternative perspectives. Some researchers make use of both, and consequently adopt methods associated with each school of thought.

2. Some phenomenologists use forms of scientific procedures in their research. They adopt logical, methodical techniques, which may include forms of experimentation, in order to get at the meaning that people draw from events. In this sense scientific methods are not necessarily the monopoly of the positivist.

3. Generally, it is true that theories and methods are almost inseparable. Different schools of sociology have developed different types of theory. These require different methods of research.

Points of criticism

1. Some authorities (for example, Hargreaves, *Deviance in Classrooms*) dispute the view that a resolution between the micro (phenomenology) and the macro (positivism) has been achieved in a satisfactory way so that researchers can obtain more detailed insights into social behaviour. He is critical of the attempt by Sharp and Green, who work from a Marxist perspective. They claim that they can also use phenomenological methods in their work in a helpful way. Hargreaves suggests that they are too imbued with their Marxist methodologies to see phenomenology as offering anything more than an aid in description of events; they do not see it as helpful in the analysis of power and constraint, whereas Hargreaves argues that it does reveal how actors use and respond to both in their everyday interactions.

2. Liz Stanley (Manchester University study of *Social and Economic Changes in Family Life*) has also argued that the attempt to combine a traditional positivist and ethnographical methodology can result in more problems rather than more insights. In her research both were used, but it was eventually found that different methodologies produced different kinds of information and new difficulties. Researchers had problems in agreeing definitions, (a household, a family, etc.). Each group of researchers found they needed to focus on new issues, which began to fragment the project; more time and finance was required (which was not necessarily available). Much time was spent in argument during the time allotted for analysis of data, where conceptual difficulties were hard to resolve. The result was not complete failure, since new research problems were revealed, although this was not the initial aim! She also points to the danger that researchers who are funded by a government agency may be obliged to produce anodyne publications to satisfy their paymasters, who would not wish to see their money spent on purely academic debate about methodological issues.

The Phenomenological Perspective

Action theory

- **Explain and assess the view that social life is nothing more than or less than face-to-face interaction; sociology is inadequate unless it proceeds from that premise. (JMB)**
- **The primary objective of social science is the understanding of social action. Discuss. (UODLE)**

Questions such as these require a full discussion of the phenomenological/action perspective, with reference to Weber and later writers.

Weber's action theory

1. He advocated an interpretive sociology which would show how an actor planned action by taking account of the behaviour of others.
2. He said actors have motives and goals which derive from the broader cultural structure of society (the desire people have to maximise their opportunities to obtain scarce resources will be related to their social status in the society).
3. He regarded explanations which stressed only the causes and consequences of the social structure on behaviour as inadequate. They take no account of people's conscious intentions.
4. He said the aim must be to show how the social world is constructed by people in their interactions.

Meade's theory of symbolic interaction (1863–1931)

1. His work derives from Weber in that he also favoured the method of 'role-taking'; imagining oneself in the position of the person with whom there is an interaction. This helps to make sense of the person's responses and behaviour.
2. This ability is the origin of one's own 'self-concept'. We learn who we are through interacting with others. We develop concepts, thoughts and the ability to direct our own action in a way that has meaning and consequence.

Ethnomethodology

1. This a recent perspective in sociology. It arose from the work of Austrian philosopher and sociologist Schutz. It has more recently been developed by Garfinkel.
2. It means the study of the methods used by people to make sense of their everyday lives.
3. People try to establish rational patterns in events which occur in their lives. This is true even when the events are bizarre or weird. Studies on the TV programme *Candid Camera* illustrate this. People are able to impose some apparent order and sense even where there is chaos around them.

Criticisms of ethnomethodology

1. It is excessively individualistic and focuses only on small-scale interactions.
2. The researcher may often rely on the reports of people who are not trained observers.
3. It is difficult for the researcher to know when the principles on which a person is acting have been uncovered.
4. It may provide much description but not very much wide-ranging theoretical explanation.

Strengths of ethnomethodology

1. It does focus on a small area and show the rule-making process in social situations.
2. The perspective does help to show how rules emerge and how they are applied to make the social world orderly where no other explanations are available.
3. It does help to provide insights which other methods do not; e.g. how people cope socially without instruction or previous experience in particular situations.

4. Ethnomethodologists wish to uncover the rules that people apply in such situations, when there has been no socialisation or training in how to respond.
5. In their studies they devise ways of challenging securely held common-sense assumptions about the world so that interaction no longer makes 'obvious sense' to them.
6. Their studies show how when dissonance occurs (lack of harmony between expectations and facts) then people try to impose some rational explanation for the events to make them understandable.
7. The aim of ethnomethodology, therefore, is to reveal the general nature of social processes, not to try to change society.

Examples of their studies

(a) Students are asked to pretend to be boarders in their own homes. This forces them to consider the taken-for-granted rules of daily life. It caused much anger among parents, who were mystified by such bizarre behaviour; many thought their children were ill.

(b) Students assumed they were being given genuine advice from an apparent 'expert' about social problems. They received random yes/no answers, many of which were contradictory. Yet they were able to 'make sense' of the advice and see that it fitted a general helpful pattern.

Consider how you might answer the following questions making use of an interpretivist perspective (in all its forms: action theory, symbolic interactionism and ethnomethodology.) Remember, you must apply the ideas to the question you are answering. It is not enough simply to list facts.

- **Analyse in detail how social actors can be said to manage themselves and others in face-to-face interactions. What factors should be borne in mind when evaluating this particular sociological approach? (JMB)**

The Observational Method

- **Why is participant observation a central method of ethnographers?**
- **Participant observation provides a licence for unverifiable subjectivity. It has no place in sociology. Is this assessment justified? (UODLE)**

Ethnography

Mitchell (*A Dictionary of Sociology*) says it is usual to refer to the descriptive account of the way of life of a particular people as *ethnography*. Herskovits (*Man and his Works*) defines it as 'the description of individual cultures'. McNeill (*Research Methods*) says it can be taken to mean 'writing about a way of life'.

Ethnography derives from anthropological studies undertaken to observe the social and cultural behaviour of people in pre-literate societies and provide descriptions of them.

Participant observation

Becker and Geer ('Participant Observation and Interviewing in Qualitative Methodology') state that it is that method in which the observer participates in the daily life of the people under study, either openly or covertly in some disguised role.

Kluckhohn says that 'its purpose is to obtain data about behaviour through direct contact and in terms of specific situations in which the distortion that results from the investigator being an outside agent is reduced to the minimum.'

Types of observation

Complete participation

The observer becomes a completely integrated member of the group observed: Whyte (*Street Corner Society*) lived in an Italian slum district in the 1930s and observed the lifestyles and subcultural values of street gangs. He took on the role of secretary of the Italian Community Club.

Overt observation as participator

The observer informs the group that they are being observed: for example, Leibow (*Tally's Corner*). He studied the world of black street-corner men. He said 'they knew I was observing them, yet they allowed me to participate in their activities and take part in their lives to a degree that continues to surprise me.'

Non-participant observation

The observer stands apart from the group and observes in a detached way: for example, Collins ('Researching Spoonbending'). He describes his unobtrusive observation of an experiment through a one-way screen.

Criticisms of the method	Advantages of the method
1. The presence of the observer may change the behaviour of the group.	1. The observer can check to see whether the behaviour is affected by his presence.
2. It relies too heavily on the interpretations of the observer. It is too subjective.	2. The observer does not introduce subjective assumptions into the findings. The subjective element is located within the group observed. The observer must reveal these to show their influence.
3. The observer may become too involved with the group observed and fail to locate the meanings.	3. The observer can seek to increase reliability and validity by conducting observations at different times and places.
4. There can be no retesting of results since the behaviour is not observed under controlled conditions.	4. The observer does not set out with established hypotheses; these may develop in the course of the study.
5. The researcher can never be sure that the real motivations and interpretations have been uncovered to explain the behaviour.	5. McNeill makes the point that the ethnographer's central concern is to provide a description that is faithful to the world-view of the participants in the social context being described: 'what makes the work scientific is the care taken to avoid error, to be thorough, exhaustive and to check and re-check all findings.'
6. The method lacks the scientific rigour of positivism which deals in quantifiable facts.	

Why participant observation is used

1. The researcher wishes to know the meaning of events for those involved.
2. The method seeks to produce an account of the lives, behaviour, values, etc. of people in their normal environment.
3. Other methods may be unsuitable for certain investigations (for example, why gang members behave in aggressive ways).
4. It may be necessary to 'be there' to understand the dynamics of the situation being observed (for example, crowd violence).
5. The observer must look at the events with a fresh eye, uncontaminated by personal preference or experience.
6. The method may help reveal explanations for behaviour which the actors themselves could not explain.
7. Ethnomethodologists disrupt 'normal behaviour' to reveal the taken-for-granted rules about 'correct ways of behaving'.

Sociology: Art or Science?

Related to questions about major perspectives are some which ask quite specifically about the status of sociology as a discipline in terms of methods used.

It would be quite possible to tackle these using the material presented so far. However, another line of argument is possible. You should therefore consider the following.

■ **Is sociology more of an art than a science?**

■ **To what extent is modern sociology an attempt to combine the methodological procedures and objectivity of physical sciences with the speculation, imagination and subjectivity of the arts?**

The main difficulty with such questions would perhaps be dealing with the relationship between art and science.

1. Nisbett ('Sociology as an Art Form') considers that sociology is closer to art than science. He argues:
   (a) The key ideas of Weber, Durkheim and Marx are related to the great art movement of the nineteenth century known as Romanticism: concepts like anomie, ideal types, alienation, etc. are abstract and largely utopian.
   (b) Such terms are also non-scientific in that they are not easy to quantify or measure.
   (c) The sociologist, like the artist, can always learn from re-reading earlier writers. There is a limit to what the physicist can learn from re-reading Newton.
2. Dr Bronowski (a scientist) says there is a likeness between the creative acts of mind in art and in science: 'The discoveries of science, like works of art are explosions of hidden likenesses.' He is claiming that science is not unlike art.
3. Kaplan (*The Conduct of Enquiry*) argues that in science valid discoveries can be made by non-scientific procedures. These include imagination, inspiration and intuition. He concludes that it is a mistake to draw too fine a line between what is considered to be 'science' and what is not. This leads to the view that practitioners in the social sciences should also use any methods that provide insights and discoveries about the behaviour they are studying.
4. Many phenomenologists would accept that sociology may not be scientific, but that it doesn't matter if it isn't.

■ **Criticisms that sociology is not scientific are based on a mistaken view of what science is. Discuss.**

1. It is helpful to clarify your understanding of the question. For example:
   (a) The natural scientist works on the assumption that everything that exists does so in some quantity which is capable of being measured objectively.
   (b) The scientific method is seen as the process of using specific rules of procedure to gain knowledge, test hypotheses and analyse data to produce

new explanatory theories. Science produces objective and accurate information and develops our understanding of the natural world.

(c) The belief in the possibility that sociology can be scientific arises from the view that the logic and method of natural science are applicable to social science.

(d) Critics argue that such quantifiable techniques are not possible in sociology to the same high degree of accuracy so that prediction is impossible. Human behaviour constantly changes.

(e) However, there is debate about this argument based on the view that it rests on a mistaken impression about the objective processes of the scientific endeavour.

2. The debate.

(a) *Positivists* argue that it is possible to follow the model of natural science.

(b) *Interpretivists* argue that it is not necessary to do so.

Cicourel (*Method and Measurement in Sociology*) argues:

(i) Modern natural science works more with notions of probability in the statistical sense than with an absolutely certain universe; and

(ii) The social world is different from the natural world; people can act on their environment, rebel, innovate, etc. Therefore other methods are required (especially those of empathetic observation).

Kuhn (*The Structure of Scientific Revolutions*) argues:

(i) Scientists work with a scientific paradigm (that is, a model or theory) which is widely accepted by others in the field. This determines how they proceed. (For example, the earth is flat; a sick person can be cured by bleeding them, and so on)

(ii) In fact the world studied by science is created by the scientists studying it (For example, chemists become concerned about solving problems related to specific issues defined by others in the field and often on behalf of governments or other institutions with an interest in the outcomes).

(iii) Occasionally, new problems are found and scientific revolutions occur. This causes the paradigm to be revised. (For example, how to explain evolution; refute the theories of Newton; or the significance of a round earth.)

(iv) He concludes that even in science all procedures and all knowledge are relative not objective (that is, they see the world differently after each scientific revolution; they approach problems in new ways).

(v) What we regard as the scientific method is simply the result of being absorbed into the current paradigm. This defines current interpretations of what science is and what it does.

Kaplan 'The Logic of Enquiry' in Worsley (ed.), *Modern Sociology* has said:

(i) Traditional scientific enquiry has been concerned with discovery. Yet many are made by chance, guess, inspiration. It is not dissimilar to the ways that artists make great art.

(ii) He attacks the idea that scientists write 'incontravertible rules of procedure' which become 'accepted methodologies'. In fact, they are only advisers and should recommend methods appropriate to need. Imaginative procedures may be inhibited because they do not conform to the scientific ideal

(iii) He concludes that it is unwise to define too closely what is meant by 'the scientific method'. It is best to say that the researcher 'has no other method than doing his damndest'.

Conclusions

(a) Much sociological research has been conducted on the basis that it is possible to use objectively quantifiable methods; whilst it is difficult to make definite predictions about future behaviour it is possible to make strong generalisations based on findings (more children from Class 5 will perform less well in school than those from Class 1). The scientific method is applicable.

(b) There is a school of thought which argues that it is mistaken to draw a clear line between what is scientific and what is not. Researchers are justified in using any method which produces insights, including non-scientific types.

(c) Kuhn has argued that science itself is flawed and does not provide the objective model which it has been assumed to be the case.

(d) Marcuse (a Marxist) has said that science is ideological. It is based on values which serve the interests of the ruling elite. It rejects apparently unscientific concepts such as alienation or anomie, and claims that poverty, inequality and so on cannot be measured accurately. This is why sociology itself is seen, by the New Right, to be a subversive and unnecessary discipline.

The Comparative Method

■ **The Comparative Method is the equivalent in the social sciences of the experimental method in the natural sciences. Discuss. (UODLE)**

Giner (*Sociology*) says that the analyses of social change in history are carried out with the help of several methods. One of the most favoured is the comparative method. This entails the study of different groups and institutions in order to examine similarities and differences. The feature under examination may occur in the same society, for example a comparison of rates of mobility between different classes. They may appear in different societies; for example, rates of mobility may be compared between societies.

1. Fox and Miller (*Occupational Stratification and Mobility*) state that in making comparisons among nations, a leap of courage must be made. 'Many of the difficulties of individual studies are compounded in comparative perspective. Some national studies are of poor technical quality, but we have no choice of substitutes if we wish to include a particular nation in a comparison. Time periods differ in various studies; occupational titles and ratings are not fully comparable'. They conclude that it is important to remember that any comparisons 'are at best only approximations'.

2. Murdock (*Social Structure*) used cross-cultural research methods to examine the structure and function of the family. He sampled 250 societies, from simple to economically complex. He found that some form of family existed in every one. In particular he found evidence of the universality of the nuclear family 'either as the sole prevailing form of the family or as the basic unit from which more complex forms are compounded'.

3. Thompson (*Emile Durkheim*) says that Durkheim drew up classifications of behaviour (for example, suicide rates) to make it possible to test hypotheses about the relationship between social phenomena. The typology could be used when making comparisons. This is 'the nearest thing to an experimental method in sociology'. Durkheim favoured the comparative-historical approach because sociologists could not carry out experiments and had to rely on the method of indirect experiment (the comparison of similar cases in a systematic way). Thompson comments that this was, for Durkheim, 'the core of sociological methodology'.

The Experimental (Laboratory) Method

The experiment is an operation in a controlled situation in which the researcher tries to discover the effects produced by introducing one new variable into an experimental group and not into an otherwise identical control group. If the behaviour of the experimental group changes and that of the control does not, then the change can be attributed to the introduction of the new variable. This is a method favoured in the natural sciences. Laboratory conditions enable the experimenter to control all the variables. However, there are examples in sociology of 'field experiments'. These take place in the 'real world' and not in a laboratory. Those whose behaviour is studied in response to 'actors' engaged by the researcher do not know that a study is being conducted. Some of these types of research studies have certain of the characteristics of the comparative method.

1. Daniel (*Racial Discrimination in England*) wished to discover the extent of racial discrimination in Britain in 1965. He arranged for three applicants to seek jobs, accommodation and insurance cover. These were an Englishman, a West Indian and a Hungarian. Each was given 'identical qualifications', they were of similar age and had good command of English. The findings showed that it was the Englishman who did best in every aspect of the test, followed by the Hungarian. The West Indian always had the least success.

2. Myerson ('Experiments without Rats') asks, 'Have you ever walked into a café and noticed where people sit when they come in? Have you ever tried to see what happens when you try to share a table when there are other ones free? If so, then you have been carrying out an experiment of the sort that has recently become popular within a particular area of sociology'. She describes some studies which have been conducted to 'invade territory' in such public places and to 'violate expectations' of the unsuspecting public to uncover the rules of taken-for-granted life in libraries, cafés and so on.

Conclusions

1. Giner says that even if a research project is not specifically comparative, it is advisable that it should be put into perspective and its results contrasted with those of similar studies in other areas.
2. Although there are some examples of small-scale experimentation in sociology, the comparative method is the most frequently used means of explaining processes of change, especially on a large scale and of drawing attention to particular cultural and structural features of a society in relation to others.
3. McNeill makes the point that 'any sociologist who is trying to identify the causes of social events and behaviour is going to be involved in making comparisons, whether by means of surveys among different groups or by conducting experiments'.

Sociology, Social Problems and Social Policy

- **Examine the relationship between sociology and social policy. (AEB)**
- **Has sociology exercised any influence on the development of social policy? Illustrate your answer with specific examples. (UODLE)**

Sociology and sociological problems

(a) We live in a social world which has social and legal rules together with many institutions, all of which form the structure of society.
(b) Sociologists investigate these features of social life to understand how and why people behave as they do.
(c) They adopt various perspectives and make use of many theoretical structures in their investigations.
(d) Sociological problems are questions of investigation of the phenomena that exist around the sociologist. They exist and so can be studied, just as a physicist's 'problems' are those which relate to the physical world which he wishes to investigate.

Social problems

(a) A social problem is something which has been labelled by some individual or group as being socially undesirable. It may then become the subject of wider concern so that pressures are brought to remedy it in some way.
(b) Some may argue that the term 'problem' is attached by those who have a specific interest in the matter (usually powerful people who 'set' the social agenda).
(c) Sociologists are sometimes accused of generating problems as a result of their investigations.
(d) Although much sociological research is concerned with issues that have been designated 'problems'

Examples of sociological problems, social problems and social policy

Sociological perspectives	*Sociological problems*
1. Positivist method	1. How to investigate the social factors associated with suicide.
2. Phenomenological	2. How does a death come to be defined as suicide?
Social problem	The increasing number of drug-related suicides.
Social policy	What agencies or organisations can be introduced to combat the number of drug-related suicides?

(poverty, race, crimes, strikes etc.) some is also interested in how issues become defined as problems and the processes by which they reach the public consciousness.

Social policy

The drawing up and implementation of social policies involves political decisions.

1. In drawing up a social policy a government bases its decisions on its philosophy of how a society ought to be run.
2. Social scientists are often called on to undertake a programme of research because they are trained in the technique required.
3. Examples of research which was commissioned by a government department and on which social policy was later based:
   (a) Kelsall (*Women and Teaching*, 1965). The study looked at the number of women teachers who had left the profession, their reasons for doing so and the chances of recalling them later if necessary.
   (b) Rose (*Colour and Citizenship*). This was undertaken for the Institute of Race Relations. The aim was to uncover the problems faced by ethnic minorities in Britain and to suggest remedies.
   (c) Equal Opportunities Commission, 1975. This body encourages research to see how well the package of Acts in 1975 to increase the equality of women in British society is working and to advise the government accordingly.
4. Shipman (*The Limitations of Social Research*) makes the point that commissions are set up to examine crucial issues without social scientists being represented. Yet it is rare for evidence from social science to be ignored in the final report.
5. One of the most important contributions the sociologist can make is to reveal the gap between the real situation and that assumed by the general public. How problems are remedied is not for the sociologist to decide, but the agencies which implement social policy.

Suggested Reading

Works noted in this chapter

S. Ackroyd and J. Hughes (1981) *Data Collection in Context*, Longman

M. Atkinson (1978) *Discovering Suicide*

H. Becker and B. Geer (1957) 'Participant Observation and Interviewing in Qualitative Methodology', *Human Organisation* 16 (Fall) pp. 28–32

R. Blythe (1982) *Akenfield*, Penguin

A. Cicourel (1976) *Method and Measurement in Sociology*, Heinemann

P. Cohen (1968) *Modern Sociological Theory*

H. Collins (1984) 'Regarding Spoonbending', in *Social Researching*, ed. W. C. Bell and H. Roberts

W. Daniel (1957) *Racial Discrimination in England*, Penguin

R. Davie *et al* (1972) *From Birth to Seven*, Longman

J. Douglas (1964) *The Home and the School*, MacGibbon & Kee

T. Fox and S. Miller (1965) *Occupational Stratification and Mobility*, Studies in Comparative International Development, Vol 1.

R. Frankenberg (1957) *Village on the Border*

H. Gans (1962) *The Urban Villagers*, Free Press

G. Gardner (1978) *Social Surveys for Social Planners*, Open University Publications

H. Garfinkel (1962) *Studies in Ethnomethodology*, Prentice Hall

S. Giner (1972) *Sociology*, Martin Robertson

D. Hargreaves *et al.* (1975) *Deviance in Classrooms*, Routledge & Kegan Paul

M. Herskovits (1951) *Man and his Works*, Knopf

H. Kaplan (1972) *The Conduct of Enquiry.*

R. Kelsall (1963) *Women and Teaching,* HMSO

G. Kluckhohn (1940) in *American Journal of Sociology*

T. Kuhn (1971) *The Structure of Scientific Revolutions*

T. Lane and K. Roberts (1971) *Strike at Pilkingtons*, Fontana

P. Laslett (1983) *The World We Have Lost,* Methuen

E. Liebow (1967) *Tally's Corner,* Little, Brown, Boston

R. Lynd (1929) *Middletown*, Harcourt Brace

P. McNeill (1985) *Research Methods*, Tavistock

R. Meighan *et al.* (1979) *Perspectives on Society*, Nelson

G. Mitchell (1980) *A Dictionary of Sociology*

G. Murdock (1949) *Social Structure*

J. Myerson (1979) 'Experiments Without Rats', in R. Meighan *et al*., *Perspectives on Society*, Nelson

Self-Test Questions

Study the following material and answer the questions below.

Item A

"The methods of conducting sociology are often categorised as either quantitative or qualitative. The former includes questionnaires, social surveys and structured interviews; while the latter refers to unstructured interviews, non-participant and participant observation.'

The prevailing assumption of some sociologists is that qualitative methods are overwhelmingly associated with the social action perspective and quantitative methods are linked with the functionalist and conflict perspectives. Undoubtedly, there are substantial links between the theoretical perspectives and the various research methods. Most sociologists, however, use whatever method suits their purpose best, irrespective of their particular theoretical standpoint. Thus, a wide variety of methods are often used in the course of a single piece of research, with functionalists using participant observation, and questionnaires used in conjunction with the social action perspective."

Source: Adapted from C. Court, *Basic Concepts in Sociology, Checkmate*

Item B

The following passage describes the methods used in Simon Dyson's study of mentally handicapped children, conducted between April 1982 and April 1983.

"The children (twelve boys, eight girls) were aged between two and twelve when the parents (or foster parents) were interviewed in April–May 1982. The interviews were taped in the parents' homes and focused on any difficulties the parents had with practical problems, services or information. The files held by professionals on the same twenty children were also looked at. These included the files kept at the school; the Schools Psychological Service, the General Hospital; the Community Health Services. Only the Social Services refused permission for me to see the relevant files. Finally, various meetings between parents and professionals were taped. In addition, a fieldwork diary was kept which recorded informal conversations which took place with parents and professionals as well as details of other schools, clinics, training-centres and social work meetings visited."

Source: Adapted from S. Dyson, *Mental Handicap, Croom Helm.*

Item C

"A major dimension of unemployment research which can be identified in the literature is the qualitative approach. This research aims to 'let the unemployed speak for themselves' and is concerned with conveying the experience of unemployment. By far the best known of this type of work is that of Jeremy Seabrook and another good example is Marsden. The latter has explained the goal of this type of research in the following terms: '. . . we wanted a range of interviews which would offer a coherent if incomplete "mental map" of situations and feelings which are shared by many of the workless'."

Marsden's approach was severely criticised by one of the leading quatitative researchers, W. W. Daniel. He claimed that Marsden's approach risked distorting the picture of unemployment by selecting untypical cases for interview. In reply, Marsden pointed out that the in-depth interviews were good for demonstrating the effects of unemployment on the relations between the unemployed and their families and friends and on unemployed people's view of themselves. He went on to express the view that this approach was complementary to the statistical surveys carried out by writers such as Daniel."

Source: Adapted from M. McCullagh: *Teaching the Sociology of Unemployment, Social Science Teaches*

1. Suggest reasons why Dyson adopted four different methods of research in his study (Item B). *(5 marks)*

2. Referring to Item C, explain in your own words Daniel's criticism of Marsden's approach to the study of unemployment. *(1 mark)*

3. State briefly what sociologists mean by quantitative and qualitative methods of research (Item A, line 2). *(2 marks)*

4. Using material from the passages and elsewhere, assess the relative advantages of both quantitative and qualitative research. *(9 marks)*

5. The author of Item A (lines 10 and 11) states that sociologists 'use whatever method suits their purpose best, irrespective of their particular theoretical standpoint'. With reference to this statement, evaluate the importance of the various factors which may affect choice of method. *(8 marks)*

Source: AEBC (June 1991).

J. and E. Newson (1965) *Patterns of Infant Care*, Penguin
R. Nisbett (1975) 'Sociology as an Art Form', in Thompson and Turstall (eds), *Sociological Perspectives*
J. Patrick (1973) *A Glasgow Street Gang Observed*, Eyre Metheun
G. Philo, Glasgow Media Group (1976) *Bad News*, Routledge & Kegan Paul
——*More Bad News*(1980) Routledge & Kegan Paul
R. Rose (1969) *Colour and Citizenship*, Penguin
A. Schutz (1932) *The Phenomenology of the Social World*, Heinemann
E. Shils and M. Young (1956) *The Meaning of the Coronation*, in E. Shils, *The Torment of Secrecy*, Free Press
M. Stacey (1960) *Tradition and Change*, Oxford University Press
L. Stanley (1987) *Social and Economic Change in Family Life*, HMSO
S. Taylor (1990) *Social Science Review, Vol. 6, no. 2*
K. Thompson (1982) *Emile Durkheim*, Tavistock
D. West (1967) *The Young Offender*, Penguin
W. Whyte (1955) *Street Corner Society*, University of Chicago Press
C. Willet (1966) *Criminal on the Road*, Penguin
P. Willmott and M. Young (1960) *Family and Kinship in East London*, Routledge & Kegan Paul
P. Worsley (ed.) (1972) *Modern Sociology*, Penguin
E. Wrigley (1973) *Population and History*, World University Library
F. Znaniecki (1958) *The Polish Peasant in America*, Dover

Works for further reading

C. Bell and H. Newby (1977) *Doing Sociological Research*, Allen & Unwin
C. Bell and H. Roberts (1984) *Social Researching*, RKP
C. Brown (1979) *Understanding Society*, John Murray
C. Cuff and Payne (1984) *Perspectives in Society*, Allen & Unwin
J. Eldridge (1980) *Recent British Sociology*, Macmillan
M. Shipman (1981) *The Limitations of Social Research*, Longman

2

THE SOCIOLOGY OF KNOWLEDGE

There are quite specific questions set every year by some boards. These will make use of the phrase 'sociology of knowledge' in the question. However, there may be an opportunity to make use of your understanding of this subject matter in answering questions from other boards which relate to such topic areas as education and religion.

The specific questions relate primarily to the following areas:

1. The Marxist view which relates the sociology of knowledge to the social structure.
2. The phenomenological view which relates it to the process of interaction.
3. A more general question which asks you to show the contribution made by the sociology of knowledge to any one area of social life (for example education, religion).

It is preparation for this type of question which may enable you to answer a question from another board from this perspective.
For example:

- **'It has been suggested that education is the most important means of activity maintaining capitalist relations of production.' What do you understand by this claim? How adequate is it as an explanation of the role of contemporary educational institutions? (JMB)**

To answer questions on this topic you must:

(a) know a definition of the sociology of knowledge;
(b) be able to explain its significance and meaning;
(c) be able to refer to some examples of analysis undertaken using these ideas (especially from a Marxist and a phenomenological perpective); and
(d) be familiar with some of the strengths and weaknesses of the perspectives.

Overview

Philosophers have asked 'how is knowing the world possible?' Sociologists have answered the question by stressing the social context in which people claim to know about society and the use to which their knowledge is put.

In his *New Introductory Reader*, O'Donnell makes the point that much sociology is, in a sense, the sociology of knowledge. 'This is because the sociology of knowledge is concerned with explaining how different groups and individuals perceive and understand the world in often radically different ways'.

- **Examine critically the contribution made by one sociologist or group of sociologists to the sociology of knowledge. (AEB)**

Explanations of the sociology of knowledge

(a) Mannheim (*Ideology and Utopia*): 'The sociology of knowledge is the study of the relationship between knowledge and existence.'
(b) Berger and Luckmann (*The Social Construction of Reality*): 'The sociology of knowledge must concern itself with everything that passes for knowledge.'
(c) Coser and Rosenberg (*Sociological Theory*): 'The branch of sociology that concerns itself with relations between thoughts and society.'
(d) Marx and Engels (*German Ideology*): 'The class that has the means of material production at its disposal has control at the same time of the means of mental production, so that thereby, generally speaking, the ideas of those who lack the means of mental production are subject to it.'

The implication of these definitions

1. Knowledge is seen to be social in its production.
2. There is a relationship between the social structure and knowledge.
3. Knowledge can be used in the interests of those who possess it.
4. To have knowledge is to have power. This point can be illustrated in the following example.

In a society people make sense of everyday events in terms of the norms and values which they have absorbed as members of it. This is the source of their knowledge and understanding. Sudden and unexpected illness may be explained by the fact that someone has broken important social rules. If there are particular expectations about how to behave and these rules are not followed then severe consequences may be predicted. In pre-industrial societies such events may be explained by withcraft. The wrong-doer is bewitched. Those who control the patterns of behaviour (witch doctors or shamen) can use their knowledge of social rules to their advantage. They may cure or explain the death of the bewitched person. This ability gives them and those they may serve, power over others. Consider the following questions:

- **The sociology of knowledge attempts to relate knowledge to social structure. Offer a critical account of any one contribution to this branch of sociology. (AEB)**
- **Examine the similarities and differences between the major approaches to the sociology of knowledge. (AEB)**

Theories of the Sociology of Knowledge

Marxist interpretation

'The ideas of the ruling class are in every epoch the ruling ideas.' By this Marx implies that all knowledge is *ideological.* It consists of and reflects all those ideas and beliefs which justify class division and ruling-class power. The economic *infrastructures* determine the way that people think and behave in a society. By controlling their social *superstructure* and the norms, values and beliefs that relate to it, the ruling class ensure that their dominance is maintained.

The following writers use a Marxist perspective based on the sociology of knowledge to analyse the educational system.

1. Althusser (*Ideology and Ideogical State Apparatuses*).

(a) The education system is part of the superstructure.
(b) It operates to serve the interests of the *ruling élite.*
(c) The educational system will be used to reproduce the kind of labour force required: producing many low-skilled workers who can endure boredom and routine.
(d) Control is both by sanctions and punishments, but also through the imposition of ideological beliefs about the normality and inevitability of these everyday patterns.
(e) These ideological beliefs are imposed through such 'state apparatuses' as the mass media, religion, the family etc.

2. Bourdieu (*Reproduction in Education, Society and Culture*).

(a) One of the major aims of the educational system is the transmission of the dominant values of the society. In effect this is the culture of the dominant ruling class.
(b) It becomes defined as the most valuable and worthy of all cultures.
(c) He refers to this as 'culture capital' because when shared it can lead to the accumulation of wealth and power.
(d) Those who fail to do so are those who fail in the education system. This justifies their low-class position. They do not have knowledge and so a label of 'low IQ' is attached.

Phenomenological perspective

The following sociologists adopt a *phenomenological perspective* to the sociology of knowledge. Their emphasis is on the way that knowledge is socially constructed by people in the process of *interaction.* Their aim is to show how people construct their reality and make common-sense explanations of their perceptions clear.

1. Keddie 'Classroom Knowledge.' She says that the important aim for sociologists is to:

(a) Examine the meanings that lie beneath 'what counts as knowledge' in the classroom.
(b) Discover the methods by which teachers evaluate a child's knowledge. (She notes that knowledge presented in an abstract form is considered superior to concrete forms, for example.)
(c) Discover how children are *labelled* in terms of their ability, which is based on the teacher's 'knowledge' of them in the process of classroom evaluation.

2. Berger and Luckmann (*The Social Construction of Reality*). They look at religion in terms of the sociology of knowledge to see what part it plays in helping people to make sense of and know their society through their social experience.

They start from the assumption that every society has a body of beliefs, knowledge and values which they refer to as 'universes of meaning'. Members absorb and learn these meanings in their everyday social relationships.

(a) The universes of meaning help people make sense of their lives.
(b) People must know how their beliefs can be justified as 'true' and worthwhile, otherwise life would be without meaning.
(c) Religion is one of the important institutions which provides some evidence for the beliefs.
(d) The religious beliefs are also rooted in the structures of society. These give them 'plausibility' (the presence of churches, clergy and church-related rituals.)
(e) People can make sense of the mysteries of life by reference to the structures and the beliefs they engender and sustain.
(f) By these means people come to know and understand their own society.

Summary

The Marxist view

1. The use of a macro-perspective entails an analysis of how people know their society, its rules and values, by looking at the ways in which the ideology of the ruling class is sustained in every major social institution.
2. The superstructure of society is said to operate in the interest of this élite. Ideas about the class structure, differences in ability, the legitimacy of the social hierarchy, etc. are all imposed and reinforced through such institutions as education, family, religion, mass media, etc.
3. By accepting such knowledge people's lives are shaped and controlled.

The phenomenological view

1. The use of a micro-perspective entails an analysis of how people know how to behave and respond in the processes of interaction. It also examines how people acquire knowledge of each other in their interpersonal relationships.
2. This leads, for example, to an analysis of how teachers know what to expect of particular pupils, and pupils of teachers; how labels become attached; how we know who the deviants are and how to develop knowledge of what causes their behaviour. ('He's been a trouble-maker from the day he walked into the school . . . what more can you expect?')
3. It may help show how people justify and rationalise their knowledge by reference to wider institutions.

Some of the strengths and weaknesses of the views:

The Marxist view

Strengths

1. It provides explanations of why the poor accept their low-status positions and do not press for major social change.
2. It illustrates how knowledge can be seen to be man-made to promote particular political ends.
3. It explains why some forms of knowledge are more highly regarded than others at particular times (because they fit more closely with prevailing élite ideology).
4. It explains the relationship between power and knowledge and why it is difficult for those from the lowest classes to obtain power.

Weaknesses

1. It is an explanation that is itself grounded in a particular ideology.
2. It tends to produce explanations about beliefs which cannot easily be tested or refuted. (Those who disagree with the argument can be accused of false class consciousness.)
3. It suggests that there is a conspiracy to discourage people from seeking the knowledge which will enable them to achieve improved social position.
4. Weberians would argue that it may not be true to say that people are deliberately denied power. They claim it is available to all who seek it.

The phenomenological view

Strengths

1. Those who adopt it do not rely on the view that there is a dominant ideological view-point being imposed on people.
2. They look at people in the process of interaction to see how they extract meanings and assume 'knowledge' of events.
3. It corresponds more closely with 'common-sense' views that people do make use of stereotypes in order to develop a knowledge of what someone is like (by looking at clothes, manners, speech).
4. It illustrates the dangers of such assumptions and the problems that can ensue (e.g. from using knowledge of behaviour to label a person).

Weaknesses

1. Where the wider social structure is not taken into account it could be argued that knowledge gained is limited and partial. Class factors, for example, may be important in explaining aspects of behaviour.
2. Phenomenologists generally rely on interpretive methods to see how people obtain the meanings which form their knowledge. Such techniques are open to the methodological criticisms which can be levelled at all such analyses (see page 27).
3. Whilst opposing the deterministic view of the Marxists, this perspective can lead to a relativistic view in which all beliefs and knowledge are equally valid.

Question

Examining photograph 9.

(i) Suggest how Marxists would claim that the ways in which these children know the world is influenced by the power of religion, priests, etc. to impose values and explanations on them.
(ii) Suggest how Phenomenologists would argue that the children's knowledge of appropriate behaviour, norms, values, etc. arises from a process of interaction.

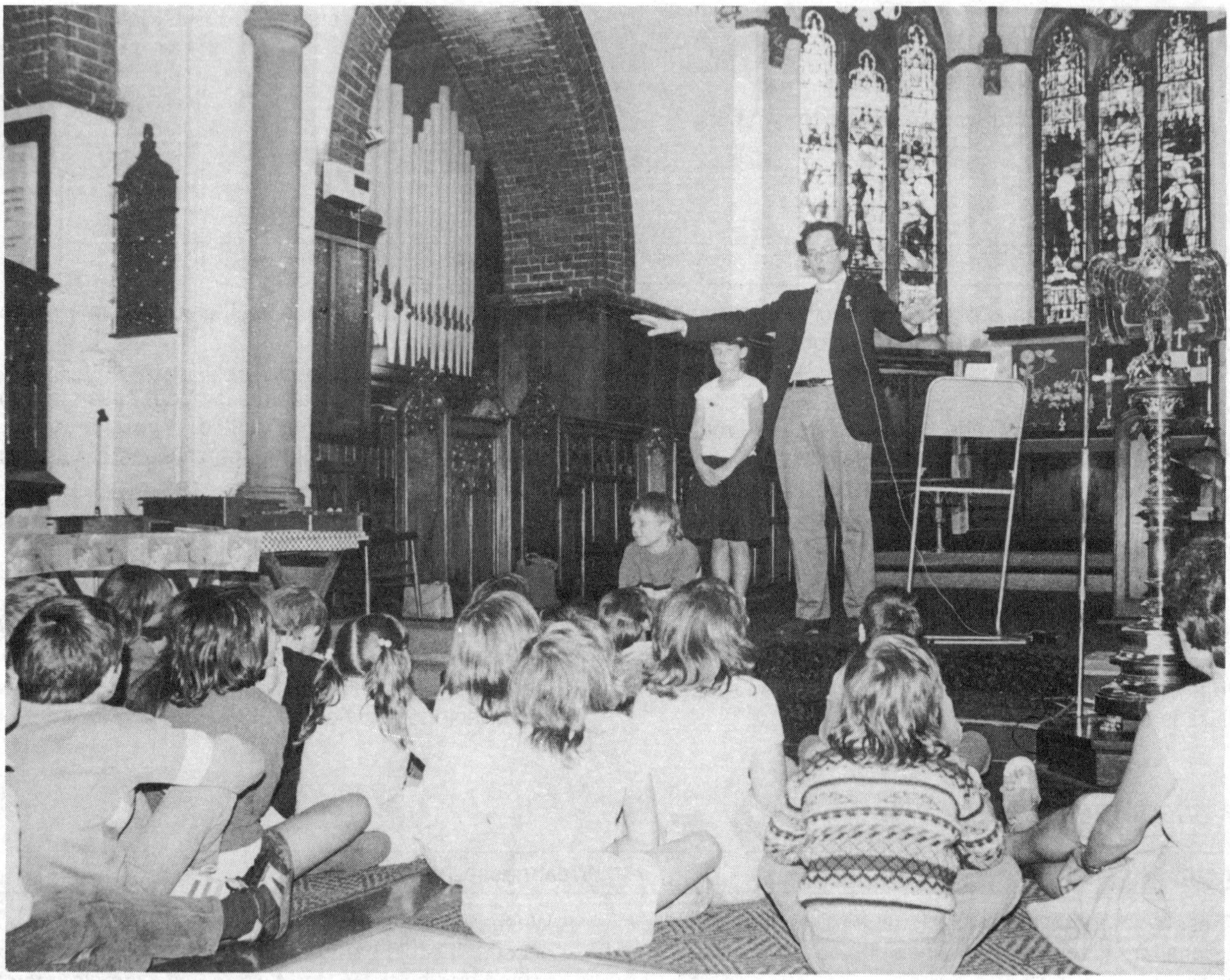

9

Source: Alec Gill

Suggested Reading

Works noted in this chapter

L. Althusser (1972) 'Ideology and Ideological State Apparatuses', in *Education: Structure and Society*, Penguin

P. Berger and T. Luckmann (1976) *The Social Construction of Reality*, Penguin

P. Bourdieu (1977) *Reproduction in Education, Society and Culture*, Sage

L. Coser and B. Rosenberg (1976) *Sociological Theory*, Macmillan

K. Mannheim (1960) *Ideology and Utopia*, Routledge & Kegan Paul

N. Keddie (1971) 'Classroom Knowledge', in Young, *The Myth of Cultural Deprivation*, Penguin

K. Marx *The German Ideology*, R. Pascal (ed), International Publishers

M. O'Donnell (1983) *New Introductory Reader*, Harrap

Works for further reading

N. Abercrombie, *Class Structure and Knowledge*, Basil Blackwell (1980)

P. Berger and B. Berger (1974) *The Homeless Mind*, Penguin

G. Bernbaum (1977) *Knowledge and Ideology*, Macmillan

P. Trowler (1989) *Further Topics in Sociology*, UTP

Self-test Questions

Consider how you might introduce a discussion of the sociology of knowledge into the following questions:

1. Religion and the mass media constitute a major source of knowledge and belief for members of industrial societies. Examine the view in relation to either the mass media or religion. (AEB)

2. Discuss the view that education in Britain is concerned with the creation and maintenance of an adequate and efficient labour force of men and women. (WJEC)

3. The major role of the educational system is to legitimise the inter-generational transmission of cultural capital. Explain and evaluate this view.

3

THE WELFARE STATE

A variety of questions on this topic appears on exam papers set by all boards. Some relate specifically to the welfare state, others combine a discussion of poverty and the distribution of income and wealth.

The main topic areas in relation to the welfare state are:

1. The aims of welfare provision:
   (a) To eliminate major social evils.
   (b) To increase equality.
   (c) To eliminate poverty.
   (d) To provide for those who fall on hard times as a result of factors beyond their own control.

2. The welfare state – analysis of issues in terms of different perspectives and theories: *functionalist*, *Marxist* and *Weberian*.

3. The welfare state and the family.

The Aims of the Welfare State

- **Why was the welfare state introduced in Britain? Have the main aims been achieved?**
- **Assess the contribution of the welfare state in achieving equality in Britain.**

To answer these types of question which test a general understanding of the aims, structure and consequences of the welfare state you need to know:

(a) something of its origins;
(b) some of the organising legislation; and
(c) some studies, statistics, etc. in order to discuss the levels of success that have been achieved. (These details will be fundamental to almost any question on the topic since you will need to discuss changing numbers in poverty, statistics relating to distribution of wealth, and income in many other related questions).

Definition The acceptance of total responsibility by the state (central government) for the welfare and well-being of all its members by the provision of appropriate social policies. The government provides minimum standards of livelihood as a right of citizenship. It includes the National Health Service, a free education system, and a range of benefits including pensions, unemployment and sickness benefits.

The origin of the welfare state in Britain

Leslie Paul (*Where After Welfare*) says that its development was a response to the perception that welfare provision should be based on social needs rather than on the individual's moral failure. Marsh (*The Welfare State*) says that attempts to relieve poverty have been made for over three centuries, but it is only recently that the concept of the welfare state has been introduced.

1601 Poor Law denied help to the able-bodied poor and kept those who received assistance at a standard below that of the poorest independent worker. The pauper's parish was responsible for providing relief.
1834 Poor Law Amendment Act introduced workhouses for the destitute.
1905–9 The Poor Law Commission produced two reports:

(a) The Majority Report supported the existing legislation.
(b) The Minority Report said the emphasis should be removed from the individual's moral failure to that of the community and the state which failed to cope with such problems adequately.

1906–13 The Liberal Government introduced the first limited benefits for the needy.
1909 Beveridge wrote *Unemployment: A Problem for Industry* in which he said there should be a move towards the redistribution of income to help abolish poverty. 'There should be bread for everyone before cake for anybody.'

The introduction of the modern welfare state

1942 The Beveridge Report was published: 'Social Insurance and Allied Services'. This produced a scheme to deal with the five giant evils of Want, Squalor, Disease, Ignorance and Idleness. His scheme was based on a system of contributions for insurance against hardship. The payment would be made by employers and employees so that all citizens would have a right to benefit if they fell on hard times. Assistance would be available from 'the cradle to the grave'.
1946 Bevan introduced the National Insurance Act which provided unemployment and sickness benefit; retirement pensions, widows' pensions and maternity grants.
1948 National Assistance Act which provided benefits for anyone whose income fell below a set level (replaced by Supplementary Benefit in 1966).
1946 National Health Service Act introduced a free health service with no prescription or other charges.
1942–8 This period marks the introduction of the modern welfare state. In addition to the reforms in social security there was also the major reform in the education system with the 1944 Education Act which introduced three stages of free education (see also page 129). There have subsequently been many developments and changes in the structure and organisation of the system with a gradual move away from the original intentions of Beveridge as more benefits became subject to means tests.

In order to discuss the issues in the questions on page 39 you must consider some of the evidence to decide whether or not its main aims have been achieved.

Has squalor been eliminated?

Beveridge saw this as a problem which related both to the needs of people and the ability they had to control their environment.

He was concerned about the quality of housing, for example:

(i) In the 1960s high-rise blocks, which have subsequently been criticised for their quality, replaced slum dwellings.
(ii) In 1981 the English Housing Conditions survey showed that there were 18 million dwellings in England and Wales, of which 1.1m were unfit for human habitation and 900 000 lacked basic amenities. Also, 1m required repairs costing more than £7000.
(iii) In 1986 the survey showed that improvements were slow. About 1.2m dwellings were in serious disrepair and more than 1m were unfit for habitation.
(iv) In 1990 only 1 per cent of homes did not have access to a bath or shower.

Table 3.1

1945–54	10 000
1960–64	70 000
1981–82	12 000

Source: English Housing Conditions Survey (1982).

Has idleness been eradicated?

In his plan, Beveridge assumed that there must be an employment policy which would eradicate idleness. 'The maintenance of employment is wanted for its own sake and not simply to make a plan for social security to work more easily'. He wished to ensure that those who could not work should not be unduly penalised.

Since the early 1970s there has been a decline in world trade, changes in technology and in economic policies in Britain. Unemployment rates have increased. Benefits are maintained at levels intended to discourage idleness. Critics argue they are too low to maintain families in basic comforts.

Table 3.2 Unemployment rates (millions)

1935	2.0
1945	0.1
1955	0.4
1965	0.3
1975	0.6
1980	1.7
1985	3.2
1991	2.5

Source: Social Trends, 22.

Has disease been controlled?

Table 3.3 Notification of infections diseases (000s)

Year	TB	Whooping cough
1951	50	195
1961	22	27
1971	10	19
1981	7	21
1991	4	17

Source: Social Trends, 22.
Infectious diseases have caused fewer deaths in recent years (although there are occasional epidemics).
A report by the water regulator Ofwat in 1993 showed that since 1988 there had been a threefold increase in the number of dysentery cases in England and Wales, from 3692 to 9935 in 1922. Hepatitis increased from 3379 cases in 1987 to 9020 in 1992.

Table 3.4 Infant mortality rates, (deaths of infants under 1 year, per 1000 live births)

Years	Rates
1870–72	150
1900–02	142
1910–12	110
1920–22	82
1930–32	67
1950–52	31
1960–62	22
1970–72	15
1980–82	12
1990–92	8.9

Source: Social Trends, 22.
Improved medical care and health facilities have reduced infant mortality rates and increased life expectancy.

Table 3.5 Life expectancy

Year	Male	Female
1901	46	49
1931	58	62
1951	66	71
1961	68	74
1971	68	75
1981	71	77
1991	73	79
2001	75	80

Source: *Social Trends* (OPCS).

Table 3.6 Infant mortality by social class of father, 1989 (deaths per 1000 live births)

Class	Deaths (000s)
1. Professional	6.0
2. Intermediate	6.1
3. (a) Skilled non-manual	6.6
(b) Skilled manual	7.8
4. Semi-skilled	9.9
5. Unskilled	11.0
Average all infant deaths	7.9

Source: Social Trends 22.
Infant mortality rates have fallen although differences remain between the social classes.

Table 3.7 Numbers employed by NHS

Years	Nurses	Administrators
1989	508 500	149 600
1990	502 200	159 200

Source: *Social Trends*, 22.
Although the NHS employed fewer nurses, more patients were being treated in fewer hospital beds.

Has ignorance been eliminated?

Table 3.8 Percentage of 16–18-year-olds in education and training after minimum leaving age, international comparison (1987)

Country	Minimum leaving age	Percentage of full-time students
UK	16	37
Belgium	14	82
Denmark	16	73
France	16	69
Germany	15	49
Italy	14	47
The Netherlands	16	77
Spain	15	50
Australia	15	50
Canada	16/17	75
Japan	15	77
Sweden	16	76
USA	16/18	80

Note The proportion varies between societies, but the UK rate is lower than the others, although the figure improves if part-time courses are included. *Source: Social Trends*, 22.

Table 3.9 Qualification of school leavers 1970–89 (%)

	1970–71		1980–1		1988–9	
Qualifications	Boys	Girls	Boys	Girls	Boys	Girls
2+ A-Levels (3 + H Grades)	15	13	15	13	18	19
1 A-Level (2 H Grades)	4	4	3	4	4	4
5+ GCSE (A–C) No A-Levels	7	9	8	10	12	15
1–4 GCSE (A–C) No A-Levels	17	18	25	28	26	29
No GCSE grades above Grade D	57	56	49	44	40	33

Note Although a high proportion of school leavers (especially boys) leave without formal qualifications (or with low grades) a higher proportion are beginning to achieve success.
Source: Department of Education and Science.

Table 3.10 Number of students in higher education (including universities, polytechnics, and colleges of higher education)(000s)

	1938–9	1970–1	1980–1	1989–90
Males	38	274	318	369
Females	12	183	216	320
Total	50	457	534	689

Source: Social Trends, 22.
There has been a steady increase in the numbers. This has resulted from improved standards in education, more opportunities to acquire qualifications, expansion of institutions offering degree courses and demand for well-qualified employees. The evidence points to improved education standards since 1944.

Has Want been eliminated?

The aim of Beveridge was to produce a scheme to ensure that everyone in the community would always be free from want. This is why he advocated three systems of benefit:

(a) social insurance payable on a contractual basis;
(b) social assistance payable on a test of need; and
(c) children's allowances payable to all without means test.

To achieve these ends the plan was:

(a) universal, covering every citizen regardless of size of income;
(b) equal benefit to all for equal contribution;
(c) those whose needs were not met through the social insurance scheme would be able to claim extra benefit if they could prove need. He assumed that such a group would gradually diminish. By these means he hoped that his plan would eliminate poverty, help in the redistribution of income and increase social equality.

There were some studies in the early 1950s (notably Rowntree) which suggested that this may have been the case, but later work in the 1960s and subsequently into the 1970s and 1980s (especially Townsend) has seriously questioned this view. For details see: poverty, page 247; distribution of income and wealth, page 228; and social equality, page 42.

■ **Is the welfare state necessary?**

The answer you give to this part of the question will depend on the arguments you have presented in your essay (see also the debate on equality, page 42.

■ **Has the welfare state increased equality and eliminated poverty?**

1. Consider the aim of increasing social equality.
   The answer that you give to this aspect of the question may depend on the perspective you adopt.
2. Consider the aim of eliminating poverty.

■ **Have the aims of the welfare state been achieved?**

Analysis in terms of different perspective and theories

You should notice how questions which have a similar central theme ('to what extent have the social and political aims of the welfare state been achieved?') can be phrased in slightly different ways. You must recognise the emphasis of the question to ensure that you are answering it adequately. The phraseology will often enable you to answer from a particular perspective or theoretical position. This is helpful because it enables you to impose a clear structure on your answer.

For example, some questions may put a functionalist point of view:

■ **The role of the welfare state is to maintain existing levels of social inequality in a legitimate form. Discuss. (AEB).**

This is asking: Do you think that it is true to say that the function of the welfare state is to maintain order and harmony in a society where major inequalities might otherwise cause disruption, by reducing their effects? In this way social inequalities are accepted by people as legitimate. Even those who do not do well in the system are given some help and assistance.

Some questions put a Marxist perspective:

■ **It has been claimed that the strongest continuing influence in the development of the welfare state has been the successful attempt of the dominant social groups to buttress the existing social and economic order. What do you understand by this claim? To what extent do you think it adequately accounts for the development of welfare provision?**

This question is asking you to consider the idea that the introduction of the welfare state has been to help disguise the extent and effect of social inequalities which in reality cannot be eradicated in a capitalist economic system. Welfare provisions have helped to buy off possible dis-

---

View that the welfare state has achieved this aim

1. If poverty is defined in an absolute way (see page 247) then the approved living standards and diets of most people must reduce the numbers in poverty.
2. Since the welfare state has provided people with greater security in the face of economic and other problems they may be less inclined to see themselves as 'poor'. There may be less subjective poverty.
3. Before the introduction of the welfare state the elderly and the unemployed, in particular, had no means of avoiding poverty. Now they can live above the level of destitution.
4. The poorest section of the population receive benefits which prevent complete impoverishment.

View that the welfare state has not achieved this aim

1. Townsend and other researchers have redefined poverty in their studies dating from the 1960s. They use a concept of relative deprivation. On this basis the numbers in poverty have increased steadily.
2. Even on an objective basis the numbers who claim supplementary benefit (the government's poverty line) is increasing. In 1991 government statistics showed that between 1981–91 the top 20 per cent of the population had grown richer; the bottom 20 per cent poorer.
3. The welfare state can only offer limited resources and these are generally inadequate. In 1991 a Social Services Policy Forum Report said the level of services varies between local authorities.
4. Poverty is deep-rooted and a complex problem. Coates and Silburn (*Poverty: The Forgotten Englishmen*) say it is not just shortage of money. It is a deprived lifestyle aggravated by poor housing, poor job prospects and permanent insecurity. The welfare state has not defeated these problems.

---

content. Other questions may ask for a discussion of a liberal or Weberian position:

- **Evaluate the contention that the welfare state is an attempt to resolve the divergent interests of different classes.**

Suggested Reading

Works noted in this chapter

K. Coates and R. Silburn (1970) Poverty: *The Forgotten Englishmen*, Penguin

R. Holman (1978) *Poverty*, Martin Robertson.

D. Marsh (1970) *The Welfare State*, Longman

L. Paul (1976) *Where After Welfare?*, SCM Press

P. Townsend and N. Davidson (1982) *Inequalities in Health*, Penguin

Works for further reading

W. Baugh (1983) *Introduction to the Social Services*, Macmillan

M. Bruce (1961)*The Coming of the Welfare State*, Batsford

T. Byrne and C. Padfield (1985) *Social Services Made Simple*, Heinemann

T. Cole (1989) *Whose Welfare?*, Tavistock

F. Field (1972) *To Him Who Hath*, Penguin

V. George, and P. Wilding (1976) *Ideology and Social Welfare*, Routledge & Kegan Paul

—— (1984) *The Impact of Social Policy*, Routledge & Kegan Paul

M. Hill (1983) *Understanding Social Policy*, Basil Blackwell

M. Loney *et al.* (1983) *Social Policy and Welfare*, Open University

R. Mishra (1984) *The Welfare State in Crisis*, Open University

C. Offe (1984) *Dilemmas of the Welfare State*, Hutchinson

R. Titmuss (1958) *Essays on the Welfare State*, Allen & Unwin

Theories of Social Justice

To answer the questions on page 42–3 you should be familiar with the following ideas:

Three theories of social justice and social equality: Functionalist, Marxist and Liberal/Weberian

Functionalist	Marxist	Liberal/Weberian
Social justice In every society there must be a hierarchy of power. Those at the top are the most privileged and they are responsible for the dispensation of social justice by being responsible for the welfare of those below them. Members of every social stratum have a function to fulfil. This hierarchical arrangement of power is recognised as legitimate so long as power-holders are seen to exercise their responsibilities for the welfare of others in some clear way. The structure of the welfare state is one way in which this is achieved. It is therefore functional in promoting order and harmony in society.	**Social Justice** This can only be achieved in a society when the hierarchy of power based on class differences has been abolished. The superstructure of society is organised in such a way as to promote the interests of the owners of the forces of production. From this point of view, even the welfare state operates to buttress the interests of this group by the provision of welfare for the poorest sectors of society.	**Social justice** This view, like the functionalist conservative interpretation, also accepts the inevitability of a hierarchy of power, but regards it as legitimate only if it has been arrived at from a position of initial equality. The liberal position is one which opposes privilege, but not necessarily inequality.
Social equality This is seen as an unattainable myth. It would be neither feasible nor desirable for everyone to share everything in society equally. People have different talents and abilities which help sift them into their class and status positions. The aim of the welfare state is to promote order in society, not equality.	**Social equality** Holman (*Poverty*) makes the point that social deprivation means lack of access to certain resources. Any commitment to countering these involves a belief that equality is possible. This would mean that it would be impossible for some to have advantage over others as a result of family connection, inheritance, etc. Those who suffer social and cultural deprivation lack equality. In an equal society everyone would have equal access to economic resources and to valued goals and happiness.	**Social equality** From this point of view social equality does not necessarily mean that everyone will become identical and share everything in the society equally. People have different talents and abilities. In this sense it is impossible to make everyone equal. The concept is best seen in terms of 'equal opportunity'. Everyone should start with the same chances of obtaining desired goals, but only those who show the most ability will achieve them. In an equal society, which is promoted by a welfare state, everyone should have an equal chance to develop their talents. Holman says complete equality is not possible but is a goal worth pursuing.

Questions

1. Examine photographs 10, 11, 12 and 13. It has been argued that the welfare state produces a dependency culture: there has been a move towards limiting benefits and extending the principle of repayable loans.
   (i) Specify some of the benefits available to those shown in the photographs:
      (a) mothers with young children;
      (b) the unemployed and low paid; and
      (c) The elderly.
   (ii) Consider the views that:
      (a) benefits should be increasingly selective in their availability;
      (b) repayable loans will exacerbate the problems faced by the poor; and
      (c) the function of the welfare state is to promote social order, not social equality.

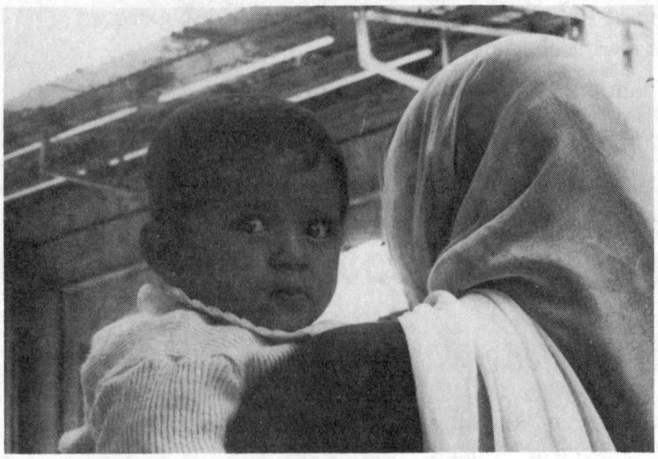

10

Source: Alec Gill

11

Source: Alec Gill

12

Source: Alec Gill

13

Source: Alec Gill

Self-test Questions

Study these extracts from newspapers and then answer the questions below.

Item A

These crimes occurred within a few days in one district of Easterhouse, a peripheral Glasgow estate where unemployment is high and where 64 per cent of schoolchildren receive clothing grants — that is, they come from families with very low incomes. The apparent connection between crime and poverty is dismissed by John Major, who attributes illegal behaviour to individual wickedness, and by the Education Secretary, John Patten, who blames parents.

Many if not most crimes in our locality are not reported. People whose flats are screwed are rarely insured. The detection rate for such crimes is low, so why bother to call in the police? Sometimes the victims know the perpetrators but are too frightened to complain. There is a connection between social deprivation and crime.

In establishing the connection, there is a danger of providing ammunition for the underclass school. New-right gurus, led by Charles Murray, claim British inner cities and peripheral estates are being taken over by a growing underclass of feckless young men, who refuse to work, and irresponsible lone mothers, who fail to bring their children up properly. This argument suggests that, supported by welfare benefits, they seek pleasure in drugs and further income from crime. He cites places like Easterhouse as examples of underclass "communities without fathers [where] the kids tend to run wild" and so become the next generation of criminals.

The underclass explanation of social problems has been gleefully accepted by politicians on the right to argue that social security benefits should be cut so as to drive the unemployed into low-paid jobs, that welfare should be transferred to a private market which can create those jobs, and that social workers should be more ready to coerce the young "barbarians", as Murray calls them, into acceptable life styles. The underclass proponents thus link poverty and crime in order not to reduce poverty but in order to attack the deprived.

If Murray lived in Easterhouse he would have learnt these lessons. Young people may be unemployed but not from choice: most want desperately to work and even compete to deliver newspapers or cut grass. Most children, over 70 per cent, live with two parents. Most residents, including lone parents, care deeply about family and community life. After all, they are the ones who suffer from local crime.

Consequently, many take counter action, like the father who has never known employment but works four evenings a week in youth clubs so that children have an alternative to the street. He is not unusual. Easterhouse has more than 200 community groups. It is not being over-run by an underclass. That is a myth. The reality is of a majority of ordinary and decent citizens who yet find themselves in the midst of crime and vandalism.

IF AN underclass is not the explanation, why is social deprivation and crime connected? A partial answer is that poverty and inequality generate circumstances which facilitate rather than deter crime.

Source: From an article, by Bob Holman in the *Guardian*, 24 June 1992, p.21.

Item B

CLEAR links between family breakdown and social disorder are being ignored by the liberal establishment, according to a study today claiming a socialist perspective.

There is little evidence that poverty and unemployment, rather than the collapse of family values, were at the root of the rioting last year on the Meadow Well estate, Tyneside, the study maintains.

It has been endorsed by Professor A.H. Halsey, the former Labour Party adviser and educational sociologist. In a foreword he argues that the left must face the need to make stable and committed parenting a priority of social policy.

Prof Halsey says children of broken families "tend to die earlier, have more illness, do less well at school, suffer more unemployment, be more prone to deviance and crime, and repeat the cycle of unstable parenting from which they themselves have suffered".

The study is published by the rightwing Institute of Economic Affairs, but its authors, Norman Dennis and George Erdos, both of Newcastle upon Tyne University, are described as ethical socialists. Compared with previous generations, they say, the rioters were not poor, short of work, badly housed or lacking public services. What they lacked was commitment to a wife and children.

Mr Dennis, a reader in social studies, and Mr Erdos, a psychology lecturer, cite earlier research on 1,000 children in Newcastle as proof of a link between the presence of a committed father and a child's development. They say the liberal intelligentsia is ignoring such evidence at a time when the proportion of families headed by a lone parent has risen to one in five.

"The notable aspect of national life that has been dramatically changing at the same time as civil life has been deteriorating, is the family," the authors say.

"The change to which we direct particular attention is the progressive liberation of young men from the expectation that adulthood involves a life-long responsibility for the well-being of their wife, and 15 or 20 years of responsibility for the well-being of their children."

Families without Fatherhood; IEA, 2 Lord North Street, London SW1P 3LB; £7.95

Source: From an article, by David Brindle in the *Guardian*, 14 September 1992, p. 3.

Item C

Poverty

David Piachaud

LOOKING back, the vision, the leap of imagination, seems almost incredible. Beveridge produced a plan to eliminate want, to remove the hated means test and to end idleness. That he did so when Britain was threatened with starvation by Nazi U-boats puts to shame the conservatism of current political debate. Yet what has become of Beveridge's vision?

Has want — now usually refferred to as poverty — been eliminated? Not, certainly, for the social outcasts. Nor has want been eliminated relative to prevailing standards. To define want there must be a poverty level that rises as the average income increases.

It can be estimated that there has been at least a threefold increase in the proportion living below half the average income level between 1953 — the earliest comparable postwar study — and 1988, using the latest available Institute for Fiscal Studies estimates. Now about one in five lives below half the average income level. Want, in terms of prevailing standards, has increased.

What of means testing? Enthusiasm for Beveridge's report was due above all to the intention to remove the means test, or at least reduce it to a minor role. When National Insurance was introduced in 1948, there were one million claimants of national assistance. Now there are four million recipients of income support and 1.5 million others receiving housing benefit. Two thirds of unemployed claimants now depend on means tested supplement. Beveridge's goal has not been achieved — rather the reverse — even if in some respects the operation of means tests today is not as harsh as 50 years ago.

Has idleness — by which Beveridge meant unemployment — been ended? For 25 years after the war, unemployment never exceeded 600,000. Times have changed: the average numbers unemployed in the last four decades were:

Fifties: 338,000
Sixties: 459,000
Seventies: 976,000
Eighties: 2,714,000

With an unemployment rate currently of 9 per cent and rising, no one could claim idleness had been ended.

Source: From an article in the *Guardian*, 11 March 1992.

1. Examine Item A.

Views concerning the aims and functions of the welfare state are contrasted:

(i) Clarify the views of the author, Bob Holman, in contrast to those of the Government and the New Right theorists with regard to:
  (a) the possible causes of poverty and crime;
  (b) the functions of the welfare state; and
  (c) the images of the poor and deprived.

2. Examine Item B.

(i) Clarify the findings from the research.
(ii) Contrast these with the views of Holman in Item A.
(iii) Specify any points of agreement and disagreement.
(iv) Suggest why the Right Wing Institute of Economic Affairs may have decided to publish research by 'ethical socialists'.
(v) Consider the ways in which the welfare state may:
  (a) assist stable and committed parenting (especially by fathers); and
  (b) undermine such parenting.
(vi) The authors suggest that there has been a progressive liberation from the expectations of a life-long responsibility for the well-being of wives and children among a section of working class youth. How might an author like Holman explain this?

3. Examine Item C.

Briefly summarise the author's views on the aims and success of Beveridge, written some fifty years after the introduction of Beveridge's plan.

4. Using information from all the Items A–C and other information you might have discuss the view that the welfare state has moved steadily away from the original aims of Beveridge and has become decreasingly effective in promoting equality and stable family units, and in defeating 'want and idleness'.

4

THE CHANGING ROLE OF WOMEN IN SOCIETY

Questions on this topic tend to fall into the following broad areas:

1. The influence of culture and biology on the division of labour between the sexes in the home and in work.
2. Changes in the domestic role of women and men in modern Britain.
3. Changes in the pattern of female employment.
4. The causes of changes in the pattern of female employment.
5. Some of the consequences of the changes in the pattern of female employment.
6. Some of the problems faced by women in employment:
   (a) the equality package; and
   (b) the effects of legislation.
7. Theoretical perspectives accounting for the position of women in society.

The Effects of Culture and Biology on Social Roles

- **Distinguish between gender roles and sex roles.**
- **Are the cultural influences more significant than the biological with regard to the role of women in society?**

Kessler and McKenna (*Development Aspects of Gender*) suggest that the term 'sex' should stand for the biological differences between males and females. Gender stands for:

(a) the social and cultural differences between men and women; and
(b) the personal and psychological characteristics associated with being a woman or a man (namely femininity or masculinity). Many of these characteristics may be 'assumed' to be biological (such as natural male dominance or female intuition) although there may be some evidence to indicate the significance of cultural influences.

The debate is about:

(a) whether the biological facts of a person's sex cause their social (or gender) roles to follow a certain pattern; and
(b) the extent to which there is inequality between men and women in contemporary society and the ways in which inequalities have been shaped by social factors, including the way society is structured and people's cultural expectations.

Morgan 'Gender' points out that just as in French 'there is nothing naturally feminine about a table (*la table*) or masculine about wine (*le vin*) . . . so this should serve to remind us that in sociology we are dealing with social rather than natural classifications'.

A *role* is a pattern of behaviour associated with a person's social status or social position in a group. The individual tends to behave in accordance with what is expected of someone in that position (for example, doctor and patient; lawyer and client). Roles are learned in the family, in school and in the workplace. This is part of the *socialisation process*, which is the way in which people:

(a) gain a self-image and sense of identity;
(b) gain values, attitudes and beliefs;
(c) learn the wider values of society;
(d) learn appropriate patterns of behaviour; and
(e) learn their gender roles: that is a set of expectations about the behaviour appropriate to each gender.

There is much evidence to show that there are differences in the ways in which boys and girls are raised in families and the way that people respond to them in everyday life. But studies of the socialisation process do not necessarily explain the source of such gender differences. These may be divided between two perspectives:

Biological arguments

These are based on the view that it is the biological facts of sex difference which determine role behaviour. Stress is laid on the significance of physiological factors.

1. In the Victorian period there was a belief in phrenology: that head bumps indicated personality. Those in females indicated love, dependence and domesticity; in males, aggression and ingenuity.
2. It was believed that measures of brain size showed males to be more intelligent because of their larger brains (later shown to be inaccurate).
3. Early psychologists, such as Galton and Burt believed that women were emotionally unstable, less logical than men and had a greater facility for simple repetitive tasks
4. In more recent years the 'split brain theory' suggested that the left side of the brain predominates in women, giving them superior skills in the use of language; in males the right side predominates, giving them superiority in spatial skills (science and engineering).
5. Some anthropologists have argued that because most of man's history has been as hunter and gatherer the role of the woman was to bear children and care for them. People have become genetically adapted to this way of life. Specific patterns of behaviour have become imprinted on human nature. Any attempt to abolish gender roles would be to run against nature. Power and politics is a male province, domesticity and child care that of the females in society.
6. Some functionalist writers have accepted the biological differences as the source of social inequalities between men and women. This is because it is the most functional way of organising society. The biological differences are not genetically programmed but they have led to practical differences in the organisation of society.

Cultural arguments

These emphasise the fact that behaviour is learned in social groups. The traditional division of labour in the home and in the place of work is justified by the values and beliefs which predominate in the society. These will vary to some extent from one culture to another. Many sociologists raise objections to the biological arguments because:

1. They are too deterministic. They assume that differences are inevitable and unchangeable. They justify the *status quo*.
2. Much of the biological 'evidence' comes from animal studies and it may be unwise to generalise from this about human behaviour.
3. There may be fewer women scientists than male because the image of 'a scientist' (an eccentric in a white coat) does not match the female self-image.
4. Girls may be diverted from science as a result of teacher expectation, i.e. they are not expected to perform well and so are given less time and attention.
5. Women have not had access to higher education until comparatively recently.
6. Opponents of the biological view argue that there are examples of societies in which there is no clear-cut division of labour based on sex differences. Morgan refers to the Kung who lived in bands of about 35 people. There was much overlap in work activities. Hunting was seen as being as much a matter of luck as of prowess and the skills required in foraging for food fully recognised. He notes how in other societies knitting, weaving and cooking sometimes fall into the male province, while such things as pearl diving, canoe handling and house building turn out to be women's work'.
7. Oakley notes how in some societies there are no rules about the sexual division of labour and the roles of father and mother are not clearly differentiated. In contemporary USSR, China and Israel women are important members of the armed forces and women are involved in many heavy manual jobs.

Changes in the Domestic Role of Women

■ **Despite the dramatic changes in the position of women over the last 100 years, the family is still the primary institution through which women participate in British society. Discuss.**

There are frequent claims that women in the modern family hold a more democratic position (Willmott and Young: *The Symmetrical Family*). This suggests that men take a greater part in the domestic duties of the household. It also assumes that because of major legal, demographic and educational changes, women have greater opportunity to choose whether to spend their lives independently, as housewives, as mothers, as companions or as careerists in dual-career families.

Legal changes For example, those which have provided greater opportunities to obtain divorce or separation and to receive economic protection (even if cohabiting).

Demographic changes These have included the decline in family size; improved methods of contraception, an increase in the number of nuclear families, and greater opportunities for social mobility.

Educational changes These have resulted in better opportunities for women to improve their education. Many more have been able to gain access to higher education and therefore to worthwhile careers.

Economic changes There has been a steady increase in the number of women in the work force, which is the result of low birth rates in the 1970s and a rise in the average age at which women have children. (See Table 4.1 on page50.)
However, some writers oppose this 'democratic' image.

Oakley (*The Sociology of Housework*) emphasises the extent to which 'housework' is part of the feminine gender role even in contemporary society.

(a) She argues that a full-time housewife without children will work a 40–60 hour week; those with one child: 70–80 hours per week. If these same women were employed outside the home, she suggests they would probably spend in housework additionally, some 30, 40 and 50 hours per week.
(b) The increasing dependency on drugs, tranquillisers and the high incidence of female shoplifting are all evidence of the sense of alienation and anomie suffered by many women.
(c) Women are socialised into the equation 'feminity = domesticity'. Through this socialisation housework becomes an accepted part of their role. Yet they cannot conceive of housework as 'work' in the same sense as what their husbands do is work.
(d) This attitude is validated by society's refusal to place an economic value on housework and to assign any status to the housewife.

Oakley (*Mothers and Children in Society*) argues that major inequalities remain in the home.

(a) Time-budgets in many industrialised countries show that men are not participating in housework and child-rearing to the extent that is commonly believed.
(b) We do not live in a unisex society and most families have a division of labour, according to which running the home and looking after children remain the wife's responsibilities.
(c) The image of the ideal woman who is capable of perfection as mother, wife and employed worker is subversively presented in the mass media, particularly advertising.

J. and E. Newson (*Patterns of Infant Care*) present a more optimistic view of the role of the father in the modern nuclear family. They rated highly-participant fathers as those who would do anything for their children; those who performed three or more functions were rated as 'helping'; and those with a score of less than three as 'sometimes helping'. Classing them into groups of participant, moderate and non-participating it was found that only 21 per cent were non-participant, 27 per cent were moderate in their help and 52 per cent were highly participant. They conclude that thirty years before their study the number of fathers rated as highly participant would probably have been negligible.

Note It is interesting that this study was conducted in the 1960s before the advent of the feminist movement and its more critical attitude towards what constitutes help in the family.

Alan Warde ('*Domestic Division of Labour*') reports the result of a study which replicated research by Pahl and Wallace. This examined what males and females had done in each household surveyed. These were categorised as 'home improvements', 'routine housework', 'domestic production', 'car maintenance' and 'child-care'. The earlier study showed that the domestic division of labour was unevenly distributed between men and women; women did a disproportionate share. The later study (with a somewhat different composition of more affluent households) supported the findings. They showed 'a strongly gendered division of tasks, with women doing routine household and child care jobs, far more than their male partner'. However, men were now more likely to be involved in some child-care and cooking than before.

Changes in the Pattern of Female Employment

There are a variety of questions asked on this topic. Some are concerned with the facts and their interpretation with regard to changes over a period of time. Others may test your understanding of more specific causes and consequences of the changes; and the success or failure of legislation designed to promote equality.

■ **Outline and discuss the major changes which have occurred in the pattern of female employment since 1930 in Britain.**

There are two points of view to consider, one which sees a steady improvement in the economic position of women and another which takes a more critical view.

The improvement view

(a) The demand for women's labour has fluctuated over time but has increased steadily since 1971. It has fallen back slightly in the 1980s as a result of increasing unemployment.

(b) About 12m women of working age have a paid job.

(c) They form about 44 per cent of all wage earners.

(d) The passing of legislation in the 1970s, especially the Equal Pay Act and the Sex Discrimination Act have helped ensure an improvement in women's earnings relative to men's.

(e) Women are increasingly holding positions of importance in contemporary Britain (for example, there is a female monarch; a recent female Prime Minister, etc.).

(f) Women's opportunities in the labour market are constantly improving, although these are influenced by whether or not the women have young dependent children, as well as their social class.

(g) Record numbers of women applied for and were accepted by universities in 1989/90. Women form 47 per cent of the undergraduate total.

The deterioration view

(a) Women tend to occupy the least well-paid jobs. They are those with fewest fringe benefits and opportunities for promotion. Two out of five women are in part-time jobs, which are among the lowest paid. Studies by the Equal Opportunities Commission (EOC) (see page 53) suggest that, despite legislation women earn less than two-thirds of men's wages.

(b) Women tend to be concentrated in particular fields of work, especially textiles, catering, health, clerical and educational.

(c) Women tend to be encouraged into 'male' fields of work at times of national crisis (for example, wartime) and discouraged in times of prosperity.

(d) The following data illustrate how the proportion of women in top professional jobs and status positions remained low, between 1985–93.

Bank managers	Less than 10%
Accountants	Less than 5%
University professors	Less than 4%
Architects	Less than 8%
MPs (of 651 in the House of Commons)	Less than 6%
Conservative Cabinet Ministers 1991/2	None
Senior civil servants	Less than 7%
Senior heads of local authorities	Less than 2%
Senior executives in business	Less than 8%
Chief Inspectors of police	2 women
General surgeons	Less than 2%
Judges	Less than 4%
Judicial members of the House of Lords	None
Senior (head) teachers	Less than 25%
Medical students	About 50%
Of all undergraduates	About 47%

(e) There is much evidence to show that the equality package has not been entirely successful (see pages 50–54). Few employers are able to offer facilities to assist women with young children.

The Causes of Increasing Female Employment

■ **What are the major causes and consequences of the increasing female employment? (UODLE)**

These can be analysed in particular time periods (according to the dates which may be specified in the question) and in terms of economic demographic and social influences.

1939–51 During this wartime period and post-war rebuilding of Britain there was a high demand for labour. Women entered factories as part of the war effort and many subsequently remained. This helped set the trend which showed that women were capable of such heavy work.

1951–71 The economic boom continued. Women workers helped satisfy the increasing demand for labour. Living standards increased and there was a steady demand for new household appliances which their extra incomes could provide. Demographic changes also occurred in this period. The birthrate began to fall in the mid-1960s following the introduction of the contraceptive pill. Family size began to fall, making it easier for women to return to work earlier. Social attitudes also began to change. The Women's Movement encouraged more women to seek careers after marriage. The educational system was expanding. New universities, polytechnics and colleges of higher education were producing more women with high-level qualifications.

1971–5 The 'equality package' was introduced (see page 52). This was intended to provide equality with men for women in work. The result may have been to encourage more women to enter the work force.

1975–85 Although there was a downturn in the economy, women continued to seek work in order to supplement family incomes (especially if the husband was unemployed). The revolution in leisure which started earlier in the 1960s meant that people had come to expect frequent holidays and access to regular entertainment. The additional income that women in the household could provide enabled this need to be satisfied. Many employers preferred to take on women employees since they accepted part-time work, and loopholes in the equality legislation enabled employers to pay lower rates than males would accept. In 1984 the Equal Pay Amendment Act was passed.

1985–91 The number of women entering the labour force increased; about 43 per cent were part-time and nine out of ten women were in various service industries; rates of pay remained lower than in equivalent work by men.

1992 The EOC estimated that 90 per cent of new jobs created in the next five years will be filled by women.

Table 4.1 Percentage of women aged 15–59 in paid employment, 1971–2001

1971	43.9
1981	47.6
1991	52.8
2001	55.1

Source: Department of Employment.

Useful studies

Mallier and Rosser (*The Changing Role of Women in the British Economy*) note how, prior to industrialisation, evidence indicates that women played an essential role in agriculture and domestic production. Industrialisation led to more women being employed in factory work and domestic service and their numbers in the economy expanded:

(a) In recent years less time is spent on domestic chores.
(b) If a woman has been employed prior to marriage it is likely that she will take the opportunity of returning to work because psychological barriers are removed.
(c) Once increasing numbers of women return to work this will encourage others, setting a trend.
(d) The advent of commercial TV may have been significant in creating a more consumer-minded society in which additional income is highly regarded.
(e) A fall in birthrate and improved child-care facilities have freed more women for work (see page 214). (This point is disputed by a 1990 study; see page 58.)

J. Martin and C. Roberts (*Women and Work*). Their study was the first full government survey of women and employment since 1965. They found:

(a) Although it is the norm for women to work before and after having children, men are still the main family wage earners. Working women still do more housework and child-care than men.
(b) Most women who take part-time work are mothers with young children.
(c) Most of the wives questioned thought that it was financially important for women to work. Few worked only 'for the pin money'.
(d) Overall, an increasing number of women are spending more of their lives in employment. Few adopt the male pattern of continuous lifetime employment as a full-time worker.
(e) Only a minority of full-time women workers shared domestic work equally with their husbands.
(f) Only 20% of full-time working wives have the same or a higher rate of pay than their husbands.

An interesting and contrary point of view has been put forward. Hakim, Principal Research Officer in the Department of Employment, argues that the rise of the working woman is a twentieth-century myth:

(a) By re-analysing data she found that the proportion of women working in 1861 was the same as in 1971.
(b) The census of 1851 noted that 25 per cent of all wives and 66 per cent of all widows had a specific occupation other than domestic work in the home. Between 1901 and 1931 that declined to one in ten married women. By 1951 it had again risen to 25 per cent. This suggests that women were typically involved in work in the mid-nineteenth century and then excluded from it in the early part of the twentieth.
(c) She also argues that there has been little or no change in the type of work women have been expected to do in the work force since the turn of the century. They have always been confined to typically 'female jobs'.
(d) There is no evidence of a trend towards greater integration of the sexes in work. Much will depend on the equal opportunities legislation to reverse the problems faced by women.

Coyle (*Redundant Women*) confirmed that paid work provides women (as it does men) with an important sense of self-identity and structure to their lives. The loss of a job had a serious negative effect on their lives. They objected to having to accept dependence on their partner. In this way men's work was found to shape women's lives.

A 1991 survey urged the regulation of men's working hours as the single most effective means of promoting equality at work. The longer men worked the shorter the hours of paid employment their female partner was likely to undertake; 34 per cent of fathers of children under ten worked more than 50 hours a week.

Leighton ('*Wives' Paid and Unpaid work and Husbands Unemployment*') suggests another consequence has been to promote more independent attitudes among women, who have come increasingly to see the oppressive nature of full-time housework. Furthermore, their entry into paid work influences their husbands' chances of seeking work when they become unemployed. She notes that where both partners are at home and there is a shortage of income, this compounds and intensifies marital tensions.

Conclusions

The question can be examined in terms of economic and social factors. Some of the economic causes of increased female participation in the labour market are the demand for labour in times of economic boom and for cheap and easily dispensable labour in times of recession; the growth of service industries; the need for more household income as house prices inflate, and a husband's job becomes less secure. Some of the social factors relate to the growth of feminism and attitudes of equality; the falling birthrate and other demographic features, and improved educational opportunities. Some of the consequences that can be examined include the effects of increased independence, higher divorce rates, single-parent families, the possibility of greater social mobility, better living standards, and improved job prospects for well-educated girls. Working wives may also influences their husbands' attitudes to work. Politicians have come to target women more carefully as their areas of daily concern are perceived to have broadened.

Consequences of Changing Patterns in Female Employment

■ **This century has been described as 'the woman's epoch'. Discuss some of the consequence of increasing female employment.**

Divorce rates Some writers (for example Hart; see page 81) have suggested that the increasing divorce rate has been significantly affected by the growing numbers of women in paid employment. They can achieve greater economic independence.

Living standards Martin and Roberts have suggested that most women who work do so to improve their family income and not just for 'pin money'.

A study entitled 'Families in the Future' found that without women's earnings four times as many families would live in poverty. For one in seven retired households women are the sole or main breadwinner.

Male hostility Glucklich and Snell (*Women, Work and Wages*) found that many men continue to resent and resist the possibility of women moving into male jobs and bringing about narrowed pay differentials, especially in times of economic difficulty. The trade unions are criticised for failing to help in promoting measures to benefit women, especially those in the lowest paid sectors. (Women comprise about 60 per cent of the lowest-paid workers.)

They are the most easily discarded workers Analysis of unemployment statistics suggests that because women are more frequently employed in part-time work they are more easily made redundant as the economy becomes depressed. They are caught under the 'last in, first out' rule because breaks for child-care reduce their length of service.

Stress Cooper and Davidson (*Stress in Work*) found that women executives suffer greater stresses and stains than their male counterparts. The woman manager with children at home has to cope with the additional workload and conflicting demands of career, marriage and family. Discrimination appears as a potential cause of stress in work. This may deter many women from entering or remaining in managerial positions.

Furthermore, feminist critics have noted that government policies in the 1980s made it more difficult for some well-qualified women to return to work, for example, the policy which encouraged community care of the sick, disabled and mentally ill, and the closing of institutional wards. Since women are the most usual unpaid carers their job prospects were limited as a result of these domestic responsibilities.

The effects on children Yudkin and Holme (*Working Mothers and Their Children*) found that:

(a) The vast majority of mothers of pre-school children made adequate arrangements for the care of their children whilst at work.
(b) A review of the literature on the subject 'shows dogmatism and relatively little evidence about long-term effects'.
(c) They argue that among school children there was some evidence to show that they developed more independence and maturity when mothers worked.
(d) There was no correlation between mothers working and rates of juvenile delinquency.
(e) They suggest that combining full-time work with caring for a child under three in the home is less desirable unless very good care arrangements have been made.

An increase in the number of dual-career families Fogarty *et al.* found that:

(a) There was an increase in the number of dilemmas which faced such couples; these related to domestic duties, child-care arrangements and so on.
(b) There were often more strains on the marriage.
(c) Where the partners were well-adjusted and could compromise, then a successful dual-career arrangement was possible and successful.
(d) The proportion of dual-income households rose from 55 per cent in 1976 to 67 per cent in 1986. But a gap widened between high-income and low-income households.

Increased social mobility of women Heath ('Women Who Get On in the World') argues that:

(a) The average working-class home is now more likely than at any other time in history to have one of its members in a white-collar job and to be exposed to middle-class influences.
(b) We may be witnessing a gradual transformation of the class structure as a result of the increasing employment of women in white-collar jobs.
(c) This could also have other effects; for example, it could affect voting patterns in the future. The mobility of women may weaken traditional party allegiances and produce a more discerning electorate.

The significance of women in the economy In recent years governments are becoming increasingly aware of the significance of women in the economy. A Report in 1990 said 'employers must recognize that women can no longer be treated as second class workers. They must recognize their career ambitions and domestic responsibilities'.

Conclusion

Feminists would argue that while women have increased their presence in the labour market, it has not been entirely on terms of equality with men. Some of the consequences have been positive and some negative. Women have benefited socially and economically, but they have also encountered much prejudice, discrimination and criticism. For example, Kate Millett (*Sexual Politics*) has argued that gender inequalities both at home and in work arise from male dominance. She describes this as the process of a patriarchal social structure which has come to be accepted as a normal feature of life. Other critics (especially Marxists) argue that it is capitalism which causes the exploitation of women.

The Problems Faced by Women at Work

■ **What factors inhibit the achievement of equal employment opportunities for women in modern Britain?**

Consider this structure as a way through the question:

The views of different feminists (who may include men) often overlap and are not always clear-cut and precise. But all tend to agree that the widespread inequalities in domestic life spill over into the work place.

Consider some evidence which could be used to debate the issues. Examine the table on page 53.

(a) **The liberals** would emphasise the ways in which the pressure for equality in recent years has been effective. In particular the implementation of an equality package from 1970–84. They would argue that in time attitudes will change and the inequalities facing women will disappear.

The equality package

1. *The Equal Pay Act 1970* Equal pay for broadly similar work.

The views of feminists about the problems that inhibit the achievement of women's equality in work

The radicals	**The Marxists**	**The liberals**
They see the oppression of women resulting from male domination in every sphere of social life. Society has a patriarchal structure (domination by men) This has come to be accepted as normal. Revolutionary change is necessary so that a matriarchy can result.	They argue that inequality is inevitable in a capitalist society. It always results in the exploitation of one less powerful group by another which controls the scarce resources (wealth, jobs, power, etc.). Revolutionary change is required.	They are sometimes seen as more moderate in their views. They describe it as a cultural problem. The socialisation process imposes values of domination and aggression in men. Change can result from legislation education, etc.

2. *Employment Protection Act 1975* Women become entitled to maternity leave.
   Pregnancy is no grounds for dismissal.
   Required employers to give back jobs to mothers within 29 weeks of childbirth.
3. *Social Security and Pensions Act 1975* Abolished lower rates of sickness and unemployment pay for women.
4. *Sex Discrimination Act 1975* Stated that it is unlawful to discriminate in the following areas:
   (a) Education;
   (b) Employment;
   (c) Housing, goods and services.
   The Equal Opportunities Commission was set up to offer legal advice and assistance.
5. *Equal Pay (Amendment) Act* 1984 Stated that where a woman is employed in work which is in terms of the demands made upon her (effort, skills and decisions) of equal value to that of a man in the same employment, she is entitled to the same rates of pay. This resulted in employers considering the concept of 'equal value' in job evaluation schemes.

(b) **The radicals** would dispute this interpretation focus on evidence pointing to the existence of the patriarchal domination of society, which cannot be legislated away since it is too deeply ingrained. They might suggest that research illustrates this.
   (i) Fogarty *et al.* (*Women in Top Jobs*):
      (a) Employers tended to see women as less reliable and assumed that maternity would end their career plans.
      (b) Women in top jobs found they were not easily accepted as equals by male colleagues.
      (c) Many older men had strong and outright anti-feminist attitudes.
      (d) Women were generally less successful than men because fewer were recruited for top positions; fewer were promoted and many were confronted by hostile attitudes.

   Studies prior to 1970 showed that the majority of women workers were involved in the lowest-skilled and lowest-paid jobs.
   (ii) Glucklich and Snell (see page 52), who examine the effects of male hostility to women and the failure of trade unions to act effectively for them.
   (iii) John Major's original Cabinet of 1992 was the first for 25 years not to include a woman.
   (iv) The fact that married women invariably adopt their husband's surname (not a legal requirement) indicates their subservient attitudes, which are exploited in work.

(c) **The Marxists** would examine the effects of capitalist structures on women to show the extent to which they are an oppressed group. Together with the radicals they would point out the extent to which the legislation advocated by liberal feminists has failed.
   (i) The 2nd EOC Annual Report (1978) revealed that three years after the Act women earned on average two-thirds of men's pay and the rate of progress towards equality was decreasing; firms were segregating jobs to retain lower rates of pay for women to show they were not 'doing broadly similar work'. Of 575 firms surveyed only 39 per cent had analysed their work force by sex. About 2 per cent were acting on their findings.
   (ii) The 5th EOC Report (1980) said women continued to earn about 73 per cent of men's pay. There were too many loopholes, 'Since the war there has not been a five-year period more unhelpful to women'.
   (iii) The 10th Report (1985) showed that on average women's hourly earnings had remained around three-quarters of men's since 1975.
   (iv) An EOC Report (1988) (*Women and Public Bodies*) said the 'old boy' network is keeping women from being appointed to public bodies in significant numbers. It said there was a failure to use the talents vested in half the nation.
   (v) A local government Report (*Developing Neglected Resources*) (1989) found only one woman chief executive out of total women employees of 1.75 million. Very few councils had attempted policies of equal opportunity.
   (vi) In the 1990s a woman who believes she is being underpaid because of her gender must face lengthy and costly legal proceedings while continuing to work for the employer she is suing.
   (vii) In 1991 at Maastricht Britain was the only EEC member to opt out of the Social Chapter which promoted equality between men and women in work.
   (viii) In 1992 a Government Report showed that the majority of women earned, on average, less than £216 p w while the male average equivalent was £355. In Europe, Britain had the second highest proportion of women in the labour force and the highest earnings gap between the sexes. The hourly rate for women remains 22 per cent less than men's.
   (ix) In 1992 the Chair of the EOC said that it was turning to European law because Britain's was too complex and inefficient. There are only about twenty inequality cases processed each year. Women who work less than 16 hours a week must stay with their employer for 5 years to qualify for protection.

'She's a bit like the barmaid at the local. Not exactly pretty. Not unattractive either. But she's got that sort of odd "something". The "something" that would make you want to take her off to the woods, and sort of, see what she's like. If you know what I mean.' *Description of a motorcycle in Hondaway magazine.*

'BATTERED divorcees tend to turn their new, placid husbands into wife beaters'.

'THE cost of each shower should not exceed 3p. This is, without question, the most inexpensive method of keeping your wife and children clean.'

'IN SPITE of the fact that most candidates were girls, the maths and science results were excellent.' *Report by J. Almond of the Academic Board meeting at Hardenhuish School, Chippenham, Wilts.*

'THEY at first thought the driver was a woman as it was being reversed with difficulty and the lights had not been switched on.' *Crime report in Newcastle Evening Chronicle.*

Mr Suthee said that corruption in Thailand has three root causes: legal loopholes, power abuse and bad wives. *New Sunday Times, Kuala Lumpur.*

'. . . the new arrangement is primarily intended for the uninitiated reader who, understandably, is often put off by such mundane chapters as "The Cow" or "Women" . . .!' *N. J. Darwood's introduction to the Penguin Classics' Koran.*

'Mrs ZITA KELLY, who from today is Lady Provost of Glasgow, came across in her interview with my colleague Jessica Barrett yesterday as a quiet, gentle, self-effacing person with little interest in politics.

And these are indeed pleasing qualities in a woman.

Her husband, Dr Michael Kelly, is clean and tidy, young and personable, intelligent and articulate.' *Charles Graham, 'Scotland's most penetrating writer,' in the Glasgow Evening Times, May 8.*

QUESTIONS in the South-western CSE examining board's English comprehension paper for May:

'Women always panic more than men in a crisis.'

'It was even more difficult than usual to make women obey.'

'It was even more difficult than usual to guess how women would behave.'

'WHY is it that women are such bad drivers? . . . If you see a car travelling at twenty miles per hour along the middle of a main road so that no one can overtake, you can be sure the driver is a woman!' *Royal Society of Arts Examinations Board, passage for aural comprehension.*

Source: Gaurdian

(x) In 1992 a Report by Equity (the actors' union) found that annual average earnings for men appearing on TV were £26 466 and for women £13 178. Women also did less well in their pay for commercials.

(xi) The *Guardian*'s 'Naked Ape' column provides examples of the negative ways in which women are viewed in Britain.

Conclusions

From a feminist perspective the unequal opportunities which women encounter in paid work are largely a reflection of their inequalities in their domestic lives. The explanations vary and include the following:

(a) The patriarchal social structure (Millett).
(b) The sexual class system that derives from biology. Inequalities arise from facts of biology. Women are dependent on men at certain critical times: in pregnancy, during early child-rearing, etc., which men have taken advantage of. This has resulted in unequal power relations (Firestone).
(c) The cultural values of society which define women as inferior. (Ortner); the ideology which developed during industrialisation defined 'a woman's place as in the home'. This allowed men to see women as rivals for jobs; trade unions supported this view. The role of housewife became a dominant model for girls (Oakley).
(d) Women's domestic duties, in which males play a minimal part, make it difficult for women to pursue careers. They become a reserve army of easily discardable labour. Legislation merely tinkers (largely successfully) with a deep-rooted economic problem (Marxists).
(e) Women's opportunities in the labour market are always limited because they are forced into the often lower-status, poorly-paid jobs which are based on their domestic skills (shop, café, factory, etc.). They do not have easy access to high-status occupations. This has been described as the 'dual labour market theory' (Barron and Norris).

Each view has certain strengths and weaknesses. While throwing some light on the problems women face, they tend to focus on one issue at the expense of another. It is clear that there are a range of explanations which can be established to show why it is difficult for women to achieve equality in employment.

Suggested Reading

Works noted in this chapter

R. Barron and G. Norris (1976) 'Sexual Division and the Labour Market', in D. Barker and S. Allen, *Dependence and Exploitation in Marriage*, Longman

Cooper and N. Davidson (1985) *Stress in Work*, Guardian report

A. Coyle (1984) *Redundant Women*, Women's Press

S. Firestone (1972) *The Dialectic of Sex*, Paladin

I. Glucklich and Snell (1984) *Women, Work and Wages*,

C. Hakim (1979) *Occupational Segregation*, Department of Education

Theoretical Perspectives

Contrast sociological accounts of the position of women in society.

The Functionalist view

1. Since the isolated nuclear family is the most functional unit for modern society, in the family the woman is primarily responsible for socialising the young.
2. Mothers bear and care for the young and so have the closest and most important bond with them.
3. Roger Scrutton (a philosopher) criticises feminism as an ideology because it fosters the idea that all social institutions are dominated by males. It seeks to make a person's sex irrelevant in determing social identity.
   He says it is an inescapable and beneficial part of the human condition that the sexes are socially distinct and perceive each other differently.
4. The sexual division of labour and of social roles reflects the differences in relationships between men and women.
5. Also in entering the labour market women help to reinforce the power of the capitalist economic system. They become a 'reserve army of cheap labour'.

The Weberian view

1. Harris (*Women in the Women's Movement*) took the view that to understand the position of women in society it is best to see how women interpret their own situation. She obtained her evidence from building up a picture of attitudes through conversations, in-depth interviews and notes from discussion groups. Her conclusion is that sexism (the belief that it is acceptable to treat people differently according to their sex) permeates the whole fabric of society.
2. She says that women have internalised male definitions of themselves (i.e. that they are less able in technical matters). This is a kind of 'slave mentality'.
3. She adds that as long as women accept this view they will always be open to exploitation and manipulation.
4. As to who benefits from the present division of labour in society she concludes that it is primarily men who do so, since they hold the power.

The Marxist view

1. Female subordination in society results from the emergence of private property.
2. Monogamous marriage developed to protect the institution of private property.
3. Men need to control women to maintain power and to ensure the legitimacy of their heirs.
4. Marxists would reject the view that a woman's apparent economic independence outside the family gives her more power within it.
5. Because women tend to enter the lowest-paid occupations in the labour market this helps reinforce their inferior status in society as a whole.
6. In considering who benefits from the division of labour, the functionalist would argue that everyone does.
7. In work women are less militant than men, subject to sexist attitudes and powerless to retaliate.
8. Gender consciousness and female solidarity are necessary for change to occur.

Kessler and W. McKenna (1978) *Development Aspects of Gender, An Ethnomethodological Approach*, Wiley

A. Heath (1981) 'Women Who Get On in the World,'

G. Leighton (1992) 'Wives' Paid and Unpaid Work and Husbands' Unemployment', *Sociology Review*, Vol. 1, No. 3

T. Maillier and M. Rosser (1976) *The Changing Role of Women in the British Economy*

J. Martin and C. Roberts (1984) *Women and Employment*, HMSO

K. Millett (1970) *Sexual Politics*, Doubleday

D. Morgan (1986) 'Gender', in R. Burgess (ed), *Key Variables in Social Investigation*, Routledge & Kegan Paul

J. and E. Newson (1965) *Patterns of Infant Care*, Penguin

A. Oakley (1981) *Subject Women*, Martin Robertson

A. Oakley (1980) *Mothers and Children in Society*

A. Oakley (1974) *The Sociology of Housework*, Martin Robertson

S. Ortner (1974) 'Is Female to Male as Nature is to Culture? in M. Rosaldo and L. Lamphere (eds), *Women, Culture and Society*, Stanford University Press

A. Warde (1990) 'Domestic Division of Labour' in *Social Studies Review* Vol. 6 No. 1

P. Willmott and M. Young (1975) *The Symmetrical Family*

S. Yudkin and A. Holmes (1965) *Working Mothers and Their Children*, Sphere

Works for further reading

V. Beechey and T. Perkins (1987) *A Matter of Hours*, Polity Press

R. Crompton and K. Sanderson (1990) *Gendered Jobs and Social Change*, Unwin Hyman 1990.

J. Finch (1983) *Married to the Job*, Allen & Unwin

R. Miles 'Past Imperfect' Women and History, *Social Studies Review*, Vol.6, No.2

R. Pahl (1984) *Division of Labour*, Blackwell

J. Pahl (1989) *Money and Marriage*, Macmillan

S. Sharpe (1976) *Just Like a Girl*, Penguin

Questions

Examine photographs 14–16.

There is evidence to suggest that the equality package of 1975 has not enabled women to achieve full equality with men.

1. Consider photograph: 14
  (i) Suggest why the majority of women continue to work in the lowest-paid occupational groups.
  (ii) Why might the career opportunities of these women be limited?
  (iii) Why do some occupations remain dominated by men even though they require no special strength or skill that a woman could not master (for example, in the large company for which they work, males dominate the ownership and the management; the chef in charge of the kitchens is a man and all the goods vehicles are driven by men).

2. Contrast the possible explanations of a radical feminist and those of a Functionalist.

3. Consider photographs 15 and 16.
  (i) Explain the concept of 'gender socialisation'.

14

Source: Alec Gill

15

Source: Alec Gill

  (ii) Do the images promote dangerous generalisations about expectations of the behaviour patterns of boys and girls or is it likely that early socialisation promotes differences in job expectations?
  (iii) Suggest how an interactionist might examine the question.

16

Source: Alec Gill

Self-test Questions

I. Study these extracts from newspapers and then answer the questions below.

Item A

THE ENGLISH revolution of the 1640s and 1650s is claimed as a golden age for the publicising of women's views. Women preached in public, women published pamphlets on the issues of the day, women led and participated in demonstrations to lobby Parliament and Quaker women walked naked through city streets as a sign of their salvation. But was this not more of a swansong than the beginning of a new era for women?

From the point of view of the woman of middling status, there is much to recommend the period from the later 15th century to the mid-16th century. Foreign commentators were much struck by what they regarded as the tremendous freedom enjoyed by the English townswoman in the 16th century. Her position, her freedom of action and freedom to dispose of her property, her capacity to act independently and to have an autonomous existence were much eroded during the 17th century. She might have gained a religious voice, but she certainly gained no status in any churches, especially not the kind of status which might mean exercising authority over men.

To have been a rich, healthy noblewoman at any period of history has much to recommend it. To be a poor woman at any period is to be excluded from the very mechanisms which allow people to transcend their immediate circumstances. The life of a woman of the middling sort in 16th and 17th century England has more to recommend it than many other periods of history. But there are few compensations for the 20th century freedom from the desperate fear of another confinement and from daily anxiety about the survival of your children.

Source: Extract from an article by Laurence in the *Guardian,* August 1992, p. 19.

Item B

THE number of women running their own businesses has nearly trebled over the past decade and three out of 10 new firms are started by women, with the rate of growth of women entering self-employment far exceeding that of men.

This phenomenon is not confined to Britain. Indeed there has been an even larger increase in the number of women entrepreneurs in Germany where they account for two out of five of all new businesses.

In the US the number of women business owners increased by 74 per cent over a decade, while more than a quarter of all business owners in Finland and Sweden are women.

To these official statistics have to be added the "hidden" self-employed and business operators, such as those running bed and breakfast accommodation or "helping" their partners.

To some observers this rapid growth is evidence that women are taking the entrepreneurial route as a means of getting round the "glass ceiling".

That ceiling is the invisible but very real barrier through which women can see the senior positions for which they have the potential, experience and qualifications but which for a variety of reasons, including prejudice, they often do not achieve.

While independence is an important factor — as it is with men who start businesses — recent research has highlighted the fact that female self-employment is also often initiated as a result of the frustration women have experienced with inequality in employment opportunities.

Source: Extract from an article by Clive Woodcock in the *Guardian,* 13 July 1992.

Item C

Lack of childcare 'confines women to marginal work'

Celia Weston
Labour Correspondent

WOMEN are still segregated into low-paid, low-status jobs by the lack of childcare facilities and stereotyping by parents and schools, the Equal Opportunities Commission said yesterday.

The claim was made as the Government published Skill Needs in Britain 1990, with figures, disclosed by the Guardian this month, showing that nearly one in five employers has difficulties in recruiting skilled staff.

Joanna Foster, commission chairwoman, said: "Despite the projections of labour and skill shortages, women and men are still channelled into male and female areas, a segregation which is traced back to the classroom and the attitudes of parents."

Women make up 44 per cent of the workforce, compared with 40 per cent in 1981, but most remain in traditional female jobs — in hotels and catering and other service industries.

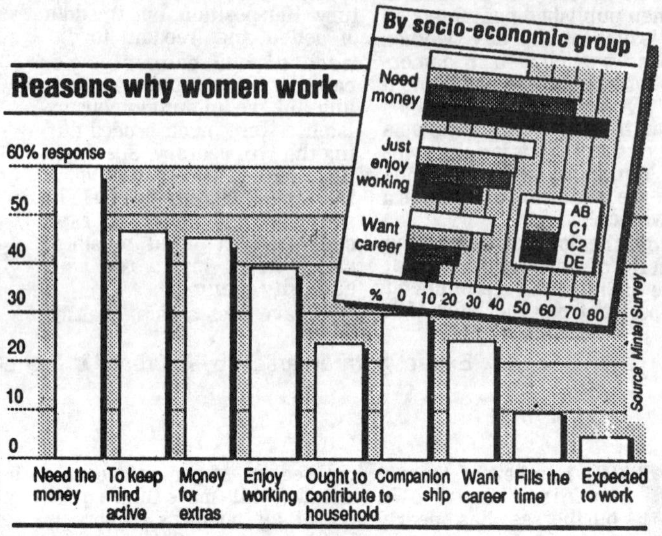

The EOC's annual statistical report on the social and economic position of women shows that only 2 per cent of children aged under five can find places in local authority and private day-care centres and nurseries, with great disparities between towns and the countryside.

It was this "pitiful lack of childcare which confines most women to part-time, marginalised, low-paid work," Ms Foster said.

The number of children under 14 was expected to increase to the end of the century, putting even greater pressure on childcare provision.

More childcare was essential if women were to bridge the skills gap and compensate for the decreasing number of school leavers.

"The nature and size of the challenge makes this much too big and complex an issue to be left to market forces," Ms Foster said. "Employers cannot afford this by themselves. The Government must help."

The pay gap between men and women has narrowed slightly, but pay for women manual workers was only 71.5 per cent of men's, and in non-manual jobs only 63.1 per cent, the EOC report says.

In 1988, out of a part-time workforce of more than 5 million, more than 4 million were women. Regionally, the percentage of women working part-time varied between 48 per cent in Yorks and Humber to 30 per cent in Greater London.

Women filled 26.5 per cent of managerial posts in 1988, compared with 24 per cent in 1983.

Women and Men in Britain 1990, Equal Opportunities Commission, Overseas House, Quay Street, Manchester M3 3HN, £6.20.

Skill Needs in Britain 1990, available from IFF Research Ltd, 26 Whiskin Street, London EC1R 0PB, £35.

Source: From the *Guardian, 27 September, 1990.*

Item D

LAST month's highly publicised and much applauded award of silk to nine women barristers, including Helena Kennedy and Patricia Scotland, underlines some painful facts about women and the system that hands out the prizes in the law. Though 10 per cent of all barristers are Queen's Counsel, only 3 per cent of the 1,170 women barristers are among them. But more serious is the shortage of women selected for the judicial training ground.

There are 1,200 part-time judges (assistant recorders and recorders), most of them practising barristers, who sit in the Crown and County courts. On average, they have between 17 and 21 years' experience as lawyers. It is from this field that full-time Crown and High court judges are selected. But fewer than 6 per cent of these are women.

Progress to the bench is a natural step for barristers. Of those called to the bar in the Sixties about half are now sitting as part or full-time judges.

Yet women who became barristers in the Seventies were significantly under-represented in the appointments made in the last five years. Throughout that period, 439 barristers were made recorders, 413 men (94 per cent) and 26 women (6 per cent). And, once in the fast stream, women did even worse. Only two women were among the 51 of these recorders who were made full-time circuit judges in the same five years. And of the 176 circuit judges appointed for the period, only eight were women (5 per cent).

As in other fields, these women appear to be better qualified than their male counterparts. They had, on average, longer post-qualification experience – nearly 23 years as opposed to the 21 years of the men. "It is only when those women who are perfectly competent but not exceptional are given the same opportunities as their male equivalents that an adequate number of women will eventually be available for consideration."

Source: Extract from an article by Sally Hughes in the *Independent,* 17 May 1991, p. 21.

1. Examine Item A.
This article suggest that there has been an historical period in which the position of some women may have been freer than in the present and therefore had much to recommend it.

(i) Discuss the conclusions concerning the view that the freedoms women have gained in the twentieth century regarding control over their fertility and the life chances of their children are ones for which there can be few compensations.
(ii) Read Item C and consider whether the details might affect the conclusions of the author of Item A.

2. Examine Item B.
This article suggests that more women are entering the entrepreneurial world as a means of breaking through the barrier of the 'glass ceiling', which often inhibits their levels of success.

(i) Consider some reasons why more women may now be running their own businesses.
(ii) In view of the information in the last paragraph of Item B consider some of the problems which women may face in becoming established in self-employment and business ownership.

3. Examine Item C
This article suggests that there are many reasons to explain why women are more frequently in part-time work than men and why they are segregated into different types of work.

(i) Outline other research evidence with which you familiar to support the reasons suggested.
(ii) Discuss some of the major differences revealed in the survey between Classes 1 and 2 (AB) and 4 and 5 (DE) as to why women work.
(iii) Various Reports by the Equal Opportunities Commission have shown that women have still not achieved equal pay with men. Outline the changes that have occurred in closing the gap since 1975.

4. Examine Item D.
This article indicates some of the facts relating to women in the legal profession and their failure to achieve high office.

(i) Tabulate the data to clarify it.
(ii) Suggest some of the reasons to explain why even well-qualified women were under-represented in legal appointments between 1986–91.
(iii) Discuss other evidence with which you are familiar to show how women's opportunities are improving in other occupational areas.
(iv) Suggest ways of assessing whether or not competent women have been given the same opportunites as their male equivalents.

II Read the following passage and answer the questions below.

'Men in the lower working class, aping their social betters, displayed virility by never performing any task in or about the home which was considered by tradition to be women's work. Some wives encouraged their partners in this and proudly boasted that they would never allow the "man of the house" to do a "hand's turn". Derisive names like "mop rag" and "diddy man" were used for those who did help. Nevertheless, kindlier husbands, especially when their wives were near exhaustion at the end of a day or in the last stages of pregnancy, would willingly do housework, cooking, washing the children or scrubbing a floor, provided doors remained locked and neighbours uninformed. Bolder spirits would even go out and shake rugs, bring in clothes and clothes lines, clean windows and swill flags, always at the risk of scoffing onlookers. One quiet little street in the village where several husbands dared to help their wives regularly became known in the pubs as "Dolly Lane" or 'Bloody-good-husband Street'. A marital phenomenon observed with much puzzlement by some in this virile society was the woman who pushed open the vault door of a tavern and with cold eye and beckoning finger caused her husband (he could be a known "fighting man", even) to put down his beer and follow her on the instant.

The male weakling in certain households, often known even through manhood as "Sonny", could be a subject of whispered concern among neighbours. He was usually "delicate". In pub and workshop there was plenty of talk, about the unspeakable. The proletariat knew and marked what they considered to be sure signs of homosexuality, though the term was unknown. Any evidence of dandyism in the young was severely frowned on. One "mother-bound" youth among us, son of a widow and clerk in a city warehouse, strolled out on Sundays wearing of all things gloves and carrying an umbrella! The virile damned him at once – an incipient 'nancy' beyond all doubt, especially since he was known to be learning to play the violin. Among ignorant men any interest in music, books or the arts in general, learning or even courtesy and intelligence could make one suspect. This linking of homosexuality with culture played some part, I believe in keeping the lower working class as near-illiterate as they were.'

Robert Roberts, *The Classic Slum: Salford Life in the First Quarter of the Century*, University of Manchester Press

From your examination of the above passage:

(i) What does the passage tell us about relationships between men and women in this community? (*4 marks*)

(ii) What part does social class play in the author's analysis of 'virility'? (*2 marks*)

(iii) Indicate *two* ways in which this community enforced expectations about proper masculine behaviour. (*4 marks*)

(iv) You wish to investigate contemporary attitudes towards masculinity among young people. Describe your approach to the research, and the method or methods you would use. What problems would you expect to meet? (*15 marks*)

Source: WJEC (June 1991).

5 THE FAMILY

Questions on this topic cover a wide range of areas:

1. Problems of definition:
   (a) Cross-cultural studies.
   (b) Analysis of different types of family structure.
2. Changes in the structure of the family in industrial societies:
   (a) Research studies illustrating variant forms.
   (b) Historical and contemporary perspectives.
3. Family relationships:
   (a) The significance of family networks.
   (b) The significance of social class.
4. Some feminist perspectives on the family.
5. Theories of the family:
   (a) Functionalist.
   (b) Marxist.

Problems of Definition

- **'The major problem of any comparative study is that of arriving at an agreeable definition of the family.' Discuss. (ULSEB)**
- **How universal is the family as a social institution? (WJEC)**

Definition 1

Murdock's definition: The family is a social group characterised by common residence, economic co-operation and reproduction. It includes adults of both sexes, at least two of whom maintain a socially approved sexual relationship, and one or more children, own or adopted, of the sexually cohabiting adults.

Problems of this definition

(a) It does not allow the use of the term 'family' about those headed by one parent.
(b) Those in which a couple have no children.
(c) Parents who live in a commune (such as a kibbutz) where the children grow up separately from them.

Comment: Whether or not the family is a universal institution depends to some extent on the definition that is used. If 'a family' is defined in a specific way, then there will be examples drawn from cross-cultural studies to indicate that it is not a universal institution. If it is defined more broadly, then it is harder to find exceptions.

Definition 2

A family is a social unit made up of people related to each other by blood, birth or marriage.

Problems of this definition It allows a married couple without children to be described as a family, but not an unmarried couple who are living with each other in a permanent union.

Comment This wider definition does meet the problems arising from Murdock's description.

Definition 3

A family is a social unit made up of people who support each other in one or several ways; for example, socially, economically or psychologically (in providing care, love, affection, etc.) or whose members identify with each other as a supportive unit.

Problems of this definition It is now so broad that it is difficult to conceive of exceptions to the existence of some form of family in every society.

Comment This wider definition would allow the term 'family' to be applied to:

(a) A cohabiting couple of the same sex.
(b) Unrelated members of a cohabiting group, such as a children's home, commune, etc., whose members regard themselves as 'a family'.

Examples from cross-cultural comparative studies

The nuclear family in Britain

(a) The small size of the unit, living independently of wider kin, is related to economic factors: income, housing and job opportunities. Children are emphasised more for what they can achieve rather than for their economic value.
(b) The main advantages of living in small units is in terms of the economic structure of advanced capitalist societies where there is emphasis on geographical and social mobility.
(c) The concept of monogamy is built into the Christian moral code and supported by the existing legal system. It is assumed to be 'the correct and best' system.
(d) The independence of young married couples and of the elderly also results from the expectations and norms which people share in modern Britain. This ethic of 'independence' is sustained to some extent by the existence of the welfare state which provides support for people.

The nuclear family in pre-industrial society

Firth (*We, the Tikopia*) describes family life on the island of Tikopia.

(a) The average population of a village is about fifty persons. There are strong incest taboos; marriage with a closer than second cousin is frowned upon.
(b) The nuclear family is always a recognisable unit. Even when two families live together in one household, each has its own section of the floor, and 'when visits are paid to other households it is this little group that moves together'.
(c) Husbands and wives who work in the gardens or fishing co-operate in the preparation of cooking meals and also in the care of children.
(d) Overall authority and the ownership of land is in the hands of the male since it is a patrilineal society.
(e) However, there are strong ties of extended kinship in the society also. The links with kindred by marriage tie members into a clan which provides strong subjective family associations. These ties of kinship are more widely used than in contemporary Britain where tasks beyond the nuclear family are carried out by institutions that are not associated with kinship.

The extended family: Yorubaland, Nigeria

(a) The extended family is the norm. Families consist of as many as a hundred people, all closely related kin, sharing homes in close proximity to each other.
(b) The family structure is based on polygamy. There are two main advantages:
   (i) *Economic*: the people are mainly farmers who require a large, cheap labour force.
   (ii) *Status*: in this society a man who can support many wives has high social prestige.
(c) The existence of an extended family system has many advantages:
   (i) There is no welfare state. The extended family provides welfare, assistance, training, etc.
   (ii) It helps reduce the level of social conflict. Problems are resolved in the family and not by law.
   (iii) People develop a strong sense of attachment and identity to a group and an area.

The family in a commune

About 4–5 per cent of the population of Israel live in *kibbutzim* settlements. They have been in existence for more than sixty years.

(a) No money changes hands on a kibbutz. Members are provided with food, accommodation, clothing, etc.
(b) All wealth produced from the sale of goods goes to finance the kibbutz.
(c) Marriage is monogamous.
(d) Children are generally raised apart from their parents, in 'age groups' with other children. They are cared for by trained nurses and other staff.
(e) Children grow up with a greater commitment to 'the community' and the kibbutz than to the individual family.
(f) Although this does not meet Murdock's definition of 'family' it could be seen as 'an extended family' from a more subjective perspective.

Concluding points

The view that the family (especially the nuclear family) is a universal institution is based on the argument that every society has some social organisation which regulates the permanent relationships between adults so that important functions are fulfilled:

(a) The reproduction of the population.
(b) The care of the young.
(c) The stabilisation of relationships between adults.
(d) The transmission of the social culture from one generation to the next.

The view assumes that the structure of the institution of the family is always broadly the same in every society. However, critics point out that:

(a) There is no universal definition of the family.
(b) It may not be the case that every society has an institution which is recognisable as a family. For example, in some, the relations between adults is not based on a permanent conjugal arrangement (for example, the Ashanti of Ghana). In others, the child's parents may have no understanding of how children are procreated and therefore they feel no need to care for them as a 'family unit' (for example, the Nayar of India and the Trobriand Islanders of the Pacific).
(c) While there are institutions concerned with various aspects of domestic life they vary in structure from one society to another.

Changes in Family Structure

- **How has the structure of the family changed in Britain over the last hundred years? Indicate the social implications of the changes. (WJEC)**
- **The modern nuclear family is uniquely well adapted to meet all the requirements of industrial society. Examine this proposition and evaluate the evidence for it.**

The nuclear family

There is debate as to whether the nuclear family developed as a result of industrialisation in the eighteenth and nineteenth centuries from a pre-industrial extended type, or whether both have always been and continue to be significant family structures.

The View that the Nuclear Family has Become Dominant

Parsons ('The American Family') writing in 1956 argues that the American family structure has been undergoing a process of major change.

(a) There has been an increase in divorce rates.
(b) There has been a change in social and moral values.
(c) There has been a decline in birth rate.
(d) The family in industrial societies has fewer functions to serve.
(e) The nuclear family is becoming the typical structure in industrial societies.
(f) Relationships with wider kin are based on choice not obligation.
(g) There is a functional relationship between the isolated nuclear family and the economic structure.
(h) The nuclear family becomes the most functionally suitable structure. This is because family members are increasingly socially and geographically mobile; the nuclear family is small and economically self-sufficient.
(i) The extended family cannot be functional in an industrial society since it tends to tie members to a specific area; conflicts can arise in a family where sons achieve higher status than the father in an inflexible and immobile family unit.
(j) He concludes that the structural isolation of the nuclear family ensures that it remains functional for an efficient industrial society.

Linton ('The Family in Urban Industrial America') writing in 1959 also argues that in modern industrial society the extended family has lost its traditional functions. This is because:

(a) There have been major changes in geographical and social mobility.
(b) New technologies have been developed requiring higher levels of skill.
(c) New systems of transport have made mobility easier.

He suggests that kinship ties are ignored when people can do without them. 'City dwellers recognise extended ties only in sending Christmas cards and occasional visits'.

The effects on the nuclear family have been:

(a) To weaken marriage ties. There are fewer pressures on people to conform to traditional norms.
(b) Life in urban areas is more anonymous and marriage breakdown more socially acceptable than in smaller, close-knit communities.

He points to a series of factors which have helped to undermine the traditional family structure:

(a) Increased *urbanisation*, which provided the chances of better houses and jobs.
(b) Increased *industrialisation*, which enabled more women to enter the work force and encouraged smaller families.
(c) Increased *secularisation*, which meant the decline in the influence of the Church in people's lives, allowing contraception, divorce, etc. to become more widespread and socially acceptable.

He concludes that the family may now be less stable than before, adding 'the revolutionary effects of these ... on the family ... can scarcely be overrated'.

Willmott and Young (*The Symmetrical Family*) in 1975 put forward a theory to describe the development of the family from pre-industrial to contemporary times. They discuss four stages of development:

(a) *Stage 1 – the pre-industrial family*: the family as a unit of production; all members work as a team. This type was displaced by the Industrial Revolution, although some examples persist to the present day.
(b) *Stage 2* – the family of the Industrial Revolution: individual members were employed primarily as wage earners. The family became a support unit for its members, especially the least successful. Among the poor in urban areas, the extended family again became a significant structure. This only declined with the improvement in living standards and the development of the welfare state. Some examples remained, however, as Willmott and Young found in their study *Family and Kinship in East London*.
(c) *Stage 3* – the nuclear family with which we are familiar in contemporary Britain has emerged from Stage 2 and become the dominant type. The authors argue that it originally epitomised the emerging middle-class family structure. But since the norms of those at the top of the social hierarchy gradually influence those at lower stages, then this structure predominated throughout society. This stage describes the symmetrical family in which husbands and wives take an equal share in the domestic duties of the household.
(d) A possible Stage 4 family is described, which is asymmetrical. They suggest that the attitude of those at the top of the occupational hierarchy towards work is that it is a central life interest. These values are likely to filter through society so that families will become less privatised as more men become involved in responsible and absorbing jobs and wives revert to a more domestic role.

Critics of this study have argued:

(i) Studies of the affluent workers suggest that they do not absorb the attitudes and norms of those in higher social classes.
(ii) This part of the theory is based on a small sample of 190 managers.
(iii) Statistics indicate that in the 1980s there are more, not fewer, women entering the work force.
(iv) Studies suggest that the workers whose jobs are affected by new technologies are not necessarily finding them more rewarding (see pages 302–5).
(v) Increasing levels of unemployment are likely to increase the levels of home-centred activities.

■ **Has the extended family been replaced by the isolated nuclear family? (UODLE)**

The View that the Extended Family Remains Significant

Historical perspectives

Laslett (*The World We Have Lost*) based his work, published in 1965 on an analysis of parish registers from between 1564 and 1821 and showed that:

(a) Only about 10 per cent of households contained kin beyond the nuclear family in the period.
(b) There was no evidence that the extended family was the dominant structure which was replaced by the nuclear type as a result of the Industrial Revolution.
(c) He suggests that it may have been the presence of the nuclear family which enabled the Industrial Revolution to develop rather than the reverse (for example, members of small family units were already potentially more geographically mobile).

Anderson ('Family, Household and the Industrial Revolution') argues that among the poor sector of the population the Industrial Revolution tended to encourage the strengthening of ties with wider kin. He found in his study of Preston in 1951 that about 23 per cent of households contained kin wider than the nuclear family. This was probably because families needed to support each other in times of depression. The family acted as a welfare system. This is the type of structure found by Willmott and Young in Bethnal Green in the 1950s.

Contemporary perspectives

Rosser and Harris (*The Family and Social Change*) confirmed in their study of Swansea in the 1960s that there were high levels of contact between related kin who were dispersed widely in an urban area.

(a) They found a form of extended family system operating. Kin were in contact by visits, letters and the telephone.
(b) Services were exchanged beyond the nuclear family, both economic and social.
(c) This was true for both working and middle-class people. The extended family provided a focus of identity in a similar way to those reported by the respondents in the Bethnal Green studies.

Sussman and Burchinal (*The Kin Family Network*) argue that the views expressed by Parsons and Linton rest on a theoretical analysis. This is coloured by their functional perspective. Sussman and Burchinal present evidence to show that the extended family (or a form of it) continues to operate in industrial America. They challenge the view that the isolated nuclear family has resulted from the urban Industrial Revolution.

(a) Most people do receive various forms of aid from kin after marriage. Even among upper-class families substantial financial aid flows from from parents to offspring (that is, nuclear families are not isolated).
(b) Other gifts, advice, job opportunities may flow from other kin members.
(c) Kinship visiting is a primary activity of urban dwelling.
(d) Desire for kinship visiting is strong, especially among middle-class families.
(e) The extended family structure still performs important recreational, ceremonial and economic functions.
(f) The view that the extended family disintegrates because of lack of contact is unsupported by evidence.

Litwak ('Geographic Mobility and the Extended Family'), 1960 has developed the concept of a *modified extended family* to deal with the difficulty of describing the family structure of contemporary industrial societies. It is composed of nuclear families bound together by affectional ties and by choice. The modified extended family functions to facilitate the achievement and mobility goals of the various families involved. He concludes that the extended family as a structure does exist in modern urban society in the sense that family members may not live in close proximity to each other, but they do have frequent contact and supply mutual aid to each other. Sussman and Burchinal comment that this concept of a modified extended family should now emerge as the one to replace the misleading one of the isolated nuclear family.

Barrow (*West Indian Families*) showed how the families she studied displayed many similar characteristics to those of the white population. However, she notes that because of the problems black males often have in gaining and retaining a job, the wife is often the dominant figure. If there are no local kin to call on in times of difficulty then more informal networks develop among friends and neighbours. Among other minority groups there were often different patterns which have been identified by other researchers. Families from Southern Asia displayed stronger kinship ties with family members, often sharing the same household or living in very close proximity, thereby forming traditional extended family units.

Werbner writing in 1992 ('Social Networks and the Gift Economy Among British Pakistanis') notes how distinctive cultural practices help bind the family members in Britain and also those still in Pakistan.

(a) There is an active attempt to promote the sense of individual and family identity by making active connections between kinship, neighbours and work colleagues.
(b) As they accumulate capital they convert some into gifts through which they ritualise family and social connections.
(c) A gift implies permanent debt and reciprocal trust. It is a way of establishing durable social bonds.
(d) By this means family unity is strengthened, reputations in the community are established and links with family and friends in Pakistan are also revitalised and renewed.

Conclusion

The Functionalists (see page 70) tend to argue that the extended family has become redundant in its traditional form in modern industrial societies. But if the definition is broadened to include family members in close relationships through visits, letters etc then it can be said to retain relevance. Also families in ethnic minorities still tend to retain cultural values which place importance on maintaining close family unity (although this may be changing to some extent among third and fourth generation members.) Ballard (*South Asian Families*) has noted how many families who have settled in Britain still retain close contacts with kin both in Britain and in remote villages in their places of origin. The same may be true of other minority groups, including Cypriots and West Indians.

- **The phrase 'the typical British family' is stereotypical and is misleading.**
  (a) Why is this so?
  (b) What are the consequences of this use of this stereotype? (AEB)
- **Examine the view that significant changes are taking place in the family in contemporary Britain.**

When people use stereotypes they are building an image which they believe to be true, of the person, group or institution. It is based on a few pieces of information and helps to make a complex issue simple and understandable. The stereotype of 'the typical British family' in the last quarter of the twentieth century would be two parents and one or two children living independently of their relatives. The family unit is democratically managed with a proportion of wives going out to work.

Mount (*The Subversive Family*) presents a strong defence of the modern family and is critical of forces which undermine it. He argues that:

(a) The family is the basis of the good society.
(b) The nuclear family is the basic co-operative unit in human society which stands as a bulwark against the tides attacking free enterprise.
(c) The family is subversive because it stands as a polar opposite to the state, which promotes bureaucratic and impersonal institutions.
(d) He rejects the interventionist doctrines of the welfare state and describes social services as an intrusion on domestic privacy.
(e) He see the extended family as a myth in modern industrial society.

The stereotype of the Victorian family is of a large family unit, stable and unified, headed by the oldest male. This is misleading because research suggests that there has never been a time when there has been a 'typical' structure.

1. See Laslett (page 64).

2. Anderson examined six popular myths about the family in the Victorian period:

(a) The view that in that period the community was more stable. The 1851 Census showed that more than 50 per cent of the population were not living in the community in which they were born.
(b) The view that the family was more stable. He suggests that death created about the same proportion of broken homes as divorce does today. There were probably more broken families with dependent children in 1826 than in 1983.
(c) The view that there was more affection towards children in that period. He argues that before the late eighteenth century there was little love and affection in relations between spouses, and parents and children. The novels of Dickens suggest that children had many problems in this respect in the nineteenth century.
(d) The view that Victorians were more moral. He suggests that the illegitimacy rate was about the same as today. Also, approximately 60 per cent of women bearing their first child in the early nineteenth century had conceived before marriage.
(e) The view that all Victorian families were large. In 1750 the average household contained 1.8 children; in 1850, 2.0 children; and in 1970, 1.1. (These figures are lower than birth-rate statistics because in earlier periods there were higher infant mortality rates; and a large number of children left home early to go into service or to find other work). But in the 1850s approximately 8 per cent of households contained three or more generations. In 1970 about 4 per cent contained three generations. In 1991 it was 1 per cent.
(f) The view that the modern family has less concern for the elderly. In 1906 about 6 per cent of the population over the age of sixty-five were in poor law institutions. The majority were looked after by relatives. In 1983 about 5 per cent were in institutions.

3. Chester describes variant forms of family structure which add weight to the view that there is no 'typical' British family. In 1979 12 per cent of families were one-parent type, of which 95 per cent were female-headed. In 1991 it was 19 per cent.

Divorce is one of the major causes of variant forms.

(a) At the community level such families tend to suffer many problems: they are more likely to be stigmatised; to be more vulnerable to intervention by neighbours, officials, etc.; to suffer social isolation; and to have low living standards.
(b) The reconstituted family: remarriage is the commonest outcome of divorce. But where children are concerned this creates step-relationships. These, too, have problems of social credentials. They may appear 'odd' through an incongruous collection of children or because of complications of surnames and kin networks.
(c) He concludes that failure to adapt to the consequences of these changes means that confusions and ambiguities in concepts of the family which produce social problems will remain.

4. Many sociologists are critical of the traditional family sociology, which assumes a clear and unambiguous definition and a stereotypical image.

(a) Gubrium and Holstein (*What Is Family?*) argue that this traditional view also:
  (i) Emphasised identifiable functional values.
  (ii) Permitted critics to see divorce as a deviation which destabilised society rather than as a functional way of re-establishing a more stable unit.
  (iii) Encouraged the view that Western nuclear families were superior to those seen in other cultures, including ethnic minorities.
  (iv) Resulted in an assumption that the domestic role of women and the power of men were socially correct and necessary.
(b) Bernades ('Do We Really Know What the Family Is?') has also rejected the picture of the normal family. He favours one which describes how people actually live their lives.
  (i) His analysis of 1981 Census data shows that few families meet the 'normal' stereotype.
  (ii) He notes the success of feminist writers in exposing the complex power structures and negotiation processes in ordinary family life.
  (iii) He complains that traditional family sociology may have perpetuated much pain and misery for its members (who may have succumbed to the 'normal' image) and become constrained by fear of public opprobrium, to complain about violence, abuse or discuss the desire to separate. It may also have helped justify criticism of the family structures of ethnic minorities, since they appeared to be different.

Table 5.1 Illegitimacy ratio (percentage of live births to single women, UK)

1951	5
1961	6
1971	8
1981	12
1991	30

Source: Social Trends, 22.

He would be critical of writers such as Mount, on the grounds that the job of social science is not morality, but reality. Therefore he rejects the concepts of the 'good', 'normal' family and recommends research which reflects the complexity of the daily life of its members

Family Relationships

- **What are the factors which affect the conjugal role relationships in the modern family?**
- **Using information drawn from any studies describe and account for the relationships which sociologists have observed between family life and social-class membership.**

Bott (*Family and Social Network*) analysed different relationships between husbands and wives in relation to their family networks. These are the connections that each spouse has with friends, organisations, place of work, etc. She distinguishes between two types:

(a) *Segregated roles* in which husband and wife carry out most of their leisure activities independently of each other.
(b) *Joint conjugal roles* in which they share most activities and equality in all their dealings. In the home there is much division of labour, shared interests and friends in common.

Factors affecting role relationships and patterns of behaviour in the family

1. Network theory suggests that the degree of segregation in role relationships varied with the connectedness of the family networks. The more this was connected, the greater was the segregation of roles. The more this was dispersed, the greater was the likelihood of joint or shared roles between husband and wife.

Points of criticism

(i) The sample was very small (twenty families in Greater London).
(ii) Measures of connectedness are hard to establish.
(iii) The class factor may be relevant in analysis.

2. Many studies have been conducted to try to establish the significance of social class in conjugal relationships.

Working-class families

1. Willmott and Young (*Family and Kinship in East London*) noted that localised working-class extended family groups spread over two or more nearby houses was a distinctive feature of kinship in the East End. Families had long-standing roots in the area. There was a strong stress on the mother–daughter tie, manual workers seeming to have more need for the extended family as 'a woman's trade union'. Roles were largely segregated.

2. Kerr (*The People of Ship Street*) notes how the pattern in this working-class area was for the woman to take her husband home to live with or near her mother. 'I couldn't get on without me mother . . . I could get on without me husband. I don't notice him'.

3. Klein (*Samples from English Culture*) says that just as industrial conflict is endemic, so is conflict in the home in lower-working-class families. Disagreements were often found to be concerned with money. The wife's role was defined in terms of her husband's convenience, much as his role was defined in terms of management's convenience. She noted that there tended to be a lack of give and take in relationships and an unusually rigid division of labour in the household.

4. In 1989 Murray (a political scientist) discussed some of the possible consequences for those families trapped in the lowest social class groups. He describes the emergence of an underclass which results from increasing numbers becoming alienated from the central and dominant value system of society. He uses as his measure facts relating to rates of illegitimacy, violent crime and unemployment.

However, he notes that there are major differences between the classes. (Rate for Classes 1 and 2 per 100 children born in 1991 was 10–15 per cent; for Classes 4 and 5, 40–46 per cent.) It is his argument that since members of Classes 4 and 5 are also more likely to be involved in crime and be unemployed some of them are becoming a disaffected and potentially destabilising sector of society. He says that this sector is defined not only by its poverty but also by its refusal to integrate into mainstream society.

5. Prosser and Wedge (*Born to Fail*; see also page 228) showed that children were adversely affected in their social development where they grew up in poor quality housing, with impoverished parents who were often sick and out of work, and with a large number of siblings. The effects accumulated to produce major disadvantages. Murray implies that the consequences are being felt in the 1990s.

Question

Examine photograph 17.

(i) Consider the similarities and differences between the views of Willmott and Young and those of Murray.

(ii) How might the child-rearing practices vary between the family in the photograph and that of a small, middle-class family unit in affluent circumstances? (See Newson p.132.)

(iii) What predictions might you make about the educational standards of the children in the family in the photograph?

(iv) How might such predictions be tested? What problems might be involved in undertaking such a project?

17

Source: Alec Gill

Middle-class families

1. Willmott and Young (*Family and Kinship in East London*) included in their study an analysis of middle-class families and conjugal relationships in Woodford. They noted that far fewer people there lived close to their parents. There was less day-to-day interaction between them. The population was more geographically mobile and relationships between spouses more democratically based.

2. Hubert (*Kinship*) found that the informants (and particularly the women in the sample) tended to be independent of parents before they married. This contrasted with the working-class situation, in which a girl tends to live at home until married. He suggests that middle-class children are taught the virtues of independence at an early age, which encourages mobility.

3. Bell (*Middle-Class Families*) He also found that young middle-class couples asserted their independence, making help between mother and daughter less likely, but a greater sense of companionship between spouses more so.

4. Leighton (*Social Studies Review*) discusses research which examined conjugal relationships in times of economic stress, when the middle-class husband had lost his job. She found:

(a) Wives with fewer qualifications tended to be more traditional in their ideas about a wife's role. The husband was seen as the natural breadwinner.
(b) Those who were full-time housewives were concerned that if they took work it might affect their husband's benefits.
(c) Those with full-time jobs became more determined to hold on to them, although they saw it as an additional stress and pressure on them.
(d) Wives in paid work were found to influence their husbands' attitudes. These husbands tended to remain out of work for shorter periods than those of wives who were not in paid work. Wives in paid work provided more incentive to their husbands.
(e) Economic power gave the working wives more positive attitudes. Housewives were more deferential.
(f) A working wife was able to challenge the usual assumption of the husband that he should maintain financial controls of the household; but disorganised relationships affected the economic organisation of the home which often led to increased marital tensions.

Concluding points

1. There is a danger of over-stating the differences between middle-class and working-class families. Rosser and Harris (see page 64) found little difference in patterns of behaviour between the two groups.
2. The concept of class is a complex one and authors need to specify more clearly which social groups they are including in their categories.
3. Although 'independence' from kin seems to be a dominant norm among middle-class families, Lupton and Wilson (*The Social Background of Top Decision-Makers*) have shown that among upper-class families kinship ties are important and 'alliances' between rich families are frequent through marriage.
4. In child-rearing, Classes 1 and 2 are likely to be better informed and more able to seek advice and act on it, and to attend parent–teacher meetings, etc.
5. It is a complex problem to interpret the effects of social factors on behaviour but there is evidence to show that class values do vary and that the differences have important consequences for the relationships between husband and wife and parents and children.
6. Some feminist writers dispute the extent to which conjugal roles have become more democratic, even in middle-class families.
7. Leighton suggests that there were many advantages which strengthened the conjugal roles among middle-class couples where a wife was in paid work. The most discordant relations were generally between unemployed husbands who objected to their wives working, and in the homes of long-term unemployed men with a wife not in paid employment. She notes that the study casts doubt on the Parsonian model of the harmoniously functioning family unit.

Some Feminist Perspectives on the Family

■ **'The most important influences in the sociology of the family in recent years have come from the work of feminist writers.' Outline and discuss some of their contributions.**

It is helpful to distinguish between different types of feminist argument (see also pages 53).

1. Radical feminists

Oakley (*The Sociology of Housework*) has presented a range of arguments in several of her books and articles which seek to explain the exploited position of women in contemporary society:

(a) She presents evidence to show that gender roles are culturally, not biologically, determined.
(b) There is no evidence to show that there are some tasks solely performed by women in all societies (except giving birth).
(c) Although there has been a steady growth in the number of women in the work force they are still expected to maintain their role as housewife, which has remained their primary role.
(d) The role of men has always been more important outside the home, so encouraging their position as 'breadwinner'.
(e) Women's primary role as 'housewife' ensures that they remain subordinate to men, making it difficult for them to pursue careers.
(f) This also leads to the increasing geographical and social immobility of women.
(g) The housewife role, which is exclusively allocated to women, has no status, is unpaid and alienating, and takes precedence over all other roles.
(h) Her conclusion is that the only way that women will gain freedom and be able to develop fully as individuals in society is for the abolition of the role of housewife, the sexual division of labour, and the family itself as it is presently understood and structured.

Delphey (*Close to Home*) too would not necessarily see the issue of the difficulties facing women in the family in traditional Marxist terms. She argues:

(a) it is simply a matter of men exploiting women for their own ends, especially through the institution of marriage.
(b) her conclusion is that women should combine to overthrow the patriarchal structures which exist to oppress women.

Friedl (*Women and Men*) sees the power of men in the family resulting from biological and cultural factors. She uses anthropological data. The implication is that gender is a major source of identity for people.

(a) She notes that in societies where certain tasks are assigned to males they carry more prestige than those assigned to females.
(b) She argues that male dominance arises from the fact that they have greater access to highly valued roles in the society and they can control the exchange of goods and materials.

2. *Marxist feminists*

Margaret Benston, for example, in *The Political Economy of Women's Liberation* argues that:

(a) Capitalism is an economic system which operates by exploiting a group who perform essential labour in the cheapest way.
(b) This occurs among the paid in work and the unpaid in the home. Women contribute to both sectors.
(c) Women form an indispensable labour force who help prop up the exploitative system.
(d) The family system disadvantages women, acts in the interests of men and employers, and promotes individual concerns at the expense of the community.
(e) Men must seek to maintain their jobs to support their families.
(f) Women become the scapegoats for the problems which men face in their employment.
(g) The family socialises its members into this value system.
(h) In this way the economic system survives largely unchallenged, occasionally meeting the demands of workers for improved wages and conditions.

3. *Liberal feminists*

They would wish to encourage both women and men to recognise the factors which inhibit their individual freedoms. Men could be better educated to be aware of the problems women face.

Sharpe (*Just Like A Girl*) discusses the significance of the educational system in shaping a girl's self-image:

(a) The school curriculum is gender based.
(b) Girls are discouraged from studying science subjects by the attitudes of teachers as well as of male pupils.
(c) The girls in her sample were inhibited by the dominant norms of what was and was not considered to be 'women's work'.

Buswell (*Social Studies Review*) also notes how school subjects are gendered, both in terms of their personnel and also in the ways they are used in employment.

(a) Traditionally the education received by working-class children has been vocationally oriented. But girls were also encouraged to become skilled in domestic labour.
(b) The result was that part-time work was the best that most could consider outside the home. The majority of women continue to be employed in the lowest-paid sector of the economy.
(c) She is not confident that in the future the compulsions of the National Curriculum will necessarily mean that girls will either identify with or achieve success in scientific subjects. This is because the educational experience of girls continues to be shaped by the expectations of the dominant culture, images of 'femininity' being disseminated by the popular media.

Bernard (*The Future of Marriage*) sees the role of housewife as the key factor in limiting the potential of women:

(a) Marriage is particularly beneficial for men. They are more likely than single men to have successful careers, high incomes and high-status occupations.
(b) Wives, on the other hand, are found to express marital disatisfaction more frequently than men, since they gain least. They suffer more illness than single women. They initiate divorce proceedings more frequently than men.
(c) It is invariably the wife, rather than the husband, who makes adjustment and compromises in marriage. Her self-image deteriorates as she accommodates to her husband's needs at the expense of her own.

Some writers have suggested that ideally, men and women could spend half a day in paid work and the other half fulfilling domestic responsibilities. Where this is not feasible, one partner could be paid a wage to be the full-time carer for home and children.

Others have argued that a collective or commune system should be encouraged in which child-rearing is shared among a small group, allowing all its members to work in paid employment if they wish. It has been suggested also that since parenting and child-rearing is largely an amateur and untrained process, it may be better to train professionals to act as parents, uncles, aunts, and so on.

Conclusions

Different feminist writers have presented much new data and new interpretations about the effects of domestic labour on women's lives:

(a) They see this as limiting women's occupational chances.
(b) They dispute the view that men are taking more responsibility in the home to free women for career development.
(c) Warde (*Social Studies Review*) confirms that his study found that women were doing a greater share of domestic work even when in paid employment.
(d) Radicals and Marxists advocate revolutionary change; liberals concede that the family remains a useful institution that can benefit all members if organised efficiently.

Critics of such views argue:

(i) They focus too much on the role of women at the expense of other family members.
(ii) The concept of a patriarchal structure is too generalised.
(iii) The implication that all women are exploited is overstated.
(iv) They may undermine the rights of parents to rear their children in the way they choose.

However, the feminist perspective has presented an alternative to the more traditional family sociology which saw women as providing the necessary expressive function and in a more subordinate role than that of the breadwinner husband.

Theoretical Perspectives

■ **The picture of the family as functional both for its members and for society has come under strong criticism. Outline the functionalist analysis of the family and discuss major critisms of this analysis.**

The functionalist perspective

1. The effectiveness of the family is seen in relation to its ability to carry out functions which are essential to the maintenance of the stability and perpetuation of society.
2. The *essential functions* include:
   (a) caring for the emotional needs of members;
   (b) the provision of a secure home;
   (c) the socialisation of the young;
   (d) the reproduction of the species; and
   (e) the stabilisation of adult personalities.
3. As society becomes more highly evolved so institutions specialise in fewer functions. The state introduces specialist organisations which remove some functions from the family (for examples, schools, hospitals).
4. The social system is in harmony when all the parts function efficiently. There is said to be a functional relationship between the isolated nuclear family and the economic system. This is considered to be the most functional unit for modern industrial society.
5. The isolated nuclear family provides a socially and geographically mobile work force to meet the changing economic needs of society.
6. It is also functional in that members gain status from their levels of achievement and success. These are crucial in an industrial society. In a 'static' extended family differentials in levels of achievement between family members could give rise to conflict, which would be dysfunctional.
7. The role of the woman in the family is functional when she plays an 'expressive' role, providing care and affection for members.
8. Because the family is isolated from wider kin this ensures closer and warmer relations between husband and wife (joint conjugal roles).
9. The family becomes more specialised in its functions (although some writers, such as Fletcher (*Family and Marriage*) have argued that the family's functions have increased in modern society since there are more duties and obligations to be fulfilled).

Points of criticism of the functionalist view

(i) The concept of the isolated nuclear family may be overstated (see Litwak, page 64).
(ii) There is evidence to show that the extended family has not disappeared in the way predicted by functionalists in modern society (see Sussman and Burchinal; Rosser and Harris, page 64).
(iii) It may be that industrial societies do not require greater geographical mobility than non-industrial societies. Many workers commute long distances to their places of work.
(iv) There is some evidence to suggest that there were large movements of population in pre-industrial times.
(v) Some research suggests that levels of social mobility are limited in modern industrial society, especially in times of high levels of unemployment.
(vi) Short-range social mobility may have been more common in pre-industrial times than functionalists assume.
(vii) The view that there is greater joint conjugal role relations in modern industrial society may be overstated (see comments of Oakley, page 68).
(viii) There is evidence that the nuclear family was a prominent form of family organisation in pre-industrial England (see Laslett, page 64).
(ix) The view presents a conservative stance and suggests that the nuclear family must be the best possible organisation. Such authors start from a committed defence of the family.

The Marxian view

■ **How far do you agree with the claim that the nuclear family is a bourgeois entity based on private gain and oppression?**

1. During the earliest stages of human development the forces of production were communally owned and the independent family unit did not exist. The society was the family.
2. As a result of evolutionary development the family slowly emerged as a social institution together with the concept of private property and class divisions.
3. The defence of the family by religious doctrines and legal enactments was encouraged by the ruling élite. Structures were necessary in order to ensure the transmission of wealth, usually through the male line, to direct family members. The male domination of the family helped ensure the paternity of offspring.
4. In contemporary society the family is seen by Marxist writers as a means of producing a supply of labour; women remain a particularly exploited group working to maintain the home and in the lowest-paid occupations in the economy.
5. The role of the woman is to maintain the household and to ensure that her husband works efficiently. She helps absorb his frustrations and disappointments in work.

6. The need to support a family ensures that workers act in responsible ways. They have duties and responsibilities.
7. The home provides a place in which the worker can relax away from the dangers and discontents of work.
8. Children are socialised into the norms of the capitalist system. They learn to be passive and not to be critical of the social structure.
9. In recent years some attention has been focused on the extent to which the blue-collar worker has become more 'privatised' (home-centred). This can also be interpreted by Marxist writers as a means of ensuring the survival of the existing society. Lack of interest in communal activities inhibits the possibility of frequent, dangerously unsettling collective action.

For Marxists, the solution may lie in:

(a) Changing the family structure. Leach (*A Runaway World*) argues that what is needed is a more communal type of structure in which children could grow up in larger units with more emphasis on the community.

(b) Changing the social structure. Cooper (*The Death of the Family*) argues that the family acts as 'an ideological conditioning device' and that an exploitive family produces an exploitive society. He suggests that only in an egalitarian society can people be truly free to develop themselves and their talents fully.

Points of criticism

(i) All Marxist writers start from an ideological position that condemns the family as an agency of capitalist values.

(ii) There is always an emphasis on the needs of the society rather than the family unit.

(iii) Such writers advocate a new social order without specifying how social life will be organised when this is achieved.

(iv) The view assumes that there will be a natural orderliness in social relations arising out of those previously imposed by forces of exploitation.

(v) All the social ills of society are seen to stem from the destructive aspects of the family system, which is an institution operating in the interests of the ruling class. This can be regarded as a narrow view of the sources of disorder.

(vi) The view does not explain the similarities in family structure in capitalist and non-capitalist societies, and why divorce and violence occur in them also.

Suggested Reading

Works noted in this chapter

M. Anderson (1971) 'Family, Household and the Industrial Revolution' in M. Anderson (ed.), *The Sociology of the Family*, Penguin

M. Anderson (1983) *Family Structure in Nineteenth Century Lancaster*, Cambridge University Press

C. Bell (1968) *Middle-Class Families*, Routledge & Kegan Paul

M. Benston (1972) 'The Political Economy of Women's Liberation' in N. Glazer-Malbin and H. Waehrer (eds) *Women in a Man-made World*. Rand McNally, Chicago. 1972

J. Bernades (1985) 'Do We Really Know What the Family Is?', in P. Close and R. Collins, *Family and Economy in Modern Society*, Macmillan

J. Bernard (1976) *The Future of Marriage*, Penguin

E. Bott (1968) *Family and Social Network*, Tavistock

C. Buswell (1991) 'The Gendering of School and Work', *Social Studies Review* (January)

R. Chester (1985) 'The Rise of the Neo-Conventional Family', *New Society* (9 May)

P. Close and J. Collins (1985) *Family and Economy in Modern Society*, Macmillan

D. Cooper (1972) *The Death of the Family*, Penguin

C. Delphey (1984) *Close to Home*, Hutchinson

R. Fletcher (1966) *Family and Marriage*, Penguin

E. Friedl (1975) *Women and Men*, Holt, Rinehart & Winston

J. Gubrium and Mayfield J. Holstein (1990) *What is Family*?, Mayfield Publishing

J. Hubert (1966) 'Kinship', in E. Butterworth, and D. Weir, (eds.) *The New Sociology of Modern Britain*, Fontana

M. Kerr (1958) *The People of Ship Street*, Routledge & Kegan Paul

J. Klein (1965) *Samples from English Culture*, Routledge & Kegan Paul

P. Laslett (1983) *The World We Have Lost*, Methuen

E. Leach (1967) *A Runaway World*, BBC Publications

G. Leighton (1992) *Social Studies Review*, Vol. 1, No. 3

R. Linton (1959) 'The Family in Urban Industrial America', in M. Anderson (ed.), *The Sociology of the Family*, Penguin

E. Litwak (1960) 'Geographical Mobility and the Extended Family Cohension', *American Sociology Review*

T. Lupton and C. Wilson (1973) 'The Social Background and Connections of Top Decision-Makers', in J. Urry and Wakeford, *Power in Britain*, Heinemann

F. Mount (1982) *The Subversive Family*, Counterpoint

G. Murdock (1949) *Social Structure*, Macmillan

C. Murray (1989) 'Underclass', *Sunday Times* (November 26)

A. Oakley (1974) *The Sociology of Housework*, Martin Robertson

T. Parsons (1959) 'The American Family', in (ed.) M. Anderson *The Sociology of the Family*, Penguin

H. Prosser and P. Wedge (1973) *Born to Fail*, Hutchinson

R. Rosser and C. Harris (1965) *The Family and Social Change*, Routledge & Kegan Paul

S. Sharpe (1976) *Just Like a Girl*, Penguin

M. Sussman and L. Burchinal (1962) 'The Kin Family Network', in M. Anderson (ed.), *The Sociology of the Family*, Penguin

A. Warde (1990) 'Domestic Division of Labour', *Social Studies Review* (September)

P. Werbner (1992) 'Social Networks and the Gift Economy Among British Pakistanis', *Sociology Review* (February).

P. Willmott and M. Young (1975) *The Symmetrical Family: Family and Kinship in East London*, Penguin

Self-test Questions

Study these extracts from newspapers and answer the questions below.

Item A

About sexual morality, do you think :

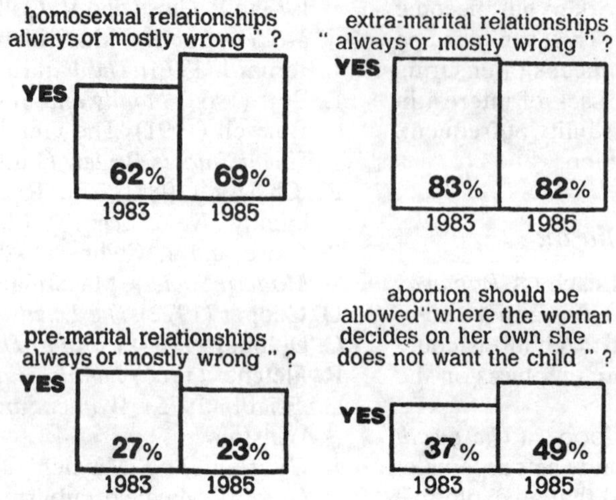

● **British Social Attitudes is the third successive annual survey. It shows " how we think and feel as a nation rather than who we are or what we do."**

Designed to complement official government reports like social trends it is financed by charitable, government and private sources.

The survey involved 1,700 people nationwide. It was carried out by Social and Community Planning Research and edited by Roger Jowell, Sharon Witherspoon and Lindsay Brook.

British Social Attitudes: the 1986 Report is published by Gower, price £25 hardback and £12.50 paperback.

Source: Extract from an article by Martin Kettle and Malcolm Dean in the *Guardian*, 29 October 1986.

1. Examine Item A.
Draw some conclusions from the findings of the survey concerning changing attitudes towards the family and the relationships of its members between 1983 and 1985.

Item B

Traditional view of family life 'held by minority of people'

	ALL %	MEN %	WOMEN %	AGE 18-34	AGE 35-54	AGE 55+
1 a) For a family with children under 5 years old, which of these statements comes closest to your own view?						
It is important that one parent is non-working, in order to look after the children	47	48	46	39	45	58
It is reasonable for both parents to work, as long as one only works part-time	30	29	32	30	34	27
It is reasonable for both parents to work and make other arrangements for looking after their children	18	18	18	25	19	10
Don't know	5	5	4	6	2	5
1 b) And for a family with children in their early teens, which of these statements comes closest to your view?						
It is important that one parent is non-working, in order to look after the children	14	15	12	10	11	20
It is reasonable for both parents to work, as long as one only works part-time	41	39	43	34	42	47
It is reasonable for both parents to work full-time and make other arrangements to look after their children	41	41	41	51	44	27
Don't know	4	5	4	5	3	6

2 a) If one parent stays at home to look after children under five is it...						
Normally better if the mother looks after the children	53	57	49	38	52	70
Normally better if the father looks after the children	*	1	0	1	*	0
Likely that both parents would be equally suitable	44	39	49	59	46	28
Don't know	2	3	2	2	2	2
2 b) If one parent stays at home, or works only part time, to look after children in their early teens, is it...						
Normally better if the mother looks after the children	33	36	31	23	30	47
Normally better if the father looks after the children	2	2	2	1	1	3
Likely that both parents would be equally suitable	62	58	65	73	66	45
Don't know	3	4	2	3	3	5
3 a) Do you think female homosexual couples should be allowed to adopt a baby...						
Under the same conditions as other couples	13	16	12	20	14	7
Under stricter conditions	18	16	20	24	19	10
Under no circumstances at all	62	63	62	49	61	77
Don't know	7	6	7	7	6	7
3 b) Do you think male homosexual couples should be allowed to adopt a baby...						
Under the same conditions as other couples	9	10	7	13	9	3
Under stricter conditions	13	10	16	19	13	6
Under no circumstances at all	72	75	70	61	71	86
Don't know	6	6	7	7	6	6
4 Please tell me whether you agree or disagree with each of these statements						
a) If a couple split up and one parent refuses to make any payment towards bringing up the children, the Government should have the powers to find that parent and deduct payment from his/her wages						
Agree	91	90	93	88	94	93
Disagree	5	6	4	7	4	3
Neither/Don't know	4	4	3	5	2	4
b) The problem of poverty among one-parent families will not be solved until the Government spends more money helping them						
Agree	63	65	62	75	63	52
Disagree	23	23	24	13	24	32
Neither/don't know	14	12	14	12	13	16

■ *NOP interviewed a representative sample of 1,634 adults aged 18 and over at 108 sampling points throughout Great Britain between 11 and 13 August 1990.*

2. Examine Item B.

(i) What is the traditional view of family life which the survey suggests may be changing?

(ii) Examine Q1 (a) and (b) in the survey. In what ways do attitudes vary between different age groups?

(iii) Examine Q2 (a) and (b) in the survey.

(a) Explain the general view of the role of the father in child-care among the older and younger members of the sample.

(b) Suggest why only a small majority (53%) think that it is normally better if the mother looks after young children.

(c) How would you interpret the fact that 62% think that both parents are equally suitable when the children are teenagers?

(iv) Examine Q3 (a) and (b). Suggest some reasons for the pattern of answers to this question.

(v) Draw some conclusions concerning the differences in attitudes among the different age groups to some of the changes that are examined in the survey.

3. Using data from Items A and B, discuss some of the ways in which the traditional view of the family has changed in recent years. Outline some future trends that may be predicted.

4. Time to End the Slander of the Innocents

'In 1988, one in four children were born illegitimate in the UK, a 12 per cent rise over the previous year; a threefold increase since the early Sixties. "Bigamy is having one husband too many," someone once wrote. "*Monogamy* is the same." Have women, wholesale arrived at the same conclusion? Has that cornerstone of society – a couple and 2.2 children – really received irreparable damage?

The Family Law Reform Act 1987 has removed most of the differences between legitimate and illegitimate children and it will improve the rights of the natural father (at present non-existent). So logically, this piece of legislation should make the very word illegitimate redundant. But the response to statistics underlines that for Government, no matter what the facts, *the illegitimate child and the lone parent remain in the camp of the the undesirable.* However varied their circumstances, they have all been lumped together: *symbols of degeneracy.* Where once we had the social security scrounger as the public's bogey, now we have Sharon, aged 17, and her baby, Jason; struggling to survive without love or money: the cause of all society's woes.

In truth, the new statistics on illegitimacy don't tell nearly such a corrupt or simple tale. On the contrary, they read as a vindication of those very forces which have given 'the family' such resilience – the need to live in stability and security with another adult and rear a child. Over a half to two-thirds of illegitimate children last year were born in stable partnerships. One of the biggest increases has come in illegitimate children born to women of 30 and older, a rise in 20 years from 5 per cent of the total to 13.4 per cent. Again, while some men unquestionably do flee from parental responsibility, others do not: over 70 per cent of illegitimate births in 1988 were jointly registered with the parents living at the same address.

The illegitimacy figures indicate that what is now being displayed is not less responsibility on the issue of parenthood, but more; children as a choice, not a coercion. *The ideology of the family* may be undergoing change (and that is what the government really mistrusts) – a move away from white weddings and *traditional roles – but the family's structure and the powerful pull it holds for individuals remain as strong.*

If teenagers are choosing pregnancy for the state social security benefits – and no research yet supports this assertion – then one has to ask why are we producing a generation of females with such low expectations? The income for an 18-year-old mother and child is not much over £50 a week; housing, if it's available at all, is abysmal. If we push motherhood as a natural role, why do we then express surprise when working-class girls with little else on offer, opt for it? And an impressive number even do it well.'

Source: Adapted from an article by Yvonne Roberts in the *Observer*, 1 October 1989.

(a) Give a brief explanation of each of the following:
(i) monogamy;
(ii) traditional roles *(2 marks)*

(b) Briefly explain what is meant by:
(i) symbols of degeneracy;
(ii) the ideology of the family. *(4 marks)*

(c) Identify and explain *two* ways in which 'the family's structure and the powerful pull it holds for individuals remain as strong'. *(4 marks)*

(d) How might sociologists explain an increased rate of illegitimacy? *(7 marks)*

(e) Briefly outline any research methods which you might consider appropriate to investigate: *either* to what extent 'the illegitimate child and lone parent remain in the camp of the undesirable';
or whether teenagers are choosing pregnancy for the state's social security benefits. *(8 marks)*

Source: ULSEB (June 1991)

Works for further reading

Women and Poverty

C. Buswell (1987) 'Training for Low Pay', in Glendinning and Millar, *Women and poverty*

J. Finch (1989) *Family Obligations and Social Change*, Polity

D. Gittings (1985) *The Family in Question*

C. Glendinning and J. Millar (1987) *Women and Poverty*, Wheatsheaf

D. Morgan (1985) *Family Politics and Social Theory*, Routledge & Kegan Paul

J. Pahl (1989) *Money and Marriage*, Macmillan

R. Pahl (1984) *Divisions of Labour*, Blackwell

A. Pollert (1981) *Girls, Wives and Factory Lives*, Macmillan

L. Segal (1983) *What is to be Done About the Family*?, Penguin

6

MARRIAGE AND DIVORCE

The questions on this topic tend to relate to the following areas:

1. The social significance of marriage:
   (a) Pre-industrial societies.
   (b) Industrial societies.
2. The problems of assessing the stability of marriage in modern society.
3. Factors affecting increasing divorce rates:
   (a) Opportunities to escape marriage.
   (b) Increased conflict in families.
   (c) Changing values with regard to marriage.
4. Variations in divorce rates between different groups:
   (a) The factors associated with these variations.
   (b) The possible consequences of divorce.
5. Trends in divorce:
   (a) Contemporary data.
   (b) Theoretical perspectives.

The Significance of Marriage

■ **From a comparison between at least two different types of societies what would you say is the sociological significance of marriage? (ULSEB)**

Every society must have its population replaced by new generations. Marriage is an institution which ties two people (in some societies where polygamy is practised, more than two) by legal or customary bonds which establish rights and duties between them. It is a means whereby the population is reproduced in a socially acceptable way in some societies. In others (for example, Tikopia) a marriage follows the birth of the first child. When the woman becomes pregnant then the couple settle down in a permanent and recognised union.

Non-industrialised societies

1. In some, marriage serves the interests of the entire family group. It helps to establish alliances between families and to ensure their survival. (This may also be true to some extent among the very rich families of industrial societies. See Lupton and Wilson, page 68).
2. In societies where marriages are arranged and the husband's family must pay a large sum for his wife to her family, then the marriage bond may be even more significant. Such marriages are difficult to break because of the complications in their arrangement.
3. In some patrilineal societies, such as Tikopia, a marriage is important as a means of ensuring offspring, who help to expand kin groups. All land is passed through the male line. When a man has left behind him sons who have settled down and have left descendants, the group is recognised as 'a house'.
4. In other patrilineal societies there is a custom called the 'levirate'. If a married man dies his widow may be taken over by one of his brothers or some other close kinsman. The wife is still regarded as being married to her dead husband and any children she may later have are regarded as his. If the wife dies at a young age then one of her sisters may be taken as a replacement.
5. In such societies marriage is important as an institution which serves the interests of the social group not those of the individual.

Marriage in industrial society

1. In modern Britain the emphasis is on the benefits for the individuals concerned.
2. Attitudes towards marriages are different in that people expect emotional gratification, companionship and security, rather than simply the production of heirs. These expectations are not always met, which may help to account for the high divorce rate.
3. However, where there are children these may be raised by both parents, in a democratic arrangement; by a single parent; or by the mother and daughter in close harmony (as described by Willmott and Young).
4. Statistics from OPCS show that 95 per cent of women and 91 per cent of men have been married by the age of forty.
5. In Britain monogamous marriage ('a voluntary union of one man with one woman for life') has traditionally been defended by the Christian moral code and the

legal system. It is therefore significant as a long-standing central institution which affects social roles, attitudes and behaviour. It is marked by a wide-ranging set of rituals.

6. The Finer Committee on One-Parent Families (1974) commented that 'marriage must be drawing into the institution large numbers who lack any evident vocation for it.'
7. The popular and stereotypical image of the family as a married couple with one or two children is mistaken. This now only represents about 25 per cent of all households. About 15 per cent of households are occupied by single pensioners and about one in eight families are one-parent households.
8. Although marriage remains a popular institution (the proportion of marriages involving the previously divorced was one in three in 1985), nevertheless there is evidence that an increasing number of people are choosing to cohabit rather than marry (see page 83).

Concluding points

Marriage serves different functions in different types of society. Its strength and fragility may also vary. In pre-industrial societies marriage is primarily a means of strengthening links between kin groups. In industrial societies the needs of the individual are more to the fore. The stability of the marriage may be related to the lack of expectations about love, affection and companionship; for example, where the marriage is arranged and large sums of money are involved. Instability is more likely in marriages which link individuals in a more personal way; in relationships based on choice. This may be unfortunate in view of the norm that most married couples are expected to produce children.

The Stability of Marriage in Modern Britain

■ **Assess the view that increases in rates of divorce, illegitimacy, the growing acceptance of pre-marital sex, and common-law marriages are all indicative of the impending breakdown of family life in modern society.**

It is always difficult to assess the extent to which marriage and family life is more or increasingly less stable now than at some time in the past. The main problems are:

(a) Finding an adequate measure of stability.
(b) Knowing enough about families of the past in order to make useful comparisons.
(c) The difficulty of using statistical measures in that they may be hard, if not impossible, to obtain. For example, it is doubtful if the number of common law marriages is recorded. Also where these common law marriages are recorded data may not have been collected for very long, making comparisons with earlier historical periods almost impossible.

Changing attitudes towards marriage

1. Urwin (*Can the Family Survive*?) wrote 'the family in the modern world, by many signs and tokens, is in a perilous state. Critical observers declare that it is disintegrating and tending to disappear'. He saw the disintegrating influences as the demand that women were making for equality in work, the 'modern pre-occupation with sex . . . almost amounting to an obsession . . . and the decline in the influence of the church.'

   These comments suggest that every generation is concerned that the family is becoming less stable.
2. Divorce rates have increased for many reasons (see page 79). But it cannot be assumed that marriages were necessarily more stable when there were fewer divorces. We do not know how many unhappy and unstable marriages existed which were not broken by divorce.
3. Other measures may be equally difficult to interpret.

There are many different details presented in Table 6.1. You would not be expected to recall all of them. But it would be helpful to be familiar with some, and with the general trends which are revealed. You would need to refer to some facts in a question of this sort. Remember that statistics are open to many interpretations. But as far as the question regarding the breakdown of family life is concerned the following points could be made:

1. Divorce rates remained comparatively low until 1969 (Divorce Reform Act). They have increased rapidly ever since, having doubled since 1971.
2. Most divorce petitions are filed by women (about three times as many as by men). The stigma of divorce has diminished.
3. The annual number of marriages increased steadily between 1901–1971, reaching a peak as changes in the divorce law became effective. It then declined, fluctuated and in 1991 fell back to the level of the early 1960s. This change in the popularity of marriage may reflect both the impact of easier divorce and the popularity of cohabitation.
4. There is an increasing number of remarriages; the rate for men is higher than for women. (Suggesting that marriage remains a popular institution.)
5. Average family size remains below 2. (The birth-rate among women from the New Commonwealth countries has also fallen, from 3.8 in 1971 to 2.5 in 1991.)
6. Patterns of family building are also changing. In recent years couples waited longer to start a family. This was most pronounced in Classes 1 and 2.
7. The proportion of women in the work force has risen steadily, causing some observers to suggest that their increased economic independence is one factor that helps to explain the decline in marriage and the increase in divorce.

Again, if the question you are tackling mentions specific issues, it is helpful to have some data to use in your discussions. The interpretation you place on them will depend on whether you are seeking to argue that the family is less secure or whether you wish to argue that the statistics are inconclusive.

Note some of the points that could be raised:

1. The proportion of conceptions terminated by legal abortion outside marriage has doubled since 1971, to 15 per cent. There has been a slight fall in the number inside marriage (Table 6.2).

Table 6.1 Comparative data showing changes in rates of marriage, divorce, births, family size and women in the labour force, 1901–2000

	1901	1921	1951	1961	1971	1981	1989	1991 (est.)	2001
Decrees absolute granted (UK) (000s)	1	3	30	27	80	157	164	165	
Marriages (000s) (UK)	300	360	400	397	459	398	392	390	
Percentage of remarriages	13.1	14.8	18.1	14.6	20.2	34	36	37	
Live births (000s) (UK)	1000	800	797	944	902	731	777	800	769
Crude birth rate (UK) per 100 live births	28.6	23.1	15.9	17.9	16.1	13.0	13.6	13.9	13.0
Average family size (UK)	3.3	2.2	2.3	2.2	2.0	2.0	1.9	1.8	
Women workers percentage of labour force	19	29	30	32	36	42	43	44	45

Source: *Social Trends, 22.*

Table 6.2

	1971	1981	1989
Percentage of conceptions ending in abortion (England and Wales)			
Legal abortions inside marriage	5	6	4
Legal abortions outside marriage	7	11	15
Percentage of live births outside marriage (UK)	8	11	27

Source: Social Trends, 22.

2. These statistics indicate that there has been a fairly steep rise in the number of extramarital conceptions and births since 1971, from about 5 per cent to 27 per cent in 1989. This may be related to:
(a) More independent attitudes developing in younger women.
(b) Legal changes which provided more protection for common-law wives.
(c) An increase in the proportion of young single women in the population following the baby boom of the 1960s.
(d) Changes in attitude towards marriage, so that cohabitation has become increasingly favoured. Dyer and Berlins (*Living Together*) suggests that couples marrying in the late 1970s were three times more likely to have lived together before marriage as couples who married at the beginning of the decade. They estimated that one in ten of all non-married couples were cohabiting. However, marriage frequently becomes an acceptable option when they decide to have children. Data from OPCS (1992) suggests that for women who married in the 1980s the proportion who had previously cohabited reached 50 per cent in 1987.

Conclusions

A writer such as Urwin and others adopting a more traditional functionalist approach may well use the statistical data to interpret a decline in the stability of the family. Murray (see page 66) sees the outcome of the increases shown as resulting in the growth of an underclass. Some feminist writers (see page 53) may interpret them as indicating that the patriarchal structures in society are being broken down as women take greater control of their lives. Bernades (see page 65) argues that social scientists should not moralise about family life but describe how ordinary lives are led in all their complexities.

Note You need to make clear your own interpretations of the data you use.

Violence in the Family

How can violence in the family be explained sociologically?

1. Dobash and Dobash (*Violence Against Wives*) argue that:

(a) Attacks by husbands on wives are increasingly common. About 25 per cent of all serious assaults in the criminal statistics of indictable offences are of this type.
(b) The statistics may underestimate the full amount since many attacks may go unrecorded.
(c) The police are often reluctant to intervene in domestic disputes.

Questions

Examine photographs 18–20.

1. Consider photograph 18.
There is evidence that marriage, especially in a Registry Office, remains popular even though divorce rates are increasing.
- (i) Suggest some of the functions of wedding rituals in contrast to the mutual arrangements of cohabitation.
- (ii) Suggest the possible significance of the role of bridesmaid for the young children involved.

2. Examine photographs 19 and 20.
There is some evidence to suggest that divorce rates may be higher in some occupations than others (see page 82).
- (i) What predictions would you make about the divorce rates of:
  - (a) The fishermen?
  - (b) The members of the armed forces?
- (ii) Suggest a hypothesis that could be tested with regard to high or low divorce rate and:
  - (a) The occupation of a spouse.
  - (b) The class background of each spouse.
  - (c) The age of each spouse.

18

Source: Paul Selfe

19

Source: Alec Gill

20

Source: Alec Gill

(d) The penalties for such attacks are relatively low.
(e) Such violence could be explained in terms of 'power relations' in a marriage. In using aggression of a physical sort men are displaying their power. This is supported by widely-accepted social norms which tend to imply that the male is, and ought to be, the dominant partner. The association between masculinity and self-esteem in a working-class culture promotes sexist attitudes to women in the home.
(f) Violence against women can also be seen as a reflection of the wider social inequalities that exist in the society between the sexes.
(g) This would be a line of argument supported by such writers as Oakley and Freidl (see page 68–69) and one that runs counter to the views of Willmott and Young in *The Symmetrical Family* (see page 63).

2. Laing (*The Politics of the Family*) argues that violence in a family can stem from the complicated relationships that develop. He is particularly concerned with the psychological violence that results in the destruction of personalities. Bizarre behaviour may be the individual's response to an intolerable social situation. It is labelled as 'madness' because it makes no sense to observers, although it may have meaning for the actor.

3. Leach (*A Runaway World*) puts forward the view that the stress and conflict between husband and wife and parents and children arises from life in small nuclear families with their 'narrow privacy and tawdry secrets'. He argues that the result is that when parents and children are forced to live in this oppressive way, they take too much out of each other: 'the parents fight, the children rebel'. His theme was directed to the conclusion that contemporary family life incubates hate, which finds expression in conflict. Writing more recently (1982) he confirmed his earlier view when he wrote of present family life resulting in 'claustrophobia for all' and that 'the English continue to rear their children cooped up in boxes like battery hens'.

4. NSPCC Report, 1985. This stated that marital conflict was the biggest single factor in child abuse. Parents often seemed ignorant of the effect of their quarrels. Between 1977 and 1983 the NSPCC found that marital discord featured in 57 per cent of their cruelty cases.

5. See also the points raised in the theoretical perspectives (page 84).

Factors Affecting Increasing Divorce Rates

■ **Examine the major causes of the increasing frequency of divorce in Britain.**

There are four categories of marital breakdown:

Divorce This is the legal termination of marriage following a decree absolute. The couple are then free to remarry.

Legal separation The partners separate but the marriage continues to exist. There are no reliable statistics available.

Desertion One partner leaves the family. The marriage remains until a decree absolute is obtained. Reliable figures for desertion are also difficult to obtain, but Chester (*Divorce*) suggests that separations and desertions are both increasing.

Empty-shell marriages The couple live together but there is no love, affection or economic support provided by either partner.

In answering any question it is always useful to look for a structure which you can impose on the question in order to ensure your material is well organised. In this case there is a useful analysis by Hart (*When Marriage Ends*) which offers such a structure. She suggests that there are three factors to consider in an analysis of increasing divorce rates:
(i) The opportunities to escape marriage.
(ii) The opportunities for increased conflict and stress.
(iii) The changing values concerning marriage.

The opportunities to escape marriage

Increases in trends in divorce have tended to follow changes in divorce legislation. At the turn of the century divorce was still comparatively expensive and therefore available mainly to the rich. The poor tended to rely on separation orders.

1909 The Royal Commission on Divorce recommended a simplification of procedure and an extension of grounds for divorce.
1923 Matrimonial Causes Act enabled a wife to obtain a divorce on the grounds of her husband's adultery, without having to prove some other offence in addition, which had been the case since 1857.
1937 The Herbert Act further extended grounds to include incurable insanity, cruelty, and desertion for three years or more.
1949 The Legal Aid Act enabled those with low incomes to be provided with assistance to cover legal costs.
1950 Matrimonial Causes Act introduced new grounds for a decree of nullity of a marriage (for example, non-consummation; being of unsound mind).
1969 Divorce Reform Act. This introduced the concept of the 'irretrievable breakdown of marriage'. This occurs when:

(a) The partners have ceased to cohabit for two years and neither objects to a divorce.
(b) They have separated for five years and one person has objected to a divorce. This objection is then overruled.
(c) Where there is conduct which a husband or wife cannot reasonably be expected to endure.
(d) But the Act states that no divorce can be obtained until the court is satisfied that the best possible arrangements have been made for the children of the marriage.

1970 The Matrimonial Proceedings and Property Act. This provides guidelines to judges in the award of financial settlements. It is based on the idea that the parties should be placed in the financial position in which they would have been if the marriage had not broken.
1984 The Matrimonial and Family Proceedings Act. This removed some of the maintenance obligations on husbands to former wives. Now maintenance may be for a set

period and may relate to the conduct of the parties. Under this Act there is an absolute bar of one year (rather than 3 years) before any couple can apply for a divorce. The main consideration remains the welfare of the children.

1991 The Law Commission Report suggests that legal processes may rush couples into divorce.

1992 Davis and Murch (*Grounds for Divorce*) found that:

(a) More than a third of the men and a fifth of the women in the sample wished that they had stayed married.
(b) About 50 per cent of remarriages ended in divorce.
(c) They support some of the fears of the Law Commissioners.

Comments

It is not so much that legislation causes divorce rates to increase but more that the increase results from the fact that couples who are not happily married can now obtain grounds for a divorce. The new law provides a solution to a marriage that has already disintegrated.

Opportunities for increased conflict and stress

These could be examined under the following headings:

Industrialisation The adaptation of the family to the requirements of an industrialised economic system may have generated more stress.

Work may be increasingly difficult to obtain; for those in work it may lack intrinsic interest; expectations for higher living standards may increase; there may be more pressure on women to run a home and seek employment.

Urbanisation Cities are often overcrowded and housing is unsatisfactory. There are problems in travelling to work and school on busy roads. There may be less sense of community and greater alienation and anomie in cities (see page 201). See also comments of Leach and Laing (page 81).

Secularisation The decline in the significance of religion in people's lives may have helped divorce to become more socially acceptable. Marriage loses its 'sacramental' quality. In 1977 there were more civil than church weddings for the first time since records started in 1832. In 1992 the figure was about 50 percent.

Changing values concerning marriage

There are some functionalist writers (For example, Fletcher, *The Family and Marriage*) who argue that people are increasingly expecting more from marriage than couples did in the past. There is an emphasis on companionship and shared experiences. Those who fail to achieve these may be more inclined to break the marriage in order to attain them with another partner. In this view a high divorce rate reflects the high standards which people have of marriage.

Oakley argues that the benefits that men and women gain from marriage are different. While there is inequality in wider society then there will be inequality in the home. One result is that women's changing role is also a significant factor in the rising divorce rates. Women file more than two-thirds of all petitions for divorce. Ross and Sawhill, conducting research in the USA, found that the higher the wife's annual income the greater the probability that the couple would separate.

Comments

It could be argued that it is not the employment of women that necessarily causes divorce. It may be more likely that this makes it possible, in that women who are unhappy in their marriage are more likely to look for satisfaction in their occupation. Having a well-paid job gives them economic independence which makes divorce feasible if the couple are unhappy in their marriage.

Variations in Divorce Rates

■ **Account for variations in the divorce rates between different groups. What have been the major social consequences of these increases?**

The occurrence of divorce is unevenly distributed in society. It affects different classes, age groups and occupational groups in different ways. These variations can be discussed in terms of the social structure of society. The problems of the consequences of divorce are open to different interpretations according to the perspective from which they are viewed. Functionalists may have one answer and Marxists another.

Variation in divorce rates

Age at marriage The younger the age of marriage the higher the rate of divorce. Teenage marriage is especially vulnerable.

(a) Young married couples face greater economic difficulties than older people.
(b) A high proportion of these marriages are to legitimate a pregnancy.
(c) As they grow older they may be more inclined to grow apart, with different interests and expectations.

Class differences The highest divorce rates occur among those groups at the bottom of their respective social classes. The highest rates are found in the lower middle class and lower working class. This may be because members are subject to more economic and social pressures.

Cultural differences The chances of marital breakdown are increased if spouses have different social or cultural backgrounds. It may be difficult for cross-class or cultural marriage partners fully to appreciate or understand aspects of behaviour, belief, etc.

Occupation Studies have indicated that there is a relationship between occupations requiring frequent separation from a spouse and high divorce rates (e.g. travelling salesman, lorry driver etc.). It may also be true among those who have a high involvement in their work and a low involvement in their home life (e.g. executives, lecturers, artists etc.).

Children in the family There is debate among researchers as to this factor. Thornes and Collard (*Who Divorces?*) found that marriages which end up in divorce were twice as likely to be childless as those which did not. However, Dominion and Abrams (*Marital Breakdown*) suggest that there is a sharp fall in happiness once children arrive, which is never recaptured; where partners have developed high expectations of companionship in marriage, babies do not necessarily cement such a union.

The possible consequences of divorce

Chester (*Divorce*) argues that society has never fully accommodated itself to the consequences of mass divorce because it has not resolved its attitudes towards the phenomenon. Governments seem undecided about how to cope with the fact that life-long monogamy is no longer pursued by about one-third of the population. The result, he says, is a succession of contradictory policies.

1. There is a need to restructure social services to meet the needs of mass divorce; although it could be argued that this could be seen as the abandonment of the family.
2. Social security schemes seem uncertain as to whether they should encourage remarriage, employment or the full-time care of children.
3. From a functionalist perspective, the family may be seen as less stable since individuals are not able to find security, identity and *emotional satisfaction*.
4. Studies by Bloom and Lynch in the USA claim to have found correlations between broken marriages and high levels of stress; increased health problems; and increased psychiatric problems, as well as higher rates of alcoholism and suicide.
5. Wallerstein and Kelly (*Surviving the Breakup*) note high levels of disturbance in young children whose parents divorce. They claim that in the USA, of children appearing in psychiatric clinics, more than 80 per cent come from broken families.
6. Illsley and Thompson (*Women from Broken Homes*) argue that the term 'broken home' must be interpreted with care. There is no general agreement as to what constitutes a broken home. It can result from death, desertion, separation, imprisonment, hospitalisation or divorce. Some are broken permanently, some for brief periods. Little is known about the extent or significance of these different types of broken home. Effects may vary between age, sex and type of broken home.

   As far as the consequences of divorce are concerned they argue that:

   (a) Broken homes of this type do not possess the monopoly of childhood unhappiness.
   (b) Some children may be better off when removed from an unhappy home atmosphere and placed in a stable one-parent family.
   (c) In general, where parental relationships are disturbed then those between parents and children are also likely to be unsatisfactory.
7. There will be an increase in the number of one-parent families. In 1984 one family in eight (including 1.5 million children) was of this type. Also numbers in care increased from 62 000 in 1961 to 105 000 in 1981. In 1991 the proportion of births outside marriage exceeded 30 per cent: in 1981 it was 12 per cent.
8. A further consequence of the increase in the divorce rate may be to increase the tendency to avoid marriage.

   (a) Dyer and Berlins (*Living Together*) conducted a survey which indicated that there was an increasing tendency towards cohabitation rather than marriage. Their survey estimated that in 1979 more than one-third of a million couples were living together unwed. Nearly a quarter of single women and two-thirds of divorced women marrying between 1977 and 1979 had lived with their husbands before marriage. For women married in the 1980s, the proportion reached 50 per cent in 1987.
   (b) Chellin (*Marriage, Divorce and Remarriage*) also notes the rise in cohabitation, not only in Britain but other European countries also. In Denmark, one in three of all people in their early twenties are living with a partner. The figure is higher in Sweden. In the USA it is estimated that there was a 40 per cent increase in the numbers between 1977 and 1979.

   Their explanations for these changing attitudes include:

   (a) A loss of belief in the value of marriage.
   (b) Marriage is no longer seen as the ultimate objective in a relationship.
   (c) Financially, it can pay to remain 'single'. The tax system works to their advantage.
   (d) A break in such a relationship is easier to achieve than the complications and expense of a divorce.
   (e) Having children is seen less and less as a reason for marrying.
   (f) There is now less opposition and social stigma attached to cohabitation.
   (g) Common-law wives can claim a share in the family home following a break in the relationship, if they can show that they have made a contribution to it, by paying a part of the mortgage, for example.
9. Chester concludes that the main problem facing Britain is not the high rate of divorce but the failure of our society to organise itself to meet the problems raised by marital breakdown.

Trends in Divorce

■ **Outline some of the trends in divorce in recent years. Is divorce functional?**

To answer any question on the trends in divorce you must be familiar with the statistics (see page 79). Apart from relevant points already mentioned you should also note the following details:

1. In recent years the rate of increase in divorces has slowed (one marriage in three).

   The reasons include:

   (a) Fewer teenage marriages.
   (b) Fewer early births in marriage.
   (c) Increased rates of cohabitation.
   (d) The high rates of unemployment in the 1980s and 1990s may be making separation or divorce difficult, since jobs, housing etc. are hard to obtain.

2. In 1981, for the first time in thirty years, the number of marriages involving at least one divorced person dropped. In one marriage in six both partners were remarrying. In 1991 there was a higher rate of remarriage for males.
3. There is a continuing trend towards later marriage (men 24.1, women 21.9 years). This has resulted in a decline in birth rate and in an increase in births to older women.
4. Between 1971 and 1981 the median duration of marriage ending in divorce remained at about ten years. In that period there was about a 4 per cent increase in divorce among those over thirty-five.
5. In 1980 more than £5 million was paid out each week in supplementary benefit to about 250 000 families unsupported after separation or divorce.
6. The OPCS (1984) noted that the divorce rates among the unemployed were almost double the national rate among those under the age of forty and nearly four times the national average in families where a husband lost his job within fifteen years of retirement.

In order to answer the second half of the question it is useful to contrast two theoretical perspectives:

The Marxist view of divorce

1. In a capitalist economic system it is women in particular who are exploited. Divorce is an important means of escaping from the limitations of marriage.
2. In such an economic system, people's material aspirations are raised, which encourages more women to go out to work. This places more stresses on the relationship and leads inevitably to conflict and divorce.
3. Children would not suffer the traumas of divorce if they were brought up in a more communal environment rather than in independent nuclear families where they often become a pawn or scapegoat in the battle between the parents.
4. Marriage is seen as a bourgeois concept which is the product of the need in a capitalist society for a stable work force, in which the ideology of the ruling class is transmitted from one generation to the next. Divorce is seen as a necessary institution.

The functionalist view of divorce

1. Divorce is functional in that it allows unhappy people to separate in a socially accepted way, providing protection for the partners and the children. It would become dysfunctional if the divorce rate reached exceptionally high levels, since it might then lead to social instability.
2. In general, policies are needed to protect the family and marriage in order to ensure a balance between the needs of the individual and those of society.
3. Vogel and Bell (*The Emotionally Disturbed Child as the Family Scapegoat*) argue that family conflict may be functional in that where it is directed at an emotionally disturbed child it provides a scapegoat for parental tension. Although this may be harmful to the child, the relations between husband and wife may be strengthened. They can then perform their normal roles in the community. The problems their child is causing may draw them closer together.

Suggested Reading

Works noted in this chapter

E. Butterworth and D. Weir (1975) *Sociology of Modern Britain*, Fontana

R. Chester (1975) 'Divorce', in Butterworth and Weir, *Sociology of Modern Britain*, Fontana

A. Chellin (1985) *Marriage, Divorce and Remarriage*, Harvard University Press

G. Davis and M. Murch (1992) *Grounds for Divorce*, OUP

R. Dobash and R. Dobash (1980) *Violence Against Wives*, Open Books

J. Dominian (1969) *Marital Breakdown*, Penguin

C. Dyer and M. Berlins (1985) *Living Together*, Hamlyn

R. Fletcher (1966) *The Family and Marriage*, Penguin

N. Hart (1976) *When Marriage Ends*, Tavistock

R. Illsley and J. Thompson (1975) 'Women from Broken Homes', in E. Butterworth and D. Weir (eds), *The Sociology of Modern Britain*, Fontana

R. Laing (1976) *The Politics of the Family*, Penguin

E. Leach (1967) *A Runaway World*, BBC Publications

T. Lupton and C. Wilson (1973) 'The Social Background and Connections of Top Decision-Makers', in J. Urry and J. Wakeford, *Power in Britain*. Heinemann

A. Oakley (1974), *Housewife*, Allen Lane

Thornes and Collard (1985) *Who Divorces*?

E. Urwin (1944) *Can the Family Survive*?, SCM Press

E. Vogel and N. Bell (1968) 'The Emotionally Disturbed Child as the Family Scapegoat' in *A Modern Introduction to the Family*, Free Press

J. Wallerstein and J. Kelly (1985) *Surviving the Breakup*, Grant McIntyre

P. Willmott and M. Young (1975) *The Symmetrical Family*, Penguin

Works for further reading

C. Harris (1983) *Family and Industrial Society*, Allen & Unwin

J. Pahl (1989) *Money and Marriage*, Macmillan

Self-test Questions

Study the following material and answer the questions below.

Item A

'Rutter pointed out that the number of stresses a child has to contend with is significant. Children with only one chronic family stress generally coped well, but with two or more stresses the psychiatric risk increased (Rutter and Quinton, 1977). They isolated six family adversity factors which seemed to be correlated with emotional and behavioural difficulties in children:

1 Father in unskilled/semi-skilled job.
2 Overcrowding or large family size.
3 Marital discord or "broken home".
4 Mother depressed/neurotic.
5 Child "in care".
6 Father – any offence against the law.'

Source: L. Stow and L. Selfe, *Understanding Children with Special Needs* Unwin Hyman. 1989.

Item B

'Illsley and Thompson argue that the term "broken home" must be used with care. There is no general agreement as to what constitutes a broken home. They can be broken in many ways (e.g. by death, desertion, separation, imprisonment, hospitalisation or divorce).

1 Little is known about the extent and significance of these different forms of broken home in the population.
2 Studies need to examine the different effects on children by age and sex in relation to each type.

They conclude:

a. Homes broken by divorce do not possess a monopoly of childhood unhappiness.
b. Some children may be better off removed from an unhappy home atmosphere into a stable one-parent family.
c. Generally, where parental relationships are disturbed then those between parents and children are likely to be unsatisfactory.

Herzov (a child psychiatrist) says that whether or not children are affected by divorce depends on:

a. How well they can adjust to new social and economic circumstances. (Parents may remarry or remain as single-parent families).
b. Their age, sex, temperament and they way they can cope with the stresses of the divorce processes. (Young, pre-school children may be at greater risk and so more vulnerable, since they may become more confused and distressed. Older children may be able to cope better.)
c. How the children are treated by the parents during the divorce proceedings. Often a child becomes a pawn or scapegoat in the battle between the parents and suffers as a result.

Wallerstein and Kelly in their book *Surviving the Breakup* are less optimistic. They argue that parents must be more aware of their significance for their children. They remain vital to a child's development (even if separated). For this reason they advocate the increased use of "joint custody". This would discourage the attitude of "having won the children". This often contributes to the bitterness between parents and so harms the children. At present in England and Wales only 2½ per cent of such children are the subject of joint custody orders.'

Source: P. Selfe, *Sociology*, Pan. 1987.

Item C

Live births outside marriage (as percentage of all births)

1901	4.0
1911	4.5
1921	5.0
1931	4.5
1941	4.0
1951	5.0
1961	5.0
1971	8.0
1981	10.0

Source: OPCS.

(**a**) Examine Item A and Item B.
The authors point to the significance of home background in behavioural difference in children. Discuss the problems of defining and assessing the significance of
 (i) 'a broken home'; and
 (ii) 'marital discord'.

(**b**) Examine Item B.
 (i) Summarise the debate between Herzov, and Wallerstein and Kelly in about 50 words.

(**c**) Examine Item C.
 (i) Suggest some reasons to account for the increase in the number of births outside marriage in recent years.
 (ii) Suggest some factors which might help change cultural values and expectations, so that birth outside marriage becomes less usual.

(**d**) Using all the items (and other information you may have) consider whether there is evidence to suggest that marriage is a less popular and less valuable institution and that divorce is functional for society and its members.

7

STRATIFICATION

Questions on this topic tend to fall within the following areas:

1. Forms of stratification.
2. Ways of assessing class membership.
3. Changes in the occupational structure.
4. Changes in the class structure:
   (a) The fragmenting class structure.
   (b) The position of white-collar workers.
   (c) Changes in the working class.
   (d) Changes in the middle class.
5. Theories of social stratification:
   (a) Marxist.
   (b) Weberian.
   (c) Functionalist.

Forms of Stratification

■ **How do slavery, caste and estate differ as forms of social stratification? (UCLES**

Cuber and Kenkel (*Social Stratification*) define stratification as 'a pattern of superimposed categories of differential privilege'. Mayer (*Class and Society*) defines it as a system of differentiation which includes 'a hierarchy of social positions whose occupants are treated as superior, equal or inferior relative to one another in socially important respects'.

These definitions indicate that stratification describes a society which is divided into different strata of groups whose members share similar levels of status, power or privilege. There exists a system of social inequality between the groups forming the various strata.

A society can be stratified according to a number of factors, of which class division is one associated particularly with industrialised societies; in pre-industrial societies caste, slavery and estate are predominant.

Caste stratification

(a) The most developed case is found in Hindu India (although there are examples found elsewhere). Caste is sanctioned by religion. This legitimises the concept of 'pollution'. This means that those in an 'unclean caste' have come into contact with others in a higher caste, whose purity is thus violated. Religious rituals are necessary in order to become cleansed.

(b) In India the main castes are the Brahmins, Rajputs, Vaishyias, Sudras and the untouchables. A person's caste determines every aspect of life: their place in the division of labour, whom they may marry, where they may live and so on.

(c) A member of a caste is never allowed to break through its rigid social and economic barriers.

(d) In the southern states of the USA and in South Africa caste-like structures are found, and in Japan there remains a group who suffer from being regarded as social outcasts, known as the Burakumin. In Britain, many gypsies are regarded as a 'pariah' group.

Estates stratification

(a) Estates were found in feudal systems of stratification.

(b) Feudal society was characterised by a hierarchy of authority headed by a king (or emperor or pope in Europe) followed by the nobility and the commoners. These formed the three main estates.

(c) These estates were legally defined (members having specific rights and duties); they had specific functions to perform in the society and they had political significance.

(d) Although the system had religious backing, this was less prominent than in the case of caste society.

(e) The system was transformed in Europe into a class system as feudalism fell into decline. Intermarriage and individual mobility between the estates was possible.

Slave society

(a) This was found in Ancient Greece and Rome. It also became a lucrative business in the sixteenth century

when Europeans transported thousands of Africans to the USA.
(b) Slaves have no legal rights. They are the chattels of their owners.
(c) The system represents an extreme form of legal and social inequality.
(d) Slaves performed important economic functions, providing free forced labour.
(e) Slavery fell into decline as it became recognised as an inefficient and immoral method of organising labour. It was abolished in British colonies in 1834 and in the USA in 1865.

Social class

(a) MacIver (*Society: Its Structures and Changes*): 'any portion of a community which is marked off from the rest . . . by a sense of social distance'.
Weber (*Economy and Society*): 'classes are aggregates of individuals who have the same opportunities of acquiring goods and the same exhibited standard of living'.
Hughes (*The Concept of Class*): 'a class is simply some collection of things grouped on the basis of at least one characteristic held in common by all members of the collection or class'.
Reid (*Social Class Differences in Britain*): 'social class is a grouping of people into categories on the basis of occupation'.
(b) In summary, there is stratification by class whenever the population is divided into groups which can be ranked in superior or inferior positions on the basis of some difference of power, privilege or status. The concept of class implies something about social relationships, values, lifestyles and life chances. There is some mobility between the classes on the basis of achievement, which is not possible in a caste, slave or feudal society.

Ways of Assessing Class Membership

■ **How far is social class position determined by level of income? Illustrate your answer with empirical evidence.**

■ **How far is occupation the major determinant of both social class and status in industrial societies?**

Assessing a person's social class is a complex matter. In using the term 'social class', sociologists are referring to broad groups of people who can be ranked in socially superior and inferior positions on the basis of some criteria. The difficulty is agreeing on the criteria to be used. The three significant rewards of high social class are power, privilege and prestige. There are several factors which could be considered: occupation, income and wealth, status, lifestyle and life chances, family background.

Occupation

The major criterion that has been used in most research is occupation. This has been found to be correlated to most other factors associated with class.

(a) Occupations are differentially rewarded.
(b) A person's occupation is a good indicator of his or her economic situation.
(c) It takes up about two-thirds of a person's life and places the individual in social situations in which there is interaction with others of a similar social type.
(d) It is likely to determine people's type of home and place of residence.
(e) It tends to influence leisure activities, favoured entertainments and so on.
(f) It may influence the type of clothing worn.
(g) Knowledge of a person's occupation helps us to 'make sense of them'. We 'know' how to treat them and what to expect of them.
(h) It influences the kind of role a person plays in society and this in turn influences patterns of behaviour.

In these ways occupation is a good single indicator of a whole range of characteristics. Knowing that someone is 'a doctor' or 'an unskilled labourer' helps us make good guesses about their level of education, their likely voting behaviour, their lifestyle, life chances, income and wealth, family background and so on.

For the purposes of research, class structure is normally assessed in terms of the Registrar General's classification. Since the Census of 1911 occupational groups have been grouped into a number of broad categories. (See Table 7.1.)

Some modifications are sometimes used which provide a finer gradation and a more comprehensive classification (see Table 7.2).

Some surveys do take account of other factors. For example, the National Survey of Health and Development classified respondents by the father's occupation as well as the social background of the mother.

Income and wealth

There are wide differentials of income and wealth in Britain (see pages 89 and 228). However, it is difficult to assess a person's class purely on the basis of this factor.

(a) Many low-status occupations may provide higher rates of pay than those more highly classified by the Registrar General (for example, skilled manual workers may receive more than clergymen, nurses, teachers and so on.)
(b) High income may give high status in a particular social environment but this is not necessarily the same as high social class (see page 96).
(c) Class is a complex concept which involves norms, values and attitudes. These cannot be changed or absorbed by someone overnight, so that to win the pools may not mean a change of class.
(d) Some research studies suggest that this is recognised by the public: Butler and Stokes asked a sample to describe the characteristics which best established a person's class (see Table 7.3).
(e) Atkinson (*Unequal Shares*) argues that income and wealth are good indicators of class membership. He shows that the top 1 per cent of wealth-holders own

Table 7.1 Registrar General's classifications

			1981
Class 1	Professional	Accountant; architect; clergyman; doctor; lawyer; university teacher.	3.7
Class 2	Intermediate	Aircraft pilot; chiropodist; MP; nurse; police officer; teacher.	20.9
Class 3a	Skilled non-manual	Clerical worker; draughtsman; secretary.	21.9
Class 3b	Skilled manual	Driver; butcher; bricklayer; cook.	24.3
Class 4	Semi-skilled	Bus conductor; postman; telephone operator.	13.0
Class 5	Unskilled	Labourer; messenger; cleaner; porter.	6.4
		Inadequately described	4.8

Source: *Census*, 1981.

Table 7.2 Occupational status level

1. (a) Higher professional
   (b) Landed proprietors
2. (a) Intermediate professional
   (b) Substantial farmers
3. (a) Lower professional
   (b) Small proprietor
4. (a) Supervisory, service employee
   (b) Self-employed (no employees)
5. Skilled manual
6. Relatively skilled manual
7. Semi-skilled manual
8. Unskilled manual

Source: Adapted from Goldthorpe *et al.*, *The Affluent Worker.*

Table 7.3 Characteristics which establish class

Middle class	% of respondents	Working class	% of respondents
Occupation	61	Occupation	74
Income	21	Income	10
Attitudes	5	Attitudes	5
Manners	5	Manners	5
Education	5	Education	5
Others	3	Others	3

Source: Adapted from Butler and Stokes.

Table 7.4 Distribution of wealth income and shares, 1963–90 (UK)

	1976	1989
Share of income going to wealthiest fifth of population (post-tax)	37	44
Percentage of wealth held in dwellings	23	37
Share of wealth held by richest 10% of population	50	53
Percentage shares held in private hands	*1963* 58	*1990* 20

Source: *Social Trends 22.*

Table 7.5 Distribution of marketable wealth, percentage 1976–89 (UK)

Marketable wealth: distribution		1976	1981	1989
Wealthiest	1%	21	18	18
	5%	38	36	38
	11%	50	50	53
	25%	71	73	75
	50%	92	92	94

Source: *Social Trends, 22.*

Table 7.6 Occupational class and industrial status 1951–71 (GB)

	1951		1971	
	Male	Female	Male	Female
Higher grade professionals	2.5	0.52	4.8	0.55
Employers and proprietors	5.7	3.2	5.0	2.7
Administrators and managers	6.8	2.7	10.9	3.5
Lower grade professionals	3.1	8.1	5.9	10.9
Clerical workers	6.35	20.4	6.38	27.0
Supervisors and foremen	3.2	1.1	5.0	1.8
Skilled manual	30.3	12.7	29.0	8.4
Semi-skilled manual	27.9	43.1	20.8	32.9
Unskilled manual	13.8	7.9	11.8	12.0

Source: Adapted from Routh, *Occupation and Pay in Great Britain.*

Table 7.7 Employment by sex and occupation, 1990.

Occupational group	Males	Females
Managerial and professional	36.3	28.7
Clerical	5.6	30.6
Other non-manual	6.2	9.3
Skilled craft manual	25.5	27.5
Semi-skilled and other manual	25.0	3.8
Unskilled labourers	0.9	0.1

Source: *Social Trends, 22.*

25 per cent of all the wealth in Britain. The top 5 per cent own 25 per cent of all the wealth. The bottom 90 per cent own about 35 per cent. These great wealth-holders form the highest social classes and hold power as a direct result of their wealth and income.

(f) Lockwood (*The Black-Coated Worker*) suggests that income is not so relevant in assessing class position. In his study he wished to see how the position of the clerk had changed over time. Between 1900 and 1930 clerks earned more than manual workers. But since that time their financial position has deteriorated. Nevertheless, the clerk retains a higher social class position. He has better job security, shorter hours and more fringe benefits.

(g) More recently, Townsend (*Inequality in the United Kingdom*) confirmed that manual workers, although often high earners, continue to suffer major disadvantages in the work place in comparison with lower paid white-collar workers.

(h) The details given in Table 7.4 show that there has been little change in the overall distribution of marketable wealth between 1976 and 1989. The share of the richest 1 per cent has fallen slightly (see Table 7.5) but that of the richest 25 per cent has increased. The richest 10 per cent still own more than half the marketable wealth of the UK. There has been a decline in private share ownership between 1963 and 1990.

Comments

1. The authors of *Social Trends*, 14 comment that there were substantial reductions in the shares of marketable wealth of the richest groups in the early 1970s (largely because of the fall in the prices of stocks and shares). During the following years there was little change in the pattern of ownership of wealth.

2. Atkinson and Harrison argue that between 1924 and 1972 there was a trend towards greater equality in wealth distribution. This trend has been reversed since 1979.

3. Atkinson (*Unequal Shares*) argues that where there has been redistribution it has been primarily between the very rich and the rich. It is his view that the reason why wealth remains more unequally distributed than income is because of the significance of inherited wealth in the pattern of wealth-holding.

4. *Social Trends*, 22 (1992) indicates:

(a) The gap between the top 10 per cent of wage earners and the bottom 10 per cent is widening, especially for manual employees.

(b) The share of income going to the top 20 per cent of households has increased (1977, 37 per cent; 1988, 44 per cent).

(c) For households as a whole, social security benefits are the second most important source of income.

(d) The top 10 per cent of tax payers were paying a larger proportion of tax in 1991 than in 1976.

(e) There had been little change in the overall distribution of marketable wealth between 1976 and 1989.

Changes in the Occupational Structure of Britain

■ **Assess the effect of changes that have occurred in the occupational structure of Britain on the class structure.**

Key issues:

(a) What changes have occurred?

(b) What have been some of the effects?

You would need to produce a few statistics for such a question to show you are familiar with the trends.

For purposes of analysis the British class structure is usually examined in terms of the occupational structure which can be compared over time. Although there is no absolute agreement on the classifications used, Routh (*Occupation and Pay in Great Britain*) has made a detailed investigation which shows changes between 1951 and 1971.

(See Table 7.6). See also the statistics from *Social Trends*, 22, shown in Table 7.7.

Comments on the statistics

The general trends that can be identified include:

(i) Higher grade professions: there was an overall increase in the numbers of both males and females. However, few women reach the top jobs even in the 1990s (see page 50).

(ii) Employers and proprietors: there was a slight decline in the number of both males and females in this category.

(iii) Administrators and managers: there was an increase in the number of males in this group and a smaller rise among females.

(iv) Lower grade professionals: the numbers of both men and women in this category increased steadily.

(v) Clerical workers: there was a small increase in the number of males but it is an occupational group which has seen the greatest increase in the number of women employed.

(vi) Supervisors and foremen: the number of men and women in this group increased. *Note*: Table 7.7 (Labour Force Survey, 1990 published in *Social Trends*, 22) shows that 48 per cent of men and 69 per cent of women in employment were in non-manual jobs. These percentages had not changed much since 1981.

(vii) Skilled manual: the number of skilled workers remained fairly constant until 1971 when it dipped below 30 per cent for the first time. There has been a marked decline in the number of females in this group.

(viii) Semi-skilled: there has been a steady decline in the numbers in this group, especially among female workers in recent years.

(ix) Unskilled labourers: there has been a decline in the numbers of unskilled workers as educational standards have improved and demand for this work has fallen. *Note*: 51 per cent of men and 31 per cent of women were in manual occupations in 1990.

Some of the possible effects of changes in the occupational structure 1951–91

1. There may be more upward mobility into white-collar jobs as traditional manufacturing declines. The number employed in this area fell by 3 million. The amount of downward mobility may have increased during the periods of recession in the 1980s and 1990s when unemployment passed 2.5 million.
2. The proportion of people in Classes 1, 2 increased between 1971 and 1991; males by 7 per cent and females by 5 per cent.
3. The clerical sector has expanded, causing more women to enter the work force. Their experiences has led to a rise in feminist demands for equality (see page 53).
4. There is some evidence to show that those with fewest skills and qualifications have fallen further behind those who have more. An underclass has been identified by some researchers (see pages 253 and 282).
5. The distribution of wealth has become more unequal in recent years (see page 89).
6. A powerful ruling business class has been identified, (see pages 90; 107; 147).
7. The decline in traditional working-class industries has led to the view that the British class structure is fragmenting, as more people enter the various middle-class strata (see page 95).
8. There has been a growth in the number of professional workers. They have been seen as an élite who can most easily maximise their rewards at the expense of others (see page 89).
9. There has been a decline in the power of trade unions as heavy industries have disappeared; but there has been a growth in white-collar unionism (see page 323).
10. The changes in the class structure have given rise to sociological analysis of embourgeoisement (see page 94) and proletarianisation (see page 93).
11. The changes have affected the fortunes of the Labour Party, which lost four consecutive elections between 1979 and 1992, partly because their traditional support had been eroded and undermined as manufacturing industry and trade unionism declined (see page 321).
12. Some have argued that the changes have made the distinctions between manual and non-manual workers irrelevant, because new sectional distinctions have emerged, taking the place of class in shaping people's behaviour (for example regional variations in occupational chances; housing tenure, etc.). These also include widely shared beliefs in:
    (i) 'instrumentalism': based on an acceptance of capitalist values; work is increasingly seen as an instrument to attain other needs; and
    (ii) 'Privatism': with less demand for collective action and more concentration on private self-interest. (These ideas were first presented in the 1960s by Lockwood and Goldthorpe; see page 292.)

Conclusion

The class structure has undergone major changes between 1951 and 1991, in terms of the occupational organisation of society, as new technologies and new economic theories have been introduced. The consequences have been varied and there is debate as to whether Britain's class structure has become more fluid (the Weberian view) or more polarised, as gaps between the well-paid in secure jobs and the poor in low-income households widens (the Marxist view).

Marshall (*Social Science Review*) disputes the view that social class is becoming a less important factor in understanding patterns of social behaviour; on the contrary, even though there have been changes in the occupational structure, it remains important as a souce of social identity.

Note: You would need to decide where you stand in this debate and conclude according to the weight of the evidence you select.

Changes in the Class Structure

■ **Is the British class structure becoming increasingly fragmented or is it becoming more polarised?**

Central issue

The view that classes are becoming more fragmented and less easy to identify is held by functionalists and Weberians. The view that it is becoming more polarised, with clearly defined membership, is presented by Marxists.

(a) Marxists have argued that society is becoming increasingly divided between extremes of wealth and poverty, between the bourgeoisie and the proletariat (see also page 251).
(b) Functionalists have argued that class divisions, although inevitable and functionally useful, have narrowed and become increasingly blurred (see also page 97).
(c) Weberians have argued that classes are so flexible that long-term cohesion is never likely. Even people in the same class do not share the same values. People move in and out of classes according to the demand that exists for their skills in the open market (see also page 96).

The view that classes are becoming more fragmented

1. Dahrendorf (*Class and Class Conflict in Industrial Society*) examines changes in the occupational structure and notes increased levels of upward mobility, the growth of the white collar sector, improved incomes and living standards, etc. He concludes that the traditional working class is disintegrating and the class structure is fragmented.

2. Lockwood (*Black-Coated Worker*) and Goldthorpe (*Social Mobility and the Class Structure*) have identified a number of different white-collar groups who may have different aspirations and opportunities according to their skills (see also their class categories, page 89). They also differ from manual workers in several respects. The authors' examined these in terms of:

(a) differences in job opportunities and prospects;
(b) differences in work relationships; and
(c) differences in status and prestige.

3. Marshall *et al.* (*Social Class in Modern Britain*) support the view that even low-level white collar workers involved in routine and repetitive work are clearly distinguishable from routine manual workers. They found that over 90 per cent of their sample thought they had not been de-skilled by technological changes (although those involved in personal service work, on check-outs, etc. thought they had been disadvantaged). They also supported the view that working class people were stratified according to the skills they possessed.

4. Hill (*The Dockers*) found that in his sample there was little evidence for class consciousness. Although they were an example of the traditional working class and saw their work in instrumental terms, they had home-centred private lives and did not emphasise collective action.

5. Roberts *et al.* (*The Fragmentary Class Structure*, see also page 95) have identified four different groups of middle-class people, each of which has a different perspective and value system.

The view that the classes are polarising

For Marxists, class consciousness means that members of the proletariat become fully aware of their common identity and the levels of exploitation they face. In becoming a 'class for itself', revolutionary action to obtain change becomes possible. They interpet the evidence to show a process of polarisation:

1. Westergaard and Resler (*Class in a Capitalist Society*) argue that:

(a) A ruling class exists which controls the wealth of the society. This is concentrated in a few hands (see page 228).
(b) The difference between people in both working and middle classes is small compared with the differences between them and the ruling class. Those who fail to recognise this are deluded by the power of ruling class manipulation (the media, Church, etc.).
(c) There is evidence to show that gaps between rich and poor have been widening since the 1970s (see page 228).

2. Scott (*The British Upper Class*) identifies a remarkable business or capitalist class whose rich and powerful members interconnect through their control of large companies, banks and other financial institutions. Their shared interests range throughout the economy. They are not adversely affected by competition because they have so many assets in common. This class is the source of real power in society. Its members intermarry and it is sustained by the public school system, the prestige of Oxbridge, the patronage of the Conservative Party and the deference shown by people towards wealth. The only constraints on it are through the Labour Party (when in power), the trade unions which can mobilise working people, and competition from foreign companies. He argues that this class holds a disproportionate amount of power and will continue to do so while divisons remain among the bulk of the population who are not and are unlikely to be members of the business class. It is they who 'participate in the strategic control of the enterprises which form the monopoly sector of the British economy'.

3. Braverman (*Labour and Monopoly Capitalism*) argues that increasing numbers of traditional white-collar jobs, especially those in offices, are becoming de-skilled and routinised. Workers in these jobs lack job satisfaction and become alienated, having extremely tedious and repetitive work. They have weak bargaining positions and are turning more to unions for support. They are therefore seen as moving into the proletariat.

4. Crompton and Jones (*White Collar Proletariat*) support this view. They also describe how changes in office technology (which has become increasingly automated and machine-based) has affected the class position of the large numbers of female workers involved. They have diminishing opportunities for upward mobility.

5. Giddens (*The Class Structure of Advanced Societies*) on the other hand, says that routine white-collar workers should be seen as part of the middle class. He sees this as a unified section of society which coheres around possession of valuable social talents. The middle class is distinguished by possession of educational and technical qualifications. Unlike the working class, they have more to offer employers than just their labour.

Points of criticism

There are problems of methodology in assessing whether classes are fragmenting or polarising.

(i) Most studies rely on the use of questionnaires and unstructured interviews to assess attitudes. These may be hard to obtain from people in their work situation. (For example: Who provides the questionnaire? Under what conditions do interviews take place? Is discussion and clarification of issues possible?) Also, they often require subjective assessments on the part of respondents.
(ii) Answers may be open to a range of interpretations. These may depend on the ideologies of the interviewer as well as on the meaning inferred by the respondent.
(iii) The sample size may be small.

Conclusions

Those who argue that the class structure is fragmenting say:

(a) There are many studies supporting the view that there is a decline in class consciousness, especially among the traditional working class. Workers are increasingly privatised, interested in family and home, and lacking interest in wider political and class issues.
(b) Where class consciousness exists it is seldom in clear and coherent form. Even if people identify with a class their activities are seldom consistent with their beliefs. The 1985 miners' strike failed to unify all the miners in a concerted effort to win their case. Many miners continued to work throughout the year-long dispute.
(c) Few people seem to believe that the social system can be changed or that class action is the basis for such change.

Those who see an increasing polarisation argue:

(a) Working-class attitudes and cultural values are deeply ingrained. Members do retain interests in wider political issues and they do have a sense of class identity. This is seen in the papers they read, films and TV programmes they watch, etc.

(b) This sense of identity is increased in times of economic depression when they often do recognise the need for collective action (for example, in 1990 the anti-poll tax demonstrations were effective in changing the law).

(c) Class remains a relevant concept because people do recognise inequalities in distribution of wealth, income and power; although some argue (for example Marshall *et al.*) that people often need to be politicised in order to draw issues and their significance to their attention.

■ **Technological change has transformed the office worker into a white-collared proletarian. Do you agree with this assessment of the current class position of the white-collar worker?**

There has been much debate about the class position of certain white-collar workers, especially those clerical workers who tend to be classified in Class 3a of the Registrar General's scale. Are they part of the middle class or the working class?

The proletarianisation thesis

The view is put by Marxist writers that there are groups of workers whose class position is objectively working class (because they do not own the means of production) even though they may appear to be in bourgeois occupations (such as clerical workers) and have middle-class identifications. The opponents of the view argue that self perception is an important aspect of class identification, as well as the fact that the work of such groups is largely different from that of manual workers in factories.

1. Westergaard and Resler (*Class in a Capitalist Society*) argue that low-level white-collar workers are among the broad mass of ordinary labour 'and indeed are often well down towards the bottom of the pile'. They dispute the view that changes in the occupational structure have led to any major changes in the class structure of modern Britain. They would accept that the modern office worker is a white-collared proletarian, and focus particularly on the more negative aspects of technological change in the office.

Some disadvantages of technological change

1. Braverman (*Labour and Monopoly Capitalism*) has suggested that there has been a great increase in the number of white-collar workers over the past century. But the skills they originally required have been undermined by changes in technology. They have lost status and their jobs have become more proletarian.

2. Crompton and Jones (*White Collar Proletariat*) support the view that there has been an increase in proletarianisation among clerical workers. They suggest that less than 3 per cent of women achieve high-level managerial posts. Some men were achieving success at the expense of women, although they argue that even their success had ceilings of responsibility and skill. Many of the men had not achieved true middle-class status because many of the jobs to which they were promoted carried little responsibility, power or status.

(a) Modern office equipment often requires fewer skills in its use.

(b) There is often much noise and impersonal work conditions in large open-plan offices, where people are tied to their desks, often doing repetitive tasks.

(c) Personal skills (shorthand, personal relationships, etc.) are often minimised and there is less contact between a secretary and the professional for whom she works.

(d) Modern technology may reduce the demand for secretaries with much training or hopes of promotion.

Opponents of the proletarianisation thesis

1. Lockwood (*The Black-Coated Worker*) argues that the number of clerical workers has steadily increased throughout the century (see data on page 89). However, the clerk appears to be in an intermediate position, trapped between classes. Although there are some similarities between the work of the clerk and that of the manual worker, Lockwood suggests that the clerk has a stronger identification with the middle class, although he accepts that the position of the male clerk in particular is an ambiguous one.

2. Stewart *et al.* (*Social Stratification and Occupations*) argue that, for men, the low-level white-collar job in an office is invariably used as a stepping stone. Few remain long in these occupations, since they tend to be upwardly mobile and achieve more senior management positions in time.

3. Weir (*Wall of Darkness*) notes how white-collar workers have always put high emphasis on secure and steady jobs which provide adequate income and chances of promotion. These attitudes tend to distinguish them from the more instrumental attitudes of blue-collar workers.

4. Weir and Mercer tested the thesis in a study of white-collar clerks in Hull. They indicate dual findings. For many of the women workers there was some evidence of proletarianisation, especially where they had low qualifications and suffered many of the disadvantages of the modern office. They tended to have little contact with the professional management. However, for the majority of males the reverse seemed to be true. They were more likely to enjoy chances of promotion and to identify with and have more middle-class contacts. They were less likely to be involved in routine work.

Some possible conclusions

1. From a Functionalist Weberian perspective it could be argued that for women from a working-class background with minimum qualifications and skills, the new technologies in the office do not enhance chances of upward mobility. For others with more qualifications and skills, working in a modern office where these are valued and utilised, the chances of upward mobility are increased. This is particularly true for males.

2. From a Marxist perspective such arguments would be seen as examples of false class consciousness.

■ **There is no working class in Britain. There are only different groups of working people. Discuss. (UODLE)**

The answer to the question depends on the perspective that is adopted.

1. Marx predicted that the working class in industrial societies would become more unified as exploitation increased. Therefore working people who do not own the means of production form the proletariat or working class.

2. Those sociologists who tend to follow the Weberian perspective in their analysis would accept the implication of the question that the whole class structure (and not just that of the working class) has become more fluid and heterogeneous.

(a) There have been major changes in the occupational structure, which has resulted in the traditional working class becoming divided into several categories whose members have little in common. Each has a different status and degree of power in the market place.
(b) Dahrendorf (*Class and Class Conflict in Industrial Society*) argues that traditional class divisions are disappearing. There has been a decline in traditional working-class industries and there has been a growth in middle-class occupational groups, especially among the bureaucrats and professionals. All this makes the class picture more complex.
(c) Butler and Rose put forward the embourgeoisement thesis to suggest that as affluence increased among the traditional working class, so the classes were likely to merge. Increased mobility may therefore have increased the flexibility of the class structure (see page 149).
(d) Lockwood (*The Black-Coated Worker*) emphasised the importance of the subjective element in class identification. Often people identify with a class to which objectively they may not appear to belong, but nevertheless this may help to shape their behaviour (for example, voting).
(e) There have been both economic and social changes in the lives of people in Classes 3b, 4 and 5 which may have affected their self-perception and to some extent their objective position. For example, many have improved living standards, the opportunity to buy their own homes (including council houses); they have access to more material goods, greater legal protection in work, and higher expectations about their opportunities and quality of life.
(f) At times of high unemployment many people may suffer downward mobility. That is, they may take work for which they are overqualified. The question then arises, are they in the class established by their present occupation or that of their first job?

These arguments lead to the view that it is not possible to speak of 'the working class', since this would encompass about 55 per cent of the population (Classes 3b, 4 and 5). Within these categories there are range of attitudes, values and social norms.

Arguments that the classes have not merged

1. Some critics argue that all manual workers tend to suffer similar problems even though they may not have developed a unified class consciousness. They are more likely than white-collar workers to be made redundant, laid off or put on short time. Unemployment rates are higher. They have more serious illness: for example, in 1982, 35 per cent of males and 42 per cent females in the unskilled category reported long-standing illness compared with 23 per cent of males and 21 per cent of females in the white-collar section.

2. Sennett and Cobb (*The Hidden Injuries of Class*) are critical of the claim that workers are melting into a homogeneous society. They describe the emotionally damaging effects of social class on blue-collar workers in the USA. They note the low self-esteem with which many manual workers describe themselves: 'These feelings amount to a sense that the lower a man defines himself in society in relation to other people, the more he seems at fault'.

3. Lockwood and Goldthorpe (*The Affluent Worker*) reject the embourgeoisement thesis. This claims that the more affluent sections of the working class are losing their identity as a social stratum and are becoming merged into the middle class. They argue that all the factors that contribute to a person's social class have not been taken into consideration. They say that income and wealth are not in themselves useful measures of class position. The other factors to be considered are:

(a) The *economic aspect*: manual workers have less job security, etc.
(b) The *relational aspects*: there is no social intermixing.
(c) The *normative aspect*: manual workers do not share the same norms or values as the white-collar workers.
(d) The *political aspect*: the manual workers tend to see the Labour Party as the party of the working class.

The main areas of convergence between the classes are in terms of their shared preference for increasingly privatised lifestyles and instrumental attitudes. These workers are described by the authors as 'the new working class'.

4. Marshall (*Social Science Review*) also argues that even though there is evidence of increasing sectional interests among different groups of workers 'class continues to be a major factor structuring contemporary British society'. For example, it remains important in shaping voting intention (especially for Labour). However, he concludes that Britain is not a nation of class warriors seeking class objectives.

Conclusion

(a) The Weberian view would emphasise the flexibility of the concept of class. Workers seek economic gain and they make use of their different skills in the market place to secure the scarce resouces they value. As these demands change over time, so class group composition changes. Some neo-Weberians (for example, Goldthorpe) argue that classes cannot polarise into mass categories, such as 'the middle class' because aspiration change and there are few long-term goals held in common.

(b) The Marxist view emphasises the similarities held by all those who do not own the means of production, their levels of exploitation and alienation, which can only be overcome by major social revolution. They can identify a clearly definable working class which exists in opposition to an upper and a middle class, whose members have unfair advantages in society.

■ **It is now more realistic to talk about the middle classes rather than the middle class. Explain and discuss this view.**

This question, like the previous one, invites a discussion between those sociologists who argue that there is an increasing polarisation of the classes, so that they are becoming more homogeneous, and those whose dispute the view and argue that they are becoming more heterogeneous.

The view that the middle class is becoming more fragmented

1. Roberts *et al.* (*The Fragmentary Class Structure*) put forward the view that it is not realistic to speak of *the* middle class since there is an increasing division into a number of different strata.

(a) The results of their survey indicated that 27 per cent of respondents had a 'middle-mass image' of society. They saw themselves as part of a middle class which made up the bulk of the population. They were trapped between a small and powerful upper class and a comparatively poor lower working class. They were mainly in the middle range income bracket.
(b) 19 per cent saw themselves as a 'compressed middle class'. They perceived themselves as a narrow, threatened group, who were squeezed between two powerful classes above and below. This view was held mainly by small businessmen.
(c) 15 per cent subscribed to a type of class imagery in which the social hierarchy was portrayed as a 'finely graded ladder'. No single stratum was recognised as numerically dominant. This view was most common amongst the more highly educated respondents.
(d) 14 per cent held a 'proletarian image'. They tended to define themselves as working class and saw themselves as part of the largest class at the base of the stratification structure. Those holding this image were mainly routine white-collar workers. The authors argue that it is unlikely that workers will become more bourgeois in the future:
   (i) Whilst it is true that there are factors which favour the development of middle-class attitudes amongst manual workers, none is sufficiently powerful in isolation to guarantee a bourgeois outcome.
   (ii) The appearance of middle-class attitudes only becomes possible when a constellation of favourable circumstances coincides, but their interconnection is rare. In the researchers' sample there were only eleven such cases: for example a worker was affluent, an owner-occupier had few close friends in work and had strong white-collar connections.
   (iii) While some of these features are likely to become more widespread, there seemed no grounds for believing that other favourable circumstances were increasingly common.

They concluded that the trends were not so much towards increasing middle-class attitudes and values among affluent workers, as the maintenance of working-class ethics with less emphasis on class awareness.

2. Goldthorpe (*Social Mobility and the Class Structure*) analyses class in terms of a person's:

(a) work situation (for example, promotion chances, job satisfaction, responsibility); and
(b) market situation (demand for skills, qualifications, intellect, etc.).

He notes wide variations among different white-collar groups at different times, in relation to these factors. He concludes there cannot be a united middle class; instead, there are various strata, which can be subdivided between Higher and Lower Professions who form a 'service class' and Routine Non-Manual, the Self-employed and Supervisors, who form an 'intermediate class'. A person's position therefore changes in a fluid way as their work and market situation changes with movements in the economy.

Abercrombie and Urry (*Capital, Labour and the Middle Classes*) have described this situation as resulting in the upper (service class) group moving socially in one direction whilst the other (intermediate class) becomes more proletarian.

The view that there is a coherent middle class

Marxist writers (for example Westergaard and Resler) would identify the middle class as 'the petite/petty bourgeoisie'. They are those with non-manual occupations whose jobs require the use of the intellect. While they do not own the means of production they do ally themselves with the ruling class and act in their interests. They are a cohesive class because they have values and aspirations in common and require a subservient working class over whom they exercise their power.

Conclusion

The debate is complex. Some writers (for example, Roberts *et al.*) see a clear process of middle-class fragmentation, with many strata emerging. Others suggest that the picture is simpler than this, since the features dividing them are less significant than the things which unite them into a coherent class (for example, educational qualifications; valued social and intellectual skills; power; responsibility; access to scarce resources; high social status).

Note: Again, conclude in terms of the evidence you have used, showing the direction in which it points in answer to the question.

Theories of Social Class Stratification

The Marxist perspective

■ **The origin of class is in the division of labour. Discuss.**

1. It is the economic infrastructure which is the foundation on which the social superstructure is built.
2. The group which controls the forces of production controls the form of the superstructure.
3. Classes arise from inequalities in the economic structure of society. When the means of production are in private hands this is the group which holds power.
4. Classes appear where there is the production of surplus goods in the economy whose distribution is controlled by the non-producers for their own gain.
5. Where there are no surpluses, as in simple societies, no classes can develop.
6. In a capitalist economic system the exploitation of the work force is known as *alienation*. Although the worker is legally free (compared with those in slave society) the workers are controlled by the employer, the pace of the work and the technology of production. There is the seed of class division in alienation.
7. Class is rooted in the economic structure of society and class conflict becomes a major source of social and historical change.
8. Class therefore refers to a whole set of relationships (economic, social and political) which determine the individual's position in the whole society.
9. Membership of a class is an objective fact, but it requires class consciousness to develop in order for people to act in a unified way to seek change.

Points of criticism

(i) There is much evidence to suggest that the manual workers of Classes 3b, 4 and 5 do not form a homogeneous group; nor do they have common status, common interests or live in similar ways with similar norms and values. They do not have a common enemy in an all-powerful ruling class.

(ii) In contemporary society there is an increasing level of cultural homogeneity, in that there is a common culture which cuts across classes, through television, radio, newspapers, etc. The mass media help to impose shared values.

(iii) Marx oversimplified a complex situation by combining together a large number of disparate people called 'the working class' (proletariat) and the 'bourgeoisie'. In fact different strata have distinctive qualities, as shown by Roberts *et al.* in *The Fragmentary Class Structure*.

(iv) Marx presents a model based on economic determinism. He does not allow for subjective impressions nor for the effects of status differences influencing opportunities in society.

The Weberian view of class and status

■ **The concentration of power in early capitalist society has given way to a contemporary diversity of competing groups among which none is supreme. Examine and evaluate this view.**

1. Classes arise from the inequalities in the distribution of power (that is, the ability to achieve desired ends against the opposition of others).
2. Power varies between people in three key spheres:
   (a) Economic.
   (b) Social.
   (c) Political.
3. A person's class is determined by the position held in the economic sphere. This market position is important in explaining why some people have greater access to scarce resources than others.
4. People are in the same class when they share the same chances in the market of obtaining the scarce resources of jobs, income and property.
5. This view allows for the existence of many classes whose membership frequently changes. For example there may be:
   (a) *Property classes* (as described by Rex and Moore, see page 275).
   (b) *Acquisition classes* (these will arise where people can exploit their particular skills in the economic market).
   (c) *Educational classes* (where people can exploit their intellectual skills in the market).
6. It also leads to the view that there are various types of working and middle-class groups which emerge according to their skills and levels of power. The class position of their members is not based on any hereditary rights; it is a fluid and flexible process.
7. There are no necessarily permanent groups. The market is a place of transitory goals; groups dissolve once they are able to achieve their ends.
8. Class conflict is not an inevitable feature arising from a desire to produce a more equal society.
9. The Weberian view leads to a more pluralistic view of class than the Marxian.

Weber's concept of status

1. This refers to differences in the social sphere. It relates to a person's prestige in the eyes of others.
2. A person's social power is determined by social prestige.
3. 'Status groups are stratified according to the principles of consumption of goods as represented by special styles of life'.
4. Class and status are different facets of the stratification system. A person with high economic power does not necessarily have high social status.
5. A person's status may be more relevant than his or her class in obtaining important scarce resources. Two people in the same class may have different levels of social status. It may be that the person of higher status is able to obtain the job or house.
6. Groups are not likely to form in a permanent way around status factors.

Points of criticism

(i) Weber's concept of pluralistic classes may be thought to reduce the significance of class as a tool of social analysis, since it becomes difficult to make any clear statement as to distinctions between the life chances of middle-class and working-class groups.
(ii) His emphasis on the subjective element in class analysis means that it is the subjective perception of the individual that is relevant in assessing class membership. If people doing unskilled, low-status work claim to be middle class, then this must be considered to be relevant.
(iii) Weber assumes high levels of social mobility in industrial societies, making class cohesion unlikely. However, at times of high unemployment mobility is limited, which might suggest that class consciousness will develop.
(iv) Although Weber wishes to distinguish between class and status, critics would argue that the two correlate closely in the economic and social spheres of everyday life.
(v) See also Scott (page 92).

■ **Examine the view that social stratification and social inequality are permanent, necessary and inevitable features of human society. (AEB)**

Notice how this question raises arguments about the functionalist perspective. You must remember that this is only one possible interpretation. You must therefore present the functionalist views, but also some points of possible criticism, and then reach a conclusion.

The functionalist view

Consider the following points:

1. The various parts of a society must be seen in relation to the whole to see how they contribute to the maintenance of the entire system.
2. A society has certain needs which must be fulfilled to ensure its survival. Even a system of stratification must be functional, otherwise it would not exist.
3. The system of stratification derives from common social values. It is a social norm that some people are valued more highly than others. Those who perform the most important functions most effectively will gain the highest rewards and greatest esteem.
4. Stratification is an inevitable feature of all human societies. Different forms of stratification result from the way that people are ranked according to the values of the society.
5. Such systems are valuable because they are examples of shared social values and they provide a means by which people can be motivated to achieve higher esteem in their society.
6. Inequalities in power are legitimate and socially necessary; without them societies would be inefficient.
7. Social stratification by class is the device by which the most important positions in society are filled by the most able and best qualified people. Since some positions in society are more functionally important than others, they require more skill and technique. These positions must therefore have higher rewards attached to them.

Points of criticism:

(i) Critics ask how it is possible to assess which positions in society are the most functionally important? Is someone earning £50 000 p.a. five times more important than someone who earns £10 000 p.a.?
(ii) There are many people in low-paid jobs who are functionally very important for society (for example, nurses).
(iii) Differentials in pay seem more likely to be related to differences in power rather than functional value.
(iv) It may be that social stratification actually inhibits mobility rather than being a source of encouragement. (The unskilled worker may believe he lacks the ability to improve his social position.) The functionalist view tends to assume that it is easy for someone to step outside their cultural norms and respond to 'the incentives of the market place'.
(v) Social stratification may not integrate people more closely into their society, but widening inequalities may become dysfunctional, encouraging conflict and distrust.
Thomas (Guildhall Lecture, 1982) said that Britain should prevent an underclass being created in its cities. He pointed out that in the USA such a group, largely comprising members of minorities, had emerged despite progress in racial advancement in the past two decades. People were trapped in a continuing web of poverty; the members could become a menace to people and property, and hostility to all underclass stereotypes was created.
(vi) Consider a Marxist interpretation, which denies that class divisions are inevitable or necessary (page 96).

■ **The analysis of the social class structure of modern Britain has ignored the position of women. Discuss.**

1. In any such question you need to clarify the concept of social class:
   (a) It is usually defined for research purposes in terms of occupational membership (rewards gained help shape lifestyle, life chances, etc.).
   (b) The Registrar General's classification is useful in this respect (although it has been elaborated and refined by many researchers, for example, Goldthorpe *Social Mobility and the Class Structure*; see page 107).
   (c) These systems of classification have relied on data relating to head of household, who is normally considered to be the male.
2. Establish the central issue in the question. It seems to be true that where the class membership of households is being established the position of women is generally ignored, but is the omission significant?

(i) **The view that it is not significant:**

The Conventional Model (Westergaard and Resler; Goldthorpe, *In Defence of the Conventional View)* This rests on the argument that the class position of a wife is determined primarily by her marital relationship. It is the husband's employment which shapes her lifestyle as well as that of other family members. Therefore it is acceptable to retain the conventional model. Some proponents, however, accept that the highest-class partner could be used to assess the class position of the family.

Point of criticism: it assumes that the family is the main unit of stratification rather than the individual: it rests on the traditional view that the male is the main breadwinner; it neglects the female's contribution to the household economy, and input on values, etc.

(ii) **The view that a woman's position should be taken into account:**

(a) The Cross-Class Model (Britten and Heath *Women's Jobs Do Make a Difference*). This view takes account of the problem which arises when two adults have different types of job, for example, a wife is a nurse and a husband a mechanic, yet the household is classified as working class. They argue that the position of the wife in the occupational structure must have a significant effect on features of family life (for example, social attitudes, voting patterns, lifestyle, family status, etc.). This model argues that women should be recognised in class analysis.

The main criticism: it places less significance on the husband's occupation as an influence on household behaviour and presumes that even low-level white-collar work may distinguish a woman's class from that of a husband in skilled manual work.

(b) The Individual Model (Stanworth, *Women and Class Analysis*; Marshall *et al.*, *Social Class in Modern Britain*). They resolve the problem by arguing that class should always be assigned to an individual rather than to a family since there is evidence that it is only in about 20 per cent of households that working men are the sole providers of economic support for the family. Also 'class fates' were found to be more affected by the class of individuals than their families.

The main criticism: in assigning class on present occupation it does not classify people not in employment; also, there are many women with young families who may be well qualified, but who are not classified; on the other hand, the single, childless woman is more likely to be employed in a high-status occupation.

(c) The Feminist Model (Delphy, *Close to Home*). Radical feminists see the patriarchal structure of society as the source of female inequality. Some have argued that women form a 'sex class' resulting from biological factors (see also page 48). They argue that gender stratification becomes significant in explaining why women are often ignored in the analysis of the class structure. Since women are either predominently housewives or in low-paid occupations, their class position is also likely to be low or non-existent. They are exploited in every area of social life, in work and in the home.

Main criticism: it is based on a clear feminist ideology and may be subject to research bias.

(d) The Class Accentuation Model (Bonney, *Gender, Household and Social Class*). This is the other side of the coin of the Cross Class Model. It suggests that most people tend to marry into the same class as their partner and seldom across class lines. This is particularly noticeable at the extreme ends of the social scale (that is, it is unusual for a Class 1 man to marry a Class 5 girl and vice versa). He notes from his research that high-earning female workers tend to have high-earning partners. The consequence is that class differences may become accentuated and patterns of inequality intensify as dual-income households become the norm.

Main criticism: it proposes a much more complex model of the class structure, since at times of high employment incomes may be high even in low-status jobs, and lower in high-status occupations; other measures of class difference may therefore be required.

Conclusion

Bonney notes that:

(a) it does seem to be the case that the Conventional Model does not take enough account of the changing role of women in the social and occupational structure.
(b) Consequently, much more careful research is needed.
(c) The models open to most criticism are the Individualist and the Feminist.
(d) The Cross Class and Class Accentuation models show the most promise for future analysis.

Suggested Reading

Works noted in this chapter

N. Abercrombie and J. Urry (1983) *Capital, Labour and the Middle Classes*, Allen & Unwin

A. Atkinson (1974) *Unequal Shares*, Penguin

N. Bonney (1988) 'Gender, Household and Social Class', *British Journal of Sociology* (March)

H. Braverman (1974) *Labour and Monopoly Capitalism*, Monthly Review Press

N. Britten and Heath (1983) 'Women, Men and Social Class', in E. Garmarnikow, *Gender, Class and Work*, Heinemann

N. Britten and A. Heath (1984) 'Women's Jobs Do Make a Difference', *Sociology*, Vol. 18, No. 4

D. Butler and R. Rose (1959), *The British General Election of 1959*, Frank Cass

R. Crompton and Jones (1984) *White Collar Proletariat*, Macmillan

J. Cuber and W. Kenkel (1954) *Social Stratification in USA*, New York

R. Dahrendorf (1959) *Class and Class Conflict in Industrial Society*, Routledge & Kegan Paul

E. Garmarnikow (1983) *Gender, Class and Work*, Heinemann

A. Giddens (1973) *The Class Structure of Advanced Societies*, Hutchinson

J. Goldthorpe (1980) *Social Mobility and Class Structure in Modern Britain*, Clarendon Press

S. Hill (1976) *The Dockers*, Heinemann

J. Hughes (1945) 'The Concept of Class', *American Sociological Review* No. 3

J. Goldthorpe *et al.* (1969) *The Affluent Worker*,

J. Goldthorpe (1983) 'In Defence of the Conventional View', in *Sociology*

D. Lockwood (1958) *The Black-Coated Worker*, Allen & Unwin

R. MacIver (1950) *Society: Its Structures and Changes*,

G. Marshall *et al.* (1988) *Social Class in Modern Britain*, Hutchinson

G. Marshall (1987) 'What is Happening to the Working Classes', *Social Science Review* (January)

K. Mayer (1956) *Class and Society*,

I. Reid (1977) *Social Differences in Britain*, Open Books
K. Roberts *et al.* (1977) *The Fragmentary Class Structure*, Heinemann
J. Scott (1982) *The British Upper Classes*, Macmillan
R. Sennett and J. Cobb (1977) *The Hidden Injuries of Class*, Cambridge University Press
M. Stanworth (1984) *Women and Class Analysis*
Stewart *et al.* (1980) *Social Stratification and Occupations*, Macmillan
P. Townsend (1979) *Inequality in the United Kingdom*, Penguin
D. Weir (1973) *Wall of Darkness*, Fontana
Westergaard and Resler (1976) *Class in a Capitalist Society*, Penguin

Works for further reading

C. Delphy (1984) *Close to Home*, Hutchinson
R. Hyman and R. Price (1983) *The New Working Class (A Reader)*, Macmillan
Walby (1986) *Patriarchy at Work*, Polity Press

Questions

1. Examine photographs 21–24.
Functionalists argue that the most able fill the most functionally important jobs and are therefore most highly rewarded. Discuss the problems of.
   (i) assessing the class position of the pop star, the dustman, the crane driver and the shop keeper.
   (ii) assessing their functional value to society.
   (iii) assessing their levels of social status and prestige.

2. Using the photographs 21–26:
   (i) Consider some of the problems which arise from the use of the Registrar-General's classification with regard to these workers and the assumptions made about the social background of their wives.
   (ii) What attempts have been made to overcome such problems by some researchers?

3. Examine photographs 25 and 26.
   (i) Explain the concept of an underclass (see pages 66 and 232–3).
   (ii) Does it usefully describe the lifestyle and life chances of the people in these photographs?
   (iii) Consider labelling theory in relation to the little girl; what points would such theorists make about the way such a child might be perceived by teachers, other pupils, the police, etc.?

4. Using the photographic material consider the view that 'we are all middle class now'.

21

Source: Alec Gill

22

Source: Alec Gill

23

Source: Alec Gill

24

Source: Alec Gill

25

Source: Alec Gill

26

Source: Alec Gill

Self-test Questions

Study the following material and answer the questions below.

1

Item A

The Measurement of Class

'Although sociologists constantly refer to social class as a major dimension of people's lives, it is not always easy to determine which class a person is in. There are two major types of definition of class: objective and subjective. The main objective indicator of class is occupation and the most used classifications of occupations are the Hall-Jones' and the Registrar-General's. However, there are serious draw-backs to using these two scales, not least of which is that they ignore the subjective dimension of class. Which class people think they are in is important, because it is likely to affect the way they act.'

Source: Adapted from T. Lawson, *Concise Sociology*, Bell & Hyman.

Item B

Changes in Occupational Structure of Britain

'Higher grade professions; predominantly male. There has been an overall increase in the number of males in this category, especially between 1951 and 1971. The number of females has remained fairly static, showing a slight increase in the decade 1961–71.

Employers and proprietors; predominantly male. There has been a decline in the number of males in the category and a slightly smaller decline in the number of women within it.

Administrators and managers; mainly male. There has been an increase in the number of males in the group, but the number of females declined between 1921 and 1931 and subsequently increased in recent years.

Lower-grade professionals; more men than women. There has been a steady increase in the number of males in this category, especially after 1951. There has been a similar increase in the number of women employees.

Supervisors, foremen; both men and women in roughly equal proportions. There has been a steady increase in the number of males and females in this category.

Clerical; predominantly female. There has been a very small increase in the number of males but it is an occupational group which has seen the greatest increase in the number of women employed.

Sales personnel and shop assistants; predominantly female. The employment of males has fluctuated and numbers have declined since 1931. For women, there has been a steady increase until 1961 when a small decline became apparent.'

Source: Adapted from P. Selfe, *Advanced Sociology*, Pan.

Item C

Personal wealth: distribution among adults of marketable wealth

	1966	*1979*	*1984*	*1985*
Percentage of wealth owned by:				
Most wealthy 1% of adults	33	22	21	20
Most wealthy 5% of adults	56	40	39	40
Most wealthy 10% of adults	69	54	52	54
Most wealthy 25% of adults	87	77	75	76
Most wealthy 50% of adults	97	95	93	93

Item D

Fragmentation has occurred within the middle class; three major groupings can be identified. The first is the traditional middle class. These are the owners and top managers of businesses and the traditional professions like doctors and lawyers, who have high status and income. The second group are the 'new' professionals or intellectual middle class such as teachers, social workers, university lecturers, etc. These are mainly found in the public sector rather than the private. The third group is the routine white-collar or non-manual middle class which has been growing in size since the Second World War. These workers are sometimes put with the lower professionals such as the nurses and technicians

1. With reference to Item A, name two social characteristics other than occupation which might be used as objective indicators of class. *(2 marks)*

2. What criticisms, other than those raised in Item A, could be made of the Hall-Jones' and Registrar-General's classifications of occupations? *(6 marks)*

3. What explanations have sociologists offered for the differences between male and female patterns of non-manual employment, as shown in Item B? *(6 marks)*

4. What pattern can be identified in Item C about the changing distribution of marketable wealth among adults? *(1 mark)*

5. The author of Item D suggests that the middle class in Britain is fragmented. Assess the argument that Britain's class structure *as a whole* is increasingly fragmented. *(10 marks)*

Source: AEB (1991).

2

Item A

'The working class of today, far from being a homogeneous group of equally unskilled and impoverished people, is in fact differentiated by numerous distinctions. Within the labour force we have to distinguish at least three skill groups: a growing stratum of highly skilled workmen who increasingly merge with white collar employees, a relatively stable stratum of semi-skilled workers and a dwindling stratum of totally unskilled labourers who are often newcomers to industry (such as immigrants). These three groups differ not only in their level of skill, but also in other attributes and determinants of social status. As with the capitalist class, it has become doubtful whether speaking of the working class still makes much sense.'

Source: Adapted from R. Dahrendorf, *Class and Class Conflict in Industrial Society.*

Item B

Immigrants into the UK from the West Indies and India and Pakistan.

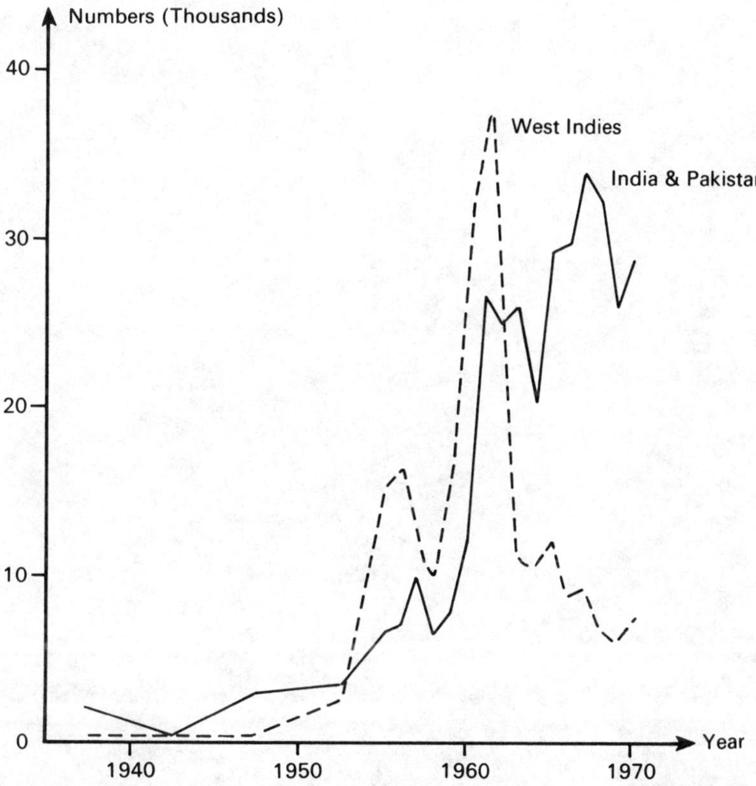

Source: Adapted from The Runnymede Trust and the Radical Statistics Race Group, *Britain's Black Population.*

1. Suggest one reason why the stratum of unskilled labourers may be dwindling (Item A, lines 6–7). *(1 mark)*

2. Why might some sociologists have expected the working class of today to be 'a homogeneous group of equally unskilled and impoverished people' (Item A, lines 1–2)? *(4 marks)*

3. Assess the view that the 'merging' of skilled workers and white collar employees represents a process of proletarianisation (Item A, line 5). *(9 marks)*

4. Suggest three reasons for the patterns shown in Item B. *(3 marks)*

5. Assess the view that ethnic minorities are over-represented in unskilled jobs largely because they are recent immigrants (Item A, lines 7–8, and Item B). *(8 marks)*

Source: AEB (1991) (AS level).

8

SOCIAL MOBILITY

Questions on this topic cover the following main areas:

1. The problems of definition and of measuring the extent of mobility.
2. The trends in mobility (statistical details).
3. The effects of mobility on the class structure.
4. The influence of education on mobility patterns.
5. Theoretical perspectives: is Britain an open society?

The Problems of Assessing the Extent of Social Mobility

■ **Define social mobility. Examine the problems that sociologists face in studying patterns of social mobility.**

In some systems of stratification people tend to be chained to a role and a category entered into at birth (for example, caste). In others the social system appears to offer opportunities for social movement, either up or down the social scale.

Social mobility refers to any movement in the class structure over a short or long period of time. It can involve either upward or downward movement. There are normally two main types identified:

Intergenerational mobility The position of a son or daughter is compared with that of their parents. This is movement *between* generations, based on occupation.

Intragenerational mobility The positions of individuals are compared at particular points in career to see whether they are moving up or down the social scale. This is movement *within* a generation.

There is third type that has been discussed by some authors:

Stratum mobility While an individual may not be mobile, his social stratum might be. For example, without leaving his social class the working-class son of a working-class father may be in a social stratum which is improving its social position relative to other groups. By raising levels of admission to the occupation it may achieve higher social status.

Problems in Measuring Mobility

1. *Intergenerational mobility* raises the following difficulties:

(a) Individuals do not necessarily have stable patterns of development throughout their careers. There are not likely to be consistent increases or decreases in income or status. This makes it difficult to know at what point to make the comparison between the generations.
(b) People constantly encounter changes of fortune in their careers. Careers are often quite erratic, shaped by unforeseen developments and subject to crises which may divert them into different directions from those intended at the outset.

2. Measuring *intragenerational mobility* raises the difficulty of deciding at which point in a person's career the comparison should be made:

(a) *With their first job*: but this may have been of a temporary nature in a relatively low-status occupation that would give a false impression of the extent of mobility.
(b) *With their first regular job*: this may have been the prelude to a career which required experience and further qualification and which was at the bottom of a ladder subsequently climbed.

Table 8.1 The social class of fathers of men in Class 1, 1949

Class of father	Percentage
Class 1	49
Class 2	16
Class 3	12
Class 4	11
Class 5	14
Class 6	0
Class 7	0

Source: D. Glass.

Table 8.2 Percentage of men having fathers in the same class as themselves, 1949

	percentage
Class 1	49%
Class 2	25%
Class 3	20%
Class 4	24%
Class 5	50%
Class 6	24%
Class 7	25%

Source: D. Glass.

Table 8.3 The social class of fathers of men in Class 1 (1972).

25% of respondents had fathers in Class 1
13% of respondents had fathers in Class 2
11% of respondents had fathers in Class 3
11% of respondents had fathers in Class 4
12% of respondents had fathers in Class 5
16% of respondents had fathers in Class 6
12% of respondents had fathers in Class 7

Source: Origins and Destinations.

Table 8.4 % of men (1972) having fathers in the same class as themselves.

Class 1	25
Class 2	12
Class 3	11
Class 4	27
Class 5	17
Class 6	42
Class 7	37

Source: Origins and Destinations.

(c) *At the height of their career*: this may have been in an exceptionally high-status position which was not subsequently maintained.
(d) *At the end of their career*: the person may have become disillusioned by this stage and failed to develop all his or her potential.

3. The problems of measuring *stratum mobility* are:

(a) How to assess the extent to which a group has increased (or lost) status over time.
(b) Comparison between occupational groups in terms of their relative status over time is also difficult because from time to time there are official reclassifications of occupation status. This occurred in 1961. The result was an apparent change in the social structure of Britain. Of 25 per cent of Class 1 who were reclassified, 20 per cent went into Class 2 and 5 per cent went into Class 3.

Concluding points

(a) The amount of mobility may depend on the measure used.
(b) The measure used depends on the operational definition used in the research project.
(c) Care must be taken when making comparisons over time, between generations and between what appear to be occupations of similar social status in those time periods.

The Trends in Social Mobility

■ **Examine the trends in social mobility in Britain since 1945.**

Lipset and Zetterberg (*A Theory of Social Mobility*) have pointed out that from Plato to the present, occupation has been the common indicator of stratification. Occupations are differentially esteemed and studies show a remarkable agreement as to how they rank in esteem. There is also substantial agreement among the rates from different areas of the country, different sizes of town, different age groups, different economic levels and different sexes. There also appears to be a great deal of international consensus about the occupational prestige classes.

Some useful studies

A Glass (*Social Mobility in Britain*); an intergenerational study. He used the following classification of class groups:

Class 1:	Professional and administrative
Class 2:	Managerial and executive
Class 3:	Inspectional, supervisory and other non-manual higher grade
Class 4:	Inspectional, supervisory and other non-manual lower grade
Class 5:	Skilled manual and routine non-manual
Class 6:	Semi-skilled manual
Class 7:	Unskilled manual

His analysis revealed the following:

Comment

1. Recruitment within a class was highest in Class 1 and Class 5.
2. It was lowest in Class 3.
3. The highest levels of social mobility were in Classes 2, 3, 4, 6, and 7.
4. Extreme movement across class lines was rare. Only 3 per cent of sons of fathers in Classes 1 and 2 had joined Classes 6 and 7.
5. None of the sons in Class 1 had fathers in Classes 6 and 7
6. There was more mobility within class groups (for example 5–7; 1–4) than between them.

B Harris and Clausen (*Labour Mobility in Great Britain 1953–63*) They conducted an intragenerational study and used the Registrar-General's classification (see page 89). They studied the careers of 4062 men and 1304 women and found:

Class 1:	94% remained in the class and 3.5% moved into Classes 2 and 3a.1% went into Class 4.
Class 2:	86% remained. 0.5% moved into Class 1.7% went into Class 3a. 6.5% moved into the manual working class.
Class 3a:	76% remained in the class. 12% moved into Classes 1 and 2.12% moved into Classes 3b, 4 and 5.
Class 3b:	78% remained in the class. 9% moved into Classes 3a, 2 and 1. 13% moved into Classes 4 and 5.
Class 4:	73% remained in the class. 7% moved into Classes 2 and 3a. 14% moved into 3a and 6% into Class 5.
Class 5:	68% remained in the class. 2% moved into Classes 2 and 3a. 30% moved into Classes 4 and 3b.

Comment

1. There were high rates of self-recruitment in Classes 1 and 2. There was little downward mobility into manual working classes.
2. Mobility in 3a was balanced between upward and downward movement (12 per cent in each direction).
3. There was greater downward mobility from Class 3b.
4. Only 7 per cent moved into white-collar occupations from Class 4.
5. There was even smaller movement from Class 5. Only 2 per cent moved into white-collar work.
6. In general, most movement was found to be short-range and within rather than across class lines.
7. There was very little long-range mobility from the top to the bottom of the class structure or vice versa.

The mobility of women

Class 1:	There was only a small representation of women in this class in 1953 (4%) and the numbers remained much the same over the ten-year period. 1% moved into Class 2.
Class 2:	86% remained in the class. 7% moved into manual occupations.
Class 3a:	84% remained in the class. 6% moved into Class 2 and 8% moved into manual occupations.
Class 3b:	65% remained in the class. 9% moved into white-collar work. 26% moved into Classes 4 and 5.
Class 4:	8% moved into white-collar work but 9% moved into Class 5.
Class 5:	70% remained in the class. 5% moved into white-collar occupations. 25% moved into Classes 3b and 4.

Comment

1. Women in Classes 1, 2 and 3a tended to remain secure.
2. Women already in manual occupations tended to move between classes rather than across them.
3. There were comparatively high rates of downward mobility among the women. This may be because they lacked opportunities, there was discrimination against them in promotion, etc., and they were more likely to have breaks in their work for child-rearing, which made it difficult to make progress in a career.

C Halsey (*Origins and Destinations*) and Goldthorpe (*Social Mobility and the Class Structure in Modern Britain*) produced data based on an intergenerational study. The class categories they used were:

Class 1:	Higher professional, higher-grade administrators, managers in large industrial concerns and large proprietors
Class 2:	Lower professionals, higher-grade technicians, lower-grade administrators, managers in small businesses and supervisors of non-manual employees
Class 3:	Routine non-manual, mainly clerical and sales personnel.
Class 4:	Small proprietors and self-employed artisans
Class 5:	Lower-grade technicians and supervisors of manual workers
Class 6:	Skilled manual workers
Class 7:	Semi-skilled manual workers

Their studies revealed the following:
Respondents were classified according to their present occupation while their fathers were classified according to the occupation they held when the respondent was fourteen.

Short-range mobility was defined as any movement in or out of Classes 3, 4, 5 or 6 (since they are all much at the same level).

Long-range mobility is that from the top to the bottom and vice versa.

Comment

1. It is difficult to make direct comparisons with the 1949 study because the researchers have not used the same system of classification, although some general conclusions may be drawn.
2. It appears that in 1972 there was more long-range mobility.
3. There appeared to be more chance to enter Classes 2, 3 and 4. This may be the result of the falling birth rate, especially in the highest classes.
4. There is a picture of a more open class structure than earlier, although other research suggests that Class 1 remains more highly self-recruiting than others. For example:

   (a) Giddens (*An Anatomy of a British Ruling Class*) examined the educational background of people holding top jobs in Britain in 1979. A high proportion went to a public school:

   85% of bishops of the Church of England;
   86% of high-ranking military officers;
   85% of top judges; and
   76% of Conservative MPs.

   (b) Scott (*The British Upper Class*) argued that there is evidence of an elite within the professional and managerial class which is closed to most outsiders. It consists of individuals with close familial and business links who control most of the important financial institutions and the most powerful companies in the country.

   (c) The wealthiest 200 people in Britain (according to

a *Sunday Times* analysis in 1989) owned £38 billion, 8 per cent of GNP, and consisted of:

57 landowners (owning 3.3m acres or 7 per cent of total land in the UK);
55 who went to the same school – Eton;
41 aristocrats (the Queen, 14 earls, 11 dukes, 9 viscounts, 6 marquises);
31 property developers;
25 who served in the same regiment (Brigade of Guards);
12 women; and
4 pop stars.

Conclusion

(a) The number of positions which are of high status and which are more highly rewarded has expanded in the occupational structure since 1945, although according to several authorities (for example Scott) there is a powerful élite whose membership is largely closed to outsiders.
(b) The proportion of white-collar workers from manual family backgrounds has reached about 50 per cent (partly due to the expansion of the clerical sector).
(c) In 1972 there was evidence of high levels of self-recruitment into the lowest social class groups (having fathers in the same class) The position of women is largely ignored (see pages 97–98).
(d) The amount of mobility may depend on the number and size of the categories distinguished. The greater the number of class categories devised the higher the possible rates of movement from one to another. Heath (*Social Mobility*) comments that the fewer the categories the less chance of long-range mobility (that is, it is hard to move from a manual occupation into professional category, but reasonably easy to move from unskilled to semi-skilled category).
(e) It is likely that intergenerational mobility, resulting from improved educational opportunities, has become more common.
(f) There remains evidence that long-range mobility (from the Registrar-General's Class 5 to Class 1 or 2) is unusual, whereas movement within Classes is the norm (for example, between Classes 3b, 4 and 5 and between 3a, 2 and 1).
(g) The evidence suggests that qualifications improve a person's chances of obtaining better-paid and higher-status jobs. Families from the middle and upper ranges of the social structure seem more able to secure these or to find alternative routes for members who fail the first time, by use of informal networks.

Some have argued that a more socially mobile society has resulted in a more open society (that is, higher-status occupations have become more accessible to more people). Patterns of voting, expenditure on consumer luxury goods and on more expensive leisure and holiday activities may also have changed, becoming more similar. There may also have been an increase in shared attitudes towards capitalist values and on private self-interest as people identify with others in terms of their similarities as property owners, non-welfare claimants and members of the securely employed in prosperous areas. This could be seen as producing a process of embourgeoisement.

However, others (for example Goldthorpe, Marshall, etc.) have refuted this view, arguing that in most classes self-recruitment is the norm and although people can move, short-range mobility is more common than long-range. They do not see an increase in class consciousness.

The Effects of Mobility on the Class Structure

■ **What has been the effect of changes in mobility on the class structure of Britain since 1945?**

Kerr (*Industrialism and Industrial Man*) argues that the industrial society is an open community encouraging occupational and geographic mobility. In this sense industrialism must be flexible and competitive.

The view is that industrial society must be 'open' and 'meritocratic'. There must be increasing opportunities for movement into higher social status levels. The emphasis is on *achieved* rather than *ascribed* status. However, there are critics of this view.

In debating the question, consider the following points:

1. Class stratification involves social inequality.
2. If a society has a system of social mobility this does not necessarily remove the inequalities.
3. Entry to a social class is a complex matter, involving changes of value, belief, attitude and patterns of behaviour.
4. It is likely that classes do become more distinct when there is limited mobility. Therefore, an 'open' society should make distinctions less clear.
5. From 1945 to 1979 there did seem to be some evidence of a trend towards greater economic equality in Britain (see data on page 89).
6. The mobility studies of 1949, 1963 and 1972 indicate that there is not a great deal of long-range mobility. However, there is debate as to whether the stratification system in Britain is becoming more homogeneous or more heterogeneous. Goldthorpe (*Social Stratification in Industrial Society*) suggested that there was evidence with the emergence of a new working class, that the system of stratification was becoming less well integrated. 'There is evidence of cultural and in particular of "social" barriers still widely existing between "working class" and "middle class" . . . middle incomes have not resulted in the generalisation of middle-class ways of life or middle-class status'.
7. Roberts *et al.* (*Fragmentary Class Structure*) located a fragmented middle class, but also a 'proletarian' working class located at the foot of the social scale who saw society as divided between 'us' and 'them'. They held fairly radical political views. They were strongly integrated into their local community, were often members of trade unions and lived in council housing. They were immersed in a blue-collar network and seemed unlikely to be subject to the effects of social mobility.
8. Scase (*Conceptions of the Class Structure*) conducted a comparative study in England and Sweden to compare attitudes. He noted how Swedish workers considered an individual's class position was determined by economic circumstances and level of education. Among English workers there was more emphasis on family background. Education was given less weight. Asked

Question

Examine photograph 27. Suggest ways of investigating whether a group of people have been upwardly or downwardly mobile in the course of their working lives.

(i) How could mobility be measured?
(ii) What problems might be encountered in the course of such a study?

27

Source: Alec Gill

whether they thought that many people moved from one class to another, 70 per cent of the Swedish workers answered yes, compared with 42 per cent of the British sample. He concluded that in Britain the class structure is still largely seen to be shaped by a number of traditional factors and there was less belief in the possibility of mobility than in Sweden.

Concluding points

(a) Social mobility may not have a direct effect on the class structure. It depends how much mobility is available.

(b) It is convenient to measure mobility by comparing occupational positions at various points in a person's career or by comparing one person's occupation with another. But there are difficulties in doing this.

(c) Rates of mobility are affected by the extent to which particular occupations are accessible. (Some become more inaccessible as entry qualifications become more demanding.)

(d) At times of high unemployment mobility may become more limited and the occupational class structure less open.

The Influence of Education on Mobility Patterns

■ **Assess the influence of education on mobility. (UODLE)**

1. Miller (*The Concept and Measurement of Mobility*) argues that patterns of mobility are not understood simply in terms of the occupational structure and occupational opportunities. It is also necessary to consider more variable aspects of the social structure, such as its educational institutions. One of the interests in research into mobility has been the factors which promote or restrain mobility, as well as the extent to which modern stratification systems are open or closed. Generally, in modern industrial societies, there is increasing emphasis on achievement rather than ascription, for which education is assumed to be a prime source.
2. Runciman (*Relative Deprivation*) points out that having a designated number of years' schooling is relevant to individual mobility only if it is accompanied by an increased availability of more privileged positions to which the education will gain preferential access.

Functionalist view

1. The dominant ideology of mobility is that everyone has an equal chance of mobility since this is based on achievement.
2. Education is a primary source of such mobility.
3. A primary reason for wishing to see high rates of mobility is to increase economic and social efficiency.
4. Societies must allow for the most able people to fill the most important positions.
5. The class structure is an open system, a ladder of opportunity exists. People can choose the rung to which they wish to ascend.
6. A fluid society is an open society. The level of mobility is therefore a good measure of how open it is.
7. Miller has said that a society which is relegating to lower status groups sons born in an advantaged stratum is more open than one which safeguards the privileges of the already advantaged.

Weberian view

1. Relatively high rates of social mobility are important in a society because they provide a political safety valve, diminishing frustration and conflict.
2. Class conflict becomes less likely when educational and occupational opportunities exist to increase levels of status and power.
3. People have the chance to influence their desire for improved status by joining power groups, such as trade unions etc.
4. Class solidarity is also unlikely in a fluid open society because people form and disperse around short-term aims in competition for scarce resources.
5. Evidence for the openness of a society is the extent to which educational survival rates of children from different backgrounds is increasing in the society.

Marxist view

1. There is no strong evidence of long-range mobility across class lines. It is primarily short range and within classes.
2. Upward mobility into the ruling elite is impossible since this is a closed group.
3. There is evidence that the lower working class is increasingly homogeneous and there is no embourgeoisement process underway.
4. There is also a large sector of the middle class which has an identification with the proletarian sector.
5. Bowles (*Unequal Education*) argues that unequal schooling reproduces the division of labour. It does not compensate for inequalities generated elsewhere in the capitalist system.
6. Distinctive class subcultures remain. Those at the bottom are unable to improve their social position because there is an unequal distribution of political power.

3. Raising educational levels ought to generate greater mobility as new technologies increase opportunities and demands for greater skills in the market place.
4. If occupation in a society is determined largely by education and education by social-class background, then the chances of increased mobility will be reduced if educational opportunities are not available in an expanding economy.
5. Stratification will become increasingly closed unless there is a sufficient expansion of opportunities to develop high-level skills and to utilise them. In some societies (for example South Africa) a closed stratification system is maintained by limiting the educational opportunities of black children. This can help to develop the emergence of an underclass of those who have no hope or chance of mobility. It can also help to develop greater class consciousness.
6. From a functionalist perspective, since the reorganisation of secondary education, further education and higher education, the opportunities have been greatly increased for people to improve their qualifications and their social status. The *tripartite system* (1944), the *comprehensive system* (after 1964), the *expansion of universities and Colleges of Higher Education* (including the *Open University* for those with no formal educational opportunities) must have increased chances of mobility.
7. Neave showed that the number of children from working-class backgrounds who entered university was increasing with the development of comprehensive education.
8. Halsey (*Towards Meritocracy: The Case for Britain*) argues that if a person's father is drawn from the highest managerial classes, that person stands an eleven times greater chance of getting a university degree than someone from Classes 4 or 5 (Registrar-General's scale).

   Industrial societies are reducing the proportion of unskilled jobs required and expanding professional and technical occupations. The direct effect of the class hierarchy of families on educational opportunity has risen since 1945.

   He concludes that the expansion of educational opportunity on its own is not enough to make significant inroads into the class-biased educational disadvantages: 'Social and educational policies have not successfully seized on the enlarged occupational opportunities since 1945 to realise either an egalitarian or a meritocratic society.'

Theoretical Perspectives

- **Is the rate of social mobility a satisfactory indicator of the openness of society? (ODLE)**
- **Account for changes in mobility rates since 1945 and discuss some of the consequences.**

1. Outline some of the changes by reference to statistical data (see page 106).

2. Present some reasons for the changes:

(a) Changes in the occupational structure (see page 102). Potentially, there is more room at the top.

(b) Differentials in fertility rates: average family size tends to be higher in working-class groups; hence they have more opportunity to fill vacancies in the middle-class occupational sector.

(c) Changes in educational structure have given people better opportunities to gain qualifications and skills valued in the economy.

3. Useful studies:

(a) Oxford Mobility Study: using Goldthorpe's class categories (see page 107) the authors note that:

(i) There was no significant increase in the openness of the British class structure for those born between 1938 and 1945 than there was for those born between 1908 and 1917.

(ii) It was still much easier for a boy born into the service class to remain there than for one born in the working class to achieve this status.

(b) Goldthorpe ('Trends in Intergenerational Mobility') conducted a follow-up and found:

(i) Little change from the earlier study, even though jobs in the service class had expanded.

(ii) The total amount of mobility had increased, but the comparative chances of those from different areas of the social structure of reaching higher positions than those into which they had been born had not changed. Upward mobility from other classes was possible but still difficult.

(iii) In times of economic depression downward mobility rates also increase.

Points of criticism

(i) The studies tend to ignore the existence of the business élite, access to which is especially difficult to anyone not connected through family, wealth or business contact.

(ii) They also tend to ignore the question of the mobility of women in the class structure. Heath in his study has suggested that women of Class 1 and 2 origins were more likely to be downwardly mobile than men of the same class origins (because of large numbers who enter Class 3a); also, women from the lowest class groups were more likely to be upwardly mobile than males of the same origin because of their ability to enter the clerical sector.

Possible consequences of changes in mobility rates

(a) If mobility rates have increased it may produce less class conflict, since there is less class cohesion. This would act as a political safety valve.

(b) The middle class will become increasingly heterogeneous in terms of its composition, and more conservative in attitude.

(c) It has been suggested that even the downwardly mobile would become more conservative, accepting their decline as their own failure to compete, while anticipating a future change in their position.

(d) The Labour Party may lose support as its traditional voters change allegiance.

(e) Traditional class solidarity may be undermined as new

sectional interests emerge to unite new groups and divide old (for example, housing tenure; regional location; welfare dependence, etc.).

(f) Giddens argues that a 3-class society has emerged as a result of changes in mobility. It is hard for those at the bottom of the class structure to reach the top. Therefore, those at the bottom become more identifiable as a class (because their mobility is restricted). Those in the intermediate buffer zone (routine non-manual) are not integral members of the middle class. They move both up and down. The more secure group at the top (professionals) have a culture which must be adopted by those wishing to join them. Social mobility thereby lessens the cultural distinctiveness of the class from which the upwardly mobile come.

Conclusion

(a) There is less than perfect mobility.

(b) More mobility has occurred since 1945; the Labour Governments placed more emphasis on the concept of equality. This was encouraged through changes in the educational structure (comprehensive schools, expanded higher education) which provided more opportunities to gain qualifications; the Conservative Governments have emphasised attitudes of competitive self-help, encouraging small businesses, share ownership etc.

(c) White-collar occupations expanded as traditional industries declined.

(d) The increase in unemployment and economic depression led to more downward mobility for the less skilled.

For some observers, significance has been in terms of the successful retention of power by the Conservative Party 1979–92; the possible decline in class consciousness; and the growth of more sectional interests.

On the other hand, Marshall notes that his 1988 study showed that class membership remains relevant in people's lives as a source of identity and attitude formation.

Suggested Reading

Works noted in this chapter

S. Bowles (1972) 'Unequal Education', in A. Coxon and C. Jones (eds) *Social Mobility*, Penguin

A. Giddens (1979) 'An Anatomy of a British Ruling Class', *New Society,* 4 October

D. Glass (1954) 'Social Mobility in Britain', in A. Coxon and C. Jones (eds) *Social Mobility*, Penguin

J. Goldthorpe (1966) 'Social Stratification in Industrial Society', in R. Bendix and S. Lipsett, *Class, Status and Power*, Routledge & Kegan Paul

J. Goldthorpe (1980) *Social Mobility and the Class Structure of Modern Britain*, Clarendon Press

A. Halsey (1977) 'Towards Meritocracy: The Case for Britain', in J. Karabel and A. Halsey (eds), *Power and Ideology in Education*, Oxford University Press

A. Halsey *et al.* (1980) *Origins and Destinations*, Oxford University Press

A. Halsey (1981) *Changes in British Society*, Oxford University Press

A. Harris and R. Clausen (1966) *Labour Mobility in Britain 1953–63*, HMSO Report 5333

A. Heath (1981) *Social Mobility*, Fontana

C. Kerr *et al.* (1962) *Industrialism and Industrial Man*, Heinemann

S. Lipsett and H. Zetterberg (1966) 'A Theory of Social Mobility', in R. Bendix and S. Lipsett (eds), *Class, Status and Power*, Routledge & Kegan Paul

S. Miller (1956) 'The Conceptual Measurement of Mobility', in *Social Mobility*, Penguin

G. Neave (1973) *How they Fared*, Routledge & Kegan Paul

K. Roberts *et al.* (1977) *Fragmentary Class Structure*, Heinemann

W. Runciman (1966) *Relative Deprivation*, Routledge & Kegan Paul

R. Scase (1974) 'Conceptions of the Class Structure', in F. Parkin (ed.), *The Social Analysis of Class Structure*, Tavistock

J. Scott (1982) *The British Upper classes*, Macmillan

P. Selfe (1987), *Advanced Sociology*, Pan

Works for further reading

T. Bottomore (1965) *Classes in Modern Society*, Allen Unwin

J. Goldthorpe, and C. Llewellyn (1977) 'Class Mobility', *British Journal of Sociology*, Vol.28, No.3

J. Goldthorpe and Payne (1986) 'Trends in Intergenerational Mobility', *Sociology*, 20

G. Marshall *et al.* (1988) *Social Class in Modern Britain*, Hutchinson

C. J. Richardson (1977) 'The Problem of Downward Mobility' *British Journal of Sociology*, Vol.28, No.3

Self-test Questions

Study the following material and answer the questions below.

Item A

'In designing the follow-up to our original large-scale study of mobility, the importance of investigating people's subjective experience was apparent to us. In critiques of mobility research, as undertaken by standard survey techniques, the question has been raised of how far people who have been measured by those techniques as moving up or down a social class scale devised by the sociologist actually feel that they have moved at all. And indeed evidence has been produced to suggest that the degree of this correspondence may in some instances be so low as to call into question the validity of the research.

While recognising then the need to give some place in our analysis to our respondents' own understanding of their mobility, it was not possible to use our preferred method, that is, open-ended questions followed up by "informed" probing. Perhaps the most obvious solution was to use structured interviews. However, we decided against this because of the doubts that we felt about the data that would be generated.

The material would therefore have to be collected in some other way. The method that came most readily to mind – as indeed the classic alternative to the interview – was that of the "personal document" in the form of the individual "life history".'

Source: Adapted from J. Goldthorpe 1980, *Social Mobility and Class Structure in Modern Britain*, Clarendon Press.

Item B

Changes in the occupational structure, Great Britain, 1911–71, by sex (in percentages)

	1911		1971	
	Men	Women	Men	Women
Non-manual				
Higher professionals, employers, proprietors, administrators and managers	13.1	7.6	21.2	7.6
Lower-grade professionals and technicians	1.4	5.8	5.5	10.8
Clerical workers, sales and shop assistants	10.1	9.7	10.0	37.4
All non-manual above	24.6	23.1	36.7	55.8
Manual				
Skilled manual (inc. foremen and supervisors)	34.8	24.8	33.9	10.5
Semi-skilled manual	29.1	47.0	21.2	27.3
Unskilled manual	11.5	5.1	8.2	6.4
All manual above	75.4	76.9	63.3	44.2
Total above	100.0	100.0	100.0	100.0

Source: Adapted from A. H. Halsey, *Change in British Society*, 2nd edn, Oxford University Press 1981

1. (i) Give an example of 'standard survey techniques' as used by sociologists. (See Item A, line 3) *(1 mark)*
   (ii) Give *two* reasons why sociologists use these techniques in social mobility research. *(2 marks)*
2. What is meant by 'validity'? (See Item A, line 7) *(2 marks)*
3. Why did the researchers in Item A choose to use life-histories rather than structured interviews in their follow-up study? *(4 marks)*
4. How have sociologists explained the changes in the non-manual workforce in the twentieth century as indicated in Item B? *(8 marks)*
5. What are the limitations of mobility studies for an understanding of the class structure of modern Britain? *(8 marks)*

Source: AEB (June 1990) (AS Level)

9

THE MASS MEDIA

Questions on this topic include the following main areas:

1. The ownership and control of communication media.
2. Theories:
   (a) Marxist;
   (b) Functionalist.
3. The impact of the media:
   (a) Attitude formation.
   (b) Reporting news.
   (c) Deviance amplification.
   (d) Violence and TV.
4. The mass culture debate.

The Ownership and Control of the Mass Media

Some questions asked on this topic require a general discussion of ownership and control:

- **Examine the relationship between the ownership, control and production of mass media. (AEB)**
- **To what extent does ownership of a national daily or weekly newspaper or large shareholding in a radio or TV channel influence its content?**

Others can be interpreted from a specifically theoretical perspective:

- **'Control of the mass media is an important part of élite power'. Discuss. (AEB)**

This is putting a Marxist view for discussion.

- **'The mass media constitute an important source of knowledge and belief for members of society'. (AEB)**

This question could be examined from a functionalist viewpoint, or in terms of the sociology of knowledge.

Definition The mass media are those communication media by which information, ideas, opinions and knowledge are transmitted to large numbers of people in the population at the same time and which have been introduced since the development of mechanical and electronic technologies. Gould and Kolb (*A Dictionary of the Social Sciences*) define mass media as 'all the impersonal means of communication by which visual and/or auditory messages are transmitted directly to audiences. Included among the mass media are TV, radio, cinema, newspapers, magazines, books and advertising.'

The mass media clearly include a range of different mediums but those most frequently discussed in terms of the question of control and influence are the press, and to a lesser extent TV. The audiences for these are very large and in terms of their political, economic and social influences, their potential is very great.

Useful detail

1922 The BBC established as a private company.
1926 The BBC reconstituted as a public corporation funded by licence fees and government subsidies.
1955 Commercial TV introduced. Many newspaper owners become major shareholders.
1964 BBC2 established.
1973 Local commercial radio introduced (many of the companies rely on the heavy investment of large corporations, including Australian multinationals).
1982 Channel 4 broadcasts, funded from advertising and providing more opportunities for independent programme producers.
1993 Channel 3, also funded by advertising, will appear. Sixteen regional areas are covered, licences having been awarded in 1991 on objective criteria.

Perspectives on the issue of ownership and control

1. Marxists argue that:
   (i) Power is held and used by those who dominate the economic structures of society. The wealthy owners of press, TV stations and film companies can influence the presentation of events, images and knowledge. Their gatekeeping role (often exercised by their managers, editors and so on) controls access to the media.
   (ii) Sheridan and Gardner (*Media, Politics and Culture*) argue that:
      (a) The concentration of power has been misused; journalists are inevitably influenced by the owner they work for in the material they produce and in its presentation.
      (b) Several independent TV stations are partly owned by one of the major newspaper companies, which heightens the concentration of power and provides wider audiences.
      (c) The need to satisfy the demands of advertisers for massive audiences lowers the standards of quality and maintains the wealth of the owners.
   (iii) Murdock and Golding (*Capitalism, Communication and Class Relations*) argue that:
      (a) Multimedia, multinational companies have steadily increased their dominance by enlarging their holdings in various media outlets.
      (b) The quest for large audiences and readerships has narrowed the range of viewpoints available.
   (iv) The Glasgow Media Group also argue that there is a great amount of similarity in the way that news events are reported on all channels. They do not compete to present alternative explanations or interpretations. They conclude that news presentations structure the attitudes and opinions of audiences; they lead rather than follow public opinion.

2. Weberians argue that:
   (i) Presentation of news in the media is not necessarily a consequence of ownership. Large organisations such as newspaper offices and TV companies must be organised rationally. Power is delegated to managers and editors.
   (ii) Such staff are appointed as part of the rational system designed to select and present news to the public. They do so by reference to those news values which are relevant to the audience they seek to attract. They are not part of a conspiracy.
   (iii) Managers are appointed to exercise particular news values in order to structure the news so that it can be presented clearly to the public.
   (iv) Choices must be exercised as to priorities. Some events will be regarded as more newsworthy than others. This is a matter of objective decision-making on the part of the manager/editor.
   (v) The more dramatic events receive higher priority than those which evolve slowly over time.
   (vi) Specialist staff are appointed, based on their objective educational and specialised knowledge of particular topic areas. Decisions about which stories to use are therefore made by editors exercising news values and the specialists advising them. In such a rational system, the owners do not exercise direct power to control content.

3. Functionalists argue that it is functional for social stability to have a wide range of mass media from which people can choose. They also accept that there is a separation between ownership and control. Control of output is in the hands of professional journalists. The owners simply manage the financial aspects of the company. They emphasise that consumer sovereignty must always be respected.
   (i) Whale (*The Politics of the Media*) says 'ownership is no more a dominant force in commercial broadcasting than it is at the BBC'. He implies that the ultimate arbiter is the consumer, who can always choose a different paper or channel.
   (ii) On this view it could be argued that large, complex organisations do not necessarily wish to maximise profits above everything. They may support moral issues or others they see as socially desirable, and alienate some of their regular audience or readership at the expense of profits. Some Conservative-supporting papers employ Labour-supporting feature writers to supply material and vice versa.
   (iii) Powerful shareholders and other investors and advertisers may also exert influence over content and policy against the views of the owner.
   (iv) A study in 1984 (*Attitudes to the Press*) showed that:
      (a) Many respondents were critical of the standards of journalism.
      (b) Many people do not buy their newspaper for its political content. They may favour its general entertainment value and be unaware of its political support.
      (c) There was little knowledge or concern about the ownership and control of the press.

Conclusions

(a) Some writers are critical of the apparent concentration of ownership among a few powerful media companies that are frequently controlled by rich and powerful men. They claim that:
   (i) They can ensure that news is reported in ways which meet with their ideological approval.
   (ii) The most influential control the high-circulation tabloid press. For them the profit motive remains paramount. Trivia dominates at the expense of the analysis of serious issues.
   (iii) Even the broadsheets, which are often controlled by the same individuals, play down alternative views that might offend the Conservative Government, which they tend to support uncritically.
   (iv) They conclude that the extent of their control is total since it can be exercised either through their own power and connections or through their appointed managers and editors. For example, Harold Evans claimed he was dismissed as editor of the *Sunday Times* by Rupert Murdoch, owner of News International, for failing to support his employer's political views in leading articles. In his 1992 autobiography, Ian Gilmour, an ex-Conservative Cabinet Minister, says that Mr Murdoch

Table 9.1 Media owners and related interests

	Percentage owned	Circulation (in millions) March 1992
1. Maxwell Foundation.		
Chief executive (until November 1991): R. Maxwell		
A National newspaper interests		
Daily Mirror and Daily Record		3.607
Sunday Mirror		2.801
Sunday People		2.096
Sunday Mail	51.0	
Sporting Life		
The European	100.0	
New York Daily News	100.0	
B Television interests		
Pergamon Media Trust	100.0	
Central TV	19.8	
Border TV	15.0	
MTV	25.0	
Maxwell Cable TV		
C Publishing interests		
Pergamon journals		
British Magazine Corporation		
Maxwell Communication Corporation		
2. Lonhro		
Chief executive (1992): T. Rowland		
A National newspaper interests		
The Observer (until May 1993)		0.545
B Provincial papers		
Glasgow Herald		
Evening Times		
Scottish and Universal Newspapers		
C Magazine interests		
Geo. Outram & Co. Ltd.		
D Radio interests		
Radio Clyde	4.5	
3. Hollinger		
Chief executive (1992): C. Black		
A National newspaper interests		
Daily Telegraph	83.0	1.042
Sunday Telegraph		0.557
B Magazine interests		
Spectator		
Publishing interests		
United Newspapers	3.3	
4. News International Corporation		
Chief executive (1992): R. Murdoch		
A National newspaper interests		
The Sun		3.629
News of the World		4.788
Sunday Times		1.182
The Times		0.391
Today		0.521
B Other publications		
Times Educational Supplement		
Times Literary Supplement		
Times Higher Education Supplement		
C Television interests		
B Sky B		
D Magazine interests		
Murdoch magazines, including:		
New Woman		
TV Guide		
Sky Magazine	50.0	
E Publishing House, interests:		
Times Books		
HarperCollins		
Reed	3.8	
Pearson	18.0	
5. Guardian		
A National newspaper interests		
The Guardian		0.428
The Observer *(1993)*		
B Provincial newspaper interests		
Manchester Evening News		
Rochdale Observer series		
Lancashire and Cheshire newspapers		
Surrey Advertiser series		
C Magazine interests		
Specialist magazines		
D Radio interests		
Picadilly Radio	17.0	
Red Rose		
Red Dragon		
Radio Aire		
E Television interests		
Anglia TV	5.0	
Broadcast communications	14.0	
6. Pearson		
A National newspaper interests		
Financial Times		0.288
B Other press interests		
Westminster Press: (8 dailies; 69 weeklies)		
FT Business Information		
Investors Chronicle		
Economist	50.0	
C Publishing interests		
Penguin		
Longman		
Ladybird		
Pitman		
Viking		
Michael Joseph		
Hamish Hamilton		
Puffin		
D Television interests		
Yorkshire TV	20.0	
B Sky B	13.0	
Pickwick Group	21.0	
7. United Newspapers		
A National newspaper interests		
Daily Express		1.538
Sunday Express		1.719
Daily Star		0.816
B Regional newspaper interests		
Scottish Daily Express		
Scottish Sunday Express		
8 other dailies		
95 weeklies		
C Magazine interests		
40 consumer		
94 business		

Table 9.1 *Cont.*

	Percentage owned	Circulation (in millions) March 1992
18 business directories		
4 advertising periodicals		
E Radio interests		
Yorkshire Radio Network	9.4	
8. Daily Mail and General Trust		
Chief executive (1992):		
Lord Rothermere		
A National newspaper interests		
Daily Mail		1.682
Mail on Sunday		1.978
B Regional newspaper interests		
Evening Standard		
13 provincial dailies		
17 provincial weeklies		
27 free newspapers		
Bristol Evening Post	23.8	
Bristol United Press	40.0	
Portsmouth and Sunderland Newspapers	5.0	
C Publishing interests		
Burlington Publishing (5 titles)		
D Radio interests		
Swansea Sound	18.0	
GWR	8.0	
Crown Communications	9.3	
Essex Radio	6.9	
Gloucester Broadcasting	7.7	
North Staffs & South Cheshire	10.4	
9. The Independent		
Chief executive (1992):		
A. Whittam-Smith		
A National newspaper interests		
The Independent		0.374
The Independent on Sunday		0.385

Licence	Awarded to
Channel 3 Licences 1991	
Borders and Isle of Man	Border TV
Central Scotland	Scottish TV
Channel Islands	Channel TV
East, West, South Midlands Independent TV	Central
East of England	Anglia TV
London Weekday	Carlton TV
London Weekend	LWT
North of Scotland	Grampian TV
North East England	Tyne Tees TV
North West England	Granada TV
Northern Ireland	Ulster TV
South & South East England Broadcasting	Meridian
South West England	Westcountry TV
Wales and the West	HTV
Yorkshire	Yorkshire TV
National Breakfast-time	Sunrise TV

Sources: *Guardian*; *Social Studies Review*, September 1989; *Spectrum*, Winter 1991.

hated liberals and 'nagged his editors into being as sycophantic as possible to Mrs Thatcher'.

(b) Others see no conflict arising from the personal ownership of vast multinational media empires and argue:
   (i) That the rich are not necessarily able to influence the content of papers or TV channels. (Lord Thompson, once owner of *The Times*, said 'I have my views ... but never see them appear unless the editor agrees with them'.) They claim that there are plenty of checks and controls to prevent such abuse.
   (ii) The managers, professional journalists, shareholders and advertisers as well as the consumers determine output and quality. They would conclude that the extent of control of the owner is minimal, especially as far as radio and TV output is concerned.

Theories

- **Control of the mass media is an important aspect of élite power. Discuss.**
- **Assess the view that it is the media professionals, and not the owner, who control media output.**
- **What factors affect the selection of news items on TV and in the press?**

Such questions could be answered by reference to theory; some factual details would be necessary in the discussion of ownership.

1. Marxist/Manipulation theory rests on the view that 'the class which has the means of production at its disposal also has control over the means of mental production'. Therefore the ability to determine content, although apparently in the hands of professional journalists and editors, invariably reflects the interests of the owners and the class they represent. (Hence three-quarters of national daily and Sunday newspapers support the Conservative Party.)
   (i) Editors exercise a powerful 'gatekeeping role'

The Marxist view	**The Functionalist view**
1. The majority of the national press and television news editors report events in terms of the *status quo*. There is wide support for the Conservative Party. Serious matters are not dealt with adequately: there is emphasis on the trivial. Those who control the media mould public taste and opinion.	1. The media are not allied to one party nor do they necessarily sensationalise or trivialise. Journalists cater for what people want. The media, therefore, reflect events, attitudes, tastes, etc.
2. Because the media operate in the interests of a ruling élite the audience has no real chance to assess competing ideologies (e.g. Northern Ireland).	2. In a free market people do have choice and there is a range of papers from extreme left to extreme right.
3. Advertisers largely determine the content of papers and TV programmes. This accounts for the low level of serious content.	3. A a major outlet for advertising, the media keep people informed as to the availability of products, and competition ensues.
4. Those who own and control the press and TV stations are likely to be men whose ideological values range between conservative and reactionary. The content of the media will reflect these views, ensuring that negative attitudes will be attached to those people and events defined as 'hostile'.	4. It is a mistake to assume that those who own media of communication necessarily control the content of the messages that are disseminated.
5. The media propagates a bourgeois concept of reality. It describes a picture of the world which fits that of a particular class. Any apparent sense of freedom to select alternative models of action or belief is illusory.	5. Fearing (*The Influence of the Movies*) suggests that in the cinema the individual learns to reaffirm the norms of his culture or group; the area of significant meanings is enlarged, as is an awareness of the range of possibilities.
6. There is seldom any account of the evolution of major events in media reports. They tend to appear as random eruptions of conflict. Their causes (often arising from exploitation) are seldom discussed.	6. Rosengren and Windahl (*Mass Media Consumption as a Functional Alternative*) argue that the media serve important functions as a source of news, facts, information, etc. which enables people to make informed judgements.
7. Critics argue that the Conservative media use the term 'Marxist' as one of abuse. It conveys illegitimacy and a powerful image of an alien force. It is a means of suggesting threat, subversion and hostility. Most people are unfamiliar with the philosophies or ideals of Marxism. Myers (*Media Hits the Pits*) argues that those who own and control the means of mass communication were marshalled in opposition to the NUM. The Glyn Report (see page 318), which put the union position, got little mention during the dispute.	7. The media help to provide a greater sense of commitment to the society by promoting cultural values and by identifying areas of conflict and opposition. The function of entertainment is an important one, helping people to relax after work and refreshing them. Those who wish to express dissenting views can do so and such reports are available for those who wish to read them.
8. The Glasgow Media Group (see page 120) argue that they have found strong evidence of right-wing bias in the content and presentation of news stories on TV.	8. The GMG is accused of being too ideologically biased, failing to examine their data with sufficient impartiality.

(determining who has access to their medium; usually those whose opinions they favour) and an 'agenda-setting role', whereby they determine what issues are important.

(ii) Althusser describes the media as 'an ideological state apparatus'; this enables editors to use their power to conceal levels of exploitation by emphasising the negative images of trade unions, strikers, Labour-controlled councils and so on.

Point of criticism

(Chibnall, *Law-and-Order News*) has pointed out that

(i) this is a highly conspiratorial view. It assumes all editors are puppets and ideologically biased; and

(ii) there is evidence of many papers and TV programmes uncovering scandal and illegal acts among the rich and powerful.

2. The Market/Functionalist/Pluralist view argues that selection of news output rests with professional editors, who select according to their audience; they merely meet public demand.

(i) News is selected in news conferences. Bulletins result from available material, especially if it has powerful accompanying pictures. Information used is also governed by relevance, time, etc.

(ii) Power is dispersed among many groups, resulting from free competition in the market place.

Point of criticism

This is said to be a naïve view since:

(i) Market forces can sometimes kill off papers which have reasonable circulation but which cannot attract advertising.

(ii) TV programmes critical of the rich and powerful are often relegated to channels and times when they attract tiny audiences. The BBC/ITV policy of catering for 'the consensus' middle ground is said to be itself an ideological position.

(iii) Butler and Stokes (*Political Change in Britain*) found the press did affect voting intentions in their study (73 percent increased their support for the party supported by the paper they read).

Conclusions

(a) Market theorists argue that there is a complex set of mutual influences between the media and the public.

- (i) Different newspapers and TV programmes appeal to people for a variety of reasons.
- (ii) Readership may influence the content.
- (iii) The same messages can be received and interpreted in different ways so their outcomes cannot be predicted. Negative news items may have unintended consequences (for example, details of Paddy Ashdown's private life in the 1992 Election may have increased his popularity).

(b) Manipulation theorists would conclude that:

- (i) 'Due impartiality' in the selection of TV news is a myth, since the journalists, editors, etc. must have values (almost certainly middle-class) which will affect their choice of items and the interpretations placed on them.
- (ii) The professional's news values and definitions of what is newsworthy will inhibit the use of material which seriously challenges the status quo.

The Impact of the Media

Attitude formation

■ **Do the mass media of communication change, or merely reinforce, attitudes and behaviour?**

Questions are sometimes asked which focus on attitudes towards race, politics, violence, etc. In such cases you must ensure that you relate your material to the specific issue raised in the question.

An *attitude* is a unified set of beliefs which are strongly held. It helps the individual to explain and make sense of events. To hold an attitude implies:

(a) an *emotional response* (a person *feels* strongly about something;
(b) a *rational element* (the person has a *reasoned belief* based on evidence; or
(c) a *behavioural response* (the person *behaves* in accordance with beliefs).

Those who wish to change attitudes include politicians, advertisers and reformers. They are faced with the problem of changing existing attitudes from positive to negative or vice versa. This can be described as an incongruent change. Or they may wish to intensify an existing attitude that is make someone believe something more strongly). This can be termed a congruent effect.

Research findings

Research indicates that it is a complex process to form attitudes and equally difficult to change them. They are learned responses which people develop, and they become fixed over time.

Trenaman and McQuail (*TV and the Political Image*) suggest that the most common effects on an audience are either minor changes or a reinforcing tendency. This arises as a result of three factors:

(a) *selective exposure* (people are selective in their choice of newspaper, programme, etc. and tend to avoid those that might give rise to conflict;
(b) *selective perception* (people tend to perceive information which fits existing expectations); and
(c) *selective retention* (people tend to retain information which supports existing attitudes and they ignore that which presents conflicting views).

It is therefore difficult to achieve an incongruent change. The communicator would have to:

(a) be someone the audience accepts as credible;
(b) present new evidence in a clear and simple way; and
(c) raise new questions in the minds of the audience.

Conclusions

Newton (*Social Studies Review*) suggests that the debate as to whether the media change or reinforce behaviour and attitudes is largely unresolved.

(a) Reinforcement theory suggest that the media do strengthen pre-existing attitudes.
(b) Agenda-setting theory suggests that the media do not necessarily tell people what to think but they do help determine what people think about and how important different issues are. This view emphasises the constant interaction between the media and the audiences.
(c) Independent-effect theory argues that the media do have direct and independent effects on public attitudes and behaviour, even if these are only small.

Reporting news

■ **Reporting news is inevitably partial, selective and biased. Discuss.**

Much research has been conducted into the way that news is gathered and selected for communication. There is a lot of debate as to whether it is done in an entirely objective way by impartial journalists, or whether there is unintentional bias.

1. Radio and TV channels are under an obligation established by Act of Parliament to ensure fair and balanced coverage of political issues from all points of view, especially during an election campaign. (The exception is where 'the public interest is involved'.)
2. The press are not faced with similar restrictions in their reporting of such issues. They are restrained in comments only by fear of legal action and issues of national security.

Research studies

1. Philo, The Glasgow Media Group (*Bad News; More Bad News*). This group undertook a detailed content

Questions

Examine photograph 28.

Some researchers have argued that in their portrayal of daily life the popular press tend to work with news values which emphasise sensational and often disturbing events. The result is that they come to amplify problems, especially deviance, by sensitising the public to new fears and concerns.

(i) Examine the photograph and suggest how the moral panic associated with mugging (see page 126) could be developed from such a picture.
(ii) Specify some of the stereotypes which the press might emphasise in a picture such as this.
(iii) Describe how the attitudes of a group of elderly people could be influenced by the media reports they encounter (see page 124).
(iv) How might such attitudes be measured?
(v) Why would a phenomenologist argue that it would be useful to talk to the young people on the street corner? (See pages 26–7.)
(vi) What difference might it make if they assumed the interviewer to be a journalist rather than a friendly passer-by?
(vii) Consider the most suitable role for a researcher.

28

Source: Alec Gill

analysis of six months of news programmes. They are critical of the presentation of news on TV.

(a) News is reported from the point of view of management/government and seldom from the point of view of the work force or those in conflict.
(b) Causal explanations seldom appear.
(c) There is an inherent class bias among the journalists (middle-class university-educated).
(d) Strikers were generally portrayed in a negative light.
(e) The impression created was that some industries were perpetually strike prone.
(f) They found an increasing feeling among the audience that the BBC news was biased against the Left (in 1960 96 per cent thought it was impartial; in 1979 only 78 per cent thought this).
(g) The Glasgow group reject the idea that there can be objective, unbiased news reporting.
(h) They reject the claim that journalists react to audience demands. In fact, broadcasters lead the audience into new attitudes.

2. Hartmann and Husband (*The Mass Media and Racial Conflict*) argue that if the media do influence events they seldom do so directly, but more through the way people think. They suggest that direct effects on attitudes following short-term exposure to media material are unlikely. But the media do play an important part in defining for people what the important issues are: 'they set the agenda for discussion'. As far as race is concerned this is in terms of 'numbers' (that is, numbers entering the country each year). They also determine how people should think about them and interpret them. Because of the gate-keeping role of the news media some people have greater access to the media than others.

(a) The British cultural tradition contains elements derogatory to foreigners (especially blacks). This stems from the colonial past.
(b) The media operate with the culture and use its cultural symbols. This is exemplified in the use of cartoons, jokes, etc.
(c) Journalists work with specific news values: the criteria by which information about events is gathered, selected and published. The dominant values are those of conflict, threat and deviance. Events are more newsworthy when they can be interpreted within a familiar framework of existing images and expectations.

They conclude that the media tend to reinforce existing attitudes. The media do not intend to report in a biased way, they are simply following their normal procedures and applying their usual news values criteria. The authors suggest that the media should become more concerned with underlying causes and possible solutions to major issues.

Conclusion

The question asks whether it is inevitable that news reporting is partial and incomplete, selective and biased. The answer depends on the perspective applied to the analysis. Those who hold a Manipulation and Conspiratorial view, argue that it is inevitable. Serious issues are trivialised, over-simplified and subject to invented facts ('Loony Left Ban Black Bin Liners' was used in a story about racial issues) or they are personalised ('Red Ken'; 'Barmy Bernie'; 'Veggie Benn' have all been used to describe Labour politicians). Some journalistic critics of the Conservative party have also made use of derogatory terms. These include 'Margaret Thatcher Milk Snatcher' (when she abolished free school milk.) Norman Tebbit became known as 'The Chingford Skinhead' and more recently Virginia Bottomley is referred to as 'Nurse Bossyboots'. They would point to evidence to show the list of TV programmes that have been subject to government interference in 1980s (regarding the Falklands War; Northern Ireland, etc). In short, reporting is biased because journalists are reaching a mass audience who they believe require simplified information which meets the consensus of the majority. Those who hold a Pluralist or Market view would dispute the arguments concerning conspiratorial bias. They would argue that a full and fair coverage of news can only occur in a free market system. Anyone is entitled to own and publish a newspaper and can present the news from the perspective they choose. But the audience determines its success or failure. Television news has a duty to be duly impartial. Occasionally news reporting may be biased but it is not inevitable that it should be so. NB. (You must conclude in terms of the views you believe carry most weight.)

Deviance Amplification

■ **Examine the role of the mass media in the amplification of deviance. Illustrate with examples. (OUDLE)**

This question must also be considered in relation to a discussion of the concept of crime and deviance (see page 181).

1. Becker (*Outsiders*) has said that 'society creates deviance'. This is done by making rules 'whose infraction creates deviance'. An act becomes deviant when it is observed by someone who takes some action in relation to it and attaches a label of 'deviant' to the actor involved.

2. Wilkins (*The Deviance-Amplifying System*) has described the sequence of events which result in an action becoming perceived as a serious form of deviance. He says 'the definitions of deviant behaviour relate to the information and cultural experience of the individuals making the definitions'.

3. Cohen (*Mods, Rockers and the Rest . . .*) examined the ways in which the mass media influenced the development of the mods and rockers phenomenon in the mid-1960s. He considers how media reports:

(a) quickly shaped people's expectations;
(b) provided the content of rumours that 'something was going to happen';
(c) publicised events and made them attractive to other youngsters;
(d) established images and stereotypes of potential trouble-makers; and
(e) increased the problems by increased comment.

It is his thesis that newspapers do not intentionally exaggerate events, but in their use of sensational headlines, dramatic interviews and comment they sensitise the public to problems.

The use of stereotyped images helps people to make sense of ambiguous situations: people know who are 'the troublemakers' and a self-image develops among those so labelled.

Cohen's deviation-amplifying system

1. Initial deviation from valued norms leading to:
2. Punitive reaction by the community (which may lead to the segregation of groups and marking them as deviant).
3. Development of a deviant self-identity and behaviour appropriate to this identity.
4. Further punitive reaction, etc.

Cohen (*Folk Devils and Moral Panics*) describes the process further when he explains how the media create moral panics as the amplification of deviance begins to spiral. The reports of an initially minor event gain wide coverage; the public are sensitised; the police may become involved; there are further detailed reports, often from the courtroom confrontations; these increase public concern; troublemakers are identified as 'folk devils', who become increasingly alienated from the wider public. They are identified by dress, manner and other qualities of their 'youth culture'. Their expected behaviour leads to a 'moral panic' (concern by the public about what is seen as a serious moral and social issue).

Eventually, the panic subsides as another issue replaces it as a matter of media attention.

- **Assess the social impact of television**
- **Critically assess the view that the effects of TV are greatly exaggerated.**

There are several areas of debate concerning the impact of TV on a mass audience. These include: its effect on voters; the effects of 'televangelism'; and the effects of viewing violence.

The influence on voters

(a) Crewe (*A New Class of Politics*) analysed the results of the 1987 General Election and concluded that the media had little effect on voting patterns.

(b) Manning (*Social Studies Review*), has noted:

(i) The rise of professional public relations (PR) groups which advise clients on their appearances and media skills. These represent a more systematic approach by political parties who wish to establish new images in the imagination of the public.

(ii) The emergence of new media pressure groups which campaign for changes in the organisation and content of the media (for example, the Campaign for Press and Broadcasting Freedom). These may have impact on political broadcasting in the future.

(iii) The possible fragmentation of audiences around different issues and concerns. It is likely, then, that they will become increasingly dependent on the media for their understanding of events. The result may be an intensification of the struggle to help shape the content of news and current affairs by PR and pressure groups.

The impact of 'televangelism' Bruce (*Social Studies Review*), notes that recent legislation has opened up the airwaves and made it likely that Britain will be faced with increasing numbers of aggressive television evangelists similar to those in America. However, he suggests that the effects are likely to be minimal, for several reasons:

(i) Stacey and Shupe noted that because there are only a small number of heathens who watch such programmes, they preach to the converted.

(ii) It is almost impossible to test the claims made by TV evangelists concerning their powers to change people's lives.

(iii) Even though they use the most up-to-date technologies in their communications to establish a spurious intimacy it seems unlikely that many in the audience will shift from unbelief or even mainstream Protestantism to fundamentalism.

However, he concludes that whilst it may fail in its primary purpose it may have an important secondary or latent function. It may serve simply as a source of entertainment. These programmes are likely to have less impact in Britain than in the USA, where about 25 per cent of the population are in evangelical groups and are also prepared to pay to watch the programmes.

The effects of viewing violence Research findings include:

1. Cumberbatch and Howitt (*Mass Media, Violence and Society*). The authors made fifteen studies on 2000 children in comprehensive schools and reviewed and analysed 300 studies into media violence. They concluded that there was no direct effect, though they found much contradictory evidence in the studies. They argue that cartoons do not have a harmful effect on young viewers.

2. Surgeon-General's Report (USA) (*TV and Growing Up*) ran to six volumes and cost more than $1 million to produce. The conclusion was that TV violence does increase levels of aggression among child audiences. As many as 25 per cent may be seriously affected. Of programmes classed as 'adult', 85 per cent are viewed by young children.

3. Noble (*Children in Front of the Small Screen*) found that for a small proportion of children with aggressive personalities viewing violence had a 'cathartic effect'. (They got rid of some of their own anger and frustrations by watching violence on TV.) But there may be some danger for children where there is no opportunity to discuss issues seen, with adults. Many delinquents were found to be avid TV watchers.

4. Pye Survey found that 45 per cent of children aged 7–10 watched TV until 9 p.m. and one child in 100 watched until 11 p.m. Seventy-nine per cent of families were found to exercise 'no control whatever over the number of hours their children watched TV'. On average each child was found to spend approximately twenty-two hours per week watching TV.

5. Katz (*Violence on TV*). This BBC audience research report found that viewers do not worry much about violence on TV; 57 per cent thought there was too much but only 18 per cent actually perceived violence in the target programmes they were asked to monitor. The author suggests that perhaps the amount of violence has affected the viewers' threshold of tolerance: they were so saturated that they were no longer concerned about it. The author accepts that his report remains largely inconclusive.

6. IBA Research (*The Portrayal of Violence on TV*) suggests that the use of violence on TV may reinforce aggressive tendencies among the emotionally unstable. In a typical hour of TV programmes there would be at least two major sequences of violence involving death: one would be fictional and one real. The report states that 'TV is perhaps one of the most powerful mediums of mass communication . . . violent deaths should be reported in context and in relation to the importance of the event'.

7. A study in 1992 (*Women Viewing Violence*) found that:

(a) Women's fear of male violence can be reinforced (rather than created) and increased by watching TV violence about women.
(b) Women who had experienced violent crime were more sensitive to TV violence (including programmes such as 'Crimewatch UK' which recreate crimes realistically) than those who had not.
(c) The most profound fear was aroused in them by Hollywood films such as *The Accused*.

Conclusions

1. Dunkley, commenting on the range of research findings, points out that there are many contradictory ones. He says, for example, that the BBC report does not provide a basis for concluding either that those who criticise TV for showing too much violence are justified or that there is no cause for concern. All the research indicates that the media can never be the sole cause of deliquent behaviour. Evidence is increasing that TV tends to reinforce existing attitudes, hence TV violence may tend to affect those in the audience who are already prone to aggressive behaviour.

2. Philo (*Seeing is Believing*) argues that his research suggests:

(i) that the social impact of television is quite considerable;
(ii) TV news is the main source of information for most people; and that
(iii) our understanding is influenced by our personal history, our political culture and our class background.

Detail In his study he gave people photos of the 1984/85 miners' strike. He asked them to write news stories based on them and on their memories of events. He found a close similarity to the original items which appeared on TV news (for example, emphasis on 'drift back to work' and 'erupting violence'.) He found that some of the information used by people to understand events came from the way they were depicted (often erroneously) in the media. He points out:

(a) That it is hard to criticise presentation where one has no alternative source of information. (Those who had experienced non-violent pickets, material hardships, etc. were generally more sympathetic.)
(b) However, he concludes that we should not underestimate the power of the media to create and sustain images (especially negative ones) in the minds of the audience.

3. The impact of TV seems to vary according to the area that is being examined. It may be low with regard to religious values but more significant in shaping images, especially towards aspects of violence, political leaders and those whom Cohen has described as 'the folk devils of our time' (see page 123).

The Mass Culture Debate

■ Is there any evidence that the mass media of communication have created a mass culture?

Some writers have argued that there is a trend towards the development of a mass society. Although it lacks precise meaning the term 'mass' has come to be associated with undesirable changes in the structure of society. The suggestion is that a mass society shares a mass culture. The means by which this is disseminated among the population is the mass media. However, there are some who oppose the negative implications and argue that the media have beneficial effects.

McQuail (*Towards a Sociology of Mass Communication*) describes the debate:

1. Mass culture refers to the cultural products manufactured solely for the mass market

(a) Wilensky (in McQuail) has emphasised the fact that there is standardisation of product and mass behaviour in its use.
(b) McQuail has emphasised the view that mass mass culture refers to a whole range of popular activities; especially to entertainment, spectacles, music, books, and films and has become identified with the typical content of the mass media, with fictional, dramatic and entertainment material.

2. The *pessimists*, who associate the mass media with unwelcome societal tendencies:

(a) *Kornhauser* sees the development of a mass society in which democratic institutions are threatened and the conditions for totalitarianism result.
(b) *Bell* describes the increase in alienation, the erosion of traditional values as the ordered community and social life of the past breaks down. There is a decay in the popular art of a more stable society.
(c) *Arendt* thinks the mass production of new cultural objects and consumer goods has resulted in a loss of originality.
(d) *T. S. Eliot* deplores the growth of mass culture because it threatens the existence of 'high culture', the culture of excellence. Mass culture is the culture of mediocrity.
(e) *MacDonald* says mass culture mixes and scrambles everything together . . . producing what might be called 'a homogenised culture'.
(f) *Tumin* says it encourages a 'cult of happiness'.
(g) *Rosenberg* says 'at its worst mass culture threatens not merely to cretinise our taste, but to brutalise our senses'.

3. The *optimists*, who do not see such dangers in the mass media:

(a) *Halloran* argues that the debate is marked by confusion as to the meaning of terms: 'high culture', 'mass culture', 'low culture'. This leads to confusion and ambiguity, making consensus difficult.

(b) *Shils* suggests that the attack on mass media and mass culture is politically motivated and presents a one-sided critique of US society.

(c) *Williams* argues that 'majority culture' may not necessarily be in low taste. People are not sufficiently familiar with it; judgements as to what is good and bad depend on the values of a small minority of 'critics'.

(d) *Hoggart* makes the point that working-class culture may be just as valuable as middle-class culture but its qualities may not be recognised.

Conclusion

The pessimists fear that in a mass society people become less concerned with the serious aspects of everyday life. Democratic values are threatened because people have less interest in them and they are therefore open to greater manipulation. Individuality is minimised. The traditional culture is replaced by one shared by the majority in the society. Tastes become more uniform. There is less interest in 'serious' culture. In a mass society, there is a mass culture and mass behaviour. People will act in a collective way: fashions, trends, etc. predominate. People will act as a mass when there are similar needs or problems to be faced.

The optimists reject these views and see confusion arising out of a failure to establish the meanings of terms as well as the fact that the media can bring many benefits and introduce new values to the audience.

■ **Outline the changes in media sociology and indicate which have been the most fruitful perspectives.**

Many different and some interelated theories have been developed to explain the effects, impact and significance of the the mass media. Some have been more useful than others:

1. *The Hypodermic Theory*. This developed in the 1920s–1930s. It assumed a direct effect, like an injection. The behaviour of the audience was believed to be influenced by what it saw or read. It is still frequently used by critics of TV violence, as explanations for behaviour patterns.

Criticism It is considered too narrow and deterministic as an explanation; it assumes an entirely passive audience.

2. *The Two-Step Flow Theory*. This developed in the 1940s–1950s. Katz and Lazarsfeld (*Personal Influence*, 1955) suggested that information flows from a media source (for example, a radio programme) to opinion leaders in the community who then influence the attitudes of others on a face-to-face basis (for example, discussion in a pub). This theory places more emphasis on the significance of group relationships.

Criticism It divides people too easily into leaders and the led. It operates with a limited view of who has the power to influence and the effectiveness of individuals to influence others in a permanent way.

3. *Uses and Gratifications Theory*. This emerged in the 1960s–1970s. McQuail *et al.* (*The Television Audience*) suggested that in order to understand the effects of the media, it would be fruitful to ask what use do people make of them and what satisfactions they gain from them. They conclude that the same medium may serve different functions for different people. For some violence on TV may be cathartic, for others the source of a 'great' film, and for others non-existent. It assumes that the selected programmes or newspapers fulfil particular needs in different people and that they are selective in their choices.

Criticism The fact that some people are immune to the message does not mean that others may be harmed by it. It is also hard to identify which basic needs are being fulfilled.

4. *Cultural Theory*. This also developed in the 1960s–1970s. Cohen (*Folk Devils and Moral Panics*) examined the ways that meanings are created and interpreted by the audience and passed into the culture. This view suggests that the images created by the media, of, for example, deviant youth, help to sensitise the public to a problem (see also page 122). It accepts that the audience is not passive but actively interprets material it receives.

Criticism It throws up methodological problems, since to understand people's interpretations of the media messages they receive, careful analysis must be made of the media content, and the social background and experiences of all audience members, in order to understand differences in response.

5. *Feminist Theories*. These emerged in the 1980s: for example, Butcher (*Images of Women in the Media*) argued that there is much material that is derogatory to women in the media; most of it supports the interests of men and helps to maintain their power and control over women. Her critical examination of women's magazines and journals suggests that women's views of themselves and their place in society is reinforced by the dominant themes which run through them. These include those of romantic love and improving domestic skills. The heavy emphasis on femininity has helped restrain women from tackling work in scientific and technological fields.

Criticism This represents a particularly powerful ideological perspective.

6. *Media Organisation Analysis*. Researchers in the 1960s, 1970s and 1980s have examined how news is produced. This involved analysis of the structure of media organisations, especially:

(a) The power of the owners (see page 116) and their demands to increase sales at all costs. Recent research (for example Cockburn, *The Brothers*) indicates that with the decline of traditional printing technology and the growth of computers the power of the owner may be increasing.

(b) The influence of editors, who can exert a gate-keeping role, selecting who has access to the media and which items are used. They can also help set the agenda as to what should be discussed and in what terms.

(c) The influence of the journalists. They must operate with the news values of the medium in which they are employed. The tabloids tend to use the 'four-S' formula in selecting news: that which is connected with *sex*, *sensation*, *sport* and *scandal* stands more chance of inclusion. They also have their own professional ideology which provides them with work practice guidelines.

Criticism Such views tend to play down the power of the audience which selects its news media from a wide choice and can put owners, editors and journalists out of work by rejecting their material.

7. *Content Analysis*. This method was developed in the 1970s and 1980s:

(a) From a neo-Marxist perspective (*Bad News*; *More Bad News; Really Bad News*). Philo and the Glasgow Media Group argue that careful analysis of the way news is presented, especially on TV, reveals that the audience is given a constantly misleading portrayal of events, especially those involving industrial disputes, politicians of the Left, etc.

(b) Hall *et al.* (*Policing the Crisis*) examined the way mugging became a moral panic in the 1970s. They argue that the media had central role in creating the concept of mugging (which had not existed in Britain prior to 1972) and identifying the potential mugger. It became a symbol of fear in a society undergoing change, with rising inflation, unemployment and so on.

Criticism Anderson and Sharrock argue from an ethnomethodological perspective that great care must be taken in analysing data from the media. Case studies can be misleading. We need to know more about how people actually read, interpret and make sense of messages. The interpretations of the researchers may not be the same as the wider audience.

Suggested Reading

Works noted in this chapter

R. Anderson, J. Hughes and W. Sharrock (1986) *Philosophy and the Human Sciences*, Croom Helm

H. Arendt (1969) in McQuail (ed.)

D. Bell (1969) in McQuail (ed.)

H. Becker (1963) *Outsiders*, Free Press

S. Bruce (1991) TV Observations on Mass Media Religion', *Social Studies Review* (November)

H. Butcher (1981) 'Image of Women in the Media', in S. Cilan and J. Young (eds.) *The Manufacture of News*, Constable.

Butler and D. Stokes (1974) *Political Change in Britain*, Penguin

S. Chibnall (1977) *Law-and-Order News: An Analysis of Crime Reporting in the British Press*, Tavistock

C. Cockburn (1983) *The Brothers*, Pluto Press

S. Cohen (1975) 'Mods, Rockers and the Rest . . .', in *Crime and Delinquency in Britain*, W. Carson and P. Wiles (eds) Martin Robertson

S. Cohen (1965) *Folk Devils and Moral Panics*, Paladin

I. Crewe (16th June 1987) *A New Class of Politics*, *Guardian* article

G. Cumberbatch and Howitt, *Mass Media, Violence and Society*

T.S. Eliot (1969) in McQuail (ed.)

F. Fearing (1947) *The Influence of the Movies,* in McQuail 1970

Gould *et al. A Dictionary of the Social Sciences*

S. Hall *et al.* (1979) *Policing the Crisis*, Macmillan

J. Halloran (1965) *The Effects of Mass Communication*

P. Hartmann and C. Husband (1981) *The Mass Media and Racial Conflict*, in S. Cohen and J. Young (eds) The Manufacture of News, Constable

R. Hoggart (1958) *The Uses of Literacy*, Penguin

IBA (1978) *The Portrayal of Violence on TV*,

Katz (1972) *Violence on TV*, BBC

Katz and Lazarsfeld (1955) *Personal Influence*, Free Press

Kornhauser (1969) in McQuail (ed.)

MacDonald (1969) in McQuail (ed.)

Manning (1991) 'Mass Media and Pressure Politics', *Social Studies Review* (March)

D. McQuail (1969) *Towards a Sociology of Mass Communication*, Heinemann

D. McQuail *et al.* (1972) *The Television Audience*

D. McQuail (ed.) 1976, *Sociology of Mass Communications*, Penguin

G. Murdock and P. Golding (1977) *Capitalism, Communications and Class Relations*, in J. Curran *et al.* (eds), *Mass Communcations and Society*, Edward Arnold

G. Noble (1975) *Children in Front of the Small Screen*, Pye Survey, Constable

G. Philo, Glasgow Media Group (1976) *Bad News*, Routledge & Kegan Paul

— (1980) *More Bad News*, Routledge & Kegan Paul

— (1982) *Really Bad News*, Writers and Readers

G. Philo (1991) *Seeing is Believing*, Social Studies Review, May

K. Rosengren and S. Windahl (1972) *Mass Media Consumption as a Functional Alternative*, in McQuail

Rosenberg (1969) in McQuail (ed.)

Sheridan and G. Gardner (1985) *Media, Politics and Culture*

Shils (1969) in McQuail (ed.)

W. Stacey and A. Shupe (1982), 'Correlates of Support for the Electronic Church' in *Journal for the Scientific Study of Religion*, Vol. 21

J. Trenaman and D. McQuail (1961) *TV and the Political Image*, Methuen

Tumin (1969) in McQuail (ed.)

J. Whale (1977) *The Politics of the Media*, Fontana

— (1984) *Attitudes to the Press*,

L. Wilkins 'The Deviance-Amplifying System', in *Crime and Delinquency in Britain*, ed. W. Carson and P. Wiles, Martin Robertson

R. Williams, Britain in the Sixties, Penguin

Women Viewing Violence (1992), British Film Institute

Works for further reading

W. Belson (1978) *TV Violence and the Adolescent Boy*, Saxton House

S. Bruce (1991) 'Pray TV', *Sociology Review* (November)

S. Cohen and J. Young (1981) *The Manufacture of News*, Constable

B. Dutton (1986) *The Media*, Longman

P. Elliott (1981) 'Review of More Bad News', *Sociological Review* Vol. 29

S. Frith (1983) *Sound Effects. Youth, Leisure and the Sound of Rock'n'Roll*, Constable

D. Glover (1984) *The Sociology of Mass Media*, Causeway

P. Hartmann (1974) *Race as News*, UNESCO

K. Newton (1990) 'Making News', *Social Studies Review*, Vol. 6, No. 1

Self-test Questions

Study the diagram below and answer the questions which follow.

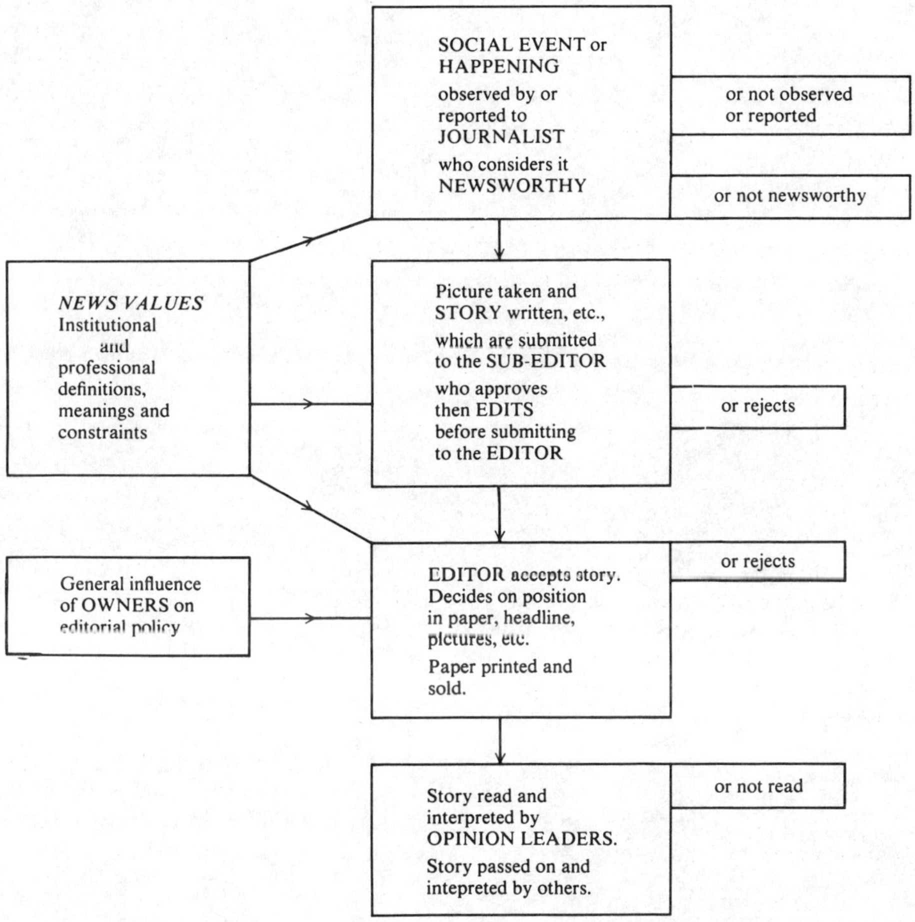

1. Give *three* examples of 'news value' which may influence the definitions of newsworthiness employed by journalists and editors: *(3 marks)*

2. Summarise the view of news and the mass media outlined in the diagram as a whole. *(8 marks)*

3. Analyse the contributions which the media makes in Britain to the formation of attitudes towards *one* particular category of events, issues or social groups (for example, strikes, race relations, welfare benefit claimants or any other of your choosing). *(5 marks)*

Source: JMB (JUNE 1984)

10

EDUCATION

There are a wide range of areas covered in this topic. They include the following:

1. The educational structure:
   (a) Mobility.
   (b) Meritocracy.
2. Theories and perspectives:
   (a) Functionalist.
   (b) Marxist.
   (c) Interactionist.
3. Factors affecting educational achievement. Arguments in the debate:
   (a) Biological.
   (b) Cultural.
   (c) The school.
4. Education and social change.
5. The curriculum:
   (a) Official.
   (b) Hidden.
6. Education and gender.

The Educational Structure: Mobility and Meritocracy

■ **Have the changes in the structure of the educational system since 1945 increased mobility and produced a more meritocratic society?**

To answer this type of question you would need to:

(a) show some knowledge of the changes in the educational structure since 1944;
(b) show some knowledge of changes in mobility patterns;
(c) be able to discuss the concept of 'meritocracy'; and
(d) reach a conclusion.

1. Changes in the educational structure:

(a) The 1944 Butler Education Act introduced the tripartite system (grammar schools, secondary modern and technical schools). This was gradually superseded by the comprehensive system (especially after the 1964 Labour Government was in office). In 1990 86 per cent of children were in such schools; there were 159 grammar schools remaining and 170 secondary moderns.
(b) There has been a slight growth in the independent sector: 1978, 5 per cent; 1983, 6 per cent; 1990, 7 per cent.
(c) The Education Act 1986 increased the power of parents and governors in the running of schools.
(d) The Education Reform Act 1988 introduced:
   (i) city technology colleges which selected pupils according to their aptitude in technological subjects;
   (ii) the National Curriculum, comprising core and foundation subjects to be taught to all pupils aged 5–16 in state schools, subjecting them to tests at 7, 11 and 14;
   (iii) some new responsibilities for the schools in managing their financial budgets;
   (iv) 'opting out': schools could apply for grant maintained status, cut their connections with the local authority and take full financial responsibility for their management, staffing, entry procedures and so on.
(e) Since 1979 there have been other initiatives affecting the structure of education with regard to improving the skills of pupils: the aim being to improve opportunities for mobility. These include Youth Opportunity Programmes (YOP); Youth Training Schemes (YTS); Technical Vocational Education Initiative (TVEI); Certificate of Pre Vocational Education (CPVE); AS level. By 1991 90 per cent of children were leaving school with some qualification.

2. Rates of mobility in Britain are difficult to assess because it depends on the measure used (see page 105). However, the general finding is that rates of long-range mobility seem fairly low. Rates of short-range mobility are higher but are mainly within classes rather than between them.

3. A meritocratic society implies that there is increasing equality of opportunity for those of similar ability. This means that people can achieve status position on merit. The educational system would act in an unbiased way to select the most able people to fill the most important positions.

Table 10.1 Destination of pupils leaving school by destination and qualifications 1989–90 (England and Wales)

	Percentage 5 + grades A–C	Percentage 1–4 grades A–C	Percentage 0–9 grades only	Percentage No results	Percentage Total
Staying on in School	72.3	30.4	14.1	7.4	38.4
Full time Further and Higher Education	17.4	24.9	13.4	2.6	17.4
Youth Training	1.5	10.5	18.7	13.7	10.0
Available for employment	5.4	21.7	35.8	34.8	21.1

Scotland (per cent)

	Full time Education	Full time Employment	YTS	Unemployed
Leavers with qualifications	32.3	31.7	26.8	5.2
Leavers without qualifications	4.3	30.2	37.5	12.8

Source: Social Trends, 22.

The table shows that in England and Wales just over 38 per cent intended to stay on at school and 17 per cent to continue in full-time or further education. In Scotland the majority of unqualified leavers went into a training scheme or into employment.

4. To a large extent the answer to the question depends on the perspective adopted.

The Functionalist perspective

(a) Educational reform which promotes greater opportunity to develop talent must be a key to a more efficient society.
(b) In modern Britain qualifications are available to all who aspire to achieve them.
(c) The previously significant 'ascribed status' has given way to 'achieved status'.
(d) Some form of social inequality is inevitable since there is a ladder of opportunity. Not everyone can climb to the top.
(e) Social mobility is greatest in a society which operates on meritocratic principles. Those who obtain them can enter occupations which provide the highest rewards.
(f) Schools help to stimulate individual talent and locate the most able people from all ranges of the class system to fulfil the most important tasks.

A more critical perspective

Although there have been major educational reforms the chances of educational success, in terms of high levels of qualification, for people of different classes, ethnic backgrounds and sexes do not seem to be achieved on merit.

(a) Reid (*Social Class Differences in Britain*) shows that the chances of going to a university became greater for the non-manual classes during the 1970s. Admission statistics showed that in the number of entrants between 1970 and 1977 the percentage for Class 1 rose from 30 per cent to 36 per cent while that from Class 4 fell from 28 per cent to 24 per cent. Private schools maintained a virtual monopoly of top jobs. They comprised approximately 86 per cent of high court judges; 83 per cent of top directors; 80 per cent of bank directors and nearly 70 per cent of Conservative MPs.
(b) Mills (*The Power Elite*) makes the point that access to top jobs is controlled by the members of the professions. They allow entry only from others in the same class. As a result levels of mobility into such occupational groups is tightly limited (see also page 107).
(c) Halsey *et al.* (*Origins and Destinations*) studied 8525 males educated in England and Wales. They found that boys from Classes 1 and 2 compared with ones from Classes 4 and 5 had: forty times more chance of attending a public school; three times more chance of attending a grammar school; eleven times more chance of entering a university. (However, since the study was conducted in 1972 the comprehensive system has become more widespread). The conclusion reached at that time was that the educational structure had not established a more meritocratic society or greatly increased opportunities of mobility.
(d) Bourdieu ('The School as a Conservative Force') also disputes the view that changes in the educational structure can have much impact on mobility or in producing a meritocracy. He argues:
   (i) In a capitalist society there is a strong relationship between economic and cultural power and educational competence.
   (ii) The majority of working-class children are excluded from access to positions of significant status and power because the school curriculum is not neutral. It is biased in favour of the already economically powerful by testing skills more usually developed in middle-class homes.
   (iii) Schools thereby act as conservative forces to maintain the *status quo* by disguising the real causes of inequality and making them seem normal and reasonable.
   (iv) He concludes that extensive social mobility is largely a myth. But its limited existence gives rise to the belief in a growing meritocracy.
(e) Research published in 1992 (from Warwick University and Bristol Polytechnic) found that recent changes to grant maintained status had not made much real impact on the quality of education or degree of choice as far as pupils, parents and teachers were concerned. The main impact had been in the emphasis on improving the school image.

Conclusions

There may be some objective evidence (for example, Halsey *et al.*) to suggest that mobility has increased over the short range (especially within classes), but selection on merit has not yet become the norm in every sphere of society. Yet subjectively people do seem to consider themselves to be potentially more mobile as they have become better educated and more able to enter white-collar occupations. (This is a development which may be harming the Labour Party in its loss of support.) But there is always the danger of assuming a universal truth from a few specific cases (such as the success of Mr Major in achieving high office from an impoverished background).

Theories of Education

- **The major role of the educational system is not to promote equality, but to legitimate inequality. Discuss. (AEB)**
- **'To understand the behaviour of children it is necessary to examine their interactions with teachers.' Discuss**

Functionalist perspective

Functionalists ask two main questions:

(a) How does the educational system promote order and stability in society?
(b) What functions does it serve for the individual?

Emile Durkheim said that society can only exist if there is a strong degree of social solidarity (value consensus). Education helps establish this by transmitting valued norms and beliefs to all pupils. These help integrate people more closely into the society. The education system also helps fulfil other needs of society by reacting to economic needs for a more skilled work force.

Parsons argues that the school is a vital secondary source of socialisation. By enabling the most able to rise to the top of the social hierarchy on merit, inequalities can be justified.

Marxist perspective

The Marxist also looks at society as a whole but examines its role in relation to the economic structure. The interest is particularly in the ways in which the values and ideologies of the ruling class are transmitted through the schools.

An example of such an analysis is: Bowels and Gintis (*Schooling in Capitalist America*).

(a) They argue that education serves to reproduce the existing social structure.
(b) The fragmentation of work is mirrored in the fragmentation of the curriculum into tiny packages of knowledge.
(c) The alienation of children in school is preparation for their later alienation in work.
(d) Pupils are organised in a competitive hierarchical structure and prevented from gaining much intrinsic satisfaction from their work.
(e) The conformists gain highest rewards.

Interactionist perspective

This perspective is based on the idea that social action arises out of interpretations and perceptions achieved in the course of interactions. The focus is on the relationships observed in the classroom.

Examples of studies using this approach include:

1. Cicourel and Kitsuse (*The Educational Decision-Makers*). They noted how teachers and counsellors evaluated students and advised them in terms of their appearance, manner and patterns of behaviour, based on reports. They were responding to images, which made equality of treatment impossible.
2. Becker (*Social Class Variations*) found that teachers assessed pupils in terms of an 'ideal type' model. They perceived the children who approximate most closely to it as the most able. They tended to come from non-manual backgrounds.

Factors Affecting Educational Achievement

- **Educational attainment varies among different sections of the population. This cannot be explained wholly by the distribution of intelligence. What other explanations are there?**
- **Critically assess sociological explanations of difference in educational achievement.**

The question that has produced a great amount of sociological research and debate is why particular groups of children (especially those in Classes 4 and 5) tend to be less successful in the educational system when there have been major changes in structure since 1944. (For differences in the educational attainments of girls compared to boys, see page 139; and for ethnic minorities, see page 276). Explanations tend to focus on three areas: biological/genetic; cultural; and the school.

Biological/genetic

Explanation

Intelligence Although there is no precise definition it is usually taken to mean: a capacity for learning or reasoning; an ability to think in abstract ways; to absorb new material quickly and process information. Some have argued that there is an IQ gene which is transmitted from parents.

IQ tests were first devised by Binet (1905) to measure mental age. Terman's index of mental development was:

Intelligence Quotient = mental age/actual age $\times$ 100.

This established the 11 + test to select children for the appropriate school under the 1944 Education Act (grammar, technical, secondary modern).

Points of criticism

1. An IQ gene has never been identified.
2. IQ tests may only measure cultural skills; they are often culture-biased.
3. They tend to measure a capacity to conform to the tester's restrictions. Only the test-makers' answer is correct. They therefore ignore creative and imaginative skills.
4. IQ scores may be improved by coaching.
5. A child's future should not be based on the results of an unreliable test.
6. Knowledge of test scores by teachers may affect the way they treat children in the classroom.
7. The results of such criticisms led to the introduction of comprehensive schools.

Cultural

Many researchers have focused attention on the cultural background of the child as being a very important factor in determining attainment. This influences the child's attitudes, expectations and beliefs about what school is like and what value it may have, before entering at the age of five. After that, there is constant reinforcement of such attitudes. The culture of origin is seen to be more significant than any other factor. See page 134.

Author summary points

1. Douglas (*The Home and the School*) noted a correlation between unsatisfactory housing, low parental interest and low levels of achievement. Middle-class parents paid more frequent visits to the school, had smaller families and exerted more choice in their child's school.
2. Prosser and Wedge (*Born to Fail*) found the disadvantaged children in their study (see page 228) were less healthy and did less well in school. Their work suggested that such children could be identified at birth so that more social and educational provision was necessary, otherwise they had no chance.
3. Halsey (*Educational Priority*) outlines a range of policies around the development of pre-schooling and community schools and their implications. He says 'not only must parents understand schools, schools must also understand the family and the environments in which the children live'. Teachers need to be sensitive to the child's social and moral climate of development.
4. Newson (*Patterns of Infant Care*) There were found to be differences in child-rearing practices between manual and non-manual classes. Middle-class practices were found to provide later educational advantages. There was an emphasis on provision of stimulating home environment; discussion of issues between parents and children, all factors which help establish patterns of appropriate behaviour in school.

Points of criticism relating to each author

1. The reason why working-class parents may appear to show less interest is because they are in employment which makes visits to school difficult.
2. It is difficult to measure 'positive' and 'negative' attitudes.
3. Such parents may have high aspirations for their children but lack the knowledge about how best to advise them.

The view that children are 'born to fail' as a result of their cultural deprivations suggests that a high proportion are 'doomed' and beyond redemption. Especially since more provision is unlikely at times of economic recession

More radical critics would argue that education cannot compensate for the inequalities in the wider social structure. 'Understanding' is not enough. There must be social change which promotes true equalities.

Interactionists would oppose the view that child-rearing patterns have a completely determining effect on future development. They would argue that people can change behaviour according to their interpretation of events in the classroom for example.

Author summary points

5. Bernstein (*Social Class and Linguistic Development*) argues that there are class differences in the use of language. Working-class children tend to use a 'restricted code'. Some characteristics:
   (a) short, grammatically simple sentences;
   (b) often unfinished sentences;
   (c) limited use of adverbs and adjectives;
   (d) meanings often conveyed more by gesture; and
   (e) emphasis more on concrete not abstract ideas and meanings. Middle-class children use a more 'elaborated code'. Its main characteristics include:
   (a) longer, more complex sentences;
   (b) more extensive use of imaginative language;
   (c) meanings more clearly stated; and
   (d) use of abstract concepts.
   Bernstein has argued that the restricted code is inefficient in formal education. The elaborated code provides the power to allow more complex ideas to be conveyed. The child who uses only a restricted code is at an educational disadvantage, especially in examinations.

Points of criticism relating to each author

(a) Rosen (*Language and Class*) argues that the terms 'elaborated' and 'restricted' may imply a qualitative difference between the classes themselves ('manual classes are inferiors'), i.e. teachers may come to assume that because they teach many working-class children they have no chance of academic success.

(b) Rosen says that working-class speech has its own strengths and is not necessarily 'deformed or underpowered'.

(c) Labov (*The Logic of Nonstandard English*) also denies that working-class children cannot express complex ideas, in his analysis of the speech patterns of black children. Theirs is also a very rich, verbal culture, and these children have the same capacity for complex conceptual learning.

(d) The emphasis on restricted language may limit research into the shortcomings of the schools.

6. Sugarman (*Social Class Values and Behaviour in Schools*) suggests that there are differences in attitude and values between the classes. In the middle classes there is an emphasis on 'deferred gratification': they are encouraged to postpone pleasures and short-term aims for long-term goals. This would explain why there are more middle-class children remaining in school or higher education than working-class children, who are socialised into an ethic of 'immediate gratification'.

(a) It may be an overgeneralisation to assume that members of the working class prefer instant gratification. Failure in school may lead to the view that things will not improve in the future, therefore it is best to take what is presently available.

(b) Families with no history of higher education or qualifications among their members will not see the relevance of these.

(c) The social norm of 'hard work' is expressed in terms of learning the job on the shop floor.

(d) For middle-class children in higher education there may be a great deal of gratification, which is not deferred.

7. Bourdieu (*Systems of Education and Systems of Thought*) writes that just as the 'formal lecture . . . defines the right culture . . . so all teaching . . . will furnish a model of the right mode of intellectual activity'. He argues that the ruling élite impose their values and meaning on others. This enables them to set the agenda in establishing what counts as knowledge or intelligent behaviour. This cultural capital is accumulated by the dominant class and transmitted to others within it. The result is their academic success. They acquire the label 'intelligent' or 'gifted'. They appear to acquire valued knowledge more easily than others. The school thereby reproduces social inequality.

(a) The theory rests on a Marxist analysis of power and domination.

(b) There are examples of children from working-class backgrounds who have no such access to the cultural capital but who are subsequently able to achieve power and status.

(c) Access to the cultural capital may assist a child in achieving an education in the private sector or in a selective school, but after that its effect may be less significant.

(d) In contemporary society the most valuable knowledge may be scientific and computer-related skills. These may be increasingly available to all social classes.

The school

This aspect focuses on the extent to which children's level of achievement is related to what happens to them inside the school – the way it is organised in terms of its goals, rules, structures – as well as to teacher–pupil relations. This has been the particular (though not exclusive) concern of the phenomenologists.

- **Assess the influence of teacher expectations on their pupils' educational performance. (UODLE)**
- **Schools do not merely react to children with varying qualities and capacities in a neutral way: they play an active part in creating children who are more or less educable, more or less knowledgeable, more or less manageable (Bilton *et al.*). Explain and discuss. (AEB)**

Author summary points	Points of criticism relating to each author
1. Hargreaves (*Social Relations in a Secondary School*) observed the normative structure of the pupils in their forms in a secondary modern school. He was concerned with the significance of the peer group in regulating patterns of behaviour. Teachers tended to assume that negative behaviour could be explained in terms of 'bad home background'. Hargreaves argues that this is an oversimplification. It ignores the crucial aspect of the pupils' sub-cultures as they develop in the process of classroom interaction. These tended to relate to the form the pupils were in and their stream. Those in the top streams had more positive attitudes than those in the lowest. He concluded that the school can be regarded as a generating factor in development of deliquency. Teachers promote deviance by their treatment of the pupils, whose negative culture was a response to the problems they faced each day in the classroom.	Whilst Marxist critics of the methods of phenomenology would not be surprised by the findings they would argue that they can be explained in other ways. Reality is objective, not subjective. The inequalities of wider society are reflected in the structure of the educational system. In school, children are differentiated and stratified by streams and ability. The perception of children as bright or dull is not just something that arises out of the interaction process; the teachers are merely operating with the accepted normative values of wider society which sees the lower working-class as less valuable members. The education system is shaped by the economic system and must produce the kind of people required by the capitalist economy. Teachers are the gatekeepers who can encourage or deter their entry into particular occupations.
2. Becker *et al.* (*Student Culture and Academic Effort*) describe some of the positive aspects of the development of cultural values among students. They state that sub-cultures develop best where a number of people are faced with a common problem and interest in the effort to find solutions. There is intensive interaction among students wondering what to learn; the worth of particular courses; how to deal with particular members of staff, etc. The culture that arises among them provides them with a perspective and a pattern of responses; it provides a system of social support and patterns of shared understandings. Student culture is the cornerstone of many of the difficulties with students; it is one of the facts of life to which teachers must make some accommodation. For middle-class students it is a culture of coping, not opposition.	Willis (*Learning to Labour*) describes how working-class sub-cultures are better described as 'counter cultures'. They evolve as cultures of opposition to the dominant middle-class values of 'academic success'. For males, these counter cultures, found in the school and the work place, are not able to replace the middle-class ethics, but they enable the working-class boy to survive. They emphasise masculinity, toughness, aggression and sexist attitudes. He defines culture as 'the very material of our daily lives, the bread and butter of our understandings, feelings and responses'.
3. A 1990 NFER Report showed that the reading ability of 7 and 8-year-olds had declined over the past five years. They argued the causes included: (a) increasing social deprivation; (b) parents having less time to help; and (c) the significance of class factors	Government spokesmen argued that the results showed: (a) poor teacher training; (b) poor classroom teaching; (c) variations in spending by LEAs; and (d) the need for reform.
4. 1992 results of the first tests of 7-year-olds showed 15% either had learning difficulties or did not speak English as a first language.	
5. Keddie (*Classroom Knowledge*) is critical of the fact that explanations for educational failure are most often given in terms of pupils' ethnic and social class antecedents. She examines the defining procedures occurring within the school itself. She used observational techniques to establish the ways in which teachers evaluate pupils and establish their levels of ability. She found that they made use of their 'knowledge' of them in the assessments. Children were perceived to be most able where they readily absorbed the material presented to them. Those who offered 'irrelevant' knowledge were perceived as 'less able'. She concluded that the failure of high-ability pupils to question what they are taught contributes in large measure to their educational achievement. Classroom evaluation of pupils and knowledge are said to be socially constructed in the interaction process.	It is difficult to prove that meanings are constructed simply in the classroom as a result of interaction, rather than being culturally derived from wider society. If this were the only source of images then we would expect more variety in these to reflect the range of interactions that occur in the classroom. It seems surprising that so many teachers arrive at the same interpretations about the same kinds of children, those from the working class being perceived in more negative ways than others. The meanings that are derived must have some origin. How do teachers know what class distinctions are likely to produce in the way of bad behaviour other than by their experiences in wider society? These expectations are carried into the classroom.

Author summary points

6. Rutter *et al.* (*Fifteen Thousand Hours*) The title refers to the number of hours spent by a child in school from the ages of five to sixteen. The study was carried out over six years in twelve inner London secondary schools. The authors examined:
   (a) attendance;
   (b) academic achievement;
   (c) behaviour in school; and
   (d) rate of deliquency outside it.

   They concluded that different schools achieved varied results with children even when background differences were taken into account. Variations were related to what happened inside the school. Success was not related to smallness of school, use of resources, age of building. What did matter was:
   (a) the spread of ability among the intake;
   (b) a reasonable spread of ability was more significant than class of origin. A high proportion of low-ability children was associated with high delinquency rates;
   (c) the ability of the teachers to create and maintain specific norms. These included encouragement; consistency; acting as a good model for pupils; and
   (d) the school ethos; rules set and enforced.

Points of criticism relating to each author

(a) Heath and Clifford (*Oxford Review of Education*, 1980) criticise the crude measures of class used: fathers' occupations were split into only three categories.
(b) The failure to consider the effects of different primary schools.
(c) The significance of class is underplayed.
(d) Ethos is very difficult to assess or measure and is unlikely to be the source of success.
(e) Action (*Educational Research*) accuses the researchers of 'cheating by putting in statistical cautions and then blandly ignoring them'.
(f) Wragg (*Perspectives: Exeter University*) argues that the schools chosen were not typical. The twelve schools had 28% of fathers convicted of criminal offences; 51% of children were in overcrowded homes; 43% of the teachers were in their posts for less than three years.
(g) Goldstein (*Journal of Child Psychology and Psychiatry*) said that the results should be treated with caution if not scepticism.

Education and Social Change

■ **The power of the education system to transform societies has been much exaggerated. Discuss. (AEB)**

Those who claim that changes in the educational system can produce changes in the structure of society would include many functionalist writers. They would argue:

1. There is a direct relationship between the educational system and the economic system. As the economy develops so an improved structure of education is required to ensure that workers have the appropriate skills.
2. The school-leaving age may be raised to retain a longer hold on pupils to prevent too many entering the labour market without appropriate talents.
3. An improved educational system produces greater chances for social mobility, so transforming the class structure.
4. Education encourages greater personal development, enabling people to extend their range of talents. This must ensure more harmony and order in society.
5. The principles of meritocracy and self-help are important values which promote the possibility of change towards a more open society.
6. The failure of many children to achieve their full potential can be explained in terms of cultural deprivation. Deficiences in culture result in poor socialisation.

Some critics argue that the concepts of disadvantage and deprivation are often badly defined. They appear to focus on poor home background and lack of adequate language development in these children. Educational programmes have been developed to try to compensate for such deficiences:

(a) Educational Priority Areas: these were introduced into Britain in the 1960s. The government provided additional finance and other resources for schools in places designated as EPAs.
(b) Operation Headstart (USA): in the early 1960s attempts were made to provide special programmes and assistance for children from poor homes (especially blacks) in their early years. It was later phased out, although some success was claimed.

Points of criticism

1. Collins (*Functional and Conflict Theories of Educational Stratification*) argues that:

   (i) The educational system does not work as closely with the economic system as functionalist writers suggest. A high proportion of skills are learned in a practical way; many people have to undertake further training, provided by their employers, once appointed.
   (ii) Many qualifications achieved by pupils are of no specific vocational use.
   (iii) Obtaining high qualifications for entry into professional occupations is the means used for controlling its membership and status. The numbers obtaining entry are very small. In 1990 there were

Questions

Examine photographs 29–30.

1 If examination test results were found to be below average in this inner-city school, (29) suggest some of the factors which a researcher may wish to study in order to find explanations.

(i) Consider both the factors external to the school as well as those within it which may account for varying levels of performance.
(ii) Relate your explanations to known sociological research.

2 Photograph 30 shows the chapel of Harrow public school.

(i) Discuss the significance for a school:
(a) Having its own chapel.
(b) Having a special and unusual school uniform.
(c) What implications might you draw about this school in comparison with that shown in photograph 29?
(d) In 1992 a list was published showing the 100 schools which achieved the best A-level results. Suggest some reasons why public schools dominated the list.
(e) What points of caution would a phenomenologist make about the interpretation of such statistics?

30

Source: Alec Gill

29

Source: Alec Gill

nearly twice as many pupils leaving school without a GCSE pass above Grade D as there were achieving 2 or more A-levels (see table 10.2).

2. Marxist writers (Althusser) argue that the educational system does not increase mobility or the chances of a meritocracy. It is a microcosm of wider society. The inequalities are reflected in the structure and organisation of the school. For the ruling class to survive, the reproduction of labour power is essential. There is evidence of a decrease in equality of educational opportunity.

3. Bernstein ('Education Cannot Compensate for Society'):

(i) He argues that the compensatory programmes would serve mainly to divert attention from the major inequalities in society.
(ii) He wrote, 'I cannot understand how we can talk about offering compensatory education to children who in the first place have not, as yet, been offered an adequate educational environment'.
(iii) Such schemes imply that something is lacking in the family and so in the child.

4. Walsey (who directed the EPAs) said the scheme was intended to assist both children and schools, but it was never properly funded and the results were disappointing.

Conclusions

Some writers have argued that changes in the way the educational system is organised can change society in radical ways:

(a) Liberals suggest that education directly affects individuals, who can learn to become more tolerant and co-operative (child-centred education).
(b) Functionalists argue that education can promote equality of opportunity and produce a more meritocratic society (Operation Headstart; Educational Priority Areas);
(c) Conservative educationalists recognising the need to produce a more technologically-minded work force introduced new 'vocational' policies in the 1980s (use of computers; new exams; national curriculum, etc).

However, critics have suggested that the power of education to change the structure of society is exaggerated:

(a) Bowles and Gintis discuss the ways in which the educational system enables the ruling class to reproduce the social structure and provide a compliant work force. All changes were to that end.
(b) Willis notes how any changes in the educational system largely bypass a disaffected section of the working class who reject school and all it represents, by maintaining a counter-culture which enables them to cope with its irrelevant tedium.
(c) Boudon believes that class stratification is the most powerful factor affecting a person's lifestyle and life chances. To achieve real equality it would be necessary to abolish class divisions.
(d) Jencks (*Inequality*) has also argued that education is not effective in achieving social change which might promote equality. He found wide status differences between people with the same educational standards. There was no evidence that educational attainment had a major influence on income. He describes schools as marginal institutions in effecting change.

The Curriculum

(See also Chapter 2 page 34.)

■ **'The curriculum includes not only clearly defined teaching of subjects but also a hidden curriculum both of which transmit to young people a series of messages'. Explain what is meant by this statement.**

The official curriculum

Bernstein (*On the Classification and Framing of Educational Knowledge*) says that the curriculum defines what counts as valid knowledge. Evaluation counts as a valid realisation of this knowledge on the part of the taught.

Young (*Knowledge and Control*) argues that the focus of attention in the sociology of education has, for some, become an enquiry into the social organisation of 'knowledge' in educational institutions.

The question arises: what counts as knowledge, especially in the classroom? The answers given depend on the perspective or ideology of the observer.

Williams (*The Long Revolution*) has pointed out that 'education is not a product like cars and bread, but a

Table 10.2 Educational qualifications of school-leavers as percentage of the relevant population: by sex

	1980–81		1988–89	
	Boys	Girls	Boys	Girls
2 or more A-levels	15	13	18	19
1 A-level	3	4	4	4
5+ GCSE/O-levels (A–C) (no A-levels)	8	10	12	15
1–4 GCSE/O-levels (A–C)	25	28	26	29
1+ GCSE/O-level (D–G)	34	32	30	26
No qualifications	15	12	10	7

Source: *Social Trends*, 22.

selection and organisation from the available knowledge at a particular time which involves conscious and unconscious choices'. 'Sociologists endeavour to relate the principles that underlie the curricula to their institutional and interactional setting in classrooms and in the wider society. Williams distinguishes four sets of educational ideologies which provide the basis for selecting the content of curriculum. These are related to the social position of those who hold them at a particular time:

	Ideology	Social position	Policy
1.	Liberal/Conservative	Gentry	The all-round educated person
2.	Bourgeois	Professionals	Education for status
3.	Democratic	Reformers	Education for all
4.	Proletarian	Working classes	Relevance; choice

Shipman (*The Sociology of the School*) notes how all societies, whether capitalist or communist, have sets of beliefs that they wish to transmit to the future generations. Schools reflect these in the curriculum and teaching methods. Of each item on the curriculum it can be asked: does it serve a useful purpose and what priority should it have?

In an endeavour to establish greater equality of opportunity some writers have suggested new approaches to the curriculum.

The hidden curriculum

■ **Whereas the official curriculum is the planned instructional activities in the school, the hidden curriculum is that which is not taught by the teachers.**

1. A National Union of Teachers (NUT) document (*Working for Equality*) suggests that the hidden curriculum includes how assemblies are run; how reward and punishment systems operate; how the register is ordered (by sex or alphabetically); how extra curricular activities are organised (are they of equal value to boys and girls?); how publicity information about the school is written (does it use stereotypes?); how staffing is structured and how responsibilities are distributed between males and females; how resources are allocated; how careers advice is organised and given; the language used in the classroom and playground; the amount of time devoted by teachers to boys and girls and the messages they give about the roles most *suited to them*.

2. Head (*Free Way to Learning*) says that the hidden curriculum describes the rules which pupils learn to survive. It is all the other things that are learnt during time in school. Children pick up an approach to living and an attitude to learning. It includes the rules for coping with problems, with delay, with teachers, with routine, etc. Children learn how to feign interest, understanding and ability where there may be none.

The Marxist view

1. The construction of a body of knowledge is inextricably linked to the interests of those who produce it.
2. The ruling élite develop their own self-justifying standards of evaluation.
3. Knowledge is what the gatekeepers of power define as knowledge. Reference to irrelevant facts in the classroom are ways by which teachers can distinguish the bright from the dull.
4. The curriculum is class-based. The Government has defined what is 'valuable knowledge' in the National Curriculum.

The Functionalist view

1. This presupposes an agreed set of societal values or goals which define both the selection and the organisation of knowledge in the curriculum.
2. The British educational system is usefully dominated by a set of academic curricula with a rigid stratification of knowledge. This provides status for the most able who are taught in ability groups and assessed by objective criteria.
3. The curriculum must change to meet changing economic needs: For example, the National Curriculum will serve this purpose.

In an endeavour to establish greater equality of opportunity some writers have suggested new approaches to the curriculum:

Argument

1. Lawton (*Class, Culture and the Curriculum*) suggests that although there are differences between classes in attitudes and values, there are also areas of similarity. Schools should endeavour to impose a common culture curriculum. This could be based on a heritage of knowledge and belief common to all.
2. Torrey (*Illiteracy in the Ghetto*) argues that where necessary lessons should be taught to ethnic minorities in their own speech patterns and they should be tested in the same way.

Points of criticism

1. The fact that there are major class differences in society makes a common-culture curriculum impossible. The dominant middle-class value system would inevitably prevail. It would not be possible to establish a consensus as to the content of a common culture within the existing social system.
2. In Britain the ethnic minority consists of less than 4% of the population which makes the culturally differentiated curriculum impractical.

The Marxist perspective

1. The hidden curriculum can be seen as a means of achieving additional control of pupils in situations normally considered to be non-academic or informal: showing deference to staff, accepting humiliating references to themselves etc.
2. Children learn to internalise a particular self-image based on the perception of teachers ('non-academic', 'slow' etc).
3. Children learn about their social-class position and what to expect in life as a result, following their grading and streaming in school.
4. They learn to accept a hierarchy of power and implicit criticism of being working-class. They learn how to cope with boredom and repetition, which will be valuable when they enter the world of work.

The Functionalist perspective

1. Children learn a great number of valuable rules about social life from contact with peers and teachers in school: to be punctual; to behave in acceptable ways in particular situations; to accept criticism; to aim for a particular occupational status in a realistic way; to be a part of a team; to be competitive; to accept defeat as well as success. Also to seek appropriate goals; to adopt appropriate roles according to sex, ability, age, etc.

3. Meighan (*A Sociology of Educating*) points out, however, that there is a problem with the definition. It is not clear whether the hidden curriculum is a concept with a recognisable content.

Conclusions

(a) The official curriculum is that which appears as timetabled subjects (of which only Religious Education was compulsory until the 1988 Education Act).
(b) 1979–87, a strong emphasis on 'the new vocationalism' appeared in the curriculum (for example, TVEI; CPVE; BTEC) for those not wishing to take A-levels.
(c) The 1988 Act imposed reforms with less emphasis on new vocational subjects but more by seeking a return to traditional values (the possibility of selection; national curriculum, with attainment targets, less course work, etc.).
(d) The hidden curriculum is all that is presented more informally to pupils as participants in a classroom and as members of a school. Bowles and Gintis say it helps produce the rules which create a passive work force; it legitimates the concept of hierarchy; promotes the beliefs in external rewards and the fragmentation of knowledge into different and often unrelated subject domains; and it helps create pupil self-image. The process sustains an underlying policy of 'divide and rule', which ultimately leads to an easily-controlled work force.

Education and Gender

■ **What differences are there between the educational experiences of boys and girls?**

Studies suggest that teachers, in the course of their work, come to develop images and stereotypes of their pupils. They then operate with what they consider to be 'professional' knowledge and understanding, based on notions of what is best for a particular type of pupil. They do, however, according to some authorities, evaluate them in terms of 'family background' or 'school record'. They are also influenced by pressures from the local community to produce 'satisfactory pupils'; from colleagues and superiors to 'maintain standards'; as well as from university departments and employers to produce 'the kind of person needed'. The result is that there are processes of selection and stratification operating in schools which may be far more subtle than crude streaming. Pupils can be persuaded to take certain courses of action and drop others because 'they are predicted failures from the start' or 'they are not the type'.

The effect operating on both boys and girls can be significant, but the following research indicates that girls are generally treated in ways that do much to discourage them from taking science subjects, entering technical careers, and, to a lesser extent, entering higher education. See Table 10.3.

Table 10.3 Ratio of pupils in each subject by sex (1978)

Subject	Boys	Girls
Physics	6	1
Chemistry	4	1
Biology	9	8
Technical Drawing	200	1
Languages	1	2

Table 10.4 Percentage of school-leavers with Grades A–C in GCSE, (GB) 1988–89, by subject and sex

Subject	Boys	Girls
English	38	52
Mathematics	38	35
Physics	23	10
Geography	20	16
Chemistry	18	13
History	15	18
Biology	14	21
French	13	22

Source: *Social Trends*, 22.

1. Meighan (*A Sociology of Educating*) says that the regular patterns that appear in the educational biographies of girls and boys in Britain include the following:

(a) Boys' and girls' achievements in school are similar up to the age of eleven.
(b) For every hundred boys leaving with one A-level or more there were ninety girls.
(c) Table 10.3 shows the ratios which existed in 1978 between boys and girls.
(d) Table 10.4 shows the proportion of boys and girls who left school in 1988/89 having achieved grades A–C (GCSE or Scottish equivalents.) Boys tended to achieve higher results in science subjects (especially physics) girls achieved better results in Biology, French, History and especially English.
(e) More boys than girls achieve entry to university and other forms of higher education (although more girls enter teacher training). In 1989–90 girls formed 47 per cent of all students on first degree courses compared with only 41 per cent in 1979–80.
(f) More girls than boys undertake courses of teacher training, nursing and catering.

2. Spender ('Don't talk, listen', *Times Educational Supplement*) argues that males dominate conversation, which is a reflection of the domination they have in society as a whole. Those without power are always the most vulnerable and tend to play a more submissive role. Girls learn this attitude in the classroom (it is part of the hidden curriculum). They discover that by avoiding a dominating role and that of the intellectual, they become less of a threat and more acceptable to their male peers. She notes how in one study girls thought it natural that male students should ask the questions and make the protests. The females should 'just get on with it' even though the work was considered tedious or pointless.

3. Nightingale ('What Katy didn't do', *Spare Rib*) found that books specifically for girls showed a preponderance of discussions about 'love, dating, romance, with side-lines in problems like spots, glasses and so on, which interfere with romance'. The tomboy's world is presented as ultimately unsatisfactory, with messages that it is perhaps better to be a girl, after all.

4. Grandall *et al.* (*Child Development*) noted how girls were brought up to be less competitive; their attitudes towards success are more likely to be mixed with doubts and lack of confidence. Girls tend to take the blame for failures and suggest that success is due to luck. Boys more readily blame others for failure and praise themselves for success.

5. Sharpe (*Just Like a Girl*) notes how girls, particularly from working-class backgrounds, are seen and see themselves as primarily aspiring girlfriends, wives and mothers, and at best aspiring typists, nurses or teachers. She argues that it is the comparatively low horizon of expectation that causes girls to do less well in school, especially at A-level, than boys. It is her conclusion that as a result of the processes of socialisation in the home (which inculcate feminine attitudes) and in school (where girls are given less of the teachers' attention and time and expected to be less able in certain fields) the sexual division of labour is reinforced and any differences that do exist are greatly exaggerated.

6. Blackstone (*New Society*) also argues that there are so few women scientists and engineers because of the impact of environmental influences on attitudes, both in the home and the school. Science and technology are seen as 'male subjects' and the acceptable female role is constantly reinforced by the media, advertising and in the course of day-to-day interactions.

7. Merrett and Wheldall confirmed from their research that:

(a) boys continued to receive more attention from teachers even where girls were achieving better exam results.
(b) Male teachers were found to praise boys for good academic work while women teachers, who were more likely to experience disruptive behaviour from boys, were more likely to spend more time reprimanding them. They conclude that teachers' responses to pupils can affect classroom behaviour and academic progress.

8. Theoretical perspectives:

(a) *Marxists/Radical Feminists* (for example, Spender, *Invisible Women*) argue that education is part of the patriarchal control system in which men control all key areas of power. Men define what is valuable knowledge. The curriculum is a sexist instrument which favours boys by placing emphasis on science and technology. Schools help maintain male dominance. Some feminists have advocated single-sex education to counter male aggression.
(b) *Functionalists* would claim that such arguments are flawed, either by their weak methodology or by inadequate data. They would point to the statistics which indicate that girls are catching up with boys in levels of educational success (see Table 10.4). In some areas (for example, leaving qualifications) they have overtaken them. The educational system is, therefore, as effective for girls as it is for boys.
(c) *Interactionists* (for example, Kelly, *Science for Girls*) has produced evidence through observational techniques to show how girls are often marginalised in science lessons by the use of textbooks which make few references to women scientists; by teachers who use examples more familiar to boys; and by other male pupils who dominate classroom activities.

■ To what extent are schools responsible for the production of deviant sub-cultures?

Points to note

(i) Deviance is a relative concept. It is defined in terms of the perceptions of others who set rules or accept them as being correct.
(ii) Deviant behaviour is that which is identified by an observer as a breach of accepted rules.
(iii) A sub-culture describes the norms and patterns of behaviour of a particular group which are different from those of the majority.
(iv) A deviant sub-culture describes the unacceptable behaviour of a group which deviates from the pattern expected in the school (or in some other social arena).
(v) The debate hinges on whether such deviant sub-cultures arise from the failure of the school to provide relevant courses for pupils, who then rebel; or

whether such cultural values are brought from outside into the school, having been learned from relatives, friends and others in the community as ways of coping with irrelevant activities.

1. The view that the school is responsible for their creation:

(a) Hargreaves (see page 134).
(b) Becker *et al.* (see page 134).
(c) Keddie (see page 134).

2. The view that its central values are imported from outside the school and inadvertently sustained within it: Willis (*Learning to Labour*) used a range of methodologies to gain insight into the lives, attitudes and behaviour of a small group of boys (PO, discussions, diaries, informal interviews).

(i) He found a specific deviant culture which involved opposition to teachers and school rules, to conformist pupils and to exams.
(ii) Members placed high value on 'having a laugh'. They were largely aimless, disruptive, frequently absent and always looking forward to the excitement gained outside school.
(iii) Their values were sexist and racist; they positively looked forward to a life of manual labour. Their rejection of mainstream success goals and values prepared them for this.
(iv) He found that the shop floor culture they duly entered was similar to that of the school sub-culture of which they had been members.
(v) The school had unintentionally reproduced their work ethics.

His conclusion: it is not the school which promotes the deviant counter-culture. Those who subscribe to it have absorbed specific ideas about the world of work from others. School is the preparation ground which is seen as totally irrelevant to their futures.

Points of criticism

(i) His sample is very small (twelve boys studied in depth).
(ii) The counter-culture he examined was extreme. Others must have existed in the school which advocated different values and with different outcomes for members.
(iii) Other analysts would see the organisation of the school, its rules, values and power structures as the more likely causes of deviant sub-cultures.

Suggested Reading

Works noted in this chapter

H. Becker *et al.* (1968) *Making the Grade: the Academic Side of College Life*
H. Becker (1971) *Social Class Variations*,
B. Bernstein (1961) *Social Class and Linguistic Development*
B. Bernstein (1971) *On the Classification and Framing of Educational Knowledge*, in Young, M. (ed.)
T. Blackstone (1980) 'Why so few girls do science in school', *New Society* (February)
P. Bourdieu (1971) *Systems of Education and Systems of Thought*
P. Bourdieu (1974) *The School as a Conservative Force*
S. Bowles and H. Gintis (1976) *Schooling in Capitalist America*, RKP
A. Cicourel and J. Kitsuse (1963) *The Educational Decision-Makers*
R. Collins (1972) *Functional and Conflict Theories of Educational Stratification*, in Cosin, P. (ed.) Education, Structure and Society, Penguin
J. Douglas (1964) *The Home and the School*, Macmillan & Ken
H. Goldstein (1979) *Journal of Child Psychology and Psychiatry*
A. Halsey (1972) *Educational Priority*, HMSO
A. Halsey *et al.* (1980) *Origins and Destinations*, Clarendon Press
D. Hargreaves (1967) *Social Relations in a Secondary School*
A. Heath and Clifford (1980) 'Fifteen Thousand Hours Reviewed', *Oxford Review of Education*
C. Jencks (1975) *Inequality*, Penguin
Keddie (1971) 'Classroom Knowledge', in M. Young, *Knowledge and Control*, Collier Macmillan
H. Kelly (1987) *Science for Girls*, Open University Press
W. Labov (1973) *The Logic of Nonstandard English*
D. Lawton (1975) *Class, Culture and the Curriculum*
R. Meighan (1981) *A Sociology of Education*, Holt
J. and E. Newson (1965) *Patterns of Infant Care*, Penguin
NUT (1988) *Working for Equality*, NUT
H. Prosser and P. Wedge (1973) *Born to Fail*, Hutchinson
I. Reid (1977) *Social Class Differences in Britain*, Open Books
H. Rosen (1974) *Language and Class*, Falling Wall Press
M. Rutter *et al.* (1979) *Fifteen Thousand Hours*, Open Books
S. Sharpe (1976) *Just Like a Girl*, Penguin
M. Shipman (1977) *The Sociology of the School, Inside a Curriculum Project*, Methuen
D. Spender (1983) *Invisible Women*, Women's Press
B. Sugarman (1970) 'Social Class Values and Behaviour in Schools', in Croft, M. (ed.) *Family, Class and Education*, Longman
J. Torrey (1973) 'Illiteracy in the Ghetto', in Young, M. (ed.) *The Myth of Cultural Deprivation*, Penguin
C. Wright Mills (1956) *The Power Elite*
R. Williams (1961) *The Long Revolution*, Penguin
P. Willis (1977) *Learning to Labour*, Saxon House
M. Young (1971) *Knowledge and Control*, Collier Macmillan

Works for further reading

S. Ball (1981) *Beechside Comprehensive*, Cambridge University Press
L. Barton and S. Walker (1984) *Social Crisis and Educational Research*, Croom Helm
I. Bates *et al.* (1984) *Schooling for the Dole*, Macmillan
B. Bernstein (1970) 'Education Cannot Compensate for Society', in Butterworth and Weir
E. Butterworth and D. Weir (1970) *The Sociology of Modern Britain*, Fontana 1970.
C. Buswell (1991) 'The Gendering of School and Work',

Social Studies Review, Vol.6, No.3, January
P. Corrigan (1981) *Schooling the Smash Street Kids*, Macmillan
R. Dale (1976) *Schooling and Capitalism*, Routledge & Kegan Paul
R. Gomm (1979) 'A Phenomenological Approach to Education', in R. Meighan, *Perspectives on Society*, Nelson
D. Hargreaves (1975) *Deviance in Classrooms*, RKP
R. Meighan (1981) *A Sociology of Educating*, Holt
K. Reynolds (1991) 'Feminist Thinking on Education', *Social Studies Review,* Vol. 6, No. 4, March
J. Salisbury (1991) 'Mucking and Mixing in Cookery Class', *Social Studies Review,* Vol.1, No.1, September
D. Spender (1983) *Invisible Women*, Womens Press
M. Stanworth (1983) *Gender and Schooling*, Hutchinson
R. Webb and H. Westergaard (1991) 'Social Stratification, Culture and Education', *Sociology Review* Vol.1, No.2, Nov.
G. Weiner and M. Arnot (1987) *Gender and the Politics of Schooling*, Hutchinson

Self-test Questions

Examine the material below and answer the questions that follow.

Item A

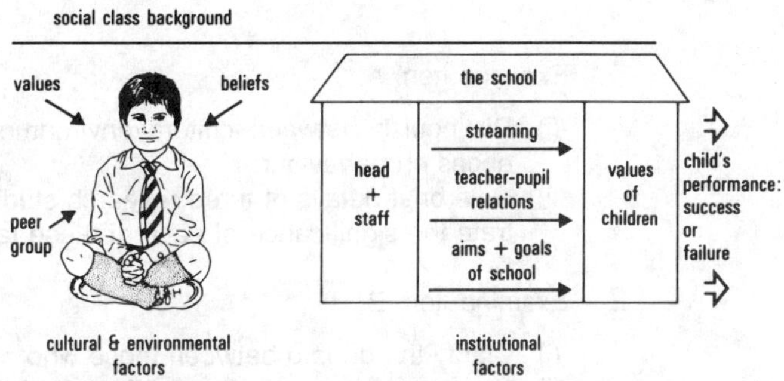

There are some factors which influence the behaviour of the child before going to school. They continue to have a significant influence on the child thereafter.

There are some factors which influence children once they attend school. They relate to the way the institution of the school is organised and structured.

Item B

'Early research in Britain and the United States (for example, Coleman, 1966; Jencks, 1972) showed consistently that a pupil's intelligence, family and community background are highly influential variables for both learning and behaviour, and the quality of school experience has relatively little effect. School resources were shown to be very poor predictors of pupil performance, as compared to the socio-economic status of parents. Schools were widely regarded at the time as ineffectual in compensating for social inequalities.

However, Rutter and Madge (1976) suggested that the measures of the quality of schooling may be at fault; rather than assessing resources, other aspects of the school environment may be influential. More recently, factors such as school organization, teacher expectations and general "school ethos" have been shown to be important variables. Many learning difficulties are probably the direct result of factors such as school absence and poor teaching, which fails to take account of the range of children's skills and abilities. There are also questions about the appropriateness of the curriculum for many children, and whether the way schools are organized helps to promote learning. Some of these factors have been closely scrutinized by research, but as yet others remain pure speculation. Because of the complexity of large schools, it is difficult to control variables, and conduct satisfactory research.'

Source: L. Stow and L. Selfe, *Understanding Children with Special Needs*.

Item C

Table 1 Pupils and their schools, 1971–90

	1971			1981			1990		
	Eng	Wales	Scot	Eng	Wales	Scot	Eng	Wales	Scot
Grammar schools	18.4	15.4	28.3	.4	1.3	–	3.4	–	–
Technical schools	1.3	–	–	0.3	–	–	0.1	–	–
Secondary modern	38.0	22.3	–	6.0	1.8	–	3.8	–	–
Comprehensive	35.0	58.3	58.7	82.5	96.6	96.0	85.9	99.2	99.9
Other	7.3	4.0	13.0	0.8	0.3	4.0	6.8	0.8	0.1

Table 2 The changing qualifications of pupils, 1970–89

Qualifications	1970–71		1980–81		1988–89	
	Boys	Girls	Boys	Girls	Boys	Girls
% 2+ A-levels (3+ H-Levels)	15	13	15	13	18	19
5+ GCSE/O-Levels (A–C No A-levels)	7	9	8	10	12	15
No GCSE/O/SCE grades	57	56	15	12	10	7

Table 3 Average class size (England)

	1977	1981	1986	1990
Primary schools	28	26	26	26
Secondary schools	22	22	21	21

Source: Department of Education and Science.

1. Examine Item A.

(i) Distinguish between cultural/environmental factors and institutional factors as influences on behaviour.

(ii) Give brief details of three research studies with which you are familiar and which illustrate the significance of each of these factors.

2. Examine Item B.

(i) Clarify the debate between those who present different explanations for ability levels.

(ii) Summarise the patterns of different educational attainment levels in Britain as revealed in some research studies with which you are familiar.

(iii) Explain why it is a difficult area to research. What are some of the important variables that need to be examined?

3. Examine Item C.

(i) Summarise briefly the evidence shown in the three tables.

(ii) Discuss how you would examine the hypothesis that as the structure of schooling has changed, levels of ability have changed.

(iii) What explanations might there be for the apparently improving ability of girls over boys in obtaining qualifications?

4. Using all the items, discuss the problems of analysing the factors which influence a child's performance in school and why care must be taken in identifying any one factor.

11

POLITICS AND POWER

Questions on this topic cover the following areas:

1. The nature of politics: What is political behaviour?
2. Power.
3. Power élites.
4. The state.
5. Voting behaviour:
   (a) the significance of social class; and
   (b) the political parties and their support.

The Nature of Politics

■ **We can be said to act politically whenever we exercise constraint on others to behave as we want them to. Discuss.**

Writers throughout history, from Plato and Aristotle to those of the present day, have speculated and theorised about the nature of politics. Aristotle said 'politics arises in organised states which recognise themselves to be an aggregate of many members, not a single tribe, religion, interest or tradition'. Politics is the master-science because it gives some priority and order to rival claims on the scarce resources of society.

Ferns and Watkins (*What Politics is About*) say that 'politics is about much more than government and administration, parties and elections. It embraces education, information, sciences, technology; in short, the totality of the human situation. Further, it is global in character'.

A sociological approach adopts a broad view of politics because political behaviour is seen primarily as power behaviour. This is the control exerted by one person or group over another in any social context. A narrower definition of political action would restrict it to the specialised machinery of government together with the administrative bureaucracy of the state. This refers more to 'party politics'.

What constitutes political action?

1. The view that political action is the ability to exercise constraint over others is that of Weber. He said that power is 'the chance of men ... to realise their own will ... against the resistance of others who are participating in the action'. This view arises from the argument that power must be examined in terms of social relationships. There is only a limited amount available and one person holds power at the expense of others who do not. Therefore they must be coerced to behave in particular ways.

From an interactionist perspective power may also be available in more subtle ways. People perceive themselves to be in inferior or superior social positions. Those in inferior situations may expect power to be exerted over them. These political realities are constructed in the process of day-to-day interactions.

2. From a functionalist perspective, Almond *et al.* (*Civic Culture*) suggest that political action occurs when decisions are made to undertake policies which promote integration and adaptation by means of the employment of threat or physical compulsion. Social liberty cannot exist without social restraint. There must be restrictions on some for others to experience freedom.

From this perspective there are inevitably unequal power relationships in society. This is because the more able are in superior positions. Those in inferior status positions must expect coercion and control so that social order is maintained. A government must have power to enforce its rules.

3. From a Marxist perspective there are unequal power relationships in society because the economic structure ensures that power is retained in the hands of a ruling élite. Political control is achieved by exerting power through force.

The constraints imposed by some over the freedom of others is the result of the exploitation of the proletariat by the bourgeoisie. In a truly free society such constraints would be unnecessary since all would be working for the common good without conflict or social division.

Power

■ **Compare and contrast two different sociological theories of the nature and distribution of power.**

Power is central to political organisation. Legitimate governments claim power to control, coerce and direct the behaviour of people in order to achieve specific goals.

There is much debate among sociologists about the origin of power and how it is distributed in society. In the seventeenth century, the philosopher Thomas Hobbes said that the power which every individual had as a citizen was devolved on the sovereign in exchange for his protection. In the twentieth century the Chinese leader Mao Tse-tung said that 'power grows from the barrel of a gun'. Those who hold illegitimate power must surrender it to those whose rights have been ignored. Leaders must hand it back to the people.

Whereas Hobbes opposed the idea of equality of power among individuals since this would lead to conflict between them, Mao stood for the opposite principle.

Power Elites

Are members of power élites also members of a ruling class?

■ **Is the concept of a political élite relevant to understanding contemporary British politics?**

Marxists argue that the political structure in Britain (and all capitalist societies) is controlled by a powerful élite who are drawn from a ruling class and who conduct their activities in the interests of their class.

Pluralists claim that those who achieve power are people who have been drawn into the political arena from a variety of backgrounds and exercise their power on behalf of all citizens.

Elites

1. From a pluralist perspective élites may be benign, having special skills, knowledge and abilities which are highly regarded in the society (for example educational or professional élites).
2. They use their abilities on behalf of others.
3. Members of power élites are those who occupy positions of total command in the society. They formulate policy, instigate it and ensure it is carried out. They may achieve their position by merit or sponsorship.
4. In society there are a range of élites (financial, political, etc.) which may compete against each other for influence and whose membership may change frequently.
5. Blondel (*Voters, Parties and Leaders*) says that in Britain political practice is a network of influences, counter-influences and compromises and is open to pressure from many interest groups. The apparent authors of policies may not be their real authors.

Ruling class

From a Marxian perspective this implies:

1. There is a small class whose members own the major instruments of economic production.
2. Members perceive themselves to be a cohesive social group.
3. They have interests in common.
4. They are in permanent conflict with the classes they exploit.
5. They also hold positions of political power.

The Marxist view

1. The distribution of power in a capitalist society reflects the inequalities that exist within it.
2. The capitalist economic infrastructure produces two main classes: the owners of the means of production and the proletariat.
3. Economic and political power are closely linked. To possess economic power is to possess political power.
4. The state is an agency of class power. There is an illusion of democracy but the reality is different.
5. The ruling élite possess the cultural capital and the ideological power which is imposed on the rest of society.
6. These values are transmitted through such social institutions as the family, education, religion, media, etc.

The functionalist view

1. Power is a special resource which enables the holder to organise the means at his disposal to achieve goals for which there is a general commitment. A government promises greater economic growth or improved living standards.
2. Although some may have to suffer in the short term, eventually the majority will benefit, so that power is used for the social good. This will help achieve greater social cohesion and integration.
3. In an efficient social system more power exists in the society because there are constantly more things to be achieved.
4. The greater the chance of co-operation the greater the chance of achieving goals.
5. To achieve goals some people must be given special authority to direct others.
6. People will accept this, so legitimating the government, because it can be seen that there will be wide-ranging benefits in the long term.

Ruling class theorists

1. Miliband (*The Power of Labour and the Capitalist Enterprise*) criticises the pluralist view. He says that capitalist enterprises enjoy a 'strategic position' in their dealings with government because they control economic resources. He argues that the power of labour (working people) is not equal to the power of capital. He sees the growth of trade unions as an essential countervailing élite which is seeking to moderate the power of business owners. This is one reason why unions get so badly attacked in the media.
2. Lupton and Wilson (*The Social Background and Connections of Top Decision-Makers*) examined the findings of the Parker Tribunal (1957). They noted the network of relationships it revealed among top businessmen and politicians of that time. They claim it showed a shared background, culture and set of customary procedures between powerful banking families and politicians. There was an interconnection between family, school, university, occupation and club.
3. Westergaard (*Power in Britain*) argues that the dominant grouping in Britain is that of a small homogeneous élite based on wealth and property. It is assured of press support, as well as that of the Conservative Party. Its members have exclusive educational backgrounds and are often united by close ties of kinship. The kind of evidence that might be used to support this argument would include the fact that, in 1970, of the 339 Conservative MPs, 51 were educated at Eton; 152 came from other public schools; 114 went to grammar schools; and Mrs Thatcher's administration included 13 members of the House of Lords (of whom 3 were in the Cabinet). Of the 22 members of the Cabinet only 2 did not go to a public school; 17 were graduates of either Oxford or Cambridge.

One of the problems that arises in accepting this model of social power is what happens when the Labour Party wins an election, since its members tend not to have the same social background as Conservatives? One view is that during such times the ruling class simply maintains its position because it has only to endure small and ineffectual changes. The Labour Party cannot introduce extreme socialist policies because it requires the support of businessmen and the City.

The pluralist view

1. Dahl (*Who Governs?*) argues that the hypothesis of the existence of a ruling class being also a ruling power élite is difficult to test. To do so:

(a) The group would have to be clearly defined.
(b) A situation must be established in which the preferences of the élite are challenged and yet they prevail.
(c) A ruling class must be shown to have members who exhibit group consciousness, coherence and conspiracy.
(d) Who is to decide the number of decisions that constitute 'power'? Who decides what constitutes a decision? Without clarification of these issues it is difficult to evaluate the extent of a group's power.
(e) The whole concept is also ideologically tainted.

2. Wakeford (*Power in Britain*) says that there is much evidence to indicate a substantial degree of the clustering of power in modern Britain. This suggests support for the pluralist perspective:

(a) Power is not located in any single centre or controlled by any specific group.
(b) Although direct democracy is not possible in a large society, there is representative democracy, in which elected representatives may hold power from one election to the next.
(c) Because there is competition for power, this ensures that it is not misused and not monopolised.
(d) It is both inevitable and necessary that power élites should exist since a society needs the most able to lead.

The State

- **How would you account for the development of the modern state? (UCLES)**
- **Sociologists have increasingly focused their attention on the role of the state in modern society. Explain why this is so and examine the major competing views of the role of the state in contemporary society.(AEB)**

Ferns and Watkins note that there are 175 nation-states in the world. They have three characteristics: a territory, a population and a government. The government is said to possess sovereign authority over the people in the state's territory. Governments differ greatly in their form and organisation, but they have one common characteristic: they are all a minority of the population they govern.

An important aspect of the study of the political organisation of society is people's efforts to organise the government of their community. Throughout history there have been debates as to the nature of the legitimate power to rule, as well as the origins and functions of the state.

Historical perspective

Plato, in the fifth century BC, said that the state originated as a means of defending the interests of the individual who is helpless and alone. An organised system of authority for promoting and defending the interests of groups and individuals is necessary.

Aristotle, in the third century BC, said that man was by nature a political animal who desired an organised social life. The city-states of Greece had the power to make and enforce decisions. The ability to make laws and exercise power on behalf of citizens of the state is the function of government.

In the Bible, St Paul explains why people should obey the state: 'Let every soul be subject unto the higher power. For there is no power but of God.'

In medieval times the spiritual base of society was still recognised. Ethical codes were backed by spiritual sanctions. The political system was seen to be divinely ordained; conformity to the rules of the state meant conformity to the rules of God.

In the seventeenth century there was a new sceptical spirit of enquiry. The philosopher John Locke explained the origin of the civil state by arguing that there had previously existed a state of nature. This was unsatisfactory because of 'a want of an established, settled known law' as well as a lack of 'an independent and indifferent judge to pronounce on conflicts between men in a state of nature'. The resulting chaos led people to realise that there were some advantages in accepting the restraints of civil society in order to preserve life, liberty and property.

In the same period, Thomas Hobbes justified the rule of the state by an absolute monarch. People entered a contract with the sovereign who would provide an environment of peace, order and security in return for unquestioning obedience. The aggregate of consenting people united under one sovereign power becomes 'the state'.

In the eighteenth century the Swiss writer Jean-Jacques Rousseau argued that the surrender of individual rights was not made to the sovereign power but to the whole of society. The contract is between all people who agree to forgo their natural freedom by constituting an organised state which is to act for all its members. People are compelled to obey common laws which make them free (from uncertainty, conflict, etc.) Every citizen has a share in the rule-making process to which each is subject.

In the nineteenth century Georg Hegel argued that 'the nation state is the highest form of social organisation. We are born into the state and it is this which gives our lives meaning. People must therefore work in a united way for the benefit of the state.'

In the same period the philosophers John Stuart Mill and Jeremy Bentham opposed these views. Mill argued that the aim of the state was to provide the conditions in which individuals could flourish. He was suspicious of a government that increased its range of activities for fear that it suppressed individual liberty. The best government was said to be least government.

Bentham accounted for man's obedience to the authority of the state in terms of the idea that its laws and rules were designed to produce the greatest good for the greatest number.

In contemporary society the heirs of these debates reach some consensus:

The modern state

In the modern state:

1. There is centralisation of power.
2. The state is the legitimate source of power.
3. There develops a bureaucracy to administer power.
4. There is increasing unity of language, currency and legal system throughout the territories administered.
5. There is a hierarchial structure of power.
6. The ideal of government should be to promote the good of all its citizens.
7. Subjects, in obeying laws, are seldom conscious of clear rational motives. Political obedience is a form of 'social compliance'.

The Marxist view

1. To control the economy is to control the state.
2. The state organises relationships between different interest groups. It helps maintain power in the hands of the ruling class, which controls the economy.
3. The state is 'the committee of the whole bourgeoisie' in capitalist society.
4. In a truly socialist society there would be the abolition of the state's repressive controls. Then, as Lenin said, 'every cook would rule the state'.
5. Later, neo-Marxists have argued that the state is relatively autonomous in that it is not staffed entirely by the bourgeoisie. If it were, it might become divided by sectional interest and open to greater working-class criticism.
6. The concept of democracy is a myth. The benefits of power are too tempting.

The pluralist/functionalist view

1. No single individual or group controls the state in a democratic society.
2. There are many groups competing for power in open elections. Also, the activities of interest groups act as a means of limiting the power of any one group.
3. The state takes account of the needs of all its citizens; if it did not there would be constant disruption (as in South Africa).
4. Socialist societies are often noted for use of repressive controls.
5. Access of power and authority in the administrative bureaucracy of the state is open to all on the basis of qualifications. The most able reach the highest positions and obtain the highest rewards.
6. Forms of representative democracy operate fairly effectively.

Conclusions

Remember that it is important to summarise and reach a conclusion:

(a) A major concern of sociology has been who has the power and how it is used.
(b) The state represents political power: policies can be enforced by law.
(c) Sociologists also wish to understand the relationship between economic and political power.
(d) The major perspective by which analyses are made are those of Marxism and pluralism: the distinction between a single power élite and many groups who share political and economic power. These may be summarised:
(e) Some contemporary writers argue that both perspectives contain some truth. Pahl has suggested that more research should be focused on the power of bureaucracies and the decision-making processes in key state agencies, especially national government.

Marxist view	Pluralist view
1. The state serves the interests of the ruling class.	1. The state is impartial. It seeks to maintain order and stability.
2. The state promotes conflict by promoting capitalist values.	2. The state manages conflict by promoting liberal values.
3. Mills (*The Power Elite*) said that in the USA power was in the hands of political, military and business men.	3. The state provides agencies which manage the competing demands of groups.
4. The state promotes the illusion of political and economic freedoms.	4. The state is composed of a plurality of interests; people have many different allegiances so that different groups emerge and disappear according to goals.

Voting Behaviour

- **How far does class explain allegiance in modern British society? (Cam)**
- **Describe the major changes in the relationship between social class and voting behaviour in Britain since the Second World War. Examine the sociological explanations of deviant voting behaviour. (AEB)**

Social class

Butler and Stokes (*Forces Shaping Electoral Choice*) quote Pulzer, who says 'class is the basis of British party politics, all else is embellishment and detail'.

Objective social-class membership has been described by many writers as the most important factor influencing voting behaviour, the traditional alignment being for middle-class groups to vote Conservative and the working-class sector to vote Labour (the party founded by the trade unions in 1906). But since the majority of people in Britain fall into classes 3b, 4 and 5 there must be cross-class voting, otherwise there would not be any Conservative victories. See Table 11.1, 11.2 and 11.3.

Table 11.1 suggests a clear line of support for the major parties between manual and non-manual workers who intended to vote. It also indicates that about one-third of manual workers intended to vote Conservative.

The figures in Table 11.2 suggest that the decline in class alignment and voting behaviour continues to change. The Conservatives increased their support among the skilled manual sector (3b).

The data in Table 11.3 show that Labour still gains most of its strength from Classes 4 and 5. Although the Labour party almost doubled its support among Classes 1 and 2 (the fastest growing groups) Class 3b remained more faithful to the Conservatives, as did Class 3a.

There has been much research into the behaviour of the working-class Tory: between 1951 and 1964 the Conservatives won three consecutive elections. This led some observers to suggest that there must have been some major change in the class structure in this period:

1. Butler and Rose put forward the *embourgeoisement* thesis. This stated that the more prosperous sections of the working class (3b) are losing their identity as a social group and are becoming merged into the lower middle class. This influences their voting behaviour.

Table 11.1 Percentage of each social class by voting intentions, General Elections, October 1974

Party	*Class 1*	*Class 2*	*Class 3a*	*Class 3b*	*Class 4*	*Class 5*
Conservative	68	60	46	30	25	34
Labour	14	20	28	50	59	52
Liberal	19	19	23	18	14	12

Source: Gallup Polls.

Table 11.2 Voting by class in 1983 General Election

Party	*Classes 1 and 2*	*Class 3a*	*Class 3b*	*Classes 4 and 5*
Conservative	62	55	39	29
Labour	12	21	35	44
Alliance	27	24	27	28

Source: Gallup Polls.

Table 11.3 Voting by class, 1992 General Election

Party	*Classes 1 and 2*	*Class 3a*	*Class 3b*	*Classes 4 and 5*
Conservatives	59	52	41	29
Labour	20	24	38	50
Liberal Democrats	19	20	17	17

Source: National Opinion Polls (NOP) survey based on a sample of 4963 electors.

2. Lockwood and Goldthorpe (*The Affluent Worker*) tested the thesis and rejected it because, they said, class is a complex concept and is not determined by income alone. They used four criteria (*norms*, *relationship*, *economic factors* and *political factors*) in their study, but found that major class differences existed between blue- and white-collar workers with regard to each. They pointed to the emergence of a new working class whose members shared some of the materialistic aspirations of the middle class but whose values and identity were still with the working class.

3. Nordlinger (*The Working-Class Tory*) found that many working-class voters preferred the candidate who had high ascribed status. Some voted Tory for pragmatic reasons; they believed that Conservative policies offered them more than those of Labour.

4. McKenzie and Silver (*The Working-Class Tory in England*) reach similar conclusions. They argue that the pragmatic voters (whom they term 'secular') are more concerned about party policy than the deferentials. Such working-class Tories were generally better informed than traditional Labour voters. There were a high proportion of women among the deviant working-class Tories, probably because they had more regard for traditional values, family, religion, etc. More recent research suggests that more women are supporting the Labour Party.

5. Crewe (*The Disturbing Truth Behind Labour's Rout*) says that it is not age or sex but class that continues to structure party choice, but this has steadily weakened over the past twenty-five years. Labour remains the party of a segment of the working class. The implication is that there is much pragmatic voting occurring now which cuts across traditional class lines.

6. Heath ('Social Class and Voting in Britain'), writing before the outcome of the 1992 General Election discusses the extent to which political preferences are shaped by class or by political party policies and party images. He notes:

(a) Traditionally class has been the basis of political choice.
(b) In the nineteenth century religion influenced choice (Church of England and Tory vote; Methodist and Liberal vote).
(c) In the early twentieth century the new Labour Party captured the working-class vote.
(d) By 1983 the Labour Party's claim that it remained the party of the working classes was threadbare.
(e) Critics noted that the class structure had fragmented in new ways:
    (i) there was now a traditional middle class (private sector: predominantly Tory-voting) and a new middle class (public sector occupations: fewer Tory voters); and
    (ii) traditional working class (strong Labour support) and a new working class (affluent manual workers providing high level of Tory support).

Conclusion

Class divisions remain a significant feature of British society. There is evidence to show that the relationship between class and voting has changed. Some see the process of fragmentation as highly significant (for example, Robertson; *Class and the British Electorate*, said, 'class in anything resembling the overall ideological sense is vanishing from British politics'). Others (for example, Marshall *et al.*, *Social Class in Modern Britain*) and Heath, using data from national representative sample surveys conducted after every election since 1964, argue that the divisions within the classes are not new; they have always existed.

They suggest that the connection between class position housing, religion, education) and voting behaviour will be influenced at any time by the specific policies of the parties: by their image and the extent to which there is consensus or dissention between members of a class on issues and how they will be affected by them.

■ **'The Labour vote largely remains working-class but the working class has ceased to be largely Labour' (Crewe). Explain and discuss this statement in the light of recent election results?**

Crewe analysed Labour's losses of the 1979 and 1983 elections. He agrees that:

1. Although the Labour Party relies heavily on a working-class vote (classes 3b, 4 and 5) there is evidence to show that the working class has become fragmented and voting patterns less easy to predict.
2. The Conservative landslide (144 majority in 1983) was partly the result of an even split in the non-Conservative vote.
3. The Conservative Party must have obtained a high proportion of its votes from working-class electors (this remained true in the 1992 Election).
4. The evidence is that the Labour Party cannot rely on a solid working-class vote as it could up to 1979.
5. The support for the Labour Party among working-class voters has fallen from about 70 per cent in 1966 to 43 per cent in 1987 and to 44 per cent in 1992.
6. It appears to be increasingly the middle classes (Classes 1, 2 and 3a) whose votes reflect class consciousness and solidarity.

1979–87: Factors working against Labour

(a) The spread of home ownership (including the sale of council houses).
(b) The contraction of public-sector employment (privatisation).
(c) The decline of blue-collar trade-union membership. Between 1970 and 1984 there were 1 million more white-collar trade-union members, 1 million fewer blue-collar members and 500 000 more women members.
(d) An ageing electorate (the Labour Party had a higher level of support among the over-65).
(e) The Party was divided over policies (defence, nationalisation, etc., causing the emergence of the SDP/Liberal Alliance).

Consequences

(a) The Labour Party needed a swing of more than 8 per cent to gain a working majority in the 1992 Election. It needed the support of the skilled manual workers.
(b) Even high levels of unemployment failed to produce class polarisation. The year-long miners' strike (1984/85) may have alienated many supporters.
(c) A large proportion of the Labour vote was lost to the Alliance, formed by defecting members of the former Labour Cabinet.

Table 11.4 Total share of the votes for each parts, 1979–92, General Elections

Election year	Tory %	Labour %	Lib. Dem. (SDP) %
May 1979	43.9	36.9	13.8
June 1983	42.5	27.6	25.4
June 1987	43.0	32.0	23.0
April 1992	43.0	35.0	18.0

Source: MORI

Table 11.5 Conservative Party's share of the vote, 1955–92 (percentage)

1955	*1959*	*1964*	*1966*	*1970*	*1974(Feb.)*	*1974(Oct.)*	*1979*	*1983*	*1987*	*1992*
49.3	48.8	42.9	41.4	46.2	38.8	36.7	44.9	43.5	43.3	43.0

Source: *Social Trends* (1–22)

(d) In 1979 Labour had lost the support of 55 per cent of voting trade-unionists. In 1983 support fell to 39 per cent.
(e) Labour seemed unable to win the support of younger voters who might pass on the values; instead these values may be dying out with an older generation.

1992 Election: Factors working against Labour

In addition to the above, there was increased de-alignment in Party support. King (Professor of Government at Essex University) noted

(a) the new working class (affluent, home owners) were driving out the old: 57 per cent of manual workers were owner occupiers; 30 per cent were council tenants.)
(b) manual workers are a declining proportion of the work force.
(c) a declining proportion of them regard Labour as 'their' party.
(d) Labour's narrowing basis of support is disproportionately located among the 'old working class' (those living mainly in the north of England and in Scotland, still involved in heavy industries, living in council houses and belonging to trade unions).

Consequences

(a) The majority of manual workers did not support Labour in the election.
(b) This was the third election in which more than 50 per cent of all working-class voters rejected Labour.
(c) Labour was not gaining ground among middle-class voters (even in the public sector, who might be regarded as hostile to a Conservative Government).
(d) Although Labour's support among manual workers remains at a historically low level, there was a modest swing among manual workers as a whole. Labour led the Tories by 5 points among the skilled workers (C2s)
(e) The Conservatives regained their lead among the university educated. In recent elections more had supported the Alliance Party (about 27 per cent voted Labour).
(f) The decline of the Alliance Party may have assisted labour in increasing its MPs from 229 (1987) to 271 (1992).

Conclusions:

Crewe has argued that:

(a) The transformation of working-class partisanship over the past twenty-five years must rank as one of the most significant of all post-war changes in the social basis of British politics.
(b) 'Labour remains the party of only a segment of the working class. That is the traditional, semi- and unskilled sector at the bottom of the social scale. It no longer represents the new working class'.
(c) Divisions within the working class following the implementation of Thatcherite policies have resulted in new attitudes and values which have produced a more volatile and less predictable electorate.

Heath has argued:

(a) That such divisions are not new; the working class has always been divided. But what is new is the change in the relative sizes of the new and old working classes.
(b) That voting patterns depend on images of party competence, specific policies presented and the extent to which there is consensus on key issues among members of a class that party policy will be to their benefit.
(c) He implies that while there is no automatic link between position in the class structure and voting behaviour, none the less the working class could be won back by Labour if they can make the right appeal in future.

Political parties and their support

■ **The major development affecting political life in recent years has been the changing pattern of support for the main political parties. Discuss.**

A political party An organisation of active political agents who are concerned with the opportunities for gaining power and who compete for popular support with another group which holds different and divergent views. The party operates with an ideology which determines its policies and activities.

1. The Conservative Party. Changing patterns of support for the Conservative Party are shown in Table 11.5.

(a) Since 1945 it has only dipped below the 40 per cent support level. It won seven of the eleven elections.

(b) In the General Elections of the 1950s there were low average swings from one of the main parties to another because there was a strong sense of 'partisan alignment' (that is, people had a strong self-image of themselves as being either Labour of Conservative).

(c) There was no major TV coverage of elections until 1959.

(d) Crewe comments that:

(i) In the 1964 election 62 per cent of non-manual workers voted Conservative (the party was led by an ex-peer, Sir Alec Douglas-Home), and 64 per cent of manual workers voted Labour.

(ii) In the 1970s and 1980s there was an increase in 'deviant voting'. The Conservative Party increased its support from manual workers and in all age groups.

(iii) Between 1971 and 1981 there was a growth of 26 per cent in professional occupations, which benefited the Conservatives.

(iv) Margaret Thatcher established herself as a strong leader (resulting in 'the Falkland's Factor'). She developed policies advocating self-interested individualism, which appealed to the skilled manual sector (even though 98 per cent of her first Cabinet had public school/Oxbridge backgrounds).

(v) In 1987 Crewe estimated that working-class support for the Conservatives was 46 per cent in the south (with 26 per cent for Labour) and was 44 per cent among the home-owning working class (with 32 per cent for Labour).

(e) In 1992 the trend was maintained, leading some observers to the view that:

(i) People were increasingly concerned with their own prosperity and believed that the Conservatives would improve it.

(ii) The factors aiding the Conservatives were the increase in home ownership, white-collar occupations and the decline in trade union membership.

(f) Thomas ('The Man Who Put Mrs Thatcher In'), argued that:

(i) Any party seeking victory must be in tune with the feelings of the skilled workers. They are affluent, potentially socially mobile, car owners, home owners and have children who increasingly enter middle-class occupations.

(ii) The Conservatives have been highly successful in this regard.

(g) They have also been more effective in their use of the media to promote their campaigns.

2. The Labour Party's share of the vote between 1955 and 1992 is shown in Table 11.6.

(a) The Labour Party lost three consecutive elections in the 1950s, but recovered to win under an effective leader, Harold Wilson, in 1964.

(b) Since 1979 the Labour Party has not broken the 40 percent support point. From 1945 to 1974 Labour was the only alternative to Conservative rule. The Liberals never achieved more than 11 per cent of the vote.

(c) This supported the view that voting followed class identification. Butler and Stokes argued that since class divisions were relatively clear, Labour claimed the vast proportion of working-class votes.

(d) In the 1970s a growing pragmatism was identified by some observers, suggesting that there was a declining influence of class on voting patterns; voters were taking policies into account. As the Labour vote began to decline, theories of embourgeoisement, deference and class fragmentation were put forward (see also page 95). Lockwood and Goldthorpe emphasised the significance of a working-class person's attachments to middle-class people and culture.

(e) King (*Observer*, May 1979) argued that Labour lost that election because:

(i) when in power in 1978 they failed to control the level of strikes;

(ii) a gap had opened between the Parliamentary Labour Party activists, who favoured radical leadership, and the general public, who preferred moderates; and

(iii) regular opinion polls showed a wide disapproval of central Labour Party policies (on defence, unions, etc.).

(f) Ryan ('The Slow Death of Labour England') argued:

(i) the traditional social basis of the old Labour Party was now dead;

(ii) the emergence of the Alliance (SDP and Liberals) took many votes from Labour;

(iii) the middle-class radicals had only a small impact on the election result;

(iv) there was no demand for extreme radicalism in contemporary Britain. The Alliance secured the middle-of-the-road image and had no class base; and

(v) the Labour Party was criticised for failing to change its appeal: its policies were seen as dated.

(g) Heath *et al.* examining the 1987 result accepted that class no longer directly affected the way votes were cast. The Labour Party has always had a small traditional base as social changes affected the occupational structure. Their presentation of an ideology which advocated freedom, security and prosperity could achieve success.

(h) Following the result of the 1992 Election observers suggest that Labour still faces many problems, including:

(i) demographic factors, a declining birth-rate and ageing population;

(ii) declining trade-union membership and heavy industries;

(iii) the increasing sale of council houses;

(iv) reduced female support and an inability to capture the youth vote;

(v) the changing geographical distribution of population, with more moving to the prosperous south and away from northern urban areas. This is likely to lose Labour up to 20 seats in the next election; and

(vi) an increasingly hostile press.

3. The Social Democratic Party (SDP) and Liberal Democrats. The SDP was founded in 1980 by key members of the most recent Labour Cabinet: Roy Jenkins, Shirley Williams, William Rogers and David Owen, all of whom have subsequently been given peerages. They were joined by other MPs (and one from the Conservative Party).

Table 11.6 Labour Party's share of the vote 1955–92.

1955	*1959*	*1964*	*1966*	*1970*	*1974 (Feb.)*	*1974 (Oct.)*	*1979*	*1983*	*1987*	*1992*
47.3	44.6	44.8	48.9	43.9	38.0	40.2	37.8	28.3	31.5	35.0

Source: *Social Trends*, 1–22.

Table 11.7 Liberal and Alliance share of the vote, 1955–92

1955	*1959*	*1964*	*1966*	*1970*	*1974 (Feb.)*	*1974 (Oct.)*	*1979*	*1983*	*1987*	*1992*
2.8	6.0	11.4	8.6	7.6	19.8	18.8	14.1	26.0	23.1	18.0

Source: *Social Trends*, 1–22.

Table 11.8 Gender, age and region of electorate, 1992

	Conservative	*Labour*	*Liberal*	*Other*
All voters	43	35	18	5
Men	42	37	17	5
Women	43	34	19	3
All voters 18–24	36	37	21	6
25–34	40	38	17	5
55+	45	35	17	2
Scotland	25	39	11	24
North of England	38	44	16	1
Midlands	42	41	15	2
South	50	26	23	2

Source: NOP poll based on 4963 electors.

(a) The Liberals became a viable third party after 1974.

(b) The Alliance between the SDP and the Liberals after 1980 produced their best result in 1983, affecting the Labour vote in a serious way.

(c) They seemed to appeal to electors across class lines.

(d) Benyon (1987) argued that even in the 1987 Election the Conservatives benefited from the votes shared between Labour and the Alliance. This led to the demand for a Rainbow Circle. This would describe a pact between them. It would establish pragmatic policies, avoiding ideological principles, and attract wide support. One candidate would fight the Tories whilst the other would withdraw from seats it could not win.

(e) Dahrendorf (*The Collapse of Class*) argued that one of the results of the rapidly changing class structure in the 1980s was to undermine traditional political loyalties. This allowed the SDP to emerge as a powerful new force.

(f) The SDP collapsed in 1990 after a humiliating by-election defeat. The two remaining MPs were defeated in the 1992 Election.

(g) The Liberal Democrats failed to achieve the 20 per cent level of support in the 1992 Election and had two fewer MPs than in the previous Parliament. They seemed to lose some of the support expected from Classes 1 and 2.

(h) The Liberal Democrats made their appeal for a pact with Labour in May 1992.

Conclusion

Heath has said:

(a) There is no longer an automatic link between position in the social structure and voting behaviour.

(b) There have been major changes in patterns of support for the political parties. These changes have been influenced by:

(i) new demographic factors affecting the class structure;

(ii) the impact of geographical and social mobility; and

(iii) increased media coverage so that the competence and effectiveness of parties and governments comes under closer scrutiny.

(c) Galbraith (*The Culture of Contentment*) has argued that the decline of parties of the Left can also be explained by the growth of a self-interested contentment which has developed in the West. People are less concerned about community values and the less prosperous.

■ **The success of the Conservatives in recent elections can be attributed to more than just partisan dealignment. Discuss.**

Note: Partisan dealignment means that the groups who traditionally supported one party in the past (especially Labour) ceased to do so in the same predictable ways after 1979.

1. The recently fragmenting class factor (see also page 95).

(a) Crewe (1988) has placed much emphasis on this factor, presenting evidence to show that:

(i) most voters were no longer loyal to one party on the basis of their class; for those in Class 3b it was not just a matter of affluence (embourgeoisement);

(ii) increased volatility and pragmatism among voters: attitudes varied between house owners/tenants; union members/non-members; and impact of party policies;

(iii) growth of self-interested individualism and an increase in the number of owner-occupier skilled manual workers, who are less deferential to union leaders.

(iv) Labour's future electoral chances were poor since they required a relatively huge 8 per cent swing to win a majority.

(b) Parkin (*Middle Class Radicalism*) has suggested that middle-class radicals tend to be found mainly in professional 'caring' occupations (public sector) because this is a haven for their radicalism. They are not interested in the concepts of 'profits' which dominate private-sector professionals.

(c) Heath *et al.* dispute the dealignment thesis and argue that:
   (i) the fragmentation of the classes is not a new feature;
   (ii) the Labour Party could win back support if it could present itself more positively to the electorate and show that it shares the same dominant ideology;
   (iii) the problems the Labour Party faces are demographic. The traditional working class has shrunk while the new middle class has expanded. There is always an element of middle-class radicalism supporting Labour;
   (iv) in the 1987 election the percentage voting for their class increased marginally. The Conservatives lost some support (about 3 per cent) among middle-class voters; and
   (v) In the 1992 Election there was a small swing to Labour among Class 3b (although the majority continued to vote Tory).

In addition to the dealignment debate, the other sociological factors to consider include gender, age and region (see Table 11.8).

(a) The only group among whom Labour had a lead were young voters 18–24 (especially in Classes 4 and 5). Labour's share of the vote among this age group generally has declined since 1987.
(b) The trend towards convergence by men and women in the distribution of votes in recent elections changed in 1992, when more women appeared to vote Conservative than men. For some, the change may be related to personalities; they preferred John Major to Margaret Thatcher, and disliked Neil Kinnock more.
(c) The narrow gap between the voters in the 25–34 age group may reflect concerns such as education, mortgages and unemployment fears.
(d) the regional differences remain; the small swing to Labour among skilled manual workers was reflected in the narrow gap between the parties in the Midlands.

Party image

(a) The Labour Party:
   (i) complained that it was unable to counter the highly negative image that was produced through the Conservative-supporting tabloid press; and
   (ii) was seen to have an untrustworthy leadership; unfair tax policies; a Presidential-type campaign, which included a triumphalist rally for 10 000 supporters before the result was known; and a lack of new 'big' ideas and policies which were not rooted in the early part of the twentieth century.

(b) The Conservative Party:
   (i) retained the support of the majority of the press throughout the campaign (although the *Financial Times* supported Labour);
   (ii) Major was always perceived to be a better leader than his adversaries, especially in the final week of the campaign;
   (iii) the election was hailed as the first in Britain following the failure of socialism in Eastern Europe, so that the Conservatives were able to dictate the new political agenda of self-interested individualism, the maintenance of the existing electoral system and the union with Scotland.
   (iv) made effective use of expatriate votes and claimed that two seats may have been won as a result: Bristol N.W. was won by 45 votes (with 53 registered expatriates voting); and the Vale of Glamorgan was won by 19 votes (64 registered expatriates voting).

(c) The Liberal Democrat Party:
   (i) gained a high proportion of support from ex-supporters of the SDP, which went out of existence after 1990;
   (ii) was able to achieve the status of an effective third party which may have held the balance of power in a hung Parliament;
   (iii) gained its highest level of support among those in Classes 1 and 2 and among the 18–24-year-olds generally; and
   (iv) was able to win wide support for the idea of electoral reform (proportional representation) and an alliance with the Labour Party to defeat the Conservatives in a future election.

The effects of the tabloid press

Some observers have argued that the Conservative-supporting press does have a significant effect on election results.

(a) Harrop (Newcastle University study) said in his analysis of the 1983 election that uncommitted voters who read the Tory press were 16 per cent more likely to end up as Tory voters than those who read a Labour paper. Those who started out as Tories were about 16 per cent less likely to defect at the next election if they regularly read a Tory paper.
(b) Miller (Glasgow University study) found that between the summer of 1986 and the election of 1987 there was an overall swing to the Conservatives of about 5 per cent. But among those who read the *Express* or *Mail* (Tory papers) regularly, the swing was 8 per cent, and among those who read the *Sun* or *Star* regularly it was 17 per cent.
(c) Aitkin (*Guardian*), commenting on the 1992 result, said that readers of the Tory press are systematically denied the facts on which to make judgements.
(d) Lord McAlpine (Tory peer) said that the Tory tabloids were the real heroes of the campaign (achieving final success through their saturation with negative Labour images). The *Sun*'s headline was 'It's the Sun Wot Won It' on the day following the election.
(e) 1992 MORI Poll found (in a sample of 22 700 voters) a 4 per cent swing to Tories among *Sun* readers, 3 per cent swing among *Express* readers and 2 per cent among *Mail* readers. This would mean about 400 000 people becoming Tory voters.
(f) Golding (Loughborough University study, 1992) noted the use of an alarmist moral panic tactic in the tabloids. The *Mail* claimed 'Kinnock Won't Curb Flood of Bogus Refugees', and the *Sun*'s headline

'Nightmare on Kinnock Street' was followed by eight pages of criticism.

The view that the effect is overstated:

(a) A 1992 *Guardian* editorial said 'evidence for newspaper influence is patchy and self deluding'. The argument is that there has always been bias and sometimes Labour has won; the message and the messenger are quite separate. The charge relies on a hypodermic model which has been largely discredited (see page 125) It implies that readers of the tabloids are too stupid to understand what is going on.
(b) In 1992 an NOP poll found that only 29 per cent of the sample said they trusted the press 'a great deal'. Most people rely on TV news for detailed information; that is regarded as being largely neutral.
(c) Some commentators concluded that the final result showing the Conservatives ahead of Labour by 8 points represented a more serious problem than just unfair media representation.

Conclusions

Most observers identify several factors at work in accounting for the success of the Conservative Party, which took as much of the vote in 1992 as it did in 1987.

(a) Harris (*Sunday Times*) commented that 'for an opposition to finish 8 points behind a Government at the height on an economic boom might be considered to be a misfortune, to finish 8 points behind in the trough of a depression is a disaster almost beyond measurement'.
(b) Some emphasise the changing social structure, with increased social mobility; some point to demographic changes which have adversely affected Labour; and others focus on the power of the media to create and destroy images and policies.
(c) It is clear that the Labour Party faces further problems in the future. The Boundary Commission reports in 1993 and is likely to recommend changes to constituencies, which may cost Labour between 12 and 20 seats; the party will require a national swing of at least 4 per cent to achieve a majority.
(d) It may be that the Conservatives in the 1980s changed the cultural expectations of the majority of the electorate, making egalitarianism, philosophies of collective help and redistributive tax policies increasingly unacceptable.
(e) On the other hand Curtice (Glasgow University) notes that a fourth term of Conservative rule may not be entirely healthy for democracy. It may become the seedbed of intellectual corruption, complacency and vested self-interest.

Suggested Reading

Works noted in this chapter

J. Aitkin (1992), *Guardian* (10th April 1992)

Almond *et al.* (1963) *Civic Culture*, Princetown University Press

Blondel (1965) *Voters, Parties and Leaders*, Pelican

D. Butler and R. Rose (1959) *The British General Election of 1959*, Frank Cass

D. Butler and D. Stokes (1974) *Forces Shaping Electoral Choice*

I. Crewe (1983) 'The Disturbing Truth Behind Labour's Rout', *Guardian* (13th June)

I. Crewe (1988) 'The Grim Challenge of the Ballot Box', *Guardian* (1st October)

J. Curtice (1988) 'Analysis', in D. Butler and D. Kavanagh, *The British General Election 1987*, Macmillan

J. Curtice (1992) 'Analysis of the British General Election 1992', *Guardian*, 10th April

R. Dahl (1959) *Who Governs*?, Yale University Press

R. Dahrendorf (1961) *The Collapse of Class*: Class and Class Conflict, RKP

H. Ferns and K. Watkins (1985) *What Politics is About*, The Sherwood Press

K. Galbraith (1992) *The Culture of Contentment*

Golding (1992) 'Loughborough University', *Guardian*, April 1992

J. Goldthorpe *et al.* (1968) *The Affluent Worker*, CUP

Harris (1992) *Sunday Times* (12th April)

Harrop (1987) 'Analysis of 1983 Election, *Guardian*, June

A. Heath *et al.* (1985) *How Britain Votes*, Pergamon

A. Heath *et al.* (1992) 'Social Class and Voting in Britain', *Sociological Review* (April), Vol. 1, No. 4

A. King (1979) 'The People's Flag Turns Deepest Blue', *Observer*, (3rd May)

Lupton and Wilson (1973) *The Social Background and Connections of Top Decision-Makers*

G. Marshall *et al.* (1988) *Social Class in Modern Britain*, Hutchinson

McKenzie and Silver (1972) 'The Working-Class Tory in England', in Worsley (ed.) *Problems of Modern Society*, Penguin

R. Miliband (1969) *The Power of Labour and the Capitalist Enterprise*, OUP

Mills, C. Wright (1956) *The Power Elite*, OUP

E. Nordlinger (1966) 'The Working-Class Tory', *New Society*, 13th October

F. Parkin (1967) 'Working Class Conservatives', *British Journal of Sociology*, 18

D. Robertson (1984) *Class and the British Electorate*, Blackwell

A. Ryan (1983) 'The Slow Death of Labour England', *New Society* (June)

D. Thomas (1983) 'The Man Who Put Mrs Thatcher In', *New Society* (May)

J. Urry and J. Wakeford (1973) *Power in Britain*, Heinemann

Works for further reading

D. Butler, and Kavanagh (1988) *The British General Election 1987*, Macmillan

I. Crewe (1986) 'How Britain Votes', *Political Studies*

I. Crewe (1988) 'The Grim Challenge of the Ballot Box', *Guardian*

B. Criddle (1988) 'Candidates', in D. Butler and Kavanagh *The British General Election 1987*, Macmillan

A. Heath *et al.* (1991) *Understanding Political Change 1964–87*, Pergamon.

A. Heath *et al.* (1992) 'Social Class and Voting in Britain', *Sociological Review* (April), Vol. 1, No. 4

F. Parkin (1968) *Middle Class Radicalism*, Manchester UP

D. Robertson (1984) *Class and the British Electorate*, Blackwell

Questions

Examine photograph 31.

Weber suggests that power is the ability to achieve aims even against the opposition of others who may disapprove.

1. (i) Marxists would argue that a powerful opposition would always resist successfully attempts to achieve change if there was disapproval of the intentions. Illustrate how this might occur with reference to the demonstration in this photograph.

   (ii) Why do people of low social and economic status generally have to unite in some powerful pressure group or party to achieve their desired ends?

2. (i) Explain the Functionalist view that demonstrations of this sort may be functional and successful.

   (ii) Why would they argue that it is inevitable that there are unequal power relationships, so that failure to achieve goals may legitimately occur?

   (iii) What would Functionalists consider determines the success or failure of the attempt to achieve power?

31

Source: Alec Gill

Self-test Questions

Study these extracts from newspapers and answer the questions below.

Item A

My post-mortem survey of the 1983 election concluded that Labour's claim to be the party of the working class was sociologically, if not ideologically, threadbare. The Labour vote remained largely working class; but the working class was no longer largely Labour. The party had come to represent a declining segment of the working class — the traditional working class of the council estates, the public sector, industrial Scotland and the North, and the old industrial unions — while failing to attract the affluent and expanding working class of the new estates and new service economy of the South. It was party neither of one class nor one nation; it was a regional class party.

The 1987 survey reinforces each of these conclusions. Labour remains the largest party among manual workers (42 per cent), but a minority party, only 6 per cent ahead of the Conservatives. The political gulf between the traditional and new working class remains (see Table 5). The Conservatives are the first party of manual workers in the South (18 per cent) among owner occupiers (+12 per cent) and non-unionists (+2 per cent) and only 1 per cent behind in the private sector; Labour retains massive leads among the working class of Scotland (+43 per cent) the North (16 per cent), council tenants (+32 per cent), trade unionists (+18 per cent) and the public sector (+17 per cent). Although the housing gap has slightly narrowed, regional differences have widened further.

Source: Extract from an article by Ivor Crewe in the *Guardian*, 15 June 1987, p. 9.

Item B

Working class electors turn their backs on the party founded for them

By Anthony King

THE LABOUR PARTY'S political problems following last Thursday's election defeat are compounded by "sociological" problems, according to Gallup's post-election survey for The Daily Telegraph.

Labour continues to draw the majority of its support from manual workers but the majority of manual workers no longer supports Labour. The April 9 election was the third in a row in which more than half of all working class voters rejected the party traditionally identified with the working class.

At the same time Labour is failing to compensate by making significant gains among middle class voters — not even among professionals employed in the public sector who might be expected to be hostile to a Conservative Government.

The Labour Party is called "Labour" because its founders in 1900 knew that manual workers constituted the great majority of the electorate and believed that in time enough could be persuaded to vote Labour to give the party a majority in Parliament.

However, manual workers today are a declining proportion of the total workforce — and a declining proportion of them regard Labour as being "their" party. Labour thus seems locked in a demographic as well as a political vice.

HOW THEY VOTED

	Con	Lab	Lib Dem	Swing to Lab since 1987
AB	57	17	20	2.5
C_1	49	28	19	5
C_2	35	40	17	6.5
DE	29	48	14	-1.5
Men	38	36	19	5
Women	44	34	16	1
18-24	37	34	21	3
25-34	36	39	17	2.5
35-44	37	37	20	8
45-64	42	34	17	5
65+	49	31	13	2

AB= Prof. and managerial, C_1= Routine non-manual, C_2= Skilled manual, DE= Unskilled manual

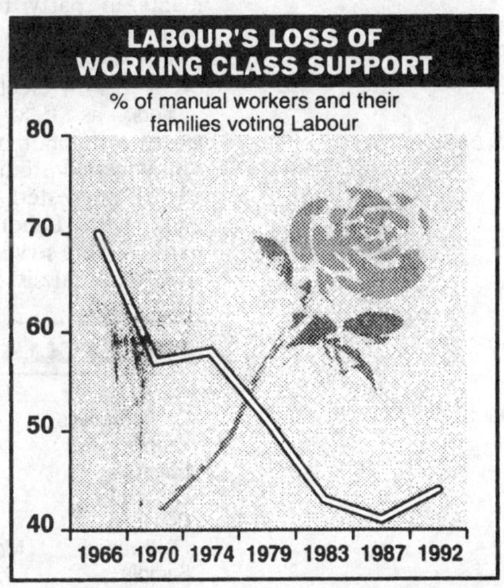

Source: Extract from an article by Anthony King in the *Daily Telegraph*, 14 April 1992.

Item C

YEAR	1945	1950	1951	1955	1959	1964	1966	1970	Feb 1974	Oct 1974	1979	1983	1987	1992
Seats	640	625	625	630	630	630	630	630	635	635	635	650	650	651
Actual %														
Con	39.7	43.4	48.0	49.7	49.4	43.4	41.9	46.4	37.9	35.8	43.9	42.4	42.3	41.9
Lab	47.7	46.1	48.8	46.4	43.8	44.1	48.0	43.1	37.2	39.3	36.9	27.6	30.8	34.2
Lib	9.0	9.1	2.5	2.7	5.9	11.2	8.5	7.4	19.3	18.3	13.8	25.4	22.6	17.9
Rest	3.6	1.4	0.7	1.2	0.9	1.3	1.6	3.1	5.6	6.6	5.4	4.6	4.3	6.0
Actual seats														
Con	210	298	321	345	365	304	253	330	297	277	339	397	376	336
Lab	393	315	295	277	258	317	364	288	301	319	269	209	229	271
Lib	12	9	6	6	6	9	12	6	14	13	11	23	22	20
Rest	25	3	3	2	1	0	1	6	23	26	16	21	23	24
Actual Maj	Lab 146	Lab 5	Con 17	Con 60	Con 100	Lab 4	Lab 98	Con 30	None	Lab 3	Con 43	Con 144	Con 102	Con 21

Source: From the *Guardian*, 15 April 1992.

Item D

Poll bias theory challenged

By Patricia Wynn Davies, Political Correspondent

THE NOTION that opinion polls contain in-built pro-Labour bias has been challenged in a review by ICM Research, which conducted polling for the *Guardian* and the *Sunday Express* during the general election campaign.

A recent suggestion by the Market Research Society, the pollsters' professional body, that polls might have underestimated the Tories' share of the vote for decades drew sharp responses from polling organisations at the time.

ICM's review, covering the first half of this year, says clear 10 and 8 per cent leads for the Conservatives over Labour shown by their May and June polls are signs that there may not have been a systematic Labour bias before the election. "Usually, such sudden movements in party fortunes follow some dramatic development," the report says. "In this case the only event was the election itself."

This, as ICM accepts, still leaves a number of possible reasons why poll predictions – virtually all suggested a hung parliament with Labour the largest party – were so wide of the mark.

ICM's analysis of recall interviews with people polled during the election campaign attributes 37 per cent of the discrepancy to failure to vote, late vote-switching, late deciders and "secret" voters – those unwilling to tell pollsters how they would vote.

Jennie Beck, an ICM researcher, said the organisation was studying poll selection criteria. Most pollsters use age, class, sex and working status to construct representative samples but factors such as housing tenure and newspaper readership might also be significant.

The organisation is also attempting to identify the kinds of people who refuse either to reveal their voting intentions or to answer any questions at all. It found a disproportionately high percentage of secret voters were Tory supporters. ICM suggested they were unwilling to vote for higher taxes, but not keen to admit it.

EXIT POLL SEAT PROJECTIONS

	ICM	NOP	Harris	Result
Cons	302	301	305	336
Labour	307	297	294	271
LDem	-			20
Pub	Sun	BBC	ITV	

FINAL POLLS AND EXIT POLLS

	NOP	Gallup	MORI	ICM	Harris	NOP	Result
Conservatives	39	38.5	38	38	41	42	42
Labour	42	38	39	38	37	36	35
LDem	17	20	20	20	18	18	18
Lab lead	+3		+1	-			
Con lead		+½		-	+5	+2	+7
Fieldwork	Mn-Wd	Tu-Wd	Tu-Wd	Wed	Exit	Exit	
Sample	1,746	2,478	1,731	2,186	20,000	18,000	
Published	BBC/Ind	Tele	Times	Guard	ITN	BBC	

Source: Article in the *Independent*, 6 August 1992.

1. Examine Item A.

   (i) Explain what Crewe means when he says that in 1983 the working class was no longer Labour, even though Labour remained largely representative of the working class.

   (ii) Suggest some reasons why the Labour Party failed to attract the affluent working class.

   (iii) Explain what the author means when he says that the Labour Party had become a regional class party.

   (iv) In what ways did his analysis of the 1987 Election result confirm his 1983 predictions?

2. Examine Item B.

   (i) Specify some of the sociological problems which the author suggests face the Labour Party.

   (ii) Outline some of the important points revealed in the two charts. For example,

      (a) Suggest which social groups are likely to form the basis of Labour support.

      (b) Suggest which groups have been captured by the Conservative Party in recent elections.

      (c) Suggest why more women support the Conservative Party.

      (d) Account for age variations in party support.

3. Examine Item C.

   (i) Make a bar chart showing the strength of each party in elections since 1945.

   (ii) Using this information and that in Item B discuss how far the result of the 1992 election confirmed or refuted the predictions of Crewe in 1983.

4. Examine Item D.

The polls proved unreliable in predicting the outcome of the 1992 election. Investigations were conducted to try to find out why.

   (i) Which polls proved most, and least, accurate?

   (ii) What are some of the major problems facing those who wish to find out how people vote?

   (iii) Discuss the view that a more secret ballot by interviewers might produce more accurate results.

12

RELIGION

Among the important topic areas on which questions are based are the following:

1. The secularisation debate:
   (a) The problems of definition.
   (b) The problems of measuring the extent of secularisation.
   (c) The causes of secularisation.
2. Sects, denominations and churches:
   (a) Examples of the typology and its value to sociologists.
   (b) Reasons for the emergence of sects.
3. Theories of religion:
   (a) Functionalist.
   (b) Weberian.
   (c) Marxian.

Secularisation

Problems of definition

■ **The concept of secularisation is used in so many different ways that it now obscures rather than clarifies the debate about the place of religion in contemporary society. Explain and discuss. (AEB)**

The secularisation debate has focused on the question of whether religion is of increasingly less significance in the day-to-day lives of people in modern society and whether it is also of less relevance as a social institution.

1. Shiner (*The Concept of Secularisation in Empirical Research*) discusses the range of meanings which writers have adopted in their use of the term 'secularisation' and shows the confusion that has resulted. He endeavours to bring the concept into focus by considering the range of possible definitions:

(a) It is used to mean *the decline of religion*: previously accepted symbols, doctrines and institutions lose prestige and influence. He points out that the problem is to find the golden age from which the decline started.
(b) It is used to mean *increasing conformity with this world*. Society becomes absorbed with the pragmatic tasks of the present. He suggests that the difficulty with this view is that there is a problem in measuring 'conformity with this world'.
(c) It is used to mean *the disengagement of society from religion and religious values*. Religion is more of an inward type with little or no influence on social institutions. There is a separation of religion from political life. He says that the difficulty with this definition is that it is not easy to know at what point secularisation has occurred. In Britain, for example, religion is still associated with political institutions: the Monarch is head of the Church of England.
(d) It is used to mean *the transposition of religious beliefs and institutions*; knowledge and behaviour once understood to be grounded in divine powers are transformed into purely human responsibility. The problem with this view is that it cannot be proved that some secular belief systems contain elements from Judaeo-Christian beliefs, for example that the capitalist ethic had religious origins.
(e) It is used to mean that *the world is deprived of its sacred character*. People and Nature become the objects of rational/causal explanation and manipulation. This definition starts from the assumption that humankind has become largely independent of religion. Some argue that human beings are incurably religious and that the sacred may/must have been temporarily pushed into the unconscious and now is finding new forms of expression.
(f) It is used to mean *a movement from a sacred to a secular society*. All theories of change become grounded in secular rather than sacred explanations. But critics argue that this is a general theory of change and does not relate specifically to religious change.

Shiner's conclusions

(a) The term has often served the special interests of the users. The result is that it is swollen with overtones and implications, especially those associated with indifference or hostility to whatever is considered 'religious'.

(b) The appropriate conclusion to draw from the confusing connotations would seem to be that the word should be dropped, and replaced with one such as 'differentiation' or 'transposition', which would be neutral.

(c) If it is used, it must be neutralised to avoid polemical connotations.

2. Martin (*The Religious and the Secular*)

He too argues that the concept of secularisation 'is the tool of counter-religious ideologies'. He rejects the use of the term because:

(a) There is the unavoidable presence of religious elements in an anti-religious position.

(b) It is difficult to interpret 'religious decline' and decline in 'religious practices'.

(c) It is unfair to make comparisons over time because they can be misleading. Attitudes and norms are relative to time and place.

3. Berger (*The Social Reality of Religion*)

He accepts that it has been employed by different writers in both negative and positive ways. Among anti-clerical writers, secularisation has come to mean the liberation of modern people from religious constraints; whereas some Christian writers (for example, Bonhoeffer) have used it to argue that secularisation is evidence for the truth of Christianity. It is a part of God's plan that people should become more mature and come of age by acting in Christian ways without recourse to 'belief' in God. However, he says, the term is useful and refers to:

(a) 'empirically available processes of great importance in modern western history. Whether these are to be deplored or welcomed is irrelevant'.

(b) It also has a subjective meaning. There is secularisation of society and consciousness. People create reality and act on the basis of their interpretations.

He describes the impact of secularisation:

(a) It is stronger on men than women.

(b) It affects the middle-aged more than the young or old.

(c) It occurs more in the cities than in the country.

(d) It affects classes more directly concerned with modern industrial production than those in more traditional occupations.

(e) Roman Catholics are more immune than Protestants and Jews.

He concludes that there is little doubt that the West has produced an increasing number of individuals who look upon the world and their own lives without reference to religious interpretations. So the concept does have some relevance.

Problems of measurement

■ **Though there is considerable evidence that participation in institutional religion has declined in Britain there is also considerble disagreement over the sociological interpretation of this evidence. Explain and discuss.**

There are some writers who argue that the empirical evidence relating to church participation shows decline in every important aspect. There are others, however, (for example, Martin) who argue that the same data can be interpreted to show it has the opposite implications. It may even suggest that the orthodox churches become leaner but healthier as they discard peripheral members for a hard core of genuine devotees.

1. Wilson (*Religion in a Secular Society*)

He describes the erosion of the institutional power of the established Churches and uses much statistical evidence to support his case. He accepts the problems of measurement but argues that the process is well under way.

2. Wilson ('The Anglican Church and Its Decline')

He develops his arguments further:

(a) The process of secularisation in Britain (as in other advanced industrial societies) affects the Church of England more acutely than the other denominations.

(b) Statistics indicate that the Church of England faces serious problems:

1966–9: a fall of 27 per cent in numbers confirmed.
1956–68: a fall of 18 per cent in numbers baptised.
1929–73: a fall of 19 per cent in numbers marrying in church.
1861: 1 clergyman to 960 people.
1971: 1 clergyman to 4,000 people.

(c) The Church is regarded increasingly as a welfare service agency, available for use in an emergency. It is used on a regular basis by about 12 per cent of the population.

(d) He concludes that on any range of indicators the facts of decline are evident. There is an increasing disposition by the public to regard Christian belief as incredible and irrelevant.

3. The Paul Report was a fact-finding report suggesting that many of the problems faced by the Church of England related to the payment and deployment of clergy. The report is criticised by Wilson, who says the weakness of the Church is the result of many factors, including:

(a) The effects of books and TV programmes by theologians (for example, Cupitt's, *The Myth of God Incarnate* and the Bishop of Woolwich's *Honest to God*) which appear to question and doubt fundamental Christian doctrine. These help undermine people's faith.

(b) The emergence of new sectarian movements which attract people away from orthodox Christian churches in large numbers, and which often provide non-Christian belief systems.

4. Paul (*The Church in Daylight*) found that in the 1970s there were just 339 clergy looking after 3 700 000 people in the 97 most densely populated parishes. In 1971, of 10 000 clergy, only 27 were under the age of thirty. Fifty-one were aged 80–92 and there was a shortage of some 3000 clergy. Subsequent data suggest that traditional British religious institutions are losing ministers and priests, whereas some of the sects are making dramatic increases. This is also true for other religions in Britain (see Table 12.2).

Table 12.1 Percentage

	1979	1989
Under 15	14	14
15–19	13	9
20–29	9	6
30–44	10	9
45–64	10	10
65+	14	13
All ages	11	10

Source: English church census.

Table 12.2 Number of ministers/priests in UK 1975–90 (in thousands)

	1975	1990
Anglican	15.9	14.1
Methodists	4.2	2.3
Baptists	2.4	2.9
Roman Catholics	8.0	7.6
Sects		
Jehovah's Witnesses	7.1	12.7
Mormons	5.3	9.8
Other religions		
Muslims	1.0	2.3
Sikhs	0.1	0.2
Hindus	0.1	0.2
Jews	0.4	0.4

Source: *Social Trends*, 22.

Table 12.3 Membership of Churches, percentage changes 1975–9

	Membership	Adult attendance	Child attendance
All Protestant churches	– 3.6	+ 0.5	– 3.9
Roman Catholic	+ 1.1	+16.7	0.0
All churches	– 1.4	– 2.4	– 2.5

Source: *Social Trends*, 22.

Table 12.4 Adult membership of religious institutions, 1975 and 1990 (millions in UK)

	1975	1990
Anglican	2.27	1.84
Methodist	0.61	0.48
Baptist	0.27	0.24
Roman Catholic	2.53	1.95

Source: *Social Trends*, 22.

Table 12.6 Sects emerging between 1949 and 1969

Year	Sect	Founder	Membership
1949	The Divine Light Mission	Guru Gi	approx. 6 000
1954	The Reunification Church	Mr Moon	2 million
1954	Scientology	L. Ron Hubbard	5 million
1968	Children of God	Moses David	5 000 (GB)
1969	Hare Krishna		1 000 (GB)

Table 12.5 Membership of two sects and other religions, 1975 and 1990 (Adult members in UK in millions)

	1975	1990
Jehovah's Witnesses	0.08	0.12
Mormons	0.10	0.15
Muslims	0.40	0.99
Sikhs	0.12	0.39
Hindus	0.10	0.14
Jews	0.11	0.11

Source: *Social Trends*, 22.

5. Wilson's view is that the clergy are losing status in modern society because they are largely redundant; and the increasing likelihood of the ordination of women is an attempt to make up the shortfall. His general conclusion is that the statistics indicate that secularisation is well advanced and that the Church of England is gradually becoming reduced to the condition of a sect. He sees the status of a sect as an irrelevant novelty and the last outpost of religion in a scientific age.

6. Others who conclude that the increase in the number of sects is evidence of the decline include:

(a) Berger, who argues that the belief in the supernatural can best survive in sectarian groups, especially among those which seek retreat from the world.
(b) Wallis (*The Elementary Forms of New Religious Life*), who suggests that for the majority of people not only is religion in decline, but sects remain a matter of 'profound indifference'.

Alternative interpretations of the empirical evidence are:

1. Martin (*A Sociology of English Religion*) argues that:

(a) It is difficult to locate a golden age when England was totally religious in attitude and behaviour.
(b) While people may not be attending churches in large numbers this does not necessarily indicate that they do not have strong beliefs in Christian doctrines. These are very difficult to measure. Some studies suggest that the numbers identifying with the Church of England amount to as many as two-thirds of the population: about two in ten with the Roman Catholic Church and one in ten with the Free Churches.
(c) Although only 12 per cent may attend every Sunday, studies suggest that about 25 per cent attend every other Sunday, 30 per cent each month and 45 per cent once in the year.
(d) People continue to have a strong sense of the supernatural. Large numbers express belief in 'subterranean theologies', belief in superstition, luck, etc. The growth

Questions

Examine photograph 32.

1. This photograph was taken at 10.00 a.m. on a Sunday morning. Consider the view that organised religion is increasingly irrelevant to young people in contemporary society. Yet they may be expressing belief in 'subterranean theologies' (luck; superstition; astrology, etc).
   (i) Consider the similarities and differences between religion and superstition.
   (ii) How do people justify their belief in superstition, astrology, etc. (which entails beliefs in untestable and unknowable forces that shape destiny) and their denial of religious faith?
   (iii) How do religious people justify their opposition to other belief systems such as astrology, etc.?
   (iv) Consider the view that the boys might hold that an hour spent church-going on a Sunday is not much different from an hour spent skateboarding. Both are pastimes.
   (v) How would you investigate any of these question?
   (vi) Suggest two different methods that could be adopted.

2. Consider the problems of assessing whether or not these boys are living in an increasingly secular society.

32

Source: Alec Gill

of fringe sects suggests that people are simply expressing their religious needs in different ways.

(e) Religion still plays an important part in daily life: there are daily services on the radio listened to by millions; churches are still used by most people in times of crisis or celebration by means of ceremonies associated with 'rites of passage'.

2. Statistics indicate that although there has been a decline in the membership of the Church of England, the Catholic Church has made some gains in numbers (see Tables 12.3, 12.4 and 12.5).

Also there has been a growth in many sectarian groups, especially those catering for ethnic minorities: the West Indian Pentecostal churches and the Rastafarian movement have increased in numbers (see Table 12.5).

3. The Ecumenical Movement, with the intention of uniting all the main Christian Churches, will greatly increase the strength of Christianity in Britain; as will the ordination of women. Also the clergy are taking a greater lead in social issues. In 1978 a Baptist conference urged members to speak out against apartheid, the National Front and other social evils. In 1982 a conference of Roman Catholic priests voted to support unilateral disarmament. In 1993 the Methodists presented a document attacking the Government's 'market-oriented, competitive, individualistic philosophy'. they wanted more concern for the disadvantaged.

Conclusion

Changes in social values and social culture have resulted in changes in attitude towards religion. But there is no complete agreement about whether such changes in Britain do amount to a decline in the significance of religion in people's lives:

(a) Wilson has argued that in a modern society knowledge and understanding is increasingly based on scientific reason rather than on mystical faith. There is less room for religion in a rational world. He claims that all the statistics support this interpretation.

(b) Berger sees the emergence of new sects as signs of decline and describes them as 'the last refuge of the supernatural'.

On the other hand, some authorities present a different view:

(a) Bellah argues that it is hard to establish an adequate measure of decline. Personal belief systems remain high even though attendance figures may be low.

(b) Martin suggests that not only are statistics open to a range of interpretation but also changes in patterns of religious behaviour are complex and their processes hard to analyse. His arguments lead to the conclusion that participation varies in different parts of Britain (just as it must in other societies in other parts of the world). It is likely to be higher where it provides a sense of regional identity (for example, Northern Ireland) and even national identity (for example, parts of Wales), and lower in urban areas where there is much geographical and social mobility and high levels of religious pluralism (so no dominant religious institution to pressurise members).

The Causes

■ How can the process of secularisation be explained?

There is much debate as to what is meant by secularisation and how it can be measured. But if it is taken to mean a long-term decline in the relevance of religion both as an institution and in the day-to-day lives of people in society, then certain explanations can be put forward to account for the process.

The proponents of the view argue:

1. The impact of science and technology has helped to make religious faith redundant. All apparent mysteries can be viewed as problems for which explanations are possible.

2. Berger (*The Social Reality of Religion*) argues:

(a) The economic process of industrialisation is a secularising force. The development of divergent lifestyles encourages a crisis in the credibility of religion.

(b) This also causes a collapse in the plausibility of traditional religious definitions of reality.

(c) The man in the street is confronted by a wide variety of reality-defining agencies that compete for his allegiance. People have greater choice as to which belief system to adopt. This helps to increase the 'secularisation of consciousness'.

3. Urbanisation: with the growth of large towns and cities people are attracted away from traditional, stable societies in which social order is related to the power of the Church. In cities life is more anonymous and there are many other activities to compete for people's time and attention. Wilson sees church-going as a leisure activity in contemporary society.

Martin has described a loss of community in society, which has resulted in increasing apathy running through the society. There is a loss of membership among a range of voluntary associations including trade unions, political parties and churches.

4. Bureaucratisation: as societies become more economically developed they produce more highly rational bureaucracies. These are the means of administering large, complex economies. As they become institutionalised the previous religious legitimations of the state lose their significance. Religion becomes more privatised, a matter of choice or preference.

5. The media: *Crockford's Clerical Directory* stated that 'one sometimes has the impression that control of the press and BBC is in the hands of men who are hostile to the Christian religion and mainly to the Church of England'. The authors complained of a loss of emphasis on moral and ethical values in favour of trivia and entertainment. For some, the media may have become the new opium of the people.

(a) Bruce ('Observations on Mass Media Religion') considers the extent to which TV may have become more important than the Church in shaping values. He notes that the recent changes in broadcasting legislation have now made evangelical TV programmes more likely, as well as the use of religious advertising. The

Church of England has considered their use. He argues that because:

(i) it is hard to contruct a measure of influence;
(ii) TV is easily ignored; and
(iii) people view selectively,

the effects are unlikely to have much impact on the process of secularisation.

(b) Stacey and Shupe have said that 'televangelism' preaches to the converted. In 1992 congregations are falling in the USA where such programmes are frequent.

6. Harvey Cox (*Secular City*) argues that secularisation is inevitable and a part of God's plan. The book is by a Harvard professor of divinity. He describes secularisation as the celebration of the death of religion and the birth of a new, true Christianity. Secularisation delivers humankind from mystical controls over their destiny. Urban, scientific humanity represents the development of maturity and responsibility. Far from being something to oppose, Christians should see it as humankind's coming of age.

7. Ecclesiastical reforms: these may have caused many traditional churchgoers to become more critical of the Churches and cause defections from them. For Catholics, the reforms of Vatican II which abolished the Latin mass and made other changes in dogma and liturgy, and for many members of the Church of England, the changes in the language of the prayer book, destroyed traditional strengths and assets.

Conclusions

The explanation for the process of secularisation may depend on the definition used. For Wilson it is the loss in significance of religious thinking, practice and institutions. Causes might include:

(a) the growth of scientific rationalism;
(b) the effects of the impact of subversive books, authors and media coverage of religious scandals, etc.;
(c) the growth of functional alternatives to the religious experience;
(d) the impact and power of peer group pressures among the young;
(e) urbanisation, industrialisation and decline of family stability; and
(f) the results of dissension within the Churches over issues of reform.

However, Bellah has criticised the emphasis on the decline in religious institutions. He has argued that people are simply expressing their beliefs in new non-institutional ways. The quest for meaning has become more private. Others sceptical of the wide-ranging use of the concept of secularisation include Martin (who wishes to abolish its use) and Glock, who has said that those who perceive it occurring will find evidence for its existence.

Sects, Denominations and Churches

- **Is the sect, denomination, church typology helpful in the study of religious organisations?**
- **Why do sociologists construct typologies of religious organisations?**

Typologies

The ideal *type* is intended as a means of clarifying complex concepts by extracting their key characteristics. They should serve to stimulate empirical investigation. A *model* is constructed against which researchers can compare similar items in the real world to see how far they conform to or deviate from their ideal descriptions.

1. Troeltch (*The Social Teaching of the Christian Churches*) The sociological concept of the sect was first evolved by Troeltch. He tried to give it some precision by making a comparison with the concept of the Church. He developed a continuum between the conservative Church and the perfectionist sect.

The sect	The Church
1. A protest movement.	1. A means of social integration.
2. Egalitarian.	2. Hierarchic.
3. Radical.	3. Traditional.
4. Appeals to outcasts.	4. Appeals to higher classes.
5. Opposed to the state.	5. Works with the state.
6. Members show total commitment.	6. Members exercise choice.
7. No specialist priests.	7. Specialist priests, teachers, etc.
8. Emphasis on fellowship.	8. Emphasis on relationship between the individual and the institution.
9. Status by achievement (members must qualify).	9. Status by ascription (members are born into the Church).
10. Non-institutionalised.	10. Highly institutionalised.

Wilson is critical of this typology because he says that the sect should not necessarily be understood in direct contrast with the Church. He says the sect may appeal to those opposed to the state secular institutions of society or other groups within it. It is not necessarily just opposed to the established Church.

2. Niebuhr (*Social Sources of Denominationalism*) tried to establish how sects became denominations. Later writers have introduced distinctions between a sect, a denomination and a Church. Broom and Selznick suggest:

The sect	The denomination	The Church
1. Concerned with purity of doctrine. 2. Depth of religious feeling. 3. Emphasis active participation. 4. Intolerance towards other groups. 5. Critical assessment of the secular world.	1. Limited membership. 2. Limited aspirations. 3. Children inducted at a young age. 4. No great demands for high levels of commitment. 5. Reflects belief in separation of Church and state.	1. Highly institutionalised. 2. Offers integration with social and economic order. 3. Members born into the Church. 4. Routinised participation. 5. Deepest commitment is provided by specialists.
Other distinctions that have been suggested include:		
1. Usually of recent appearance (e.g. Scientology, 1954). 2. Represents only a small minority of devout believers. 3. Often advocates unorthodox ideology (salvation only for sect membership). 4. Expulsion is possible. 5. Emphasis on charismatic leadership.	1. Of longer existence (e.g. Methodism, eighteenth century). 2. National membership with regional differences. 3. May specify some limitations on behaviour (no alcohol). 4. Expulsion unusual. 5. Some charismatic preachers.	1. Very long existence, highly organised structure. 2. Represents the majority in society. 3. Salvation is available to all (no sense of exclusiveness). 4. Expulsion rare. 5. No emphasis on charismatic leadership.

3. Yinger (*Types of Religious Organisation*) produced a classification that focuses on the degree of institutionalisation which distinguishes different types of religious organisations. He identifies five categories: *cults* (religious groups whose main preoccupation is an esoteric belief or form of worship: there is much secrecy and the exclusion of outsiders); *sects* (of recent origin); *established sects*; *denominations* and *Churches*.

Wilson argues that classifications must avoid being culture-bound (for example, centred on Christian organisations). They must use categories that recognise the similarities of social processes in different contexts and provide methods of analysis which have wide applicability.

4. Wilson (*Patterns of Sectarianism*) argues that it is important to explain the relationship between doctrine, organisation and form of association and action, all of which may change independently of each other. The categories must not be from the Christian tradition alone and from only one historical period. He examines a series of sectarian organisations. He accepts that the elements fused in any sect are always a unique combination of variables which may not be distinctive of one sect alone. For him the principal criterion of classification is 'response to the world'; how the question 'what shall we do to be saved?' is resolved.

He has analysed a range of sects and noted that different types makes a different kind of appeal at different times.

He identifies seven types of sect and the message each offers:

(i) *Revolutionist*: God will overturn the world.
(ii) *Introvertionist*: God calls us to abandon the world.
(iii) *Reformist*: God call us to reform the world.
(iv) *Utopian*: God calls us to reconstruct the world.
(v) *Convertionist*: God will change us.
(vi) *Manipulationist*: God calls us to change our position.
(vii) *Thaumaturgist*: God will grant us powers and will work miracles.

He says these represent a complex orientation to the wider society and its cultural values and goals. They all represent ways of attaining salvation.

5. Wallis (*The Elementary Forms of New Religious Life*) produces a typology distinguishing three types of sect based on their relationship to non-sect members, institutions and cultures. He suggests that a sect can reject, accommodate or affirm the non-sectarian world.

(a) *World-rejecting sects*
  (i) (for example, Moonies; Children of God; Rastafarians). These promote: an ideology critical of the non-sectarian world, and their members wish to achieve a change in it.
  (ii) *Millenarians*, who anticipate divine intervention in the social order, expect God (or gods) to impose and effect the change (for example, Cargo Cults, Jehovah's Witnesses).

  Such movements are generally puritanical and impose strict rules on members' life styles.

(b) *World-accommodating sects* (for example, Pentecostalists; Elim Four Square):
  (i) These are often related to an existing major religious organisation.
  (ii) They are mainly concerned with heightened spiritual experiences not obtainable in the church from which they have split.
  (iii) Such values help them cope with difficult day-to-day issues (for example, racial prejudice).
  (iv) They emphasise moral purity, but members mix with non-members in wider society.

(c) *World-affirming sects* (for example, Transcendental Meditation (TM); Scientology):
  (i) These are sometimes referred to as cults with little Christian content.
  (ii) They make specific claims to their members about how to achieve mystical experiences.
  (iii) They may not have specific places of worship or organised ceremonies.
  (iv) Insight and salvation are achieved on an individual basis by following prescribed methods.

(v) They seek wide membership which usually involves financial involvement.

Wallis suggests that the changes such sects undergo depend on external events (their image and level of acceptance in wider society), and their own internal organisational structures. While they may change from one type into another they do not necessarily progress to the status of a denomination (although some, like Pentecostalists, may be considered so).

Conclusions

The value of typology in sociology:

(a) It establishes models. These can be tested in the real world.
(b) They also assist in the process of classification and in clarifying complex social phenomena.
(c) The sociologist can begin to make more accurate statements about how people express their religious beliefs; why these expressions take different forms and why some organisations appear at different times and others fade.
(d) Their different functions, values and ideologies can be made clear.
(e) The results may be open to criticism, comment and refinement. By such means can sociological analysis progress.

■ **Why do so many religious sects emerge and flourish in an apparently secular world? (UCLES)**

■ **To what extent can the growth of religious sects be seen as a response to conditions of social disorganisation and change? (AEB)**

Sects in society

Wilson (*Religion in a Secular Society*) says that sects are not static. They undergo change. Some attributes may recede in importance over time. They provide examples of attempts by people to construct their own societies in which they establish new norms and values, often in opposition to those of mainstream society. They have a carefully ordered structure of social relationships and patterns of behaviour.

Possible explanations for their emergence:

1. They fulfil basic human needs of their members, who are:

(a) given strong group support in crisis;
(b) presented with a sense of enlightenment;
(c) provided with definite answers to problems;
(d) subjected to strict disciplines; and
(e) provided with a 'father figure' as leader.

2. Mainstream Churches do not meet basic needs. The vacuum is filled by new sects.

3. Yinger (*Sociology Looks at Religion*) argues that sects offer hope, status and understanding for the underprivileged members of society whom they frequently attract. They enable those who wish to express their opposition to the social structure to 'orient them to the new order in a way that helps individuals and groups to maintain a sense of control and dignity'. In the USA the Black Muslim sects developed in the 1960s as protest movements for improved rights. The sects offered a means of providing solutions to problems of underprivilege.

4. They are likely to attract those of low status or those who feel they have little access to the scarce resources of society. The sect provides ways of coping as well as explanations, with the promise that one day things will be different for those who are marginal in society. The Rastafarian movement arose in the slums of Jamaica out of unemployment and social disadvantage. Members believe that one day they will return to Africa; that the promised land is Ethiopia and the late Haile Selassie is the Messiah. They believe that the Bible contains the truth about their future but that its message has been distorted by white people to conceal the truth that they are the true children of Israel and God's chosen people.

5. Some sects also attract more middle-class membership (for example, Christian Science). These may include some who are intellectually dissatisfied with orthodox ideologies and others who feel relatively underprivileged.

6. Sects provide a universe of meaning. People may turn to sects at times of social change and upheaval. Pentecostal sects provide a strong appeal for West Indians. They provide a meeting place for those recently arrived from other societies; they are a source of group support, integration and stability.

7. Wallis points to the impact of rapid social change occurring in the 1950s and 1960s which may help to account for the growth of:

(a) World-rejecting sects (for example, Moonies):
   (i) more young people were entering higher education, encountering new ideas and questioning the taken-for-granted world;
   (ii) youth cultures emerged which often included experimentation with new value systems (for example the Children of God); and
   (iii) there was a rejection of the values embodied in the 1960s slogan 'you've never had it so good'.
(b) World-affirming sects (for example, Mormons):
   (i) new charismatic pop groups emerged in the 1960s (for example, the Beatles) who became involved in TM, and may have become role models; and
   (ii) even the economically successful may also require insights into their personalities and motivations (for example, Erhard's Seminar Training (EST); Scientology).
(c) World-accommodating sects (for example, Pentecostalists):
   (i) these may have appealed to those already involved in orthodox religious institutions but who were dissatisfied with them; and
   (ii) In times of international tension (for example, the Vietnam War; Cuban Crisis) people may have turned to religious groups offering answers (for example, the Quakers).

8. The rapid growth in the number of new cult and sectarian movements in recent years, which include Pyramidology, the Emin, the Avatar, the Axminster Light Centre, the Aetherius Society, the Dartington Solar

Quest, suggest that people continue to have a need for the mysterious and the supernatural in a scientific age.

In 1991 a Gallup poll found that 16 per cent of women and 23 per cent of men had a strong belief in the existence of flying saucers. In 1992 Darwin College, Cambridge accepted a gift of £50 000 to establish a research fellow in parapsychology to investigate such belief systems.

9. However, the participation in bizarre sects and cults has been criticised by the Committee for the Scientific Investigation of the Paranormal in USA. They warn that the uncritical acceptance of reports of the paranormal 'fosters anti-scientific sentiment' and leads to support of 'the dangerous doctrines and virulent programmes of such sects'. In 1978, 913 followers of a charismatic leader of a cult known as The People's Temple committed suicide on the instructions of its leader, James Jones. In 1993 about 70 members of a cult known as Branch Davidian died in mysterious circumstances following the attack by the police on their headquarters in Waco, Texas after a long siege, the aim of which had been to arrest the leader, David Koresh. The Archbishop of Canterbury commented 'the tragic events remind us of the dangers of an exclusive religion . . .

Conclusions

Some of the possible explanations for the emergence of sects include:

(a) *Weber's theory of marginality*: sects appeal especially to those who have been marginalised in society. They explain underprivilege and offer members success in the near future.
(b) *Wallis's theory of community*: sects provide a place of refuge and aid in times of stress, dissatisfaction and dislocation. They give a sense of family and communal integration.
(c) *Wilson's theory of stability*: sects provide a sense of stability in the lives of people disrupted by major social change. They offer members order, knowledge and answers.

Theories of Religion

The functionalist view

- **What are the major social functions of religion?**
- **Examine the view that religion is necessarily a conservative force in society. (AEB)**

There is a problem in defining the term 'religion'. Beliefs in forms of supernatural power seem present in every society. Some definitions are so broad that they take into account any strong belief system. However, more useful definitions include:

> 'Some pattern of belief and action by means of which certain vital social functions are performed. It is a group-supported road to salvation.' (Yinger)

> 'The belief in the existence of supernatural beings which have a governing effect on life.' (Robertson)

1. Victorian evolutionists believed that the earliest forms of religion rested on beliefs in which inanimate objects were thought to contain powerful spirits. Others emphasised the supernatural powers of nature. They argued that as human societies developed, so religion became more sophisticated and adopted more organisational structure. Basic functions remained, to fulfil people's intellectual and emotional needs.

2. Durkheim (*The Elementary Forms of Religious Life*) as a functionalist is interested in the sources of order and stability in society. He argues that religion is a major source of integration. All religious activity has one major function: the celebration of the social group. Religious activity draws people together. There is value consensus in that they share common beliefs. This increases the sense of community. He concludes from his analysis of aboriginal society that religious worship is in reality the worship of society itself.

3. Parsons (*Religious Perspectives in Sociology*) argues that human behaviour is shaped by pressures of social norms. These are built into the social culture. Religion is a central part of the culture and religious values are transmitted to each new generation. These provide guidelines for acceptable patterns of behaviour. In this way consensus is maintained, and stability and order ensured.

4. O'Dea (*The Sociology of Religion*) argues that religion also functions to provide answers to questions which science cannot explain; it satisfies emotional needs in times of crisis; it provides an ethical code as a guide to conduct; and prayer and sacrifice may have a cathartic value for people.

Points of criticism

The theory neglects:

(i) the ways that religion can cause conflict;
(ii) the increase in secularisation and loss of belief; and
(iii) religion as a source of change (Weber's view).

Conclusions

(a) The early evolutionists saw the functions of religion in terms of their ability to satisfy specific human needs, for example, those of making sense of a complex world and of resolving stress, fear and uncertainty.
(b) Later functionalists emphasised the social needs of society rather than individual needs. In particular those of social solidarity and integration. Shared religious values could provide this value consensus necessary for the stability of society.
(c) The view that religion is a conservative force in society derives from a Marxist critique (see pages 170–1).

Weberian view

- **Why did Weber attach importance to the role of religion in society?**

Weber was interested in the effects on society of the interaction between people and the social institutions of society. He argued that religion can be seen as a source of social change. He shows, for example, how, when new charismatic leaders appear, they advocate change. These have a wide-ranging effect over time. He suggests that most of the radical changes which occurred in Britain in the nineteenth century were instigated by religious groups.

The Protestant ethic and the spirit of capitalism

Capitalism has been defined as: 'The pursuit of profit and forever renewed profit' and 'Rational business transactions.' The spirit of capitalism was epitomised in the writings of Benjamin Franklin in the eighteenth century: 'Time is money. Time wasting, idleness and diversion lose money.'

Weber argued that the sixteenth-century theologican, John Calvin, established an ethic, a way of life which provides duties and obligations. Weber wished to see to what extent religious values influenced the development of the spirit of capitalism.

Calvin's teaching emphasised abstinence, self-discipline and austerity. Weber says that Protestant sects were based on these principles of good conduct:

(a) a man must have a well-defined career;
(b) this must be pursued in a single-minded way;
(c) God commands man to work for His glory;
(d) success in one's calling means God has helped; and
(e) making money is a concrete sign of success.

Weber's argument is that this teaching was a vital influence in the creation of the capitalist ethic. It attacked laziness and time wasting. Making money became both religious and a business ethic which justified improved methods of production and the division of labour.

In this way religious beliefs influenced and changed social attitudes in the West. Capitalism did not emerge in the East because the religious teachings and ethics there were different.

Marshall ('The Protestant Ethic', *Sociological Review*) makes the points that:

(a) When Weber examined the relationship between the rise of capitalism and Protestantism he was examining a relationship which had been considered commonplace from the seventeenth century onwards
(b) He was the first to develop a clear theory that endeavoured to explain the factors in the relationship which promoted a particular type of outcome. In doing so, he focused on the Lutheran doctrine of 'calling', which taught that God required man not to retreat into monastic asceticism but to live a Godly life in society, rejecting worldly pleasures in favour of hard work and the accumulation of capital.
(c) He was able to explain why capitalism did not develop in China and India where the dominant religions did not promote similar values.

Points of criticism

(i) Many places in Europe have had a strong Calvinistic tradition but have not been prominent in developing capitalistic attitudes or structures in the ways predicted (for example, Scotland).
(ii) Many places had strong capitalist ethics and structures before Calvin developed his teachings. Some of these are in Catholic countries of which Weber's theory would not take account (for example, Florence.)
(iii) The success of the development of capitalism could be accounted for by other factors, for example, imperialism. Some of the most successful early capitalists may have been non-religious people, as are many of the contemporary rich.
(iv) Critics have said that he misunderstood the economic ethics of the great religions he studied and that he does not produce sufficient empirical evidence to support his theory. But, in his defence, Marshall emphasises that Weber did not claim that the theology of Calvinism was the only factor in the development of capitalism. In addition it was necessary to have:

1. a formally free and skilled labour force (which may account for why Scotland did not earlier develop a successful capitalist economy);
2. the separation of business and household capital;
3. rational book-keeping and technology;
4. a rational structure of law and administration; and
5. the rational spirit within the culture.

Conclusions

(a) Weber argues that action must be understood by recognising the meanings that people derive from their observations. Hard work is seen as a virtue.
(b) The ways in which people make sense of the world and act in it result from processes of socialisation. One important agency is that of religion. This lays down principles of salvation.
(c) His analysis examines the ways in which the economic values of capitalism were derived both from the ethics implicit in ascetic Protestantism and sustained by the existence of appropriate social structures.
(d) He shows how religious values can thereby influence economic values. Religion can be a force for social change.

Marxian view

■ **Assess the view that 'religion is a kind of mystified reflection of relations of economic dominance in society'.**

Marxists argue that religious institutions and organisations are a part of the social superstructure. This operates in the interests of the ruling class who thereby use religion as a means of social control:

1. Religion serves to legitimate power which is held by the ruling élite.
2. Rulers promote the myth that their position is divinely ordained (the monarch is crowned in a cathedral and the anthem says 'God save the Queen').
3. Religion serves the function of justifying the exploitation of the proletariat and the *status quo*.
4. People are blinded to reality; they are alienated and deluded by religious indoctrination.

5. In that religion is an illusion which eases the pain caused by exploitation it is 'an opium of the people'.
6. 'Religion is the sign of the oppressed creature, the sentiment of a heartless world'. The reality is that God did not create humankind, rather humankind created God.
7. Religion promises heaven to those who have nothing on earth, and it makes poverty more tolerable by offering long-term rewards in heaven. It deters people from seeking changes which would destroy the stability of society ('Blessed are the poor . . .').
8. Religion is an essentially conservative force which inhibits social change. It is an effective source of social control.

Points of criticism

(i) Kibbutz societies are religious organisations and which have adopted socialist principles. The two do not appear to conflict.
(ii) Some Roman Catholic priests in South America adopt Marxist principles in their support for social change.
(iii) Some powerful leaders do not appear to make particular use of religious organisations as a means of support or legitimation (for example, Adolf Hitler).
(iv) Turner (*Religion and Social Theory*) disputes the view that religion has been important as a source of ruling-class exploitation:
  (a) He argues (from historical data) that religion was not central in the lives of peasants.
  (b) Religion did, however, play an important part in the lives of nobility in supporting rules of marriage and inheritance.
  (c) Religion and religious institutions provided an important source of occupation for later-born sons of wealthy families whose first-born inherited land and estates.

Conclusions

Marxists see religion as a mystified reflection of relations of economic dominance in society in the sense that:

(a) Religion is described as a drug administered by the powerful to prevent poorer people seeing the reality of their inferior position and unhappy conditions of life.
(b) Religion is a tool in the hands of the ruling class to oppress and exploit. It helps distort a true picture of reality. It justifies hierarchy and inequality of power.
(c) The most socially deprived turn to religion for solace. They accept their situation as inevitable, give support to governments which do not act in their true interests (promoting false class consciousness) and they adopt belief systems which sustain inequality.
(d) Religion has therefore been an important part of ruling-class control by establishing hegemony of ideas and beliefs that are accepted unquestioningly by those in poverty.

Suggested Reading

Works noted in this chapter

R. Bellah (1976) 'New Religious Consciousness and the Crisis in Modernity' in C. Glock and R. Bellah (eds) *The New Religious Consciousness*, University of California

P. Berger (1969) *The Social Reality of Religion*, Faber and Faber

Bishop of Woolwich (1963) *Honest to God*, SCM Press

L. Broom and P. Selznick, *Sociology, Readings*, Harper International

S. Bruce (1991) 'Observations on Mass Media Religion', *Social Studies Review* (November)

H. Cox (1965) *Secular City*, Penguin

D. Cupitt (1980) *The Myth of God Incarnate*, CUP

E. Durkheim (1961) *The Elementary Forms of Religious Life*, Collier Books

D. Martin (1967) *A Sociology of English Religion*, Heinemann

——— (1969) *The Religious and the Secular*, RKP

H. Niebuhr (1929) *Social Sources of Denominationalism*, Henry Holt

T. O'Dea (1963) *The Sociology of Religion*, Free Press

L. Paul (1973) *The Church in Daylight*, Geoffrey Chapman, London

T. Parsons (1965) 'Religious Perspectives in Society', in Lessa and Vogt, *Reader in Comparative Religion*, Harper and Row

R. Robertson (1970) *The Sociological Interpretation of Religion*, Blackwell

R. Shiner (1971) 'The Concept of Secularisation in Empirical Research', in K. Thompson and J. Tunstall eds.

W. Stacey and A. Shupe (1982) 'Correlates of Support for the Electronic Church', *Journal for the Scientific Study of Religion*, Vol.21

E. Troeltch (1931) *The Social Teaching of the Christian Churches*, Allan & Unwin

B. Turner (1984) *Religion and Social Theory*, Humanities Press

R. Wallis (1984) *The Elementary Forms of New Religious Life*, RKP

B. Wilson (1966) *Religion in a Secular Society*, Penguin

B. Wilson (1974) 'The Anglican Church and its Decline', *New Society* (5 December)

B. Wilson (1967) *Patterns of Sectarianism*, Heinemann

J. Yinger (1969) *Sociology Looks at Religion,* Macmillan

J. Yinger (1971) 'Types of Religious Organisation in Sociological Perspective', in K. Thompson and J. Tunstall (eds.), Penguin

Works for further reading

P. Berger (1967) *The Sacred Canopy*, Doubleday
J. Brothers (1967) *Readings in the Sociology of Religion*, Pergamon
S. Bruce (1991) 'Pray TV', *Sociology Review*
J. Hadden and A. Shupe (1988) *Televangelism*, Holt
G. Marshall(1982) *In Search of the Spirit of Capitalism*, Hutchinson
——— (1991) 'The Protestant Ethic', *Sociology Review* (September), Vol. 1, No. 1
R. Shiner (1971) 'The Concept of the Secular', in K. Thompson and J. Tunstall, *Sociological Perspectives*, Penguin
B. Wilson (1970) *Religious Sects*, Weidenfeld & Nicolson
——— (1974) 'The Anglican Church in Decline', *New Society*

Self-test Questions

Study the items below and answer the questions that follows.

Item A

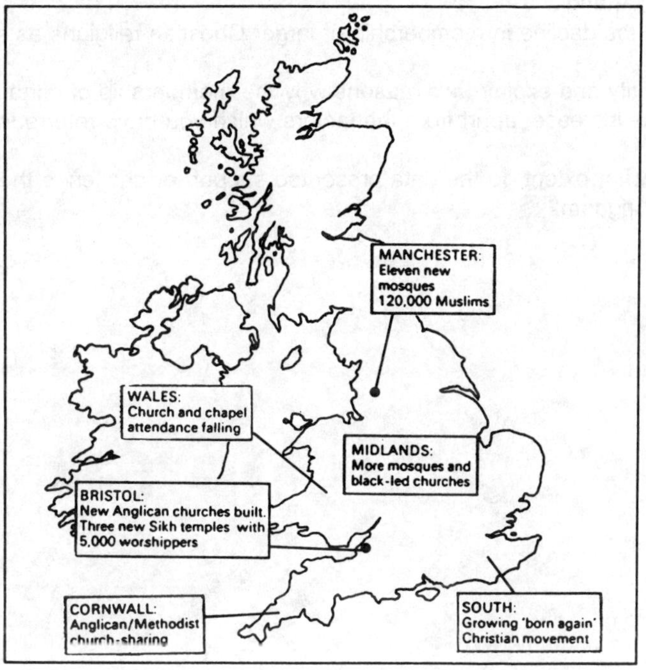

United Kingdom *Source:* Adapted from M. Denscombe, *Sociology Update*, Hyperion, 1989.

Item B

	1975	1985 (projected)	1990
Protestants	5 290 000	4 650 000	4 300 000
Roman Catholics	2 540 000	2 160 000	1 990 000
Mormons 80 000	80 000	80 000	
Jehovah's Witnesses	80 000	100 000	110 000

United Kingdom Source: Adapted from *Social Trends*, HMSO, 1988.

Item C

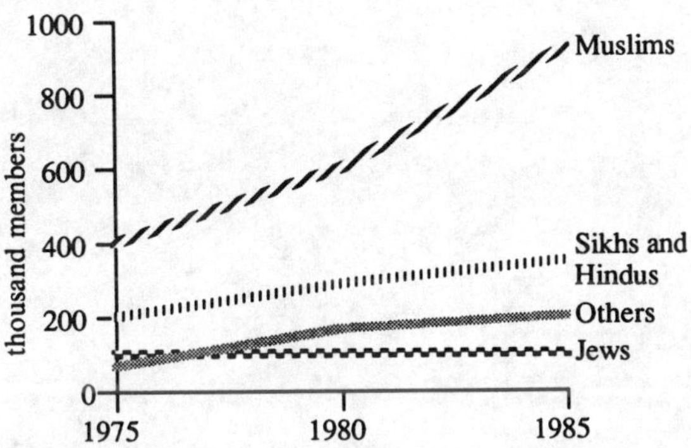

United Kingdom *Source:* Adapted from *Social Trends*, HMSO, 1988.

1. Examine Items A, B and C and describe and explain the main trends presented by the data. (*8 marks*)

2. Offer *two* brief explanations for each of the following:

(i) the apparent religious revival in certain regions of the United Kingdom as shown in Item A; and

(ii) the decline in membership of larger Christian religions as shown in Item B. (*4 marks*)

3. Identify and explain *two* reasons why the membership of certain religious groups seems to be on the increase, apart from the factors which you have referred to above. (*4 marks*)

4. To what extent do the data presented support or challenge the secularisation thesis in the United Kingdom? (*9 marks*)

Source: ULSEB (JUNE 1991)

13

CRIME AND DEVIANCE

The questions on this topic tend to fall into the following broad areas:

1. The criminal statistics: problems of interpretation.
2. The age and sex of offenders.
3. Theories of crime:
   (a) Functionalist.
   (b) Marxist.
4. White-collar crime.
5. Theories of deviance:
   (a) Interactionist perspective: distinctions between crime and deviance.
   (b) Labelling theory.

Criminal Statistics

■ Do the increases in serious crime indicate a crime wave?

'Crime' has a specific meaning. Every society has rules which the state says should not be broken. In England and Wales there is a distinction between serious crimes (known as notifiable offences), which require trial by jury and are subject to more severe penalties, and less serious crimes, which are normally tried in magistrates' courts.

Positivists make use of the statistics as social facts about the extent of social problems and disorder. *Phenomenologists* argue that sociologists must do more than describe social facts. They must take care over their use and interpretation. They emphasise the need to explain how people become criminals; they ask who collects the statistics and why and how they are interpreted in particular ways.

Table 13.1 Total number of notifiable offences recorded by the police in England and Wales 1951–91 (millions)

1951	*1961*	*1971*	*1981*	*1991*
.5	.8	1.6	2.9	5.3

Source: *Social Trends*, 22.

Table 13.2 Number of notifiable offences in England and Wales 1971 and 1990 (thousands)

Offence	*1971*	*1990*
Violence against the person	47	185
Sexual offences	24	29
Burglary	450	1007
Robbery	7	36
Drugs trafficking	–	10
Theft and handling stolen goods	1003	2374
Fraud	100	148
Criminal damage	27	553
Others	6	21
Total	1664	4363

Source: *Social Trends*, 22.

Comments

1. The number of recorded offences increased from about half a million in 1951 to over 5 million in 1991.
2. The number of crimes recorded is always greater than the number of people eventually found guilty.
3. In 1981 theft and handling stolen goods accounted for about 50 per cent of all serious offences. In 1991 crimes against property accounted for about 90 per cent of all offences.
4. The number of sexual offences is always comparatively small. Between 1989 and 1990 the number recorded fell by 2 per cent.
5. The risk of being a victim of any crime is higher among ethnic minority groups.
6. Reconviction rates remain high. About 44 per cent of adult males are reconvicted within two years of their release from prison.
7. Police clear-up rates fluctuate: 1971, 45 per cent; 1981, 38 per cent; 1991, 32 per cent.

Problems of interpretation

Wiles (*Criminal Statistics and Sociological Explanations of Crime*) argues that statistics of crime may be imperfect as instruments from which to draw definite conclusions about the state of a society. There are major problems in their interpretation. He disputes the idea that they indicate that there is an increasing crime wave.

The 'dark figure' of crime

This refers to criminal acts that are not reported. They are known to exist, as a result of admissions from both observers and victims.

The British Crime Survey (1982) found that:

(a) There may be as many as fifteen or twenty times as many crimes committed as are recorded.
(b) Most of the unreported offences are less serious types.
(c) Crime may not be reported where the observer does not perceive the act to be an offence; where the observer has a close relationship with the offender; where the observer justifies non-reporting on the grounds that 'it's nothing to do with me'.
(d) There are anomalies in the recording procedures: for example, if five bottles of milk are stolen, five offences are recorded. If a cheque book is stolen and fifty thefts occur, only one offence is recorded.

The authors conclude that the crime which is recorded is only the tip of an iceberg. We do not know with any precision how much goes unrecorded.

Conclusion

Apparent increases may be the result of the following factors:

(a) Changes in reporting behaviour.
(b) More policemen being asked to police areas suspected of having high rates of crime. The result is more arrests.
(c) It has become easier to report offences as the number of telephones has increased. There are also more policemen.
(d) There is more opportunity to commit offences (for example, supermarkets).
(e) The police are more efficient in recording offences (use of computers).
(f) The statistics do not take account of the 'meaning' of the offence to the offenders. Many people offend by chance. Increases in crime may represent more of the 'iceberg' being revealed.

■ **What problems are there for sociologists in the use of official crime statistics?**

Notes

(a) You will require reference to some statistics to answer this question.
(b) You could make use of detail from Wiles (see above). But in addition consider the following:

1. Lewis (*Social Trends*, 22) notes the following points:

(a) All official statistics are used by different groups for different purposes (for example, authorities use data to inform, guide and justify policies; critics use them to attack government policies, etc).
(b) Criminal statistics are particularly vulnerable to misinterpretation because their publication makes headline news. While changes in the law redefine crimes (for example, attempted suicide is removed, and the keeping of certain breeds of dog is included as a crime), changes in public attitudes make some crimes more newsworthy than others.
(c) The more newsworthy crimes (for example, child abuse, rape) may result in greater levels of reporting, leading to the view that there is a crime wave in specific activites (the number of reported rapes increased from 1200 in 1980 to 3300 in 1990).
(d) Most people's direct knowledge of crime is limited, but they are informed by the experiences of friends and by the media portrayal of crime, often in misleading ways (for example, the elderly may fear being out at night although attacks against them are comparatively rare).
(e) 'True crime' is a different concept from 'recorded crime'. The former describes all the crimes committed, whether or not they are reported. Recorded crime requires an observer/witness, a person to report it, and an acceptance by the police that it is genuine (it could later be deleted if an error is found).
(f) Victim surveys, which were first carried out in the 1980s, suggest that the amount of recorded crime is a major underestimation of the true amount committed. One survey showed that in 1988 60 per cent of all crimes encountered by a sample of people had not been reported to the police (too trivial, not wanting to get someone into trouble, etc.).
(g) Analysis of the ways the police deal with crime showed that changes in recording levels can occur without an actual increase in the number of incidents, for example, some crimes are complex and are subject to counting rules which define the number of different offences committed.
(h) The number of recorded crimes in an area may be related to:
 (i) the proportion of young males (15–25) in the population;
 (ii) the extent to which it is an urban rather than a rural area; and
 (iii) the perception of the police in the area.

2. Young (*Rise in Crime in England and Wales 1979–90*) noted the following:

Table 13.3 Percentage of 1950 crime rate, when 500 000 crimes were recorded

	1951–64	*1964–70*	*1970–74*	*1974–79*	*1979–90*
Conservative Government	12		18		32
Labour Government		11		15	

Source: *Social Trends*, 22.

He concluded:

(a) recorded crime rose twice as fast between 1979 and 1990; and
(b) the average rise in crime during a Labour administration was 3.2 per cent and during Conservative 7.2 per cent.

But note possible criticisms of the study:

 (i) the statistics are considered at their face value;

(ii) the short periods of Government in 1970/74 and 1974/79 allowed no time for policies to come to fruition; and
(iii) Young heads a team which has been termed 'new Left realists' and who are likely to be critical of Conservative policies.

Conclusions

Sociologists who warn of the problems associated with the interpretation of statistics argue from a phenomenological perspective that:

(a) The information contained in them is the result of a social process (that is, they are gathered for specific purposes; they vary in reliability).
(b) Distortions are not necessarily deliberate. They may arise out of the impact of the media in sensitising people to particular issues.
(c) It may be dangerously misleading to base explanations on statistics (for example, 'people are becoming more criminally minded'). There may be more laws to break; not all breaches are intentional.
(d) Official statistics only give a partial picture of the world. (Some people may be more able to avoid inclusion in the statistics; middle-class offenders may be less easy to catch and punish.)
(e) The recording and interpretation of statistics must be seen as the outcome of interaction between people (the witness, the reporter, the police). Note how Atkinson (see page 16) has shown how coroners make interpretations as to which acts are suicide and which are accidents.
(f) Care must be taken in assessing the validity of the statistics; it may be necessary to ask who is using them and for what purpose (for example, to justify new policies, to criticise existing policies).
(g) The effects of new legislation must be taken into account. Changes in the definition of burglary occurred in 1968, making it difficult to compare data before and after that date.

The Age and Sex of Offenders

■ **Account for the differences in the rates of male and female delinquency. (UODLE)**

Cowie *et al.* (*Delinquency in Girls*) make the point that the literature on the subject of delinquency in girls is not more than a small fraction of that relating to offences committed by males.

They suggest that the reasons are:

(a) The delinquent girl is a rarity.
(b) She is criminologically much less interesting. The offences for which she is likely to be charged are shoplifting and sexual misdemeanours. Delinquency in the male is more varied, dangerous and dramatic.

Comment

Data in *Social Trends*, 22 (1992) suggests that:

1. The peak age for male offenders in 1961 was 14, and in 1990, 18. The peak age for female offenders in 1961 was 14, and in 1990, 15. Relative to male offenders, females were most likely to offend between the ages of 14 and 15, and least likely at the age of 18.
2. The number of girls aged 15–20 in penal institutions was 860 in 1983. In 1990 there were 1800 women in prisons and 50 000 men (of all ages).
3. Home Office Research estimates that whereas 33 per cent of males will have a conviction for a serious offence before the age of 31, only 7 per cent of females are likely to do so.
4. Over 60 per cent of offences for which male and female offenders under the age of 17 were found guilty or cautioned in 1989 were property-related.

Studies:

1. Belson (*Juvenile Theft*) found in his 1975 study that by the time the average boy in London left school he had committed a hundred thefts. Only 13 per cent had been caught.
2. Cambell (*New Society*) found evidence that adolescent girls admitted to nearly as much deviance as males.
3. Mayhew (*New Society*) says:
   (a) Little attempt has been made to see how the social patterning of women's lives determines the chances they have of committing crime.
   (b) There are few situations in which males and females have equal opportunity to offend and it is difficult to measure these in a simple and reliable way.
   (c) In the case of shoplifting he found that there was no difference in the proportion of men and women who shoplifted, which was statistically significant. Men and women appeared, on the basis of the results of three studies, to be equally likely to commit this offence.
4. Cowie *et al.* suggest that the factors associated with higher rates of delinquency in girls were: low-income family; large family; parents having low levels of intelligence and also having a criminal record. (These were similar to the findings of West (*Delinquency, Its Roots, Causes and Prospects*), who studied 400 delinquent males aged 8–24).
5. Wilkinson, in a study in the USA (1983) found in California a 'near epidemic' of cases which involved women in embezzlement. Of one hundred cases, eighty were women. He suggests that this is because more women are engaged in those high occupational positions where they are able to control a company's finances.
6. Research and Planning Unit Bulletin (1985). This report outlined the factors which related to levels in delinquency among boys and girls:

Boys

1. Having delinquent friends.
2. Not feeling guilty about stealing.
3. Going out a lot.
4. Not having a close relationship with his father.

Girls

1. Having delinquent friends.
2. Poor parental supervision.
3. Not regarding stealing as serious.
4. Not having a close relationship with her father.
5. Having friends who would not be worried about stealing.

Possible explanations for the increase in female offenders

1. With more mothers at work there is less supervision of children in the home.
2. With more marriages ending in divorce there is more disruption to family life and less opportunity to develop a close relationship with the father, for security and discipline.
3. One-parent families are likely to face more financial hardship.
4. The feminist movement has encouraged women to become more autonomous and to seek wider goals (see Merton's theory, page 179).
5. Girls may be more likely to become attached to youth cultures which tolerate and encourage deviant behaviour.
6. It may be that there is not necessarily an increase in female deviance but that there is a dark figure (see page 176) of which more is being uncovered.

Possible explanations of why females offend less than males

1. Girls are socialised into roles which promote conformist attitudes.
2. They are less motivated to commit serious crime.
3. They are less often in situations which are conducive to crime (for example, less likely to fight; to get drunk).
4. Church attendance: although evidence is very limited there seems to be some (Wootton: *Social Science and Social Pathology*) suggesting that regular church attendance is relatively uncommon among offenders. Girls are more likely to attend than boys.
5. Truancy from school is also associated with delinquent behaviour. (One third of juvenile offences are committed in school hours). Girls are better attenders than boys.

Conclusions

Frith ('The Sociology of Youth') argues that he is not happy with the ways in which most studies have focused almost exclusively on male delinquent behaviour. This has resulted from the implication that the statistics can be taken at their face value. He raises the following points:

(a) The differences in rates of delinquency between males and females remain to be explained. Girls also experience status frustration; marginalisation; exploitation; alienation; and anomie, but their responses are seldom adequately examined.
(b) Because their patterns of deviant behaviour do not fit easily into those theories presented to explain male deviance, it is largely ignored or seen as the province of the psychologist. Cowie *et al.* see deviant behaviour in girls as related to abnormal hormonal balance.
(c) Since the statistics indicate that girls frequently get into trouble over some sexual offence, their sexual activity is treated as 'a problem' whereas that of males is not.
(d) He suggests that it may be that fewer girls appear in delinquent statistics because the attitudes of observers towards female deviance may be different from that towards male deviance. (A girl may be told to go home while a boy may be charged.)

From a Marxist perspective there is always selective enforcement of laws, to reinforce ruling-class ideology and maintain the image that most crime is located among working-class males, who remain the most easily identifiable folk devils. Girls who are involved in deviant activities are treated as having sexual problems or as abnormal.

Theories of Crime

The functionalist view

- **Examine the view that crime occurs as a result of the discrepancy between aspirations which society has socialised into its members and the ways their society provides for realising such aspirations.**
- **Is crime normal? Discuss.**

Functionalists look for the source of deviance in the culture and structure of society and examine the agencies of socialisation. Writers such as Emile Durkheim argue that crime is normal and helps to sustain conformity and stability. Crime is inevitable because many people are badly socialised.

Durkheim (*The Division of Labour*) says 'crime brings together upright conscience'. He notes how 'when some moral scandal has been committed . . . people stop each other on the street . . . they talk of the event and wax indignant.' The effect is to develop a sense of solidarity among people as they become sensitised to a social problem, which they are agreed requires a solution. The identification and punishment of a deviant helps to unify the community.

Other functions include:

(a) The social rules of the society are made clear when someone can be identified as having broken them.
(b) By uncovering deviance and establishing why it is 'a crime', undesirable behaviour can be identified and the young socialised to perceive it as such.
(c) Undesirable types of people ('criminals') can also be identified.
(d) Social rules can be clarified, maintained and if necessary modified. (Some may be dysfunctional in that they increase the number of law-breakers because the law is badly drafted.)
(e) There is justification for sanctions and punishments imposed on deviants. They are potentially disruptive and socially irresponsible. Moral values can be established and upheld.

It is in ways such as these that the collective sentiments of society are maintained at a strong level.

Theorists who emphasise structural and cultural factors

1. Merton (*Social Theory and Social Structure*) argues that deviance arises from the way society is structured.

(a) The majority of people share similar values as to what are the most important goals in social life.
(b) Unfortunately, there are differences in the opportunities available to people to achieve them.
(c) In the USA the 'American dream' is to attain material success. This includes getting a good job, owning a

house and having all the material goods needed for a successful life.

(d) Those who cannot attain these may suffer anomie. To resolve this their response may be one of the following:
  (i) *Conformity*: they will seek success through orthodox channels.
  (ii) *Ritualism*: they seek more modest goals.
  (iii) *Retreatism*: they are resigned to failure.
  (iv) *Rebellion*: they advocate a re-modelled society.
  (v) *Innovation*: they turn to deviant means to achieve the goals.

(e) Merton concludes that it is more likely to be members of the lower social classes who will innovate.

2. A. Cohen (*Deviance and Control*) opposes Merton's view that the motivation for deviant behaviour arises out of the frustrations of failing to achieve success by legitimate means. He discusses the sub-cultural values of deviants.

(a) He notes that delinquent acts are not always undertaken as an individual response to frustration.
(b) Many delinquent acts are not undertaken for financial gain, but are 'non-utilitarian and malicious.'
(c) He sees the cause of much delinquency as status frustration.

Success goals are replaced with an alternative set which provide a means of gaining prestige in the eyes of their peers. These are the values of a lower-working-class, delinquent sub-culture into which such boys are socialised.

Points of criticism;

(i) Merton's theory does not take account of non-financial acts of deviance of working-class offenders.
(ii) Cohen's theory does not account for middle-class offences and for only a small minority of working-class crimes.
(iii) Cohen's theory may overemphasise the extent to which deviants belong to 'delinquent gangs'.
(iv) There must come a point when too much crime is dysfunctional and causes social disharmony.

Conclusions

(a) Functionalists examine society as a whole; the analysis of crime is in terms of the structure of society. Quetelet (1869) said, 'society bears in its womb the embryo of every crime that is ever committed . . . the criminal is merely the tool'.
(b) Crime can be considered normal in the sense that it is inevitably present in all types of society at all times. Not every one will be socialised and integrated into the acceptable values of the society. Someone is bound to break a social and legal rule. When social problems are identified, social change can occur.
(c) The existence of crime may also justify the imposition of new rules and structures to help maintain order. Some analysts have suggested that crime rates increase when there are high levels of unemployment (although Box, 1987, found conflicting evidence) and an alienated sector among the young.
(d) If social deprivation, lack of commitment to community values and inability to achieve accepted goals results in increased crime then new social policies may emerge to deal with such problems.
(e) The structural and sub-cultural theorists present the view that people turn to crime as a response to their failure to achieve the mainstream goals of society in legitimate ways.

Marxian perspective

■ **Discuss the contention that most crime is committed by members of the working class. (UCLES)**

1. The Marxian analysis of crime is based on the view that:

(a) It arises because of the private ownership of property and the exploitation of one group by another.
(b) The high rate of crime in Western capitalist societies represents a protest against alienation and powerlessness.
(c) Capitalism is a competitive ideology; people are encouraged to become aggressive and hostile. In such a society, criminal behaviour is understandable.
(d) Chambliss and Mankoff (*Whose Law? What Order?*) examine laws from a colonial and historical perspective. Acts are defined as criminal which serve the interests of the colonial rulers to so define. The law is always used to control the work force and to maximise profits.

2. Young (*Mass Media, Drugs and Deviance*) argues that the mass media are always supportive of the *status quo*. Although the only concessions to working-class people in legal rights have been gained by united labour movements, such as trade unions, these come to be seen in a negative light. Strikers are portrayed as deviants. He also notes a different level of social reaction to the use of drugs: 72 million tablets are used legally each year; but there is a widespread sense of condemnation about the use of certain drugs by teenagers, hippies, etc. In *The Drug Takers* he suggests that they come under police surveillance because those who reject the values of capitalist society are seen as a potential threat.

3. Pearce (*Crimes of the Powerful*) sees organised crime as a tool of the ruling class. Gangsters have been known to assassinate political opponents, break strikes, etc. He also argues that there are few prosecutions of powerful companies and very rich people because they have the power to control the legal processes. Yet there are major infringements by them (tax evasion) which are often regarded as legitimate. This also creates the impression that such activities are minimal.

The merits of this approach

(a) It provides an explanation for why so much crime is related to the desire for material goods (most serious crime is theft).
(b) It provides an explanation for the fact that most offenders who are prosecuted come from the lowest social classes, although studies suggest crime is committed by all classes.
(c) The prison population exceeded, 50 000 in 1992 the majority of whom may be described as 'the poor and the powerless'.

The weaknesses of the approach

(a) It is based on a specific ideology. Marxists are committed to major social changes. They see the law as an instrument of class control.
(b) The theory does not explain the presence of crime in socialist societies in which there is no private property and the ownership of the means of production is communal.
(c) The theory does not easily explain the fact that there are middle-class offenders who are prosecuted.

4. Hughes (*Sociology Review*) discusses the views of the New Left Realists' (NLR) explanations of working class crime. This group emerged in the 1980s. The aim was to 'take crime seriously without the moral hysteria of the right'. Their analysis suggests:

(a) Changes in the crime rate are related to the changing class structure over the last 200 years. Particular groups have become increasingly marginalised (in recent years unskilled, inner-city blacks).
(b) NLR draws on:
  (i) Subcultural theory to explain links between marginalised individuals and the growth of street crime. This suggests that working-class criminal values are much the same as those which are accepted as the dominant values of capitalist society (aggressive, acquisitive and selfish behaviour).
  (ii) Relative Deprivation Theory to explain the growth in street crime and disorder among the most relatively deprived working-class youth. Riots are seen as acts of protest.
(c) The causes of crime are located in the brutalising effects of an exploitative social system.
(d) Its value is seen as moving beyond doctinaire Marxism and reviving old but valuable sociological concepts.

Points of criticism

(i) NLR offers a structural sociological explanation but fails to provide a sociology that can account for the way individuals give meaning to their acts and provides little examination of different motivations.
(ii) It focuses heavily on class at the expense of such features as gender, ethnicity and community.
(iii) There is strong focus on street crime at the expense of other types.

Conclusion

The Marxist sees crime as an inevitable feature of a capitalist economic system which promotes self-interest and greed. Emphasising the more sensational crimes usually committed by working-class people helps to maintain ruling-class ideology and power. The view that the most serious offences are committed by the working class is promoted through media reports. Law enforcement agencies are said by Marxists to be employed not to reduce crime but to manage it.

White-collar Crime

■ **What is white-collar crime? What is its significance for the sociology of crime?**

Definition Sutherland (*The Professional Thief*) says that white-collar crimes are those 'committed by persons of respectability and high social status in the course of their occupations'. Although these can include clear breaches of the law, such as tax evasion or breach of Factory and Company Acts, there are some actions which may be interpreted as bribery or as 'extravagant gifts'. Taking a broad view of such activities in the world of business and company transactions, Sutherland suggests that such practices are widespread (for example, the Poulson affair, in which an architect bribed councillors to obtain planning permission and wider political patronage).

Mays (*Crime and the Social Structure*) says that 'some of the so-called perks which businessmen enjoy are legalised forms of theft'.

Carson (*The Sociology of Crime*) argues that the study of white-collar crime raises crucial questions about how and why certain kinds of laws are enacted, confronting the investigator with the need 'to cast his analysis not only in the framework of those who break laws, but in the context of those who make laws as well.'

Research findings

1. Carson (*White-Collar Crime*) sampled 200 firms in the south-east of England. He found that every firm had committed some violation in the four and a half years studied, but the offences were rarely prosecuted. Official warnings were the most usual means of dealing with infringements.

2. Sutherland sampled seventy large corporations in the USA and found many types of violation were accepted practice. They were successful because:

(a) they were hard to detect;
(b) there were seldom any victims;
(c) they were often seen and justified as 'normal business practice';
(d) the public was seldom aware that an offence had been committed; and
(e) even when detected there was seldom a prosecution, which may have encouraged others.

He concludes that there is a constant bias involved in the administration of criminal justice under laws which apply to business and the professions and which therefore benefits the upper socio-economic group.

3. Mars (*Cheats at Work*) describes the 'normal crimes of normal people in the circumstances of their work'. He suggests that the nature of 'fiddling' varies with the nature of occupations. In jobs in which people's activities are highly controlled by management and in which they are often isolated from each other by noise or by distance, then their work fiddles may involve a single type of offence, for example, checkout staff overcharging customers. In fact these may even have arisen because of managers attempting to set the books right by encouraging fiddles at times of stocktaking. However, in jobs where the individual has more freedom to apply different levels of skills, fiddles cover a wider spectrum and involve a more complex range of illegal activities.

4. Pearce (*Crimes of the Powerful*) examined the criminal activities of large US business corporations and says that in monetary terms the activities of working-class offenders are a drop in the ocean. A more recent study in Sheffield (Levy) points out that middle-class crime is often more difficult to detect because it is more sophisticated. Middle-class offences such as tax evasion have been estimated to cost ten times more in losses than social security fraud by working-class people.

Some conclusions

Carsons raises some of the issues relating to white-collar crime:

(a) Why do the infringements by companies appear to enjoy substantial immunity from the legal process?
(b) Is there legislative bias in dealing with such irregularities?
(c) Studies indicate it is widespread and should undermine the myth that law-breaking is primarily a working-class phenomenon.
(d) How and under what circumstances can the law deal with such crime and so function as an instrument of social change? 'The efficiency of repressive criminal law in this respect, is an issue on which sociologists, like contemporary politicians, are by no means agreed.'

Deviance

■ **Distinguish between crime and deviance. Why are some deviant acts classified as criminal and others not?**

Crime A crime is a breach of the criminal law. There are two main types: *indictable* (notifiable) which are serious offences normally tried in a Crown Court and punishable by imprisonment or fine. A *non-indictable* offence is a less serious breach (for example, motoring) and is normally tried in a magistrates' court.

(a) Many acts defined as crimes are related to the social culture (what is regarded as a crime in one society may not be in another). In Eskimo society the ritual killing of the elderly was socially and morally acceptable, since food supplies were scarce.
(b) There is little evidence that there is behaviour which is condemned in every society.
(c) The concept of the meaning and significance of punishment also varies between cultures.

Deviance This is a more relative term that avoids the legal meaning attached to the term 'crime'. Deviance has both a legal and a non-legal usage. There is no absolute way of defining behaviour as deviant in a society, whereas it is possible to define an act as criminal.

(a) It implies behaviour which incurs public disapproval.
(b) It is behaviour which departs from the norms of a group.
(c) Whether an act is deviant depends on who commits it, who sees it and what action they take about it. The same act may be considered deviant when committed by one person, but not by another: an observer may define it as 'deviant' to cause trouble in a football ground; the troublemakers may regard it as 'normal'.
(d) Erikson (*Notes on the Sociology of Deviance*) says that deviance is not a property inherent in certain forms of behaviour; it is a property conferred by the audiences who witness them: 'The critical variable in the study of deviance is the social audience rather than the individual actor'.
(e) Taylor (*Deviance*) says that the explanations for deviant behaviour are to be found 'inscribed on the cultural map which belongs to the actor and his community'. The key concepts for interpreting this are those of 'role', 'interest' and 'expectations'. These change over time and help to shape behaviour.

Identifying deviants: labelling

■ **What are the strengths and weaknesses of the labelling approach to social deviance?**

Becker (*Outsiders*) has said that *deviance* is rule-breaking behaviour in which someone is labelled as 'deviant'. Deviance is not a quality that lies in the behaviour itself, but in the interaction between the person who commits an act and those who respond to it.

The process of labelling:

(a) To be successful there must be an audience or group who perceive others as being in some way different from themselves.
(b) There must be a group or an individual to receive the label.
(c) The label affects the status of both groups; the differences between them are made clear. The label 'deviant' produces a negative image of those labelled ('football hooligans') and develops a negative self-image in those labelled ('non-academic').
(d) Once the label is confirmed, either by someone of high status (the headmaster) or by further observations, then it becomes more firmly fixed.
(e) The effect is to establish *stereotyped images* which reduce uncertainty about those observed; the label makes the world more consistent. It makes predictions about future behaviour easier. ('He's always been a troublemaker. . . .')

Research findings

1. Cohen and Short (*Juvenile Delinquency*) note that middle-class offenders do not get as far as lower-working-class boys in the legal process when apprehended. Even though the offence is similar, they are less likely to be charged, or convicted and sentenced. This is because the label 'deviant' is less likely to be attached effectively to boys in the upper middle class. Therefore, there are different expectations about them.

2. Vincent (*Unmarried Mothers*) notes that the reaction of the local community to 'illicit pregnancy' is likely to be much more severe as far as the mother is concerned, whereas the unmarried father tends to escape much censure.

3. Hall *et al.* (*Policing the Crisis*); his work (as well as that of the authors who follow) illustrates how the enforcement agencies operate with pre-existing conceptions of what criminals and deviants are like.

The selective discrimination arises from the expectations that the police, lawyers and court officials have, which arise from the *labels* attached to certain types of people. Hall argues that this is why young black males are perceived to be deviant and treated accordingly. They have become the archetypal 'mugger'. This was a term imported from the USA in 1972. Its use in the media sensitised the public to a new problem: the headline 'Must Harlem Come to Handsworth?' appeared in a paper which warned that 'mugging' was starting in Britain (there were no cases described as mugging before 1972). This helped to establish a 'self-fulfilling prophecy'. It anticipated a problem, described the typical offender and, shortly after, the first offenders were located. The problem became amplified (see also page 122) as more black youths were arrested and there was more publicity in the press. Their own sense of alienation and anomie was increased.

4. Cohen (*Folk Devils and Moral Panics*) also shows how the label 'deviant' became attached to mods and rockers in the 1960s as a result of the publicity they gained in the popular press. He notes how some of this was manufactured by journalists. But the effect was to polarise the youth, the police and the public. The deviants developed a self-image and many behaved in accordance with it, causing further problems in more seaside resorts.

5. Cicourel (*The Social Organisation of Juvenile Justice*) shows how in the course of exercising discretion about their treatment of offenders, the enforcement agencies can produce delinquents:

(a) The police stop and question someone.
(b) This is based on their interpretation of 'suspicious character' and the fact that some areas are perceived as being worse than others.
(c) The interrogation may lead to arrest, depending on the appearance and manner of the person questioned.
(d) If arrested, further action may depend on the details learned about home background, school record, etc.
(e) If charged and prosecuted the outcome may also rest on such factors. In Britain the majority found guilty of an offence between the ages of 10 and 17 and therefore designated 'juvenile delinquents' come from Classes 4 and 5.

Cicourel concludes that what ends up as 'justice' is the result of negotiations in the interaction process.

The merits of the interactionist labelling perspective

1. It presents an alternative to the positive approach, which assumes that the 'facts' of crime are found in an analysis of the statistics.
2. The labelling theorists argue that deviant behaviour is the result of meanings derived from interaction.
3. The view argues that criminals are not different from non-criminals in that they are necessarily imbued with a criminal culture. There is unlikely to be any adult who has not committed a crime at some time in their lives.
4. Instead of searching for final causes the interactionist analyses the processes whereby behaviour comes to be defined as 'deviant'.
5. Interactionists do not adopt an absolute view of crime but present a position of moral relativism (attitudes change over time and place as to what is considered deviant).
6. There does seem to be much evidence that people develop stereotypes of others and respond to them.
7. This theory leads to the view that the witnesses or observers of the action become as much a focus of research interest as the actors themselves.

Some criticisms of the interactionist view

1. It may appear that there is too much concern for the offender.
2. It may be argued that there is too much concern for those in the most marginal areas of deviance (social deviance, drug-takers, etc.).
3. They do not explain the origin of deviance, but imply that it only arises after the label has been attached. It seems strange to suggest that deviance does not occur unless there is someone to observe it.
4. The role of the deviants is underplayed. They appear as rather passive victims of the observers of their actions.
5. The theory suggests that the deviants act without gaining pleasure or satisfaction from their behaviour. (It may be that there are some who deliberately cause trouble in football grounds for the 'excitement', 'status', etc. that it brings.)
6. It may be that observers of deviant acts actually help to cause a decrease in such behaviour (by expression of disgust, etc.).
7. Some people may deliberately seek the label 'outsider' to distinguish themselves from other groups or generations.

■ **Examine some of the theories which seek to explain deliquency, and criticisms which have been raised against them.**

Note

(i) *Delinquency* describes the criminal acts of young people aged 10–17.
(ii) Several of the questions already discussed have considered some of the theories of crime and delinquency and their criticisms. In summary, these include the following, some of which you would need to discuss and elaborate.

1. *Structural Theory (including that of Anomie) (Merton):* People are differentially placed in the social structure and some cannot achieve the goals of mainstream society. The result may be anomie, normlessness. Their response to this may result in delinquent behaviour by some young people to achieve financial gain.

Criticism

(i) this places much emphasis on delinquency as an individual response, whereas such results from group activity; and
(ii) it does not explain crime that has no financial benefit.

2. *Status Frustration Theory* (*A. Cohen*) Delinquency results from the failure of young people to achieve middle-class goals in school and in work. The result is a deliquent sub-culture. Success is achieved in deviant ways to fill the vacuum in their lives.

Criticisms

(i) this explanation would seem to apply only to a small minority, whereas deviance and delinquency

Questions

Examine Photograph 33.

Consider the facts that you would need to know before deciding whether Photograph 33 illustrates a crime or a perfectly legal activity?

(i) Explain how negative 'deviant' labels can become attached to young people by observers of even legal activities such as adding material to a bonfire.

(ii) How might a phenomenologist study this process?

(iii) Not all deviant acts are necessarily crimes. Explain this point.

(iv) Explain labelling theory and briefly discuss a study in which it has been used.

33

Source: Alec Gill

is more widespread and appears in all classes; and

(ii) it assumes that such young people cannot achieve status in other legitimate ways (for example, sport).

3. *Lower Class Subculture Theory (Miller):* This suggests that delinquency results from the power of working-class norms and values determining the response of young people which get them into trouble (aggression, toughness, being smart, etc.). These bring them into conflict with mainstream society.

Criticisms

(i) this assumes that the lower working class are insulated from the values of wider society (available through the media, etc.); and
(ii) it is a determinist view, which assumes that people are trapped by their culture.

4. *Drift Theory (*Sykes and Matza, *Delinquency and Subterranean Values*) argue that a number of supposedly delinquent values are similar to those embodied in the leisure and day to day activities of middle class society. For example, the desire for conspicuous consumption, the respect accorded to masculine values, toughness and aggression, (often demonstrated on the sports field), the high status achieved by 'those who dare'. Thus, whereas the wealthy may ski, gamble, explore, drive fast cars, travel to exotic places, indulge in dangerous sports, have a sense of comradeship with other club or regimental members, many less affluent youths turn to deviance to achieve these goals. Such quests for excitement, thrills, friendship etc are not in themselves deviant values but they can best be achieved in the appropriate circumstances. The authors conclude that juvenile delinquents suffer from bad timing and serve to reinforce the law-abiding in their positions of respectability. The values of the delinquent are far less deviant than is commonly portrayed. Hence such behaviour is found in all social classes as young people drift in and out of deviance and often express remorse and seek to neutralise their acts by saying 'but everyone does it . . . '.

Criticisms

(i) can the attempts to neutralise their actions be accepted at face value? They may, in fact, be rejecting mainstream social values, and merely seeking to minimise punishment;
(ii) the theory suggests delinquency is a widespread activity, but does not explain why working-class boys seem more likely to succumb to temptations than those of the middle class; and
(iii) It may be objected that the quest for excitement, thrills, danger etc, are not typical middle class values at all.

5. *Ecological Theory: (Chicago School)* This suggests that some young people will be more likely to fall into delinquency because of the area of the city in which they grow up. Those nearest the centre are at greatest risk. Delinquent values impress themselves in the area and are passed on from one generation to the next.

Criticisms

(i) the theory does not hold for many British cities, which developed in different ways from those in America; and
(ii) it is a highly determinist theory, suggesting that people cannot escape the power of social norms on their behaviour.

6. *Marxist Theory (Pearce):* The explanation is in terms of a rational response on the part of the delinquent to the competitiveness and inequalities of life in a capitalist society. Greed, self-interest, hostility and the quest for power are central values, which delinquents emulate in their deviant activities.

Criticisms

(i) all delinquency is said to emanate from the economic structure, but not all crime is for financial reward; and
(ii) it does not account for crime in non-capitalist societies.

7. *Labelling Theory (Becker):* This argues that delinquent acts result from the process of labelling a person as a deviant, following the observation and reporting of their behaviour to others. The result can be a self-fulfilling prophecy, causing more people to commit delinquent acts.

Criticisms

(i) it is deterministic. It suggests that once a label is attached, the young person is propelled into more deviance; and
(ii) it does not seem to allow for the deviant acts that occur when no one sees them and before labels are attached.

In addition, Frith makes the criticism that none of the theories adequately explain female delinquency (see page 178)

Suggested Reading

Works noted in this chapter

H. Becker (1963) *Outsiders*, Free Press
W. Belson (1975) *Juvenile Theft*, Harper and Row
B. Cambell (1977) *New Society* (June)
W. Carson (1970) *The Sociology of Crime*
—— *White-Collar Crime*, in W. Carson and P. Wiles, *The Sociology of Crime and Delinquency in Britain*, Martin Robertson
W. Chambliss and M. Mankoff (1976) *Whose Law? What Order?*, John Wiley
S. Cohen (1985) *Folk Devils and Moral Panics*, Paladin
A. Cohen (1966) *Deviance and Control*, Prentice-Hall
A. Cohen (1956) *Delinquent Boys*, RKP
J. Short (1965) *Group Processes in Gang Delinquency*, University of Chicago Press
J. Cowie *et al.* (1971) *Delinquency in Girls*, Heinemann
E. Durkheim (1947) *The Division of Labour*
M. Erikson (1963) *Notes on the Sociology of Deviance*
S. Frith (1985) 'The Sociology of Youth', in M.

Haralambos, *Sociology: New Directions*, Causeway
S. Hall *et al.* (1979) *Policing the Crisis*, Macmillan
M. Haralambos (1985) *Sociology: New Directions*, Causeway
G. Hughes (1991) 'Taking Crime Seriously', *Sociology Review* (November) Vol. 1 No. 2
G. Mars (1982) *Cheats at Work*, Allen and Unwin
C. Mayhew (1977) *New Society* (June)
J. Mays (1967) *Crime and the Social Structure*, Faber
R. Merton (1968) *Social Theory and Social Structure*, Free Press
W. Miller (1962) 'Lower Class Culture as a Generating Milieu of Gang Delinquency' in Wolfgang *et al* (eds) *A Critique of the Ideology of the Poverty Movement*
F. Pearce (1976) *Crimes of the Powerful*, Pluto Press
G. Sykes and D. Matza (1964) 'Deliquency and Subterranean Values', *American Sociological Review*, 26
E. Sutherland (1937) *The Professional Thief*, University of Chicago Press
I. Taylor (1973) *Politics and Deviance*, Penguin
J. Young (1971) *The Drug takers*, Paladin
D. West (1969) *Delinquency, Its Roots, Causes and Prospects*, Heinemann
B. Wootton (1959) *Social Science and Social Pathology*, Allen and Unwin
P. Wiles (1971) 'Criminal Statistics and Sociological Explanations of Crime', in W. Carsons and P. Wiles (eds) *Crime and Delinquency in Britain*, Martin Robertson
J. Young (1992) *Rise in Crime in England and Wales 1979–90*), Middlesex Polytechnic

Works for further reading

W. Carson and P. Wiles (1971) *Crime and Delinquency in Britain (Readings)*, Martin Robertson
Chibnall, S., *Law-and-Order News*, Tavistock 1977.
A. Crawford *et al.* (1990) *The Second Islington Survey*, ESRC
Criminal Statistics, England and Wales, Com. 1332, HMSO 1990.
S. Field (1990) Trends in Crime, HMSO
S. Frith (1985) 'The Sociology of Youth', in M. Haralambos, *Sociology New Directions*, Causeway
P. Gilroy (1987) *There Ain't No Black in the Union Jack*, Hutchinson
R. Kinsey (1986) *Losing the Fight Against Crime*, Blackwell
J. Lea and J. Young (1984) *What Is to be Done About Law and Order?*, Penguin
D. Matza (1969) *Becoming Deviant*, Prentice-Hall
D. Mayhew *et al.* (1988) *The British Crime Survey*, HMSO
P. Rock (1989) 'New Directions in Criminology', *Social Studies Review* (September)
J. Solomon (1988) *Black Youth, Racism and the State*, CUP
—— (1988) 'Recent Developments in Criminology', in M. Haralambos, *Developments in Sociology*, Vol.4

Self-test Questions

Read the following extracts and answer the questions which follow.

Item A

'Some sociologists see deviance as inevitable and even functional for all societies. Deviance is the inevitable outcome of any society that has a shared normative structure. If a society's values are not strong then deviance becomes disruptive. Widespread anomie and eventually social collapse are the inevitable consequences of a social system that fails to counter growing levels of deviance by either adapting or reasserting central values.'

(a) How can deviance be seen as functional for society? (*6 marks*)
(b) Choosing *one* institution of your choice, and using the perspective in the passage, demonstrate how social change can create deviant behaviour. (*6 marks*)
(c) Taking *one* area of social life discuss how society might try to adapt or reassert central values. (*6 marks*)
(d) How might other sociologists criticise the view of deviance outlined in the passage? (*7 marks*)

Item B

'Some sociologists see deviance as the outcome of strategic interactions which involve the ability of some individuals to negotiate and define situations in certain ways and impose their definitions upon others, thus labelling them as deviant. Deviant labels are therefore the outcome of some socially powerful individuals or groups imposing their definitions, not inherent in the act itself.'

(a) Explain and illustrate what is meant by 'deviance is the outcome of strategic interactions'. (*6 marks*)
(b) Taking *one* area of social life show how powerful groups have defined and labelled acts and actors as deviant. (*6 marks*)
(c) Choosing *one* institution, and using the perspective in the passage, demonstrate how deviant behaviour is related to social change. (*6 marks*)
(d) How might other sociologists criticise the view of deviance outlined in the passage? (*7 marks*)

Item C

'Some sociologists see deviance as a device for directing attention away from the activities of ruling and powerful groups within society. Fears about drug abuse, sexual permissiveness, declining moral standards, street violence and hooliganism are consciously produced in order to divert less powerful groups from the truth: that the powerful daily commit crime, pervert justice and influence the definition of social rules in order to maintain their dominant social position.'

(a) Explain and illustrate what is meant by deviance as a device for directing attention away from ruling and powerful groups. (*6 marks*)
(b) Taking *one* area of social life show how some sociologists might argue that powerful groups 'daily commit crime, pervert justice and influence the definition of social rules'. (*6 marks*)
(c) Choosing *one* institution, and using the perspective in the passage, demonstrate how deviant behaviour may be seen to threaten the position of powerful social groups. (*6 marks*)
(d) How might other sociologists criticise the view of deviance outlined in the passage? (*7 marks*)

Source: JMB (JUNE 1990)

14

YOUTH AND AGE

There are questions on this topic which relate to:

1. The social construction of age:
   (a) Childhood.
   (b) Adolescence.
   (c) Old age.
2. Youth cultures:
   (a) Functionalist perspective.
   (b) Structuralist explanations: working-class sub-cultures.
   (c) Interactionist perspective.
   (d) Middle-class youth cultures.
3. Soccer hooliganism.

The Social Construction of Age

- **What comparative evidence is there to suggest that terms such as childhood, adulthood and elderly refer to expectations about how individuals should act rather than the number of years they have lived? (ULSEB)**
- **Societies vary in their expectations of children, adolescents and old people. Does evidence from both pre-industrial and industrial societies support the claim that the various stages of the family cycle are a matter of social definition?**

Sociologists are interested to study the way that people are treated in terms of their age in society. Although ageing is a biological process there is evidence to show that cultural interpretations of its significance and meaning are relevant and important.

There is evidence, too, to suggest that in pre-industrial societies the terms childhood, adulthood and the elderly do tend to refer to expectations about how people should act, rather than the number of years they have lived. In Western industrial societies the terms have meaning in both respects.

Childhood

1. Aries (*Centuries of Childhood*) says that this is a phenomenon of the twentieth century. In medieval times, the idea of childhood did not exist. Children became the companions of adults as soon as they were considered capable of doing so without mothers or nannies. This could have been as early as the age of seven.

2. Musgrove (*Youth and the Social Order*) says that in the late eighteenth and early nineteenth centuries parents began to value children largely because they became an economic asset. The new industries were heavily dependent on the skills and ability of the young. Children presented an insurance against misfortune in later life and old age. The birth-rate after 1870 slumped with the first Education Act: as Musgrove says, 'By the early part of the twentieth century children were no longer central to the economy; they were moving to the periphery, into marginal and relatively trivial occupations'.

3. Malinowski, Meade, Maddock and other anthropologists have shown how transitions from one age group to another in pre-industrial societies are usually marked by initiation rites and ceremonies. The traditions and customs of the society are transmitted from one generation to the next and their new roles made clear.

4. Barnouw (*Anthropology*) says that 'different societies hold up contrasting ideas of the growing child, ranging from the proud, self-assertive warrior to the mild, self-effacing citizen'.

5. The problems facing children in contemporary Britain were highlighted

(a) in a report published in 1983 (*Children Today*). This stated that there were:

(i) more than 100 000 children in care;
(ii) about 2 million in low-income families;
(iii) 1.5 million in one-parent families;
(iv) 25 000 homeless families with children; and
(v) 20 000 children in care awaiting adoption.

(b) National Society for the Prevention of Cruelty to Children (NSPCC) data for 1989 showed over 36 000 children in England and Wales were recorded as either having been abused or giving rise to grave concern. (However, Taylor (*Measuring Child Abuse*) points out that there are problems in measurement, and bias may occur.)
(c) The Children Act (1991) recast the law on caring for and protecting children in England and Wales.
(d) *Social Trends*, 22 showed that in 1990:
(i) there were about 67 000 children in care (down by a third since 1970);
(ii) an increase of 19 per cent in the proportion of lone mothers (1 per cent in 1971);
(iii) about 46 000 children on the Child Protection Register; and
(iv) about 104 000 homeless families with dependent children.

Adulthood

While childhood and old age are clearly differentiated, it is more difficult to clarify the specific features of adulthood.

Rosser and Harris (*The Family and Social Change*) have described the family cycle in contemporary Britain:

Family phase

1 Home-making
From marriage to the birth of the first child
2 Procreation
From the birth of the first child to the marriage of the first child
3 Dispersion
From the marriage of the first child to the marriage of the last child
4 Final phase
From the marriage of the last child to the death of the original partners

They accept that these do not represent clear and distinct milestones in the progress of an individual family through the typical cycle. But they are able to identify particular patterns of family behaviour with each phase.

The period of adulthood might be taken to be the time between phases 1 and 3, from the ages of 25 to 45, before the time of the onset of 'middle age'.

In the West it is a time when careers are established; children produced; marriage relationships established; and the family becomes more privatised. It may also be a time of increasing frustrations if careers or marriages fail and new relationships form. Children may come to be seen as 'problems'.

In simple societies there are initiations into adulthood. For boys this may involve separation from their mothers and closer association with adult men. The rites help to celebrate and reinforce the bonds of male and tribal solidarity. Boys may be given new names, new privileges and new status in society.

Brown (*A Cross-Cultural Study of Female Initiation Rites*) found that no initiation ceremony takes place for girls in societies where they leave home upon marriage since the act of leaving marks that change. But in societies where the girl remains in the same social setting after marriage, a ceremony may be performed to mark her change of status, especially in societies in which women make a notable contribution to subsistence.

There are many cross-cultural anthropological studies which emphasise the significance of socialisation and training for adult roles rather than the influence of biological factors.

Old age

Old age can also be said to be socially constructed in the sense that in Western societies we tend to treat people differently when they reach 'old age'. They are perceived as 'pensioners' or 'senior citizens'.

This perception affects our treatment of them:

(a) Their roles change when they are no longer economically active.
(b) Their income falls on retirement.
(c) They are seen to be less active.
(d) They are believed to be out of touch with the values of a younger generation.
(e) Their status tends to fall.
(f) The family remains the chief source of support for the elderly. About 6 per cent of those over 60 are in residential homes, hospitals, etc. One of the chief roles undertaken by the elderly is that of 'grand-parent' whereby they may regain some status in the family.
(g) In 1990 about 18% of the population (10.4m) people were of pensionable age. It is estimated that by the year 2030 there will be 14m.
(h) In 1991 Age Concern Survey reported that people's perception of old age varied according to their own age. 43% of those asked who were in the 16–24 age group said 'under 60', whereas only 4% of those over 75 agreed. The survey also showed widespread fears among the sample about ageing because of loss of income, health and independence.

Conclusions

(a) Comparative evidence from anthropologists and sociologists shows that in every society people have a status and a role which are ascribed (by family, gender, age, etc.).
(b) People move through age categories that are seldom closely defined, through babyhood, childhood, young adult, mature adult to elderly adult following prescribed norms and expected patterns of behaviour.
(c) Different societies may define such age groups in different ways; in pre-industrial societies there may be rites of passage indicating that a person is being admitted from one category to another and that their behaviour must change. Those classified as 'old' may achieve higher status as guardians of secret knowledge; in industrial societies the status ascribed to the elderly may be less satisfactory and result in greater disengagement from mainstream society.
(d) In industrial societies that are more bureaucratically organised entry into adulthood is marked by legal requirements (for example, the right to vote, to marry, to drive, etc.) although there may be no agreement as to the specific age for each right. But the general expectation is that behaviour should become 'more mature'.

(e) The durations of different life periods are socially defined. They correspond only roughly to biological stages of development. Each socially-defined group has expected patterns of norms to follow. To infringe them results in criticism.
(f) Sociologists conclude that to understand the different ways in which different societies treat the process of ageing it is necessary to examine the different norms and expectations that exist in them.

Youth Cultures

- **Why have youth cultures received the attention of sociologists? Discuss critically some of the theories presented.**
- **In what ways are youth cultures functional for their members?**

The concept of youth cultures is a relatively recent one analysing behaviour patterns of young people in Western industrial societies. It has been used particularly since the emergence of groups in the 1950s such as the Teddy Boys and the Beats; in the 1960s, the Mods and Rockers, the Hippies, Skinheads and Greasers; in the 1970s, the Punks, New Romantics, Rastas; in the 1980s, Goths, Heavy Metal and so on.

1. *Functionalists* emphasise changing patterns of social life to explain the emergence of a distinct culture of youth: particularly the effects of affluence, following pre-war and wartime austerity; the expansion of education and the effects of the mass media which helped to spread a mass culture. They focus on the positive values of a youth culture. Some suggest that youth tends to share a general culture, almost as a classless tribe, members passing through a peer group holding stage before entering the serious phase of adulthood.

2. *Marxists* have placed emphasis on the significance of class differences among youth which affect the form the cultures take. Explanations have emphasised the need to 'read' the signs and symbols of youth cultures in relation to those of competing cultures. Particular attention has been paid to lower-working-class sub-cultures, which are seen as attempts to cope with the deprivations of an exploitative society.

3. *Interactionists* have examined the way youth cultures are manufactured by the media reports which help to bind the participants into an amplification spiral. This serves to promote the values of the culture and to polarise its members from others in society.

The functionalist view

1. Parsons (*Essays in Sociological Theory*) explains the emergence of modern youth culture in terms of the impact of changes that occur in modern industrial societies. There is more self-interested action and less concern for the individual as bureaucratic institutions develop and social roles become more specific. Membership of youth peer groups in which there is a shared culture may be seen as a useful period of transition and as a means of coping with the marginal status of adolescence.

2. Eisenstadt (*From Generation to Generation*) argued:

(i) youth is a time of instability. The shared youth culture provides meaning, friendship and shared experience; and
(ii) in meeting the needs of the youth of society the culture promotes stability in their lives and facilitates their gradual assimilation into wider adult society as they pass through the phase of experimentation.

The view that youth cultures can be dysfunctional

3. Martin (*A Sociology of Contemporary Cultural Change*) describes the emergence of a 'counter-culture' (a culture of opposition) which developed in the 1960s as 'a cultural revolution among a small minority of crusading radicals'. This culminated in 'altering some of our deepest and therefore most customary and commonplace habits and assumptions'. She says it was a search for 'liminality'. This represented an attempt by young people to counter the restrictions of social life by moving to the thresholds of 'no man's land', the edge of the 'abyss' and to embrace a state of anomie for the sake of creative possibilities that it offered.

She is critical of the movement because:

(a) It was based on romantic values which emphasised the needs for self-fulfilment and experiential richness at the expense of the individual's commitments to wider society.
(b) The search led people away from a sense of social integration.
(c) It was excessively individualistic, which went against the traditional values of social solidarity.
(d) The group that acted as the main carrier of these expressive values was a cultural élite, namely middle-class radicals.
(e) The movement could only prosper as a result of the freedom and affluence of Western societies, and yet it was critical of these societies.
(f) The quest for a boundary- and rule-free utopia is a fruitless one.
(g) The need for rules and order is deeply rooted in mankind.
(h) The expressive youth culture has had a dangerous effect in wider society because others have inadvertently been affected by them. The boundaries of good taste, moral values, etc. have all been pushed back. It was an attempt to make all life 'an evening of freedom' in which rules, roles and conventions were abandoned.

However, she notes that there have been some attempts to oppose the counter-culture with the regeneration of religious values.

Points of criticism

(i) Functionalist theories developed particularly to describe the early youth groups in the 1950s (especially in USA), with low levels of unemployment and in societies of growing affluence.
(ii) The view that youth cultures are essentially classless has been questioned, especially by

Marxist sub-cultural theorists, who focus on working-class cultures.

(iii) There is evidence to support the notion that some youth cultures can be dysfunctional, failing to promote stability and community. For increasing numbers of young people the norm is to turn to drug and alcohol use (Mori, 1992 found that more than 50 per cent of 17-year-olds have had a hangover; ICM, 1992 found that 33 per cent of 18–24-year-olds had lost confidence in the police; Bynner, 1992 found that Britain's young people constitute a generation of political illiterates. Only 37 per cent of 17–18-year-olds were interested in politics, and most of these were educational high achievers. A report in 1992 showed that 1000 teenagers a week were suffering from severe hardship because of the government's failure to guarantee a training place for all under 18, while withdrawing benefits from them.)

Marxist sub-cultural theory

This suggests that emerging youth cultures represent ideological forms of resistance. They seek to challenge the ruling class's power. They symbolise a refusal to accept their marginal status and limited power, and the economic problems of low income and high levels of unemployment. They are seeking more control over their own lives.

Points of criticism

(i) They present a hightly deterministic view; the sub-cultures emerge from environmental pressures. Marsland has disputed the view that class is the key variable in the analysis; the problems faced by young people are complex and arise in all social classes.

(ii) They tend to focus almost exclusively on working-class sub-cultures and pay less attention to those of middle-class youth.

(iii) There remains a problem in explaining why many working-class youth cultures oppose each other (Mods versus Rockers; Skinheads versus Greasers and so on).

(iv) If punk culture was one of opposition to the conventions and expectations of middle-class society and musical forms, etc., why has it also appeared in socialist societies?

Interactionist theory

1. This view is based on the argument that behaviour is not determined entirely by environmental factors, but is shaped by people's response to events as they occur and are perceived. What is important is the meaning events have for participants. See, for example:

(a) Cohen (*Folk Devils and Moral Panics*) (see page 123).
(b) Hargreaves (*Social Relations in a Secondary School*) (see page 134).

Such studies show that culture grows out of an interaction between individuals as well as from a set of events that frequently gain wide media publicity.

2. Labelling theory shows how labels precede deviant behaviour by sensitising the public.

(a) Youth groups are easily identified and their activities become newsworthy.
(b) Those labelled as outsiders (Becker, see page 181) adopt the patterns expected of them and fulfil the concerns of the observers. Their shared patterns of behaviour have meaning to the actors, however bizarre they may appear to observers.
(c) To obtain insights into patterns of behaviour it is necessary to take account of the views of the actors to produce explanations of the culture. Even 'hanging about on street corners' can be seen by participants as doing something.
(d) Ryan (1985) complains of the effect of the media in stereotyping young people collectively as 'yobbos and scroungers' and alienating them.

Points of criticism

(i) They place much emphasis on the power of the media to label and stereotype.

(ii) Becker suggests that cultures arise quickly in response to the needs of a group to cope with specific problems of the moment, and dissolve quickly. But many cultures have a permanence and importance in the lives of members and seem to be more than just short-term coping mechanism.

(iii) A criticism which all the theorists face is that there is little attention paid to young people who do not appear to identify with any specific youth culture and regard themselves as conformist youth (while facing many of the problems of those who do). Nor do they look closely at the involvement of girls in youth cultures.

Conclusions

(a) The attention which sociologists have paid to youth in recent years has resulted from the fact that the period of time between childhood and adulthood has widened. The time spent in school and college prior to entering the world of work has increased for more young people.
(b) Youth cultures have emerged which describe the patterns of belief and behaviour associated with young people (whose precise age group is hard to define).
(c) Shared activities and values which they wish to explain and analyse are always of interest to sociologists.
(d) These attempts have varied according to the perspective adopted.
(e) There are constant changes going on. Frith argues that the distinctive nature of youth culture must be explained not simply by reference to leisure activities, but also young people's position in work and family which shape their attitudes and behaviour.

Theories of working-class sub-cultures

1. Miller (*Lower-Class Culture*), writing in 1962, described a distinctive cultural system associated with lower-working-class youth. These values included 'toughness', being 'smart' and seeking 'excitement'. There is also concern for 'masculinity' in the face of physical threat. To be smart means being able to outwit, dupe or 'con' others.

Questions

Examine photographs 34–37.

1. (i) Consider photograph 34 and suggest the ways in which childhood can be described as a twentieth-century phenomenon.
   (ii) What documentary or other evidence would you seek to investigate this view?

2. Examine photographs 35 and 36.
   (i) Most youth cultures promote a deep interest in specific types of music and sport:
      (a) Is there evidence that youth cultures are classless, or do different cultures appeal to young people of different classes?
      (b) How would you research this question?
   (ii) What functions does the support of the team play in the lives of these fans?
      (a) Why do the young fans make their support clearer than older fans?
      (b) What is the significance of music for youth cultures?
      (c) How would you investigate the belief that new developments in pop music tend to result in new moral panics?

3. Examine photograph 37.
   (i) Consider some of the problems in defining the elderly.
   (ii) What are some of the major problems facing the elderly in contemporary society?
   (iii) How might problems vary between the elderly in different social classes?
   (iv) In which class would you place the couple in the photograph? What criteria are you using?
   (v) Suggest how you would conduct a research project into the ways in which old age is socially constructed.

4. Can any significant distinctions be drawn between working-class and middle-class youth cultures?

35 Source: Alec Gill

36 Source: Alec Gill

34 Source: Alec Gill

37 Source: Alec Gill

Excitement involves the search for thrills and is found in gambling, the use of alcohol and so on. All these can be obtained when with the peer group. Miller argues that the concern is to find enjoyment as a compensation for the dull routine of work. These cultural values are always likely to lead a working-class youth into acts of deviance.

2. Clarke (*The Skinheads and the Magical Recovery of Community*) argues that skinhead culture represents and an attempt to recreate the working-class culture of the East End which has been lost.

The emergence of the culture can be seen in terms of the skinheads' exclusion from existing sub-cultures and because they perceived themselves to be under attack and subject to the authority of others.

(a) Their need for solidarity derived from the solidarity of their working-class community.
(b) This had been lost as a result of slum clearance, etc.
(c) The result has been an exaggerated 'style'.
(d) Support for local football teams helped emphasise the importance of 'territory' and provided a sense of identity.
(e) He concludes that territoriality, solidarity and masculinity are all ways of re-creating a sense of community and become significant aspects of the culture of the East End youth.

3. Hall (*Resistance Through Rituals*) argues that working-class sub-cultural activities are an attempt to resist middle-class values being imposed on them. This is achieved by developing a pattern of behaviour and a cultural style that distinguishes them from those they oppose.

(a) The style is evident in the clothes they wear, the music they listen to and the language they use.
(b) Such styles carry the youth culture to which they adhere.
(c) The culture often encourages ritualistic behaviour, especially at football matches.
(d) Aggressive behaviour is interpreted as a means of compensating for loss of status and power.
(e) In some cases, aspects of the culture have been incorporated by the media into the mainstream of society (for example, punk dress becoming 'fashionable').

4. Corrigan (*Schooling the Smash Street Kids*) argues that working-class youth seek to construct and control their own activities and avoid or oppose anyone who threatens to stop them doing so. This is why much time is spent 'hanging around' street corners, which in effect offers the possibility of making something happen. They reject the idea of conformity to school norms and the idea of obtaining qualifications.

5. McRobbie and Garber (*Working-Class Girls and the Culture of Femininity*) argue that girls are subject to the subordination of both their class and their gender.

(a) Their destiny as adults is to do low-status work, since they are discouraged from achieving high qualifications.
(b)They share an anti-school culture and may gain status from deviant activities.

6. Willis (*How Working-Class Kids Get Working-Class Jobs*) showed how anti-school sub-cultures are carried over into the work place. He noted how 'the boy's culture provided criteria for the kind of work the lad is destined for, basically manual and semi-skilled work. Because these criteria arise from a culture, and because the school-based culture also has profound similarities and continuities with the work place . . . once the kids get onto the factory floor . . . they feel at home.'

7. Cashmore (*Rastaman*) discusses the significance of youth cultures for black youth, especially involvement in the Rastafarian movement.

One of the most important factors relating to every example of youth culture is music (jazz; rock; New Wave) and for black youth in particular, it is reggae music. This stems from the sub-culture of Jamaica and is a product of deprivation and poverty. The music grew out of a specific context of slavery and colonialisation. The music makes constant reference to these roots, together with biblical sources. The slave-owners had used Christianity as a method of control.

Rastafarianism, founded by Marcus Garvey, uses biblical prophecy to show that when the Millennium comes there will be peace and brotherhood among blacks and whites. The saviour is the late Haile Selassie of Ethiopia and the promise is that the Rastas will one day return to their cultural home in Africa.

These ideals are expressed through reggae music:

(a) Both the music and religion are important for black youth because they provide a source of popular nationalism, an identity with Jamaica.
(b) It is a source of black consciousness and takes them back to their African roots.
(c) It has a social significance in that it is the religion and the music of poor blacks.

The music therefore has a strong ideological content, although it has developed into a highly commercial sound which nevertheless reaffirms and resurrects the culture of Jamaica for the audience. It has been described as a dialogue between Black Africans and dispossessed Jamaicans.

Theories of middle-class youth cultures

Functionalist theorists have been criticised for presenting too generalised an account of youth culture and for failing to consider the significance of class and gender differences.

Theorists of working-class sub-cultures have been criticised for concentrating on a small section of working-class youth whose behaviour is atypical of the majority.

Less attention has been paid to middle-class sub-cultures. (Marxists would argue that this is because it is not the middle-class radicals who will be the agencies of revolutionary change.)

1. Marcuse (*One-Dimensional Man*) argued that society is a confidence trick offering high standards of material comfort in exchange for slavery to the industrial machine. The only people likely to rebel against this are the unbribed poor, racial minorities and the young. Marcuse argues that violence lurks behind the liberal façade. He provided intellectual justification for student movements which advocated revolutionary change. His appeal was to the radical university students of the 1960s, who staged major demonstrations to try to raise people's level of political consciousness.

2. Touraine (*The French Student Movement, May 1968*) argues that the world-wide student movement arose from symptoms of post-war confusion. It reflected crises within the capitalist states in which grievances had to be aired by those with access to the greatest privileges in it: young, middle-class students. He claims that its significance in France was that it presented a challenge to the ruling classes since there was no longer a consensus about the future.

3. Frith ('The Punk Bohemians') argues that punk culture was the product of middle-class art students, not working-class dole queues. It was not a product of simple commercial manipulation; rather it has a firm place in the history of radical British Art. He says that art schools have always been the basic source of British youth cultural symbols. They played their part in punk, providing key musicians, gigs, audiences and fashion. They have always encouraged students to question and innovate.

4. Rosak (*The Making of a Counter Culture*) suggests that in the 1960s an attempt developed among some middle-class young people to produce a counter-culture opposed to that of the technological age in which they lived.

(a) It was compared by him to the Romantic Movement in the nineteenth century. They both sought to oppose dehumanising influences on social life.
(b) In the new youth culture (which came to be identified with the 'flower-power hippy movement'), members experimented with drugs and new kinds of religious experience.
(c) It was was based on 'creativity, opposition to the impersonal forces of technology, and on a spiritual vision, making for a new heaven on earth'.
(d) It was criticised by Wilson (*Youth Culture and the Universities*), who said it was a revolution by urbanites who were clearer about what they were against than about what they were for. He says their life style was a reaction against middle-aged, middle-class values. They were largely a political personal revolutionaries: 'The millennium of the socialist society was too remote for their enthusiasm'. Their literary spokesmen were in *Oz*, *Time Out* and *Rolling Stone*.

5. A Survey in 1988 by Ann Holt sampled 1400 young people. She found that there was emphasis on industrial enterprise and high reward in work, among both boys and girls. She concludes that the entrepreneurial urge is not particularly middle-class or overwhelming masculine. It appeals to a section of both sexes hoping to enter skilled manual jobs.

6. The view that it was middle-class youth which provided the richest of the literary aspects of youth cultures dates from the late 1950s when *On the Road* by Jack Kerouac was published. It was described by the *New York Times* as 'a book likely to represent a generation'. It described the experiences and attitudes of a restless group of young people 'mad to live, mad to talk, mad to be saved'. They were members of the 'beat' generation (beat meant beatitude: a state of being emptied out, receptive to everything and impatient with trivialities).

Conclusions

(a) Some of the earliest analyses of youth cultures in the 1950s and 1960s saw them as classless. It was functional for all young people to indulge in a period of experimentation prior to adulthood.
(b) Later, delinquent sub-cultures have been identified as predominantly working-class phenomena. They are seen as forms of resistance to the dominance of middle-class norms and values.
(c) Middle-class cultures have been seen as emerging in parallel to those of working-class youth, but promoting different values.
   (i) Frith says that middle-class cultures were radicalised by working-class youth behaviour.
   (ii) They tended to have a stronger political and literary content and were based around different musical tastes.
   (iii) They also advocated a more self-conscious counter-culture.
   (iv) They may also have been the seed-bed for groups such as the ecology movement; women's rights; gay rights; agit-prop theatre groups; animal rights, etc. They argued that existing power structures could be attacked and attitudes changed.
(d) The recessions of the 1980s and 1990s in which there was increasing youth unemployment may have widened the gap between the cultural values of different youth groups.

■ Critically examine the sub-cultural theory of youth culture.

Sub-cultural theory first appeared in USA in the 1950s. Explanations were presented to account for the emergence of teenage delinquent groups, using ethnography and observations (see page 26).

1. The theory said that such behaviour was:

(a) Normal, and determined by cultural norms.
(b) It was predominantly group behaviour.
(c) The cultural norms of fighting, quest for excitement, etc. satisfied focal concerns relating to status, power and so on.

2. In Britain, theorists added a Marxist perspective and emphasised the significance of class factors to examine the relationship between sub-cultures and society. Hall *et al.* (*Resistance through Ritual*) argue:

(a) Deviant youth cultures are primarily working-class in membership.
(b) They explain these cultures in terms of their styles.
(c) These styles (of dress, attitudes, musical tastes, etc.) represent:
   (i) gestures of rebellion against parents;
   (ii) a means of confrontation with middle-class authority figures (teachers, police, etc.) This rejection was essential to their meaning;
   (iii) deviant styles and behaviour are a visible, public and collective commitment to resistance. Their shared problems include those of marginal status, lack of power, economic security, etc.: and
   (iv) the significance of the cultures is that they mark out territory and focus on key occasions of

social interaction: the disco, the weekend, the match.

(d) The sub-cultural styles help members make sense of the impacts of social change in which the working class experienced fragmentation in their traditional work place solidarity, community and family life. The solution was to develop a form of group leisure in a world of competing values.

(e) S. Cohen described these as 'ritual solutions to cultural contradictions'; their challenge of dominant ideas provokes moral panics.

Points of criticism

1. Redhead (*Social Studies Review*) argues that the sub-cultural theory has not been useful or appropriate in the analysis of some recent youth cultural movements. He considers its application to the examination of 'Acid House' or 'Rave' culture of the late 1980s. He argues that:

(i) Some youth cultures (such as Acid House) are a part of a long history of casual (and insignificant) style. This (like Punk before it) is a hybrid of media manufacture and authentic desire to adopt oppositional values.

(ii) Many youth cultural movements (especially those closely related to pop stars such as David Bowie and Gary Glitter) were the products of media manufacture. Yet sub-cultural theory assumes that there is some authentic meaning behind the surface phenomena which is distorted by manufactured press and TV images and their use of stereotypes.

(iii) Redhead argues that they are wrong to assume that this meaning can be understood by 'looking beneath the shimmering mediascape' in order to interpret the style and the symbols attached to it, since there is none there.

(iv) For him it does not constitute a new sub-culture. It arose from questions of legality relating to venues of youth pleasure in the night-time economy of major cities, and the ensuing public concern.

2. Frith questions the view emanating from sub-cultural theory that deviant youth cultures represent resistance to existing power structures. He asks:

(i) Whether Teds, Skinheads, Rockers, Punks, etc. were more politically conscious than their 'normal' peers?

(ii) How the theory accounts for the many young people who are deviant but who do not publicise their revolt by turning it into a public style.

(iii) In what ways do bizarre clothes, hair-styles, etc. achieve political resistance?

3. Feminists (for example, McRobbie) argue that females seem to be largely excluded from the sub-cultural theorists analysis, although they must surely be involved.

Conclusions

1. Hebdige (*Subculture: The Meaning of Style*) accepts that the interpretation of sub-culture is always in dispute, and says 'style is the arena in which the opposing definitions clash with most dramatic forces'.

(a) Such theorists argue that sub-cultures arise as a response to collectively experienced problems and rapidly changing events.

(b) The emergence of oppositional counter-cultures (such as those of New Age Travellers in the 1990s) represent challenges to bourgeois respectability.

(c) They argue that by describing, interpeting and deciphering the style and forms the cultures take, the impact of the history of social change since the Second World War can be understood; including, for example, the history of race relations, educational change, unemployment, loss of working-class communities, and changes in family structure.

2. Critics complain of the failure of the sub-cultural approach to:

(a) Explain the wide gap that must exist between the accounts that the actors might give and those of the theorists whose views are often based on limited research.

(b) Recognise the long history of casual style which has characterised youth cultures since the 1950s.

(c) Appreciate the individual joy among youth of dressing up, inventing an image and striking a pose.

Soccer Hooliganism

■ **Give a sociological account of soccer hooliganism. (ODLE)**

1. Marsh Rosser and Harre (*Rules of Disorder*) applied a range of techniques, including observation and interviews, in their analysis of violence in football grounds. They say that 'we have come to see it through the eyes of the people who take part in it'. They conclude that by sharing the excitement of the fans they are able to feel what it is like to be in that situation. The day-to-day existence of the fans is generally dull; the football match provides an experience worth talking about. It becomes a part of the group culture. Saturday becomes an important day of the week. There is a build-up of group activity and excitement. The crowd develops particular norms and rules of behaviour. To be a fan serves an important function. It provides an identity and dictates the rules governing forms of aggression. Ritualising aggression becomes a way of channelling it in a comparatively safe way. They do not excuse the behaviour but show how events can be construed in other ways. There are rules of disorder.

2. Robbins argues that by the mid-1960s the first generation of ex-urban youth were expressing dissatisfaction with the shortage of public leisure amenities and were seeking ways of achieving the kind of group solidarity they had known as children. Communities and neighbourhoods had been lost in the process of redevelopment. One of the strongest ways of achieving solidarity was in support for football teams. These became the focal points for exiled teenagers. Around spectacular match-day activities a whole under life grew up, involving group allegiances and territorial alliances. Robbins suggests that 'if you are out of work, a student failure with little to do and nowhere to go, there is a great appeal in joining up in a supra-local army with a national reputation'.

3. Seabrook (*Landscapes of Poverty*) says that soccer hooliganism may be a rather tormented reassertion of needs that may have found an earlier outlet in a sense of class identity, which on the whole has always been very temperate in Britain, with its reasonable labour movement, its readiness to compromise and its modest claims to a share in the country's riches.

4. Dahrendorf (in a letter to *The Times*, 1985) says that in some places soccer has turned from a working-class game into an under-class game. This is a group which combines desolate living conditions and lack of traditional bonds, even of class, with low skills and hopeless employment prospects. The result is cynicism towards the official values of a society bent on work and order.

5. Pearson (*A History of Respectable Fears*) has said that because we are frightened of violence we find it hard to comprehend. We are subject to the idea that violence is some kind of epidemic sweeping the country like a pestilence. 'We imagine some earlier golden age in which the streets were safe and a Dixon of Dock Green pounded every beat . . . In fact the belief that we live in a mounting crime wave is likely to do with the changes in the reporting of crime and the attitudes of the courts.'

6. Redhead and McLaughlin ('Soccer's Style Wars') describe how contemporary troublemakers at football grounds have been increasingly concerned about group style and structure. They dress in expensive clothes and travel to matches in luxury coaches or by inter-city express trains. They adopt such names as Inter-City Firm, Anti-personnel Firm, Main Line Crew. They have no visible club identification or chant, which makes them difficult to identify or detect. These regional style wars have resulted in increasing levels of organised violence both inside and outside the ground. They have become a more serious problem since the groups are not subject to the 'the rules of disorder' described by Marsh. As a result there could be more serious injuries in less ritualistic patterns of behaviour.

7. In the early 1990s the problem of football hooliganism appeared to decline as a moral panic. There was less media coverage of disturbances, although the sport remained an important leisure interest for a high proportion of young males:

70 per cent of the 15–17 age group attended matches in 1987
52 per cent of the 16–17 age group attended matches in 1988
34 per cent of the 17–18 age group attended matches in 1989

During the 1990/91 season attendances rose for the third consecutive time. In 1992 a study by the London Business School found that only ten League Clubs consistently made a profit without endangering the quality of their team. Others required wealthy patrons or luck for success. The implications are that inequalities between the clubs could reduce interest in the sport, lead to disillusionment and promote more aggressive attitudes among supporters.

Conclusions

The question of football hooliganism can be viewed from various perspectives:

1. *Phenomenologists* argue that we make sense of behaviour by categorising it. We distinguish between different types of event by our definitions and interpretations. Pearson (*Hooligans*) shows how youth has been seen as a 'social problem' for more than a century.

(a) The problem of deviance among youth can be seen as a projection on to the young of adult concerns. The labellers (or witnesses of 'hooliganism') become of as much interest to the sociologist as the actors. It is they who construct and interpret the behaviour as deviant.
(b) Negative labels are more easily attached to some behaviours than others. Football supporters are easier targets than undergraduates. But in 1992 Oxford University put an end to post-examination celebrations after four people were injured. In 1986 rules were introduced to stop champagne-spraying and egg-throwing in public places. Such activities would usually be reported as 'high spirits'.
(c) Hebdige notes how reports in the media of sub-cultural activity make it both more and less exotic than it actually is. The media can trivialise youth cultures or sensationalise them. They select the latter approach in their coverage of football hooligans. The hooligans are said to act in ways that are beyond the bounds of common decency. The media sensitise the public to the typical offender and assist in the process of deviance amplification (see page 122).

2. *Conflict structuralists*, using sub-cultural theory (for example, P. Cohen) would focus on the ways in which many young working-class fans:

(a) Seek means of expressing their independence and their power.
(b) Utilise their free time to make gestures of defiance against grievances about which they feel strongly (their school, work, their team, the opposition, etc.).
(c) Defend their territory, both real and symbolic.
(d) Are preoccupied with territory and masculine values which may lead them into conflicts with the police and the public.
(e) Are seeking to recover a lost sense of working-class community.

Suggested Reading

Works noted in this chapter

P. Aries (1962) *Centuries of Childhood*, Jonathan Cape
V. Barnouw (1979) *Anthropology*, The Dorsey Press
J. Brown (1963) 'A Cross-Cultural Study of Female Initiation Rites', *American Anthropologist*, 65:837–53
E. Cashmore (1979) *Rastaman.*, Unwin
J. Clarke (1976) 'The Skinheads and the Magical Recovery of Working-Class Community' in S. Hall *Resistance Through Rituals*, Hutchinson
D. Hargreaves (1975) *Deviance in Classrooms*, RKP
D. Hebdige (1981) *Subculture. The Meaning of Style*, Methuen
P. Corrigan (1981) *Schooling the Smash Street Kids*, Macmillan
S. Eisenstadt (1956) *From Generation to Generation*, Free Press

S. Frith (1978) 'The Punk Bohemians', *New Society* (9 March)
S. Hall (1976) *Resistance Through Rituals*, Hutchinson
H. Marcuse (1972) *One-Dimensional Man*, Abacus
Marsh, et al. (1978) *Rules of Disorder*, RKP
B. Martin (1983) *A Sociology of Contemporary Cultural Change*, Blackwell
W. Miller (1962) *Lower-Class Culture*, in Wolfgang *et al.* (see p. 185)
A. McRobbie and Garber (1978) *Working-Class Girls and the Culture of Femininity*, Centre for Contemporary Cultural Studies
F. Musgrave (1965) *Youth and the Social Order*, Methuen
T. Parsons (1964) *Essays in Sociological Theory*, The Free Press
G. Pearson (1983) *Hooligans, A History of Respectable Fears*, Macmillan
S. Redhead and McLaughlin (1985) 'Soccer's Style Wars', *New Society* (16 August)
S. Redhead (1991) 'Rave Off: Youth, Subcultures and the Law', *Social Studies Review* (January) Vol. 6, No. 3
T. Rosak (1971) *The Making of a Counter Culture*, Faber
R. Rosser and C. Harris (1965) *The Family and Social Change*, RKP
A. Ryan (1985) *New Society*
J. Touraine (1970) *The French Student Movement, May 1968*, Penguin
S. Taylor (1992) 'Measuring Child Abuse', *Sociology Review*, Vol. 1, No. 3
P. Willis (1977) *How Working-Class Kids Get Working-Class Jobs*, Saxon House
B. Wilson (1970) *Youth Culture and the Universities*, RKP

Works for further reading

J. Barrett (1977) *The Rastafarians*, Heinemann.
H. Becker (1963) *The Outsiders*, Free Press.
M. Brake (1980) *The Sociology of Youth Culture* RKP.
A. Cohen (1955) *Delinquent Boys*, Free Press.
S. Cohen and I. Young (1973) *The Manufacture of News*, Constable.
N. Cohn (1970) *Awopbobaloobob Alopbamboom*, Paladin.
S. Cosgrave (1989) 'Acid Enterprises', *New Statesman and Society* (13 October).
M. Davis (1991) *City of Quartz*, Verso.
Eisen (1969) *The Age of Rock*, Random House.
S. Frith (1976) *The Sociology of Rock*, Constable.
S. Frith (1983) *Sound Effects*, Constable.
S. Frith (1985) 'The Sociology of Youth' in M. Haralambos, *Sociology New Directions*, Causeway.
G. Greer (1970) *The Female Eunuch*, Paladin.
J. Kerouac (1957) *On the Road*, André Deutsch.
D. Lain (1969) 'The Decline and Fall of British Rhythm and Blues' in Eisen.
D. Leonard (1980) *Sex and Generation*, Tavistock.
A. McRobbie (1978) *Women Take Issue*, Hutchinson.
G. Melly (1972) *Revolt into Style*, Penguin.
G. Mungham (1976) *Working Class Youth Culture*, RKP.
J. Parker and J. Burchill (1978) *The Boy Looked at Johnny*, Pluto Press.
N. Polsky (1971) *Hustlers, Beats and Others*, Penguin.
D. Robbins and P. Cohen (1978) *Knuckle Sandwich*, Penguin.
H. Thompson (1967) *Hells Angels*, Penguin.
D. Willis (1978) *Profane Culture*, RKP.

Self-test Questions

Study the following extracts from newspapers and answer the questions below.

Item A

YOUNG people today have terrible PR. Is their public image one of caring concern, industry and responsibility? It is not. They are generally portrayed as unruly, selfish and a menace to society, the sort of people you'd cross the street to avoid, particularly if they are hanging around street corners in groups. Government ministers portray them as degenerate and use them to illustrate the dreadful fate of a society that turns away from the hell-fire of biblical sanctions.

Yet who would be a young person today? A report published yesterday by the British Youth Council paints a bleak picture of life for people aged between 16 and 25. Poverty, homelessness and a lack of jobs, education and training opportunities are increasing for this age group. Unemployment, for example, is running at 16 per cent for the under-25s compared to the national average of nine per cent; young people now represent 32 per cent of the out-of-work population in the UK. According to Low Pay Unit figures, in May 1992 18 to 20-year-olds earned only 53 per cent of average earnings compared with 61 per cent in 1979.

Yet only 22 per cent of young people out of work can get any state benefits. Income support for most 16 and 17-year-olds was abolished on the grounds that youth training places would be provided for them. The Government, however, has failed to honour this promise and consequently many young people now have no job, no training place and no benefit.

According to Youthaid, there are now 103,000 unemployed 16 and 17-year-olds, of whom 80,000 are getting no benefit at all on the assumption that, in Mrs Thatcher's words, they had to stand on their own two feet or go back to mother. Unfortunately, there often isn't a mother or a family life worth the name to go back to. Not surprisingly, more than 150,000 16-19-year-olds are thought to become homeless every year, 41 per cent of them having been in care. Alcohol and drug abuse are on the increase; most young adults classify themselves as regular drinkers and nearly 20 per cent of 17 to 19-year-olds have used cannabis. Someone under 25 calls the Samaritans every four minutes, and more and more young people are killing themselves.

Source: An article by Melanie Phillips in *The Guardian*, 10 July 1992, p. 20.

Item B

THE AVERAGE British 16-year-old drinks alcohol at least once a week and eats only cereal or toast before going to school, according to a major survey of Britain's youth.

In addition, teenage love is growing younger with nearly one in three 11-year-olds claiming to have a regular boy or girlfriend.

In the survey by the Health Education Authority's schools health education unit at Exeter University, 32.6 per cent of boys and 31.2 per cent of girls aged 11 to 12 said they had a regular partner. By the age of 16, the number rose to 41 per cent for girls against 31 for boys.

Shortlived relationships

The survey, which questioned 18,002 pupils at 88 schools last year, found 22 per cent of the boys and 14.6 per cent of 11 year old girls said their relationships had lasted more than a year, against 14 per cent of boys and 20 per cent of girls in the 16 year old group.

Nevertheless, most youngsters said their relationships were shortlived, with between a third and a half saying their current relationship had lasted only a few months.

Some 51.9 per cent of 16 year old girls and 54.3 per cent of boys of the same age feel uneasy when meeting new people of the opposite sex, while 9.4 per cent of boys and nine per cent of girls feel very uneasy.

Source: Extract from an article by Clare Hargreaves in the *Daily Telegraph*, 6 November 1987, p. 12.

1. Examine Item A.
   (i) Discuss the concept of a stereotype in relation to the comments made.
   (ii) Discuss some of the dangers involved in using stereotypes to assess behaviour.
   (iii) Tabulate the data in the article to make them clear.
   (iv) Consider the views of Clarke and Miller, (see pages 190, 192) that working-class youth cultures inevitably differ from those of middle-class youth and that patterns of behaviour involving unemployed youths on street corners are a means of resisting middle-class values.

2. Examine Item B.
   (i) Tabulate the data presented in the article to make them clear.
   (ii) Consider the Functionalist view that adolescent patterns of culture and behaviour are normal ways of growing into adulthood among people of all classes.
   (iii) Functionalists have been criticised for presenting an over-generalised view of youth behaviour. Discuss this point in relation to the survey.
   (iv) Discuss some of the problems which the researchers are likely to have encountered in the course of this large-scale study.
   (v) Which issues in Items A and B may indicate that some aspects of youthful behaviour could be potentially dysfunctional to social stability?

3. Using the points in the newspaper extracts above and other data, discuss the view that it is likely that youth cultures vary between classes according to age and the specific types of problem faced by them while growing up in contemporary Britain.

15

THE COMMUNITY

The questions which arise on this topic include the following areas:

1. The community:
   (a) Problems of definition.
   (b) Loss of community.
2. The urban–rural continuum debate:
   (a) The types of distinction that have been suggested.
   (b) Their validity.
3. The city.
4. The suburbs.
5. The distribution of population in cities:
   (a) The social factors; ecological models.
   (b) The processes that sustain segregation.

Community

- **Assess the notion that community has become too much of an overworked and value-laden term to be of any objective social scientific use. (ULSEB)**
- **A spirit of community depends on shared values and interests. As cities become socially mixed, maintenance of community spirit becomes impossible. Discuss. (UODLE)**

Sociologists have been interested in the concept of community since the discipline was established in the 1830s. This is because the earliest writers were concerned about the nature and effect of social change; in particular what happened when a society changed from rural to urban in structure.

Subsequently, many sociologists have developed *typologies* to illustrate the differences between types of society, and theories to explain the processes of change. The result has been a range of definitions and models which some critics complain has caused more confusion than clarification.

1. Tönnies (*Gemeinschaft und Gesellschaft*, 1887). He used an *ideal type* based on Gemeinschaft (community) and Gesellschaft (association) and said that the trend in human history was a movement from community to association. He described typical relationships related to each:

Gemeinschaft

1. Intimate.
2. Enduring.
3. Personal.
4. Based on ascribed status.
5. Based in a homogeneous culture.
6. Enforced by moral custodians (e.g. church; family).
7. Upheld by traditional values.

The result is a strong sense of territoriality; a sentimental attachment to a beloved place.

Gesellschaft

1. Few important primary relationships.
2. Contractual and calculative.
3. Impersonal.
4. Based on achieved status.
5. Based in heterogeneous culture.
6. There is no widely agreed source of moral values.
7. There are no sustaining traditional values.

The result is no sense of attachment to place; increased isolation; anonymity and alienation.

He sees the *loss of community* resulting from the effects of industrialisation, urbanisation and the growth of capitalism.

2. Durkheim (*The Social Division of Labour*) also discussed this issue but used different concepts. He described a move from simple mechanical societies to complex

Mechanical	Organic
1. Simple, traditional society.	1. Complex, modern, industrial.
2. Rural.	2. Urban.
3. Little division of labour.	3. High degree of division of labour.
4. Homogeneous culture, population.	4. Heterogeneous culture and population.
5. Cohesion based on shared norms.	5. Cohesion based on contract.
6. Law based on repression.	6. Law based more on restitution.

organic types. He was concerned with the question of social order in times of change: how can *social solidarity* be maintained where the pattern of life is subject to rapid change? His answer was the social division of labour. This helps to bind people more closely into their society since it increases their dependence on each other.

Later research, especially in the USA, revealed the problems of clearly defining the concept of community. Debate centred on the question of whether community implies the existence of a basic unit or structure which can be objectively defined and located. Some believed that it did, others, more recently, see it as a more flexible and less easily defined concept.

Community as a basic unit

1. Redfield (*The Little Community*) describes community as having four key qualities:

(i) distinctiveness;
(ii) small size;
(iii) self-sufficient economy; and
(iv) homogeneity of inhabitants.

This has been criticised because such groups are impossible to find in the real world. If communities are identifiable units then everyone ought to know to which community they belong. In fact, most people can identify several, which may overlap.

2. McIver and Page (*Society, an Introductory Analysis*) define community as a term we apply to a pioneer settlement, a village, a city, a tribe or a nation: 'Wherever the members of any group, small or large, live together in such a way that they share . . . the basic conditions of a common life, we call that group a community.' The problem with this definition is that it also emphasises a limiting boundary within which a community is formed, whereas other writers prefer a wider interpretation.

3. Wirth (*Urbanism as a Way of Life*) argues that historically, community has been an expression that emphasised the unity of common life of a people or of mankind; and that community must have a territorial base. It must be possible to locate the centre and boundaries of community. The loss of community has resulted from the rapid growth of urban life, which introduces qualitatively new forms of social existence.

Community as a more flexible concept

1. Arensberg and Kimball (*Family and Community in Ireland*) say that in Ireland the rural community is not defined by a geographical area. 'Kin are scattered . . . the farmer attends church in one parish and sends his children to school in another . . . They have a variety of interests or sets of interests and they are liable to pursue them within a series of different communities which do not necessarily add up to a clearly defined whole.'

2. Seeley *et al.* (*Crestwood Heights*) describe a prosperous upper-middle-class suburb of Toronto. The adult males in the population spend little time in the area since they work in the city. Yet they describe the area as their community, 'because of the relationships that exist between people . . . revealed in the functioning of the institutions they have created'. Participation in the community is largely related to the central life interest of child-rearing.

3. Durant (*Watling: A Survey of a New Housing Estate*) points out that community life flourished while new residents fought against external authority, 'but might perish when the battles for gardens, tarmacadam and street lights had been won'. Conflict acted 'as a stimulus for establishing new rules, norms and institutions'.

Comment

(a) Such studies suggest that communities are not necessarily 'basic units', but consist of overlapping groups.
(b) They involve social relationships and these can change according to the factors giving rise to the sense of community.
(c) The source of community may not be harmony, but conflict.
(d) Redfield, Wirth, etc. said that communities could not exist in amorphous urban and suburban areas.
(e) Pahl (*Patterns of Urban Life*) argues that the meaningful social area which people inhabit depends on class, life-cycle characteristics, length of residence, career pattern, etc.

Conclusions

There is no doubt that the word community has been subject to a vast range of definitions and interpretations:

1. Hillery reviewed ninety-four definitions and stated 'beyond the recognition that people are involved in community, there is little agreement about the usage of the term.'

2. Wirth (*Towards a Definition . . .*) has said 'community . . . has been used with an abandon reminiscent of poetic licence'.

3. Dennis (*The Popularity of the Neighbourhood Community Idea*) said 'in the vocabulary of the social scientist there must be few words used with either the frequency or looseness of 'the community'.

4. Pahl (*Patterns of Urban Life*) says that 'the word community serves more to confuse than illuminate the situation in Britain today'. He suggests a solution to the problem is to use the phrase 'a locality social system'. This is related to the local distribution of power, status and facilities. These are open to empirical investigation and would allow more specific statements about patterns of social relations to be made and more useful conclusion to be drawn.

The Rural–Urban Continuum Debate

■ **What contrasts have been drawn by sociologists between urban and rural societies?**

In their attempts to understand how patterns of behaviour change in different social situations, sociologists have endeavoured to construct systems of classification. Some of the early writers developed ideal type models (for example, Tonnies and Durkheim). These theories of contrast led to the view that where people live influences how they live. The work of a number of American sociologists starting in the 1920s developed the concept of rural–urban distinctions. Empirical studies were undertaken to show that these existed and significantly affected patterns of life.

More recently attempts have been made to construct a continuum to show the different stages in social life between rural at one end and urban at the other. The continuum is used to show the differences in social life as rural areas become infected with urban values.

Criticisms have been made of both approaches by sociologists in recent years.

Theories of contrast: polar types

1. Redfield (*The Little Community; Folk Society*) claimed that there are clear-cut differences between urban and rural societies. Community is an identifiable unit found only at the rural end.

2. Wirth (*Urbanism as a Way of Life*) claimed that:

(a) Urbanism characterises modern society.
(b) Urbanism is unnatural and breaks with tradition.
(c) Modern culture is urban culture.
(d) The city is the centre of innovation.
(e) Urbanism has changed every aspect of social life.
(f) The city and the country are two opposite poles.

He said that urbanism has distinctive characteristics:

(a) The size of population:
  (i) there is more differentiation by class and social area;
  (ii) utilitarian relationships prevail based on contract; and
  (iii) anomie develops.

(b) Increased density of population:
  (i) social and economic differences between people are accentuated;
  (ii) there is greater competition for scarce resources;
  (iii) there is more social friction, overcrowding and crime; and
  (iv) there is the 'lonely crowd' effect, in which people feel isolated and alone in a crowded city.

(c) Heterogeneity of population:
  (i) it is more varied because of the increasing division of labour;
  (ii) there is a more complex class structure; and
  (iii) there is a fluid mass society in which there is more mobility.

His conclusions are that urban life has many negative qualities which can be contrasted with the more positive features of rural life.

Points of criticism

(i) Many empirical studies indicate that theories of contrast are mistaken because there are many examples which do not fit the predictions:

Examples of urban studies

1. Seeley *et al.* (*Crestwood Heights*). This study shows how an 'interest' community existed in a suburb.
2. Willmott and Young (*Family and Kinshik*). They found *Gemeinschaft* relationships existing in an urban area.
3. Gans (*The Levittowners*) found people living on housing estates experiencing a sense of community which they found satisfying.

Examples of rural studies

1. Lewis (*Life in a Mexican Village*) went back to Tepoztlan, a village studied by Redfield, on which he based his findings. Lewis found class conflict, anomie and tension where Redfield found the opposite.
2. Littlejohn (*Westrigg*) found social disharmony and class divisions in a remote Cheviot village.
3. Weightman (Small-Town Life) says that Lewes is not one community, but several mutually exclusive social groups.

(ii) Pahl (*Readings in Urban Sociology*) says 'for a long time polar typologies . . . served as justification for . . . the uncritical glorifying of old-fashioned rural life'. He questions whether there are fundamental differences between urban and rural.

■ **Some sociologists have constructed a continuum based on various characteristics of urban and rural life: how useful is this concept?**

1. Frankenberg (*Communities in Britain*) says 'towns and cities make more sense if they are seen as part of an evolutionary process in which the progression from a simple to a diversified technology is accompanied by certain sociological changes'.

He reviews studies of communities in a rough order of increasing economic complexity:

(a) truly rural;
(b) the village in the country;
(c) the town that is a village;

(d) small town communities in cities; and
(e) urban housing estates.

From his analysis he ends with a typology based on some of the key differences between the polar extremes. Some of these include:

Urban (less rural)

1. Association.
2. Overlapping role relationships.
3. Diverse economy.
4. Organic solidarity.
5. Loose-knit networks.

Rural

1. Community.
2. Multiple role relationships.
3. Simple economy.
4. Mechanical solidarity.
5. Close-knit networks.

2. Southall (*An Operational Theory of Role*) suggests a continuum could be based on social role differentiation:

(a) number of persons in a particular area;
(b) type of role played;
(c) inequalities in role distribution;
(d) number of roles played over a period of time; and
(e) number of roles an individual perceives as being open to him.

Points of criticism

1. Benet (The Ideology of the Urban–Rural Continuum) says that this continuum was a figment of the imagination, but it helped to develop an anti-urban mentality.

2. Pahl (*Patterns of Urban Life*) says of Frankenburg that 'he asserts rather than explains by convincing argument'.

3. Pahl (*Urbs in Rure*) says that his study of commuter villages indicates that they do not fit easily into the urban–rural continuum. The commuters were frequently resented by local manual workers and this caused a breach in community feeling.

Conclusions

1. Studies from other areas of the world cast doubt on the usefulness of the concept of the continuum. African studies referred to by Pahl indicate that tribal and urban can exist side by side, with migrant workers moving between the two worlds. In the city they wear Western clothes and work as clerks; in the village they change into traditional clothes and behave as villagers.

2. Banton (*Social Alignment and Identity in a West African City*) argues that there are 'urban villages' in Africa where urban values have permeated the countryside. He says that the rural–urban continuum must remain open to empirical investigation.

3. Pahl concludes that 'I find little evidence of a rural–urban continuum. More important is a distinction between the "local" and "the national"; the "large-scale" and the "small-scale" society'. He suggests that both the theories of contrast and the theories of a continuum are no longer fruitful. He suggests they can be largely abandoned in favour of concentration on the processes of change; more comparative work on patterns of community leadership and further analysis of the concepts of role and social networks.

The City

■ **Discuss the contribution of urban sociologists to our understanding of the city.**

Note: In answering the question you need to be aware of areas of debate: Pahl has said, 'the city cannot be defined and so neither can urban sociology'. This is because the subject matter for analysis is so diverse and interrelated with other disciplines in the social sciences. But it can be taken more generally to refer to sociological research which focuses especially on life in large towns and cities.

Slattery has said that the urban revolution, the movement into large cities from rural areas, has both altered *where* people live and *how* people live. The effects have been:

(a) shifts of population;
(b) the development of new environments;
(c) the growth of new social relationships and bureaucratic structures;
(d) the emergence of new ways of life;
(e) some possible advantages of city life are that they become centres of government, law and culture; and
(f) some possible disadvantages are that they become places of isolation, alienation, congestion and social problems, lacking community.

The city has become the centre and focal point of much sociological research to discover the effects of the changes on people's behaviour and to see how far the images of the city are true or false.

The views of theorists

1. *The Founding Fathers*

(a) Durkheim (see also page 199) feared the transition from rural to industrial would intensify the problems of anomie, since there were fewer forces of integration.
(b) Marx saw the city as a place of progress in which class consciousness would be heightened as social differences became more apparent. It would be the arena for social revolutions.
(c) Weber saw the development of the city from its mediaeval origins as the cradle of modern society; it required the emergence of a rational bureaucracy, a new merchant class and new social structures.
(d) Tönnies saw the city as the death of community.
(e) Simmel saw the city as a liberating place which freed the individual from traditional constraints. It was the centre of complexity and calculative relations.

Critics have said that some of these views are ambiguous and others start from preconceived assumptions ('the city is bad').

2. *The Ecological and Community Studies Schools*

(a) Park wished to explain the underlying laws of urban life. The city was seen to be like a social organism with a life of its own and in which there was a struggle for space, the most powerful obtaining the most favourable parts.
(b) Burgess developed the concentric zone theory which described how different parts of cities were inhabited by different social groups. The inner city was identified as a source of social problems.
(c) Wirth focused on the cultural factors which shaped city life. He said its characteristics were those of size, density and heterogeneity of population. These promote social segregation and impersonality. It becomes the source of dangerous phenomena. People become alienated as urbanism becomes a way of life.

Such writers helped develop the urban–rural continuum debate (see page 201).

Critics have said that:

(i) Chicago in the 1920s (the city on which the theories were based) was not typical. There are many which have similar characteristics but in which rates of disorganisation are low.
(ii) Gans argued that the key factors in determining ways of life were social class and stage in the family cycle.
(iii) The basic framework of the community studies school was seen to be based on an anti-urban bias.
(iv) Studies revealed the existence of community in the city (see page 201).

3. *Radical perspectives*

By the 1960s the Ecological and Community Studies Schools were under criticism. There was a move back to the Founding Fathers for new analysis. In particular there was an examination of the distribution of power in cities.

(a) *Neo-Weberians* such as Rex and Moore examined the way the housing market operated. They analysed the city in terms of power, class and conflict.

Critics have said that the type of house a person occupies is the *effect* of their position in the social hierarchy, not the *cause*. They do not identify which people exercise the most significant power nor how they come to control the distribution of urban resources.

(b) *Neo-Marxists* such as Castells examined particular issues, such as urban riots.

(i) Castells saw them in terms of problems of urban planning, mal-distribution of wealth, housing, education and jobs. Increasing class consciousness led to politicisation and militancy of ordinary people.
(ii) Harvey (*Social Justice and the City*) explained such events in terms of the activities of property developers and speculators, who do not invest in housing but in office blocks and shopping centres. It is the internal contradictions of the economic system that cause urban crises.
(iii) Jewison (*Sociology Review*) argues that capitalism not only creates cities, it also destroys them. There is constant demand for new markets, technologies, commodities, etc. This results in great disruption and change. He describes three phases of city development:

(i) *The industrial city*, which in Britain developed between about 1800 and 1880, in which new urban ways of life appeared. There was little government planning or control.
(ii) *The metropolis*, which occurred between about 1880 and 1960. There was increased centralisation of economic and political institutions; growing bureaucracies and managerial intervention. There were more specialised geographical areas in the city for industry, housing, etc., more property speculation and a decline in working-class communities.
(iii) *The megalopolis*, which developed from about 1970. This arose when the city began to sprawl as a decentralised urban area grew. The old central areas began to lose their appeal and the inner city areas decayed. Planning legislation was relaxed and ethnic groups became more isolated. One of the consequences was the riots which represented an explosive expression of the citizens' experience of capitalist cities.

Critics have said that such commentators use obscure language and vague definitions of protest movements, and overstate the significance of these in their explanations. Even socialist societies face crises in their cities from time to time.

Conclusions

1. In recent years the focus of attention has been the way power is obtained and used in cities.
2. Urban sociology has fragmented into a variety of themes and perspectives and has made use of the insights of other social sciences.
3. There have been new approaches and more specific areas of research. These include studies of:
   (a) *Urban politics and economic problems*: Saunders has examined urban voting patterns; the control of local councils; and the effects of policies of central government.
   (b) *Central government policies*: Hall has examined the impact of free market policies on the process of revitalising depressed areas of cities.
   (c) *Urban planning (procedures and outcomes)*: Donnison has examined the power of managers and their ideologies.
   (d) *Urban housing and environmental problems*: Lambert *et al.* have examined the power of those controlling the housing market, whose methods are often secretive and outside normal public knowledge.
   (e) *Urban households*: Pahl has noted that it is differences in household size and membership that is mainly responsible for the class divisions and inequalities that exist in cities. Gaps widen as unemployment increases; charity shops, car boot sales and other types of informal economy develop. Rex and Moore have looked at ethnic groups.
4. While the earlier assumptions and approaches to the study of the city have been rejected in recent years, many of the original methods of ethnography and

participant observation have been retained (for example, *Endless Pressure*, Pryce's study of Bristol).

5. There has been a move away from the view of the city as having a distinctive life of its own to the view that it reflects organisations and structures of wider society. The study becomes that of both the forces that go on inside it and those which affect it from outside.

The Suburbs

■ **Examine the sociological contribution to our understanding of suburbs.**

Although doubts have been cast on the view that there is a clear distinction between urban and rural lifestyles and relationships, some writers continue to search for a particular way of life associated with a specific type of social environment, especially in the suburbs.

1. People are initially attracted into cities because there are better opportunities for work, housing, welfare, entertainments, etc. Wirth argued that as the city develops and expands, the population becomes more socially segregated.

2. Burgess (*The Growth of the City*) helped to develop the *Ecology School* of analysis. He argued that population in a city is distributed according to specific factors, in particular 'the struggle for space'. There was competition for the scarce resources available. As a result, new suburbs became attractive to particular social groups. They were able to leave behind the poorest section in the *zone of transition*.

3. The suburbs also offered improved facilities: better living environments; new housing; better leisure opportunities, etc.

4. In recent years there has been an attempt to encourage industrial relocation into suburban areas, in special industrial estates. The effect has been to encourage the growth of the suburbs with new housing and shopping areas. It is this process which North (*Independent*, 17 April 1992) suggests is starting to destroy the rustic ideal for those who dislike the city and who aspire to the rural life. It is the price of suburbanising country life for those who want privacy without loneliness.

5. To try to counteract the decline of the city and especially the decline of the inner-city areas which have fallen into decay, governments have made more money available for redevelopment; for example, in 1984 Liverpool, with 20 per cent unemployment, received £140 million under an urban aid programme; £110 million from the Department of Trade, £134 million from the Docks and Harbour Board, and £96 million from the Manpower Services Commission (MSC).

6. Wirth predicted the major problems and dissatisfactions with urban life in his writings between 1928 and 1938. He argued that in urban areas people become increasingly depersonalised, alienated and isolated. Primary group relationships are replaced by impersonal secondary relations. He described the city as the prototype of mass society.

(a) The crowding of different types of people into small areas led to the development of separate neighbourhoods.
(b) Lack of physical distance between people led to the 'melting-pot' effect. This would lead to a breakdown of primary relationships.

7. Later, these ideas were taken up by Whyte (*The Organisation Man*). He believed that the suburbs attracted a particular type of person, who would quickly adapt to the new suburban lifestyle. This was likely to be the upwardly mobile white-collar worker. This was now seen to be the home of the modern *alienated man*.

Points of criticism

1. Berger (*Working-Class Suburb*) argues that a myth of suburbia has developed in the USA. This relates to the social and cultural ramifications that are believed to have been present in the exodus, often depicted as presenting 'a new way of life'. It is assumed:

(i) The suburbanites are the upwardly mobile.
(ii) They are predominantly young.
(iii) They are well educated.
(iv) They will lead a hyperactive social life.
(v) They have a maximum of similar interests.
(vi) They are increasingly 'classless'.
(vii) The central interest is child-rearing.
(viii) They are primarily commuters to work in cities.
(ix) There is a voting shift to the right.

He argues that if any of these are true they relate only to the middle-class suburbs. The reports on which they are based are highly selective. Large numbers of blue-collar workers are moving away from inner-city areas and on to estates, and there is no evidence to show that a shift in location is causing them to adopt a new way of life.

2. Gans ('Urbanism and Suburbanism as Ways of Life') produces a severe critique of the views of Wirth. Among the points he makes are:

(a) People do not necessarily adopt new ways of life in their move from city to suburb. The range of house prices attracts a range of different social types with different cultural values.
(b) Ways of life are not the result of living in a particular area but of economic factors; cultural values; stage of the life cycle, and social class. The latter two are particularly important.
(c) People's behaviour relates to the choices they have and the roles they play according to occupation, etc.
(d) He rejects the ecological model and emphasises the cultural factors. A young married couple are directed to modern suburban estates because they have little capital and high incomes. Therefore they can obtain a mortgage more easily.

Conclusion

(a) The effects of social change have always been of central interest to sociological analysts.
(b) They have used a variety of different types of social and geographical areas, both rural and urban, to test the theory that where a person lives influences how they live.
(c) In the 1960s, writers such as Gans and Berger began

to undermine the view that the suburbs imposed a specific type of lifestyle on their inhabitants, who were primarily in the young, upwardly mobile managerial class.
(d) They revealed widely varied suburban lifestyles which were shaped mainly by class and family cycle factors rather than by absorbing a mythical suburban culture.
(e) They concluded that it is fruitless to attempt to tie the patterns of social relationships to specific geographical areas.
(f) Dewey said (more cautiously) that such differences in behaviour patterns are real but relatively unimportant 'There is no such thing as urban culture or rural culture, but only various culture contents somewhere on the rural–urban continuum.'

The Distribution of Population in Cities

■ **What factors determine the pattern of residential segregation in cities? (UODLE)**

Sociologists have examined the spatial distribution of population in terms of the determining social factors and also the social processes which are inherent in the patterns. These two approaches are closely interrelated.

The social factors

1. The Ecological School of sociology was established in Chicago in the 1920s. This describes the relationship between people and their environment. Burgess described Chicago in terms of five zones, each of which had distinctive social and physical characteristics. There were particular subcultural values dominant in each. They concluded that the main factor that helped the appropriate people to decide to live in their appropriate areas was competition based on the struggle for space. (Those in the most powerful economic position controlled the most valuable parts of the city.)

2. Collison and Mogey (*Residence and Social Class in Oxford*) made use of three zones in their analysis. They described how the pattern of residential development spread out in wedges from the centre for historical and social reasons.

(i) Classes 1 and 2 were mainly represented in the northern wedge and also close to the city centre, where the university is situated.
(ii) Class 3's numbers increased when moving from the centre, especially to the east, where they were attracted by the chance of cheaper homes and easier access to the industrial areas on the outskirts of the city.
(iii) Classes 4 and 5 were concentrated close to the centre, but in the southern sector. This was because the poorest housing was in an area known as St Ebbs.

3. Chombart de Lauwe (*Paris et l'agglomèration parisienne*) described seven concentric zones in his analysis, similar to those of Burgess. He notes the significance of class differences in areas of residence. There is a contrast between the bourgeois west with its broad streets and open spaces and the proletarian east. This has narrower streets, less regular patterns, much industry and poorer quality housing.

Segregation in cities

Some sociologists have examined the ways in which patterns of social relations within the different zones of the city are sustained in daily life.

Pahl makes the point that people are distributed more as a result of the constraints that operate on them in the choices they make rather than being distributed according to chance.

Economic constraints The rich can exercise more choice than the poor; the employed more than the unemployed.

Social constraints People tend to seek a home according to their income, occupation and stage in the family cycle. Gans makes the point that young couples with high incomes but small amounts of capital and with young children are forced into housing estates where mortgages are available.

Racial constraints Rex and Moore (*Race, Community and Conflict*) aimed to contribute to an understanding of race relations in Birmingham. They examined the factors affecting the distribution of population in the area known as Sparkbrook. They divided the area into three zones.

(i) Zone 1 was originally an affluent middle-class area, but which had fallen into a state of decay. From the 1930s onwards the middle-classes began to move out into more desirable suburbs. The large houses were divided into lodging houses which attracted Irish and black immigrants in the 1950s.
(ii) Zone 2 was an area first developed in the 1830s which came to house the working class but not 'rough labourers'. The authors suggest it is an area similar to Bethnal Green. There was a gradual increase in levels of black immigration since property was cheap, although much was awaiting demolition and redevelopment.
(iii) Zone 3. Most of the property here was built in the 1890s by the Barber Trust. It was good quality and attracted the respectable working class. Much of the housing remained in good order and was still occupied mainly by white residents.

They note how a class struggle arises where people in a market situation enjoy differential access to property. The immigrant population, having lowest status and least power, were forced into the poorest-quality housing in Sparkbrook. The zone of transition is characterised by overcrowding, high rents and lack of privacy: 'The Immigrant, the discharged prisoner, the deserted wife have little in common except their housing conditions'.

Conclusions

The Ecological analysis came under attack in the 1970s and sociologists returned to the views of the Founding Fathers for explanations of urban problems.

Table 15.1 Statistics illustrating the problems of inner-city life (Liverpool, Manchester, Newcastle and Sheffield, 1982)

Percentage	Average for the four cities	Country as a whole
Need for supplementary benefit	25	10
No car	50	33
One-parent families	10	5
Ethnic minorities	15	2
Unemployed	22	14
Unemployed, 16–24 age group	30	20

(a) *Neo-Weberians* (for example, Rex and Moore) explained why particular groups inhabited certain areas of Birmingham, by reference to:
   (i) their income levels;
   (ii) their ethnicity; and
   (iii) the way the housing market operated – membership of a housing class being of great importance in determining lifestyle, interests and associations.

(b) *Neo-Marxists* argue that cities are controlled by the ruling class, whose interests are maintained by housing managers, building society managers, urban planners, estate agents, solicitors, speculators and property developers.
   (i) They ensure that housing is distributed in ways that maintain social segregation.
   (ii) These theorists argue that we should not be surprised at the occasional outbursts of riots and other destructive activities in the poorest areas of major cities.
   (iii) The Free Market approach has encouraged the mal-distribution of resources in the city and high levels of homelessness.

■ **What links are there between life in the inner city and the decline of community?**

■ **What light have sociologists thrown on the problems of inner city life?**

Note

1. In order to answer such questions you should be able to define:

(i) *Inner city*: Gans (Urbanism and Suburbanism as Ways of Life) says 'by the inner city I mean the transient residential areas ... the slums that generally surround the Central Business District (CBD). In Britain they generally refer to the areas of poorest housing and quality of life in the city.

(ii) *Community*: see Tönnies and Durkheim (page 199) but note the problems in achieving a satisfactory definition. Many would argue that community can exist in an inner-city area.

2. Specify issues which have been defined as 'problems' of inner-city life. These include:

A Deprivation

(a) A Report by local government leaders from Liverpool, Manchester, Newcastle and Sheffield (1982) presented some statistics to illustrate the problems of inner city life (see Table 15.1). They claimed they were having to overspend to compensate and were being penalised by the government's capping policy as a result.

(b) The Barclay Report (*Social Workers. Their Tasks and Role*) noted that in Tower Hamlets (E. London) there were:
   (i) insufficient social workers to meet the extent of the needs;
   (ii) a high proportion of elderly people in need;
   (iii) an exceptionally high proportion of young children in care;
   (iv) a large ethnic population with special needs;
   (v) housing in poor state of repair; and
   (vi) all helping agencies including the Citizens Advice Bureau (CAB) faced cuts in grants.

B Quality of housing

(a) Most housing was traditionally rented from councils or landlords; because residents generally were unable to raise a mortgage. But Jewison notes how the inner city fares badly as part of the new megalopolis. Council-house building has been virtually halted.

(b) Much of the stock is old and of a declining standard (especially in the private sector). That built in rehousing schemes is often on large, impersonal estates, some of which may house large numbers of 'problem families.'

(c) Cheaper, sub-standard property may result in higher heating costs and problems of maintenance. The estates may also be far from places of work, increasing travel costs.

(d) Note the work of Rex and Moore (see page 205), who show how poorer families get squeezed into certain areas of cities and into certain types of housing by the pressures of the property market.

C High rates of crime

(a) In 1989 crime figures for London showed:

Sex attacks up by	23%
Violence up by	20%
Fraud and forgery up by	8%
Vandalism up by	5%
Burglary up by	4%
Theft up by	4%
Robbery down by	3%

The overall reported crime rate rose by 5 per cent to the second highest level on record; the clear-up rate was 17 per cent. Overall, there were 756 300 crimes reported and there were 111 400 arrests. The areas of highest risk included city centres late at night; public houses; car parks; and underground trains. Those at most risk of violence were young men in such areas who had been drinking.

(b) However, it must be remembered that there are problems in interpreting such statistics (see page 176). Much of the increase may result from more incidents being reported in response to police campaigns and improved methods of investigation.

(c) It should be noted that in 1991 the highest increases in recorded crime were in Cumbria (35 per cent), Kent (34 per cent) Gloucestershire (32 per cent) and Cambridge (31 per cent).

D Riots

There were a series of riots in some inner-city areas in 1981 and 1985. In 1991 and 1992 riots were mainly confined to large estates in Newcastle and Coventry. Commentators suggested a number of explanations:

(a) *Criminal greed*: criminally-minded people took opportunities to loot.

(b) *Conspiracy theory*: the riots were inspired by activists.

(c) *Social and economic deprivation*: the riots were the result of unemployment and poverty, especially on the part of black minority groups.

(d) *Police incompetence*: the riots resulted from the mishandling by police of minor events. The Scarman Report (*The Brixton Disorders, 1982*) produced some recommendations and comments:

(i) It supported the police in their desire to stop and search; to have better equipment; to be better trained; and to have powers to limit marches and demonstrations.

(ii) It was critical in its identification of racially-biased policemen; the lack of policemen from the ethnic minorities; and the need for an independent body to investigate complaints against them.

(iii) There was no strong evidence that the riots were racially motivated, since different ethnic groups were not fighting each other. Large numbers of white youths were also directly involved.

(iv) In 1991/92 explanations for the riots in Newcastle and Coventry focused back on the impact of delinquent youth cultures which encouraged 'joy riding'.

E Ethnic minorities

These groups face particular problems in some inner city areas:

(a) Housing: There are high levels of overcrowding because of discrimination in granting mortgages to ethnic minorities, preventing them from becoming home owners.

(b) Education:

(i) The 1988 Education Act gave parents the right to choose a school for their children. Many in inner-city areas are rejecting schools where there are more than 45 per cent from ethnic minority backgrounds. Some Asian parents are seeking to remove their children from schools were there are few Muslim children. The CRE (1990) said that it was concerned that state bodies may be forced to carry out racially-motivated instructions.

(ii) In 1986 a survey showed that in Birmingham more children from ethnic minorities were staying on at school after the age of 16 than British-born white children. They also had lower truancy rates and higher levels of ambition.

(iii) Driver's survey of 2300 school-leavers found the academic results of West Indian boys and girls (especially those of second and later generations) were for the most part better than those of the born white children.

(c) Unemployment:

(i) Surveys have repeatedly shown that while unemployment rates for whites had doubled, for many in ethnic groups it had quadrupled. Worst hit are teenagers.

(ii) Because ethnic groups include large numbers of young people, a high proportion are entering the economically-active age group.

(iii) There is a danger of producing a hostile generation and a deprived underclass among those who remain long-term unemployed and whose long term hopes cannot be fulfilled. (Note Merton's theory of anomie see page 179.)

Conclusions

In their analyses of the inner city, sociologists have:

(a) Established problems of definitions.

(b) Re-considered the analysis of poverty, especially the 'culture of poverty theory' which assumes that the poor suffer multiple deprivation and pass on the culture of deprivation from one generation to the next. Critics argue:

(i) deprivation seldom occurs in multiples; unemployment may be the cause;

(ii) poverty is not just a feature of the inner city and it is not always inherited; and

(iii) high rates of crime also occur outside inner city areas.

(c) Some writers reconsidered the position of ethnic minorities and found that some are very successful in school but may face problems in obtaining good jobs and satisfactory housing.

(d) Others re-examined government policies to see how far they have been responsible for the flight out by the successful and the fragmentation of traditional working-class communities by unsatisfactory rehousing schemes.

(e) Various researchers have put forward suggestions for improving inner city areas:

(i) A Reading University Report (1983) suggested greater involvement by both private enterprise and central government to recreate local communities in inner city areas.

(ii) Donnison (*The Good City*) has suggested schemes to create new jobs, develop more parks and leisure facilities, build more low-density housing and control transportation costs in the city.

(iii) Rex and Moore point to the dangers of policies which segregate populations in cities. They will lead to frustration and disharmony.

(iv) Some have argued that since 1979 Free Market policies have given a free hand to property developers, which has attracted the 'unacceptable face of capitalism'. Others on the Right have said that such policies have not gone far enough.

Suggested Reading

Works noted in this chapter

C. Arensberg and S. Kimball (1940) *Family and Community in Ireland*, Peter Smith, London

M. Banton (1965) Social Alignment and Identity in a West African City, in H. Kuper (ed.) *Urbanisation and Migration in West Africa*. University of California Press

F. Benet (1963) 'The Ideology of the Urban–Rural Continuum', *Comparative Studies in Society and History* 6

B. Berger (1969) *Working-Class Suburbs*, CUP

E. Burgess (1967) 'The Growth of the City', in R. Park and E. Burgess, *The City*, University of Chicago Press

P. Chombart de Lauwe *et al.*, *Paris et l'agglomération Parisienne*, University de France

P. Collison and J. Mogey (1959) 'Residence and Social Class in Oxford', *A.M. Journal of Sociology* 6

N. Dennis (1968) 'The Popularity of the Neighbourhood Community Idea', in R. Pahl, *Readings in Urban Sociology*, Pergamon

D. Donnison (1974) *The Good City*, Penguin

R. Durant (1959) *Watling: A Survey of a New Housing Estate*, P.S. King, London

E. Durkheim, *The Social Division of Labour*, Free Press

R. Frankenberg (1966) *Communities in Britain*

H. Gans (1967) *The Levittowners*, Allen Lane

H. Gans (1968) 'Urbanism and Suburbanism as Ways of Life', in J. Raynor and J. Harden (eds) *Cities, Communities and the Young* RKP, Open University

D. Harvey (1973) *Social Justice and the City*, Edward Arnold

N. Jewison (1991) 'The Development of Cities in Capitalist Societies', *Sociology Review* (November), Vol. 1, No. 2

R. McIver and C. Page, *Society, an Introductory Analysis*, Macmillan

R. Pahl (1970) *Patterns of Urban Life*, Longman

R. Pahl, *Readings in Urban Sociology*, Pergamon

R. Pahl (1965) *Urbs in Rure*, Weidenfeld & Nicolson

—— (1968) *Readings in Urban Sociology*, Pergamon

R. Park (1952) *Human Communities*, Free Press

K. Pryce (1979) *Endless Pressure*, Penguin

R. Redfield (1955), *The Little Community*, University of Chicago Press

R. Redfield (1947) 'Folk Society', *American Journal of Sociology*, Vol. 52

J. Rex and R. Moore (1967) *Race, Community and Conflict*, OUP

Scarman Report (1982) *The Brixton Disorders*, HMSO

J. Seeley *et al.* (1968) *Crestwood Heights*, Wiley

S. Southall, *An Operational Theory of Role*

G. Weightman, *New Society* article

P. Willmott and M. Young (1957) *Family and Kinship in East London*, Penguin

L. Wirth (1938) 'Urbanism as a Way of Life', *American Journal of Sociology*, Vol. 44

L. Wirth (1964) *Towards a Definition of the Local Community* in J. Raynor and J. Harden

Works for further reading

C. Bell and H. Newby (1974) *The Sociology of Community*, Frank Cass

E. Burney (1967) *Housing on Trial*, OUP

S. Butler (1982) *Enterprise Zones*, Heinemann

M. Castells (1983) *The City and the Grass Roots*, Edward Arnold

P. Dunleavy (1980) *Urban Political Analysis*, Macmillan

J. Fulcher (1991) 'A New Stage in the Development of Capitalist Societies', *Social Studies Review*, Vol. 1, No. 2

P. Hall (1981) *The Inner City in Context*, Heinemann

P. Harrison (1983) *Inside the Inner City*, Penguin

N. Jewson (1989) 'No Place like Home . . .', *Social Studies Review*, Vol. 4, No. 4

N. Jewson (1990) 'Urban Riots', *Social Studies Review*, Vol. 5, No. 5

C. Jones, (ed.) (1979) *Urban Deprivation and the Inner City* Croom Helm

M. Kettle and L. Hodges (1982) *Uprising*, Penguin

C. Lambert and D. Weir (1982) *Cities in Modern Britain*, Harper Row

O. Lewis (1951) *Life in a Mexican Village: Tepotzlan Revisited*, University of Illinois.

J. Littlejohn (1979) *Westrigg*, RKP

M. Lovey and M. Allen (1979) *The Crisis of the Inner City*, Macmillan

S. Lukes, (1974) *Power: A Radical View*, Macmillan

H. Newby (1977) *The Deferential Worker*, Allen Lane

R. Redfield (1930) *Tepotzlan*, University of Chicago

J. Rex and S. Tomlinson (1979) *Coloured Immigrants in a British City*, Routledge & Kegan Paul

B. Robson (1988) *Those Inner Cities*, Clarendon Press

P. Saunders (1979) *Urban Politics*, Hutchinson

P. Saunders (1981) *Social Theory and the Urban Question*, Hutchinson

M. Smith and J. Feagin (1987) *The Capitalist City*, Blackwell

J. Solomos (1990) 'Changing Forms of Racial Discourse', *Social Studies Review*, Vol. 6, No. 2

M. Stacey (1969) 'The Myth of Community Studies', *British Journal of Sociology*, 20

R. Williams (1973) *The Country and the City*, Chatto & Windus

Questions

1. Examine photographs 38, 39 and 40.
   (i) List some of the major problems in defining 'a community'.
   (ii) How might Redfield's definition be applied to the caravan dwellers?
   (iii) Why might he be surprised at the location?
   (iv) How might the views of Seeley *et al.* (p. 200) be applied to photograph 39?
   (v) Suggest ways of testing such a hypothesis that community exists in suburbs.

2. Examine photographs 39 and 40.
   Consider the view that:
   (i) the growth of suburbs is a response to the flight from the problems of the inner city?

3. Examine photograph 38.
   (i) Why might observers have been led to the view that where you live influences how you live?
   (ii) Gans suggests that ways of life in suburbs are influenced more by the stage people have reached in the family cycle, as well as economic and class factors, than the place in which they live. How might this view be tested?

38

Source: Alec Gill

40

Source: Alec Gill

39

Source: Alec Gill

Self-test Questions

Study these newspaper extracts and answer the questions below.

Item A

Church group urges low-cost homes to halt rural decline

THE RURAL idyll is a myth and there are significant tensions between traditional village communities and affluent newcomers who have fled the city, according to a report from the Church of England published yesterday.

The Archbishops' Commission on Rural Areas report, ***Faith in the Countryside***, paints a grim picture of life in Britain's rural areas, with a lack of affordable housing, dwindling public transport and agriculture in trouble.

It says: "Local village employment has declined; housing has become more difficult; local shops, post offices and halls have been under threat of closure; local transport has declined to the point of uselessness in many areas." The commission, chaired by the former Cabinet minister Lord Prior, calls on the Government to increase substantially rented and low-cost housing, particularly for young people in rural communities who have been priced out of the market.

In particular, it proposes the removal of restrictions that prevent local authorities using funds from the sale of council homes to provide affordable low-cost housing.

Newcomers to village life were often resistant to new forms of employment in the area if it changed their idea of village life. Lord Prior cited the conversion of underused farming facilities to light industrial use. "What too few appreciate is that they are entering a society which to maintain its balance, and cohesion needs local skills and a working environment to survive," he said.

This was not being allowed to happen in many "gentrified" areas, he said, and people had to accept "a working countryside". The report also says the Government should commission a review of transport facilities in rural areas with a view to connecting all settlements of more than 1,000 people with accessible and well-publicised services. It argues that the Department of Employment should make special provision to provide for the training and re-training of the rural work-force.

"We are looking to the Government to change the emphasis of all the money going into the inner city. Some money should be going to rural areas." Lord Prior said.

In almost 150 recommendations, more than two-thirds are directed at the church, suggesting that, with more land at its disposal than anyone except the Queen, it realises that it has to put its house in order too.

Other recommendations in the report:

- Every parish should carry out a housing need survey;
- Programmes to close hospital services should be critically reviewed;

Source: Extract from an article by Martin Rowe in the *Independent*, 12 September 1990.

Item B

ON a hot summer's evening, the tension is palpable around the dismal streets of Benwell. Groups of young people, from their early teens to twenties, gather on corners or on waste ground, occasionally whistling at the young constable on his beat, muttering abuse or hurling a missile.

Many houses are boarded up, burned out, or roofless. Shops are often vacant and shuttered. A newish council estate, overlooking Britain's flashiest shopping centre barely half a mile away, lies deserted and semiderelict, bricks carpeting the overgrown walkways — the ultimate "void", in the apocalyptic jargon of the housing manager.

This is the West End of Newcastle upon Tyne, 10 months after a spate of mobbing and petrol bombing brought riot police on to the streets of the city for the first time.

YET after a decade or more of pumping billions into the development of new towns on green fields, the problems were actually recognised in the late 1960s, long before the rioting, with the first legislation designed to bring cash into inner cities. By 1971 a new Tory government called for a "total approach" to the problems of urban decline after a series of studies highlighted a flight of capital and skilled labour from city to suburb.

Since then we have had a white paper on the inner cities (1977), an Inner Urban Areas Act (1978), two docklands development corporations (1981), City Action Teams (1985), Tasks Forces (1986), eight more development corporations (1987-88) and a new City Challenge programme (1991). But instead of the "total approach" advocated in 1971, we have had a series of ad hoc measures and little coordination, with councils often pushed to the side.

Meanwhile, our city ghettoes, like Benwell, are festering. Jeremy Beecham, the Newcastle council leader, says "material conditions" in the area, which is by chance his own electoral ward, are worse than last year. Surely, he asks, a nation which can organise so efficiently for war, from the Gulf to the Falklands, can mobilise an emergency programme to tackle the urban horror in its own backyard before it is too late.

But government priorities now dictate more economies. Newcastle is axing £30 million annually from its budget over the next five years already, with cuts in the national job training programme no doubt a foretaste of what is to come.

Source: Extract from an article by Peter Hetherington in the *Guardian*, 11 July 1992, p. 22.

1. Examine Item A.

(i) Redfield (see page 200) suggested that rural life was the source of community. Suggest some points raised in the article which could be used to criticise the view.

(ii) Consider how the points raised may confirm the view of Lewis (see page 201).

(iii) Suggest some ways in which the points raised in the article add to the debate concerning the problems of analysing the concept of community.

2. Examine Item B.

(i) Suggest some reasons to explain why such problems have arisen in many inner-city areas in recent years. Apply different theoretical perspectives.

(ii) Discuss the points raised in the article in relation to the views of Wirth and Simmel (see pages 201 and 202).

3. Using the data in the articles, discuss:

(i) 'The sense of community is not the monopoly of rural areas and may even be found in the most deprived urban areas.'

(ii) 'Social problems in rural areas are no less serious than in urban areas.'

4. How would you undertake a research project to assess the possible existence of community, its value as a concept, or its demise? Discuss methods, hypotheses, places and people to be studied. What problems might you anticipate?

16

POPULATION

Questions on this topic include the following areas:

1. Factors affecting the birth rate.
2. Factors affecting the death rate.
3. Factors affecting population trends:
   (a) Social factors.
   (b) Comparative data.
4. Class differentials:
   (a) Mortality
   (b) Fertility
5. Immigration and emigration

Factors Affecting the Birth Rate

■ **What factors would you take into account in explaining the long-term decline of the birth rate in Britain?**

■ **Describe and account for patterns of fertility in any one society in the last thirty years.**

Crude birth rate The number of live births in one year per 1000 people. It is an important determinant of population growth.

Fertility rate The number of live births in one year per 1000 of women of child-bearing age (15–45). Age-specific rates would be the number of children born each year per 1000 women in age groups: 15–19; 20–24; 24–29; 30–34; 35–39; 40–45.

Some useful statistics are shown in Tables 16.1 and 16.2. The birth rate has declined steadily; the slight increase in the latter part of the last decade may be related to the fact that:

(a) Career women were delaying their families and having them at a later age.
(b) Those born in the baby boom of the early 1960s were having their own children.
(c) The number of births in the UK is projected to peak in 1994 at about 810 000.
(d) The annual number of births is projected to fall after that date as the large generation born in the 1960s passes the peak of child-bearing age.

Points to note

1. Forecasters have found predictions as to future trends very difficult:

(a) They base estimates of future fertility rates on events that have occurred before. These may not have the same effect in the future.
(b) It is difficult to predict when trends have or have not peaked:
   (i) In 1949 the Royal Commission on Population said there would be a substantial decline in the number of births, lasting until the mid-1960s, because there were fewer women of child-bearing age in the population. In fact, birth rate rose during the 1950s and early 1960s.
   (ii) In 1965, new predictions were made suggesting that the fertility rate would rise until 1975 and continue into the early years of the next century. The peak seems to have been reached in mid-1966. Decline followed until 1976, when it picked up again.
   (iii) New predictions suggest that by the year 2030 there will be more deaths than births. The UK will then have a net decrease in population for the first time since 1976.

2. The number of births in 1991 (about 800 000) was about a third higher than that of the low point of 1976 (676 000) but about 20 per cent below the high point of 1966 (980 000).

Table 16.1 Crude birth rate 1841–1990 (per 1000 of population)

1841–50	32.5
1861–70	35.2
1881–90	32.8
1901–10	27.2
1921–30	18.3
1941–50	18.0
1961–70	17.4
1971–80	13.1
1981–90	13.4

Sources: Registrar-General's *Statistical Review of England and Wales*, and *Social Trends*, 22.

Table 16.2 Live births, totals and rates 1951–91

Year	Total live births	Crude birth rate (per 1000 of population)
1951	797 000	15.9
1956	825 000	16.1
1961	944 000	17.8
1966	980 000	17.9
1971	902 000	16.1
1976	676 000	12.0
1981	731 000	13.0
1986	755 000	13.3
1991	799 000	13.9
2001	769 000	13.0

Source: *Social Trends*, 22.

Table 16.3 International migration into and out of UK (all countries) (1000s)

	Inflow	Outflow	Balance
1975–79	186.6	207.7	−21.1
1980–84	186.3	213.9	−27.6
1985–89	232.1	208.0	+24.1

Source: *Social Trends*, 22.

Table 16.4 Death rate and life expectancy, 1870–1980 (England and Wales)

Year	Death rate	Life expectancy (years) Males	Females
1870	23.0	41	45
1890	19.5	43	48
1910	13.5	52	55
1930	11.4	59	63
1950	11.8	66	72
1970	11.8	69	76
1980	11.7	71	77
1990	11.1	73	78

Source: *Annual Abstract*.

Table 16.5 Death rates for males and females, 1961–81 (UK)

	Death rate (per 1000)			Total deaths (000s)		
Year	Males	Females	Average	Males	Females	All
1961	12.6	11.4	12.0	322.0	309.8	631.8
1971	12.2	11.1	11.6	328.5	316.5	645.0
1981	12.1	11.4	11.7	329.1	328.8	657.9
1991	11.2	11.1	11.1	314.6	327.2	641.8

Source: *Annual Abstract*.

Table 16.6 Infant mortality rates 1931–91 (deaths of infants under 1 year of age per 1000 live births)

1931	70
1951	32
1961	23
1971	18
1981	10
1991	8

Source: *Social Trends*, 3 and 22.

Table 16.7 Infant mortality rates in Classes 1–5 (1988/89) (deaths of infants under 1 year of age per 1000 live births)

Class 1	(Professionals)	6.0
Class 2	(Intermediate)	6.1
Class 3a	(White collar)	7.0
Class 3b	(Skilled manual)	7.5
Class 4	(Semi-skilled)	10.4
Class 5	(Unskilled)	11.0

Source: OPCS.

Conclusions

(a) Population increases by the fact of more people being born than dying and by more people moving into a country than leaving it (see Table 16.3). For demographic purposes a migrant is defined as someone who, having lived abroad for at least 12 months declares an intention to reside in the UK for at least 12 months.

(b) The definition of an emigrant is the reverse of this. Births to mothers born outside the UK fell from 12.2 per cent of all live births in 1981 to 11.0 per cent in 1990.

(c) Population does not increase by regular and unvarying amounts each year, which would make predictions easy.

(d) There appears to be a tendency to defer having children until later in marriages in the 1990s.

(e) There is no clear explanation of why patterns of family building change.

(f) Projections into the future are always suspect because it is so difficult to identify trends. Should a fall over a few years be considered or an overall rise over a longer period? In 1970 the government's Actuary Department said: 'a large element of personal judgement has to be exercised in projections . . . and it seems doubtful whether the prospects for predictive accuracy are improving'.

(g) In the mid-1800s the number of live births per 1000 of the population was about 35. In the mid-1900s it was 12.5. In 1985 it was 11.5. In 1885 a smaller proportion of women were producing more children.

(h) From 1970 to 1976 the population of the UK grew about half a million. Most of this took place before 1974. Between 1975 and 1985 it was stable. Between 1989 and 1990 the population increased by about 174 000. This was similar to the average annual increase between 1984 and 1989.

(i) The annual number of births is projected to remain higher than the number of deaths over the next forty years, leading to a natural increase in population.

Factors affecting a decline in the birth rate

1. Economic
   (a) High cost of housing.
   (b) Lack of job opportunities.
   (c) Children not economic assets.
2. Normative
   (a) Where class norm is for small family.
   (b) Childlessness is socially acceptable.
   (c) Large families socially unacceptable.
   (d) Rising age of marriage.
   (e) Increasing frequency of cohabitation.
3. Social and medical
   (a) War or other major social crisis.
   (b) New efficient methods of contraception.
   (c) Abortion Act (1967).
   (d) Improved education (especially for women, offering better career chances).
   (e) More women in paid employment (see page 250). In 1900 25% of women bore a child every year. In 1930 it was 10%. Overall fertility rates fell between 1971–81 in England and Wales and have since remained stable. In 1980 a woman aged 20 spent 7% of her remaining years child-bearing.
   (f) Improved medicine, welfare and child-care limit the need for a large family as survival rates increase.
4. Immigration Emigration.
   Between 1975–85 there was a net outflow of population although this reversed 1985–89; fertility rates for overseas-born women have in general continued to fall since 1981. Rates for women born in the old Commonwealth countries halved between 1971–90.

Factors affecting an increase in the birth rate

1. Economic
   (a) Economic boom: more houses available.
   (b) More jobs available.
   (c) Children are an economic asset.
2. Normative
   (a) Class norms encourage large families.
   (b) Childlessness carries stigma.
   (c) Large families provide high status.
   (d) Falling age of marriage.
   (e) Delayed family building brings later increases in birth rates.
3. Social and medical
   (a) End of war or other social crisis.
   (b) Changes in attitude towards family planning (growing religious oposition).
   (c) Decline in number of women in paid employment.
   (d) Having gained qualifications and career more women may increase family size.
   (e) New medical techniques may enable more women to have children who previously could not do so.
4. Immigration: because the ages of a high proportion of women in ethnic minorities is young their birth rates are initially high.

(j) The total UK population is projected to increase to about 59 million by 2001 and 61 million by 2025. The death rate may begin to exceed birth rate after 2030.

(k) Patterns of fertility can be examined in terms of changes in economic factors, changing norms and social mores, the impact of advances in medicine, and patterns of immigration and emigration.

In 1987, the over-60s (27 per cent) outnumbered the under-30s (25 per cent) for the first time. In 1991 there were 600 000 fewer 18–24-year-olds and 200 000 more over-60s.

Factors Affecting the Death Rate

■ **What have been the major changes that have occurred in mortality rates in Britain since 1900? How would you account for the changes?**

Crude death rate The number of deaths per year per 1000 people.

Infant mortality rate The annual number of deaths of infants aged 0–12 months per 1000 live births in the same year.

Mortality patterns These show the trends in deaths. In Britain the mortality rates for all age groups have declined (see Tables 16.4 and 16.5). Although the number of infant mortalities has declined for all social classes there are still differentials between those in the highest and lowest classes. Health still appears to be related to family environment.

Comment

(i) The crude death rate has remained fairly stable since the turn of the century. Men tend to have higher mortality rates than women. Birth rates are usually higher than death rates, which accounts for the steady growth in population, even though birth rates are falling. Population has grown more slowly in recent years as birth and death rates have become more finely balanced. The only year in which there were more deaths than births was 1977.

(ii) Research (1985) by the Royal College of Physicians stated that the number of centenarians in Britain has increased at least tenfold between 1955 and 1985. This has been the result of such factors as clean air legislation, use of antibiotics and improved standards of care for the elderly. The chance of a woman reaching the age of 100 is nine times better than that a man.

(iii) There were declines in death rates for all age groups of both sexes between 1961 and 1991. Men had the higher death rate at all ages. The most dramatic falls were in the under-1 age group and the over-80s.

Changing infant mortality rates (deaths of children in the first year of life per 1000 live births) (see Table 16.6).

(a) In the mid-nineteenth century rates were very high: 1850–1900: an average of 150.
(b) They began to fall below 70 after 1930.
(c) Between 1950 and 1990 there were only two occasions when the rate increased from one year to the next.
(d) Although infant mortality rates have fallen there remain variations between different social classes (see Table 16.7).

Conclusions

Mortality rates have fallen steadily and population has continued to increase. Such knowledge is important for policy-makers in planning for schools, hospitals, work and pension schemes.

1. A government report (*Employment for the 1990s*) noted that there will be a shortage of young workers in the future.

(a) The population is ageing as people are living longer. In 1931, life expectancy for males was 58 and for females 62. By 2001 it will be 75 for men and 80 for women.
(b) The shortfall may be offset by the increased recruitment of women.
(c) There may be problems in the future in financing old-age pensions and schemes of social security if there are fewer economically-active people supporting more retired people.

2. The main causes of the changes are:

(a) Economic factors:
  (i) There has been greater prosperity, resulting in more affluence, better housing and better nutrition.
  (ii) Improved conditions of work, shorter hours, more safety-conscious employers.

(b) Social factors:
  (i) Improved living standards, better amenities, etc., which make life healthier and more satisfying.
  (ii) Increased state provision of welfare, town planning, etc.

(c) Medicine:
  (i) Improved medicine has helped reduce disease and infection.
  (ii) The advances of medical science: vaccination, sanitation, pure water supply, midwifery, etc.

(d) Education:
  (i) This has produced a better-informed public who have pressed for reforms in welfare, hygiene, etc.
  (ii) Parents have become better informed about child-care, diet, etc.

Population Trends

■ **Are human population trends socially determined? (UCLES)**

The question is asking you to discuss the social factors which might operate in a society to help control the growth of population. If population size is related to changing social norms, then are specific population policies necessary?

A report of the Select Committee on Population (1971) argued that the government ought to act to prevent the consequences of population growth making the everyday conditions of life intolerable. It was pointed out that although Britain had a slow-growing population, if the rate of growth continued the population would reach 980 million by the year 2500. To stabilise the growth the report said that every three families needed to have one fewer child between them.

Among the *consequences of overpopulation* are:

(a) Pressure for accommodation.
(b) Demand for greater employment opportunities.
(c) Pressure on education services.
(d) Pressure on medical and social services.
(e) Increased environmental problems.

Among the suggested means of *stabilising population* were:

(a) Improved methods of birth control.
(b) The government should talk, tax or legislate the average family down from 2.5 children to 2.1.
(c) Removal from the welfare system of any features which appear to encourage families increasing.
(d) Encourage more women to go out to work.
(e) Provide benefits for those who do not marry or who do not have families.

Research findings

1. Turnbull (*The Demography of Small-Scale Societies*) examined the ways in which small-scale societies manage to control their levels of population and suggested that large-scale societies (complex industrial) may have similar methods of control based on social factors.

He accepts that many of his points are speculative, since non-literate societies have no specific records or data to which to refer. Anthropologists rely mainly on observation and discussion.

Population control operated on the following bases:

(a) Marriage of young girls to much older men.
(b) Ritual taboos prevented sexual relations between partners for up to three years after the birth of a child.
(c) There was wide-ranging acceptance of homosexuality.
(d) Ritual groupings between members of the same sex made contact between men and women less frequent.
(e) There were powerful stipulations as to possible marriage partners (often exogamy i.e. marriage outside the tribal group) was encouraged.
(f) Infanticide may be acceptable where a child is deformed, etc.
(g) Twins are often unacceptable and one child may be abandoned.
(h) There are high mortality rates among infants.

Questions

Examine photographs 41 and 42.

Although the birth rate has declined the population has increased.

(i) Explain this statement.
(ii) Discuss some of the advantages and disadvantages of:

(a) a population with a high proportion of young people in it; and
(b) an ageing population in which there are fewer young people because of very low birth rates and falling death rates.

42

Source: Alec Gill

41

Source: Alec Gill

He suggests that a complex industrial society is also quite sensitive in its adjustment to environmental demands to maintain levels of stability and equilibrium. This hypothesis does seem to be supported to some extent by the fact that population increase has slowed in recent years, making many of the suggestions of the Select Committee of 1971 unnecessary.

2. Gilje and Gould ('Population Growth or Decline?'), writing in 1973, noted the continued fall in fertility rates since 1964 and argued that a decreasing population ('or at least one that's not growing') was a possibility for the future.

They examined the difference between the government's Actuary Department projections (GAD) and the Greater London Council (GLC) projections as to future population trends.

The GAD projections did not assume that reproduction rates would fall below replacement levels for the next forty years. GLC projections assumed a falling rate which would result in a stable replacement level within a few years.

Fertility patterns are the product of several factors:

(a) The number of women in the fertile age groups (15–49).
(b) Current norms about ideal family size.
(c) Actual family size (the extent to which the ideal is realised).
(d) Rate of family formation (spacing between births).
(e) Changes in marriage patterns (whether people tend to delay age of marriage; 97 per cent of births are to women under the age of 30).
(f) The number of marriage eligibles (the higher birth rate in the late 1950s and early 1960s was a product of the population bulge that occurred after the Second World War ended).

Factors affecting the size of families:

(a) Changing norms as to ideal family size.
(b) The couple's estimate of their ability to maintain a family of a particular size.
(c) GAD suggested that there was a trend towards deferred child-bearing until later in marriage. GLC argued that fertility rates were declining, not just being deferred.
(d) Spacing between children increased.
(e) Improved contraception made family planning more accurate.
(f) More women continued to enter the work force.
(g) More emphasis on companionship in marriage.
(h) More emphasis on higher living standards in preference to a larger family.

Conclusion

These research studies provide support for the view that social norms and pressures do help to control 'automatically' population size, in accordance with Turnbull's thesis based on small-scale societies, suggesting they are socially determined to some extent.

■ **Population control is necessary to maintain social stability. Discuss.**

Thomas Malthus, writing in 1794, argued that food production could not support uncontrolled growth in population, which would therefore result in starvation and social catastrophe. Since that time demographers have debated the view. It has become of particular significance in recent years following a series of world-wide economic disasters.

Areas of concern

1. World population:
   - 1950: 2.5 billion (bn)
   - 1992: 5.4 bn
   - 2025: 8.5 bn (est.)
   - 2100: 14.0 bn (est.)
2. Population of Britain:
   - 1794: 10.0 million (m)
   - 1901: 38.0 m
   - 1951: 50.0 m
   - 1991: 57.0 m
   - 2001: 59.0 m (est.)
   - 2020: 61.0 m (est.)

3. Between 1990 and 2010 it is estimated that 90 per cent of births will be in poor countries: for example, in South America, Asia and Africa.

4. The world population will rise by an estimated 97 million people a year for the next decade.

The views of the neo-Malthusians

(a) Ehrlich (*Population Time Bomb*) has argued:
   - (i) Food production has fallen behind population growth in two thirds of developing countries between 1978–89.
   - (ii) There has been famine, civil war and social catastrophes in Ethiopia.
   - (iii) The rapidly increasing population of USA is a major threat to long term world stability because of their consumption patterns and use and control of environmentally harmful technologies.

(b) Harrison (*The Third Revolution*) has suggested that in a world of 11.5bn people, all consuming resources at US rates, would result in entire reserves of copper and oil being used up in four years; natural gas in one; all of which would require the immediate development of new energy sources.

An over-populated world also faces a crisis of pollution, threats of global warming and the destruction of forests, causing ecological disasters.

The views of the anti-Malthusians

(a) Julian Simon (US economist) suggests that:
   - (i) Malthus omitted the factor of human ingenuity in his analysis; that is, human beings responding to crises and new problems with ingenious solutions. Epidemics, famine and wars may decimate populations (65 million people were killed in the two world wars) but improved medicine, technology and biological skills ensure that replacement and growth occurs.
   - (ii) The predictions of Ehrlich in the 1970s have proved to be wrong. Reserves of finite mineral and fossil fuels and valuable metals have not been exhausted. Bigger reserves were

uncovered as exploration increased. Food production has kept pace as a result of improved biological skills. In the developing world a 'Green revolution' has occurred, in which high-yielding rice and wheat crops have been developed.

(iii) He notes the example of the island of Mauritius, which in the 1960s had the fastest growing population in the world. It was projected to increase from 500 000 to 3 million in forty years. It has a finite land mass and had a single cash crop, sugar. Whereas Malthus would have predicted catastrophe, the ingenuity of the Mauritian government has coped with a population of double the size by use of new technologies, improved education and living standards, better management of land and better use of crops.

(iv) Other countries which have coped with rapidly expanding populations include Kenya (which grew at 4 per cent p.a.) and Japan, which has become one of the richest in the world.

(b) Preston (US economist) argues that we could now feed a world of 25–35 billion people to a high and satisfactory nutritional level. He says there is no possible agreement as to an optimum population level beyond which catastrophe would occur. However, he accepts that the quality of life may suffer.

(c) Zaba (geographer) has examined land use to see whether there is a correlation between population growth and the new uses of land. She found that this was not the case. More significant were the effects of war, government policies and climatic change.

Conclusions

(a) Neo-Malthusians argue that:

(i) The world's resources are being depleted by a rapidly growing population. The result will be destabilisation of the societies in which competition for scarce resources occur.

(ii) Economists who dispute this are using short-term models not long-term perspectives.

(b) Critics dispute this view:

(i) Human populations cannot be controlled by coercive methods in democratic societies. Such attempts in India have failed.

(ii) Functionalists and free market theorists argue that in developed societies where populations have expanded they have been accompanied by indicators of well-being: improved education, life expectancy and per capita income levels. Population growth may be an asset.

(iii) Conflict theorists argue that concern about population is a smokescreen for the real issues which are the over-consumption of goods in developed countries, which consume four-fifths of the world's resources and cause 70 per cent of the world's pollution (especially among some of the Eastern European countries with comparatively small populations).

(iv) George (*How the Other Half Dies*) argues that it is likely that populations will decline automatically as people are better educated, health care improves and poverty is attacked. People in developing societies tend to have children because they protect the parents against poverty. If women had fewer than two children each (as in Europe) the world population would decline after 2050. (But if they have more than two the population is estimated to reach more than 21 billion in the twenty-second century.)

(v) We could have fewer people in the world and still have social and environmental problems or we could sustain a much larger population if the planet is managed properly.

Suggested Reading

Works noted in this chapter

P. Ehrlich (1968) *The Population Time Bomb*, Ballentine

S. George (1977) *How the Other Half Dies*, Penguin

E. Gilje and T. Gould (1973) 'Population Growth or Decline?', in D. Potter and B. Sarre, *Dimensions of Society*, University of London Press and Open University

P. Harrison (1992) *The Third Revolution*, Tauris

D. Potter and B. Sarre (1973) *Dimensions of Society*, University of London Press and Open University

C. Turnbull (1972) 'The Demography of Small-Scale Societies', in D. Potter and B. Sarre

Works for further reading

Eurostat (1992) *Demographic Societies*, Eurostat.

HMSO (1992) *Birth Statistics*, HMSO.

HMSO (1992) *International Migration Statistics*, Series MN, HMSO.

HMSO (1992) *Key Population and Vital Statistics* (US/PPI), HMSO.

HMSO (1992) *Labour Force Survey* HMSO.

HMSO (1992) *Mortality Statistics for England and Wales*, Series DH1 2, 3, 4, 5, 6, HMSO.

HMSO (1992) *Population Projections* 1989–2029, Series PP2, 17, HMSO.

HMSO (1992) *Population Trends*, HMSO.

HMSO (1992) *Regional Trends*, HMSO.

R. Kelsall (1970) *Population*, Longman.

G. Myrdal (1970) *The Challenge of World Poverty*, Penguin.

OPCS (1992) *OPCS Monitors* OPCS.

C. Turnbull (1972) 'The Demography of Small Scale Societies', in Potter and Sarre, *Dimensions of Society* ULP.

United Nations (1992) *Demographic Year Book*, UN.

B. Ward and R. Dubbos (1972) *Only One Earth*, Penguin.

E. Wrigley (1969) *Population and History*, World University Library, 1969.

Self-test Questions

Study these items and answer the questions below.

Item A

Even in a developed country like Britain, few demographic factors stay constant

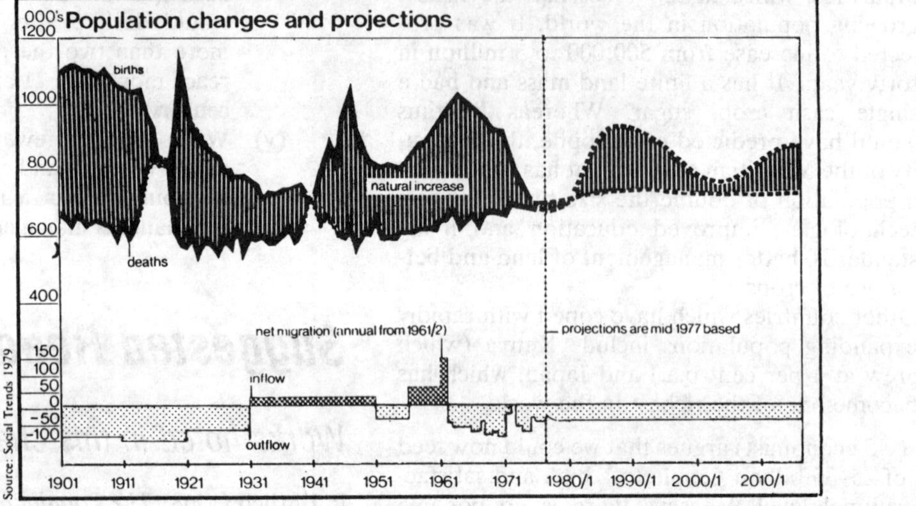

Source: New Society, 1 November 1979.

Item B

WOMEN will be able to pick and choose their husbands more carefully in future, because men now outnumber women in the marriageable age groups by 3 per cent.

Researchers are predicting that the change will alter the power balance between the sexes and lead to men taking more trouble to attract women, to ensure they are not left on the shelf.

New figures to be released by the Office of Population, Censuses and Surveys next month will show that the trend is becoming more pronounced and that, by the year 2025, the imbalance could reach as much as 5 per cent (105 men to every 100 women).

Traditionally, women have been in the weaker position because they have outnumbered men in the normal marriage years as a result of wars, emigration and a higher death rate among boys. In consequence, many women never married and the phenomenon of the maiden aunt was common.

With lower infant mortality rates and a prolonged period of peace, however, the preponderance of boys at birth is continuing into later years. Boys outnumber girls at birth by more than 5 per cent and, if present trends continue, the disparity could still be evident into the twenty-first century, when today's children are reaching their twenties.

Men now outnumber women in the 16-35 age group by 212,000 and in the peak marriage years of 20-24 by 59,000, or 3 per cent. By contrast, in the census year of 1921, women outnumbered men in the 20-24 age group by 15 per cent, and still outnumbered them by 5 per cent in the 1951 census year.

Melanie Henwood, research officer in the Family Policy Studies Centre, an independent research body, said: 'There is always a time lag between reality and people's attitudes and behaviour. But things will change.

Source: From an article by Annabel Ferriman and Tim Walker in the *Observer*, 10 July 1988, p. 3.

Item C

THE definition of old age is moveable — the older you are the later it gets, a survey by Age Concern has found.

The survey was commissioned as part of Age Concern's Golden Years appeal, which aims to raise £10 million over the next three years to fund projects for the elderly.

"It is shocking to think that so many people should dread later life," said Sally Greengross, director of Age Concern.

"Ageing is something that happens to us all, and it is particularly sad that the survey also reveals that young people have the most negative views."

In 1990 there were 10,490,000 people over pensionable age living in the United Kingdom, 18 per cent of the total population. By 2030 there are expected to be 14 million people of pensionable age.

The number of those between 60 and 74 is expected to rise by 36 per cent, and those aged 75 or over by 44 per cent.

Source: From an article by Chris Mihill in the *Guardian*, 22 January 1992.

1. Examine Item A.

(i) Account for the major peaks and troughs in the birth and death rates shown in the figure.

(ii) Suggest why the projections made in the mid-1970s indicate that peaks and troughs will also occur in the future.

(iii) Check recent *Social Trends* to see how accurate the projections have been (including immigration and emigration data).

(iv) Make a simplified figure using a few dates; comment on the trends revealed.

2. Examine Item B.

(i) Present some hypotheses based on the possible consequences of the excess of men over women in the future.
Consider:
(a) Choice of marriage partners.
(b) Attitudes towards marriage and cohabitation.
(c) Caring roles in society.
(d) Changing age of marriage.
(e) Family size.
(f) Career attitudes of women.
(g) Marriage and divorce rates.

3. Examine Item C.

(i) Discuss some of the possible consequences of an ageing population.

(ii) Why might governments wish to conduct frequent surveys among the elderly in society?

4. Using data in Items A, B and C discuss the view that population changes and projections, although not always precise, are important in order that governments can develop policies to cater for future social change.

17

HEALTH

The questions which appear on this topic include the following:

1. Key concepts (definitions and explanations of terms: health; illness, etc.).
2. Theories of health:
   (a) Marxist (structuralist).
   (b) Functionalist.
   (c) Interactionist.
3. Inequalities in the distribution of health and medical care.
4. Class differences in mortality rate.

Key Concepts

- **Cross-culturally, health and disease have different meanings. Compare these between at least two different types of society and show their implications for what is done to cure people. (Lon)**
- **There is no general agreement as to what is meant by health and illness. Explain, with examples, why this is so.**

To answer such questions you must be able to define and explain the significance of the key concepts referred to in them.

Cross-cultural definitions

Different societies place different meanings on terminology. Words like 'health', 'illness', 'disease', may have different meanings within different cultures. It is important to recognise the conceptual differences in order to make sense of different approaches to health and illness that can be identified. Without such awareness there can be a danger of an ethnocentric bias, assuming that one's own cultural definition is somehow superior to that of others.

1. In the West, medicine operates in a tradition which stresses scientific methods of analysis. The patient is viewed as an isolated object. There is a tendency to ignore different levels of experience. The aim is to isolate the cause of a specific physical illness and produce a cure. If there is uncertainty each new hypothesis is tested in turn until a solution is reached.
2. Wilson (*Magic and the Millennium*) notes how in societies where medical practice has been intimately involved with religious ritual and where modern medical services are scarce, then religious cults have been concerned with healing as well as with death.
3. Other observers have noted how in such societies the *shaman* ('medicine man', witch doctor) combines the roles of what in Western society would be described as 'priest' and 'psychotherapist'.
4. He or she operates with a detailed knowledge of the healing properties of plants as well as 'tribal psychology'.
5. Patients are treated in terms of their spiritual and psychological needs as well as in terms of their physical illness.
6. The shaman works with traditional beliefs about the world and its creation as well as with knowledge of how breaches of morality can cause illness.
7. The causes of illness are therefore seen to be associated with a complex pattern of relationships that exist between the patient's personal, social and moral life and his relationship with the well-being of the tribe itself.
8. Illness is seen as the possible result of witchcraft or a spiritual failing as much as a physical or biological problem.
9. Recovery relies on antidotes. These involve a complex set of ceremonies which may last many days. The problem of recovery relies on overcoming the spiritual and social dysfunctions and by seeking a means of reintegrating the patient into society.

10. Such ceremonies may serve important cathartic functions. Not only may they cure the patient but in providing remedies for social reintegration (assuring him of the affection of friends and family) they help to increase tribal solidarity and cohesion.

Conclusion

1. Cross-cultural studies confirm that there are different frameworks for understanding health in different societies (and within societies).

(a) In the West, where there has been a predominantly scientific view, good health is seen as a state which can be assessed in terms of soundness of body and mind; freedom from disease; and a sense of well-being. Illness is seen as a condition which can be diagnosed when the patient experiences the abnormal effects of some disability. It results from identifiable causes in the environment. Medicine prevents and cures such disabilities.

(b) Anthropologists have shown how in some pre-industrialised societies where there is no access to scientific knowledge, illness or other social disaster is often seen as the consequence of witchcraft.

(c) Such problems are usually dealt with by a shaman, whose job is to communicate with spirits and provide explanations for such problems. Shamans make use of charms, spells and dramatic events to persuade the patient that they are in competent hands.

(d) In some non-literate societies the shaman makes use of an accurate knowledge of the chemistry of local plant life. Plotkin (a conservation biologist) suggested at the Earth Summit Conference in Rio (1992) that as Amazon Indians abandon traditional ways, the death of a Shaman is like a library burning, with the loss of knowledge of potentially valuable pharmaceutical plants.

(e) Even in technologically-developed societies some see a mystical or religious explanation for illness. They see it as 'God's plan' that someone suffers, to test their faith and that of others around them (for example, Snake Sect members in the Appalachian Mountains of USA), and may refuse the use of medicines or treatment other than prayer to effect recovery.

2. Critics of the Western model have argued that scientific medicine often fails to take account of a patient's emotional and spiritual needs and is often supported by bureaucratic and impersonal organisations.

3. Critics of the approaches which emphasise unconventional methods argue that scientific analysis of illness and treatment are the safest ones.

Theories of Health

■ **Social work and medicine are best described as part of the apparatus of state control, a means of making individuals conform to society. Discuss.**

The Marxist perspective

This is based on the view that people's lives are shaped by the economic infrastructure of their society. In a capitalist society illness is defined as the inability to work.

1. Definitions of illness are in the hands of middle-class professional medical workers. They diagnose and establish who is and who is not ill. Working-class people are more likely to be perceived as malingerers. Their opportunities to receive time off through illness with pay are less than those of middle-class workers.
2. The state has taken an interest in the health of workers to ensure a healthy work force.
3. High levels of illness among working-class people is a reflection of their poor working conditions, stress and alienation.
4. For the same reasons there are higher levels of mental illness among working-class people. Working-class women are particularly prone to psychiatric illness as a result of their exploitation as workers and housewives.
5. Because profits come before health, consumption patterns among working-class people are determined by capitalist exploitation (white bread, cigarettes, alcohol, etc.: the diseases of affluence).
6. Unemployment rates are highest among those in Classes 4 and 5. Studies indicate that there is more ill-health among the long-term unemployed. They have higher mortality rates and suicide rates as well as higher divorce rates. This is also related to stress and discontentment.
7. By encouraging the assumption that ill-health is an objective physical ailment which strikes the population at random, this diverts attention from the class-based inequalities of illness and disease. People claim that their health is not under their own control.

Points of criticism

(i) The state is constantly seeking to improve health care. The fact that working-class people appear to be less healthy may be because they fail to make use of the facilities available.

(ii) As soon as an industry is regarded as hazardous it is subject to stringent health laws.

(iii) Capitalism has assisted the poorest sectors of society to improve their living conditions.

(iv) High rates of mental illness among women may be the result of their spending more time in the home, isolated from wider society and with more limited opportunities for careers.

(v) The capitalist market does not determine what people buy: it provides opportunities for choice. It is not just working-class people who suffer from diseases of affluence.

(vi) There is some statistical evidence to suggest that unemployed women have longer life expectations than those who are employed full time. It may be that the unemployed subjectively feel more ill because they have more time to ponder ill-health and to visit doctors.

(vii) People's health could be improved by better education so that individuals become better-informed about how to lead healthier lives.

Conclusions

1. Marxist analysis emphasises the health differences that exist between different social classes. The poorer levels of health among working-class people is explained in terms of the exploitation they suffer:

(a) The work they do tends to be more dangerous and more injurious to health.
(b) They consume larger quantities of the more dangerous commodities produced by capitalism (tobacco, alcohol, etc.).
(c) They are forced into poorer-quality housing in poor areas by the pressures of the housing market that is controlled by those with more wealth and more power (see page 205).
(d) They suffer higher levels of unemployment and consequently more stress and more severe economic problems.
(e) The power of capitalism to create illness is disguised to some extent by the provision of an efficient medical system.

2. Critics argue that there is no clear evidence to show that socialist societies are healthier than those in which capitalism is the dominant economic system.

■ **Consider the view that ill-health is normal in society.**

The functionalist perspective

This is based on the view that every institution in a society serves a function. Among the most important are those which help maintain stability and the integration of the individual in society. The state must provide a means of welfare to ensure that people can obtain the necessary care and advice when they are ill. Medicine is therefore seen as a device to ensure the adequate performance of important social roles.

Main points:

1. Since it would be dysfunctional to allow everyone to be absent from work simply because they 'felt ill', it is necessary to have an organised system of diagnosis and control. Doctors serve this important function. They can issue certificates to those they regard as genuinely ill. This system must operate in all societies, whether capitalist or socialist.
2. The role of the doctor is a highly professional one. It is subject to training, qualification and control by a professional organisation. It is a position achieved on merit. This is an example of the need for a hierarchical social system in which the most able reach the top and the least able remain at the bottom. (About 75 per cent of doctors come from Classes 1 and 2.)
3. The claim that medicine does and should have scientific status is justified.
4. As far as the patient is concerned one function of illness is to allow the individual to escape activities which are stressful or unpleasant for a period of time.
5. Vogel and Bell (*The Emotionally Disturbed Child as the Family Scapegoat*) argue that it may be functional for parents to have a disturbed child in the household since it enables them to release their tensions and draws them closer together. This helps to stabilise the family unit by enabling the parents to perform their roles in society more effectively.
6. Health care and health chances are distributed in a rational way in contemporary society. People have a choice as to which services to use and when to use them. Private medicine increases this choice. If there appears to be inequality in distribution it is only because some people make better use of the facilities than others.
7. The groups in poor health are declining as medical welfare improves.
8. Upward social mobility ensures that more people are leaving the dangerous, unhealthy jobs. New technologies will eventually see their eradication.

Points of criticism

(i) The organisation of occupations into professions is a way in which particular groups maintain their privileges and power. Gomm points out how doctors often develop 'deterrent strategies' to cope with what they consider to be abuse. They may keep lists of suspect patients or 'shelter behind a fierce receptionist, refuse home visits or adopt a cold attitude.'
(ii) The professionalisation of medicine is an example of capitalist self-interest in which power is passed on from one generation to the next. Those at the bottom have no real chance of reaching top professional positions.
(iii) Illich (*Medical Nemesis*) attacks the view that the medical profession confers scientific benefits on society. New drugs are introduced but they have harmful side effects. Their increasing use means that people are less likely to face pain, which would strengthen them and the whole culture. Medicine engenders drug addiction and ill-health, which produces a weaker society. He concludes that the medical establishment has become a major threat to health. Health has improved as a result of better diet, not drugs. Medical treatment is a means of convincing those who are subject to poverty and hardship that it is they who are ill rather than allowing them to see that their society is sick.
(iv) There can be dangers in allowing a person to accept the label 'invalid' about themselves since this can lead to negative patterns of behaviour.
(v) The views of Vogel and Bell place the interests of the family as a whole over that of the individual child whose chances of becoming an adequate parent in the future may be limited as a result.
(vi) Programmes to improve people's awareness of their rights with regard to health will have little effect because they do not affect the fundamental economic inequalities in society. The Court Report (see page 228) suggests that those parts of the country with greatest need get the worst provision of welfare services.
(vii) Prosser and Wedge (*Born To Fail*, see page 228) showed that there remain an increasing number of disadvantaged children suffering major health problems, especially in Classes 4 and 5.

(viii) High rates of unemployment inhibit upward mobility. Most mobility from Class 5 is into Class 4 and mortality rates have not improved in this class relative to others.

Conclusions

1. The Functionalist argues that society requires institutions and structures to maintain social stability. Definitions of good and bad health are taken to be objective and open to statistical measurement:

(a) Ill-health is seen as normal, in that people are bound to become ill from time to time and the different patterns of social and economic ill-health must be identified and resolved in order to satisfy the needs of the majority.
(b) This justifies the high status of professionals such as doctors, surgeons, dentists, etc., who service patients.
(c) Sickness is functional and normal because:
  (i) it promotes increased family integration when there is a sick person to care for, especially that of the parents where a child is involved; and
  (ii) it allows people to withdraw legitimately from their normal, often stressful, roles for a short period.
(d) High levels of sickness, or long-term withdrawal through self-diagnosed illness could become dysfunctional; the role of the doctor is to monitor the patient and limit absence from normal family and work roles to a minimum.

2. Critics argue that:

(a) The use of medicine in a capitalist society is as an agency of social control to maintain the existing power structures in society and to ensure that ill-health does not become a political issue.
(b) The medical statistics are open to similar criticisms as those of crime statistics (see page 176: Lewis 1(a)).

■ **At first sight 'health' and 'illness' appear to be simply medical issues. In what ways have sociologists contributed to an understanding of these aspects of human behaviour? (JMB)**

The interactionist perspective

This view is based on the idea that action develops from negotiated meanings which are constructed in the course of social interaction. People derive meanings from events and act on their interpretations.

1. Roth (*The Treatment of TB as a Bargaining Process*) wrote his findings based on field notes kept while he was in the roles of patient, an attendant and as a social observer. He spent time 'hanging around' the hospital wards and offices, attending conferences, making rounds and listening to doctors discussing their 'problems' with one another.

He argues that the treatment relationship may be conceived of as a conflict for control of the patient's behaviour, a conflict usually resolved by bargaining. Through their observations and pooling of information, patients learn appropriate behaviour patterns.

Roth is arguing that what happens to patients in a hospital is not a matter of objective fact relating to illness, but more a matter of subjective interpretation on the part of patient, nurse and doctor.

2. Goffman (*The Effects of Inmate Status*) used similar observational methods to describe how a mental patient starts by clinging to his memories and knowledge of his past. He gradually gives up this effort at anonymity and enters the hospital community. This is regarded as 'settling down' by the staff. He then undergoes further 'humbling moral experiences' as he becomes socialised into the patterns of hospital life and accepts his new persona as a 'mental patient'. He is presented with new models of behaviour, both by the staff and other patients. He comes to accept the reasons for his hospitalisation.

Points of criticism

(i) This perspective focuses on the micro-level of analysis. It does not take much account of the individual in relation to wider class or cultural values.
(ii) Staff would no doubt be surprised to be informed that they were teaching someone to become a 'mental' or a 'hospital' patient. They would have a different interpretation.
(iii) The views are also open to the criticism of all interactionist research, that it relies on the skills and accuracy of the observer, who draws on his own observations and interpretations of events, rather than on 'objective' scientific data.

Conclusions

1. The interactionist argues that people create meanings in their lives through symbolic communications and interpretations to make sense of the world.

(a) Health and illness are not seen as just medical issues, but as social constructs; they result from labels attached by professionals following a process of negotiation.
(b) The labelling process is effective because of the power doctors and other medical staff have.
(c) The work of sociologists adopting this perspective shows how doctors manage their patients by restricting the flow of information about their illness and their treatment; and how they manage their time, often giving more to middle-class patients than those from the working class.
(d) Goffman, Roth, etc., have shown how patients in hospitals must conform to the role of 'patient', often undergoing 'mortifying' and alienating processes, and changing their self-perceptions, from 'healthy' to 'ill'.
(e) The approach helps to make sense of the ways in which health and illness are created in a society and why the use of health statistics must be viewed and interpreted with care.

2. (a) Marxist critics argue that interactionist theories fail to take sufficient account of power structures in wider society or how the organisation of medicine is related to the economic structure of society and the interests of the ruling class.
(b) Functionalists argue that health statistics are a useful source of data, and definitions of health and sickness are objective facts not just social constructs.

■ **Outline and evaluate the sociological insights provided by viewing health as a *social construct*.**

Traditionally in Britain, it has been assumed that 'good' or 'bad' health was an objective physical characteristic. However, some sociologists have raised questions as to the validity of this view. How is good health to be measured? (Most people complain of some ailment from time to time without visiting a doctor.) What is 'illness'? At what point does it start and finish?

Two people may suffer the same ailments. One claims to be ill and is off work, the other does not and continues to work.

1. Gomm (*Social Science and Medicine*) argues that illness and disease, as well as health, are social products. The processes that distribute health chances are social processes. Definitions of terms, their diagnoses and treatment vary from place to place and time to time.

2. The process of becoming defined as 'ill' is a complex one. People have their own self-perceptions and can make decisions about what to do about them. Others in a family may seek to impose the role of invalid on an individual, in order to care for them, protect them, etc. In the case of mental illness, some writers such as Laing and Cooper suggest that this can have disastrous consequences (see pages 71 and 81).

3. There is a range of culturally derived knowledge about illness and health and how to respond to it. In Britain it may be 'having a temperature' and 'going to bed and calling a doctor'. In a tribal society it may be the failure of crops and the death of animals.

4. In Western societies the process of acquiring a label which defines the individual as ill is complex. It is not necessarily a matter of objective facts, but more a social process by which a person claims illness, is diagnosed and treated by a professional (or family amateur) and then comes to adopt the characteristics of illness (lethargy, distress, etc.). The work of Roth and Goffman (see p. 226) illustrates how patients in hospitals learn their roles and appropriate patterns of behaviour.

Conclusions

1. It is primarily Interactionists who see health as a social construct. They argue that they show how:

(a) The process of defining someone as 'healthy' or 'ill' requires a person to attach the label. This is normally a person in the society with the power and status to impose their definition on another.
(b) The person labelled 'ill' must adopt the appropriate role if treatment is to be successful.
(c) It makes the practices of medicine in pre-industrial societies more understandable, however bizarre they may appear.
(d) It makes us question some of the assumptions about scientific medicine:
    (i) that it is objective and precise;
    (ii) that health can be measured accurately; and
    (iii) reminds us that health statistics must be examined and interpreted with care, (that is, if more people report for medical treatment, this may reflect increased medical concern and awareness among particular social classes and the availability of treatment which may vary between regions).
(e) It makes us more concerned to question what health means and reminds us that it can have a range of meanings in different societies.
(f) It allows the idea that ill-health can have many causes outside those resulting from infection; our constant assessment of the health of others may affect our perception of our own.
(g) It makes us consider the role of doctors, their status and training, and their power to define health.
(h) It makes us aware of the processes which result in health differences between classes.

2. Critics of those who emphasise the view that health is a social construct (rather than an objective physical fact) argue:

(a) The view makes health and ill-health a relative concept (that is, a person becomes 'ill' if so defined by others).
(b) It encourages the methods of scientific medicine to be questioned and any bizarre remedy to be considered on the grounds that it will affect the patient's emotional and spiritual well-being.
(c) It encourages a range of untestable hypotheses to explain ill-health and untestable remedies to be used.
(d) It makes it hard to identify 'genuine' ill-health and undermines the position and status to the qualified doctor.
(e) It renders the use of health statistics as largely invalid and thereby may help restrain much valuable social policy which is often based on this data.

Inequalities in the Distribution of Health and Medical Care

■ **The social distribution of good health closely reflects the social distribution of wealth and income. Discuss.**

■ **The availability of good medical care tends to vary inversely with the needs of the population served. Discuss.**

1. There is evidence of unequal distribution of wealth in Britain (see Table 17.1).

Material welfare is unequally distributed and there is evidence that this affects life styles and life chances.

2. In 1985 the Low Pay Unit reported that some workers were earning less than £1 per hour. In 1983 the *Sunday Times* noted that the Duke of Westminster had an income estimated to be about £10 800 per hour. In 1989 he was reported to be the second richest person in the UK (worth £3200 million, in a study which showed that the 200 richest people owned about £38 billion (8 per cent of Britain's gross national product GNP).

Table 17.1 Distribution of wealth in Britain

Marketable wealth owned by:		1976	1981	1989
Wealthiest	1%	21	18	18
	5%	38	36	38
	50%	92	92	94
Poorest	50%	8	8	6

Source: OPCS.

Table 17.2 Infant mortality rates (UK), 1989 (per 1000 live births)

Class 1	6
Class 2	6.1
Class 3a	7.0
Class 3b	7.1
Class 4	9.0
Class 5	10.6

Source: OPCS.

Table 17.3 Standardised mortality ratios (SMRs) of men, married women (by husband's occupation) and single women, aged 15–64, by social class, 1971

Group	Class 1	Class 2	Class 3	Class 4	Class 5	All
Men 15–64	76	81	100	103	143	100
Women 15–64	77	83	103	105	141	100
Women (single)	83	88	90	108	121	100

Source: Quoted in I. Reid, *Social Class Differences in Britain*, Open Books, 1977, p. 125.

Table 17.4 Comparison of social class standardised mortality ratios (SMRs) for selected causes in men and married women, aged 15–64, 1971

Cause	Class 1		Class 2		Class 3		Class 4		Class 5	
	Men	Women	Men	Women	Men	Women	Men	Women	Men	Women
Tuberculosis	40	41	54	61	96	102	108	112	185	178
Coronary	98	69	95	81	106	103	96	107	112	143
Bronchitis	28	33	50	51	97	102	116	118	194	196
Cirrhosis	106	94	136	132	86	92	85	92	137	115

Source: I Reid, *Social Class Differences in Britain*, Open Books, 1977 p. 115.

Table 17.5 Infant mortality rates by social class, 1921–90 (per 1000 live births)

Year	Class 1	Class 2	Class 3	Class 4	Class 5
1921	38	55	76	89	97
1950	17	22	28	33	40
1970	12	14	16	20	31
1980	9	9	10	13	16
1990	6	6.1	7.4	10.4	11.0

Source: OPCS.

3. Recent editions of *Social Trends* fail to give much information about health inequalities, making it hard to obtain up-to-date information. There are differences in infant mortality rates (see Table 17.2).

4. Earlier research suggests that the poorest sector suffered more ill-health and had least access to welfare facilities:

(a) The Court Report, 1973. This was set up to examine health services for children. It found:
  (i) the parts of the country with greatest need got the lowest provision of services;
  (ii) there was no evidence that the areas that needed better provision actually got it;
  (iii) the reverse was true: in regions with a high birth rate, a high proportion of children in the population, or high infant mortality, the numbers of GPs and local authority medical staff were low.
  (iv) The Report found that poverty and ill-health are fellow travellers, particularly in childhood.
  (v) The provision of health services had moved in the opposite direction. In areas with high living standards, health was better and more was spent on medical facilities.

(b) Prosser and Wedge (*Born to Fail*). This 1973 publication showed that nearly 900, 000 children were growing up disadvantaged and faced an accumulation of adversities. (They were considered disadvantaged if growing up in a large family or with only one parent, with low income and poor housing.) Such children were found to suffer more health problems; were less likely to be immunised against serious illness; 1 in 3 never attended a welfare clinic; there was a great prevalence of infection; and, in the sample their general physical development was less good by the age of eleven than those not disadvantaged.

(c) The Black Report, 1980 (*Inequalities in Health*) also pointed out the major inequalities in health and health services. Death rates vary between social classes, suggesting that it may be desirable to re-allocate resources and provide more for those in greatest need. The recommendations are set out in this report (edited by Townsend and Davidson).
(d) Fox (*Unemployment and Mortality*) found that in 1981 unemployed men (compared with others in the sample of the same age) were more than twice as likely to commit suicide; 80 per cent more likely to have a fatal accident and 75 per cent more likely to die from lung cancer. The death rate was 36 per cent higher among such men than it should have been.
(e) Platt (*Leeds University Report*, 1984) said that the evidence of an association between unemployment and suicide was overwhelming. He concluded that health and social policy should be devised on the assumption that unemployment endangers health. Present policies are based on the opposite assumptions. Unemployment tends to be concentrated in large families where the parents are unskilled. In 1982, 96 per cent of professional husbands had a job whereas only 67 per cent unskilled workers were employed.
(f) *Faith in the City* (1985) suggested that the poor tend to suffer greater loss of dignity, have less power and are generally treated less well. Inequalities (including those of poorer health) followed them throughout life.
(g) Wicks (*A Future for All*) noted that:
   (i) While wealth and income increased throughout society in the 1980s (more people became home owners, had more consumer durables, and more children left school with more qualifications), none the less there remained two nations: the lowest 50 per cent of the population own about 6 per cent of all marketable wealth.
   (ii) About 70 per cent of the unskilled manual working class were tenants; 90 per cent of Classes 1 and 2 were owner-occupiers.
   (iii) Although it is hard to ascertain, it seems likely that the inequalities in health noted by earlier research remain.

Conclusions

1. Those who argue that there is a correlation between inequalities in the distribution of wealth and that of health claim:

(a) Although it is increasingly hard to obtain, there is statistical evidence that wealthier people are more likely to avoid illnesses that cause high mortality rates in the working class.
(b) The author of the Inverse Care Law suggested that the less affluent members of well-paid occupations tend to suffer more illness.
(c) The Black Report was firm in its view that material deprivation was a major cause of inequality in mortality rates between the classes.

2. Critics argue that:

(a) If such inequalities existed the classes would have polarised. They do not appear to have done so, so it seems unlikely that poor health results from material shortages of goods necessary to sustain health.
(b) Interactionists would argue that health statistics are hard to interpret. Trends are complicated, for example, by changes in the class structure over time and frequent modifications of the Registrar-General's scale.
(c) Some researchers argue that it is not so much inequality in distribution of wealth and income that causes inequalities in health provision and standards. Rather, it is differences in class norms. The working class (often involved in hazardous or dangerous manual work) also retain outmoded values that are injurious to good health (for example, smoking and drinking heavily, and indulging in unhealthy diets).

Class Differences in Mortality Rates

■ **Describe and account for the social differences in mortality rates in Britain in this century.**

1. Analysis of differences in mortality rates rests on the use of statistical data which positivists claim provides clear factual information (a view disputed by interactionists).

2. Gomm ('Social Science and Medicine') argues:

(a) There is repeated evidence to show that the risk of death before the age of 65 is much greater for unskilled manual workers (especially men), and even diseases popularly associated with overworked executives in fact cause a higher mortality rate among those in Class 5.
(b) The middle classes have also reduced their risk of premature death more rapidly than has the working class.

3. The evidence: see Tables 17.3 and 17.4.

Comments

(i) To make comparisons between classes more meaningful, SMRs are produced:

$$\frac{\text{observed deaths}}{\text{expected deaths}^{*}} \times 100$$

The SMR for any given population is taken to be 100.

(ii) The trend for growing inequality between the social classes is established.

(iii) The single women's rates show a shorter, more level distribution (from 83 in Class 1 to 121 in Class 5, compared with 77 to 141 for married women).

(iv) Women live longer than men (see page 214) but women suffer more ill-health (especially in Classes 4 and 5). They may suffer more problems as a result of their dual roles as mother and worker; also the manual work they often undertake may be unhealthy.

---

* 'Expected deaths' is the number one might expect to find in a particular social clan if the age specific death rate for the population (15–64) was replicated in the group in question.

Questions

Examine photograph 43.

In the 1970s studies (for example, *The Court Report*) suggested that health care in Britain varied inversely with the needs of the population it served.

(i) Explain this statement.

(ii) Discuss the possible problems faced by an elderly widower in a poor inner-city area in contrast with one in a prosperous area. What particular differences might emerge if the inverse care law still applied?

(iii) Consider how you would conduct research to discover whether it remained true at the present time.

43

Source: Alec Gill

3 Analysis of Registrar-General's Reports (1961, 1971) confirms that life chances were worse in the lowest social classes (for example, those in Class 5 had 2.5 times more chance of dying before retirement age than those in Class 1). See Table 17.5.

Comment

1. Morris and Heady analysed 80 000 stillbirths (deaths in the first week of life), neo-natal deaths (deaths in the first four weeks) and post-natal deaths (deaths in the first year of life) between 1949 and 1950 and compared the results with data for 1911. They found:

(a) There was a reduction in infant mortality rates in all social classes, but differences remained between each one.
(b) Rates for infants born into the homes of unskilled workers were about forty years behind those whose fathers were in Class 1. (This has now fallen to about thirty years.)

2. House of Commons Social Services Committee, 1985. Their report revealed the following:

(a) Babies born into unskilled working-class homes are almost twice as likely to die in the first week of life as those from Classes 1 and 2.
(b) Class differences widened in the years 1978–82, as a result of: the economic recession; poor nutrition among lower-working-class mothers; inadequate health care in inner-city areas; and the failure of GPs to encourage their patients to check into ante-natal clinics early in pregnancy.

3. The differentials in rates between the classes was maintained in data for 1990. In addition to the issues noted in section 2 above, in the latter part of the 1980s the economic depression took firmer hold; unemployment reached 2.8 million, with those in Classes 4 and 5 facing the greatest hardship; more homes were repossessed; and more children were born to single mothers. Fox (1984) found a link between unemployment and mortality.

4. Suicide rates.

(a) Reid noted that data for 1971 showed that suicide rates for men increased between Class 1 and Class 5. For women it was highest in Classes 1 and 5.
(b) In 1992 a Report in *British Medical Journal* noted that while suicide rates were falling generally, among the old they were static but among the young they were increasing. The suggested causes included unemployment and family breakdown. However, these were seen as part of a complicated matrix of factors.
(c) But note the views of Atkinson (page 16).

5. Wicks (*New Statesman and Society*) points out that recent editions of *Social Trends* omit details of inequality. Many sections portray Britain as a classless society, even in those areas (such as health) where class is a determinant of life chances.

Possible explanations for the social differences in mortality rates

1. *Marxists* would argue that they are:

(a) The result of the way the capitalist economic system operates. It favours the middle class and exploits the remainder.
(b) Classes 4 and 5 are employed in dangerous and stressful work. They suffer more accidents, and are generally more affected by problems of unemployment.
(c) The social distribution of health is seen to be as unequal as the distribution of wealth, income and material advantages.
(d) There are cultural variations in the lifestyles of the classes. Heavy drinking and smoking may be used by those in Classes 4 and 5 to help them cope with the stresses they face. Their rejection of good health messages may reflect their sense of powerlessness and the working-class ethic that the future is not in their own control.

2. *Functionalists* would argue that:

(a) Inequalities are inevitable in every aspect of social life, not least in health.
(b) Not everyone is socialised to be health-conscious or to take the advice of health experts.
(c) Ill-health is functional in legitimising brief exclusion from stressful roles and for identifying areas of social concern.
(d) As social mobility increases, so health will improve. The fittest will move into higher social classes, improve their material standards and climb out of poverty.

3. *Interactionists* would stress:

(a) Health differences are matters of social construction and social process.
(b) The ways in which health matters are negotiated and dealt with by doctors and other health professionals.
(c) Doubts on the value of the health statistics as objective facts.

Suggested Reading

Works noted in this chapter

Black Report (1980) *Inequalities in Health*, Penguin
D. Cooper (1972) *The Death of the Family*, Penguin
A. Fox (1981) *Unemployment and Mortality*
I. Goffman (1973) *The Effects of Inmate Status: Asylums*, Pelican
R. Gomm (1979) 'Social Science and Medicine', in R. Meighan *et al.*, *Perspectives on Society*, Nelson
I. Illich (1975) *Medical Nemesis*, Calder and Boyers
R. Laing (1976) *The Politics of the Family*, Penguin
R. Meighan *et al.* (1979) *Perspectives on Society*, Nelson
R. Morris and Heady in P. Worsley (ed.) (1970), *Modern Sociology*
A. Platt (1984) *Faith in the City*, SCM
H. Prosser and P. Wedge (1973) *Born to Fail*, Hutchinson
I. Reid (1977) *Social Class Differences in Britain*, Open Books
A. Rose (ed.) (1972) *Human Behaviour and Social Processes*, RKP
J. Roth (1971) 'The Treatment of TB as a Bargaining Process' in A. Rose (ed.), *Human Behaviour and Social Processes*, Routledge and Kegan Paul
E. Vogel and N. Bell (1968) 'The Emotionally Disturbed Child as the Family Scapegoat', in N. Bell and E. Vogel (eds) *A Modern Introduction to the Family*, Free Press
M. Wicks (10 February 1989) 'The Vanishing Poor', *New*

Statesman and Society
M. Wicks (1989) *A Future for All*, Penguin
B. Wilson (1973) *Magic and the Millenium*, Paladin

Works for further reading

C. Carter and J. Peel (1976) *Inequalities in Health*, Academic Press
A. Coote (1983) 'Death to the Working Class', in M. O'Donnell (ed.), *Readings in Sociology*, Harrap
Department of Health (1992) *Statistical Bulletins* Department of Health, Honey Pot Lane, Stanmore HA7 1AY
L. Doyal and I. Pennell (1979) *The Political Economy of Health*, Pluto Press
E. Evan-Pritchard. (1937) 'Witchcraft, Oracles and Magic', in M. O'Donnell, M. (ed.) (1983) *Sociology*, Harrap
M. Haralambos (1985) *Sociology: New Directions*, Causeway
N. Hart (1935) 'The Sociology of Health and Medicine', in M. Haralambos, *Sociology: New Directions*, Causeway
T. Hart (1971) 'Inverse Care Law', *Lancet*, I
HMSO (1992) *Mortality Statistics*, HMSO
HMSO (1992) *Population Trends*, HMSO
HMSO (1992) *Regional Trends*, HMSO
K. Kesey (1973) *One Flew Over the Cuckoo's Nest*, Pan
V. Navarro (1976) *Medicine Under Capitalism*, Croom Hel
G. Stimpson and B. Webb (1975) *Going to See the Doctor*, RKP

Self-test Questions

Study these extracts from newspapers and answers the questions below.

Item A

■ The first AIDS video for schoolchildren was launched yesterday amid controversy about its explicit references to sexual acts.

Leaders of the Inner London Education Authority, which made the film, denied it broke the law requiring children to be taught about sex in a moral context. They also rejected criticism over the inclusion in the video of an 18-year-old student at an ILEA college who described himself as "a gay man".

Source: Extract from an article by Oliver Gillie in the *Independent*, 1 October 1987, p. 4.

Item B

Sir Donald said it was only after the first Aids advertisements appeared in March 1986 that ministers "began to feel that they might themselves tiptoe into the limelight".

He admitted the early advertisements were amateurish but said they were an important breakthrough because they showed the public was willing to receive advice about unpleasant aspects of a taboo matter if it was given in good faith.

Sir Donald, who is now special adviser to the World Health Organisation in the former Yugoslavia, said there was no vaccine or cure against the disease and it was unlikely that there would be one within the next 10 years.

He said there was a worrying rise in cases of the disease in homosexual men and a small but steadily growing number of heterosexual infections.

A recent study in America of young people aged 16 to 21 in inner cities had found infection rates of one in 300. "I quote this example from the United States not because we can read across directly from the American experience to our own growing underclass of homeless young people but because the situation there shows that within at least one developed Western country the epidemic remains unstable."

He said that recent studies in Britain "demonstrate beyond a shadow of doubt the existence of a small but growing pool of individuals who have become infected as a result of sexual intercourse with a person within the UK who themselves acquired the infection from heterosexual intercourse — so-called second-generation cases.

"It is understandable but worrying that because these people by definition have no idea that they have been at risk they tend to be diagnosed later when they are already ill and probably have been infectious for some time."

Looking to the future Sir Donald said: "It seems to me inevitable that HIV from this small heterosexual pool will continue to spread at first almost imperceptibly.

"What is certain is that we have an infection with a latent period of 10 years.

"We have to take a very long view indeed of this epidemic — a view which takes account of our children and grandchildren as well as ourselves."

Source: Extract from an article by Chris Mihill in the *Guardian*, 27 August 1992, p. 6.

Item C

THE PUBLIC SECTOR has always faced difficult choices about which services to provide, and how to deliver them. Health authorities are leading the way in a novel approach to this problem: asking the public, through opinion polls and other surveys.

In January the NHS Management Executive circulated a document entitled *Local Voices*, which called for "a radically different approach" to consultation, involving the broader community in decision making. Although it is not yet obligatory, it is a clear indication of government thinking for the whole of the public sector. Health authorities are encouraged to be involved in a wide range of continuing consultation procedures to establish the public's service priorities, and to try to reflect these in the decisions taken. Recognising that opinion polls cannot be regarded as infallible, other consultation methods are also advocated including user panels, focus groups and patient satisfaction surveys.

The rationing of health care is potentially the most emotive issue on which to consult the public. Dr Bobbie Jacobson is director of public health at the City of Hackney, in east London, which is conducting a survey of local views on service priorities. She says there are enormous ethical problems involved, especially in an area as poor as Hackney, where very few people can exercise the choice of using private health services. "We asked people to put 16 choices into categories of importance, but they had difficulties, because people in Hackney can't go private if they want an abortion, for example."

Those using the results have to be aware that the wording of questions and their context strongly influence the answers given. In an early Hackney survey respondents said that intensive care for premature babies weighing less than one and a half pounds should be a top priority. When the question was reworded and asked again, indicating the low survival expectations, this became the lowest priority.

Source: Extract from an article by Paul Gosling in the *Independent*, 6 August 1992, p. 16.

Item D

More babies born below safe weight

MORE babies are being born with low weight that makes them acutely vulnerable to cot death, government figures revealed yesterday. The marginal rise, against expectations, will be seen as evidence of the growth of poverty and poor health among pregnant women.

The rise emerged as statistics showed the continuing gap between north and south in baby deaths. Last year, a baby in Bradford was almost three times as likely to die within a year as one in the health district of North Hertfordshire.

Officially a low-birthweight baby is below 2,500 grams, or 5.5lb. Such babies account for 60 per cent of all stillbirths and 50 per cent of infant deaths, within a year of birth.

The proportion of babies classified as low-birthweight in England and Wales rose to 6.9 per cent in 1991 from 6.8 per cent the two previous years.

The rate of perinatal mortality, or deaths of foetuses after the 28th week of pregnancy and of babies under a week old, was 8.0 deaths per 1,000 live births for England and 7.9 for Wales. Five of the 14 English health regions — Northern, Yorkshire, Trent, West Midlands and South West Thames — show a rise in perinatal mortality between 1990 and 1991, as does Wales, and two regions — Northern and Oxford — show a rise in infant mortality.

The Office of Population Censuses and Surveys, which publishes the figures, says the fairest district comparisons are over three years.

Bradford has the worst infant mortality rate for 1989-91, of 12.1, although the worst for 1991 alone is Central Manchester, with 13.8. The best three-year average is that of North Hertfordshire, with 4.3, and of the best 10 districts only Chester, with 4.7, is not in the south.

Infant mortality: 1989-91

10 Worst Districts	**Rate per 1,000 births**
Bradford	12.1
Central Manchester	11.8
Calderdale	11.5
West Birmingham	11.5
Hartlepool	11.2
Wolverhampton	11.2
Rhymney	11.2
South Birmingham	11.1
Blackburn, Pendle, Rossendale	11.0
Coventry	10.7
10 Best Districts	
North Herts	4.3
Chester	4.7
North West Herts	4.7
Huntingdon	4.9
Chichester	5.0
Somerset	5.0
East Surrey	5.1
Winchester	5.1
Mid Downs	5.4
Mid Essex	5.4

OPCS Monitor DH3 92/1; Information Branch (Dept M), OPCS, St Catherine's House, 10 Kingsway, London WC2B 6JP; £2.

Source: Extract from an article by David Brindle in the *Guardian*, 3 September 1992.

Item E

A SEARCH was launched yesterday to fill Europe's first professorial chair of alternative medicine by early next year.

The £50,000-a-year post at Exeter University will aim to bring scientific rigour to non-orthodox therapies.

The chair is being funded through a £1.5 million donation from Sir Maurice Laing, president of the building company John Laing. He has been interested in complementary medicine for more than 30 years.

For the past five years an Exeter centre for complementary health studies has been offering post-graduate qualifications in certain disciplines to doctors, nurses, and suitably-qualified alternative medicine practitioners. It concentrates on homoeopathy, osteopathy, chiropractice, acupuncture, and herbalism and eschews the more eccentric fringe therapies.

The professor is expected to be qualified in orthodox medicine but also experienced in at least one alternative discipline.

Source: Extract from an article by Chris Mihill in the *Guardian*, 29 June 1992.

1. Examine Items A and B.

(i) Discuss the effectiveness of using the mass media:

(a) to try to influence and change cultural attitudes and values; and

(b) to inform the public about new and complex issues.

(ii) What problems are likely to be encountered in seeking attitude changes in the case of AIDS?

(iii) How could any changes in attitude and level of knowledge be measured?

(iv) Is there evidence that the attempts have been successful?

2. Examine Item B.

The evidence is that at present there is no cure for AIDS. Discuss the view that it is a disease which requires careful sociological analysis as well as medical expertise and that it cannot be defeated by science alone.

Consider:

(a) Problems of poverty.

(b) Class factors.

(c) The feminist views on the position of women.

(d) The views of religious commentators.

(e) The problems of changing sexual attitudes and values.

(f) Attitudes towards marriage and cohabitation.

(g) The impact of media sterotypes.

(h) The role of the media.

3. Examine Item C.

(i) Explain some of the problems that Health Authorities may encounter in seeking the views of the public on the ways that health-care should be rationed.

(ii) Clarify the ethical problems that may be encountered.

(iii) Suggest how the same question (relating to the priority that should be given to premature babies) may have been worded in two different ways to produce two different answers.

(iv) Give examples of where opinion polls have been shown to be fallible in other sociological research.

(v) Explain how the other methods suggested may provide useful qualitative if not quantitative information.

4. Examine Item D.

(i) Draw a bar chart to show the differences in mortality rates between the five best and five worst districts listed

(ii) Suggest some reasons to account for the differences in rates.

(iii) Distinguish between infant mortality and perinatal mortality rates.

5. Examine Item E.

(i) To what extent is the high status of orthodox practioners based on their exclusive access to medicines, drugs, knowledge and skills beyond the layperson?

(ii) Consider the view that to increase the status of non-orthodox medical practioners, who are not qualified doctors, may undermine the professional authority of the highly-trained orthodox GP.

(iii) Discuss the social significance of the growth of non-orthodox medicine in an increasingly scientific age.

18

DEVELOPMENT

Questions on this topic cover the following areas:

1. Key concepts:
   (a) The meaning, definition and problems associated with terminology; for example, development; underdeveloped; Third World; modern; modernisation; traditional societies.
   (b) The sociology of modernisation.
   (c) The sociology of underdevelopment.
   (d) Possible measures of development.
2. Theories of development:
   (a) Functionalist views: modernisation theory.
   (b) Marxist views: underdevelopment: dependency theory.
   (c) Weberian views: diffusion theory.

Key Concepts

- **Some societies are described as *developed* and others as *undeveloped*. Explain what these terms mean and why they are of interest to sociologists.**
- **What are the main differences between modern *industrial* societies and *Third-World* countries?**
- **How far is a distinction between *traditional* and *modern* valid and useful in classifying societies?**
- **Distinguish between a sociology of *underdevelopment* and *modernisation.***
- **What is meant by *development*? How can it be measured?**

To answer any of these questions you must be clear as to the possible definitions of terms and some of their implications.

1. 'Development' may be used to describe:

(a) Changes within specific institutional forms, for example, 'the development of capitalist society';
(b) The move from one type of social structure to another, for example, 'the development of capitalism from feudalism'.

Note: There is a danger in assuming that some form of development is necessarily beneficial for a society and that all societies should aspire to 'development'.

2. Developed, industrialised, modern 'First-World societies': have well-organised, long-standing industrial bases, which are the source of wealth and high living standards (for example USA; Britain).

3. Second-World countries: those subject to effective industrialisation; but the term is generally used to describe the former Communist countries in the Eastern bloc. The distinction between First and Second Worlds is primarily a political one.

4. Third-World countries: characterised by a low per capita income, an abundance of unskilled workers, a lack of investment capital and an economy that relies on a few main crops, which may fail, causing great hardship.

5. The sociology of modernisation: the process of modernisation from underdeveloped to developed is advocated by many writers (especially in the Functionalist school). Such sociologists as Parsons and Moselitz have been interested in the debate as to the processes involved in a society becoming developed and modernised. They have been concerned with:

(a) the speed of social development;
(b) ways that development can be encouraged;
(c) factors which inhibit development.

For such writers, development implies the following:

(a) The ability to sustain increased population, providing sufficient food, housing and work.
(b) A more complex social life emerges providing a hierarchy of power and authority.
(c) Industrialisation reaches 'take-off' point. Machine-based production replaces agriculture as the major source of the production of wealth in society.

(d) Living standards are raised.
(e) Urbanisation occurs in a planned and organised way.
(f) There is division of labour producing more goods more cheaply for wider markets.
(g) There is the development of specialist institutions for education, welfare, leisure, etc.
(h) There are more complex forms of bureaucracy for purposes of government and administration, which ensures greater efficiency in all aspects of society.

6. Underdeveloped societies: There is no general agreement as to how societies develop and change; whether there are developmental stages or what precisely constitutes an underdeveloped society.

(a) One feature they may share in common is a colonial past.
(b) There is an implication that such societies are economically 'backward'. They are sometimes described as 'Third-World' countries, such as those of South America, and parts of Africa and Asia. They have some potential for growth and change but have not yet achieved the point of 'take-off'.
(c) The term 'Fourth World' has also been introduced by some writers to describe those that are even further behind in economic development and which appear to be stagnating (for example, Haiti; Ethiopia).
(d) Modernisation theorists suggest that such underdeveloped societies can be assisted towards development and modernisation by specific policies, and by becoming more exposed to the values and ideologies of advanced Western societies.

Note: There are equally difficult problems in the use of this terminology. The use of the term 'a developing society' may convey a sense of optimism that the society is progressing towards an idealised Western model. In fact, for many such societies their internal problems may be increasing and any economic benefits may be reaching only a small élite.

7. The sociology of underdevelopment:

(a) This has tended to be the area of interest for Marxist (or materialist) sociologists and economists. Marxist writers have examined the cause of underdevelopment in terms of the exploitation of Western capitalist societies.
(b) Marxists argue in their analysis of underdevelopment that obstacles to development are externally created by the exploiting powers.
(c) They see change resulting not from increased aid but from internal class struggle, leading to the overthrow of repressive élites.

Possible measures of developments

Measurement is obviously difficult since there is no precise agreement as to what constitutes an underdeveloped or a developed society. However, the following factors could be considered:

Economic It should be possible to calculate the levels of national and personal wealth in a society. These could be used to establish minimum levels below which a society could be described as underdeveloped. However, it is difficult to make such international and cross-cultural comparisons.

Political It may be possible to establish levels of development on the basis of answers to such questions as: Is there a democratic form of government? Is there an organised bureaucratic administrative structure?

Social Living standards could be assessed: opportunities to obtain housing, its quality, running water, electricity, etc. Also life expectancy, average family size, opportunities for education, levels of literacy, etc.

Legal The legal system in a developed society may be based on a long-standing accepted structure which offers justice, opportunity for appeal, etc.

By comparing levels of development and underdevelopment according to some criteria it may be possible to make judgements about standards in and between societies. Where there are deficiencies then policies could be directed to those problem areas.

Points of criticism

1. There is no universal agreement about what constitutes development or underdevelopment.
2. There is no consensus about how it can be measured.
3. There is also no agreement about how it occurs or what forms are most desirable.
4. Terms like these can be misleading, since they tend to divide the world into two or three camps which appear to be independent of each other and which may be ranked in terms of inferior and superior positions. In fact, most societies of the world are interlinked in a variety of ways.

Comments

1. The idea that underdeveloped societies can and ought to be modernised is part of the 'modernisation theory' favoured by functionalist writers.
2. The view that they can become modern (but not that they necessarily will) but they may be held up by lack of necessary leadership or social institutions, fits into a Weberian perspective on development.
3. The view that such societies ought not to follow the Western capitalistic pattern of growth is the view of the Marxist writers on the subject.
4. It is easy to adopt an ethnocentric position and view other societies in comparison with one's own.
5. While different schools of sociology tend to focus on different aspects of questions about development and underdevelopment, there are some divisions within each school, differing in their views of the major forces of social change.
6. A major difference between the theorists is that the Marxists tend to make use of mono-causal theory (based on economic factors) whereas others prefer multi-causal explanations.

Theories of Development

Modernisation theory

Associated mainly with Functionalists.

■ **Examine the view that modernisation theory offers too simple a model for understanding the problems of development. (AEB)**

■ **What are the major obstacles to modernisation in underdeveloped societies today? (UCLES)**

■ **Can societies be said to have evolved over time?**

Main points

1. Underdeveloped societies are said to be economically backward. They have the characteristics of *Gemeinschaft* societies: there is emphasis on ascribed status, primary relationships, and attachment to a locality. There is little social mobility.
2. Development and modernisation are based on a series of changes leading from one type of society to another higher, form which is more complex and economically sophisticated.
3. Any obstacles to development are the result of the maintenance of traditional elements in the society, which hinder rationalisation.
4. Development involves changes in the economic, political, family and religious institutions of society. These are a major part of the social system. To induce development it is necessary to obtain changes in the structure of society.

Evolutionary theory

Early functionalist perspectives

1. Comte and Spencer said that societies developed from simple to complex structures.
2. The evolutionary principles of the natural world could be applied to the social world.
3. The assumption was that societies developed in a fixed way, following the path of those already more advanced.

Points of criticism

(i) It is not possible to generalise from the pattern of the development of one society to that of another.
(ii) Every society is faced with specific problems in the course of change, and the solutions adopted by one may not be appropriate to those of another.

More recent Functionalist views:

1. There is a rejection of traditional evolutionary theory.
2. It is accepted that not all societies have an equal potential for development.
3. It is agreed that developmental change can take many forms. That which appears in Western Europe is only one type.
4. Since obstacles to development vary from one society to another, major radical change (rather than evolutionary change) may be necessary to achieve modernisation.
5. Also major structural changes may be necessary. For example, the abolition of primitive religions; the introduction of efficient schools and universities; the encouragement of the nuclear family; the imposition of more democratic political structures; more capital investment; improved transport and communication systems; more financial aid from rich Western societies.

Points of criticism

(i) Such views tend to ignore the effects of the colonial past and the effects of the negative attitudes which may have been imbued (for example, the effects of slavery).
(ii) Societies which have long-standing social structures based on traditional values, customs and beliefs cannot be 'reformed' in a simple way.
(iii) There is an assumption that 'the West is best' (that is, that the social and economic structure of developed societies is an ideal model for all underdeveloped societies to follow).
(iv) There is evidence that programmes for modernisation have not been successful. Forster (*The Vocational School Fallacy in Development Planning*) argues that to provide technical, vocational and agriculture instruction in schools has often failed because such experts cannot be absorbed into the economy. He says there is always the problem of 'generalised unemployment'.

Dependency theory

Mainly associated with Marxists.

■ **We should be less concerned with the sociology of development and much more with the sociology of underdevelopment.**

Underdeveloped societies remain poor as a result of long-term exploitation in international relations (especially through colonialism and imperialism). It is capitalism which has produced the dependency of the poor societies on the rich industrialised countries.

Early Marxist views

1. There are laws of social development which could be scientifically established to show that all societies move through a series of stages. These are: *simple*; *primitive*; *ancient*; *feudal*; *capitalist*; *socialist*; and *communist*.
2. Social development is related to economic factors. As the economic infrastructure changes so societies develop and new forms emerge. The highest form of social life is the final stage of communistic society in which there are no contradictions or inner weaknesses.

More recent neo-Marxist views

1. The rich Western societies have increased their wealth by exploiting and controlling the poor countries.
2. This has continued into the twentieth century. The power élites in these poor societies have aligned themselves with the interests of the West.
3. The result will be internal conflict as class divisions emerge and ultimately revolutionary changes will occur to promote the interests of the proletariat.

Points of criticism

(i) Not all underdeveloped societies can be explained in terms of capitalist exploitation. Many are underdeveloped and have no contact with the West.
(ii) Some societies remain underdeveloped even though there is aid from the West, and it would seem in the

interest of the industrialised societies that they should develop rapidly (for example, Mexico and Turkey).

(iii) The wealth of the advanced societies comes from advanced methods of technology and trade. It may also come from investment in other rich societies.

(iv) Rich countries with interests in poor ones do not necessarily have power over them.

Conclusions

In recent years some writers have presented a new interpretation of the direction and consequences of social change.

1. Bell (*The End of Ideology*) argued that the failure of Marxism in the USA meant that ideological differences had come to an end. There was, thereafter, likely to be consensus about political organisation and institutions. What was happening in America would happen elsewhere.

2. Fukuyama (a political scientist) (*The End of History*) has argued similarly that with the collapse of Eastern European Communist societies in the 1980s and 1990s there is an end to ideological conflict and therefore an end to history. By this he means that historical development has reached its end point in liberal democratic structures as exemplified in Western societies. He reinterprets the Marxist view concerning the evolutionary process of history and sees it ending not in a Communist utopia but in the system operating in late-twentieth-century America, which he describes as the culmination of human achievement. This embodies the principles set down in the French Revolution of 1789, which advocated liberty and equality. All other social systems are stages on the route to the liberal democracy which satisfies the majority because it promotes consumerism and the human desire for self-esteem.

Criticism

(i) The values of other ideologies, such as socialism or Islam will always retain some appeal to some people.

(ii) Why should liberal democracies not evolve into a new form of social organisation in the future?

(iii) The demands for liberty and equality are always in tension and the pull towards one at the expense of the other may lead to disequilibrium.

Diffusion theory

Mainly associated with Weberians.

- **Examine the major competing explanations for some societies remaining underdeveloped.(AEB)**
- **Critically examine a theory which explains how a society may change from being underdeveloped to developed.**

Main points

1. Underdeveloped societies remain poor until the values of a particular group, an innovationg élite, usually inspired by a charismatic individual, predominate in the society.
2. For change to occur it is necessary for a rationalisation process to develop. Bureaucratic organisation is the predominant characteristic of modern industrial society.
3. Affective and traditional action indicates that individuals have no real understanding of why they act as they do. They are guided by emotion and custom. These are the characteristics of underdeveloped societies.
4. Rational action involves clear knowledge of specific goals; it involves assessing a situation and following logical means to attain the goals. This is the dominant mode of procedure in industrial society.

Progress towards development

1. The main ways of achieving development are to encourage access to developed societies so that their values and ideas are absorbed.
2. Obstacles to development are lack of contact with developed models as well as lack of appropriate progressive institutions.
3. The progress of social development can never be foreseen or predicted in the way that Marxists claim is possible. This is because development is largely the product of processes of interaction, which cannot be prophesied.
4. Patterns of social change are in the hands of individuals whose ideas, beliefs and actions can influence events.

Points of criticism

(i) This view argues that a new religious creed or particular type of family structure could cause the development of a new economic system, which could result in developmental changes. However, some critics have asked whether the economic system creates the conditions for the new religious creed or for changes in the family structure. (In Britain, did the Protestant ethic help develop capitalism, or vice versa?)

(ii) The view is thought by some to overemphasise the significance of powerful leaders to impose new values on a large, traditionally minded population. Once they have disappeared it is likely that the society will revert to its traditional form.

(iii) To maintain change the society also requires a rapid growth in disciples of the leader, raw materials, fuels, markets and a political structure which is viewed favourably by Western societies, who provide other aid. Shared values may not be enough.

(iv) Many underdeveloped societies have had access to Western models as a result of colonial influence but they have not necessarily adopted Western values because they are not appropriate. They may also have rejected the values as unacceptable. Charismatic leaders may take the society in different directions and in some cases back to more traditional roots (Iran).

- **Contrast different sociological theories to explain the problems facing Third-World countries.**
- **To what extent have the theories of the sociology of development proved to be helpful in the analysis of the Third World?**

	Underdevelopment theorists (primarily Marxist)	Modernisation theorists (primarily functionalists)	Modernisation theorists (primarily Weberian)
Explanations for why the Third World remains poor	The exploitation by the rich colonial powers.	1. Lack of capital investment. 2. Failure to develop products for export. 3. Lack of stable political structures. 4. Failure to reform traditional social structures.	1. Lack of an ideology of social and economic progress. 2. Lack of trained, literate administrators. 3. Lack of an ethic of rationality.
Factors affecting the process of development	Failure to escape the influences of Western exploiters will inhibit change.	1. The ability of developed societies to exert influence. 2. The acceptance of highly developed Western societies as appropriate models for change.	1. The introduction of well-organised educational structures. 2. The presence of an educated modernising élite to impose new values on the society. 3. Charismatic leadership.
Attitudes towards the development of Third-World countries	While the capitalist societies continue to exert influence on them there is little chance of social change.	1. The influence of Western developed societies can only be beneficial. 2. The technology and ideology of free enterprise will speed development.	The chances of introducing progressive ideologies is good because the benefits can be seen through the media (e.g. Live Aid concert to raise funds for famine relief was viewed by 1500 million people in 140 countries in July 1985).

Points of criticism

Foster–Carter 'Development Sociology, Whither, Now?' is critical of the way development sociology has become too concentrated on particular theories and, he says in doing so it has become too restricted. He argues that:

(i) The crisis of the semi-collapse of the Second World of Communism in Eastern Europe in the late 1980s renders the term 'Third World' inaccurate.
(ii) Modernisation theory and dependency theory present too simplistic a dichotomy and are based on dated material.
(iii) While development sociology has been helpful in drawing attention to specific issues (for example, poverty, growth, change), it has been less successful in presenting solutions. There has also been an unhelpful overemphasis on deprivation.
(iv) He therefore advocates new approaches which would entail a broadening of the perspectives used.

Possible new approaches include a return to:

1. *Social anthropology*, which emphasises the importance of:
   (a) Social culture in analysis of behaviour.
   (b) The perceptions of the actors.
   (c) The micro-social which focuses attention on communities and individuals as they are affected by broader social forces.

2. *Comparative and historical sociology*, which:
   (a) Draws on evidence from a wide range of different societies over time.
   (b) Does not concentrate on 'want' and 'deprivation'.
   (c) Does not focus specifically on the Third World but more on geographical context.

3. *Modernisation theory*, on the grounds that:
   (a) There have been some interesting variations and interpretations by writers such as Berger and Giddens.
   (b) Areas such as the collapse of Communism and the rise of Eastern Asia would be usefully examined from this perspective. The success of Japan, Hong Kong, etc. seem to undermine the view that tradition (for example, Confucianism) is an obstacle to modernity.

4. *The globalisation of sociology*, which would entail:
   (a) A greater acceptance of the interconnectedness of other social sciences and increase the need for the use of the comparative method.
   (b) Accepting that knowing about the sociology of

Questions

Examine photographs 44, 45, 46, 47, 48, 49 and 50.

1. Some of these were taken in Britain and some in poor parts of Eastern Europe and Asia.
   (i) Using the photographs as examples, explain why it is difficult to assess from these which are the developed First-World societies and which are Second- or Third-World societies?
   (ii) Explain why the concept of development requires careful analysis.
   (iii) What further information would you require in order to establish which are the developed and which the underdeveloped societies?

2. Consider photograph 48. Why would Marxists claim that some societies remain underdeveloped because of a colonial past?

3. Consider photographs 44, 45, 47 and 50. Functionalists suggest that overall, social development and modernisation requires major changes in the social structure. What obstacles might a functionalist suggest inhibit changes in the life-style of these people?

4. Consider photograph 46. Under what conditions might custom and tradition inhibit the processes of societal development and when might it be an enriching part of the culture of a developed society?

5. Examine photograph 49.
   If this is interpreted as an historic part of a British city it may be accepted as part of the heritage and agreed that it should be listed for preservation. If, on the other hand, it is seen as a poor area of a Third-World city it may be seen as a slum ready for demolition. Explain how care must be taken
   to avoid ethnocentric attitudes in discussing the problems of undedevelopment and the Third World.

44

Source: Alec Gill

45

Source: Alec Gill

46

Source: Alec Gill

47

Source: Alec Gill

48

Source: Alec Gill

49

Source: Alec Gill

50

Source: Alec Gill

Britain and generalising from it is not enough. This perspective could become sociology's fundamental unit of analysis in the future.

Conclusions

Foster-Carter suggests that

(a) Development sociology has been helpful for the discipline in putting on the agenda issues of practical urgency (for example, deprivation).
(b) It has been of analytical value in seeking to explain the uneven development of different societies.
(c) It now needs to invigorate itself and mingle with other areas, perspectives and social sciences.
(d) In particular, he argues, a varied comparative sociology is required for for the future.

Suggested Reading

Works noted in this chapter

A. Foster-Carter (1991) 'Development Sociology. Whither. Now', *Sociology Review* (November), Vol. 1, No. 2

D. Bell (1961) *The End of Ideology*, Free Press

P. Forster (1979) The Vocational School Fallacy in Development Planning, in Meighan, R. *et al.* (eds), *Perspectives in Society*, Nelson

F. Fukuyama (1992) *The End of History*

Works for further reading

H. Alvi, and T. Shanin (eds), (1982) *Introduction to the Sociology of the Developing Societies*, Macmillan

E. Boserup (1970) *Women's Role in Economic Development*, Allen & Unwin

J. Burton (1972) *World Society*, CU

A. Foster-Carter (1985) 'The Sociology of Development' in M. Haralambos, *Sociology: New Directions*, Causeway

D. Gregory and J. Urry (1985) *Social Relations and Spatial Structure*, Macmillan

A. Giddens (1990) *The Consequences of Modernity*, Polity Press

A. Gilbert and J. Gugler (1982) *Cities, Poverty and Development*

M. Haralambos (1985) *Sociology: New Directions*, Causeway

P. Harrison (1981) *Inside the Third World*, John Wiley,

N. Long, and A. Long (eds), (1992) *An Actor Struggles* and *The Social Construction of Knowledge*, Routledge & Kegan Paul

W. Rostow (1971) *The Stages of Economic Growth*

J. Roxborough (1979) *Theories of Under Development*, Macmillan

L. Sklair (1991) *The Sociology of Global Systems*, Harvester

T. Skocpol (ed.), (1984) *Vision and Method in Historical Sociology*, CUP

B. Turner (1990) *Theories of Modernity*, Sage

A. Webster (1984) *An Introduction to the Sociology of Development*, Macmillan

Self-test Questions

Study these items and answer the questions below.

Item A

HAVE

- 25 per cent world population
- 80 per cent consumption of energy
- Average US citizen uses 12,000 tonnes of coal (equivalent) a year
- 86 per cent of world industry
- Five countries control 60 per cent of industry
- Water use 350-1,000 litres per day
- 40 per cent water used for industry
- 500 million earn more than $20,000 per year
- 250,000 die on roads a year, 10 million are injured
- Consumes 70 per cent fossil fuels
- Consumes 85 per cent chemical production
- Consumes 85 per cent military spending
- Consumes 90 per cent automobiles
- 8 per cent work in agriculture
- More than 80 scientists per 1,000 people
- For every 100 teachers 97 soldiers
- Military spending 1991 $762 billion
- Rich nations pay 4 % interest on foreign debt

HAVE NOT

- 75 per cent population
- 20 per cent consumption of energy
- Average Ethiopian consumes 55lbs coal (equivalent) a year
- 14 per cent of world industry
- 44 least developed countries 0.21 per cent of industry
- Water use 20-40 litres a day
- 93 per cent water used for food production
- 2 billion suffer chronic water shortage
- 3 billion earn under $500 per year
- 800 million illiterate people
- Diarrhoea kills 4.6 million children a year
- Ratio cars to people 1:10,000
- 14m children die malnutrition per year
- 40 countries poorer than in 1980
- Has 12.9 per cent of world trade
- 700 million unemployed
- 100 million affected by famine 1990
- Military spending $123 billion.
- Poor nations pay 17 % interest on debt

Sources: UN; UNDP; World Bank; UNEP; Global Commons Institute, World Development Movement.

Item B

The South now subsidises the North and can never repay its loans. Crippling interest repayments mean many countries are forced to produce and export at the expense of their national health, wealth and environment

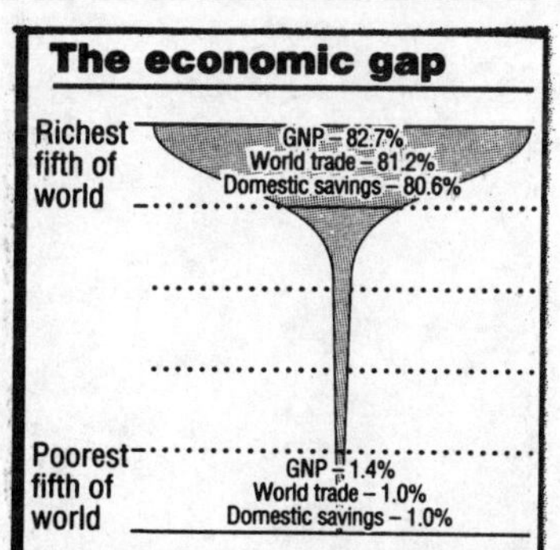

1. Examine Item A.
   (i) The table distinguishes between the rich (*Have*) and poor (*Have Not*) countries. Suggest and justify five points which help explain why the latter have such difficulty in modernising.

2. Examine Item B.
   (i) This suggests that countries in the northern hemisphere are wealthier and more prosperous than many poor countries in the southern hemisphere. Some sociologists have argued that by a process of evolution all societies follow the same path of progress towards modernisation. What factors make it difficult to close the economic gap?
   (ii) What points of criticism might be raised against the evolutionist assumptions?

3. Using the data in Items A and B:
   (i) Discuss how Marxists might argue the case for the exploitation of the poor countries by the rich.
   (ii) Suggest why many of Marx's predictions have not been fulfilled.
   (iii) Suggest how the discussion of development and modernisation is often made difficult by the introduction of ethnocentric values.

19

POVERTY

Most of the questions on this topic relate to the following areas:

1. Problems of defining poverty.
2. Who are the poor?
3. Theories to explain the causes and persistence of poverty. Analysis in terms of functionalist, Marxist and Weberian theories.
4. The contribution of sociology to the analysis of poverty.

Problems of Definition

■ **'Defining and measuring the extent of poverty in Britain is inevitably a value-laden exercise.' Discuss and explain. (AEB)**

To answer the question:

1. You must know at least three different ways of defining poverty.

Absolute or subsistence poverty This is measured by estimating a list of the basic necessities of life. They may include the number of calories and amount of protein to sustain life; quality of accommodation; availability of medical facilities to maintain good health, and even the availability of educational, leisure and cultural facilities.

Relative poverty This is measured in terms of assessments by people in society as to what is considered to be an acceptable standard of living at a particular time. Lafitte says it must be assessed in the context of the community's prevailing standards. Townsend says people could be poor where their resources are so seriously below those commanded by the average person that they are excluded from ordinary living patterns. Holman (*Poverty*) says it is concerned with the lowest incomes, being too far removed from the rest of the community.

Subjective poverty This refers to the subjective attitudes of people with regard to poverty. Do they feel themselves to be poor? How do they perceive themselves in relation to others in the society and how do their patterns of behaviour relate to their sense of being poor?

2. You need to know the details from studies or results from research which have produced some measurements of poverty using these definitions:

(a) Rowntree used *an absolute method of analysis* and found in 1901 that per cent 15 per cent of people in York has an income insufficient for them to achieve the minimum necessary for the maintenance of life. His last study in 1950 suggested that this had fallen to about 1.5 per cent.
(b) Townsend (*Poverty in the UK*), using *a relative concept*, says that over 50 per cent of the population of Britain are likely to experience poverty at some stage of their lives as a result of failure to enjoy the normal expectations of modern society.
(c) Using *a subjective analysis* of poverty, MORI researchers found that between 5 and 12 million people were living in poverty in 1983. More than 5 million said they considered themselves to be poor all the time and nearly 12 million said they were poor some of the time.

3. You must consider the meaning of 'inevitably value-laden'. This implies that some or all of the following points are true:

(a) The choice of definition is related to the values of the researcher (see page 22).
(b) The results produced may be biased by the values of the researcher.
(c) The interpretation of the results may be biased.
(d) The word *inevitably* suggests that it is impossible to conduct research into the topic without this occurring.

You must decide your views on the issue before entering the exam room. It would be possible to argue, for example, that sociologists who choose a relative definition of poverty are likely to be committed to liberal or radical views and a concern about the least well-off in the society. While this may not in any way cause them to be less than careful in the collection of their statistics, they may interpret their results to emphasise the extent of the problem.

■ **Assess the merits of different definitions of poverty.**

You are being asked to state the strengths of the three ways of defining poverty. (It would be reasonable in such a question to include some of the disadvantages, since this will help you to reach a conclusion.) Examine the merits and the weaknesses listed below.

Conclusions

Lister ('Concepts of Poverty') has considered the language of poverty. She argues that:

(a) Conventional definitions of poverty often obscure the different meanings experienced by certain groups such as women, black minorities and other ethnic groups.

(b) Academic distinctions between absolute and relative poverty have been blurred. They lack explicit recognition of how the meaning and reality of poverty and marginalisation might be different for different groups. Leech and Amin argue that blackness and poverty are more correlated in the 1990s than they were in earlier years. Members of black ethnic minorities often face the added burdens of unemployment and low pay.

(c) Women are particularly vulnerable to poverty and its attendant problems because their economic position is closely tied to dependency on men, who may not share income fairly.

(d) Hidden poverty may not be picked up by traditional measures which lump a couple's income together and assume they all share the same financial experiences.

(e) Other critics have noted that the official government statistics are not kept stable, either in absolute or relative terms, and so are not reliable measures. The figures of those living on incomes at or below benefit levels have not been published since 1988.

Who Are the Poor?

■ **Discuss the view that the major causes of poverty are illness, handicap and old age.**

■ **Unemployment has replaced old age as the major cause of poverty. Discuss. (UODLE)**

■ **The poor are always with us because there are always low-paid and disadvantaged families in society. Discuss.**

Questions such as these embrace the main categories of people whom research has suggested are the most likely to fall into poverty (either from a subjective or an objective point of view.)

Questions may ask you to assess which of the factors

Some of the merits

1. Absolute poverty:
(a) This helps to present a clear line between those who are and those who are not in poverty.
(b) It is possible by using this definition to show that poverty is being defeated as standards improve in the society.

2. Relative poverty:
(a) It presents a picture of a society as having serious problems, which may help to keep policy-makers more alert to deprivation.
(b) It is helpful in that it presents a comparison between people in the same society at the same time period.
(c) Townsend says that only by deciding on accepted living standards and lifestyles can we decide on the extent of poverty. Any definition must be related to the needs and demands of a changing society.

3. Subjective poverty:
(a) It is important to know what people believe, subjectively, about themselves and their relationships to others. This helps us to understand their behaviour.
(b) It is also a way of assessing general attitudes at a particular time. If an increasing number of people feel themselves to be in poverty they may become more active in seeking to change their environment.

Some of the weaknesses

1. Absolute poverty:
(a) Even within an absolute definition the numbers in poverty will vary according to which 'necessaries' are included.
(b) In showing that poverty is disappearing because living standards are improving this may disguise the existence of other forms of deprivation.

2. Relative poverty:
(a) This definition may be thought to overstate the extent of the problem and cause some to become more critical of those who complain.
(b) This definition makes it hard to see how poverty can ever be defeated since there is always going to be someone who is poor in relation to others.
(c) It is difficult to decide what an acceptable living standard is. Mencher says 'standards become so fluid that no definition of need satisfies the ever-changing expectations of modern life'.

3. Subjective poverty:
(a) Some people may be objectively in very deprived circumstances but they may not perceive themselves as being 'poor'.
(b) The failure of some to recognise their poor situation in relation to others may prevent them from applying for all the benefits to which they are entitled.
(c) Others may claim that they are poor when objectively they do not seem to be so.

Table 19.1 Numbers of people of pensionable – age 1951–91 (millions)

1951	*1961*	*1971*	*1981*	*1985*	*1991*	*2031*
6.6	7.5	8.8	9.6	9.7	10.5	14

Source: *Social Trends*, 22.

Table 19.2 Numbers claiming supplemantary benefit (millions)

1975	*1985*
1.7	3.0

Source: Social Trends, 22.

Table 19.3 Reported long-standing illness or disability by class, 1989–90 (per 1000 people)

Class 1	*Class 2*	*Class 3a*	*Class 3b*	*Class 4*	*Class 5*
291	*325*	*349*	*370*	*416*	*478*

Source: Social Trends, 22.

Table 19.4 Total numbers claiming invalidity benefit (GB) (thousands)

1976–7	*1981–2*	*1986–7*	*1989–90*
510	660	935	1190

Source: Social Trends, 22.

Table 19.5 One-parent families as a percentage of all families

1965	*1985*	*1988*	*1990*
9.3	*12.5*	*13.0*	*15.0*

Source: OPCS.

Table 19.6 Unemployment (millions)

1965	*1972*	*1975*	*1978*	*1982*	*1985*	*1990*	*1991*	*1992*
0.5	0.7	0.8	1.3	2.7	3.1	1.6	2.5	2.9

Source: OPCS.

Table 19.7 Gross weekly earnings of full-time employees, 1971–90 (£ mean)

	1971	*1981*	*1986*	*1990*
Males	32.4	138.2	207.5	295.6
Females	18.4	92.0	137.2	201.5

Source: OPCS.

(i) old age,
(ii) handicap and disablement,
(iii) one-parent families,
(iv) unemployment or
(v) low pay

is the major cause of poverty.
To answer such questions you must be able to suggest reasons to support and sustain a particular view.

Examples

1. Old age

1. People over retirement age lose their economic power. Most have to rely on state benefits for survival. Since these are fixed, pensioners face particular difficulties in times of high inflation. Numbers in the category have steadily increased (see Table 19.1).

2. Many old people fail to claim benefits to which they are entitled, making their economic position more serious. It is estimated that in 1985 this was almost one million (see Table 19.2).

3. The number of people of pensionable age has increased over the past forty years and the trend is projected to continue. In 1990 there were 10.5 million people in this category, a rise of 1 million since 1971. Numbers are expected to reach 14.5 million by 2031.

4. In 1988 23 per cent of pensioners' income came from occupational pensions, 60 per cent from state benefits.

2. The handicapped and disabled

1. Those in this category have lost economic status and power. They rely on benefits, which may often be inadequate.

2. **1974**: 570 000 were living within the range of supplementary benefit plus 20 per cent.
1975: 225 000 received supplementary benefit.
1981: 3.5 million were estimated to be handicapped or disabled.
1982: 29 per cent of households in Britain were thought to be affected in some way by such disadvantage.
1984: 1.25 million were registered as disabled.
1985: 5.5 million were estimated to be qualified to claim for various benefits.
(Source: Royal Association for Disability and Rehabilitation Survey.)

3. A 1988 study by OPCS (*Prevalence of Disability among Adults*) found that there were 6.2 million disabled

adults in Britain. The largest group (1.2 million) have mobility problems.

3. *One-parent families*

1. These include families broken by divorce, separation, death, imprisonment, etc.
2. Nine out of ten are headed by a woman who is faced with the problem of raising a family and holding a job. Poverty may be particularly severe for children of an unmarried mother without work and from a low socio-economic background.
3. Numbers in the category are increasing (see Table 19.5).
4. In 1988 there were about a million one-parent families caring for 1.6 million children.
5. In 1989 about 25 per cent of all children were born outside marriage. In 1991 the figure was 31.2 per cent (*Population Trends*, 68).
6. The National Council for One Parent Families reported that less than a quarter of one-parent families received maintenance in 1991 even when a court order had been made. (There are more than 80 000 enforcement proceedings in the courts every year.) Severe economic problems were found when maintenance was not forthcoming.

4. *The unemployed*

1. This group has increased most rapidly since 1965 (see Table 19.6).
2. The unemployed have no economic status or power. They rely on benefits. The numbers claiming have steadily increased. Some may also have been poor whilst in work as a result of low income.
3. The number of long-term unemployed (out of work for more than twelve months) has also increased, from about 150,000 in 1973 to 1 million in 1985. In 1991 a quarter of unemployed males and one in five unemployed females had been out of work for more than one year.
4. Daniel suggested that the types of worker most likely to become unemployed include:

   (a) the low skilled;
   (b) the low paid;
   (c) black workers;
   (d) women;
   (e) older and less fit workers.

5. Piachaud ('Problems in the Definition and Management of Poverty') said that:

   (a) High levels of unemployment have resulted in at least a threefold increase in the proportion of people living at below half the average income level between 1953–88.
   (b) There are 4 million recipients of income support and 1.5 million others receiving housing benefit. Two-thirds of unemployed claimants now depend on means-tested supplements.

5. *The low paid*

1. Low pay is usually defined as approximately two-thirds of the national average wage (see Table 19.7). The Low Pay Unit found that in 1991, 10 million adult workers (half of them part time), earned less than £5.15 per hour.
2. Increasing numbers of low-paid workers.

   (a) The number of low-paid workers has risen since 1979, when about 15 per cent were in the low-pay category.
   (b) In 1992, figures based on an analysis of the government's new earnings survey and the Council of Europe's 'decency threshold' gave the UK figure of £193.60 per week. They showed the percentage of workers who earned less than £180 p.w.:

Women manual workers:	74.8%
Women non-manual workers:	37.9%
Men manual workers:	24.5%
Men non-manual workers:	11.3%

   The main reasons for these figures were the changing composition of the work force, with greater participation by women, and increases in part-time and service sectors.
   (c) The low-paid have had virtually no real increase in pay between 1983 and 1991, while the earnings of the highest-paid 10 per cent have risen by a fifth in real terms. In 1987 the highest paid businessman earned £2.5 million.
   (d) The research notes that the earnings of the lowest-paid manual worker, when compared to the average, were lower in 1991 than in 1886 when records began.

3. Berthoud and Kimpson (*Credit and Debt*) found that in 1989 there were approximately 2.5 million households in debt. Most of these were low-paid.

Conclusions

Lister (*The Exclusive Society*) has argued that:

(a) Millions are barred from full citizenship because they fall into one or more of the categories most frequently found to suffer poverty.
(b) She claims that 'inequalities run like fault lines through society to shape the nation's civil, political and social spheres. Poverty spells exclusion from the full rights of citizenship, undermining their ability to fulfil the obligations of citizenship'.
(c) She calls for a 17-point charter for full citizenship, including a statutory minimum wage, an increase in child benefit and an end to homelessness.

Theories of the Causes and Persistence of Poverty

■ **Examine the implication of the statement that 'poverty is a class phenomenon, the direct product of the social pattern of class inequality'. How does this view compare with other sociological explanations of poverty? (JMB)**

It is useful to approach this type of question by reference to the major theoretical perspectives adopted by sociologists (see page 251):

■ **What explanations can sociologists offer for the persistence of poverty? How adequate are these explanations? (JMB)**

The Functionalist view

1. The function of inequality is to enable the most able to achieve their full potential in the competitive social world.
2. Poverty persists because only a few can achieve success. The less able are left behind and fill the bottom ranks of the hierarchy. It is among this group that the poor are found.
3. Inequalities in society also act as incentives. Those at the bottom should seek to improve their position. But they should never be given more than the minimum in case they lose their will to improve themselves.
4. The welfare state can be justified as a safety net to catch those unable to look after themselves. It serves the function of maintaining stability when people may otherwise become dissatisfied or totally dejected.
5. Poverty thereby helps create jobs for those who serve the poor.

The Weberian/Liberal view

1. A person's class position depends on their market situation: i.e. on the amount of power held by them to influence the chances of obtaining scarce resources. Also on the rewards that the person's skills and expertise can command in the competitive market place. From this point of view groups such as the old, the disabled, one-parent families, the low-paid and unemployed have little or no economic power. Therefore, they receive little economic reward. This is why they remain poor.
2. The poor are also among the weakest groups because they lack access to power. They are often non-union, low-paid workers and without the sympathy of the community.
3. The welfare state is important for them as a source of protection. It may also serve as a platform from which to improve their status.

The Marxist view

1. Poverty is an inevitable characteristic of a capitalist society. Wealth is concentrated in a few hands (those who own the forces and means of production).
2. Capitalism requires a motivated work force. This is achieved through inequalities and differentials in pay and conditions of work.
3. Poverty continues because it is in the interests to the ruling élite, which requires a submissive work force at all times.
4. To abolish poverty by increasing the real wages of the low-paid and all the benefits to those who cannot work and by ensuring full employment, would, this view, undermine and destabilise the whole of the capitalist economic structure.
5. The welfare state, although necessary, may generate false class consciousness by deluding people about the level of equality in society

---

There have been several explanations for the persistence of poverty:

1. The Culture of Poverty. This suggests that:

(a) The life style of the poor results in deprivation, which is transmitted from generation to generation.
(b) It has become a way of life or 'a design for living'.
(c) The poor share key characteristics: they are feckless; have marginal status; a sense of helplessness; view the future as beyond their control; and maintain a strong dependence on others, especially the welfare state.
(d) Those sharing the culture do badly in school, marry early and have large families, who in turn do badly in school, etc.
(e) Their social life is characterised by failure to integrate into mainstream values and failure to participate actively in important social activities, including those of education, politics, the work place or the local community.
(f) A culture of deprivation develops and enmeshes people, making it impossible for them to escape. For some observers, failure to achieve mobility also reflects the fact that in an openly competitive society the poor are not well placed to achieve much success, although a few well-motivated people may do so.

Points of criticism

(i) There is evidence from Third-World societies that many are poor without their sharing the central characteristics identified by the culture of poverty theorists.
(ii) Madge and Brown found from their study in Britain that different groups in poverty did not share the same characteristics. Nor did they find that people necessarily reared their children in the same ways as they had experienced.
(iii) The concept of culture has been criticised for implying deeply embedded values which are not susceptible to change. Whereas there is much evidence of people becoming socially mobile over time.

2. A Functionalist analysis would explain the persistence of poverty by arguing that:

(a) It is impossible to achieve complete equality, so there will always be some who are poor in relation to others.
(b) It is functional for poverty to exist. If it did not, it would be dysfunctional for the more successful members of society.

Points of criticism

(i) Marxists would argue that this view illustrates how the poor are exploited in a capitalist society. It is an inevitable consequence of capitalism.
(ii) It is a view that justifies the *status quo* and makes extreme inequality justifable.

3. Marsland (a supporter of the New Right views established in the 1980s) argues ('Universal Welfare Provision') that poverty persists because the poor have developed a culture of dependency.

(a) Low income is the result of the dependency on the welfare state, which does not encourage the poor to become self-sufficient.

(b) Benefits are not targeted efficiently on those in greatest need.
(c) The effect has been to undermine community bonds and the strength of the family to support its members.

Points of criticism

Lister argues that:

(i) Such views revive a moral attitude to poverty. It encourages a pathological image of people in poverty who are different from the more successul members of society.
(ii) It gives rise to the concept of a feckless 'underclass' which in reality is not easy to define or identify.
(iii) Poverty does not result from an over-generous system of welfare which inhibits self-sufficient attitudes, but one which is too mean to set people on their feet.

4. Conflict theorists tend to explain the persistence of poverty in terms of of the impact of social and economic constraints on people.

(a) These arise from the impact of low income, unemployment, ill-health, old age or impoverished family background.
(b) The view suggests that the poor are no different from others in better economic situations, but they suffer more constraints.
(c) Poverty is seen to be rooted in the structure of society, with class inequality at its core.
(d) Weberians emphasise how certain groups become more vulnerable because they lack the valued market skills that would enable them to compete successfully for the resources needed to escape poverty (a good job, home, etc.). But an individual can effect change in his or her life chances by acquiring valued skills.
(e) Marxists emphasise the extent to which poverty is inherent within the capitalist economic system. Change will occur when the exploited become politicised and class-conscious, and act in unison.

Points of criticism

(i) The view implies that the welfare state has been totally ineffective in alleviating poverty. (A view held by supporters of the New Right, who see the Welfare State as one of the causes of poverty.)
(ii) Functionalists would argue that the aim to eradicate poverty and achieve equality is wasted effort. Equality is an ideological myth.

The Contribution of Sociology to the Analysis of Poverty

■ **What light has sociology thrown on our understanding of poverty in contemporary Britain?**

1. Sociologists have clarified the range of possible definitions of poverty.
2. Much research has indicated the extent of poverty and how its range varies according to the definition used:

1965 Townsend and Abel Smith indicated that the poor consisted of:

(a) the unemployed (7%);
(b) the low paid (40%);
(c) the elderly (33%);
(d) the disabled (10%); and
(e) one-parent families (10%).

1967 *Circumstances of Families* showed that about 500 000 families (including 1 million children) were living below supplementary benefit level: about 10 per cent of parents were in low-paid jobs.

1976 Supplementary Benefit Commission found that about 5 million people were dependent wholly or partly on supplementary benefit.

1983 A MORI poll found that 7.5 million people could be said to be living in poverty, from a relative and subjective point of view. People were asked what they considered to be necessary for a decent life from a list of thirty-three items. Two-thirds saw such things as heating for living areas, indoor lavatory, a damp-free home, a bath, enough bedrooms for children, money for public transport and three meals a day for children as essential. The poll found that 3 million people cannot afford to heat their homes and 4 million live in damp homes. They conclude that at least three quarters of a million people are living in intense poverty.

3. Such research has also focused on the problems facing the poor:

(a) The poor are often housed a long way from city centres, on estates. This can result in high travelling costs.
(b) Housing may be of poor quality.
(c) They have poor job opportunities and generally lack skills and qualifications.
(d) High levels of stress may result in poor health.
(e) They lack good-quality clothes and are frequently in debt.
(f) They have poor life chances and lifestyle.

Government statistics published in 1992 found that:

(a) The number of people living on social security who faced deductions from Income Support payments to meet debts rose by 65 000 in the autumn of 1991.
(b) More than one in ten relying on Income Support faced pre-payment deductions to meet debts for fuel and other bills.

4. A Report by the National Institution for Social Work in 1992 found that provision for those in need varied between different areas and on circumstance. Those in rural areas, and black and other ethnic minority groups were often found to be badly served.

5. An EOC Report in 1992 found that elderly women were more likely to suffer from poverty than men because they had worse pension prospects. Only those who had made full National Insurance contributions for 39 years were entitled to a full pension at the age of 60. Most had broken records of employment while child-rearing; those who had worked for less than ten years got nothing.

6. A study entitled *Severe Hardship* found that more than 1,000 teenagers a week were suffering severe hardship because of government failure to guarantee training places for all under-18s. A call was made to remove the ban on 16- and 17-year-olds receiving Income Support.

7. The work of sociologists in establishing increasing areas of concern and the large numbers of people living in varying levels of poverty resulted in the reopening of the debate concerning the existence of an underclass in British society:

(a) Weber first described this as a group whose poor position in society was the result of its low status in the economy. The group lacked power, prestige and status and included the elderly, the chronically sick and the long-term unemployed.
(b) In the 1970s and 1980s many observers (especially in the USA and those in Britain who supported the views of the New Right) began to discuss the ways in which an underclass was developing in Britain. Murray used the term to describe a type of poverty. It included those whose culture accepted high levels of illegitimacy, unemployment, violent crime and other 'deplorable behaviour' He advocated not more welfare for them but more social engineering to give poor communities 'a massive dose of self government'.
(c) Field (*Losing Out*) defined the underclass as those who are largely excluded from the normal rights of citizenship by virtue of their poverty; for him the solution is a new and improved welfare state.
(d) Ormerod and Salama (*The Rise of the British Underclass*) argued that it was lack of training and investment that produced an impoverished sector in society. They also blame taxation policies for widening inequalities in the distribution of income and wealth. It is estimated that 10.25 million people of working age have no significant qualifications; this produces a skills underclass. The problems of poverty may thereby intensify in the future.
(e) Rex and Tomlinson (*Colonial Immigrants in a British City*) discussed the specific problems faced by ethnic minority groups that resulted in large numbers falling into poverty. The prejudice and discrimination they suffered caused many to subside into an underclass.

Points of criticism

1. There is no agreed way of measuring poverty and so the level it reaches can be exaggerated or reduced according to the measure used.
2. The welfare state is seen by many as an adequate safety net for those in difficulty; although the debate as to whether benefits should be more selective or more universal remains.
3. Critics of the concept of an underclass include:

   (a) Lister ('Concepts of Poverty') who argues that:

   (i) It is seldom well defined and therefore hard to identify its members since there is no obvious stability among them as a group.
   (ii) Its use results in an emotive image of the poor, seeing them as being different from others and to be feared because their response to their situation is often regarded by observers as 'deplorable'. (In fact, such behaviour may stem from lack of opportunities to achieve mobility. It may not be that they choose not to take jobs but rather that they cannot obtain them.)

   (b) Pilkington ('Is There a British Underclass?') who argues that:

   (i) The term has become too freely used (often by non-sociologists) to describe the notion of a group whose cultural behaviour seems far beyond the normal (for example, 'Panorama' discussing car theft and 'hotting' on estates followed by attacks on the police in 1991). Yet it remains nebulous and imprecise.
   (ii) The most frequent use of the term originated in the USA, to describe groups seen as a subordinate and dangerous stratum, but it is unwise to make direct comparisons with events in Britain.

Conclusions

1. Piachaud has argued that the study of poverty is ultimately justifiable if it influences individual and social attitudes and actions.
2. Sociologists, using predominantly positivist methods, have identified causes and consequences of poverty and groups most prone to its impact. Some have recommended improvements in welfare provisions, others have seen these as the cause of the emergence of a dependent underclass
3. A wide debate has emerged concerning the validity of this view. Pilkington concludes that Britain has become a more polarised society in terms of the distribution of resources, wealth and income and their attendant implications, but he is not convinced that this has resulted in a distinct underclass. Analysis of the way it has been used raises doubts about its utility.

Suggested Reading

Works noted in this chapter

R. Berthoud and E. Kimpson (1992) *Credit and Debt*, IPSI, 100 Park Village, London NW1 3SR
Circumstances of Families (1967) *Severe Hardship* (1992), NACAB, 115–125 Pentonville Road, London
W. Daniel (1983) *Workplace Industrial Relations in Britain*, Heinemann
F. Field (1989) *Losing Out*, Basil Blackwell
R. Holman (1978) *Poverty*, Martin Robertson
F. Lafitte (1970) 'Income Deprivation' in R. Holman (ed.) *Socially Deprived Families in Britain*, Bedford Square Press
K. Leech and K. Amin (1988) *A New Underclass*, CPAG, 1–5 Bath Street, London EC1V 9PG
R. Lister (1990) *The Exclusive Society*, CPAG
——— (1991) 'Concepts of Poverty', *Social Studies Review* (May)
D. Marsland (1989) 'Universal Wealth Provision', *Social Studies Review* (November)
S. Mencher (1972) 'The Problem of Measuring Poverty', in J. Roach and J. Roach (eds), *Poverty: Selected Readings*, Penguin
C. Murray (1989) 'Underclass: A Disaster in the Making', *Sunday Times* (26 November)

Photograph Question

Examine photographs 51, 52, 53, 54, 55 and 56.

1. The people in the photographs are representative of groups who are most frequently found in relative poverty; they include the elderly, the low paid, the unemployed, the sick or disabled and the homeless.
   (i) Discuss some of the problems in assessing whether people in such categories really are poor.
   (ii) Consider the view that poverty is inevitable and functional because:
      (a) not everyone is socialised adequately;
      (b) some people are morally inadequate;
      (c) some people are inevitably unfortunate in life; and
      (d) some people are born into a culture of dependency and deprivation.
   (iii) Consider the view that the cause of poverty lies in the structure of the capitalist society itself:
      (a) because there is no commitment to equality; and
      (b) the poor are an expolited group.
   (iv) Consider critically the view that poverty can adversely affect life chances and lifestyle.

52

Source: Alec Gill

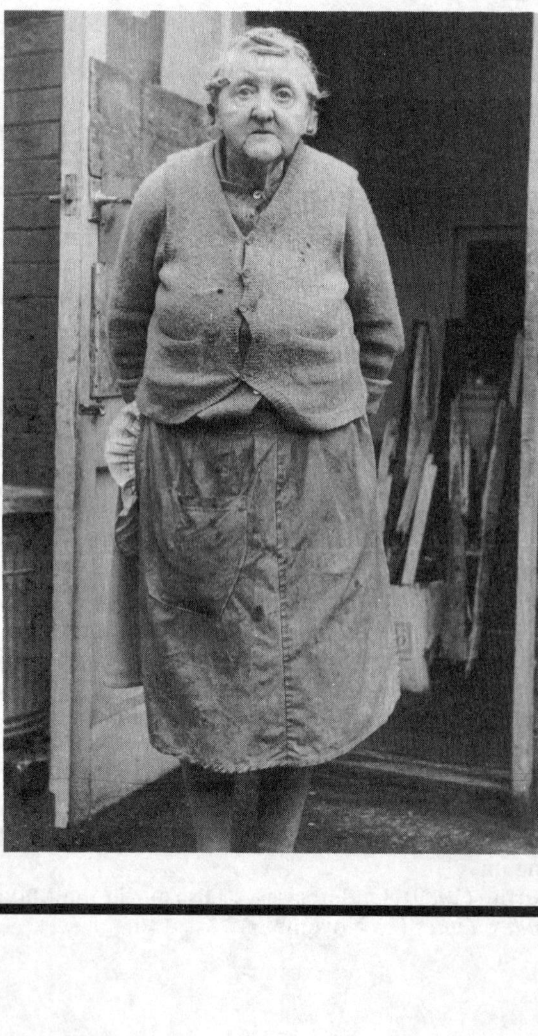

51

Source: Alec Gill

55

Source: Alec Gill

54

53

56

OPCS (1988) *Prevalence of Disability Among Adults*, HMSO

P. Ormerod and E. Salama (1990) *The Rise of the British Underclass*

D. Piachaud (1987) 'Problems in the Definition and Measurement of Poverty', *Journal of Social Policy*, 16

A. Pilkington (1992) 'Is There a British Underclass?', *Sociology Review* (February)

J. Rex and S. Tomlinson (1979) *Colonial Immigrants in a British City*, Routledge & Kegan Paul

B. Rowntree (1901) *Poverty: A Study of Town Life*, Macmillan

P. Townsend and B. Abel-Smith (1965) *The Poor and the Poorest*, Penguin

P. Townsend and A. Walker (1991) 'Poverty and the Underclass', in M. Haralambos, *Developments in Sociology*, Causeway

Works for further reading

K. Auletta (1982) *The Underclass*, Random House

G. Grieve-Smith (1990) *Full Employment in the 1990s*. PPR, 30–32 Southampton Street, London WC2

B. Jordan (1973) *Paupers. The Making of a Claiming Class*, Routledge & Kegan Paul

J. Mack and S. Lansley (1985) *Poor Britain*, Allen & Unwin

Self-test Questions

Study these newspaper extracts and answer the questions below.

Item A

A City banker earning £2.5 million a year - over £48,000 a week or £6,883 every day - has emerged as Britain's highest-paid businessman.

The banker, though not officially named, is widely assumed to be Mr Christopher Heath, a 41-year-old executive of the bankers Baring Brothers, who sells stocks and shares to the Japanese.

Source: From an article by Michael Smith in the *Guardian*, 7 October 1987.

Item B

BRITAIN'S managing directors rode out recession-hit 1991 with increases in their total pay, perks and bonuses averaging 21 per cent, nearly three times the going rate on the shop floor, a survey showed yesterday.

Average basic pay for chief executives of £105,000 is more than doubled once benefits, stock options, bonuses, and pensions are taken into account.

Source: From an article by Dan Atkinson in the *Guardian*, 21 September 1992.

Item C

Britain's 1.3m single-parent families figure is highest in EC

BRITAIN has the highest proportion of one-parent families in the EC, with single parents in charge of almost one in five families with children under 18, a report for the Family Policy Studies Centre, an independent research body, said yesterday.

This figure compares with one in seven in Denmark and one in eight in Germany and France.

The proportion in Greece, Spain and Italy is about one in 20. Britain also has the most single parent families in the EC, with about 1.3 million parents living with 2.1 million children, the study found.

The report's author, Jo Roll, said that over the past decade the growth in single-parent families was generally due to a rise in divorce and separation rates. "But in Britain in the late 80s there also seems to have been an increase in the number of younger unmarried women deciding to have children and living alone without their partners," she said.

"This compares with Denmark, for example, where the proportion of children born outside marriage is much higher but there the parents are much more likely to co-habit."

Source: From an article by David Brindle in the *Guardian*, 29 July 1992, p. 8.

Item D

CHILDREN, blacks and other minorities continue to suffer disproportionately from the effects of America's economic problems and their plight worsened last year, according to new US census bureau figures.

The bureau's report said the number of Americans living below the official poverty line rose by 2.1 million to 35.7 million in 1991 — at 14.2 per cent of the population, the highest figure since Lyndon Johnson launched his "war on poverty" in 1964.

The census figures showed clearly that among those people classified as poor — a family of four earning $14,000 (£7,000) or less annually, or an individual earning $7,000 or less — there were wide variations related to social origin and age.

The poverty rate among blacks, who account for about 12 per cent of the population, was 32.7 per cent, among Hispanics 28.7 per cent. Slightly more than 40 per cent of the poor were children.

Twenty-two per cent of all American children are now living below the poverty line. And the trend is worsening: one in every four children aged under six is in poverty.

Source: From an article by Simon Tisdall in the *Guardian*, 5 September 1992, p. 9.)

Item E

ONE IN FOUR children is living in poverty, according to official figures published yesterday which confirm that the gulf between rich and poor widened massively during the decade of Conservative government to 1989. They show that the poorest families suffered a 6 per cent cut in real income.

The figures, released on the eve of the parliamentary recess, estimate that in 1988/9, 12 million people were living below half-average income, the nearest thing to an official poverty line. In 1979, when the Tories took office, the equivalent total was 5 million.

The data show that 25 per cent of all children were living below this line in 1988/89, compared with 10 per cent in 1979, indicating that almost 3.2 million children are in poverty.

Critics seized on the figures as proof of the failure of the vaunted "trickle-down" effect, by which ministers have defended widening income inequality. They have argued that growing prosperity of the better-off would trickle down to improve the lot of the poor.

Source: From an article by David Brindle in the *Guardian*, 16 July 1992, p. 1.

Item F

'Low pay' plight of 10m workers

Keith Harper
Labour Editor

MORE than 10 million adult workers, half of them part-time, earn less than £5.15 an hour, says a report published yesterday by the Low Pay Unit.

The figures are based on an analysis of the Government's new earnings survey and the Council of Europe's "decency threshold" which gives a UK figure of £193.60 a week, or £5.15 an hour, for the current year.

They show that 74.8 per cent of women and 24.5 per cent of men manual workers earn less than £180 a week, and 37.8 per cent of women and 11.3 per cent of men doing non-manual jobs.

The report says there is ample evidence of a continuing pay divide between north and south, and a wide gap between gross weekly earnings in Greater London and the rest of the country, particularly Wales. Earnings have fallen most in Yorkshire and Humberside.

Adult employees on low pay
% below £180 a week or £4.92 per hour in 1991/2

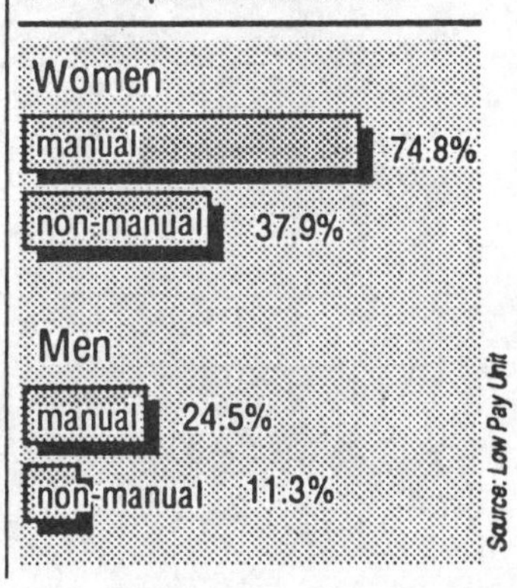

The number of low-paid workers has risen rapidly since 1979, when 38 per cent earned less than the Council of Europe's threshold. Now it is 46 per cent. The main reasons are the changing composition of the workforce, with greater participation by women and increases in part-time and service sector work.

The report says government policies have also contributed. Unemployment, it argues, has been used to discipline unions in pay negotiations, and policies unfavourable to manufacturing have helped destroy industries which traditionally paid good wages.

The research says the earnings of the lowest paid manual worker compared with the average were lower in 1991 than in 1886, when records began.

The report blames recent legislative changes which have removed pay protection from the most vulnerable workers — the young, the unskilled, and those in traditionally low-paid industries.

It says benefit rule changes mean the young and unemployed are offered no protection against exploitation in the labour market.

Allowances of £3,000 a year for staff working in central London are commonplace. A study by Incomes Data Services among 170 organisations says the highest levels are paid by finance sector operations, with £3,765 a year the highest at Allied Dunbar.

Source: From an article in the *Guardian*, 14 January 1992.

1. Examine Items A, B and F.

(i) Consider the functionalist view that it is necessary to have major inequalities in earnings in order to promote competition, skills and incentives.

(ii) Consider the Marxist view that such inequalities present a source of potential conflict.

2. Examine Items C, D and E.

(i) Tabulate the data in each to clarify the main points.

(ii) Suggest some reasons to account for the variations in the number of children in poverty within and between societies.

(iii) Outline some of the social problems that arise from an increase in the number of one-parent families and which face their members.

3. Examine Item F.

(i) Tabulate the data to make the points clear.

(ii) Discuss some of the problems arising from low pay and unemployment.

4. Examine Items C, D, E and F.

(i) Suggest some different definitions of poverty and explain why it is hard to define with precision.

(ii) Consider the view that the low paid are less likely to fall into poverty than one parent families or the unemployed.

(iii) Suggest some explanations to account for the fact that some members of society have very low levels of income on which to subsist.

5. Using data from all the Items A–F explain how data can be interpreted in various ways: government spokesmen argue that prosperity is generally increasing and the trickle-down effect will occur; the poor are often feckless; critics suggest that gaps between rich and poor are widening; the poor are a powerless group subject to economic factors beyond their control.

6. Suggest research projects which would seek to resolve the debate. Note some of the problems that might be encountered.

20

ORGANISATIONS AND BUREAUCRACY

Areas on which questions are asked include the following:

1. Why do bureaucracies develop? How can they be analysed?
2. The process of bureaucratisation; types of organisation: formal and informal.
3. Weber's analysis.
4. Advantages and disadvantages of bureaucratic organisations.
5. Weber's critics and supporters.
6. Organisations and level of democracy.
7. Total institutions.

- **Contrast different theories of bureaucracies.**
- **What explanations have been put forward to show why bureaucracies develop and how they can be analysed?**

(a) Every society requires some form of efficient administration. Even in pre-industrial societies there are many examples of organisations designed to provide systems of irrigation, the collection of taxes, etc. As societies become more complex and industrialised the size and scope of organisations grows.

(b) In contemporary Britain everyone has contact with some type of bureaucratic organisation in the course of their lives; either in their work or in their social lives, for example, in relation to education, religion, medicine, work, politics, the law, the armed forces, social welfare.

(c) In an industrial society the division of labour becomes a dominant feature in every aspect of work. Each person employed in an organisation does a different specialist job which contributes to the success of the whole enterprise. One result is that the organisation becomes carefully structured.

(d) Complex organisations are features of industrial societies over the past 200 years. They involve people in relationships to achieve common goals. The relationships are:

(i) relatively enduring over time;
(ii) based on control, power and coordination; and
(iii) contractually organised with legal force.

Reasons for the Process of Bureaucratisation

1. With the emergence of new democratic institutions in industrial societies there was a need to replace old aristocratic traditional institutions of administration. These relied on patronage and wealth for membership and control.
2. Such old traditional institutions were inefficient and contained incompetent people.
3. As societies developed and changed there was a need for efficient organisation to administer the economic and social policies of the government.
4. In business new professional managers emerged to reorganise their companies to increase their profits.
5. New techniques were introduced by social scientists to improve managerial and organisational efficiency.

(a) The scientific school of management advocated providing special tools and techniques for employees to increase their output and the profits of the organisation.

(b) New models of efficiency were advocated, such as the effectiveness of the Army as a hierarchical organisation making use of specialist staff and strict rules.

(c) The Human Relations School of Management, which emerged in the USA in the 1920s and 1930s was the first to modify the views of the scientific managers by emphasising the need to understand and make use of the informal norms of behaviour that developed among staff at various levels.

Efficiency and effectiveness in work could be improved by taking account of the aims and goals of work groups. The Hawthorn Plant studies illustrated this view. (When friendship groups were disrupted, output decreased. See page 262.)

Some of the aims of the sociology of organisations

(a) To examine and understand the effects of the growth of bureaucratic organisations on social and political life.
(b) Blau (*The Dynamics of Bureaucracy*) said his aim was to analyse processes of organisational development on the basis of an examination of the daily operations of employees.
(c) To see how organisations vary between societies.

Three analytical approaches

1. The Founding Fathers.

(a) Weber's contribution to analysis was.
 (i) to establish an ideal type of bureaucratic organisation against which different examples could be assessed to see how far they are similar to or different from the ideal form;
 (ii) to promote research and new theories and explanations; and
 (iii) his view that a rational bureaucracy created a new and superior type of organisation, in which all workers would become more efficient.

(b) *Marx* argued that:
 (i) the central feature of the capitalist mode of production was the bureaucratic organisation; and
 (ii) this was used by the ruling class to control the lives, power and output of the working classes.

(c) *Durkheim* argued that:
 (i) since the process of industrialisation was causing fragmentation of communities and families, organisations were required to promote integration; and
 (ii) he saw the possibility of bureaucratic organisations promoting social solidarity.

Points of criticism

(i) Most of the work was highly theoretical and not based on much empirical research; and
(ii) the ideas expressed were based largely on secondary analysis of existing data.

2. Analysis of the formal structure and function of the organisation: Among those who adopt this approach are: Weber, Michels, Lipset *et al.*, Selznick, Gouldner. Such writers use a 'systems' approach, based on the idea that an organisation can be viewed rather like a machine that has evolved from a simple to a complex form over time. It will produce satisfactory end results so long as it is maintained and serviced

(a) In the 1950s and 1960s, inspired by Weberian ideas, the focus of attention was on specific organisations, the aim being to see how far they met the predictions of the researchers.
(b) The work of Gouldner, Selznick and Blau produced some important case studies.
(c) They also emphasised the need to produce more precisely quantified data.
(d) Some research began to show how bureaucracies could sometimes be unexpectedly inefficient. Other work (for example, Blau) showed how efficiency was not always achieved by following prescribed rules, since they may be inappropriate for particular problems that arise.

Points of criticism

(i) Glenn Morgan ('The Sociology of Organisations') has argued that:
(a) Such approaches tended to give limited consideration to the choices and conflicts that existed within the organisation.
(b) They were seldom interested in the issues of wider social change and development.
(c) They sometimes uncovered problems but were unable to prescribe solutions (for example bureaucrats seem to gain increasing power over people's lives in modern societies and are often not accountable to the public for their decisions). See page 268.

3. Advocates of other approaches

(a) Some writers (for example, Salaman, *Class and the Corporation*) advocated:
 (i) a 'return to a Marxist approach to organisations; but one which incorporated elements from the Weberian tradition'; and
 (ii) he recommended that the sociology of organisations demonstrated their class nature and their underlying sustaining ideologies.

(b) Others (for example, Goffman, Roth, Blau and Benson) advocated the use of more interpretive methods:
 (i) since organisations consist of groups of people in significant work relationships who interact with each other, aims, goals and methods of achieving them will vary and fluctuate; and
 (ii) they argue that the conscious actions of the actors can be important in shaping behaviour and the changes which occur within rational organisations. It may not be just the needs of the economic system to have effective bureaucratic structures in place which determine outcomes. Changes frequently occur as a result of the continual processes of negotiation among employees and clients.

Points of criticism

(i) The return to a Marxist approach may overemphasise the extent to which those employed in large-scale organisations are controlled and exploited by groups external to their organisation.
(ii) Much of the research of the interpretists has been undertaken in unusual settings (for example, mental hospitals) which may not be typical of bureaucratic organisations. Negotiations with patients may be more feasible than with prisoners, or military or other administrative personnel.

More recent developments

Morgan notes that some researchers have begun to examine new issues.

1. *The internal organisation*: how the organisational culture operates in relation to wider society: for example, the significance of gender and sex within the organisational culture; the extent to which male culture dominates the organisation.

The value of this approach

(a) It shows that all kinds of goal-oriented behaviour exists: rational, irrational, emotive, habitual.
(b) Braverman showed how managements seek to control and direct the culture.
(c) Knight *et al.* showed how tight systems of control and rigid hierarchies reduce individual motivation.
(d) It integrates theories about the distribution of power and control in society and different management practices.

2. *Comparative analysis of organisations*: how similar organisations operate in different social and economic cultures and with what consequences.

The value of this approach

(a) Clegg has revealed how different societies have different expectations about how organisations and management should be structured.
(b) Similar forms of organisation can differ radically, even between successful capitalist economies (for example, Japan, Hong Kong, Korea).
(c) It has raised questions about the relationship between multinationals, national governments and supranational institutions such as the Economic Community (EC).

Conclusions

(a) Large-scale organisations predominate in modern industrial societies. They are important as administrative systems for dealing with large numbers of people in terms of the distribution of important resources, controlling behaviour and maintaining order.
(b) The classic theories of bureaucracy were established by its founding fathers.
(c) Subsequent analysis was borrowed from these writers, while new perspectives were also advocated: especially interpretive methods, greater focus on the organisational culture and comparative analysis.
(d) Blau (writing in 1953) said he believed the door was opening on a new phase in the sociology of formal organisations that would see a proliferation of interest in the field. Morgan suggests that in the 1990s it faces a host of threats, challenges and opportunities. These rest on whether it can make itself more widely relevant to areas of public debate, while retaining a distinctive identity.

- **Contrast formal and informal organisations.**
- **Discuss some of the strengths and weaknesses of Weber's theory of bureaucracies.**

Formal organisation

1. It has specific goals to achieve. An organisation is set up by the government to administer benefits to those in need.
2. The rights and duties of all are specified in written regulations. Those who apply for benefits must meet the special rules of the organisation. The rules must be administered according to the written regulations.
3. Members must have the appropriate qualifications. The staff are qualified and are part of a hierarchy of power, each member being subject to the authority of the Head of Department. The staff are also trained and may achieve promotion over time.
4. Positions of authority are ordered systematically. A bureaucratic organisation of this type is concerned with administering policies of the government. It cannot be held in private hands and employees cannot buy their position. They must achieve any success they obtain through their own efforts. Relationships between staff and clients must always remain impersonal.
5. Those with more power supervise those lower in the hierarchy.
6. Office-holding is based on training.
7. Promotions are regulated and based on contractual agreement.
8. There are fixed monetary salaries.
9. There is separation between the employee's official work and private life.
10. The employee cannot own the 'means of administration' nor appropriate the position.

Informal organisation

1. Usually created by those working within the formal organisation to cope with particular problems (e.g. unpleasant boss; strict teacher; boring work, etc.). In school, children may develop strong friendship groups.
2. There may be no direct planning in their creation; they arise to meet specific needs. Some may become a major problem in the classroom especially where their values oppose those of the teacher.
3. Control of such informal organisations is not based on written rules but more on social norms. Particular children may become labelled as 'troublemakers' and acquire status in the eyes of their peers. These may become 'stars of attraction' whom other children admire and follow.
4. There will be no elected power-holders but some in the group will become opinion leaders. Children who adopt the values of the group may then behave in accordance with the expectations of its members who share the culture.
5. The power of such informal organisations can be difficult to defeat where it is perceived by the formal organisation as a threat since it may be sustained by a shared group culture.

Type of action	Based on	Type of authority	Example	Source of legitimacy
Traditional	Custom ingrained habit	Traditional and customary loyalty	Power of kings in feudal Europe	Inherited status and personal affection
Emotional	Loss of temper. Appeal by an orator	Charismatic: followers devoted to a leader	Jesus; Napoleon Mohammed	Special qualities of the leader
Rational	Agreed goals: Control Profit Advice	Bureaucratic	Civil Servants Managers Administrators	Professional qualifications

Advantages

1. Weber said that 'the decisive reason for the advance of bureaucratic organisation has always been its purely technical supremacy over other forms of organisation. The fully developed bureaucratic mechanism compares with other organisations exactly as does the machine with non-mechanical modes of production.' (From Gerth and Mills, *Max Weber: Essays in Sociology*.)
2. It employs trained specialists.
3. It operates on a rational rather than a traditional or emotional level.
4. It is normally successful in achieving long-term goals.
5. The hierarchy of officials ensures efficiency, order and discipline. Weber said 'more and more the specialised knowledge of the expert became the foundation for the power of the officeholder'.
6. The growth of many bureaucracies should help to decentralise power. 'The monarch is powerles against the bureaucracy'.

Disadvantages

1. Bureaucracies are rule-bound and treat people in impersonal ways: (e.g. if a social security claimant does not meet the specifications laid down in the rules then benefit will not be available).
2. Because officials are employed to perform specific tasks their opportunities to develop wider skills may be limited.
3. It is not easy to change the goals of a bureaucracy to meet short-term needs (the education system is difficult to change to increase the chances of working-class children reaching higher education).
4. Since membership of a bureaucracy requires qualifications this gives rise to status and class differences and possible conflict and disharmony.

Types of organisation

Formal organisation

A formal organisation is called a bureaucracy.

Weber was the first writer to conduct a major analysis of such organisations. He identified specific characteristics in his ideal type. (For a discussion of ideal types see page 263, 267 and 325).

Studies

Elton Mayo (*Human Problems of Industrial Civilization*), describes studies carried out in the USA between 1927 and 1932 which were intended to inform management about sources of employee satisfaction and dissatisfaction at work. His team looked at the informal processes.

Roethlisberger and Dickenson (*Management and the Worker*). They found that informal norms developed among work groups that established what was considered to be a reasonable day's output. This may not have coincided with the views or desires of management. The solidarity of the group in the Hawthorne Plant, where the study was carried out, was maintained so long as they agreed on levels of production. When management tried to introduce scientific methods to increase output (by improving lighting, ventilation, etc.) they were unsuccessful. They could not defeat the norms of the group. The conclusion for the management of the formal organisation was that it needed to become more 'employee centred' and to listen more to the needs and problems of the work force.

Weber's analysis of bureaucracies

His theory

Bureaucracies are necessary in modern societies to help establish control over economic resources of the society by means of rationally organised administrations. The main features of a bureaucracy are:

(a) specialisation of role by ability;
(b) rational decentralised rule; and
(c) efficient implementation of rules to achieve goals.

His theory of social action

All human behaviour is directed by meanings drawn from social situations. To understand action it is therefore necessary to understand the meanings which underlie them.

(a) *rational action* is goal-directed;
(b) *affective action* is based on emotional responses; and
(c) *traditional action* is based on custom.

For Weber, the bureaucratic organisation is the perfect example of rationality. Rationality is the decisive feature of modern social life. It is the 'attainment of an end . . . by means of precise calculation'.

Key concepts

Bureaucratic organisations are systems of control. In order that the control is effective it must be regarded as *legitimate*. Different types of *authority* give rise to different types of legitimacy.

■ **Bureaucracy is the most efficient type of administrative system. In what circumstances is this true and when is it false? (UODLE)**

■ **The main advantage of large-scale bureaucratic organisations is their insistence on rules. Discuss. (UODLE)**

To answer such questions you must be familiar with some of the important advantages and disadvantages of bureaucracies as well as some studies in which these are discussed. Note the details on pages 262 and 264.

Conclusions

Weber saw both advantages and disadvantages in bureaucracies. The benefits were its technical superiority; lack of equivocation; written rules; continuity; sense of discretion; uniformity of operations; the concentration of the means of administration; and the fact that it established a rational–legal type of organisation that provided a set of authority relationships which became permanent and indispensable.

He was critical in that people were likely to become trapped in their impersonal specialist roles: such people would become small cogs in a giant machine; and the bureaucratic machine was in the process of destroying all the traditional values and methods of the society by its power and ruthless efficiency. He was also concerned that a bureaucratic state would control every aspect of a citizen's life and reduce levels of freedom and choice: even the elected leaders may become the servants of bureaucrats. (In a speech in 1985 Mr Enoch Powell said that the TV programme 'Yes, Minister' was an accurate and unexaggerated guide to the way the British Government worked).

■ **Weber's concept of bureaucracy is important as an example of an ideal type, not because it tells us of reality. Discuss with reference to an example. (UODLE)**

Weber attempted to define a 'pure type' of bureaucratic organisation by building a model or 'ideal type' specifying its key characteristics. This was to act as a measure against which different types of organisation could be compared and assessed. He was producing an abstract conceptual scheme rather than a concrete description. His model has subsequently been used by writers as the basis for research into organisations. In the debate some have tended to stress the positive aspects of his ideas, others the negative. (See the example of formal organisation page 263.)

Weber's critics and supporters

■ **Oligarchy is inevitable in any large-scale organisation. Discuss. Why is it difficult for large organisations to be democratic?**

Michels (1876–1936) (*Political Parties*; *1911*) was concerned to show how democracy (the opportunity that people have for electing and dismissing leaders, expressing views freely and implementing majority decisions) is inconceivable in a large modern state without effective organisations. But the irony is that as soon as people join such organisations as political parties, pressure groups and so on, the result is hierarchical bureaucracy and the chances of achieving true democratic procedures is lost. Direct democracy, in which everyone is consulted, is impracticable. The only possibility is representational democracy.

Delegates represent the masses

Michels examines the deficiences of organisations which employ full-time officials and experts. There are more rules to be followed and there is increasing inflexibility. Decisions are taken by executive committees and the masses are excluded from decision-making processes. He concludes that 'bureaucracy is the sworn enemy of individual liberty'. Organisations inevitably produce oligarchy, and rule by a minority or a small élite. This is the 'iron law of oligarchy'. Selznick (*TVA and the Grass Roots*, showed in his study how even an organisation introduced by the American Government in 1933 to combat poverty in seven southern states lost its democratic principles in order to achieve specific goals. He argued from a functionalist perspective that organisations have needs, especially for survival. Anything which threatens the central goal (even the need for democratic procedures) will be displaced. Hence, he concludes 'ideals go by the board when competing realities of organisational life are permitted to run their course'. He says that the scheme ended up serving the interests of the farm leadership rather than the general public.

A study which opposes the view that bureaucracies cannot be democratic is that by Lipset, Trow and Coleman entitled *Union Democracy*.

They examined a craft printers' union in the USA and found the following:

1. The union contained a structure which enabled a careful system of checks and balances on power and power-holders.
2. There were frequent elections for national and local officials.
3. There were frequent referenda by which rank-and-file members could express their opinions.
4. There was a high degree of participation of rank-and-file members in the day-to-day running of the union.
5. There was a strong sense of 'community' existing between members: they shared leisure pursuits, etc.
6. The union had a long history of democratic procedures which members were keen to retain.
7. Union representatives did not have special benefits which would make them want to cling to power at any cost.

However, the authors accept that this may be a special and unusual case and that most large organisations do not share the qualities that encouraged democracy in the union they studied.

Studies which oppose some of the predictions in Weber's ideal type, that bureaucracies are always the most efficient types of organisation because they are rule-bound, and provide discipline and precise procedures for action, include the following:

1. Gouldner (*Patterns of Industrial Bureaucracy*) studied the organisation of a plant in the USA which was mining gypsum and making wall boards, of which the gypsum was an ingredient.

He found the following features:

(a) There was less bureaucratisation in the mine than in the factory. In the mine the miners often made their own decisons as to procedures. Not all duties were clearly defined.
(b) In the plant, on the surface there were strict rules of procedure; there was division of labour and a hierarchy of power.

He noted how attempts to impose greater bureaucratisation on the miners by management was rejected because of the strong norms of solidarity which developed among them.

2. Burns and Stalker (*The Management of Innovation*) suggest that it is useful to clarify Weber's ideal type by distinguishing two types of bureaucratic organisation. (See below.)

3. Blau (*The Dynamics of Bureaucracy*) studied a Federal law enforcement agency and an employment agency in the USA. He found:

(a) There were many unofficial practices used by employees which actually increased their efficiency. For example, having private discussions with colleagues about problems rather than consulting with supervisors, which was the approved procedure.
(b) There was more success in the employment agency in finding clients jobs where the employees adopted informal and cooperative methods.

In order to develop greater efficiency in the allocation of scarce jobs, interviewers were assessed according to the number of people they placed. As a result, competition developed among interviewers, but many applicants were not placed in the most appropriate jobs. Where interviewers were encouraged to co-operate rather than to compete there was greater and more effective productivity.

Blau showed that official procedures do not always maximise efficiency. His work shows the importance of examining informal bureaucratic structures.

- **Goffman's analysis of 'total institutions' differs from previous approaches to organisations because of its emphasis on the understanding of action in terms of meaning. Outline Goffman's concept of 'total institutions'. Examine his distinctive approach and show how it can be used in the study of such organisations as asylums, prisons or boarding schools.**

- **Using a range of case studies, illustrate the concepts and ideas which interactionist sociologists have used to study organisations. Point out the distinctiveness of the interactionist approach.**

To answer questions such as these you must be familiar with:

(a) the interactionist perspective (see page 25);
(b) the methods of the Interactionists (see page 26);
(c) some relevant studies, especially Goffman; and
(d) organisation theory (see page 261).

Some relevant studies

1. J. A. Roth ('The Treatment of TB as a Bargaining Process'). In this paper he explains how he used an interactionist perspective to illustrate how members of the same organisation could have different goals and how they set out to achieve them, with varying levels of success; also how aims were changed and modified over time.

His data were obtained from his own observations as a patient, an attendant and later as a sociological observer. He explains how in his last role he spent much time 'hanging about' the hospital wards and offices, attending therapy conferences, making rounds with doctors and listening to staff discuss their problems, and patients discuss theirs.

(a) The goals of the professionals in the hospitals and those of the patients were never entirely the same. Often they were in conflict. For example, the patients

Two types of bureaucratic organisation advocated by Burns and Stalker:

Type of bureaucracy	Characteristics	Features of bureaucratic organisation
Mechanistic	Stable market Standardised product. Steady demand. Example: the car industry.	Hierarchy of power. Chain of command for supervison and discipline. All staff have clearly defined roles. Little initiative or responsibility.
Organic	Unstable market. Changing product. Fluctuating demand. Example: the electronics industry.	No hierarchy of power. No chain of command for supervision and discipline. Staff do not have clearly defined roles. All contribute to problem solving.

generally wanted more privileges and greater freedom; the staff wished the opposite.

(b) Conflicts were usually resolved by 'bargaining'.

(c) He illustrates how patients, through their own observations and pooling of information, learned which nurses were likely to give certain drugs and nursing services. They learn how to manipulate the restrictive system to maximise freedom and choices.

(d) The process of anticipation and modification of behaviour and goals continues so long as the process of interaction is maintained.

(e) He concludes that the bargaining process is not a matter of open threats and the development of power positions; it is much more subtle.

2. Goffman (*Asylums*) He also uses an interactionist perspective to show how behaviour of people in the organisation results from their perception of events and the meanings they derive from processes of interaction.

Total institutions

These are organisations which place barriers between themselves and the outside world. These barriers may include 'locked doors, high walls, barbed wire, cliffs, water, forests or moors'.

The types of institution and setting he has studied include: mental hospitals, prisons, monasteries and army barracks.

Central features

1. All aspects of life are conducted in the same place or under some authority.
2. Each phase of the life of each member is conducted in the company of others.
3. There is a tight schedule in daily activities.
4. The activities are justified as part of a rational plan to fulfil the aims of the institution.
5. There is a clear distinction between 'staff' and 'inmates'.
6. Inmates are excluded from decision-making.

Significance in society

1. They are controlling organisations. They control and supervise large numbers of people as 'blocks'.
2. Their goals are often determined by ideological considerations and the aim may be to prevent inmates from being contaminated by unacceptable beliefs in the outside world (for example, religious organisations).
3. Some total institutions may serve useful social functions, in caring for those with special needs.
4. Others, such as mental hospitals, may, in Goffman's words, 'serve as storage dumps for inmates'.

In his paper, 'The Moral Career of a Mental Patient' he describes how, through a series of humiliating interactions with staff and other patients, the inmate comes to establish a new role and a new self-image which explains his predicament. He learns how to become a mental patient.

Points of criticism

(i) As always, observational studies rely on the skills of the observer and his or her ability to interpret evidence. Goffman, interestingly, draws his evidence from a wide range of sources including novels (for example, Kerkhoff, *How Thin the Veil*), autobiography (T. E. Lawrence), and his own observations.

(ii) The question arises, can the observer be sure that the interpretation of events offered is the 'true' explanation?

(iii) The studies are invariably on a small scale, from which it may be difficult to make wider generalisations.

(iv) Researchers are sometimes accused of ignoring events outside the organisation studied which may affect behaviour inside.

Summary

1. A distinction can be made between *formal organisations* (bureaucracies) and *informal organisations* (which arise, for example, among groups sharing similar norms and cultural values).
2. Organisations can be studied from a *functional/positivist* perspective or from an *interactionist/phenomenological* perspective.
3. Weber presented an *ideal type model* which is a useful measuring rod. It helps to generate research and theory building.
4. He saw an increasing trend towards bureaucratisation in modern industrial societies, although he saw some possible dangers in the process.
5. Some writers have subsequently produced some support for his concern that bureaucracies were likely to reduce people's freedom and choices (Michels).
6. Others have argued that all large organisations tend to become undemocratic structures. Their main goal always is survival at the expense of all others (Selznick).
7. Some researchers have found evidence that this may not always be the case (Lipset *et al*).
8. In their debate with Weber, some writers suggest that bureaucracies may not always be efficient and rational in their pursuit of goals (Gouldner).
9. To clarify this point further some researchers have distinguished between types of organisation: *mechanistic* and *organic*. The suggestion is that the structure of the organisation varies with its type. In the organic type the goals of workers and management may diverge yet the organisation does not collapse (Blau).

11. Another school of sociology (related to the organic perspective) focuses more on the organisation in terms of the processes of human action within them, rather than on the goals (Goffman). This view holds that organisations are made up of people and they change and alter methods, goals, etc. according to people's actions and reactions.

Questions

Examine photographs 57 and 58.

1. Consider how long-stay patients in hospitals become subject to the bureaucratic rules of the institution:
   (i) Suggest some rules in relation to sleeping, waking, exercise, medication, personal objects, dress, etc.
   (ii) What effects might these rules have on the behaviour of the elderly?
   (iii) What effects might they have on young children?
   (iv) What are the likely attitudes of the staff?

2. Contrast the major features of a total institution with those of other, more liberal, types.

3. (i) Construct a continuum showing a range of organisations from 'highly bureaucratic' to 'low level of bureaucracy'.
   (ii) Note the criteria on which you make your assessment.
   (iii) Has the list you have made resulted in a helpful typology? Clarify the concept of a typology.

4. Suggest how a study could be conducted which examines the ways in which hospitals or other institutions achieve conformity among their members (see references to the work of Roth and Goffman).

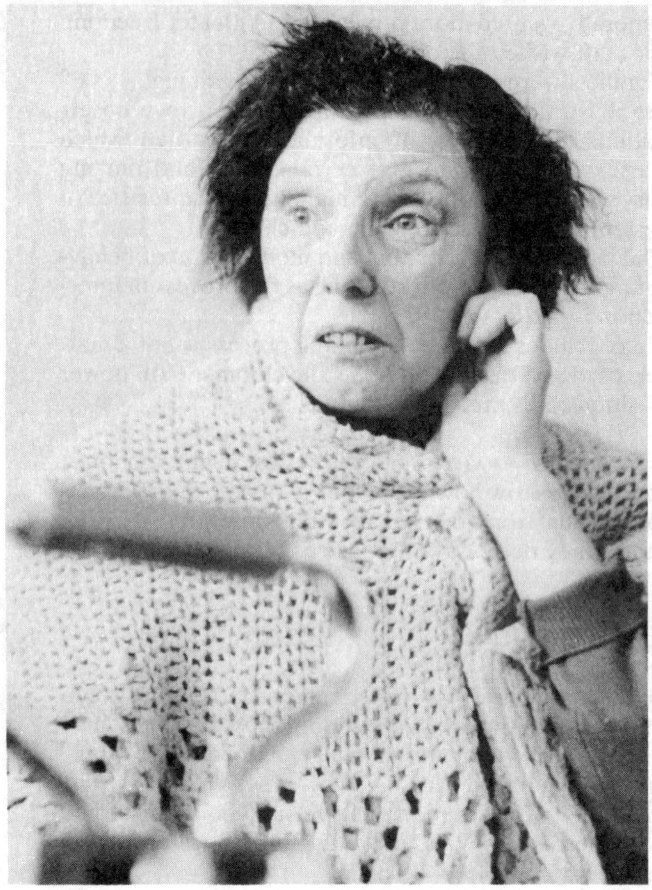

57

Source: Alec Gill

58

Source: Alec Gill

Suggested Reading

Works noted in this chapter

P. Blau (1953) in Merton *et al.* (eds), *A Reader in Bureaucracy*, Free Press

P. Blau (1973) *The Dynamics of Bureaucracy*, University of Chicago Press

H. Braverman (1974) *Labour and Monopoly Capitalism*, Monthly Review Press, New York

T. Burns and G. Stalker (1966) *The Management of Innovation,* Tavistock

S. Clegg (1990) *Modern Organisations*, Sage

I. Goffman (1968) *Asylums*, Penguin

A. Gouldner (1954) *Patterns of Industrial Bureaucracy*, Free Press

D. Knight *et al.* (1989) *Labour Process Theory*, Macmillan

S. Lipset, M. Trow and J. Coleman (1956) *Union Democracy*, Free Press

E. Mayo (1933) *Human Problems of Industrial Civilisation*,

R. Michels (1949) *Political Parties*, Free Press

G. Morgan (1992) 'The Sociology of Organisations', *Sociology Review* (February), Vol. 1, No. 3

F. Roethlisberger and W. Dickenson (1939) *Management and the Worker*, Harvaid University Press

A. Rose (ed.) (1971) *Human Behaviour and Social Processes*

J. Roth (1971) 'The Treatment of TB as a Bargaining Process', in A. Rose (ed.) *Human Behaviour and Social Processes*, Routledge & Kegan Paul

G. Salaman (1981) *Class and Corporation*, Fontana

P. Selznick (1966) *TVA and the Grass Roots*, Harper & Row

Works for further reading

M. Albrow (1970) *Bureaucracy*, Pall Mall

J. Benson (1977) 'Organisations', *Administrative Science Quarterly*, 22

G. Burrel, and G. Morgan (1979) *Sociological Paradigms and Organisational Analysis*, Heinemann

S. Clegg, and D. Dunkerley (1980) *Organisations, Class and Control*, RKP

S. Clegg and D. Dunkerley (1977) *Critical Issues in Organisations*, RKP

S. Cohen and L. Taylor (1972) *The Experience of Long Term Imprisonment*, Penguin

M. Olson (1970) *The Process of Social Organisation*, Holt

C. Perrow (1988) *Complex Organisations*, Scott Foresman

D. Pugh *et al.* (1987) *Writers on Organisation*, Penguin

P. Thompson and D. McHugh (1990) *Work Organisations*, Macmillan

Self-test Questions

Study these extracts and answer the questions below.

Item A

The ABC of Sociology

BUREAUCRACY

BUREAUCRACY refers in its narrowest sense to the officials and civil servants who run today's modern government. In its broadest sense it covers all forms of administration, from the local comprehensive school to hospitals, trade unions and even the local football team—they all need people to run them. As modern government has expanded its responsibilities, it has needed to employ more and more civil servants to run such major services as health, housing and, of course, taxation. This growth in size seems to be happening to all major organisations.

Max Weber, the 19th century sociologist, believed the most efficient way to run an organisation was to choose officials solely according to their ability; to give them specific tasks or duties to be carried out only according to a specific set of rules and regulations; and to organise them in a sort of chain of command or hierarchy, with the officials above controlling those below. Thus Weber hoped to ensure organisations ran smoothly without favouritism or abuse of power.

Unfortunately "bureaucrats" are not always as efficient and dispassionate as Weber hoped. They are often criticised for being too conservative, and for creating endless printed forms, many of which are unintelligible to the general public. They are accused of being insensitive in the way they treat people, especially the homeless, the aged and unemployed, and most especially of being too powerful.

"Faceless" bureaucrats seem to be making all the decisions in society and taking none of the responsibility. This increases people's sense of powerlessness and of alienation.

. . . *is for Bureaucracy*

DRAWING BY PETER BROOKES

Source: Extract from *New Society*, 1 November 1979.

Item B

Bureaucrats battle to hide names of Euro-fraudsters

THE battle against multi-billion pound swindles in the European Community's Common Agricultural Policy is set to get increasingly bitter. Fraudsters are diving for cover, fraudbusters are fighting for the right publicly to identify swindlers and the authorities bicker about strategies.

Fraud, as *The Observer* revealed last week, costs an estimated £2.4 billion a year or £20 for every wage-earner in the EC. But last week, say senior Commission sources, Agriculture Minister John Gummer blocked European Commission proposals to fight Euro-fraud.

There is growing evidence of a split between the Ministry of Agriculture and the Treasury on the issue. Mr Gummer, whose Ministry has traditionally favoured British farmers over consumers, said on Radio 4 that the revelations in *The Observer* were a 'silly story' and 'almost all out of date and dealt with'.

But Sir John Cope, the Paymaster General, told the all-party House of Lords sub-committee on the EC last Wednesday that there was 'considerable concern' in Whitehall about the massive swindles.

Lord Aldington and Lord Benson, doyen of the accountancy profession, pressed Sir John for greater publicity to be given to the prosecution and conviction of the fraudsters.

Customs and Excise, responsible for combatting Euro-fraud in Britain, confirmed that it often dealt with fraudsters without going to court, preferring to impose fines that were kept secret because, a spokesman claimed: 'It saves the cost of prosecution.'

Source: Extract from an article by Hugh O'Shaughnessy in the *Observer*, 19 July 1992, p. 2.

1. Examine Item A.

(i) Give a broad definition of bureaucracy, using some examples of your own.

(ii) Suggest four key dimensions established by Weber in his typology.

(iii) Explain why such an organisation was considered by Weber to produce efficiency.

(iv) Weber accepted that bureaucracies were not always as efficient as his ideal type predicted. Suggest some reasons for potential inefficiency.

(v) Why might a bureaucracy be criticised or defended for being too conservative? Give examples with regard to the dispensation of welfare benefits.

(vi) What factors in Weber's typology lead a bureaucracy towards conservatism?

2. Examine Item B.

(i) Suggest why fraud might occur in a bureaucratic organisation such as the EC.

(ii) To which other bureaucratic organisations might the Minister belong?

(iii) Why might the EC bureaucrats seek to minimise the fraud or deal with it secretly?

(iv) What methods might be open to them to achieve these ends?

(v) What are some of the features of a bureaucratic organisation which may make the EC extremely effective in many of its activities?

3. Using details from the Items and by providing examples:

(i) Indicate why some bureaucratic organisations are not always as efficient in achieving goals as Weber would have predicted. Explain why in some cases they may be dysfunctional for some of their members and their clients, producing increasing levels of alienation.

(ii) Contrast the efficiency of different bureaucratic organisations with which you are familiar. Account for the differences you identify.

21

RACE RELATIONS: ETHNIC GROUPS IN BRITAIN

The areas on which questions are asked:

1. Definition of terms.
2. Trends in immigration and emigration, and the factors that affect them.
3. The problems of prejudice and discrimination facing ethnic minorities in specific areas of social life: (a) employment; (b) housing; and (c) education.
4. Legislation and its effectiveness.
5. Theories to explain racial tensions, and the class and status positions of ethnic minorities.
6. Comparative data: you will need to know:
   (a) Some basic statistics (from surveys, census returns).
   (b) Details from at least one study;
   (c) Some knowledge of recent legislation.
   (d) Some knowledge of competing theories.

Definitions of Terms

Some questions will specifically test your knowledge of the meaning of terms. For example,

- **Distinguish between racial *discrimination* and racial *prejudice*. Which do you believe to be more significant in race relations in contemporary Britain? (UODLE)**

Others may make use in a question of terms which you should not take for granted. For example,

- **Outline the position of *immigrants* in Britain in the housing market. Base your answer on relevant research. (WJEC)**
- **How have sociologists helped us understand the experiences of *ethnic minorities* in either employment or housing? (AEB)**

Some questions you may feel are ambiguous in their use of terms. For example,

- **The *coloured population* is extremely small. In no area or occupation do they form concentrations of political or economic power. . . .**
- **Outline the educational disadvantage facing *blacks* in Britain. . . .**

It is best to make the meaning that you are adopting for the purpose of your answer clear early in your essay.

Race There is no universally accepted meaning of the word 'race'. Attempts have been made to identify distinct groups on the basis of biological and physiological characteristics, which are then frequently related to skin colour. It is often used in negative and confusing ways.

Sociologists argue that beliefs about the world are socially constructed. Beliefs about 'races' are closely related to contemporary attitudes existing in society, and often serve as a label to identify differences.

Race relations One means of establishing the relative status of different social groups is by reference to their race. Those with least status tend to be the groups who, it is assumed, are the most recently arrived. They are identifiable as 'strangers', by virtue of skin colour or cultural differences. Their status can then be used to justify differential treatment and can give rise to hostility between groups.

Ethnic groups Many writers prefer this term and it tends to be used to describe groups on the basis of shared cultural characteristics (for example food, language, dress, religion, etc.).

Prejudice A person is prejudiced who holds preconceived beliefs about others and pre-judges them on this basis. It is normally used in its negative sense.

Discrimination This is the *act* of prejudice. Since 1965 it has been unlawful to treat a person less favourably on the grounds of colour, race or ethnic or national origin.

Immigrant This means anyone who has recently arrived from another society in which they have habitually lived.

It may be criticised because it is widely used to refer to non-whites rather than to EC citizens or people of British descent who have lived abroad for most of their lives. Of black people in Britain, 40 per cent are British-born.

Racism This is the dogmatic belief that one race (however defined) is superior to another and that there are identifiable racial characteristics which influence behaviour (for example the idea that white people have higher IQs than coloured people).

Racialism This means putting the beliefs of racism *into practice* so that some people become subject to discrimination, hold lower status and are deemed to have fewer rights.

Trends in Immigration and Emigration

- **Describe the major trends in immigration into and emigration from Great Britain since 1971 and discuss their implications.**

- **What have been the factors influencing the rate and composition of immigration into Britain in recent years?**

To answer such questions you must:

(a) present relevant statistics; and
(b) draw conclusions from them.

Major trends

Points to note

(a) the definition of a migrant is taken to mean someone who, having lived abroad for at least twelve months, declares an interest in residing in the UK for at least twelve months. The definition of an emigrant is the reverse.
(b) The number classified as immigrants is always much higher than the number of people actually accepted for long-term settlement (that is, allowed to stay indefinitely).
(c) Table 21.1 shows:
 (i) that the number of immigrants into the UK fell from about 200 000 in 1971 to 143 000 in 1989; and
 (ii) about 80 per cent those entering in 1989 came from EC, Commonwealth countries and the USA.
(d) Table 21.2 shows:
 (i) that rates of emigration to Australia and Canada are higher that rates of immigration from these countries.
 (ii) rates of immigration from New Zealand have increased in recent years;
 (iii) numbers entering from the New Commonwealth are higher than those returning, but numbers have remained fairly stable since 1975, with some evidence of a decline in recent years;
 (iv) between 1985 and 1989 more migrants (who include British citizens returning to live in the UK) entered than left, reversing the trend between 1980 and 1984;
 (v) the numbers entering from EC doubled between 1975–9 and 1985–9; and
 (vi) numbers entering from the USA have declined, while those from South Africa have increased.
(e) Table 21.3 shows:
 (i) that in recent years more people are entering Britain than are leaving. The figure for 1990 was the highest since 1966. In the last decade immigrants from the Old Commonwealth, EC and the USA have risen significantly (see Table 21.1); and
 (ii) the report, *International Migration*, notes that the inflow and outflow does not necessarily reflect the numbers who will finally settle here (see Table 21.5).
(f) Table 21.4 shows:
 (i) that most ethnic minority groups have a different age structure to that of the white population. There is a higher proportion in the younger age groups (having been born in Britain in recent years) and fewer in the older age groups (there being relatively few members of a third generation): and
 (ii) about one in five of the white population was over 60 in 1992 compared with one in twenty of the minority groups.
(g) Table 21.5 shows:
 (i) that numbers accepted for permanent settlement have remained at about 50 000 p.a. over the last decade;
 (ii) in that time, about 50 per cent are from the New Commonwealth and the remainder from other parts of the world; and
 (iii) of those from the New Commonwealth, 50 per cent are wives and children of men who are British citizens.

Factors affecting immigration

1. *The economy of Britain*: in the 1950s and 1960s the British economy was buoyant and immigrants came seeking work. Many were recruited by large companies (such as London Transport) seeking labour. As the economy became depressed numbers entering Britain declined.
2. *The economy of the country of departure*: most of the migrants from the New Commonwealth are seeking better prospects than they can find at home.
3. *Political and religious factors*: many migrants have come to Britain to seek escape from political or religious persecution: for example, Jews in the 1930s; Hungarians in 1956; Ugandan Asians in 1971.
4. *Educational opportunities*: some migrants may wish to take the opportunity to provide their children with a good education in Britain.
5. *Legislation*: numbers tend to increase just before the introduction of legislation which limits numbers who can be accepted for entry. In the 1950s legislation in the USA limiting the number of West Indians allowed to settle caused them to divert to Britain.
6. Many simply exercise their rights, either as British passport holders or as member of the EC, to enter and seek work.
7. Female migration has not been thoroughly researched but there is evidence that it has always been high (especially among West Indians). In 1982, 70 per cent

Table 21.1 Migrants by country of last origin (thousands)

Year	*Old Commonwealth (Australia, Canada, New Zealand)*	*New Commonwealth (Indian subcontinent)*	*West Indies*	*EC*	*USA*	*Total*
1971	52	24	5	21	22	200
1976	40	27	4	25	16	191
1979	31	33	5	23	13	195
1981	20	27	3	23	17	153
1989	35	23	3	58	26	143

Source: Social Trends, 22.

Table 21.2 International migration into and out of UK by country of last or next residence (annual averages) (thousands)

Country of last or next residence	*1975–9*			*1980–4*			*1985–9*		
	In	*Out*	*Balance*	*In*	*Out*	*Balance*	*In*	*Out*	*Balance*
1. Australia	21	28	−7	13	35	−22	18	35	−17
2. Canada	7	22	−15	6	14	−8	6	9	−3
3. New Zealand	9	10	−1	6	8	−2	11	7	+4
4. African Commonwealth	17	12	+5	14	10	+4	11	6	+5
5. Bangladesh, India, Sri Lanka	16	4	+12	15	4	+11	14	4	+10
6. Pakistan	13	2	+11	11	2	+9	9	2	+7
7. Caribbean	4	3	+1	3	3	0	3	3	0
8. Other	16	10	+6	16	16	0	17	15	+2
Total Commonwealth	103	91	+12	84	92	-8	89	81	+8
1. EC	28	36	−8	38	37	+1	58	51	+7
2. Rest of Europe	5	8	−3	7	6	+1	10	10	0
3. USA	15	23	−8	21	29	−8	26	30	−4
4. Rest of America	4	4	0	3	3	0	3	3	0
5. South Africa	11	14	−3	6	16	−10	12	4	+8
6. Middle East	10	18	−8	13	23	−10	15	15	0
7. Other	11	13	−2	15	8	+7	16	10	+5
Total Commonwealth	84	116	−32	103	122	−19	140	123	+17
All Countries	187	207	−20	187	214	−27	229	204	+25

Note: Numbers have been rounded up.
Source: *Social Trends*, 22.

Table 21.3 Migration into and out of Britain 1964–84 (thousands)

Mid-year to mid-year	*Total inflow*	*Total outflow*	*Net figure*
1964–5	223	281	−58
1966–7	232	326	−94
1969–70	224	306	−82
1971–2	196	240	−44
1973–4	183	255	−72
1977–8	162	198	−36
1980–4	187	214	−27
1985–9	229	204	+25
1990–1	267	231	+36

Source: OPCS.

Table 21.4 Population by age and ethnic group, 1987–9 (percentages)

Group in the population	*0–15*	*16–29*	*30–44*	*45–59*	*60+*
West Indian or Guyanese	24	32	17	21	8
Indian	30	26	24	15	5
Pakistani	45	23	19	10	2
Bangladeshi	47	25	14	12	2
Chinese	28	26	31	11	4
African	30	29	28	10	2
Arab	24	31	30	11	4
Mixed	53	25	12	6	4
Other	27	28	28	10	6
All ethnic minorities	34	27	21	13	5
White	19	22	21	17	21

Source: *Social Trends*, 22.

Table 21.5 Numbers accepted for settlement in UK, 1974–90 (thousands)

1974	*1976*	*1981*	*1985*	*1989*	*1990*
69	81	57	55	49	52

Source: *Social Trends*, 22.

Table 21.6 The estimated population of non-white ethnic minorities in Britain, 1966–92 (millions)

Year	*Number (millions)*	*Percentage of the population*
1966	1.1	2.2
1971	1.3	2.4
1976	1.8	3.3
1986	2.0	4.0
1992	2.6	4.7

Source: *Social Trends*, 22.

Table 21.7 Numbers of ethnic minority groups in Britain, 1992 (thousands)

Origin	*Numbers*
Caribbean	482
Africa	127
India	779
Pakistan	433
Bangladesh	112
Chinese	132
Middle East	72
Mixed	284

Source: *Social Trends*, 22.

of those accepted for entry were wives and children of those already settled. In 1992, they were 50 per cent of those accepted for settlement.

Conclusions

(a) There are many difficulties involved in studying ethnic minorities. It is hard to establish clear definitions as to the meaning of terms such as immigrant, emigrant, race, white, non-white, etc.

(b) The available data tends to cover only a proportion of all those who could be described as 'ethnic minorities' (for example, it is hard to find information about the number of Poles, Lithuanians, Maltese, etc. who reside in Britain).

(c) There tends to be an over-emphasis on trends in the immigration rates of 'non-white' minorities, or those most visible and therefore different from the indigenous population.

(d) The increase of migrants from the Old Commonwealth and Europe in recent years has been responsible for affecting the imbalance in numbers since 1985.

(e) It may be that the economic recession in the 1990s will deter migrants from seeking entry.

Problems Facing Ethnic Minorities in Britain

Employment

■ **What is the pattern of employment of Asians and West Indians in Britain? How would you account, sociologically, for this? (UCLES)**

■ **In the 1960s the major problems facing immigrant groups were associated with housing, whereas now they are associated with employment. Discuss.**

To answer such questions you must be familiar with the details from a range of studies. The following are some typical examples. Remember to use your illustrations to argue a case. In the first question, are you going to argue that the pattern has developed and changed over time, or that it has remained fairly static and unchanging? In your answer it is useful to be able to relate your facts to a theory which accounts for the position of ethnic minorities in Britain (see page 279). In the second question you must decide whether you think it is true that the *major* problem facing immigrant groups has changed from that of housing to that of employment. You may wish to argue that both problems are so closely interrelated that it is not easy to say which is the major one, or again, that the problem of employment has always been the most serious one facing immigrants to Britain. You must know which line of argument you intend to follow for the purpose of your essay before you start to write. You should therefore note points from research to help you reach your conclusion. Never list details in note form (as they appear below) but link issues together in clear sentences to try to prove your argument. The mark you receive will be based on how well you answer the question set and not on the number of unrelated authorities and their research that you can list. The following examples are therefore provided to remind you of the kind of detail you should be looking for from your reading or from your notes.

1. E. Rose (*Colour and Citizenship*, 1966).

(a) The occupational distribution of male immigrant groups in London showed a fairly widespread range over a number of occupations, with no overwhelming concentration of any in a specific job. However, there was evidence of quite large numbers of West Indian men in woodworking, transport and engineering work.

(b) In the West Midlands, the pattern for male migrants showed greater concentration and fewer differences between each group.

(c) There was some similarity between male and female patterns. Indian-born women were well represented in clerical and professional jobs in London. The most important occupations for West Indian women were in service jobs (especially engineering and nursing).

(d) In the West Midlands, all male immigrant groups were

badly under-represented in white-collar jobs. Those from India were the best represented in these occupations; West Indians and Pakistanis were hardly represented at all.

(e) He concluded that all immigrants were less well-represented than the total population in those occupations usually considered to be the most desirable, and over-represented in those least liked.

2. W. Daniel (*Racial Discrimination in England*). In 1966 his team used three actors: a Hungarian, an Englishman and a West Indian, to apply for the same jobs, houses, mortgages and insurance policies. They were all given the same appropriate qualifications. It was found that the West Indian had least chance of success. This was still the case if he was given better qualifications than the others.

3. MacIntosh and Smith (*The Extent of Racial Discrimination*) In 1975 they used thirteen actors to apply for the same jobs. They conducted 821 tests in six towns. They found that the coloured applicant suffered discrimination as follows:

White-collar work	30% of occasions
Skilled manual	20% of occasions
Unskilled work	46% of occasions

4. Campaign for Racial Equality (CRE) Report, 1980. This found that unemployment rates among ethnic minorities were at least four times greater than for whites. It said that insufficient time was spent by the government in promoting better race relations while great expenditure was provided to limit immigration. At least 40 per cent of black people are British-born and deserve more help.

5. Home Office Report (*Ethnic Minorities in Britain*, 1983). This report confirms the high level of discrimination against coloured people in contemporary Britain, especially in employment. It indicates higher levels of unemployment and lower wages among West Indians and Asians. When unemployment is rising then the number of unemployed among ethnic minorities increases more rapidly than among the rest of the population. Of the coloured labour force, 73 per cent is concentrated in the South East and the West Midlands. These suffer a disproportionate number of unemployed. The report also shows that those in work undertake longer hours and more shifts to bring their pay into line with white workers. They are increasingly concentrated in less secure jobs in older industries. As a result of their low earnings, large numbers of dependants and higher housing costs, they experience a greater degree of poverty than white households.

6. Policy Studies Institute Report (*Black and White Britain*, 1984). This presents a pessimistic picture of the social and economic position of black people in contemporary Britain. Their opportunities have scarcely changed since the 1950s. Black Britons are still largely confined to the worst jobs and housing. The increase in national unemployment has limited their chances of mobility, and black unemployment is nearly twice the rate for whites. Enormous efforts need to be made to help black people move out of the low-status and low-paid jobs that most are in.

7. Government statistics in 1986 showed that black workers were twice as likely to be out of work as whites.

(a) Unemployment rates varied among different groups. While the average was 20.4 per cent, for Bangladeshis it was 30.6 per cent and for West Indians 23.0 per cent.

(b) Black women, who formed about 3.7 per cent of the labour force accounted for 6.7 per cent of unemployed women.

8. A Report by the Employment Institute in 1990 showed that:

(a) There were about one million people from ethnic minorities in the British work force of about 28 million, but only a few have reached positions of power and responsibility. They remain more likely to suffer unemployment and redundancy.

(b) This reflects high levels of prejudice and discrimination in the work place.

(c) It calls for more efforts on the part of the government and employers to achieve greater racial equality.

Conclusions

(a) The patterns that emerge show on the one hand that a high proportion of black people continue to suffer major problems in work even though several pieces of legislation have been passed to try to limit discrimination. On the other hand the issue is complicated by the fact that different groups achieve different levels of success (see Table 21.8).

(b) Some minority groups have been more successful than others in their working lives. Africans have similar employment patterns to those of white workers.

(c) Women workers from ethnic minorities in particular show many similarities with their white counterparts.

(d) These may reflect different cultural values within the minority groups. Such values may result from religious teachings and historical factors, such as slavery and other colonial experiences. Other influences may include the different ways in which they are perceived and treated by white workers, and how they respond to such perceptions.

(e) While there is evidence of racial disadvantage the data do not indicate that the ethnic minorities are concentrated in non-skilled manual work.

■ **How have sociologists helped us to understand the experiences of ethnic minorities in any one society? (AEB)**

In such a wide-ranging question you would need to organise your material carefully. You would consider:

(a) Specific areas of social life such as housing, education, crime and employment.

(b) The debate relating to the underclass (see pages 253, 282).

(c) Some of the theoretical issues (see page 279).

However, you would need to draw on some factual evidence in the course of your answer, such as that listed below.

Point to note

There are many ethnic minorities in Britain but a large number tend to remain 'invisible' in research studies (for example Cypriots, Maltese, Eastern Europeans, etc.). The focus of attention is invariable on black ethnic minority males.

1. (Daniel, *Racial Discrimination in England*). In 1966 a West Indian, a white immigrant from Hungary and a white English person were all given identical qualifications and asked to apply for accommodation in each of six areas. The applications to landlords showed that the West Indian was discriminated against two-thirds of the time when flats which did not exclude him in advance were tested in practice. The Hungarian experienced little discrimination. There was a strong similarity between the pattern of results in all six areas. There was no less discrimination against the West Indian when he was applying for the accommodation in a 'professional role' as a hospital registrar than when he was applying as a bus conductor.

2. (Burney, *The Experience of Race Law in Housing*). She makes the point that under the 1968 Race Relations Act it became illegal to discriminate against someone on the grounds of their colour. Landlords or their agents were no longer allowed to operate a colour bar. Building societies had to remove from their application forms questions which implied less favourable treatment of people of overseas origin. Yet in 1992 the CRE ordered an estate agent in Oldham not to discriminate against Asian people in buying and selling houses, following complaints.

3. Government White Paper (1975). This stated that people should not be confined to an estate or an area, nor be compelled to leave, simply on the grounds of colour. It accepted that like many coloured immigrants to Britain over the last twenty years, many were forced into the cheapest and poorest accommodation. But it concluded that it would be neither appropriate not practicable to single out immigrants for special help, since comprehensive housing action programmes are necessary for all citizens.

4. Home Office Report (*Ethnic Minorities in Britain*). In 1984 this found that, in housing, many West Indians and Asians are subject to a 'coloured tax' by landlords and are forced to pay more for run-down accommodation. They found some evidence to suggest that there is much overcrowding, especially among Asian families. Discrimination in the private sector is still thought to be substantial. There has been some movement of West Indian families from privately-rented accommodation to council house property. This may relate to the problems they have in obtaining mortgages and finance to purchase their own homes.

5. Policy Studies Institute (*Black and White Britain*, 1984). This stated that 'the separation of the jobs and residential location of British people of Asian and West Indian origin is so firmly established that it generates among both whites and blacks assumptions, expectations and behaviour that perpetuated it . . . discrimination is still a fact of life'. In 1987 the CRE called for better access for qualified black applicants to resolve hospital understaffing. The survey found that the number of black people working in the Health Service was disproportionately high compared with the number of black people in the population.

6. A Survey by the Society of Black Lawyers found that in the 1980s:

(a) Ethnic minority students at Guildford College of Law were five times more likely to be turned down by firms of solicitors than their white colleagues.
(b) In 1992 their Report found that black defendants are being wrongly convicted by bigoted all-white juries and biased summaries by judges. They advocate multi-racial juries.

7. Reports by NACRO in 1991 and 1992:

(a) stated that black people made more complaints about rough treatment by policemen;
(b) said that people who were arrested were less likely to be allowed to contact friends, relatives or lawyers; and
(c) highlighted the limited numbers of black people in senior levels of the justice system (see Table 21.9).

Conclusions

1. Sociologists have produced much research which describes the negative experiences of members of black minority groups.
2. Apart from facts uncovered in surveys, some have noted how the language of race has changed. Solomos has examined how changing social, political and legal environments may be producing new types of discourse.
   (a) Critics such as Lewis (*Anti-Racism: A Mania Exposed*) representing the New Right, argue that the problems associated with race are over-stated.
   (b) Opposition to a multi-racial society is not necessarily irrational; prejudice and discrimination are inevitable and cannot be eradicated by legislation.
   (c) Anti-racism has become a focus of concern as an intrusion on individual freedom. It is seen as an invention of the Left.
3. Critics of the New Right argue that:
   (a) Such views have helped shift public attention from the processes of discrimination and focus it on the anti-racists who are believed to have a vested interest in claiming that Britain is a racist society.
   (b) They help legitimise the relative inactivity of the government since 1979 in the field of racial policies.
   (c) They feed into the view that ethnic pluralism raises problems for social and political cohesion.

4. Solomos concludes that sociologists should focus more on the role of political language in the debates about race relations in Britain.

A more complex question is one that takes you into a discussion involving a theoretical analysis as well as a presentation of facts. For example:

Housing

■ **Racial tension is the result of competition in the housing market. Discuss.**

One useful way of approaching this type of question is to present a Weberian analysis (see page 279) followed by an example in which the method was adopted. Remember too that it is always useful to be able to add concluding points which offer some criticism or confirmation of the arguments presented. Consider the following structure:

1. Weber's view starts from the assumption that there is always a plurality of competing groups in a society. They compete for scarce resources.

Table 21.8 Job level: all employees by ethnic group and gender (percentages)

	White	West Indian	Asian	Indian	Pakistani	Bangladeshi	African
Men							
Class 1/2	19	5	13	11	10	10	22
Class 3a	23	10	13	13	8	7	21
Class 3b	42	48	33	34	39	13	31
Class 4	13	26	34	36	35	57	22
Class 5	3	9	6	5	8	12	3
Women							
Class 1/2	7	1	6	5			7
Class 3a	55	52	42	35			52
Class 3b	5	4	6	8			3
Class 4	21	36	44	50			36
Class 5	11	7	2	1			3

Source: C. Brown. *Black and White in Britain* (Heinemanns) 3rd PSI Survey, 1985.

Table 21.9 Black people in senior positions in the justice system (England and Wales)

Year	Position	Total	Percentage/number black
1990	Police force	149 100	20%
1972–	..	20 539	122 men; 30 women
1981–	..	25 435	321 men; 86 women
1991	..	27 011	452 (total)
1991	Solicitors	55 685	92 (Afro-Caribbean)
1981	Circuit judges	334	1 (Afro-Caribbean)
1990	.. ..	427	2.. ..
1991	Court recorders	752	6 (ethnic minority)
1991	High Court Judges	83	First black woman appointed

Sources: *Social Trends* 22; *Sociology Review* (September 1991).

2. Race relations can be viewed as a form of power relationship which arises when people of different ethnic membership are in competition.
3. Each group has its own access to power by joining relevant power groups, and each shares particular life chances.
4. Any group may suffer disadvantage at one level (for example in housing) but hold power in another (membership of a union may give power in work).
5. Immigrants may well suffer disadvantage in the housing market because they tend to have low social status in the eyes of the local residents with whom they are competing. (Although this view would suggest that they are not necessarily powerless in all other spheres of social life.)

An example of a study in which the view is tested is Rex and Moore (*Race, Community and Conflict*). They conducted their study in an area of Sparkbrook, Birmingham, to examine the conditions of housing faced by various ethnic groups. They included approximately 44 per cent English; 23 per cent Irish; 16 per cent West Indian; 8 per cent Pakistani; 1 per cent Indian and 5 per cent others. They identified three housing zones. The one which contained the majority of immigrants was that with the poorest and most dilapidated property. The middle classes who once lived in the area had long since moved out to more desirable areas further from the city centre.

Rex and Moore identify a hierarchy of housing classes; the immigrants fill the lowest of these, since they are of lowest status and have fewest resources to rise into higher groups which consist of outright owners of property.

The authors conclude that the immigrants come to be seen as the creators of the decaying areas; these 'perceived' meanings about the behaviour of ethnic minorities are translated into real facts about their lifestyles and life chances. They create their own communities, cinemas, restaurants, etc. 'Being a member of a housing class is of first importance in determining a man's associations, his interests, his lifestyle and his position in the urban social structure'.

Points of criticism

(i) Davies and Taylor conducted a study (*Race Community and No Conflict*) between 1966 and 1968 in a poor area of Newcastle-upon-Tyne which showed that Asians had a very strong drive towards property ownership. This was not just the result of a desire to avoid exploitation by landlords, but more because they have an ethic of hard work and ambition. They conclude that an explanation of the behaviour of the Asians in this area couched solely in terms of 'colour discrimination' and of 'passive victims', makes little sense.

(ii) Rex and Moore imply that the housing structure is independent of the wider economic class structure, where Marxists would argue that such factors must be seen as the fundamental source of social conflicts. It is seen as a mistake, therefore, to try to distinguish many housing classes and status groups. There are either owners or non-owners; the latter are subject to dangers of exploitation.

Education

■ **The problems encountered by racial minorities in the educational system are no different from those faced by white working-class children. Discuss.**

■ **In all societies there are both similarities and differences in the experiences of various ethnic minorities compared with the rest of the population. Examine these similarities and differences in the sphere of education.**

1. Rutter *et al.* (*Children of West Indian Immigrants*) compared the educational achievements of a group of non-immigrant children from a London borough with a similar non-immigrant group on the Isle of Wight. They found that those from London had more problems and lower educational attainments. They also compared children whose parents were born in the West Indies with those of indigenous families. They found:

(a) Children of West Indian background had even more problems. They also had lower levels of attainment.
(b) The children of West Indian parents born in Britain had a reading age on average ten months above their counterparts born in the West Indies.
(c) West Indian parents fell mainly into Classes 4 and 5. Their housing conditions were often poor, and overcrowding was more frequent. Family size tended to be larger.
(d) However, they found a very warm and caring relationship between West Indian parents and their children. They conclude that much of the concern about high rates of 'problem' behaviour among West Indian parents and children is unjustified.

2. G. Driver's research in 1981 challenges the accepted belief that West Indian pupils do less well in school than white children.

(a) He sampled 2300 school-leavers and found that the academic results of West Indian girls and boys were, for the most part, better than those obtained by white children.
(b) White boys did better than white girls in their level of qualifications, but West Indian girls were ahead of West Indian boys.
(c) His evidence suggests that West Indian children may do less well than their white counterparts at primary or even at the start of secondary school, but they begin to catch up and improve later.

3. Racial Equality in Training Schemes CRE Report 1985 found that black pupils are four times more likely to be suspended than whites. The CRE blames insensitive teachers who do not appreciate cultural differences as a cause of the behaviour about which they complain. Rastafarian culture was a common source of friction.

4. The Swann Report, 1985 aimed to change behaviour and attitudes in such a way as to promote a genuinely multi-racial educational system; and to suggest policies to combat racism in education. The committee was concerned that the children of some ethnic minorities were not doing as well as they should in the present educational system (see Tables 21.10 and 21.11)

Findings

(i) Racial discrimination and social deprivation are more important factors in West Indian underachievement than IQ.
(ii) Single-sex schools may be important in multi-racial areas to encourage Muslims to keep their children in education.
(iii) Asians seem to do as well as white children despite deprivation (see Tables 21.10 and 21.11).
(iv) None of the minority groups was found to be looking for assimilation in the majority community other than in terms of being fully accepted and equal members of society.
(v) Ethnic minority children tended to come from homes suffering greater economic and social deprivation than the white children.
(vi) Racial prejudice does not have identical effects on every minority group and teacher perceptions may

Table 21.10 In all CSE and GCE O-level exams, percentage of children gaining 5 or more high grades

West Indian	6
Asian	17
Others	18

Source: *Social Trends*, 22.

Table 21.11 In CSE and O-Level, percentage gaining higher grades

	English	*Maths*	*In A-Level 1 + pass*	*University entrance*
West Indian	15	8	5	1
Asian	21	21	13	4
Others	29	21	13	4

Source: *Social Trends*, 22.

Table 21.12 Numbers passing O-Level examinations (percentages)

Origin	*Did not take exams*	*Passed 5+ (A–C)*
Indian	6	26
African Ugandan/Kenyan	10	25
Pakistani	9	18
White	22	10
Afro-Caribbean	14	5
Bangladeshi	36	4

Source: 1 LEA.

Functionalist view	Marxist view	Interactionist view
The assimilation of all children into 'the British way of life' is possible. It is a matter of time before values are assimilated and appropriate norms of behaviour absorbed. The function of education is to promote value consensus. The process is slow because it will take many generations to complete socialisation.	The underachievement of children from some ethnic minority groups can be understood in terms of the serious deprivations they face, both social and economic. Parental aspirations are low, the culture of the school is unfamiliar to them and the teachers are often hostile. It is fundamentally a class problem.	To understand why the children of ethnic minorities do not do well it is necessary to focus on the processes of interaction which occur in the classroom. If teachers perceive a West Indian child to be 'less able' and treat the person accordingly, this discrimination may force the child into negative forms of behaviour.

be significant. Reasons for the varying levels of performance between children from different ethnic groups seem likely to lie deep in their respective cultures. For example, the Asians may do better because they prefer to keep a low profile and accept an ethic of hard work transmitted through their close family ties. Teachers may assume that Asians' only difficulty is language, whereas they may perceive West Indian children as potentially 'less able'. They are treated differently, attract fewer resources and respond less well.

Recommendations

(i) Opposes the idea that ethnic minorities should set up their own schools.
(ii) Rejects the idea of bilingual teaching. This should be left to the local community.
(iii) Schools should adopt clear policies on racism.
(iv) Priority should be the learning of English.
(v) There should be a non-denominational approach to religious education.
(vi) The government should fund teacher exchanges between all-white and multi-racial schools.
(vii) Britain must be accepted as a multi-racial and multi-cultural society and all pupils must be enabled to understand what this means.
(viii) It is necessary to combat racism, to attack inherited myth and stereotypes and the ways they are embodied in institutional practice.

5. Research studies in 1988 by Bradford City Council and in London by ILEA (the Inner London Education Committee), showed that since 1983 the exam results for black pupils (mainly Asian) improved faster than for those of white pupils. In 1987, 47 per cent of Bradford's black school leavers passed 5 or more O-Levels (A–C)/CSE Grade 1 compared with 39 per cent of white children. Only 7 per cent had no passes, whereas 19 per cent of white children failed to achieve any. In 'disadvantaged schools' (where more than 20 per cent of pupils take free lunches) the performances were similar. In London schools data shows that white children were out-performed by three ethnic minority groups (see Table 21.12).

Parekh (Deputy Chairman, CRE) notes that:

(a) The poor performance of white London children may relate to the fact that the results are from inner-city schools attended mainly by working-class children.
(b) The minorities from India, Uganda and Kenya may have more middle-class backgrounds, even though living in an inner-city area.
(c) The West Indians and Bangladeshis have been less successful in establishing a middle class of their own in Britain.
(d) Class and cultural factors are significant. Hindus do particularly well. The Brahmins, the highest caste, are traditionally teachers, with a strong commitment to education and success in business.

■ **Contrast different heoretical intepretations to explain the situation of children from ethnic minorities in the educational system.**

Legislation and its Effectiveness

■ **How effective have recent legislation changes been in reducing racial discrimination in Britain? (OUDLE)**

To answer a question on this topic you will need to establish the nature and extent of the problems faced by ethnic minorities between 1948 and the present time.

You will also need to know the dates and details of various pieces of legislation that were passed and enforced in recent years.

Finally, you must decide (on the basis of research findings) the extent to which they have been successful in achieving:

(a) limitation in numbers entering the country (see page 271); and
(b) more harmonious race relations (see studies).

The major pieces of legislation and some brief points from each are listed below. For a balanced essay you should try to relate the legislation and its aims to the specific problems it endeavoured to resolve. (See details on page 278.)

Conclusions

1. There remains evidence to suggest that legislation has not been entirely successful in reducing discrimination. It still occurs in many areas of social life:

(a) The 1990 CRE Report showed that out of 1381 complaints of discrimination:
  (i) 59 cases were settled before a court hearing;
  (ii) 26 were successful after a hearing; and
  (iii) 24 cases were dismissed after a hearing.
(b) In 1991 the CRE prepared a legal challenge to the Asylum Bill on the grounds that it breached Section 20 of the 1976 Act.

Legislation to control entry

1948 (Labour) British Nationality Act. This replaced 1914 legislation. It established the right of all citizens of Commonwealth countries to enter Britain to work and settle.
1962 (Conservative) Commonwealth Immigration Act. The first Act which limited entry to those holding work permits and their close relatives.
1968 (Labour) Commonwealth Immigrants Act. This denied entry to British subjects of Asian descent who were threatened with explusion from Kenya.
1969 (Labour) Immigration Appeals Act. This gave right of appeal to special tribunals and limited the number of dependents who could enter.
1971 (Conservative) Immigration Act. Patrials (anyone with at least one British grandparent, or who had been naturalised, or had lived five years in Britain might enter freely). Also anyone closely related to them or who had been resident in Britain before 1973. Irish and EEC citizens had right of entry. All others needed permits.
1981 (Conservative) British Nationality Act. This further tightened the definition of those who can claim British citizenship to:

(a) those already settled here; and
(b) those with one British parent who were registered abroad at birth.

Those with British passports who have lived abroad and have no recent connection or residence in Britain will not be allowed to enter and settle.
1991–2 (Conservative) Asylum Bill. Government proposes to limit the number permitted to enter Britain as refugees. They may not have the right to legal aid and representation.

Legislation to protect minorities

1965 (Labour) Race Relations Act. This made it a criminal offence to discriminate on the grounds of colour, race or ethnic origin, in providing goods, facilities or services. It also established the Race Relations Board, to monitor the Act and advise complainants.
1968 (Labour) Race Relations Act. This gave more powers to the Board and it established the Community Relations Commission. This was to advise the government and try to foster better race relations in the community.
1976 (Labour) Race Relations Act. The Race Relations Board and the CRC were merged into the Commission for Racial Equality (CRE). This was given powers to make formal investigations and to prosecute offenders. Employers became responsible for the unlawful acts of their employees. The Act bans positive discrimination in favour of ethnic minorities. All services are to be offered equally to all whatever their colour. (In 1985 a Greater London Council (GLC)-funded women's group was fined £125 for deliberately hiring a black woman at the expense of a white applicant.) In the same week three national daily papers and a London evening paper were criticised by the Press Council for mentioning the colour of a 17-year-old black youth who was convicted of murder.

(c) In 1992 CRE:
  (i) launched an investigation into allegations of racism at Glasgow Dental School and in four other educational institutions; and
  (ii) forced a 65-year-old working man's club to change its rules and admit black and Asian members. The club was in an area where 50 per cent of the local population was non-white.

(d) A Report in 1992 (*Racial Justice at Work*) argued that the present law needs to be replaced and tightened. It noted that the more qualified ethnic minority members were, the more discrimination they faced.

(e) In 1992 the Department of Employment issued recommendations to employers with regard to ethnic minority employees which included extending targets for access to top positions.

(f) The CRE advocated:
  (i) the introduction of compulsory ethnic-minority monitoring;
  (ii) increasing levels of compensation which employers must pay where discrimination occurs; and
  (iii) adoption of an EC directive to outlaw racial discrimination.

(g) In 1992 a part-time judge was cautioned against making racially insensitive remarks in his courtroom.

2. On the other hand there is evidence that where it can be proved the law does have teeth:

(a) In 1990 a total of £40 612 was paid to people suffering discrimination and £121 472 was paid in out-of-court settlements.
(b) In 1991 an Industrial Tribunal ordered the UK Immigrants Advisory Service to pay £11 000 to a Ghanaian employee who failed to become Deputy Director because of racial discrimination. An Asian candidate was preferred.
(c) In 1992 two black people found to have been treated in a racist manner by the police were awarded £20 000.

Theories to Explain Racial Tension

■ **Outline two competing theories which sociologists have presented to explain racial tension in contemporary Britain.**

This type of question is inviting you to display knowledge of the theoretical issues that are associated with the views of either Functionalists, Marxists or Weberians on the question of race relations. In the same way, other questions may appear in which you can utilise the same information although the word 'theory' may not appear. For example:

■ **Where do ethnic groups fit into the British class structure? (UODLE)**

Functional segmental theory

All societies consist of various segments with their own sub-cultures. Different groups live in separate areas of cities; race has become an additional feature of segmentation. Conflict between groups is based largely on these cultural differences. People are naturally suspicious of newcomers, especially 'dark strangers': they are perceived as a threat. Differences are experienced in terms of colour, religion, lifestyle, etc.

Functional pluralism

This view adds that races do not fit neatly into the categories described by Marx and Weber, based on class and status differences.

(a) Ethnic groups cut across classes.

(b) In every society there are a variety of groups based on religious, economic, cultural and ethnic differences. Pluralists dispute the idea that immigrant groups are necessarily subject to the domination of particular classes. They prefer to describe a process in which both conflict and consensus exist, regulated by government policies. If ethnic groups suffer discrimination it may be as a result of their failure to adopt mainstream British values.

Marxist interpretations

1. Racial inequality is directly linked to social inequality.
2. Racialism is a consequence of capitalist economic structure.
3. Racial hostility reveals levels of alienation and class division.
4. Racism is a means of ruling-class control.
5. The hostility of working-class people towards ethnic minorities is evidence of false class consciousness.
6. Ethnic minorities become part of a pool of surplus labour, open to exploitation and easily dispensable. As a result they are forced to live in the poorest areas, work in specifically migrant occupations, and face high levels of unemployment at times of economic depression.
7. They are faced with constant denigration in the media, where the negative image of the 'immigrant' is deeply embedded in the culture of the host society. This derives from the time when they were subject to colonialisation.

Points of criticism

- (a) Not all members of ethnic minorities are in the lowest social classes and they do not all live in the poorest areas.
- (b) Weberians argue that power is available to all.
- (c) It presents a very pessimistic picture of race relations.

Weberian interpretations

1. Racial inequality is related to people's perceptions, which arise out of processes of interaction in everyday life. People behave in accordance with the meanings they derive from events.
2. Racial hostility is part of the construction of daily reality by which some people make sense of complex events going on around them; e.g. if they are competing for scarce resources (jobs, homes) then the presence of ethnic minorities may be seen as a threat, especially in times of economic crisis.
3. It is largely irrelevant whether or not real racial differences exist; the fact that they are perceived to exist is enough to explain the hostility that results.
4. Those with greater access to the scarce resources have higher class and status positions than those who do not. Status and class positions are constantly changing as people achieve and lose access to power.
5. An immigrant is not necessarily destined to remain in a low-status or low-class group. These are flexible groupings and subject to change.

Points of criticism

- (a) It may present an over-optimistic view of contemporary race relations.
- (b) It presents a picture of a very fluid society. In reality there may be limited chances of mobility for members of ethnic groups.
- (c) Marxists argue that it is a mistake to place more emphasis on status differences than on class factors.

Questions

1. Examine the photographs A,59, 60, 61, 62 and 63. Every society tends to have minority groups who are treated less favourably than the indigenous population:
   (i) Suggest some reasons why those in photographs 61 and 63 (caravan dwellers) may often be regarded with hostility?
   (ii) Suggest how a study could be conducted to see whether those who hold such beliefs base them on personal prejudice or on hard research evidence.
   (iii) Explain the terms 'scapegoat' and 'stereotype'; suggest how they are used in relation to minority groups.

2. Examine photograph 62. Rex and Moore suggest that members of minority groups are often forced into specific areas of cities. Consider the factors that may have influenced the parents of these children to live in a poor inner city area.

3. Examine photographs 59 and 60:
   (i) More than 40 per cent of black Britons were born in Great Britain. Discuss the problems of defining 'an immigrant'.
   (ii) Suggest some of the major problems which research suggests this lady may face in relation to:
      (a) her education;
      (b) her job opportunities; and
      (c) her housing opportunities.
   (iii) Suggest some reasons why the Conservative Party tends to produce legislation that controls entry into the country and the Labour Party tends to promote legislation to protect minorities.

59

Source: Alec Gill

60

Source: Alec Gill

61

Source: Alec Gill

62

Source: Alec Gill

63

Source: Alec Gill

Summary points

From a functionalist perspective it may be convenient to have ethnic minorities in a society since they may meet specific demands for labour in certain occupations and they may provide specific skills or services. It may also help to integrate the members of the host society more into the mainstream of their own society by being able to identify 'strangers' of a lower social status and class. Their presence may also help explain social disorders and conflicts: they may become a convenient scapegoat for such problems.

Patterson (*Dark Strangers*) argues that such conflict and misunderstanding may only be a temporary state. Such problems can be overcome in due course as the ethnic minorities come to accept the dominant values of the host society.

Points of criticism

(i) There is not much evidence yet to show that second- and third-generation members of ethnic minorities have become more accepted and integrated in British society.
(ii) The view underplays major social inequalities based on class factors.
(iii) Major social conflicts (riots, etc.) tend to be minimised.

Following the riots in Brixton in 1981 Lord Scarman produced a report. It main recommendations were:

1. The early introduction of an independent element into police complaints procedures.
2. The doubling of the length of police training.
3. A statutory framework for police–community consultations.
4. Racist marches to be banned.
5. The recruitment of police from ethnic minorities.
6. The elimination of racially-biased policemen by careful recruitment.
7. Better management training for inspectors and sergeants.
8. Racial prejudice in policemen to be an offence punishable by dismissal.
9. Improved patterns of police patrol in inner-city areas.
10. The use of plastic bullets, etc. only in grave emergencies.
11. A better coordinated attack on inner-city problems.
12. Local authorities to check housing policies for discrimination.

In 1985 riots again occurred. Writing of those in Birmingham, Cashmore (*New Society*) said that the government, in trying to rein back local authority spending, sidestepped some of the aims of Scarman: 'It has drip-fed black youth with pointless YTS schemes ... it is out of touch with the forces in modern society'. He argues that the economic insecurity, deprivation and enforced idleness of young blacks is at the core of the problem.

Harris, writing of the riots in Tottenham in 1985 (*New Society*), says 'it was not a race riot; half of those who appeared before the magistrates were white'; although, as Murji points out, the incident which sparked the events was the shooting by police of a mother of six children.

Gaskell and Smith (*How Young Blacks See the Police*) conducted a study following troubles in Toxteth in 1985, to examine the hostility felt by young blacks towards the police. (Of their sample 41per cent said they thought the police were 'bad' or 'very bad'.) They concluded that blacks feel police hostility as a kind of group experience. A folk history of unpleasant, frightening experiences with the police has 'worked its way into the shared beliefs of black youngsters'.

Reiner (*New Society*) says that inequalities in housing and employment mean that blacks figure disproportionately in the young street population. They have a group consciousness. The common experience of discrimination means that respectable adult blacks will have common cause with them. 'All this could turn an underclass into a dangerous class'.

■ **Does the theory of an underclass provide a useful explanation of the social position of ethnic minorities in Britain?**

The concept of an underclass

This term has been used by many writers, but in imprecise ways:

1. It implies the existence of a class which is below that of the unskilled working class and whose members are distinct from those immediately above them.
2. It has been applied to ethnic minorities because it has been argued:
   (a) They have been shown to suffer high levels of poverty and powerlessness as a result of prejudice and discrimination.
   (b) They have more limited levels of mobility than white people of low social class.
   (c) Their opportunities in the search to obtain scarce resources (houses, jobs, etc.) is limited.

The Weberian view

(a) His work encourages researchers to examine the way subjective meanings translate into objective consequences.
(b) Rex and Tomlinson insist that race should be taken seriously as a social issue because of the problems ethnic minorities face.

Points of criticism

(i) Marxists see ethnic minorities as integral members of the working class; the problems they face are common to a large proportion of lower-working-class people.
(ii) There are about 2.6 million black people in Britain (1992 figures) but they are not all in the same economic position.
(iii) The New Right argue that the extent of racism is overstated.

The Marxist view

(a) Castles and Kosack (*Immigrant Workers and the Class Structure of Western Europe*) argue that it is a mistake to see ethnic minorities as an underclass. They form a reserve army of labour and a lowest stratum to the working class, having been marginalised and scapegoated.
(b) Miles (*Racism and Migrant Labour*) also argues that migrants occupy 'a structurally distinct position in the economic, political and ideological relations of British capitalism, but within the boundaries of the working class'.

(c) For some Marxists, race is not a legitimate sphere of study because it assumes that the problems faced by ethnic minorities are different from those of the working class in general. It gives credibility to misleading concepts (migrant; race; underclass, etc.) and provides negative images to people assumed to be different in specifically biological ways.
(d) Others examine the ways in which racist ideologies emerge, are reproduced and change as capitalism evolves (for example, black people become identified as a threat as Jews become increasingly assimilated).

Points of criticism

(i) Data from Policy Studies Institute (PSI) surveys indicate that ethnic minorities are not overwhelmingly located in the semi and unskilled working class. For example, in 1985: there were in the Registrar General's classes 4 and 5

West Indian men and women	39 per cent
Indian men and women	46 per cent
Pakistani men	43 per cent
Bangladeshi men	69 per cent
African men and women	32 per cent
White men and women	24 per cent

(ii) It plays down the significance of problems which have been shown to be specific to black people and would thereby deny attention to its most deprived members.
(iii) Weberians would argue that by recognising the existence of an underclass their special interests can be provided for and their re-entry into mainstream society gradually achieved, through educational, housing and employment initiatives.
(iv) The theory rests on factors which are hard to prove empirically, including a ruling class conspiracy to exploit black people to sustain the needs of the capitalist system.

The Functionalist view

(a) The New Right have identified the existence of an underclass. It is said to result to some extent from the effects of the welfare state which has promoted a dependency culture.
(b) It is inevitable that some will sink to the bottom within any social hierarchy, but as they become more skilled and develop more incentives they will become more mobile. (The 1988 Asian *Who's Who* shows 720 people, highly successful in business (many of them multi-millionaires), the world of education, politics, the media, literature and sport.)
(c) The existence of an underclass is functional in that it draws attention to social problems and weaknesses in existing social structures. It justifies changes in policy; tighter limits on immigration; for example, selective welfare benefits; more emphasis on market forces that can make use of the reserve army of labour.
(d) The process of mobility and assimilation and integration will maintain social order.

Points of criticism

(i) Lister argues that the concept of an underclass is too nebulous and imprecise to be of value. Its use encourages a pathological view of the very poor.
(ii) Marxists argue that the view minimises the problems facing working-class people (including minority groups).
(iii) Weberians would also dispute the view that racism is a myth and that prejudice and discrimination are normal and natural responses.
(iv) It reduces the belief in the need for reforming legislation.

Conclusions

(a) The use of the term *underclass* has come from:

(i) Weberians concerned at the plight of the black ethnic minorities in post-war Britain. They adopt a structural approach; that is, they see the emergence of a very poor sector in society resulting from the structure of the housing and job markets; their low status and low prestige is reinforced by racist attitudes within the class structure. There is a failure of government policy to remedy the problems.
(ii) The New Right, whose supporters emphasise the existence of a culture of poverty and dependence (for example, *The Emerging British Underclass*). They argue for a return to market forces to establish a culture of independence.

(b) The Marxist view is that the concept of an underclass is misleading. The economic and social situation of black ethnic minorities are said to be not much different from that of white working-class people.
(c) Pilkington ('Is There a British Underclass?') suggests that it remains debatable whether there is a distinctive black underclass cut off from the lower-working-class and characterised by distinctive attitudes and values.

Comparative Data

- **To what extent have the problems facing women in ethnic minorities been ignored in research studies?**
- **Compare the social situation of any two ethnic groups in Britain. (UODLE)**

A question of this type could be answered by reference to the similarities and differences of their experiences in obtaining housing, work, etc. (see pages 272 and 274).

Another approach would be to include details about the cultural variations between two groups and relate these to their social experiences in contemporary Britain.

Recent researchers have noted how women have largely been ignored in analysing the social situation of ethnic minorities in Britain. Akeroyd has argued that there are marked discrepancies and differences between men and women, whether in the same ethnic minority or in different categories.

The sources of differences

(a) *Legal and administrative constraints and procedures.* These have affected different groups in different ways according to the time when they arrived and the changing laws relating to immigration.

(b) *Demographic factors* (age and family developmental cycle).
(c) *Cultural factors* (each group having a different language, religious practices and educational differences) which have had various consequences for men and women and for family units.

The problems facing women

(a) Most of the research concentrates on Asian and West Indian males. Women in all minority groups have been largely invisible in studies.
(b) They have always been at the centre of moral panic scares (for example, with regard to birth rate, arranged marriages, etc.).
(c) They have been subject to stereotyping: West Indian women appearing to dominate and often head the family; Asian women being perceived as been confined within the family, and girls subject to excessively authoritarian controls.
(d) There are differences in educational attainment between girls from different ethnic minorities, different age groups and between the sexes which are not always highlighted in discussions of minority groups.

Table 21.13 shows that:

(i) Those from Pakistani/Bangladeshi groups were among the least well qualified.
(ii) The other groups surveyed among the girls had similar profiles to their white counterparts.

(e) The position of women from minority groups has been better documented in the field of paid employment where:

(i) They are badly under-represented in professional occupations. Their position is strongly affected by legal, educational and familial factors.
(ii) There are differences in experience between different groups. Indian women are more likely to be found in skilled manual work; West Indian women do much semi-skilled for unskilled work in the health service.
(iii) Unemployment rates for ethnic minority women are double those for white women. Bangladeshi women are the least likely to be in employment for various cultural reasons. See Table 21.14.
(iv) Women in the garment industry (mainly Asians and Cypriots) work under particularly hard conditions. They are recruited through kinship networks and are subject to male domination.

Conclusion

Akeroyd comments that while the economic and social position of women might be expected to be similar to that of ethnic minority men given the shared impact of race and class, the gender factor makes their situation very different. The implication is that more detailed research is required.

■ **Discuss reasons for immigration from New Commonwealth countries into Britain since 1950. What light has research thrown on the experiences of any two groups?**

Table 21.13 Qualification level of the population by ethnic origin and sex, 1988–90 (percentages)

Males	White	West Indian	Indian	Pakistani/Bangladeshi	Other
Higher	15	6	19	8	22
Other	57	58	51	40	56
None	29	36	30	52	21
Females					
Higher	13	16	13	4	20
Other	51	52	46	28	52
None	36	32	41	68	28

Source: *Social Trends*, 22.

Table 21.14 Unemployment by ethnic group (1986) (percentages)

	Females	Males
White	10	13
Afro-Caribbean	16	25
Indian	18	14
Pakistani	28	29
Bangladeshi	52	29
Asian	21	17

Source: PSI Survey.

	Indians	Sikhs	Pakistanis	West Indians
Place of origin	Indian India; Kenya; Uganda; Trinidad; Fiji.	The Punjab (India).	Pakistan (founded in 1947 formerly part of India) and Bangladesh (until 1971 part of Pakistan).	The Caribbean islands.
Numbers in Britain	779, 000 (1992).	50% of all Indian migrants are Sikh. 350, 000 (1991).	433, 000 (1991).	482, 000 (1991).
Religion	Hindu (360, 000) Sikh (360, 000)	Sikh.	Muslim.	Christian/Rastafarian.
Historical backgroung	The British went to India in the eighteenth and nineteenth centuries as colonial administrators. They justified their presence as the 'discovers' or by military conquest.			The Spanish conquered the islands in the sixteenth century. They imported slaves to work the plantations. Later British colonists maintained slavery.
Reasons for migrating to Britain	1. Colonial connections with Britain. 2. Wartime service with British troops. 3. To improve living standards (obtain work). 4. To reunite with family members.	1. Wartime service. 2. To improve living standards.	1 Originally part of Commonwealth and holders of British passports. 2. To improve living standards.	1. Wartime service. 2. Recruitment: (London Transport; nursing, etc. 1950s). 3. As British passport holders. 4. To improve living standards.
Cultural characteristics	1. The caste system produced strong success goals in Brahmins. 2. Many migrants have experience as successful business people. Strong work ethic. 3. They maintain strong kinship connections. 4. Outstanding sportsmen (cricket, hockey). 5. Higher proportion of women in skilled and semi-skilled work than other migrant groups. Fewest in unskilled category.	Wear turbans, beards. Strong religious values; ethic of hard work and equality.	Strong extended family ties. Wives do not always have good English. Many outstanding sportsmen: cricket, hockey, squash, etc.	Share many values of Western society music, sport etc. Rastafarians seek African roots. Many outstanding sporting successes in cricket, football, athletics, etc.
Main problems faced	1. Discrimination. 2. Failure by white population to appreciate or understand their cultural norms and values.	1. Discrimination in work, housing. 2. They are clearly identifiable.	First generation developed a guest complex. Second generation more aware of problems.	1. Discrimination. 2. Subject to negative stereotypes. 3. Concentrated in manual jobs.

All members of ethnic minority groups are subject to the effects of an economy in decline. They are easily scapegoated and find it difficult to obtain jobs, housing, etc. Pakistanis may be seen by white working class as the greatest economic threat, but West Indians may be the most disappointed of the minority groups.

Suggested Reading

Works noted in this chapter

C. Brown (1985) *Black and White*, Heinemann,

E. Burney (1972) *The Experience of Race Law in Housing*, Runnymede Trust

S. Castles and G. Kosack (1973) *Immigrant Workers and Class Structure of Western Europe* Oxford University Press

E. Cashmore (1985) *New Society* (September)

W. Daniel (1968) *Racial Discrimination in England*, Penguin, Harmondsworth

J. Davies and J. Taylor (1970) *Race Community and No Conflict*, *New Society* (9 July)

G. Gaskell and P. Smith (1982) *How Young Blacks See the Police*, New Society Reader

M. Harris (1985) *New Society* (4 October)

Home Office Report (1983) *Ethnic Minorities in Britain*, HMSO

R. Lewis (1988) *Anti-Racism, A Mania Exposed*, Quartet, London

N. MacIntosh and D. Smith (1975) *The Extent of Racial Discrimination* PEP

R. Miles (1982) *Racism and Migrant Labour*, RKP

C. Murray (1990) *The Emerging British Underclass*, IEA

S. Patterson (1965) *Dark Strangers*, Penguin, Harmondsworth

A. Pilkington (1992) 'Is There a British Underclass?' *Sociology Review*, February, Vol. 1, No. 3

PSI Report (1984) *Black and White Britain*, PSI, 9 July

T. Reiner (1985) *New Society* (25 October)

J. Rex, and J. Moore (1979) *Race, Community and Conflict*, RKP

E. Rose (1969) *Colour and Citizenship*, OUP

J. Solomos (1988) *Black Youth, Racism and the State*, CUP

J. Solomos (1990) 'Changing Forms of Racial Discourse', *Social Studies Review*, November, Vol. 6, No. 2

Works for further reading

R. Ballard and C. Ballard (1977) 'The Sikhs', in J. Watson, *Between Two Cultures*, Allen Lane, London

M. Banton (1977) *The Idea of Race*, Tavistock, London

M. Barker (1981) *The New Racism*, Junction Books

L. Barton and S. Walker (1982) *Race, Class and Education*, Croom Helm

J. Bhaba *et al.* (1985) *Worlds Apart*, Pluto

P. Bhachu (1985) *Twice Migrants. East African Sikh Settlers in Britain*, Tavistock, London

B. Bryan, S. Dadzie and S. Scafe (1985) *The Heart of the Race. Black Women's Lives in Britain*, Virago, London

H. Carby (1982) *The Empire Strikes Back*, Hutchinson, London

E. Cashmore (1979) *Rastaman*, George Allen & Unwin, London

E. Cashmore and B. Troyna (1982) *Black Youth in Crisis* George Allan & Unwin, London

S. Field, 'Trends in Racial Inequality' (1986) *Social Studies Review*, March

M. Fuller (1982) 'Young, Female and Black', in E. Cashmore and B. Troyna, *Black Youth in Crisis*, George Allen & Unwin, London

S. Hall (1978) *Policing the Crisis*, Macmillan, London

R. Honeyford (1988) *Integration or Disintegration*? Claridge Press

C. Husband (1975) *White Media, Black Britain*, Arrow

S. James (ed.) (1985) *Strangers and Sisters*, Falling Wall

R. Jeffcoate and B. Mayor (1985) *Migration and Settlement*, Open University Publications

V. Khan (ed.) (1979) *Minority Families in Britain*, Macmillan, London

E. Krausz (1971) *Ethnic Minorities in Britain*, Paladin, London

B. Parekh (1978) *Asians in Britain*, Campaign for Racial Equality, London,

A. Phizacklea (ed.) (1984) *One Way Ticket. Migration and Female Labour*, Routledge & Kegan Paul, London,

A. Pilkington (1984) *Race Relations in Britain*, UTP

K. Pryce, *Endless Pressure*, Penguin, Harmondsworth, 1979.

J. Rex and S. Tomlinson, (1979) *Colonial Immigrants in a British City*, Routledge & Keegan Paul, London

M. Sarup, (1986) *The Politics of Multi-Racial Education*, RKP

Lord Scarman (1981) *The Brixton Disorders* HMSO, London

D. Smith (1977) *Racial Disadvantage in Britain*, Penguin, Harmondworth

T. Walvin (1984) *Passage to Britain*, Penguin, Harmondsworth

J. West (1982) *Work, Women and the Labour Market*, Routledge & Kegan Paul, London

A. Wilson (1978) *Finding a Voice. Asian Women in Britain*, Virago, London

W. Wilson (1987) *The Truly Disadvantaged*, University of Chicago Press

J. Watson (1977) *Between Two Cultures*, Allen Lane

Self-test Questions

Study these extracts from newspapers and answer the questions below.

Item A

"NO BLACKS need apply" signs may have disappeared from outside accommodation agencies and flats, but one in five agencies employ more subtle discrimination against minority ethnic groups, an investigation has revealed.

Sorry, It's Gone, a report by the Commission for Racial Equality, shows how agents will often deny black people access to private rented property, while readily referring white people of identical status and means.

Yesterday the CRE said these agencies were breaking the law. Michael Day, the chair, called on the Government to require all agencies to be licensed.

"A condition for holding a licence should be evidence of non-discrimination in the provision of services," he said. Unlike publicly accountable landlords, such as councils, private landlords are under no legal obligation to promote good race relations.

The London Housing Unit said the report showed that racism in the private rented housing sector helped ensure that three times more black people than white

By Heather Mills
Home Affairs Correspondent

were likley to become homeless.

In the first formal investigation of private letting, the CRE used actors to test for discrimination. White and ethnic minority actors were paired off to apply to agencies with the same requests for homes. "We were the perfect pair of tenants, single, employed with reasonable salary, no children, no pets. The only difference was the colour of our skins," one said.

Of the 13 towns and cities tested, Ealing in west London, was the worst. Nearly half of the agencies tested, 10 out of 22, contravened the 1976 Race Relations Act. The other locations were Birmingham, Blackpool, Bristol, Cardiff, Edinburgh, Leeds, Barnet, central London, Manchester, Nottingham, Southend on Sea and Swindon. Mr Day said: "The findings of this investigation are shameful, but not surprising. It confirms what we have known for many years, that people from minority communities suffer discrimination at the hands of accommodation agencies in all parts of the country."

The investigation also included landlords and landladies who advertised privately and small hotels and guest houses. Little discrimination was found among guest house and small hotel owners. "With few exceptions, most of them appeared to treat both white and ethnic minority applicants equally." One in 20 private landlords advertising vacant flats, houses or rooms discriminated against non-whites.

While blatant white racism had gone, more subtle discrimination remained "worryingly high", the report concluded.

"In many cases what we found was not discrimination at second hand, where agencies were following discriminatory instructions from landlords and landladies, but rather discriminatory decisions taken by agency staff directly, through a mixture of ignorance, racial stereotyping or plain racial bigotry."

Source: From an article in the *Independent*, 14 September 1990.

Item B

Commission calls for new laws to take on 'entrenched' racism

THE Commission for Racial Equality yesterday called for tighter legislation against racial discrimination, *writes Nikki Knewstub.*

The law needs to be able "to challenge entrenched forms of discrimination more effectively", the commission says in its second review of the 1976 Race Relations Act.

It calls for a statutory obligation on employers to carry out ethnic monitoring, and for a new definition of indirect discrimination to outlaw practices not essential for efficiency, such as word-of-mouth recruitment, apprenticeships for employees' children, and advertising vacancies internally only.

It wants legislation against discrimination in Northern Ireland, which is outside the 1976 act; legal aid extended to discrimination cases in tribunals; a discrimination division set up within the industrial tribunal system; better protection against victimisation for invoking the act; a prescribed minimum payment for injury to feelings; and compensation limits for discrimination victims raised to £30,000.

The commission also recommends a specific law against incitement to religious hatred, further consideration of a law against religious discrimination, and that the law of blasphemy be extended to other religions besides Christianity or be abolished.

Source: From an article in the *Guardian*, 10 September 1992, p. 3.

Item C

SOMALIS have fled from famine and massacres in East Africa to find themselves the ignored victims of a "social catastrophe" in the East End of London.

A remarkably self-critical inquiry into their fate by Tower Hamlets, the inner London borough that houses the largest concentration of Somalis in the country, has discovered that thousands of refugees have not so much fallen through the welfare state net as missed it completely.

Violence, near-total unemployment, homelessness and a lack of medical and psychiatric care have greeted them in Britain.

"The long-term neglect of moral and stautory duties . . . is a source of much bitterness and discontent," the council's investigators reported.

The refugees' life is far better than in Somalia. But it can still be appallingly bad by any civilised standard.

Meanwhile, the report accuses police and the council of "consistently and complacently" failing to take action against the organisers of racist attacks on Somalis and the Home Office of refusing to respond to the "acute levels of deprivation" by authorising special spending.

Indeed, the investigators discovered that to the agencies responsible for every vital aspect of life – health, security, education, housing – the East End Somalis were all but invisible. No one knew or had tried to find out how many Somalis lived in east London, used its schools or went to its hospitals. No one had collected the Somali homelessness or unemployment figures.

There was a complete absence of statistical data on which an assessment of the condition of the refugees could be based. The inquiry tried to fill the gap. It estimated that there were now 15,000 Somalis living in Tower Hamlets – about 10 per cent of the population. The overwhelming majority had fled as refugees since 1988.

Source: From an article by Nick Cohen and Mark Gould in the *Independent* on Sunday, 23 August 1992.

1. Examine Item A.

(i) Define:

(a) discrimination;

(b) blatant discrimination; and

(c) subtle discrimination.

(ii) Discuss the possible problems which high levels of discrimination impose on members of ethnic minorities.

(iii) Discuss some of the advantages and disadvantages of using actors to investigate levels of discrimination.

2. Examine Item B.

(i) Explain:

(a) direct discrimination;

(b) indirect discrimination; and

(c) entrenched discrimination.

(ii) What problems may occur from the perspective of the ethnic minorities if they become subject to ethnic monitoring?

3. Examine Item C.

(i) Explain what is meant by describing the Somalis as 'all but invisible'?

(ii) What explanations can be suggested to account for their low level of status in the market for housing, jobs, etc?

(iii) What explanations might Rex and Moore present to account for the predicament of the Somalis being restricted to the poorer sections of the area?

4. Using all the items and any other data with which you are familiar discuss the view that when comparing the findings of research in 1966 (Daniels) with that of 1990 and 1992 it suggests that the legislation to combat discrimination in housing, work, etc, has been largely ineffective.

22

WORK

The following topics are widely covered by all the examination boards:

1. The impact of industrialisation.
2. The significance of work on people's lives:
   (a) Work as a source of identity.
   (b) The functions of work.
   (c) Prior orientations and expectations about work.
3. Factors affecting attitudes towards work:
   (a) The organisation of work.
   (b) Alienation.
   (c) The impact of new technologies.

The Impact of Industrialisation

The origins of sociology lie in the attempts of early writers such as Comte and Durkheim to explain the causes and consequences of social change. They were concerned in particular with the transition from one type of society to another (from rural to urban, pre-industrial to industrial) as well as changes in social institutions. These are the special province of sociology, hence the interest in their change, especially in relation to the processes of industrialisation.

Consider the following questions:

- **To what extent is technological innovation the cause of social change? (UCLES)**
- **Examine the impact of industrialisation on the structure of the family. (WJEC)**

Industrialisation

The introduction of power to drive machines and of power-using machines made from metals. The source of wealth in the society is transferred from the farm or small cottage industries to large-scale complex economic organisations. These include factories, banks, shops, etc. The invention of improved forms of transport, electricity and other technologies all helped to modernise methods of production.

The Functionalist view of social change

1. Social change is an evolutionary process that occurs as a result of the changing specialisation in structure and function of institutions.
2. There is a constant adaptation of the impact of external factors (climate trends, military threat, etc.) and internal factors (for example, demographic changes, cultural values, religious teachings, new leadership, as well as new inventions and technologies).
3. New technologies are necessary to help produce the goods and other items required to meet the needs of the society and its members.

The Marxist view of social change

1. Change arises from the inherent conflict in the structure of society. In every society the forces of production correspond with a particular set of social relationships of production. These give rise to disruption.
2. The methods of production, the technology and the social relations generated by them are the basic feature of the society. The economic infrastructure helps to shape the social superstructure.
3. The exploitation of one group by another is the source of social change.
4. The weaknesses of the infrastructure lead to the breakdown of institutions and social organisation and the creating of a new social structure.

Industrialisation and the family

The Functionalist view

1. Families become more socially and geographically mobile in their search for work and new homes.
2. They become smaller in size with the introduction of new methods of family planning.
3. They become more independent of wider kin. The nuclear family becomes the functional pre-requisite for an industrial society.
4. They become more democratic in structure, with more wives going out to work.
5. There are improved living standards.
6. They may become less stable and more prone to divorce, separation.

The Marxist view

1. Families become the prime source of labour for the capitalist economy.
2. Family members, especially women, are exploited in a capitalist economy. They provide a source of cheap labour and they are essential for the maintenance of the home.
3. As an agency of socialisation the family becomes an important means of ensuring the transmission of the ruling-class ideology.
4. Cooper (*The Death of the Family*) says that 'an emploitive family produces an exploitive society', as the family prepares its members for their roles in society.
5. Instability and conflict are inevitable.

Weber's view of social change

1. He accepted the Marxist theory that the emerging middle classes took every opportunity to accumulate wealth and other resources and that conflict arose between groups in competition for scarce economic resources, causing some change.
2. He looked for unique factors as sources of change. He argued that one such feature was the appearance of a particular form of religious teaching, namely Protestantism, in the sixteenth century.
3. He suggests that at certain times and places change can occur from religious beliefs since these can affect economic behaviour. Protestantism preceded Western capitalism, making the accumulation of wealth both a religious and a business ethic.
4. He concludes that the major change from a feudal to a capitalist system could have occurred, with all its subsequent effects, without the appearance of Calvinism.

Conclusion

It is generally agreed that there is no single theory of social change which is seen as a normal feature of every society.

Industrialisation and social change

■ **Is there a logic of industrialism which explains social change? (UODLE)**

Main points

1. Historically, industries developed from small groups of workers who brought different skills together to form larger units. The factory system was the basis of the *division of labour*.
2. The division of labour means that many people contribute to the production of a complex item by undertaking at least one, often simple, task. It is a term associated specifically with industrialisation. The opposite is *craft production*, in which one worker is responsible for the completion of the entire product.
3. Subsequent changes in technology have had profound effects on workers and their attitudes to work. All industrial societies have problems of organising appropriate and efficient working structures.
4. Sociologists endeavour to understand the effects and impact of these productive systems. They wish to know whether there is a logic of industrialism.

Discussion of the concept.

1. Eldridge (*Sociology and Industrial Life*) says that those who want to argue that there is a logic of industrialism want to point to the similarities of structure and process which accompany industrialisation in different societies.

2. Inkeles (*Industrial Man*) says that 'insofar as industrialisation, urbanisation and development of large-scale bureaucratic structures create a standard environment . . . to that degree they should produce relatively standard patterns of experience, attitudes and values'. He suggests that from an analysis of cross-cultural studies there are certain similarities common to all industrial societies. In all, the highest levels of job satisfaction are among white-collar and skilled manual workers. The implication is that if conditions of work become increasingly alike in societies subject to industrialisation, then attitudes and values will become similar, so producing a 'homogenised culture'. He suggests that this process is already advanced in the USA and may follow elsewhere, so that in the future there may be a fairly uniform world culture.

3. Miller (*The Dockworker*) also contends that there are widely shared conditions associated with dock work which seem to produce a universal dock work sub-culture. The conditions include the casual notion of employment; the arduousness of the work; the danger; the lack of career structure; the necessity of living near the docks; and the self-perception of being a member of a low-status, working-class group. The sub-culture includes such values as: solidarity with fellow workers; militant unionism; and liberal/radical politics, but conservative views about work practices.

However, Miller does not deduce that all industrialising societies must necessarily produce a dock work sub-culture at some stage in their industrial history. This is because:

(a) Dock work is derived from the international commercial system that is always changing.
(b) Every society is subject to its cultural norms and values.
(c) Feldman and Moore (*Comparative Perspectives*) argue that while there are some common core structures in industrial societies they see the ultimate influences as being political activity.
(d) Kerr *et al.* (*Industrialism and Industrial Man*) believe the logic of industrialism will lead to a stage in which class warfare will be forgotten and in its place will be a contest between interest groups.

■ **Discuss the view that the recent social changes in Eastern Europe lend support to the convergence thesis.**

Specify some of the issues relating to the convergence thesis

1. Historical detail:

(a) Communism was established in the former USSR in 1917 and in various other Eastern European countries after the Second World War. The guiding ideology was that of Marxism, which aimed to:
  (i) end economic class distinctions;
  (ii) promote greater equality for all; and
  (iii) introduce political bureaucratic structures to prevent capitalist methods and values contaminating the new regimes.
(b) The ideological differences between capitalism and Communism suggested different lines of future social development.

2. The origin of the debate.

In the late 1950s and in the 1960s, sociologists such as Bell (*The End of Ideology*), Kerr *et al.* (*Industrialism and Industrial Man*), Rostow (*Stages of Growth*), Feldman and Moore (*Industrialisation Industrialism, Convergence and Differentiation*), Inkles and most recently in the 1990s Fukuyama (*The End of History*), have argued that:

(a) All complex industrial societies (in the East and the West) will converge in terms of their political, social and economic structures, especially as the values of Western liberal democracy become dominant.
(b) Similar types of industrial technologies must make use of similar types of employees. They require both the well-educated and the low-level manual workers, who must accept different income and status levels.
(c) Wide social inequalities are therefore inevitable and necessary in an industrialised society; stratification systems in Eastern Europe will become more clearly delineated.
(d) The most powerful class will be the professional technocrats who will be increasingly committed to the values of individual success and the competitive market. They are less likely to be interested in unionism and class solidarity, which may be seen as restraints on development.
(e) Proponents of the thesis have argued that existing systems of stratification in Eastern Europe have always been more pronounced than Marxists admitted. The political élite held great privileges which they could transmit to their children, who also inherited high status.

3. Theoretical implications:

(a) The convergence thesis emerges from Functionalist theory which suggests that the evolution of modern complex societies results in the adaptation and change of institutions which promote increased efficiency and wealth production.
(b) Growth is assisted by the emergence of certain dominant ideological values (such as ethics of achievement, individualism, intelligence, the inevitability of class division); also the development of efficient economic and political structures. These include:
  (i) democratic institutions and organisations;
  (ii) a new class of technocratic and managerial experts; and
  (iii) central economic planning.
  (iv) an efficient bureaucratic administrative structure.
  (v) new technologies which require a well educated and skilled work force.
(c) The assumption is that as these values spread through industrialised societies they will modernise and become more similar. This will be facilitated through the growth and development of an increasingly sophisticated mass media (which Marshall McLuhan described as having the effect of reducing the world to a global village).

Consider points of criticism

In the 1960s and 1970s various sociologists responded to the convergence thesis in critical ways:

(a) Marxist critics argued that in Eastern Europe the means of production were communally owned, so socio-economic classes could not exist in the same way that they did in capitalist societies. In the West, classes were polarising as new technologies deskilled workers into clearly divided groups, whereas in Eastern Europe divisions were narrow and closing.
(b) They claimed there was no evidence that other developing societies were converging because they remained subject to the exploitation of the wealthy West.
(c) Weberians (such as Goldthorpe and Lockwood) argue that stratification systems in socialist societies resulted from political engineering in which wage differentials were reduced, the peasantry was awarded higher status than other groups of workers, and that of white collar workers was reduced. While it was not possible to remove all inequalities, excesses were limited and no serious ideological conflicts existed between groups.

Consider the significance of the collapse of Communism in Eastern Europe

(a) The downfall of these Communist governments led to a reassessment of the convergence thesis because they were replaced by democratic institutions and by the intention to introduce capitalist economic systems.
(b) Rostow had argued in 1960 that 'communism was a disease of transition'. He predicted its collapse as the demand for Western democracy gained momentum.
(c) Lane ('State Socialism in the 1990s') described two major factors which have faced state socialist societies since the mid-1970s:

(i) economic decline; and
(ii) a massive expectations gap between what people expected to receive and what the economy could produce. These led to the crises of legitimacy and precipitated the reform movement.

(d) Lane concluded that in copying the processes of advanced capitalism the leadership of the once socialist societies were likely to encounter these problems:
(i) exacerbated social tensions;
(ii) rapid inflation and increased unemployment;
(iii) wider differentials in living standards; and
(iv) the emergence of a new class of business people who may come to be resented by manual workers.

(e) He concluded by giving some support to the convergence thesis. He noted that if a rapid rise in gross national productivity occurs then the working class itself will become more highly stratified, with the more affluent and skilled siding with the leadership. Politics would then become more concerned with individual interest and personal achievement.

Conclusion

(a) There is much evidence to show that major social changes have occurred in formerly Communist societies, which indicates a move towards capitalism. In 1992 the still-Communist Government of China allowed the introduction of greyhound racing for the first time; in Russia, vouchers were issued which could be exchanged for shares in privatised industries sometime in the future. It seems likely that there will be increasing areas of similarity with Western institutions and social structures, although some critics may continue to question this view.

(b) O'Donnell, discussing Swedish society in the 1980s noted that this was one in which there was a high level of social equality (as proposed by the socialist model) and high levels of political equality (based on democratic systems of the West). He concluded:
(i) convergence theory is too generalised and based on ethnocentric assumptions about the strengths of Western societies while overlooking their weaknesses; and
(ii) Swedish society lends support to Gouldner's view that people can organise society in ways which do not make technocratic or ruling class élites inevitable. They can make choices and act on them.

(c) In the second half of 1992 the Conservative Party split over the implementation of the Treaty of Maastricht, which was intended to promote greater convergence between the members of the EC. This could suggest that convergence of institutions is not necessarily accepted as a worthwhile aim even among members of Western societies.

(d) In view of the problems which faced many western societies in the early 1990s it may be that this model of social development comes to be rejected by the formerly communist societies. There were high levels of unemployment and recession as well as major social inequalities in wealth and income in Britain. A Report by the Low Pay Unit in 1992 showed that the pay gap between lowest-paid workers and average earners was the greatest since records began in 1886. It said the working poor were increasing in numbers and declining in prosperity.

(e) It could therefore be argued that, as yet, it is too soon to conclude with certainty that there is a logic of industrialism which will lead to an inevitable convergence of ideologies and values as well as social and economic structures in Eastern and Western Europe.

The Significance of Work for the Individual

Questions on this topic area are asking you to discuss:

Why do people work?
What is the influence of work on people's lives?
On what basis is work chosen: for the satisfaction it provides, for enjoyment and self-fulfilment or the opportunities it offers to enjoy life outside work?

Source of identity

- **What light have sociologists thrown on the meanings of work for people in an industrial society?**
- **What are the social consequence of unemployment?**

1. Daniel ('What Interests the Workers?') discusses some of the views put forward by writers who have tried to explain what people may want from their work.

2. Maslow (*Motivation and Personality*) said that everyone has basic needs. As one is satisfied then the next in the hierarchy becomes important. The ultimate need is to develop one's abilities, to be creative and to express oneself. In adulthood, this is sought and achieved in work. Hence, Maslow would be critical of any working structures that denied the individual these opportunities.

3. Hertzberg (*The Motivation to Work*) suggests that people seek five main goals in work which when satisfied can produce a strong sense of satisfaction. These include obtaining:

(a) a sense of personal achievement;
(b) praise and compliments in work;
(c) a degree of trust or responsibility;
(d) promotion and fresh challenges; and
(e) high levels of intrinsic satisfaction (see page 293).

Instrumental attitudes

Lockwood and Goldthorpe in their study of car workers in Luton found that the majority had a strongly instrumental attitude towards their work. They tended to see their work as an instrument for achieving a particular end, which was to obtain as high an income as possible, to increase their living standards and have plenty of leisure time. They grew up expecting that work would be tedious and unpleasant. They expected to be rewarded for doing it by obtaining high pay. Work was therefore seen as a way of making money and not as a place for developing friendships, social skills, personality development or meeting new challenges. The attitude would normally be associated with:

Table 22.1 Seasonally adjusted unemployment levels 1955–91 (millions)

Year	Numbers unemployed
1955	0.3
1965	0.4
1975	0.8
1979	1.1
1982	2.5
1984	2.9
1985	3.0
1986	3.1
1988	2.3
1989	1.8
1990	1.7
1992	2.9

Notes: Figures prior to 1971 are not comparable to those from 1971 onwards.

Source: Department of Employment.

Table 22.2 Unemployment rates, by gender and ethnic origin (percentages)

Gender/ethnic origin	1984	1986	1988	1989	1990
Males, white	11	11	9	7	7
Females, white	11	10	8	7	6
Males, West Indian	30	26	18	15	13
Females, West Indian	18	19	11	14	–
Males, Indian	13	16	11	10	8
Females, Indian	20	19	13	9	11
Males, Pakistani	33	27	24	18	15
Females, Pakistani	–	–	–	–	–
Males, Other	19	17	9	8	12
Females, other	19	17	10	8	9

Source: *Social Trends*, 22.

(a) those from a class which has come to accept such values and transmits them from one generation to the next; and
(b) those with low educational qualifications who have little job choice, and who have had unhappy work experiences.

Intrinsic satisfaction

This means that workers gain a sense of value and enjoyment from the work itself. It is important not for extrinsic reasons, but because it provides opportunities for self-development and personality growth.

The attitude would normally be associated with those who:

(a) have come from a social class which promotes such values and transmits them from one generation to the next;
(b) have remained in the educational system and obtained high qualifications. They can exercise some choice in their work; and
(c) have specific skills which they wish to use in their work.

Unemployment

Research into the effects of unemployment on those anticipating a job and seeking one, confirms that failure to work can affect an individual's self-esteem, sense of dignity and worth in the community. There are also possible consequences for the social and economic structure of society.

1. Definitions:

(a) (from 1982 onwards) 'a count of those people claiming unemployment and related benefits at Employment Service offices who on the day of the monthly count, are signed on as unemployed and actively seeking and available for work'; and
(b) 'those persons without a job who were available to start work within two weeks following the date of the survey and had either looked for work in the previous four weeks or were waiting to start a job they had already obtained'.

Numbers estimated to be unemployed vary according to the definition used. Between 1979 and 1987 the method of government calculation was changed twice. Other changes were made to the administrative system for paying benefits. It is claimed that these recalculations produce a less exaggerated and more realistic picture. Critics argue that the true figure is always underestimated.

2. Causes of unemployment:

(a) The national economy goes into recession. Workers in certain industries are made redundant as demand falls.
(b) A region goes into decline as demands for its traditional products fall.
(c) There is a change in the technology of an industry; traditional industries which employ large numbers decline.
(d) Workers lack relevant skills or qualifications; others remain geographically immobile and cannot move to obtain work where it is available (perhaps for family reasons).

3. Changing levels of official unemployment (see Tables 22.1 and 22.2).

4. The social distribution of unemployment:

(a) Unemployment rates are higher among ethnic minorities than among whites. Between 1986 and 1990, however, the fall in rates was greater among ethnic minorities than among the white groups. The fall was greatest among West Indian males.
(b) It tends to be highest in Classes 3b, 4 and 5 among men and among junior members of Class 3a; and in Classes 4 and 5 for women.
(c) Rates are highest among those under 25. In 1990, for those under 20, rates were almost double the average male unemployment rates.
(d) There are regional variations. In 1990 rates were highest in Northern Ireland, the North, the North West and Scotland.

5. Perspectives on unemployment:

(a) Conflict theorists see it resulting from the nature of the capitalist system, which inevitably goes through crisis and recession.
(b) Functionalists see it as inevitable and necessary for those lacking appropriate skills as technologies change. Its threat forces them to become more prepared to retrain or to accept the problems it may cause. The free market operates to allocate the most able to the most functionally important positions.
(c) Phenomenologists point out the problems of interpreting the statistics. Since it is impossible to measure accurately it is more useful to look at processes of categorisation and understand the meanings attached to unemployment by people and the consequences for them in their everyday lives.

6. Some of the consequences of unemployment:

(a) On social and economic life:
   (i) Unions lose bargaining power and membership.
   (ii) Inflation tends to decline.
   (iii) The work force becomes less mobile.
   (iv) Divisions between rich and poor, the successful and the unsuccessful, may widen.
   (v) Women and ethnic minorities may be scapegoated as causes of unemployment among white males.
(b) On individuals and groups of unemployed:
   (i) Their living standards fall and poverty increases. More homes are repossessed.
   (ii) There are incentives to retrain.
   (iii) There is an increase in alienation and the marginalisation of the long-term unemployed.
   (iv) Problems of ill-health increase. In 1992 a Report suggested that a big rise in tuberculosis, especially among young women, was directly related to poverty and homelessness. An examination of 300 cases in Liverpool showed that the highest levels occurred in the areas with the highest social deprivation.
   (v) Willis (*Learning to Labour*) discusses the problems of youth unemployment. He argues:

- That lack of a wage means lack of a key to the future. The direct experience of work has great importance in structuring adult identity.
- Lack of work may produce a crisis for working-class males; for women it may mean a deepening of their domestic duties and their oppression. An alternative may be pregnancy and dependence on the state, since child-rearing may offer a clear and attainable role.
- Unemployed youth may become the source of moral panics. They have more free time, low boredom thresholds and tend to congregate in public spaces where they become noisy, conspicuous non-shoppers, easily identifiable 'folk-devils'.

Conclusions

(a) Research suggests that different groups of workers place a different emphasis on the meaning that work has for them. Some seek instrumental satisfaction, others intrinsic satisfaction.
(b) Willis claims that, in general, all paid work is an enfranchisement into general, political, social and cultural adulthood.
(c) Allen and Watson have suggested that it is hard to identify precise effects relating to unemployment since there may be a complex set of interrelating factors at work.

■ **Drawing on relevant sociological evidence, assess the view that both manual and non-manual workers are now characterised only by instrumental attitudes.**

To answer this question, or its opposite:

■ **In modern society, work is performed mainly for intrinsic reward. How valid is this claim for both manual and non-manual workers?**

you must consider a range of relevant studies. For example:

(a) Lockwood and Goldthorpe (*The Affluent Worker*) suggest that the answer to the question, 'What do workers want from their work?' is a complex one. Certainly, different groups of workers seem to want different things. The shop floor workers had often deliberately chosen tedious and repetitive work because it was highly paid. They placed more emphasis on the instrumental rewards the work offered: 'Their social experiences and social circumstances were such that they had an instrumental orientation to work.'
(b) Walker and Guest (*The Man on the Assembly Line*) point out the constraints in the opportunities for social interaction according to the technology. For example, the assembly line is noisy, with little time between job cycles; it forces the worker to maintain output at the pace of the machine. They suggest that the low levels of enjoyment in this work must help explain levels of industrial conflict.
(c) Chinnoy (*Auto Workers and the American Dream*) found that where workers gained little opportunity for meaning and purpose in their work because the product was standardised and their contribution to the manufacturing process was limited, then they gained little or no intrinsic satisfaction.

Examples of studies which describe workers who gain intrinsic reward:

(a) Mumford (*Job Satisfaction: A Study of Computer Specialists*) found high levels of intrinsic satisfaction among the workers he interviewed. He comments that there can be very few jobs in industry which evoked the level of enthusiasim he found. It seems that data processing provides a continuously challenging work state (see Table 22.3). Mumford concludes that an analysis of the variety of skills required by the programmers showed that they required a multitude of skills, which was an important factor in job satisfaction.
(b) Sykes (*Work Attitudes of Navvies*) describes a participant observation study of navvies on a construction site in the north of Scotland. He describes the hard and dangerous work, the long hours and limited chances of relaxation. The labourers displayed hostility towards their employers and the management. Few

Table 22.3 Degree of satisfaction with work choice (percentages)

Q. *Have you ever regretted your decision to become programmers?*

	Yes	No	No answer
Users	13	87	–
Manufacturers	4	91	5
Consultants	3	93	4

Table 22.4 Categories of employment, 1984 (percentages)

Occupation	Full-time	Part-time	All women	All men
Professional/managerial	8	1	6	24
Professional in health	16	10	13	5
Clerical	41	22	33	6
Catering, cleaning, sales	16	54	32	7
Manufacturing, transport	17	10	14	51
Other	2	3	2	6

Source: *Women and Employment* (HMSO, 1984) (quoted in Crompton).

were members of a union. But he noted how norms of hard work and individual skills were important among them. Although they were motivated by instrumental attitudes (they wanted high wages), at the same time they drew some intrinsic satisfaction from feats of hard work, and from their ability to do the work quickly, efficiently and without much supervision.

(c) McGuire (*Threshold to Nursing*) suggests that research shows the principal attraction of nursing to be the opportunity it offers for service to others. Linked with this is the intrinsic interest of the work and the opportunity to advance the education of the entrant.

Conclusions

(a) To some extent, whether or not people find intrinsic or extrinsic satisfaction in their work relates to their prior expectations. The affluent workers expected work to be tedious but well paid.
(b) Generally, there seem to be higher levels of intrinsic satisfaction among white-collar workers, although this may vary between jobs. The modern office may be not unlike a factory for some workers (see page 302).
(c) Some low-skilled workers may gain some levels of intrinsic satisfaction but their prime motive is likely to be monetary reward.
(d) Work attitudes are also related to the way the work is organised, the influence of the technology of production being significant in this respect (see page 298).

■ **What can we learn from research of the influence of work on people's lives? Illustrate your answer with reference to specific studies in the sociology of occupations.**

The significance of work

Worsley (*Introducing Sociology*) says that work is crucial as a source of income. But it has other significant aspects. It 'gives the worker identity and status . . . When we ask the question "what is he?" the kind of answer we normally expect is a statement about the work a person does, "he's an engineer" or "he's a dentist". Such words are not merely labels which inform us about the kind of technical functions a person fulfils in society but they are also a major key to social placement and evaluation.'

Examples of research

1. Lockwood and Goldthorpe (*The Affluent Worker*) showed that the work experience affected the assembly-line workers' attitudes towards several aspects of their lives:

(a) *Their family life*: they became more home-centred (privatised). Tightly-knit work groups were rarely found. Workplace friends and friends outside work were separate social categories.
(b) *Their leisure activities*: they spent more time in family activities and less in communal association with workmates.
(c) *Their political values*: they retained support for the Labour Party, which was seen to represent their interests. These values were reinforced in the work place.

2. Parker (*The Future of Work and Leisure*) argues that a range of social behaviour is influenced by a person's occupation. As society becomes more industrialised, work often becomes less intrinsically satisfying for larger numbers of people. They may begin to seek more from their non-work (leisure) time. As work becomes less of a central life interest, so work and leisure become separate worlds.

3. Carter (*Into Work*) says that work is particularly important for school-leavers. It provides them with the money and independence that enables them to identify with a 'teenage culture' in which the excitement of motorbikes, girl and boy friends, music and dancing predominates. Willis has described the problems of failure to obtain work for young people and the consequences of having no regular income (see page 300).

4. Leighton (*Wives' Paid and Unpaid Work and Husbands' Employment*) describes the significance of work for women. She argues that gender as an analytical concept has been marginalised in research into work. Traditionally, the man has represented the world of work and the woman the world of domesticity. It has been assumed that men determine women's life chances and that women are peripheral to the class system. Her results cast doubt on the Parsonian model of a harmonious functioning family unit. She reviews studies which show:

(a) Gender is used by management as a part of the tacit control of the work force (Pollert, *Girls, Wives and Factory Lives*)
(b) When women lose their jobs they are generally resentful of having to return to a relationship dependent on their husband.
(c) Women's earnings are often a crucial component of family household income.
(d) Women tend to be involved in occupational areas that are extensions of their domestic role. They are seldom in competition with men for jobs.

The Functionalist view of work	The Marxist view of work
1. Work enables people to obtain a sense of achievement and fulfilment. 2. It enables people to become more socially mobile by means of a promotional ladder. This is a source of status. 3. It provides a sense of identity and personal worth. 4. It provides opportunities to develop personality and skills. 5. It provides an opportunity to enjoy leisure. 6. Durkheim (*The Division of Labour*) said that work helped to integrate people more closely into their community as they came to rely on each other more and more. 7. The interdependence of skills and the exchange of goods, together with the learning of moral values which guide good behaviour, all help to provide a structure for cooperation.	1. Mills (*White Collar*) says that the work that most working-class people do enables them to forget the problems of life without being able to solve them. 2. Bowles and Gintis (*Schooling in Capitalist America*) argue that for the working-class, work enables the ruling elite to control their income, opportunities and skills. 3. It seen as a source of alienation and class division. 4. Sennet and Cobb (*The Hidden Injuries of Social Class*) point out how dull, repetitive work helps reinforce in the workers the view that they lack skills and ability. It also makes it more difficult for them to use their leisure in constructive ways. 5. The hierarchy of the division of labour helps reinforce the beliefs that workers have about the inevitability of a hierarchy in society.

(e) Wives' involvement in paid work was found to influence the length of a husband's unemployment: it was shorter where wives also worked.

Crompton ('Women and Work in the 1990s') confirms that the structure of women's work is different from that of men:

(a) It remains less well paid; is less well regulated by unions, and much is part time (see Table 22.4).
(b) Part-time work seldom has any career structure and most is semi-skilled or unskilled. The effect of domestic responsibilities on women's paid work is severe. There are increasing demands on them to care also for the elderly and the sick: 'Women do not choose poorly paid part-time work but have it thrust upon them.' This is likely to increase in the future because there will be a shortfall in numbers of young people entering the labour market.

Conclusions

(a) Most researchers conclude that work is significant in people' lives, providing status, role and meaning. It also brings structure to daily life.
(b) There appear to be different responses to work according to a person's background, the expectations they bring and the experiences they have had.
(c) For women, work is significant in consolidating household income, providing them with status; freeing them to some extent from domestic responsibilities, and increasing democratic relationships in the home. There is some evidence that family structures are strengthened, especially when a husband is unemployed.

Attitudes to Work

A report by the Office of Health Economics said 'perhaps the most significant factor associated with sickness absence is job satisfaction'. Studies show that more days are lost through sickness than through strikes. Sociologists have been interested in understanding the factors that affect people's attitudes to work; how and why they are motivated in work; and how to find ways of analysing the relationship between work and the individual.

■ **What are the causes of alienation? Can it be overcome by restructuring work? Discuss with reference to empirical studies.**

Alienation

1. The Marxist view.

Alienation is the concept used to describe the consequences of the exploitation of workers within the capitalist system. It is the idea that mundane and unpleasant work alienates the workers from their true nobility and sense of worth. For the majority of working-class employees it consists of:

(a) Failure to gain any sense of personal value from the work.
(b) A constant sense of misery, unhappiness or futility in work.
(c) A lack of any driving physical or mental energy in work, and little motivation.
(d) Menial work which is humiliating and dehumanising.
(e) Immense satisfaction in leisure time.
(f) Failure to gain any intrinsic interest; but a strong sense of forced labour.
(g) A lack of autonomy and control over their own lives, which belong to the employer. The alien character of work is shown by the fact that when there is no compulsion to work it is avoided like the plague.
(h) The reduction of workers' lives to a purely economic factor. Private property is the result of alienated labour and, in the alienation of man from man, the germ of class division.

2. Blauner (*Alienation and Freedom*) describes alienation as a general syndrome made up of objective and subjective conditions. It emerges from relationships between

workers and the socio-technical conditions of employment. He defines it in terms of the following conditions:

(a) Powerlessness of the worker to exert control over the work.
(b) Meaninglessness of the work.
(c) Isolation of the worker from colleagues by noise, distance, etc.
(d) Self-estrangement of the worker, who lacks a sense of involvement.

Blauner conducted investigations among workers in various industries to see the extent to which they could be described as being alienated.

Printers Their technology required skill, judgement and initiative. They were free from much external supervision. They saw the finished product. They were not socially isolated but well integrated into their local community. They were involved in their work. He concludes that they were not alienated workers.

Textile workers They were largely machine minders. They did experience powerlessness and were subject to strict supervision. Their product was standardised and required little skill to produce. However, he concludes they were not alienated workers because they were involved in a small, closely-knit community united by ties of kinship and religion. This accounted for the low levels of self-estrangement. Subjectively, they were not dissatisfied.

Automobile workers The assembly line gave them little or no control over their work. The work was routine and fragmented, the product was standardised and they had no identification with it. They were socially isolated and there were high levels of self-estrangement. He concludes that they did not form occupational communities. They were dissatisfied, both objectively and subjectively. As a result he sees them as highly alienated workers. Blauner is led to the conclusion that mass production is an important source of alienation (although it is not inevitable). He sees automation as a way of ending this trend. It may help increase levels of consensus and work satisfaction. It would lead to a decline in class consciousness and worker militancy.

Some criticisms of the two views:

Attempts to increase levels of job satisfaction

1. Redesigning and restructuring the work:
   (a) increasing the workers' responsibility and control;
   (b) increasing the variety of work experience (for example, job rotation schemes); and
   (c) increasing chances of promotion, achievement, etc.
2. Improving the working environment:
   (a) better opportunities to rest and relax;
   (b) provision of meals, etc.; and
   (c) improved factory/office design.
3. Improving industrial relations:
   (a) better worker/management relations; and
   (b) better union/management relations;
4. Provision of new technologies:
   (a) micro-electric systems (see page 302); and
   (b) automation (see pages 301, 302).
5. Increased worker participation:
   (a) indirect (a representative is sent to board meetings from the shop floor); and
   (b) direct (worker cooperatives and full shop-floor decision-making opportunities).

Comment

Marxist critics might argue that most of these attempts to improve job satisfaction are concerned to find ways of making the workers more productive and disguise the levels of exploitation that operate. They would argue that tedious jobs are always tedious.

However, the ideas of worker participation might find more favour. An efficient and apparently effective cooperative system has been established in Mondragon in Northern Spain since 1956. It is based on the principles of Robert Owen (1771–1858) and the Rochdale Pioneers in 1884. The principle is that profits should be returned to the workers, who have shares in the enterprise.

In Britain such cooperatives have been largely unsuccessful in recent years since they lack any government support in times of crisis and it has been found difficult to

Criticisms of the Marxist view

1. Marxists assume that all workers who sell their labour to the owners of the means of production must be alienated, especially those doing tedious work.
2. Marx does not provide a clear way of measuring alienation.
3. Workers who enjoy apparently tedious work may object to the view that they are 'de-humanised' by such experiences and are deluded in failing to realise it.
4. Automation is seen as a source of increased alienation, although some research suggests it adds enjoyment for some workers (especially the low-skilled).
5. It underestimates the high levels of job satisfaction that some research has subsequently identified, even among manual workers. It minimises the need for economic incentives and the ability of individuals to adapt to the demands of the technology.

Criticism of Blauner's view

1. Mallet (a Marxist) says that automation is another way by which capitalist owners increase profits and deny control to workers.
2. Automation may heighten alienation for some workers by reducing skills.
3. Workers who enjoy tedious work may never have had the opportunity to take a responsible and demanding job.
4. Such workers would seem to be alienated from an objective perspective. Why should this not be more significant than their subjective attitudes?
5. Daniel's research (see page 301) suggests that not all workers enjoy automation. Highly skilled workers show levels of dissatisfaction and hostility.

establish the same rights for new members as are held by long-standing workers.

Conclusions

(a) Marxist views on the inevitably alienating character of work for most working-class employees have been heavily criticised by the New Right, which sees in these attitudes an exaggerated sense of dissatisfaction.

(b) However, opponents of these critics argue that tedious and repetitive work, which characterises the experiences of a high proportion of workers, reflects the distribution of power and prestige in society.

(c) Weberians argue that the work structure and the technological processes involved can be adapted and changed to prevent worker dissatisfaction and limit alienation accordingly.

■ **Critically assess the relative importance of various factors which shape the attitudes of people in their work.**

A useful approach to this question would be to structure it around the views of different theorists, noting the strengths and weaknesses of their arguments.

1. Marxists. It is their argument that people are largely conditioned to accept certain kinds of work according to their class background. They bring expectations with them, are reinforced by the work experience. For the lower working class these are usually tedious, repetitive and often dangerous jobs.

(a) Allen (*The Sociology of Industrial Relations*) has argued that:
  (i) Industrial relations occur in a 'dynamic conflict situation which is permanent and unalterable so long as the structure of society remains unaltered'.
  (ii) The conflict results from the economic structure of society; the interests of owner and worker are irreconcilable.
  (iii) Alienation is inevitable; where labour is bought and sold, and used to satisfy the needs of the owner, dissatisfaction in work is the outcome.
  (iv) No amount of tinkering with the way the work is organised will make it less tedious. A simple increase in wages will only result in the worker becoming a 'better-paid slave'.

(b) Braverman (*Labour and Monopoly Capitalism*) argues that:
  (i) Skills in work have become progressively reduced as capitalism has evolved. This has been a way of controlling the work force (for example, through mass production and the division of labour).
  (ii) Labour power becomes a commodity: a means of increasing the wealth of the owner. Workers become dissatisfied and more militant.
  (iii) Apparent attempts to make work more enjoyable are ways of making workers accept new management controls. Women are particularly subject to exploitation as their work becomes more deskilled.

Points of criticism

(i) Some have argued (for example, Piore) that in recent years employees require many more skills than in the past since we are entering a new age of computer technology.
(ii) On the other hand, some industries have always made use of a majority of semi-skilled and unskilled workers and this has not changed. Many of these do not complain of job dissatisfaction.
(iii) Weberians argue that to understand attitudes to work it is necessary to examine more closely the internal structure of the work and the technologies used. Attitudes vary.
(iv) Some feminists have argued that there is a problem in defining the concept of skill. Much work done by women (for example, cooking, cleaning and so on) requires specific talents which may not meet the conventional definition of 'skill'.
(v) Penn has argued that employees, with the help of trade unions, have often been able to resist management attempts to deskill and restructure work.
(vi) There is no evidence that workers are more fulfilled in tedious work in socialist societies.

2. Weberians. They seek to understand workers' attitudes by examining the technical organisation of production.

(a) Woodward (*Industrial Organisation and Control*) stressed the inter-relationship between technology, environment and workers' attitudes. She made use of socio-technical systems analysis. This examines the internal and external environments that affect production:

External factors
1. The market situation (size and stability).
2. Relations with competitors.
3. The location of the industry.
4. Type of product and demand for it.

Internal factors
1. The technology and methods of production.
2. The methods of payment.
3. The social structure of the shop floor (norms, etc.).
4. Worker–management relations.

She identifies three types of production:
  (i) *Unit* (craft work, with tightly-knit cohesive teams working on whole units).
  (ii) *Mass production* (continuous conveyor-belt system; high level of division of labour; few skills needed; little worker cohesion).
  (iii) *Process production* (automated work, which may require skilled supervision but little human intervention).

She argues that:
  (i) Management styles accompany firms with similar production systems. (The more complex the production the more compex the authority system.)
  (ii) Organisations using mass production tend to be more bureaucratic.

(iii) Those using craft and process systems are more flexible. These produce higher rates of job satisfaction.
(iv) Workers' attitudes vary according to the type of production system in which they are engaged.

(b) Blauner (*Alienation and Freedom*).
(i) He examined four different industries; each was representative of a different type of technology. Printing was a craft type; textile was machine-minding; motor vehicle was assembly-line; and chemical was automated process production.
(ii) He concluded from his questionnaire data that craft technology provided the greatest level of freedom for workers; this diminishes with machine-minding and assembly-line work; but increases again in process production.
(iii) It is his view that worker satisfaction can be increased and alienation reduced by changing the technology rather than the economic structure of society.

(c) Lockwood and Goldthorpe (*The Affluent Worker*).
(i) They found that workers in their sample were engaged in largely tedious assembly-line and machine-minding work, but because they did not have high expectations of their work they were not disappointed by it.
(ii) These workers were found to work for instrumental reasons; it was not important as an area of self-expression but as a source of high income, which gave freedom to do other things.
(iii) They concluded that the workers did not complain of alienation but neither did they gain intrinsic satisfaction from it.

(d) Wedderburn and Crompton (*Workers' Attitudes and Technology*).
(i) They tend to support the view that different technologies affect attitudes in different ways.
(ii) They support the view that process production produces higher levels of job satisfaction than assembly-line work.

Points of criticism

(i) Socio-technical systems analysis implies that the system being analysed can be clearly isolated, although the outside environment tends to be narrowly defined in terms of economic pressures on management. The significance of class, ethnicity, etc. are minimised.
(ii) Gallie has criticised the work of Blauner on the grounds that his methodology is weak (very small samples drawn) and there are cultural variations which must be considered. He found that differences occurred between French and British workers in their attitudes towards automation.
(iii) Marxists have argued that the workers described by Lockwood and Goldthorpe are not unlike the alienated workers they identify. They would say that the social structure may affect workers in ways that they themselves do not perceive clearly. The actors' perspective, while interesting, is not the end of the story.
(iv) Mallet has argued that automation could result in the increased politicisation of workers. They may come to see that they are the controllers of a complex industry and will question the power and authority of the owners.
(v) Even more optimistic views are presented by writers who describe the emergence of new flexible work systems that have begun to emerge with the decline of trade union power and the demands for greater rationalisation following the economic depression of the 1980s and 1990s. The result will be increased job satisfaction for more workers as they become more skilled.

Conclusions

(a) Different theorists offer different explanations to account for the way employees perceive their work.
(b) The Marxists are pessimistic and argue that under capitalism work remains unsatisfying and alienating for the majority, who gain no intrinsic satisfaction.
(c) The Weberians see the organisation of work and the technology used as significant in affecting levels of job satisfaction. These can be changed to increase enjoyment.
(d) The New Right is optimistic in seeing work moving into a new stage in which new skills are required by increasing numbers of employees.
(e) It appears that while some areas of work are becoming less skilled and subject to tighter management control, other fields are requiring more skill and more flexibility.

■ Sociological studies of work need to take more account of experiences outside the workplace to explain attitudes within it. Discuss.

Examples of studies showing dissatisfaction in work:

1. Clack (*Strikes and Dissatisfaction with Assembly-Line Work*) notes the 'propensity to strike may *be greatest in occupations which segregate* together large numbers of persons who have heavy and unpleasant jobs and least for industries where individuals are isolated or doing relatively light, pleasant work'.

2. Sayles (*Behaviour of Industrial Work Groups*) identified four types of work response:

(a) *Apathetic* (for example drill press operators, who seldom made use of strike activity. There was little homogeneity among such groups.)
(b) *Erratic* (for example welders, who became militant from time to time).
(c) *Strategic* (for example wire drawers, whose attitudes varied according to changing circumstances).
(d) *Conservative* (for example mainly white-collar workers, who never took militant action).

Examples of studies which showed satisfaction in work:

1. Thierry and Iwema found that the percentage of respondents reporting satisfaction with their work is generally high and this percentage has increased in recent times to 80–85 per cent.

2. Harding (*Contrasting Values in Western Europe)* produced a cross-European study based on a sample of 12 000 people and found that job satisfaction was higher in Britain than in any other Western European society except Denmark, Eire and the Netherlands.

But the questions arise: *Why do people enter particular types of occupation? Why do attitudes vary?* and *Is their behaviour entirely a response to the technology used?* Many studies cast doubt on this view.

Studies outside the work place. Researchers have examined various factors to see how they affect a person's job choice and people's attitudes to work.

1. The experience of school.

Willis (*How Working Class Kids get Working Class Jobs*) endeavoured to uncover the subjective meanings and definitions of the situation of a small group of white working-class boys without formal qualifications as they proceeded through their last 18 months in school and their first months of work.

(a) They were identifed as non-conformist problem children in school. Their values, attitudes, behaviour, dress, etc. constantly led them into conflict with authority.
(b) They were contrasted with a more conformist group by Willis who found in the division between the two produced different kinds of future, different kinds of gratification and different kinds of job.
(c) Affiliation to the non-conformist group affected their attitudes and expectations. The work they looked for and got had to be able to fulfil their needs for high income; where they could be open about their desires, 'their liking for booze, their propensity to "skive off", where mates could be trusted, where the self could be separated from the work task, and where pen-pushing was decried and value given to things other than work-related skills'.
(d) The non-conformist school culture thereby provided the criteria for specific kinds of work. It was an experiment 'with accommodative and cultural practices'. They recognised that the real conditions of work they would face would be grim and unrewarding.
(e) He concludes that the counter-culture of the school and the shop floor lie parallel to each other and share many of the same determinants. The common impulse is to find ways of dealing with boredom and the controls imposed on them.
(f) The implication is that the conformists were more likely to achieve high levels of intrinsic satisfaction in work.

Bowles and Gintis (*Schooling in Capitalist America*) argue that:

(a) The main role of education is to reinforce the class structure.
(b) They describe a close relationship between the social attitudes found among working-class children in school and those found among similar groups in work.
(c) This relationship results from the effects of schooling, which produces a passive and docile work force, an acceptance of hierarchy, and motivation by external rewards.
(d) The implication is that those who achieve reasonable levels of success and enjoyment in school will seek to repeat the experience in work.

Points of criticism

(i) Willis has been criticised for his methodology. He used a very small sample on which to base his theories.
(ii) He does not examine other school sub-cultures, which may have offered different values but which have the same outcomes as those attributed to the non-conformists.
(iii) He does not include any girls in his sample.
(iv) The views of Bowles and Gintis that the educational system produces a docile work force is opposite to that of Willis, who describes a subversive non-conforming working-class employee, made more so by long-term unemployment.
(v) They assume that the curriculum produces a passive and uncritical pupil and an unthinking worker, whereas most teachers would hope they are producing questioning and thoughtful young people.

2. The experience of unemployment

Willis (*Learning to Learn*), in a subsequent series of articles examines the effects of youth unemployment on the young people concerned, indicating that they may become the disaffected workers of the future.

(a) Among working class men there remain powerful cultural motors which produce the expectation of work and a masculine definition of it. The sense of 'being a man' is often tied up with the idea of physical work.
(b) The importance of being a breadwinner also runs deep in the culture.
(c) Lack of work may produce a crisis for the individual and the family. (A lack of dignity and meaning in their lives.)
(d) Among working-class women lack of work may mean a deepening of their domestic roles. The alternative is likely to be a movement into low-level part-time work.
(e) He concludes that for both men and women the problems of finding work constantly reinforce instrumental attitudes towards work.

3. The economy.

Benyon (*Working for Fords*), writing in 1972, suggested:

(a) The external environment of the car industry was comparatively unstable and the demand for the product varied seasonally. Workers could earn relatively high wages at some times of the year, but when there was a market change they could be laid off.
(b) He suggested that this was one reason why there was a history of high levels of militancy and aggressive bargaining in the industry.
(c) It was the market that affected relationships in the plant. A depressed demand for cars could lead to an atmosphere of 'war', in which supervisors could settle old scores with shop stewards who had given them trouble.

Lupton (*On the Shop Floor*) used a socio-technical systems approach and argued that behaviour (such as restricting output by workers) could be explained not by examining just the technology, but by also analysing a cluster of factors which included some external to the shop floor. He argued that management and workers should make realistic appraisals of their situation in light of economic trends and then act in accordance with them.

Table 22.5 Qualifications by class (father), 1989 (Percentages)

	Class 1	Class 2	Class 3a	Class 3b	Class 4	Class 5
Degree	38	17	18	5	4	3
Higher Education	18	16	16	12	7	6
A-Level	10	14	13	9	8	6
O-Level	20	24	27	22	20	14
CSE	4	8	9	13	13	13
No qualifications	6	17	14	37	47	54

Source: General Household Survey.

4. The home background.

Zweig (*The Worker in an Affluent Society*) described how newly-affluent, upwardly mobile individuals fixed their eyes on middle-class material standards of living; they were well-informed about family limitation; they adopted middle-class norms of wishing to ensure that their children were successful in school, co-operating with teachers and establishing long-term goals for them.

J. and E. Newson (*The Family and its Future*) may help to explain why:

(a) Middle-class children are 'future oriented'; parents appear to be more protective of them; they are expected to learn communication skills as early as possible; and they are socialised by example. Among middle-class mothers, the principle of reciprocity is seen as a practical way of life.
(b) These contrast with the values and child-rearing practices of lower-working-class parents.

Bernstein (*Education Cannot Compensate for Society*) describes linguistic differences between children of different classes:

(a) He notes that it is not that working class children lack the vocabulary of middle-class children in using a restricted code; rather there are differences in the use of language arising out of a specific context.
(b) Middle-class children are generally more able to make clear what they mean, via an elaborated language code, to the person with whom they are communicating, whereas working-class children do not do this to the same extent.
(c) Such findings suggest that middle-class children may be more successful in achieving high-level exam results, which give access to more intrinsically satisfying work. (See table 22.5).

Points of criticism

(i) Critics have noted that children from aspiring middle-class homes do not necessarily succeed just because parents urge them to do so.
(ii) Not all middle-class children enter white-collar jobs and maintain a process of upward mobility, but increasing numbers are entering such groups from working-class backgrounds, especially girls.

Conclusions

(a) There is evidence to show that work attitudes (both positive and negative) are shaped by many factors. These include the experience of work itself and the technology used (see page 298).
(b) But there are important external factors to consider. More children from middle-class homes enter top professional occupations.
(c) There is some evidence that low-level white-collar work does not always produce the level of intrinsic satisfaction anticipated, since much is routine and involves the use of noisy machines (see page 303).
(d) In 1992 a Careers Services report showed that at least 55 000 unemployed young people were awaiting a Youth Training place; 11 000 were receiving no benefit, leading to homelessness, estrangement and criminality; 75 000 were on YT waiting lists. The delay may have a negative effect on future work attitudes.
(e) Several writers argue that there is evidence to show that more people entering the work force have a positive attitude to work for its own sake and a strong belief in the possibility of upward mobility.

■ **What are the major consequences of automation for workers?**

Automation

Daniel (*Automation and the Quality of Work*) examined the attitudes of workers towards the introduction of automation in the petrochemical industry. He contrasted the optimistic view (that it helped rehumanise tedious work by integrating the operators into a management team) with a pessimistic interpretation. This suggests that automation increases alienation so that the operator becomes 'a dial watching, button pushing robot'. His findings indicate some support for the optimistic view. He noted that with few exceptions the men found the work more interesting and satisfying when it was automated.

But workers with qualifications who found themselves deskilled by the effects of automation were more dissatisfied. They had less chance to realise their abilities and they were working alongside people with no skills or qualifications. See advantages and disadvantages of automation, page 302.

■ **Does technological change inevitably lead to deskilling of occupations? Illustrate your answer with specific examples.**

■ **Assess the view that changes in technology and organisation will produce less alienating environments.**

There remains debate and uncertainty as to the consequences of new technology and work organisations.

Advantages of automation	Disadvantages of automation
1. Worker is not tied to the machine or its pace of work.	1. There may be higher levels of unemployment in automated industries.
2. Worker has to take responsibility in emergencies.	2. Many workers are deskilled since they are only required to check controls.
3. Worker may become part of the management team.	3. Less concentration is required for previously skilled workers.
4. Worker may have more time for training, education, etc.	4. The quality of output is dependent on the computer which controls the machine. The workers lose responsibility.
5. There may be a shorter working week.	5. The workers' sense of community may diminish (smaller workforce, less security, fewer unions).
6. There are fewer repetitive and tedious jobs for workers to do.	6. Costs of large manufacturing companies are reduced, smaller businesses cannot compete.
7. Preferred by the unskilled.	

Point to note

(a) You would need to specify the groups most likely to be deskilled or reskilled by the introduction of new technology, since skilled workers could be taken to mean all those with high-level qualifications and training in Classes 1, 2, 3a and 3b. This could include the majority of the working population.

(b) The main types of new technology to which the question refers include:

(i) All that uses micro-electronics (a name that applies to all electrical components made to very small dimensions). Silicon integrated circuits consist of a layer of silicon etched with chemicals. These are formed into tiny blocks called micro-chips which have the capacity to handle and store information in computers and are produced at low cost.

(ii) Automated process production, in which the input of raw materials and the output of completed goods is controlled by robots and computers with minimum of human intervention. Automation is also prominent in the home, with automatic washing machines, central heating systems, etc. It is different from mechanised production: this describes the techniques of mass production based on the division of labour around conveyor-belts and the assembly-line.

(c) There remains much unresolved debate about the impact of new technology; commentators suggest that:

(i) Office work is most open to the effects of the micro-chip. (It was mistakenly estimated in 1984 that in Germany office employment could fall by 40 per cent by 1990.)

(ii) Automation and the use of robots is likely to have most effect in large manufacturing industries (car manufacturers account for 50–60 per cent of all robot users).

1. The views of Marxists.

Alienation is the frustration of human potential through tedious work. It arises from the fact that in the capitalist system labour is sold. It occurs in the division of labour (which produces wealth for the capitalist) and in the factory system, both of which dominate the worker. It can only be overcome when labour is no longer treated as a commodity.

(a) Work will remain largely unrewarding for the majority of working-class employees regardless of the technology used or attempts to promote job satisfaction.

(b) New technologies will produce high levels of unemployment. For example, the Cambridge Economic Policy Group Report predicted that there will be 3–5 million people unemployed as a result of micro-electronics by the end of the decade.

(c) Barron describes four main effects:

(i) It will limit competition. Some companies will go out of business because they will fail to match their rivals' use of the new technologies.

(ii) There will be skill displacement.

(iii) There will be major job losses as micro-electronic processes produce goods cheaper and quicker.

(iv) Effects will vary between industries. The more an industrial sector uses micro-electronics the more it will be hit.

(d) 'The Impact of the Chip Technology', a survey by Metra International was described as the most extensive analysis so far of jobs and skills that will be affected by the new technologies in the EC, North America, Japan and Scandinavia. It identifies sectors of office work and other industries where it says that more than 50 per cent of jobs will disappear in the next ten years. The report concludes that 'it is easier to point to skills for which there is a diminishing demand than to those where people should be trained'.

The areas of work most likely to be adversely affected include: semi-skilled work, machine-tool operation, clerical work and assembly-line work, especially where the work is accompanied by the application of computer-aided design (CAD). This will further deskill the workers.

(e) 'New Technology and Women's Employment': this Report predicts that among women workers there will be a range of 10–40 per cent job losses because a high proportion of women are in part-time factory work and in offices. In 1985 the white-collar union ASTMS said 'one chip can replace 800 white-collar workers'.

(f) A 1985 Report by Warshaw (a clinical psychologist) said that research indicated that VDU (computer terminal) operators are increasingly vulnerable to stress-related disorders, at the root of which was job dissatisfaction.

(g) Cooper and Cox (Manchester University Study) compared the mental comfort of those working with visual display terminals on word processors with secretaries and copy typists who did not work with such machines. They found higher levels of job satisfaction among the secretaries and typists:
   (i) The machine operators reported more anxiety and depression; they lacked a clear definition of their work role; their equipment was often shared; and they were largely tied to a machine.
   (ii) The other workers who were not affected by the new technology felt they had better career prospects and enjoyed the contact they had with others in their typing pool.

An alternative view comes from those who argue that Western industrialised societies have now passed from the era of mass production based on the assembly-line, pioneered by Henry Ford, into a new epoch epitomised by new economic theories and new technologies:

2. The New Right.

(a) Marsland (*Bias Against Business*) and Piore (*Perspectives on Labour Market Flexibility*) would dispute the Marxist view and present a more optimistic argument about the potentials for job satisfaction. They claim:
   (i) There is too much emphasis in research on the negative aspects of industry. If the areas of services, sales, distribution and advertising are examined, levels of enjoyment are high among workers. There are also opportunities to increase incomes, profits, living standards and quality of life.
   (ii) The more developed societies are moving from an era of mass production to one of flexible specialisation, made possible by the decline of the unions, heavy traditional industries and the demands of an economy in recession.
   (iii) The introduction of computers, satellite communication, fax machines, etc. is making organisations of all sizes more flexible. There is a reduction in low-skilled tasks and more home-based working for white-collar employees.
   (iv) In modern capitalist economies free markets encourage new technological initiatives which produce increases in national wealth.

(b) Handy (*The Future of Work*) says that new technologies can increase people's skills: 'The secretary becomes an information manager, and a ticket clerk a personal travel agent.'

(c) A British Telecommunications (BT) Report (1992) showed that at the beginning of the 1990s about 1.5 million people were working from home or at a satellite office. By 1995 it is expected that there will be 2.5–3.3 million in this category.

(d) The new flexibility will mean that firms will be less hierarchical in structure; workers will be better trained and used more creatively, and their autonomy increased. Johnstone (*Who's Afraid of the Micro Chip?*) says the public has been badly misinformed about the potential of computers. They will create more work. Opposing the views of ASTMS he says, 'a chip can increase a worker's productivity by 100%'.

(e) Proponents claim that some occupations will grow rapidly as a result of the new technologies. Those benefiting include: writers, journalists, computer programmers, insurance brokers, businesses of all sizes, including shops and supermarkets, etc., who will be able to keep a closer eye on stock and replace goods more quickly and efficiently. Also, small towns may become attractive as places to open offices, connected through the new technologies.

(f) A 1985 Government White Paper denied that there was any relationship between increasing levels of unemployment and new technologies. A further £120 million was spent on encouraging their development. All schools began to introduce the use of computers in the classrooms.

Points of criticism

(i) It is unlikely that the process of flexible specialisation could benefit many, other than high-level white-collar workers. Those involved in industries that use heavy machinery are unlikely to benefit.
(ii) In the 1990s there have been complaints that young people leaving school are not receiving sufficient training in appropriate skills, thus limiting their job opportunities.
(iii) The spread of such flexibility is limited by cost. The economic depression of the 1990s may restrict its development.
(iv) The BT Report (1992) found some employees unhappy at the prospect of working from home. They missed contact with others in work; and commuting was enjoyed as 'private time' for reading, chatting, etc. Unions were concerned about possible exploitation, affecting their members' pay and hours.
(v) In 1986 a Report (*Micro-electronics Industry*) stated that more than 80 000 jobs had been lost in two years because micro-chips had begun to be used in products and production processes. It also noted that the poor level of training in industry prevented those who lost their jobs from finding new employment.

Conclusions

(a) Writers from both Left and Right perspectives complain that their opponents are ideologically biased. Marxists are criticised by Marsland for failing to recognise the crucial significance of competition in the pursuit of profit in the effective operation of the economy. It is this which others see as the source of helpful new technologies.

(b) Those on the Right are criticised for an over-optimistic view. Freeman and McLean (Sussex University) argue that the effects of the new technologies are still largely unpredictable. They suggest that no one has yet produced a decent model of technological change. There is need for much more research. We do not fully know the extent to which technologies deskill, nor under what conditions they create more jobs and more valuable skills, nor their impact on unemployment and job dissatisfaction.

■ **It is no longer work, but leisure, that is the source of meaning and satisfaction in people's lives today. Discuss.**

Questions

1. Examine photographs 64, 65, 66 and 67
   - (i) Apply Blauner's measures of alienation to the work shown and suggest which are likely to be the most and least alienated workers: the firemen, the crane driver, the lighthouse keepers or the teacher?
   - (ii) Suggest the possible effects of the introduction of new technology (automation, computerisation) on the levels of job satisfaction of those shown in the photographs.
   - (iii) Consider the view that it is increasingly leisure rather than work that provides people with a sense of worth and satisfaction in their daily lives.
   - (iv) Why might the teacher have more difficulty in defining her leisure time than those involved in the other occupations?
   - (v) Discuss some of the factors that may have shaped the decision of each person to select their particular occupation.

2. (i) Suggest ways of testing:
   - (a) Blauner's theory of alienation; and
   - (b) differences in levels of job satisfaction between occupational groups.

   (ii) Indicate some of the problems that might be encountered.

65

64

Source: Alec Gill

67

Source: Paul Selfe

66

Source: Alec Gill

Table 22.6 *Typology*

Constraint				Freedom
Work	Work obligations	Physiological needs	Non-work obligations	**Leisure** **Leisure**
Sold time	Work-related time	Existence time	Semi-leisure time	**Free time**

Source: S. Parker, *'The Future of Work and Leisure'.*

Notes:

1. Work time is that which is devoted to earning a living.
2. Work-related time is that spent on activities related to work (including travelling, meetings, reading documents, etc.).
3. Physiological needs are met in existence time and include eating, sleeping, etc.
4. Non-work obligations are activities undertaken in non-work time and include visiting, decorating, etc.
5. Leisure time is that which is free from all the contractual obligations of work and those connected with semi-leisure.

■ Occupation is an important determinant of leisure patterns but not the only one. Discuss.

Those who take the view that leisure is an increasing source of meaning and satisfaction suggest that for increasing numbers work has become more routine and tedious. People seek fulfilment elsewhere. Leisure then becomes a central life interest because people can satisfy needs and achieve goals unconstrained by the obligations of work.

What is leisure time?

(a) Distinctions could be made in terms of the following:

Characteristics of work

1. Contractual obligations.
2. Compulsory activities.
3. Legally-agreed payments.
4. Job may or may not be satisfying.
5. Specific roles imposed by work.
6. Subjective element defining work.

Characteristics of leisure

1. No contractual obligations.
2. Freedom to choose activities.
3. Payment unlikely.
4. Satisfaction high priority.
5. Little or no role imposition.
6. Leisure is subjectively known.

(b) Parker's Typology (*The Future of Work and Leisure*). He seeks to isolate qualities which distinguish various activities so that a comparison can be made with patterns of behaviour in the real world to see how far they meet the expected characteristics. He describes it as an analysis of life-space in which all activities can be categorised (see Figure 22.6).

Those who support the view

(a) C. Wright Mills (*The Power Elite*) has said that the work ethic is being replaced by the leisure ethic, which increasingly takes precedence.
(b) Burns (*Leisure in Industrial Society*) argues that leisure provides people with the chance to exercise real choice and become creative beings.
(c) Wilensky (*Work, Careers and Integration*) suggests that the worker is increasingly likely to segregate work from leisure, so they become separate worlds, and to retreat into the security of friends and kinship groups.

Points of criticisms

(i) Such views are based on the assumption that work is not a satisfying experience for increasing number of people.
(ii) Roberts (*Contemporary Society and the Growth of Leisure*) has disputed the significance of leisure for the majority. The most popular pursuits according to repeated surveys are watching TV and reading newspapers, rather than creative and active uses of time.
(iii) Some studies suggest that the unemployed (who would appear to have endless leisure time) and those who have 'enforced' spare time may actually have more difficulty in making use of it creatively. They lose social status and may have insufficient means to make constructive use of free time.
(iv) It may be that, in an ironical way, to enjoy leisure in a modern society, it is necessary to have a regular job.

Factors affecting choice of leisure activities:

1. Occupation

Parker ('The Future of Work and Leisure') said 'studies of leisure which have hitherto focused on social class differences are now developing the theme that there are occupational differences within class and status groupings which play a large part in determining the style of leisure . . . as well as more general values'. He distinguished between three types of response that people make to their work, and showed how these shaped their leisure pursuits:

(a) *The extension pattern*: for people such as child-care workers, teachers, etc., their leisure activities are frequently an extension of their work.
(b) *Neutrality patterns*: for those who were found to gain neither great satisfaction nor dissatisfaction from their work, such as bank employees, leisure was a time for relaxation.
(c) *Opposition patterns*: for those with low levels of satisfaction in work, such as miners and assembly-line workers, leisure was a time to escape its rigours and hazards.

Points of criticism

(i) He seems to ignore the significance of factors other than occupation (especially class), which he describes as the prime determinant.
(ii) Other writers have shown the relevance of such factors as family background, family structure and norms; gender and age as well as the power of the market to create new interests.

2. Family structure and life-cycle; age and gender.

(a) Roberts points out that the family acts as a normative reference group by giving guidance to members as to what is and what is not a suitable activity.
(b) R. and R. Rapoport (*Leisure and the Family Life Cycle*) discuss how leisure pursuits vary according to the stage in the family cycle: there are the stages of adolescence, young adulthood, adulthood proper, and old age. Each produces particular preoccupations which influence how free time is utilised.

Points of criticism

(i) In directing family members into particular activities (joining a tennis or golf club in which equipment is expensive) the parents may just be reflecting class norms.
(ii) The Rapoports emphasise a biological basis to the family life-cycle, whereas critics suggest that such phases are socially constructed, and shaped by the meanings which people give to them.
(iii) They have been criticised for weak methodology and failing to provide sufficient details in their data.

3. Market manipulation:
Tomlinson ('Buying Time: Consumption and Leisure') argues that:

(a) The majority of leisure pursuits are market-led. In 1992, TV-watching was the UK's most popular activity according to Henley Centre's *Time Use Survey*; second was newspaper and magazine reading.
(b) Changes in the market affect modes of consumption. In the 1980s changes pushed leisure activities more into the sphere of the home, with growth sales of colour TVs, videos, CDs, etc. These dominated the life-styles of all ages and all social groups (97 per cent of film watching was done via either TV or video).
(c) Consumption is vital for the expansion of capitalist markets. People work in them not just to survive, but to live in particular ways, to display evidence of their success and status, and to have experiences in common. The leisure markets help satisfy this hunger.

Points of criticism

(i) The implications are that people have their leisure pursuits manipulated for them.
(ii) Their choices are lacking imaginative or creative responses.
(iii) It may be that work has become more demanding in all classes and there is simply an increasing emphasis on leisure for relaxation. The process of greater private, home-based life-styles was noted in the 1960s by Lockwood and Goldthorpe.

4. Class and economic constraints.
(a) Willmott and Young (*Family and Class*) showed how some clubs and organisations weight their regulations more towards one class than another. This helps preserve their exclusiveness.
(b) Clarke and Critcher (*The Devil Makes Work: Leisure in Capitalist Britain*) argue that capitalist economics shape people's experiences of both work and leisure. It is class factors that determine people's choices:
(i) Leisure is an important setting as work for the battle between different social groups for status, power and prestige. But the powerful control the main areas in which leisure pursuits can be followed: (betting shops, clubs, pubs, etc.). Large corporations often sponsor or subsidise places of leisure to promote their goods.
(ii) This can lead to conflict for control of public spaces in which working-class youth tend to congregate in pursuit of their leisure (such as football grounds, streets on estates, etc.).
(iii) Working-class youth often become the cause of moral panics since they are perceived to have too much misspent free time.

Points of criticism

(i) They assume high levels of constraint on a person's choice of leisure activity by their class norms.
(ii) They also see a process of manipulation by the powerful to promote the profits of the leisure goods they produce.
(iii) They would seem to disapprove of the provision of services (leisure centres, etc.) for those groups whose position they are otherwise defending because these are subsidised or sponsored by powerful groups.

Conclusions

(a) There has been more emphasis on leisure as working hours have been reduced and in light of the view that much work is lacking intrinsic interest for many workers.
(b) The surveys show that the great majority seek to use leisure time in pursuit of entertainment activities.
(c) The debate about the factors which shape the way people use their free time has ranged from the singular (occupation) to the plural (family structure, etc.). Roberts cites a range of possible influences.
(d) Some writers have suggested that it is only by understanding the meaning of work that the meaning of leisure can be understood.
(e) Whereas Dumazedier (*Towards a Society of Leisure*) has concluded that since the values associated with a person's leisure have been shown to exercise a significant influence on other spheres of his or her life, it may even help in the selection of an occupation. Many may come to choose a job that gives them time for specific leisure pursuits.

Suggested Reading

Works noted in this chapter

D. Bell (1961) *The End of Ideology*. Free Press
J. Benyon (1975) *Working for Fords*, EP Publishing.
B. Bernstein, *Education Cannot Compensate for Society*, in J. Raynor and J. Harden, *Equality and City Schools,* Vol. 2. RKP OU.
S. Bowles and H. Gintis *Schooling in Capitalist America*, RKP
H. Braverman (1974) *Labour and Monopoly Capitalism*, Monthly Review Press
T. Burns (1973) Leisure in Industrial Society, in Smith, Parker and Smith (eds) *Leisure and Society in Britain*, Allen Lane
G. Cooper and Cox (1985), Manchester University Report
R. Crompton (1991) 'Women and Work in the 1990s', *Social Studies Review* (May) Vol. 6, No. 5
W. Daniel (1972) 'What Interests the Worker?', *New Society* (March)
W. Daniel (1969) *Automation and the Quality of Work*, New Society
J. Dumazdier (1967) *Towards a Society of Leisure*, Collier-Macmillan
J. Eldridge (1973) *Sociology and Industrial Life*, Nelson.
Freeman and McLean (1985), Sussex University Report
A. Feldman and W. Moore (1969) in W. Faunce and W. Form (eds) *Comparative Perspectives on Industrial Society*, Little, Brown
F. Fukuyama (1992) *The End of History*, Hamish Hameta
D. Gallie (1978) *In Search of the New Working Class,* CUP
F. Hertzberg (1959) *The Motivation to Work*, Wiley & Son
A. Inkeles (1970) *Industrial Man,* in H. Landsberger (ed.) *Comparative Perspectives on Formal Organisations,* Little, Brown
C. Kerr *et al.* (1962) *Industrialism and Industrial Man*, Heinemann
D. Lane (1990) 'State Socialism in the 1990s', *Social Studies Review* (September) Vol. 6 No. 1
G. Leighton (1992) *Wives' Paid Work and Unpaid Work and Husbands' Employment*, Feb. Vol. 1 No. 3
S. Mallet (1963) *La Nouvelle Classe Ouvrie*, Paris. Editions du Seuil
A. Maslow (1954) *Motivation and Personality*, Harper & Row
R. Miller (1969) 'The Dockworker', in *Comparative Studies in Society and History II*, 3
J. and E. Newson (1965) *The Family in Modern Society*, Oxford University
M. O'Donnell (1987) *A New Introductory Reader in sociology*, Nelson
R. Penn (1984) 'Skilled Manual Workers in the Labour Process': in S. Wood (ed) 'Skilled Workers in the Class Structure', CUP
W. Rostow (1963) *Stages of Growth*, CUP
A. Sykes (1969) 'Work Attitudes of Navvies', *Sociology*, III No. 1 (January)
C. Walker and R. Guest (1952) *The Man on the Assembly Line*, Harvard University Press
H. Wilensky (1969) 'Work, Careers and Integration', in Burns (ed.) *Industrial Man*, Penguin
P. Willis (1977) *Learning to Labour*, Saxon House
P. Willmott and M. Young (1960) *Family and Class*, RKP
P. Worsley (1976) *Introducing Sociology*, Penguin

Works for further reading

V. Allen (1971) *The Sociology of Industrial Relations*, Longman, London
R. Blauner (1964) *Alienation and Freedom*, Chicago UP,
N. Britten, and A. Heath (1984) 'Women's Jobs Do Make a Difference', *Sociology*, Vol. 18, No. 4
T. Burns, (ed.) (1969) *Industrial Man*, Penguin, Harmondsworth
M. Carter (1966) *Into Work*, Penguin, Harmondsworth,
E. Chinnoy (1955) *Auto Workers and the American Dream*, Doubleday
G. Clack (1967) *Industrial Relations in a British Car Factory*, CUP
J. Clarke, and C. Critcher, (1985) *The Devil Makes Work: Leisure in Capitalist Britain*, Macmillan, London
A. Coyle (1984) *Redundant Women*, Women's Press, London.
M. Featherstone (1990) 'Perspectives on Consumer Culture', *Sociology*, 24
J. Lockwood and Goldthorpe, *et al.* (1968) *The Affluent Worker*, Vol. 3, CUP
C. Handy (1984) *The Future of Work*, Basil Blackwell, Oxford
S. Harding (1986) *Contrasting Values in Western Europe*, Macmillan, London
Hertzberg *et al.* (1968) *Work and the Nature of Man*, Staples Press
T. Lupton (1963) *On the Shop Floor*, Pergamon
D. Marsland (1987) *Bias Against Business*, Educational Research
C. Mills (1959) Wright *The Power Elite*, Oxford
S. Parker *et al.* (1972) *The Sociology of Industry*, Allen & Unwin, London
S. Parker (1975) 'The Future of Work and Leisure' in Butterworth and Weir, *The Sociology of Modern Britain*, Fontana, London
A. Pollert (1981) *Girls, Wives and Factory Lives*, Macmillan, London
M. Piore (1986) 'Perspectives on Labour Market Flexibility', *Industrial Relations*, 45
R. and R. Rapoport (1975) *Leisure and the Family Life Cycle*, Routledge & Kegan Paul, London
K. Roberts (1978) *Contemporary Society and the Growth of Leisure*, Routledge & Kegan Paul, London
L. Sayles (1958) 'Behaviour of Industrial Work Groups', John Wiley
Thierry and Iwema (1984) in P. Drenth, *Work and Organisational Psychology*, John Wiley
A. Tomlinson (1991) 'Buying Time: Consumption and Leisure', *Social Studies Review*, JanuaryVol. 6 No. 3
M. Weir (1976) *Job Satisfaction*, Fontana, London
P. Willis (1975) *How Working Class Kids Get Working Class Jobs*, Birmingham University (CCCS)
P. Willis (1984) 'Youth Unemployment', *New Society*, (March/April
J. Woodward (1970) *Industrial Organisation*, OUP, 1970.
E. Zweig (1961) *The Worker in an Affluent Society*, Heinemann, London

Self-test Questions

Study these newspaper articles and answer the questions below.

Item A

EMPLOYMENT: More women are going out to work than ever before, while the number of men not working and not seeking a job has risen by almost half as many again since 1971.

Most of the men have left employment partly because of early retirement but an estimated 2 per cent of them (340,000) have dropped out because they do not believe any jobs are available.

The number of men regarded as "economically inactive" has increased from 9 per cent in 1971 to 13 per cent in 1986.

Unemployment rates for non-white ethnic groups, according to the Labour Force Survey 1984-86, were double those of the white population.

Unemployment was highest among the West Indian/Guyanese group and the Pakistani/Bangladeshi group while working males from India, Pakistan and Bangladesh were more likely to be self-employed.

Most of the 1.8 million women who have joined the labour force since 1971 are in part-time employment.

The proportion of women staying at home dropped from 44 per cent to 37 per cent between 1973 and 1985. Many have taken part-time jobs in service industries because they need to earn money while caring for children.

In 1985, 27 per cent of all wives were working full-time and 32 per cent part-time.

The British Social Attitudes Survey 1986 asked what people thought of working mothers. Most (76.3 per cent) thought it was best for children under five if the father worked full-time and the mother stayed at home, although 16.9 per cent thought women should work part time. But more than 80 per cent thought the mother should work once the children had reached their early teens.

The total number of employees in the UK rose by one million between 1971 and 1979, fell by more than two million during the next four years and then rose by more than half a million between 1983 and 1986.

The number of self-employed, mostly engaged in one-person businesses, rose sharply between 1979 and 1986 from 1.9 million to 2.6 million.

Strikes cost 1.9 million working days in 1986, the lowest number since 1963.

Source: From an article by Sarah Boseley in the *Guardian*, 14 Janaury 1988, p. 4.

Item B

ANOTHER 29,100 people joined Britain's dole queues last month, pushing unemployment to a five-year high and intensifying pressure on the Government to take action to stimulate the economy.

Official figures from the Department of Employment yesterday showed that the number of people out of work and claiming benefit rose by 95,776 (before seasonal adjustment). This was the 27th month in a row to show an increase, taking the total to 2,753,400 in July.

Male unemployment stands at 13 per cent against 5.3 per cent for women. The Department of Employment's regional breakdown shows that the South of England continues to have the biggest job losses. Unemployment in the South-east rose by 11,600 last month, taking the total to a record 845,300.

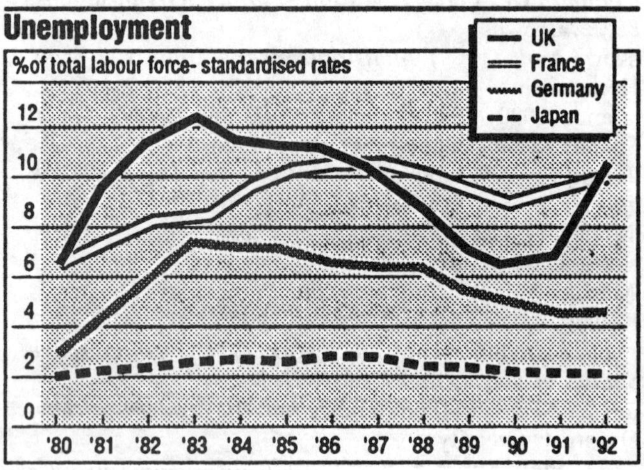

Source: From an article by L. Elliott, R. Kelly and M. Milner in the *Guardian*, 14 August 1992, p. 1.

Item C

Changing working patterns mean that already 1.5 million people are working partly or completely from home or a satellite office. Barbara Stephens, industrial adviser at the National Economic Development Office, believes many more people will opt for 'telecommuting'. 'But I don't think it's something you'll get workers doing from the age of 20 until they retire,' she says.

report, both employers and employees could benefit by teleworking. Its author, Noel Hodson, predicts that up to one in four people will eventually work partly or completely away from the main office. Other forecasts suggest that by 1995 there will be between 2.5 and 3.3 million teleworkers — about 15 per cent of the workforce.

Source: From an article by Susan Young in the *Observer*, 21 June 1992, p. 9.

1. Examine Item A.
This information comes from an analysis of a *Social Trends* publication.

- (i) Suggest why such details concerning the changes in the employment levels of different groups of people is valuable information.
- (ii) Explain the reasons for the increase of women in the economy and suggest the possible significance for the family.
- (iii) Consider the view of some feminists that the social attitudes revealed in the survey constrain women in their career opportunities.

2. Examine Item B.

- (i) Suggest some reasons for the changes in levels of unemployment in Britain between 1980 and 1992.
- (ii) Discuss the view that the different levels of unemployment in the four countries illustrated in the graph may produce different social and cultural attitudes towards work in the future.
- (iii) Discuss some of the problems which arise for individuals and societies where there are prolonged rates of high unemployment.

3. Examine Item C.

- (i) Discuss the advantages and disadvantages of changing work patterns which enable more people to work from home.
- (ii) Discuss the view that changes in technology (such as the increased use of telecommunications, computers, etc.) may increase levels of worker alienation among those who previously had high levels of job satisfaction.

4. Examine Items A and B
Discuss the problems of defining and measuring unemployment and the economically inactive.

5. Using Items A, B and C (together with any other data with which you are familiar), discuss the view that changes in the patterns of employment may cause increasing social tensions which will result in greater class polarisation as some sections of the population become more likely to be unemployed while others benefit from new technologies.

23

INDUSTRIAL RELATIONS

Questions on this topic tend to fall into the following areas:

1. Industrial conflict:
   (a) The extent of strike activity.
   (b) Statistical detail and interpretations.
   (c) Variations in levels of strike activity.
   (d) The significance of research and case studies.
   (e) Theoretical perspectives in analysing strikes and disputes.
2. Trade unions: their Structure and Functions.
3. Professions and Professional Associations.

Industrial Conflict

■ **Examine the view that industrial conflict is an inevitable feature of industrial societies.**

■ **How widespread is industrial conflict in Britain?**

1. It is hard to measure industrial conflict because it can take various forms. Discontent may evoke responses from either employees or employers:

Responses by workers
1. Strikes.
2. Overtime ban.
3. Go-slow or work to rule.
4. Absenteeism.
5. Sabotage.
6. Deliberate inefficiency.
7. Pilfering.

Responses by management
1. Plant closure.
2. Lock-out (no one allowed in).
3. Stronger controls.
4. Arbitrary disciplinary action.
5. The laying-off of workers.
6. Withholding bonus payments.
7. Withholding information about policies.

2. Every work organisation is likely to encounter one or more of these responses from time to time but some are considered more serious than others and create more publicity. These normally involve the actions of employees, although the actions of employers may be the cause (for example, laying-off workers may cause strike action).

3a. *Strikes and stoppages.*

(a) Hyman (*Strikes*) has said that there are five elements in a strike:
   (i) Work stops (for at least a full working day).
   (ii) It is temporary (although one believed to be the longest in Britain entered its seventh year in 1992 with workers carrying on a round-the-clock vigil: it was dispute about manning levels).
   (iii) It is a collective act involving a group of employees in a power struggle.
   (iv) It reflects some level of discontent.
   (v) It is calculated to achieve a particular goal through negotiation.

3b. Sabotage, deliberate inefficiency, pilfering as responses to discontent, Sabotage is a deliberate act to harm the work environment. It may occur for many reasons and range from minor to quite serious damage.

(a) Mars (*Cheats at Work*) says it is most frequent in jobs where there is tight control over employees. They lack autonomy; they cannot use their initiative; they are rule-bound. There may be no opportunity to work a 'fiddle'. They may wish to slow down the pace or impose a delay. The response may be sabotage.
(b) Taylor and Walton suggest it may be a way of coping with frustration: 'In the Christmas rush in a Knightsbridge store, the machine which shuttled change . . . suddenly ground to a halt. A frustrated salesman had

demobilised it by ramming a cream bun down its gullet.'

(c) Pilfering and 'fiddles' are discussed by Mars, who suggests they go on in most occupations, but in more major ways where the workers feel themselves to be overconstrained:
   (i) They are described as the normal crimes of normal people in the normal circumstances of their job.
   (ii) He suggests that some occupations are so 'fiddle-prone' that the workings of whole sectors of the economy cannot be understood without taking it into account.
   (iii) Most workers justify them by viewing the gain as an entitlement or 'perk'.
   (iv) Those in high-status positions often escape investigation because of their prestigious social positions. Mars notes how they achieve the position of 'shaman', whose powers must be respected. When MPs were accused of making use of their secretarial allowances without using secretaries, the criticism was brushed aside because, it was pointed out, MPs are 'honourable gentlemen' in title and practice.

3c. Absenteeism and sickness. It is difficult to measure absenteeism in terms of a response to dissatisfaction in work. Some absenteeism is legitimate, and some is not.

(a) Douglas has suggested that where a person cannot adapt their values, beliefs and attitudes to suit a job's demands, the worker can resign or struggle to continue and possibly suffer high rates of sickness and absence. This is a type of response to alienation or anomie.
(b) Sometimes a worker can use weak work structures to extend breaks between operations; in the same way, sickness absence can be extended because some systems allow two days off before a note is required.
(c) More time is lost through sickness absence than any other form of action. In 1977, 310 million working days were lost; in 1984, 9.6 per cent of the work force was absent for at least one day, and in 1990 9.7 per cent.
(d) A Report in 1992 found that British workers were second to the Dutch in having time off work through sickness (see Table 23.1).

3d. Work to rule; overtime ban; without imagination.

(a) Fox (*A Sociology of Work in Industry*) has noted how workers may impose this option where:
   (i) They are in conflict but wish to stop short of outright strike.
   (ii) They may wish to illustrate the impracticality of new management procedures. Working to particular rules can bring the organisation to a complete stand-still.

(b) Crouch (*Trade Unions: The Logic of Collective Action*) has said that there are some disadvantages to the action:
   (i) Not all work is sufficiently under their control for it to be effective.
   (ii) Overtime bans involve loss of pay, which is not always popular.

But it also has advantages:
   (i) It reduces the cost to the union of a full strike.
   (ii) It keeps negotiations open.
   (iii) It makes use of the most strategic members of the work force.

4. Managers may create conflict by the methods they use to manage, or they may respond to a situation created by the work force.

(a) Salaman (*Class and the Corporation*) notes that:
   (i) Within the enterprise employers and controllers are able to exercise control over subordinate members by virtue of their control over desired resources – money, careers, promotion, conditions, the conferring of status, approval, etc.
   (ii) They also have control over sanctions, the withdrawal of rewards, locking out workers, closing down plants, imposing tighter controls, and dismissal.

Conclusions

(a) Conflict in industry is very widespread in that it can take many forms, some being more serious than others.
(b) Mars notes that strikes are the most serious resort to action. They represent the most dramatic index of industrial discontent. But for much of the time, especially in recent years, agreements are reached quite quickly between employers and unions. They are not particularly widespread throughout industry. Most occur in a diminishing industrial sector which employs just over half of all workers in the UK.
(c) Most overt conflict is regulated and contained and has become 'institutionalised' (that is, it is structured and rule-bound).
(d) There is some problem in interpreting statistics relating to strikes. Recording procedures may vary. Some firms may not report all stoppages (to promote a good record); others may record every one (to argue for tighter legislation).
(e) Lane and Roberts (*Strike at Pilkingtons*) have argued that conflict is normal in that it is likely to occur in some form in most places of employment. However, it is more likely to take a serious form in some settings than others.

■ **Explain why the level of industrial conflict appears to vary between different industries and different societies.**

■ **Why is it difficult to analyse the extent of strikes and stoppages when clear statistics are available?**

(a) Note the problems of measuring 'conflict' because it can take many forms.
(b) As far as strikes are concerned, Jackson (*Industrial Relations*) has said that strikes are the most visible and spectacular manifestation of industrial conflict. As a result, much attention has been focused on the strike figures regularly published by the government. It is these details that allow researchers to make historical and international comparisons.

1. International comparisons
Internationally, there was a downward trend in working days lost through strikes in OECD countries between

Table 23.1 Percentage of working week lost through sickness (EC) (1991)

Netherlands	4.3
Britain	2.7
All	1.9

Source: Social Trends.

Table 23.2 Industrial stoppages: working days lost per 1000 workers in all industries, 1972–81 (international comparison)

Italy	217
Spain	949
Canada	944
Irish Republic	699
Australia	674
UK	531
USA	428
France	191
Sweden	138
Japan	99
West Germany	23
Holland	19

Source: Social Trends.

Table 23.3 Selective presentation of data showing problem of interpretation of stoppages and days lost, 1951-91

Year	Stoppages to nearest 50	Days lost (million)
1951	1700	1.7
1961	2700	3.0
1971	2250	13.6
1981	1350	4.2
1986	1050	1.9
1988	800	3.7
1990	650	2.0
1991	600	.6

Source: *Social Trends*, 3.6, 22; *Employment Gazette.*

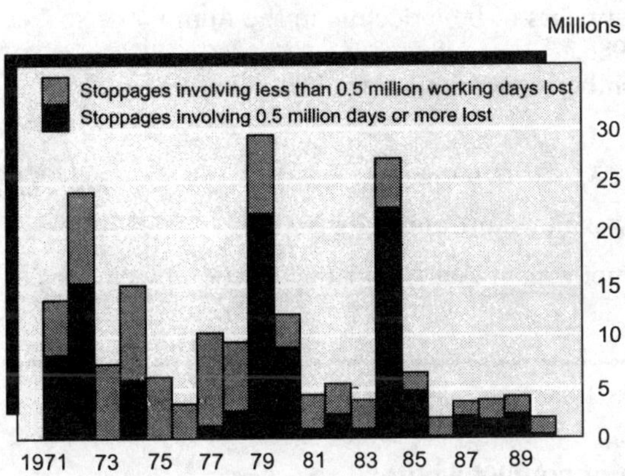

Working days lost during year

Source: Employment Department

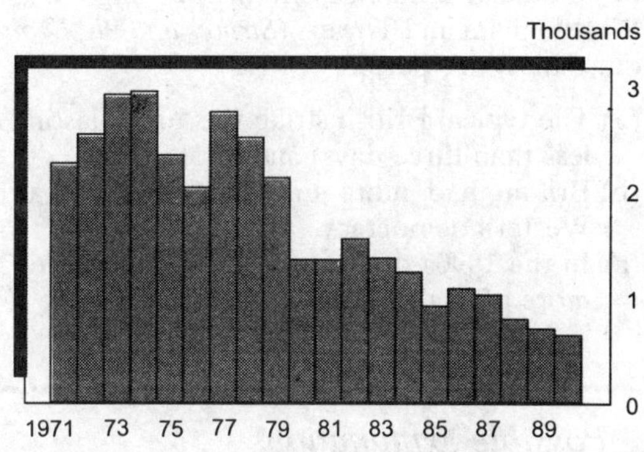

1 Small stoppages are excluded from the statistics

Work stoppages in progress during year

1976 and 1985. The highest incidence was in Spain, Italy and W. Germany; the lowest was in the Netherlands and Canada.

Points to note from the statistics

1. Britain's industrial performance is not much worse than that of other countries. During these years Britain stood a little above the middle of the international ranking lists.
2. There may be some difficulty in making direct comparisons since there are differences between countries in their definition of a strike and their thoroughness in recording events.
3. Strike rates may be lower in some societies as a result of specific cultural factors. In Japan, for example, there is a norm of deference to superiors.
4. It is important to remember that statistics must be interpreted with care. It would be important to know whether the methods used in data collection are the same in all countries.

2. Internal comparisons.

In Britain the government publishes official statistics which indicate:

(a) The number of official stoppages (those supported by a union and for which strike pay may be provided).
(b) Those which are unofficial (where the workers take action without the support of the union).
(c) The number of workers involved and the number of working days lost. (If five men strike for ten days, then fifty working days are lost.)

Unofficial strikes

Records have been kept since 1961. They indicate that between 1961 and 1981 the proportion of strikes known to be unofficial remained within the range 93–98 per cent. Whittingham and Towers (*Strikes and the Economy*) point out that in this period:

(a) The typical British strike was brief (lasting on average less than three days) and unofficial.
(b) Britain had more unofficial strikes than any other Western democracy.
(c) In the 1990s the picture began to change. There were more official strikes which lasted longer.

The analysis of the causes and consequences of strikes and stoppages is a complex matter. Phenomenologists constantly point out the problems of the interpretation of statistics.

Selective presentation of data may disguise patterns of conflict (See Table 23.3).

Conclusions

(a) The level of conflict, as measured by stoppages and days lost, varies significantly from year to year, but the number of stoppages has declined in the 1980s and early 1990s. In the 1980s the level was running at about half that of most years in the 1970s.
(b) The number of days lost does not relate directly to the number of disputes. It is more a reflection of their length. The Miners' Strike of 1984/5 accounted for 22.4 million days lost out of a total of 27.1 million.
(c) Although comparisons with other countries are difficult it appears that in terms of working days lost Britain's record has been about average. The highest incidence between 1976 and 1986 was in Spain and Italy. The lowest was in Holland.
(d) Stoppages are more frequent and widespread in some industries than others. They are seldom used by white-collar workers whereas they often occur among manual workers in heavy manufacturing industries. Between 1960 and 1979, when there were higher numbers of stoppages, 46 per cent of all days lost occurred in 64 industries.
(e) There are more days lost through sickness and absenteeism than through strikes. (About 10 per cent of the work force lose at least one day from work each year.)
(f) The interpretation of statistics is always problematic.

■ **Account for the variations in rates of stoppages between 1971 and 1991 and between different industries.**

1. The trends show fluctuations from one year to the next.
2. There appears to be a decline in the number of strikes since 1986.
3. The number of working days lost has declined.

Possible explanations

1. There was new anti-union legislation:

(a) 1980 Employment Act. Sympathetic action by employees

Possible explanations

High levels of conflict where:

1. The technology is based on assembly-line or other repetitive system (extrinsic satisfaction)
2. Workers have little autonomy or responsibility.
3. Management imposes strict controls.
4. There are no well-established procedures for consultation and negotiation.
5. Workers live and work in the area and have strong community bonds which unite them in adversity.
6. Manual workers in strong unions have pay levels that are open to frequent negotiation.
7. There are changing attitudes to work and strong extrinsic instrumental attitudes.

Low levels of conflict where:

1. The technology is based on craft or process production (intrinsic satisfaction).
2. Workers have high levels of autonomy and responsibility.
3. Management uses flexible controls.
4. There are well-established procedures for consultation and negotiation.
5. Workers commute and have little sense of local community bonding
6. White-collar workers have pay and conditions which are well structured.

in other industries made them liable for damages unless they had some close relationship with the employees in dispute.

(b) The 1982 Employment Act narrowed the definition of an industrial dispute to one which was wholly or mainly about terms or conditions of employment. All others became liable for damages. Injunctions could be granted to stop unions engaging in unlawful strikes. Failure to obey meant the imposition of very large fines and confiscation of their funds. Strikers could be dismissed by management action, which would not be regarded as unfair.

(c) 1984 Trade Union Act. This imposed secret ballots to be held before industrial action could take place. New Social Security laws limited the amount of money that could be paid to the families of striking workers.

(d) The government statistics relating to stoppages of work subsequently relate only to disputes connected with terms and conditions of employment. Stoppages involving fewer than ten workers or lasting less than one day are excluded (except where the total of working days lost exceeds 100). People laid off and working days lost through shortages of supplies are excluded.

(e) Hyman concludes that the effectiveness of the legislation, and the loss of union membership as unemployment increased, undermined the workers' collective strength and confidence.

■ **Account for the variations in rates of stoppages between between different industries in recent years.**

(a) Examine Tables 23.4 and 23.5
(b) Consider possible explanations, above.
(c) Note Table 23.6.

Tables 23.4 Industries with high rates of conflict 1987–8: stoppages of work by industry and working days lost per 1000 workers

Industry	1987	1988
Mining (coal)	1413	1691
Sea transport	109	9500
Other transport,equipment	255	3188
Motor vehicles	652	2165
Textiles	75	318
Clothing	104	50
Railways	17	88
Other transport and communication	3204	2350

Source: *Employment Gazette*, 1989.

Table 23.5 Industries with low rates of conflict, 1987–8: stoppages of work by industry and working days lost per 1000 workers

Industry	1987	1988
Agriculture, forestry, fishing	0	0
Public administration	0	0
Processing of coke, mineral oil, natural gas	0	1
Hotels and catering	1	1
Medical and health services	5	27
Paper, printing and publishing	36	7
Timber and wooden furniture	7	8

Source: Employment Gazette, 1989.

Table 23.6 Major causes of disputes, percentages of working days lost.

Causes	1911–47	1966–74	1988
Wages, hours	61	57	51
Working arrangements	30	29	10
Trade union principles	9	14	7

Source: K. Knowles, Strikes – A Study in Industrial Conflict.

Studies

Various studies have been conducted to examine some ofthe explanations presented.

1. Kerr and Siegal (*The Interindustry Propensity to Strike*) conducted a comparative study. They argued that their results showed that:

(a) The most strike-prone industries had workers living in close-knit communities where there was a solidarity in values (mining).

(b) Workers were cut off from frequent contact with other occupational groups.

(c) The industries affected are more likely to fall into decline in importance as the economy changes.

The most strike-free were found to be:

(a) Those where workers were well-integrated into wider society.

(b) They were members of occupational groups where striking was not the norm.

Points of criticism

(i) They have been criticised on methodological grounds. They relied on statistics classified by others (as to the cause of a strike).

(ii) Their study was conducted in the early 1950s. With the development of the mass media there are now fewer occupational groups who are isolated from the views of others.

(iii) Hill (*The Dockers*) found little evidence of tight community integration among the dockers he studied, although strike rates were high.

2. Lane and Roberts (*Strike at Pilkingtons*) used a social action approach and examined the strike from the points of view of the major groups participating. They found:

(a) It started over a dispute about wage calculations.

(b) It spread rapidly and unexpectedly to other departments.

(c) It took the union (which originally opposed the strike) by surprise.

(d) It was settled by negotiation after seven weeks.

They concluded that:

(a) The origins were related to changing attitudes towards work and the way that monetary values were increasingly pervading many aspects of life in the early 1970s.

(b) Different groups of workers had different views as to what the strike was about, so that a small wage miscalculation escalated into a serious stoppage affecting a wide range of workers.

(c) The same action may be interpreted differently and therefore have different consequences for people.

Table 23.7 Patterns of strikes, 1900–79

Period	Average number of strikes
1900–11	529
1912–16	894
1917–21	1123
1922–6	568
1927–31	367
1937–41	1020
1942–6	1960
1947–51	1590
1952–6	2100
1957–61	2630
1962–6	2260
1967–71	2748
1972–5	2639
1976–9	2310

Source: Quoted in Jackson (*Industrial Relations*).

Table 23.8 Pattern of unemployment, 1951–79, percentage unemployed of total number of employees

1951	1.2
1961	1.5
1966	1.5
1968	2.4
1970	2.6
1971	3.6
1976	4.2
1978	5.7
1979	5.3

Source: *Social Trends*, 3, 22.

Points of criticism:

(i) It may be that interpretations vary because different groups of workers stand in different positions to the means of production. Those with lower status may feel more aggrieved.
(ii) Their explanations relied largely on the subjective interpretations of the strikes and management.

Conclusions

Marxists would emphasise the variations in strike rates in terms of the process of alienation and class exploitation suffered by working-class people in the course of their lives inside and outside the factory.

Weberians would examine the technology of production and show how this can produce satisfied and dissatisfied workers.

Phenomenologists show how the perceptions of workers are important in defining events. For some, their interpretations will lead to conflict whereas others produce more positive meanings so that stoppages are minimal.

- **What light does research throw on industrial relations?**
- **Explain and discuss the changing patterns of strike activity and the ways that industrial relations in Britain have altered in recent years.**

1. Fulcher (*A New Stage in the Development of Capitalism*) indicates that changes which have occurred can be examined within what he describes as stages in the development of capitalist society.

(a) *Anarchic capitalism.* In this period capitalism made its breakthrough. Labour was mobile, unorganised and lacked power.
(b) *Managed capitalism.* There was growing state regulation. Deficiencies were found in unregulated capitalism. Large and effective unions emerged to protect their members' interests. After 1964 there were more agreements between governments (especially Labour) and TUC and CBI; incomes policies and negotiated industrial relations reforms were attempted. The patterns of strikes and unemployment levels in this period were as follows:

2. Durcan *et al.* (*Strikes in Post-War Britain*) describe four phases of union activity which occur in the period of managed capitalism:

(a) 1945–52 Post-war peace; austerity; decreased economic demand. There is limited union activity.
(b) 1953–9 A period of increasing prosperity; workers' demands and expectations are raised. The strike is more widely utilised.
(c) 1960–8 Changing social attitudes emphasise concepts such as equality and opportunity; in the work place there is an increasing number of small-scale unofficial strikes as people on the shop-floor utilise their power.
(d) 1969–73 The Conservatives regain power; they seek to control the unions, who respond to the challenge. Large-scale disputes became more common and more disruptive.

However, they argue that Britain is not strike-prone, rather there are particular *industries* which are. They suggest that although stoppages cause dislocation they are an unfortunate necessity in a democratic society.

3. Department of Employment Report based on research into the distribution and concentration of industrial stoppages in manufacturing industry in Britain for the years 1971–3 showed the following:

(a) The popular impression of the British worker constantly on strike is a myth. On average 97.8 per cent of manufacturing establishments were generally free of stoppages and 81.1 per cent of employees were in strike-free industries.
(b) Over the three-year period 95 per cent of factories were free of strikes.
(c) Of the 5 per cent of factories where strikes occurred, two-thirds had only one strike.
(d) Of 60 000 factories surveyed, strikes occurred in 150. They concluded that in manufacturing, Britain does not suffer from a problem of widespread industrial stoppages but from a concentration in a relatively few number of factories.

4. Fulcher describes the third stage in the development of capitalism after the Conservative election victory of 1979 as 'deregulated capitalism'.

(a) It arises following the failure of managed capitalism to stem industrial crisis.
(b) The TUC could not control the unions and the unions could not control their members; the CBI had no real authority over employers. Governments had failed to reform industrial relations.
(c) A new ideology was introduced to stimulate British capitalism and revive the economy. It was an anti-socialist neo-liberalism which went back to the period of anarchic capitalism.
(d) This emphasised the rights of the individual against the state and collective organisations. There is strong anti-union legislation (see page 315).
(e) It advocated the economics of monetarism (the strict supply of money in the economy); privatisation; internal markets in the NHS; attacks on the welfare state and provision of benefits which might limit individual initiative. (Hence loans for students and those to the poor to be repaid, restrictions on benefits, more responsibilities placed on families to take over functions from the state.)
(f) The economy became more dependent on its ability to attract mobile capital. Traditional heavy industries (coal, docks, etc.) declined. New service industries using new technologies thrived. The pattern of strikes and unemployment in this period is shown in Table 23.9.

Table 23.9 Patterns of strikes, 1980–92 percentage

Year	Number of strikes	Number of unemployed (%)
1980	1350	6.8
1981	1344	10.4
1982	1538	12.1
1983	1364	12.9
1984	1221	13.1
1985	903	13.5
1986	1074	11.7
1987	1016	10.7
1988	804	7.8
1989	701	6.2
1990	630	5.8
1991	580	11.8
1992	450	12.1

Source: *Social Trends, 22; Employment Gazette.*

Points to note

(a) The aim of the new industrial policies was to curb union power. This did not affect rates of unemployment. These fluctuated between points much higher than in earlier periods when union power was much greater and stoppages apparently more frequent.
(b) Critics suggest that there appears to be little support for the argument that union activity causes unemployment, by forcing companies to cut staff through excessive pay demands, since even when there are few stoppages unemployment rates are often high, (for example, 1985) and vice versa (for example 1957–61).

The effects of deregulated capitalism

The result has been a changing pattern in industrial relations:

(a) There is a loss of union membership as unemployment increases.
(b) There are fewer unofficial strikes as legislation takes effect.
(c) There is an influx of new industrial organisations (for example, Japanese car firms) which establish no-strike deals. Unions are forced to accept more single-union deals in large companies.
(d) There is a challenge to the traditional position, powers and functions of the unions as the economy requires a more flexible work force, including large numbers of part-time women workers.
(e) As they find it increasingly hard to recruit new membership, unions resort to merger.

Conclusions

(a) Fulcher's view is that as managed capitalism gave way to deregulated capitalism (a period described by Hyman as 'coercive pacification') a change could be observed in the pattern of industrial relations and in levels of strike activity.
(b) There was a direct assault on unions, which were also undermined by increasing unemployment, the processes of de-industrialisation and a decline in class support and sympathy for union activities.
(c) Daniel and Millward (*Industrial Relations in Britain*) suggested that this might result in fewer strikes in the future, although discontent and conflict could take other forms. They say that the incidence of strikes may no longer be an adequate measure of overt industrial conflict.

■ **Workers and employers engage in disputes for a variety of reasons, many of which are specific to their own work situation. Use case studies to illustrate this proposition. To what extent are sociological perspectives useful in analysing specific disputes?**

1. There are many explanations for industrial stoppages and strikes which may stem from the activities or perceptions of workers or employers. These include:

(a) The effects of technology (see pages 298–9).
(b) The effects of external pressures which may shape attitudes (local community norms sustaining solidarity in conflict) (see pages 314, 318).
(c) Poor negotiating procedures, skills and practices.
(d) The strength and power of the union to control membership. Where this is weak, unofficial stoppages may occur. Where it is strong, excessive demands may be made.
(e) The size and structure of the organisation. Those employing a large number of manual workers may experience more conflict.
(f) Ineffective management; unduly authoritarian methods of control.
(g) The perceptions of employees of actions by employers or vice versa; even mistaken assumptions can lead to conflict.
(h) Worker expectations may rise in times of steady prosperity and remain stable in times of austerity or economic depression.

2. Case studies. This is a method which has been used widely in social science. It provides the researcher with a detailed analysis of the complexities of a situation. The inter-relationships which develop can be examined and it does not rely just on statistical data, which may sometimes be flawed.

Gouldner (*Wildcat Strike*), using a social action approach, described the causes of a strike in a gypsum mine in a small town in the USA in the 1950s. He examined:

(a) the working procedures;
(b) the relationships between work and the attitudes of the local community; and
(c) the changes that occurred in the structure of the organisation.

The working procedures

(i) management did not supervise workers very closely; and
(ii) traditionally, workers who contravened rules were given a warning and a second chance.

Local community values

(i) most of the workers lived in the community; and
(ii) there were many shared activities between workers and supervisors.

The structure of the organisation

(i) this had been stable for many years but began to change quickly when new managers were appointed;
(ii) new technologies were introduced; and
(iii) this led to a demand for speedier work, and tighter controls were placed on the workers.

Outcomes

(a) A strike started within two years of the new changes.
(b) Workers began to show increasing resentment of the new practices and the ending of the old ones.
(c) There was a breakdown in the flow of consent. The workers no longer accepted the legitimacy of the management's procedures.
(d) The cohesion of the local community was undermined and fractured.
(e) The strike was eventually settled by establishing new, more bureaucratic procedures, which Gouldner suggested might be the cause of future problems.

He drew attention to the different perceptions of the events held by different people involved.

B. The miners' strike 1984–5
The strike started in March 1984 because the Coal Board wanted to close uneconomic pits. There ensued a debate as to the meaning of 'uneconomic' which was never resolved. The National Union of Mineworkers (NUM) decided to call out its members until the Board changed its policy. It did not do so and the NUM was ultimately forced to concede defeat in March 1985 as the union began to split and men drifted back to work.

The NUM's argument

In 1972 there were 289 collieries employing 281 000 men.

In 1984 there were 174 collieries employing 180 000 men.

They wanted to protect the jobs of those remaining in the industry.

The Glyn Report 1984 stated:

(a) Some pits described by the Board as uneconomic were in fact profitable.
(b) The social cost of closing the pits was not taken into account.
(c) It would have been cheaper to subsidise the 'uneconomic' pits rather than pay out unemployment benefits.

The Lloyd Report (*Understanding the Miners' Strike*; 1985) suggested that the strike failed because:

(a) It was started in the spring, when demand for coal falls.
(b) Public sympathy was lost through alleged acts of violence by miners on picket lines and the death of a taxi driver taking a working miner to the pit.
(c) There was strong media opposition to the miners' leaders, who were portrayed as leaders of a revolutionary vanguard.

C. The study by Lane and Roberts (*Strike at Pilkingtons*) represents another example of a case study (see page 315).

Summary

1. A strike can be viewed as a normal feature of industrial life.
2. Although unions are frequently blamed for having too much power, it must be remembered that only 5 per cent of strikes are officially backed and organised. More often the union fails to control its membership.
3. It is difficult to identify the actual causes of a strike. The real causes may be connected to social and economic changes in society, affecting the workers' expectations and perceptions of events.
4. Not all strikes successfully achieve their aims.
5. In contemporary Britain it does appear that strikes are more frequent in occupations that have certain characteristics (see Tables 23.4 and 23.5). They tend to be those that are dangerous, tedious, noisy and repetitive, and lack most of the features associated with intrinsic satisfaction.
6. Strikers often suffer hardship as a result of their action: they may not get strike pay and may not receive any social security benefits unless there is extreme hardship.
7. Researchers tend to agree that in terms of working days lost as a proportion of total working days, strikes are insignificant. They may, however, help to develop a 'bad reputation' for British manufacturers.
8. Turner (*Is Britain Really Strike Prone*?) has pointed out that whatever inconvenience is caused by a strike the extent of economic damage is frequently exaggerated by the media reports. Losses are presented in terms of the selling price of the product. The savings are not taken into account (for example, wages, fuel, power and material costs).
9. Research findings suggest that if there is a strike problem in Britain it is sectoral (located in certain industries) rather than national.

■ **How can industrial conflict be explained sociologically? Compare two theories of such conflict.**

The Marxist perspective

1. Strikes are symptoms of the conflict which arises when the owners of the means of production exploit the workers.
2. These conflicts are based on class interests.
3. In a capitalist economic system such conflict is inevitable since the interests of employers and employees are irreconcilable.
4. Employers are concerned to maximise their profits. The employees will strike when they become aware of the level of exploitation. No amount of social engineering in which tedious jobs are made to appear more interesting will prevent the conflict that is endemic to industrial organisations.
5. In times of economic depression management may manufacture strikes to save costs and reorganise.
6. For the Marxist, strikes are completely understandable in terms of class exploitation.

The Weberian perspective

1. This perspective stresses the subjective perceptions of the actors in social situations. The focus is on how these perceptions affect their pursuit of particular goals.
2. Workers have a particular perception of their work environment which will be based on a variety of influences. These include the external and internal factors (see page 300). The decision to strike will be based on how they translate their experiences into meaning.
3. Lane and Roberts (*Strike at Pilkingtons*) note that 'workers can be drawn into a strike without being conscious of a wide range of grievances . . . it can gather momentum under normal working conditions'.
4. From this perspective 'a strike is a social phenomenon of enormous complexity...which is never susceptible to complete description or explanation' (*Gouldner*).

The Functionalist perspective

1. This starts from the view that in an industrial society roles are specialised but function to maintain the stability of society.
2. Specialisation requires cooperation through agreed rules and codes of conduct. The relationships between trade unions, their members and employers have been properly institutionalised to establish a framework for negotiation. This prevents either side operating constantly in their own interests.
3. This would entail careful industrial reform rather than any radical change in the structure of society as a whole.
4. Strikes are themselves functional in that they are indications of levels of dissatisfaction among workers which need to be dealt with by management. Also, an occasional strike may act as a useful safety valve for letting off steam when discontent reaches high levels.
5. Strikes and other forms of conflict are normal and provide opportunities for restructuring industrial

Conclusions

Sociological perspectives have been useful in examining strikes and other forms of industrial conflict, especially where the case study has been adopted.

(a) This has enabled various researches to look at the detailed complexities of the events leading up to and during the dispute.
(b) The method frequently shows how events develop and spiral because interpretations placed on them by different groups within the organisation lead to different and sometimes conflicting actions and outcomes.

Trade Unions

■ **Why do workers join trade Unions? (UODLE)**

A trade union is an organisation of employees who combine together to improve their return from and conditions at work.

Chief aims

(a) To improve the working conditions of their members.
(b) To improve wage rates.
(c) To present the case of their members to management in matters of policy.
(d) To provide members with legal advice.
(e) To make educational and welfare provisions for members.
(f) To provide funds for the Labour Party from the political levy.

Types of industrial action

(a) Official strikes.
(b) Unofficial strikes.
(c) Token strikes.
(d) Overtime ban.
(e) Go-slow or work-to-rule.
(f) Sympathetic action.
(g) Blacking of goods from companies who have helped to break a strike.

Possible reasons for joining a union

(a) In some occupations people were obliged to join. This was known as a *closed shop*. (The Employment Act 1982 introduced secret ballots into closed shops; by 1992 the Labour Party had abandoned its traditional defence of this system.)
(b) Where there is choice they may join because it is the social norm among the work force to do so.

(c) Some may believe it is 'moral' to join, since any benefits obtained by the union are for all workers regardless of whether or not they are members.
(d) Some may join for the protection offered.
(e) Some may join because they are Labour Party supporters.

Types of union

The type of union that people join has traditionally depended on their type of occupation:

Craft unions Members are generally skilled, having acquired a trade or craft through a period of apprenticeship; for example ASLEF.

Industrial unions Usually found within one particular industry; for example NUR.

General union Members are often semi-skilled or unskilled. The largest is the TGWU.

Occupational, often white-collar, unions Usually attract members of a single occupation or profession. However, these are increasingly becoming general categories. There are fewer unions which fit the categories precisely. This is particularly true as unions amalgamate. For example, TASS was originally an entirely white-collar union. But in recent years it has begun to merge with non white-collar unions. The result has been to increase its membership to over 300 000 but this has diluted its original purpose to act for a particular category of white-collar workers.

■ **Describe and account for the major changes in the size, number and distribution of trade-union membership since 1945.**

(a) ExamineTables 23.10; 23.11; 23.12.
(b) Membership fell by more than a quarter from its 1979 peak of 13.3 million to 10.2 million in 1989. This has been the result of unemployment and anti-union legislation as well as a decline in popular support. The fall has continued and was 7.7 million in 1992.

The distribution of membership

(a) The largest falls in membership have been in unions operating in industrial sectors. Statistics indicate that from 1979 to 1981:
    Textiles lost 47.3%
    Clothing lost 27.9%
    Construction lost 20.6%
(b) Some unions have increased in membership. In the years 1979–81 the greatest increases were in:
    Professional and scientific 25.7%
    Services 3.1%
    Banking and insurance 0.3%
(c) There is a large concentration of members in a small number of unions. In 1973, eleven had a membership of more than 250 000. This accounted for more than 60 per cent of total membership. In 1989 80 per cent of all members were concentrated in 7 per cent of unions. A high proportion of unions have a small membership: in 1989 40 per cent of all unions had less than 500 members.
(d) The TGWU remained the largest union, although it lost 1 million members in less than 10 years. In 1989 it had 1.3 million members and the rate of decline had slowed. In 1991 it had 1.1 million members.
(e) In 1990 a document entitled *The Challenge of a New Union* presented plans for the creation of a public services' 'super union'. It recommended the amalgamation of NALGO, NUPE and COHSE over a three-year period, to create the largest union. The new union to be known as UNISON will take effect in 1993 with approximately 1.4 million members. This will become the largest union
(f) In 1992 the AEU, with a membership of just under 1 million, merged with the non-TUC Electricians' Union. It became the AEEU.
(g) Another large union was the GMB general union with a membership of 900 000 in 1992.

Conclusions

(a) Trade union membership reached its highest point in the late 1970s.
(b) The unions consolidated their position in the period of managed capitalism and extended their base among white-collar workers. The distribution of membership remained uneven, with the majority being members of a small number of large unions.
(c) They came under attack in the period of deregulated capitalism of the 1980s and 1990s. Legislation and high unemployment undermined their strength and standing in the eyes of potential members.
(d) Some authorities have used a structuralist approach in the analysis of changing union membership: trade unionism is seen as an inevitable response to the needs of workers, especially as they become more aware of the imbalance of power in society. The subsequent decline is explained by examining the way the powerful can impose new ideological values and structures to undermine them.
(e) Others have used an action theory approach to show how attitudes are shaped by perceptions and meanings. While people see more benefits than losses to be gained from membership, they will join. When the reverse is true, they will not.

■ **What problems does trade-union involvement in politics create in contemporary Britain?**

Some points to consider

1. It would be useful to consider the concept of 'a problem'. Who defines an issue as 'a problem'?

(a) opposition groups; or
(b) the mass media?

2. Can it be argued that involvement in politics creates problems for union members? If so, in what sense?

(a) It may divide the membership; for example, the NUM is divided following the strike of 1984–5. A new mineworkers' union has emerged: the Union of Democratic Mineworkers.
(b) It may divide the union leadership, some of whom wish to pursue policies which accept Conservative legislation. For example, there was much hostile debate among unions as to the acceptability of single-union deals, in which an employer could select the

Table 23.10 The membership of trade unions, 1940–92

Year	Men (millions)	Women (millions)	Total (millions)
1940	5.6	1.0	6.6
1951	7.7	1.8	9.5
1961	7.9	2.0	9.9
1971	8.4	2.8	11.1
1976	8.8	3.6	12.4
1978	9.2	3.9	13.1
1979	9.4	3.9	13.3
1981	8.4	3.8	12.2
1987	5.9	3.3	9.2
1988	5.9	2.9	8.8
1989	5.8	2.8	8.6
1990	5.6	2.8	8.4
1991	5.4	2.8	8.2
1992	5.4	2.3	7.7

Source: Social Trends, 22: TUC.

Table 23.11 Proportion of employees who are union members 1970–89 (percentage)

Year	Men	Women
1970	56.4	31.5
1979	63.4	39.5
1989	44.0	33.0

Source: Social Trends, 22.

Table 23.12 The number of trade unions affiliated to TUC

1907	1950	1955	1960	1965	1970	1977	1983	1987	1993
236	186	183	184	172	150	115	102	87	73

Source: TUC.

union they wished to represent their work force. While the TGWU had no objections, in 1992 the GMB became the first union to refuse to compete. Members were suspicious of the arrangement because they had no choice themselves. They claim the contests are popular with inward-investing companies, such as the Japanese.

3. What is the nature of the political involvement of unions?

(i) There is a traditional association with the Labour Party:

(a) It was formed in the 1900s as the Labour Representation Committee, being renamed the Labour Party in 1906. Its origins lie in the demands of the trade unions to have some party representation in Parliament. The unions provide over three-quarters of its funds from the political levy paid by members, unless they contract out.
(b) In 1974–6 the Labour Government introduced the Social Contract, in which the TUC agreed to assist in trying to limit pay claims in return for more say in Government economic policy. But in 1977–9 the contract broke down as inflation increased and many unions went on strike for higher wages. As a result of the connection, unions are perceived to be a powerful pressure group helping determine Labour Party policies.
(c) A small proportion of Labour MPs are sponsored by unions which means they defend them in Parliament.
(d) Bell (*Labour into the Eighties*) suggests that the relationship has its weaknesses for the Labour Party too. It may be discomforting to rely so heavily on a particular sectional interest, especially when the unions are not the most popular of vested interests in Britain today.
(e) The loss of four consecutive elections has forced the Labour Party to distance itself from the unions: accepting the Conservative legislation, abandoning the closed shop, changing their powers in the framing of policy, and loosening its cash links with them, so that in 1992, 50 per cent of Labour Party finances were from non-union sources.

(ii) The Conservative Party: the involvement of the unions in politics is seen as a potential danger. As a result legislation has been introduced to curb union activities. The miners' strike of 1973 helped to defeat the Government of Mr Ted Heath in the 1974 election.

(a) The Employment Act 1980 limited the number of people allowed to take part in a picket at any one place of work.
(b) The 1982 Employment Act defined a trade dispute to one that was mainly or wholly about terms and conditions of employment. Any dispute which was not covered by immunities was liable to claims for damages. Unions were subject to very large fines and confiscation of their funds. Workers could be dismissed for taking unofficial strike action.
(c) Trade Union Act 1984 stated that unions must obtain a majority of those participating in a ballot in favour of strike action to secure immunity for damages resulting from losses. Union members may request a postal ballot, the costs of which will be refunded by the government. It also allows members to vote by ballot every ten years on whether they wish the union to spend money supporting political parties or causes.

Conclusions

The main problems relating to the involvement of trade unions in political issues include:

(a) Conflicts with the elected Government of the day. However, Jackson notes that prior to the 1960s Britain was unique. Few countries in the world had systems in which there was so little state intervention in industrial relations.

(b) Attempts to deal with the unions according to ideological principles may lead to greater conflicts or be ineffectual. Hyman has argued that the role of the state in industrial relations can be linked to the prevailing economic and social philosophy:
   (i) After the 1960s the state began to intervene more decisively. Incomes policies were formulated to try to control wages and salaries, collective bargaining, conciliation and arbitration. Strikes eventually reached record heights.
   (ii) The failure of these policies in the late 1970s led the Conservative Governments which followed to act more directly against the unions themselves. Early attempts to defy the new laws resulted in heavy fines.

(c) Attempts to deal with the unions are not always successful and not all observers agree that such policies are necessary or effective.
   (i) Taylor and Walton (*The Fifth Estate. Britain's Unions in The Modern World*) have argued that unions have too little rather than too much power; they have become so enmeshed in the corporate state that their role has been reduced to that of mediators rather than workers' champions.
   (ii) MacInnes (*Thatcherism at Work*) has argued that the statistics suggest that while strikes may be diminishing in some areas of work they are more prevalent in others, where they are getting longer. This indicates that the legislation has not been successful in achieving industrial peace.

■ Are trade unions democratic organisations?

Introduction

1. The *structure of unions* in Britain has been described as being among the most complex in the world, and no other European country has a trade union movement with a structure as simple as that of Germany and the Netherlands.

(a) The national executive provides the leadership.
(b) The area committee controls the local organisation.
(c) Local branches allow members to meet to discuss problems.

2. For an organisation to be democratic, either members must be able to vote directly on every issue that affects them (*direct democracy*) or they must be able to elect representatives to conduct affairs in their interests (*indirect democracy*).

The view that Unions are democratic:

(a) All unions have a set of rules and regulations to determine the way their affairs are run. All important decisions are discussed at the annual conferences and policies are formulated.
(b) Most unions have representative democracy. Members elect, approve and appoint leaders. Some, however, are appointed for life.
(c) It is likely that union leaders would argue that their organisations are democratic in that they favour the growth of democracy in the work place. One of their aims is to encourage the extension of control and power of the worker in the working environment.
(d) Shop stewards are elected by the workers on the shop floor to act as a link with the full-time officials in the branch office, to act on the workers' behalf as their representatives.
(e) Strikes cannot now take place without a ballot that gives all workers the opportunity to make their views clear.

The view that unions are not democratic:

(a) It may be that many members of unions fail to attend meetings or to cast their votes.
(b) Some leaders once in power may seek to limit opportunities to remove them.
(c) Michels has said that oligarchy is inevitable in any large organisation:
   (i) All such groups develop bureaucratic structures. The price is the concentration of power at the top of the hierarchy and the limiting of power among those in the rank and file.
   (ii) He also said that leaders were then likely to pursue ends which were personal and different from those of the wider membership because the leaders' own status and power depend on maintaining their position.

Conclusions

(a) The views of Michels have been examined by several authorities and given some support by Lipset *et al.* (*Union Democracy*), Goldstein (*The Government of British Unions*) and Lockwood and Goldthorpe (*The Affluent Worker*). But they were writing in the 1950s and 1960s before trade union reforms developed in Britain.
(b) Some have disputed the view and said that the lack of democracy may have been exaggerated. Turner (*Trade Union Growth, Structure and Policy*) suggested that levels of democracy varied between different styles of trade union. Some display features that are highly democratic. They tend to have high membership participation, few full-time officials and little distiction between members and leaders in terms of status.

■ Account for the growth of white-collar unionism since 1945.

Definition Jenkins and Sherman (*White-Collar Unionism*) say they have a 'detestation for the semantic game of defining white-collar workers . . . the term is overtly male chauvinistic . . . women rarely wear white collars'.

Lumly (*White-Collar Unionism in Britain*) suggests that the term refers to such occupations as administrators, managers, professional workers, scientists, technologists, draughtsmen, creative occupations, clerical and office workers, shop assistants, salesmen and commercial travellers. These categories include those normally described in Classes 1, 2 and 3a.

Important points

(a) There has been a steady increase in the number of white-collar workers in the work force (see Table 23.13).

Table 23.13 Number of white-collar workers (millions)

Year	Numbers
1910	3.3
1971	10.0
1985	12.8
1991	13.5

Source: *Social Trends*, 22.

Table 23.14 Employees by sex and type of occupation (1990)

	Non–manual	Clerical	Craft
Men	48.1	6	25
Women	59.3	31	4

Source: *Social Trends*, 22.

Table 23.15 Five of the largest white collar unions (1993)

National Union of Teachers (NUT)	164,000
Banking, Insurance and Finance Union (BIFU)	162,000
Civil and Public Service Association (CPSA)	124,000
National Association of Schoolmasters and Union of Women Teachers (NAS/UWT)	121,000
National Union of Civil and Public Services	112,000

Source: TUC.
NB. Many of the larger general unions have a substantial white collar membership.

(b) Women provide the majority of clerical and teaching staff. The 1990 Labour Force Survey shows that just under half of men and two-thirds of women in employment were in non-manual occupations; 31 per cent of women were in clerical and related occupations compared with only 6 per cent of men.
(c) The Women's Movement and the equality package of 1975 may have helped to encourage more women to take collective action, although women in professional occupations more frequently join staff associations, which are less militant.
(d) This expansion in white-collar work helps explain the growth in membership of white-collar unions (see Table 23.14 and 23.15).

1. The increase in membership in the 1970s was associated with increased chances of social mobility as more workers moved into white-collar occupations from manual groups. They may have been more trade-union-minded.
2. In times of economic decline, white-collar workers become more concerned to protect their economic position; so strikes among teachers and other professionals may become more frequent.
3. Also, at times of economic depression those in the most secure white-collar jobs may become more trade-union-minded to ensure their protection.
4. Unionisation of white-collar jobs has occurred in many occupations which involve the use of machines and technology, which makes offices not unlike factories. It may be that such workers hold working-class attitudes towards trade-union membership, which emphasises the importance of collective action.
5. The decline in the status of white-collar workers may also have helped in the development of union membership among this occupational group.
6. White-collar unions have begun to recruit in the new 'high tech' industries which have developed with the growth of the micro-electronics technology. Some have also encouraged mergers with smaller unions which might otherwise cease to function.

Conclusions

(a) There has been an increase in the number of white-collar workers in the economy as a whole, but especially among public-sector workers. The public sector has become more concentrated and bureaucratised and the union may help workers to regain some control over their work situations as well as improving their pay.
(b) White-collar workers may make use of many of the other functions performed by unions, advice about retirement, grievance complaints etc.
(c) The union may provide the white-collar workers with a means of staying ahead of the manual workers, whose interests unions have traditionally protected. C. Wright Mills described this as 'status panic'.
(d) From a Marxist perspective, the white-collar workers are recognising that their livelihoods are under as much threat as those of manual workers as their status declines within the existing economic system. They are seeking strength in unity.

■ Has the changing status of white-collar workers affected the growth of white-collar unions?

Introductory point

The question could be interpreted as asking whether it is true that the reasons why more white-collar workers are joining trade unions is because their status has declined, putting them in a similar economic position to that of manual workers.

The argument that it has not affected the growth:

1. Social status is based on subjective opinion as to someone's prestige and standing in society.
2. Traditionally, white-collar workers have always had higher social status than manual workers in British society.
3. This has remained the case even though their incomes have fallen behind those of many sectors of manual workers.
4. The result is that white-collar workers tend not to join trade unions in large numbers (even though there are a high proportion of them in the occupational structure) because they do not share the same value system as manual workers. They wish to distinguish themselves from them.
5. If they do join unions it is for reasons other than concern about status.
6. It is more likely that they will join an organisation which accepts the existing social structure and which does not have an ideology of opposition; that is a professional association.

Trade unions: three perspectives

Marxist perspective

1. Trade unions are compelled to act in aggressive ways because the capitalist economic system gives rise to conflict.
2. Allen (*The Sociology of Industrial Relations*) says that trade unions result from a society which has as its main precepts the sale of labour, and divisions between buyers and sellers.
3. Miliband (*The State in a Capitalist Society*) says that compared to employers, trade unions have little power. They are a countervailing elite seeking to balance the power of the owners of the means of production.
4. Hyman (*Strikes*) says that the view expressed in the media that unions attack the 'national interest' is a smoke-screen disguising the true interests of capitalists.
5. Trade unions should be the source of class consciousness.

Functionalist perspective

1. In capitalist society power is dispersed among a variety of groups.
2. Trade unions help to provide those with the least power some chance of expressing discontent, in a democratic society.
3. In this way they help to institutionalise conflict by helping to ensure that it is dealt with through recognised methods.
4. Since conflicts in society are inevitable, these must be controlled by legitimate means. Employers and employees are two sides of a balanced struggle.
5. Trade-union membership helps provide workers with a necessary sense of unity. They become more integrated into the capitalist society.
6. They help create social order in industry embodied in a code of rights.

Weberian perspective

1. This perspective tends to be a more non-committed one. Actors are said to have goals which they seek to achieve by specific means. These goals will include some which trade unions claim to be able to achieve for workers.
2. Therefore a worker's reaction to trade union membership is a reflection of the strength of his belief that such action will help achieve desired goals.
3. There is a continuous conflict of interests in industrial relations but these are not necessarily class interests. They may be conflicts between status groups. Union membership may be perceived as a way of achieving or protecting status.
4. The growth and decline in union membership can be accounted for in terms of changing images, attitudes, motives and perceptions held by people in relation to specific goals.

7. In 1987 a new white-collar organisation was suggested, to be known as Manufacturing Science and Finance which, it was hoped, would attract the upwardly-mobile white-collar workers. Old divisions would be swept away, merging membership in one highly-skilled labour force. This came into being in January 1988 and had a membership of 604.000 (1992).

The argument that it has affected the growth:

1. Behaviour can be understood in terms of class membership. As those in white-collar jobs (especially in Classes 2 and 3a) come to suffer similar economic problems to those in the lower working classes, so they will begin to behave in similar ways.
2. The membership of a trade union provides the opportunity for collective action.
3. The more people come to perceive and accept that conflict in society is inevitable and that unions provide the individual with a range of benefits, so even formerly high-status employees become more inclined to join an appropriate union.
4. More and more white-collar workers are employed in environments that are not unlike those of manual workers.
5. Promotion opportunities for lower-level white-collar workers are diminishing and their jobs are less secure.
6. As these employees' perceptions of their social status alters so do their attitudes towards unionism; the result is that traditionally non-striking groups, such as teachers, become more militant.

Conclusions

(a) From a Marxist perspective, white-collar workers are in an ambiguous class position. They are seldom producing goods and neither are they owners or controllers of the means of production. They stand between labour and capital. They join unions for the same reasons as blue-collar workers: to protect their interests and to win benefits. Their steady loss of status has made the work of many of them scarcely different from that of factory manual workers, operating heavy office machines and doing repetitive, tedious work.

(b) Banks has argued, however, that it is unreasonable to analyse white-collar unionism in terms of Marxist concepts. These were devised to refer to a different kind of society. The system today is no longer capitalist in the sense that ownership of capital is no longer a crucial factor in deciding whether or not an individual becomes an employer of labour or an employee. People have many motives for joining such unions.

■ **Has industrial conflict been institutionalised? (UCLES)**

■ **Discuss the functions of trade unions in Britain. (WJEC)**

(a) See the table above
(b) The institutionalisation of conflict

1. Many writers (especially Marxists) have asked not why conflict occurs, but why it does so infrequently. The answer they give is in terms of:

(a) The process by which the employers' authority is seen as legitimate.
(b) The process whereby conflict becomes institutionalised (that is confined within borders which all parties accept and there is resort to agreed ways of dealing with it).

(c) Its function (so long as it is kept within bounds and there is a clear possibility of resolution) as a safety valve for the discontented.

2. Institutionalisation of conflict requires:

(a) effective trade unions to act as a countervailing élite against the power of the employers; and
(b) collective bargaining, which provides the means of negotiating the acceptable result.

3. The consequences have been to prevent a total breakdown of society at times of industrial discontent:

(a) Workers do not need to take to the streets. Instead, they allow their leaders to resolve their disputes according to the rules of negotiation.
(b) Leaders are always under strong moral pressure to achieve agreement; the media remind them of 'the national interest' and the need to settle for 'a fair day's work for a fair day's pay'.

Conclusions

(a) A critic such as Allen (*Militant Trade Unionism*) writing from a Marxist viewpoint has said that in accepting the institutionalisation of conflict the union leaders have accepted the capitalist norms of peaceful competition. At every point of their involvement the unions are accommodated comfortably in the system of distribution they are struggling against.
(b) Dahrendorf (*Class and Class Conflict*) notes the ways in which the isolation of conflict has limited overt and unrestrained violence, but argues that there are limits to the extent to which industrial discontent can be institutionalised:
  (i) many employers do not accept that they have responsibility for the dispute and see conflict as abnormal;
  (ii) not all unions are led effectively and fragmentation occurs in their representation. Then the ability to manage conflict will be weakened; and
  (iii) where the leaders are persuaded to exercise restraint, the membership may not be. This may lead to the growth of unofficial leaders and unofficial strikes, which are harder to resolve.

Professions and Professional Associations

■ What are the primary characteristics of a profession? In what sense is teaching a profession?

Greenwood's typology of a *profession* (in Nostrow and Form, *Man, Work and Society*) suggests that members have:

1. High social status because the occupation is difficult to enter (for example, medicine; law).
2. Social power and prestige (there are a high proportion of lawyers in Parliament; most top professionals are among the highest paid).
3. High academic qualifications.
4. Specialised knowledge, of which the lay person is ignorant and often legally prevented from obtaining.
5. Special code of ethics which controls behaviour. This includes confidentiality between client and practitioner. Breach of the code can cause the professional to be disciplined or prevented from practising.
6. A special culture. Members share specific norms, values and sometimes a special form of clothing (for example, wigs and gowns).
7. A controlling body or association which supervises their activities and helps ensure their immunity from critical comment by lay people (for example, the Law Society).

One way of judging the extent to which an occupational group has succeeded in becoming professionalised is to see how many of the characteristics it has which are described by Greenwood. Some, such as doctors which claim professional status, lack many of the attributes of the highly professionalised occupation. Doctors were organised into a professional group in 1858 and were given a monopoly on the practice of medicine. This gave them strong control over their market worth. Teachers, on the other hand, failed to achieve the same level of professionalism before state intervention in education in the nineteenth century. The teachers never gained control over their methods of training, standards of entry and so on. They do have some of the qualities of a profession; but lacking a controlling organisation they are more likely to join trade unions than professional associations to improve their market situation.

Note. In answering such a question notice how important it would be to go through points 1–7 and indicate which apply to teaching and which do not.

■ What are the major characteristics of professional associations?

Professional associations are independent bodies which seek to advance the economic and status interests of their members who are drawn from specific salaried occupations in various organisations. Legally, professional associations are different from trade unions in that they are normally incorporated under the Companies Act or they have been granted a Royal Charter.

Some examples:

British Medical Association (BMA)
Royal Institute of British Architecture (RIBA)
British Association of Chemists (BAC)
Institution of Professional Civil Servants (IPCS)
Chartered Institute of Public Finance and Accountancy (CIPFA)

Members of well-established professions are obliged to join their professional association (for example, doctors are subject to the BMA and lawyers to the Law Society). The association or controlling body may have the right to:

(a) Discipline members or prevent them from practising.
(b) Determine the educational standards necessary to enter the profession and set up the educational establishments to train new members.
(c) Prevent the lay person from gaining access to specific knowledge which is the province of the professional.
(d) Promote the image of the profession as being committed to public service.

The Functionalist view

1. *Integration*: Durkheim discussed the possibility of establishing a moral order in society in which concern for others was crucial for maintaining stability. Membership of a profession helps to integrate people into occupational groups. The association controls training and education, establishes proof of competence and a code of ethics.
2. *Service to the community*: professionals serve society as a whole, not sectional interests. They are trained to provide care, advice and assistance to those who require specialist advice on complex issues. This helps promote an orderly and caring society.
3. *Expertise*: professionals serve important functions for society in that they have access to important knowledge which is too complex for most lay people to master.
4. *Professional authority*: it is always necessary to have a hierarchy of power in any society. The professional is the most able and best qualified in the occupational structure. However, it is also necessary to have methods of controlling and disciplining those who fail in their social duties. If errors are made blame can be located.
5. *Professional associations*: their function is to ensure that the professionals are of the right educational standard; that they behave according to the rules of their profession. In this way clients are protected and confidence maintained.
6. *Rewards*: professionals are rewarded according to their functional importance for society as a whole. Those with access to more valuable knowledge are more highly rewarded. Work performed by professionals involves 'central values' (health, justice, etc.). It is functional for work related to these areas to command high standards.

Points of criticism

1. The integration of professionals is into a value system which promotes power and elitism. They are not really concerned about public service, since professionalism is a strategy employed by particular occupational groups to improve their market situation.
2. Professionals serve only the ruling élite, e.g. accountants and lawyers are in the service of the rich and powerful. Mills (*White-Collar*) says they are employed teaching the financiers how to do what they want within the law . . . and how best to cover themselves'.
3. Their expertise is mythical. Lawyers deliberately make the law inaccessible. Illich (*Medical Nemesis*) says that most serious illnesses were in decline before the development of the medical profession. It is the ills of capitalist society that bring bodily illnesses. By treating them as medical problems their real causes are obscured.
4. The concept of professional authority is part of ruling-class ideology to damp down opposition to exploitations by justifying differentials in reward and status between different types of occupation. Professionals are the servants of power in that they serve the interests of power élites. Their authority is musused.
5. The power that the controlling body has to determine entry ensures that the profession can eliminate competition and that the demand for their services remains high. Illich has referred to the monopoly which professions have in specific areas of social life as 'occupational imperialism'. In controlling conduct the association promotes the view that professional conduct is above reproach and that professionals are committed to public service. In fact, the occupation is controlled in the interest of its members.
6. Once groups have the power to define their services as more valuable than others then they can further their own interests. The image of public service is an ideology used by them to justify their high status and rewards. These are also high because they fulfil the needs of the rich, who make up most of their numbers.

(e) To negotiate with the government on behalf of members. (In some cases the professional association may sponsor new trade unions to carry out their protective function).

Professional associations tend to remain isolated from each other and from trade unions (even though they may have overlapping membership). They see themselves as independent and non-political bodies existing to protect their professional standing while giving public assurance that high standards and competence are being maintained.

- **Why do professionals receive higher rewards than other occupational groups?**

- **Consider the view that 'professionals are the servants of power'.**

- **Consider the view that professionals serve society as a whole.**

Note: In answering such questions it is useful to note Greenwood's typology and then use a theoretical perspective.

Rates of pay vary widely between different groups of professionals. From a Functionalist point of view this adds weight to the argument that for some the idea of 'a vocation' is more important than having high pay (although this increases with experience). From a Marxist viewpoint it is further indication of exploitation and false consciousness on the part of those accepting the position.

Table 23.16 Some rates of pay, 1992/3 (£)

Teaching	
Teacher, Scale 1	11 184
Teacher, Scale 10	18 837
Head teacher, Group 1	22 911–27 273
Head teacher, Group 6	39 153–50 181

Questions

Examine photographs 68 and 69.

1. Suggest reasons based on research why those involved in work in heavy industries, such as the welder, are more strike-prone than, for example, trawlermen.

2. (i) Suggest why union membership has fallen generally in recent years.
   (ii) Suggest why it has declined in the fields of work shown in the photographs.

3. (i) Contrast different theories which might explain levels of strike activity in these industries.
   (ii) Discuss some of the problems which researchers might encounter in investigating these issues.

69

Source: Alec Gill

68

Source: Alec Gill

Nursing	
Nurses/midwives:	
Grade A	7 000–8 570
Grade I	20 050–22 700
Medicine/Dentistry	
GP (Average nett)	40 000
Consultant (max. award)	95 445
Registrar (Senior)	21 185
Dentist (average nett)	35 815
Military	
Brigadier	52 808
Colonel	45 315
Private (4)	7 884
Government	
Cabinet minister	63 047
Lord Chancellor	106 550

Source: *Financial Times, Daily Telegraph.*

Rewards for blue-collar workers vary because of many more factors. In 1991/2 the lowest-paid manual workers received £3.41 per hour; but earnings vay according to such things as the amount of overtime worked, entitlement to bonuses, shift allowances, grade increments and other productivity and incentive payments. Subsequent pay increases may be influenced by the profitability of the employer, inflation and productivity.

Table 23.17 The highest-paid directors in industry (£) 1992

Chairman (Beechams)	1 800 000
Chief Secretary (Chairman)	1 700 000
Chairman (Glaxo)	1 000 000
Chairman (Wilkes Engineering) received £533 000 to resign in 1992.	

Note: (Payments made up of salary and bonuses based on company profits and share options.)

Source: *Financial Times, Guardian.*

Conclusion

(a) The traditional approach of examining the traits of professional work has helped in producing a definition of the qualities expected in such workers; and it has identified why they tend to obtain higher social and economic rewards than others. It suggests an objective basis to their claim to be highly competent in specific skills not available to those outside the profession.

(b) The view has been criticised on the grounds that:
   - (i) It presents a rather uncritical analysis; aspects of conflict between professionals and others is not explored.
   - (ii) In contemporary society the number of workers defining themselves as professionals has increased, making it easier to question the validity their high status. Many highly-paid directors may have few of the qualities normally associated with a professional.
   - (iii) Reward levels also vary widely between different occupational groups. More have become unionised in an attempt to improve their positions.
   - (iv) Some professionals are increasingly employed by large corporations, so removing them from the mystique of independent practice.
   - (v) Clients have begun to criticise the work of professionals more readily, especially as malpractice is publicised through media reports. Major professional bodies are criticised (for example, the Law Society for defending their 150-year monopoly over conveyancing; the General Medical Council for not reforming its antiquated complaints procedures).
   - (vi) Such attacks lead to the view that professional associations remain, as Shaw said, 'conspiracies against the laity'. They begin by seeking to protect the public from incompetence, but end up as insular, self-serving bodies promoting their own privileges at the expense of the public interest.

Suggested Reading

Works noted in this chapter

V. Allen (1966) *Militant Trade Unionism*, Merlin.

C. Bell, *Labour into the Eighties*

C. Crouch (1982) *Trade Unions*, Fontana

W. Daniel and N. Millward (1983) *Industrial Relations in Britain*, Heinemann

R. Dahrendorf (1959) *Class and Class Conflict*, RKP.

Durcan et al (1983) *Strikes in Post War Britain*, Allen and Unwin

A. Fox (1973) *A Sociology of Work in Industry*, Collier-Macmillan

J. Fulcher (1991) 'A New Stage in the Development of Capitalism', *Sociology Review*, Vol. 1 No. 2

Goldstein, *The Government of British Unions*

A. Gouldner (1954) *Wildcat Strike*, Harper and Ro.

E. Greenwood (1962) 'Attributes of a Profession' in *Man, Work and Society,* S. Nostrow and W. Form, Basic Books

S. Hill (1976) *The Dockers*, Heineman

R. Hyman (1984) *Strikes*, Fontan

I. Illich (1975) *Medical Nemesis*, Calder and Boyar

C. Jenkins and B. Sherman (1979) *White Collar Unionism*, RKP

C. Kerr and A. Siegal (1954) 'The Inter–industry Propensity to Strike', in A. Kornhouser *et al.* (eds) *Industrial Conflict*, McGraw-Hill

T. Lane and K. Roberts (1971) *Strike at Pilkington*, Fontana

Lipset *et al.* (1956) *Union Democracy*, Free Press

Lockwood and J. Goldthorpe (1968) *The Affluent Worker*, CUP

R. Lumley (1973) *White Collar Unionism in Britain*, OUP

J. MacInnes (1987) *Thatcherism at Work*, Open University

G. Mars, *Cheats at Work*, Counterpoint

R. Michels (1949) *Political Parties*, Free Press

C. Wright–Mills (1951) *White Collar,* Oxford University Press

S. Nostrow and W. Form (1962) *Man, Work and Society*, Basic Books

L. Taylor and P. Walton (1971) *Industrial Sabotage*: in S. Cohen, *Images of Deviance*, Penguin

G. Salaman (1980) *Class and the Corporation*, Fontana

H. Turner (1969) *Is Britain Really Strike Prone*?, CUP

H. Turner (1962) *Trade Union Growth, Structure and Policy*, Allen and Unwin

T. Whittingham and B. Towers (1971) 'Strikes and the Economy', *Natwest Bank Review* (November)

Works for further reading

G. Bain, *et al.* (1973) *The Growth of White Collar Unionism*, Heinemann, London

B. Barber (1963) 'Some Problems in the Sociology of Professions', *Daedalus*

E. Batstone *et al.* (1977) *The Shop Steward in Action*, Blackwell

D. Bell (1974) *The Coming of Post-Industrial Society*, Heinemann, London

Lord Bullock (1977) *Report of the Committee of Inquiry into Industrial Democracy*, HMSO, London

R. Crompton, and G. Jones (1984) *White-Collar Proletariat*, Macmillan, London

J. Eldridge (1971) *Sociology and Industrial Life*, Nelson, London

J. Hughes (1968) *Trade Union Structure and Government*, HMSO, London

S. Lash, and J. Urry (1987) *The End of Organised Capitalism*, Polity Press, London

R. Taylor and P. Walton (1980) *The Fifth Estate: Britain's Unions in the Modern World*, Pan, London

Self-test Questions

Study these extracts from newspapers and answer the questions below.

Item A

Trade unions

Sisters marching

FORGET cloth caps, shop floors, and bosses with cigars. From next July the members of Britain's largest union will be mainly female (two-thirds), brain-workers rather than brawn-workers, often part-time and usually employed in the public sector. Unison, the union in question, is being created out of a merger of NALGO, organising local-government workers, NUPE, which recruits public employees generally, and COHSE, the health workers. Assuming the proposal survives a membership ballot in all three unions at the end of this year, Unison will boast 1.5m members, outstripping the transport workers with 1.2m.

Unison offers delegates to next week's Trades Union Congress in Blackpool a glimpse of a different future. They need it. When Margaret Thatcher came to power in 1979, 53% of British workers belonged to unions. Today, the proportion is 38% and falling. Most of the big unions have lost members, though some, such as the GMB, have compensated by taking over smaller, weaker brethren. Some of the blame has belatedly been landed on the TUC's buffoon general secretary for the past nine years, Norman Willis, who is likely to be replaced by his able deputy, John Monks.

But Unison's emergence highlights the resilience of trade unions in the public services. Seven in ten public-sector workers belong to a union, compared with fewer than one in three private-sector workers. "There is no doubt that the majority of union members are now in the public sector," says Lord McCarthy, of Oxford University.

Oh brother

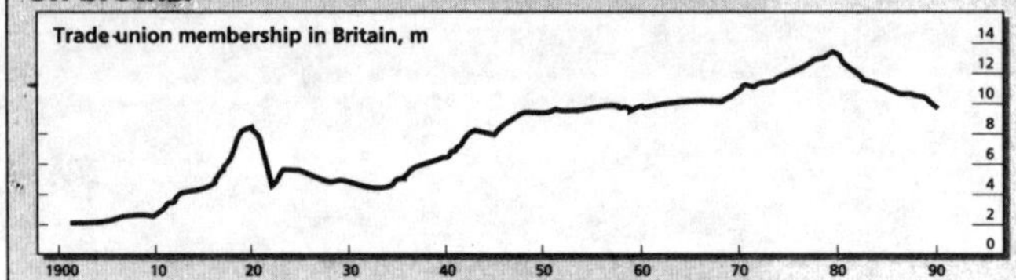

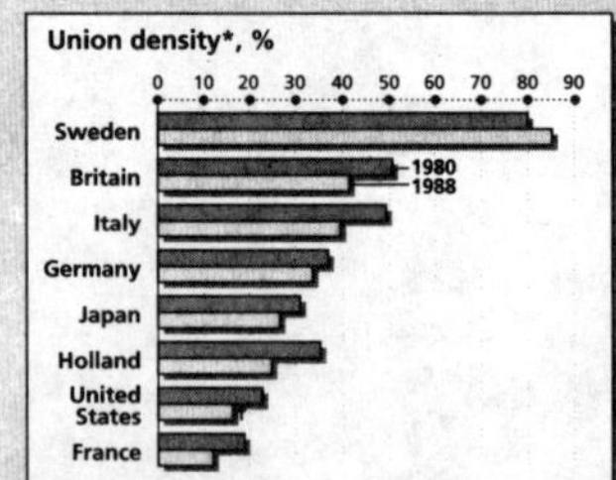

Union membership, '000s

	1981	1991	% change
Transport & Gen (TGWU)	1,781	1,224	-31
Engineering‡ (AEU)	1,102	702	-36
Gen & Municipal (GMB)	866	933	8
Local Gov't (NALGO)	796	744	-6
Public Employees (NUPE)	704	579	-18
Shopworkers (USDAW)	438	362	-17
Mfg, Sci, Fin (MSF)	427	653	53
Electricians‡ (EETPU)	395	357	-10
Construction (UCATT)	275	207	-25
Miners (NUM)	250	53	-79

*Union membership as % of employed workforce †1989 ‡Now sections of the AEEU (Amalgamated Engineering and Electrical Union)
Sources: Department of Employment; OECD; TUC

Source: From an article in *The Economist*, 5 September 1992, p. 36.

Item B

FALLING membership and failing finances yesterday forced the TUC to adopt radical changes to its organisation and workload in the wake of a fourth Tory election victory.

The future role of the 7.75 million-strong body and its general secretary, Norman Willis, has been thrown into question by the development of super-unions and the receding prospect of securing a Labour government before the end of the millennium.

Delegates agreed overwhelmingly to support a motion on employment law calling for a campaign against the forthcoming bill on trade unions and in favour of individual workers' rights, particularly the right to belong to a union.

Delegates also agreed to a general council-backed resolution which requires the TUC to in future concentrate on just six priorities: achieving full employment; promoting an employees' charter of rights; lobbying against the forthcoming trade union bill; working in Europe; helping individual unions with trade union education, health and safety and equal rights; sorting out future relations between unions.

Source: From an article *by Celia Weston and Keith Harder* in the *Guardian*, 8 September 1992, p. 8.

Item C

SPONSORSHIP of Labour MPs by trade unions is at an all-time high with 152 of the 271 parliamentary party members receiving direct financial aid.

The level of financial sponsorship typically stands at a grant of £2,000 to £3,000 towards an MP's general election expenses plus £150 a quarter paid direct to his or her constituency.

The amount is not large compared with trade union political fund payments direct to the Labour Party. But as the debate intensifies within the party over whether the introduction of one-member, one-vote democracy will break the union link it demonstrates that in one important aspect the relationship is growing closer with each election.

One critic of union sponsorship is Graham Allen, MP for Nottingham North, who organised the unions' political fund ballots campaign. He believes they are wasting their money.

"It is a relic of the past when MPs were not paid. It is very easy to misrepresent the situation and equate it with the consultancies and directorships that are received personally by Tory MPs.

"We are taking all the flak unnecessarily."

He sees little point in giving money to a safe Labour seat in South Wales which clocks up majorities of 20,000-plus.

"We could remove the MPs from the equation and sponsor constituencies directly . . . it would make more sense for the trade unions only to sponsor those marginal consitituencies it is necessary to win to establish a Labour government."

Trade union sponsored MPs 1945-1992

Union	*1945*	*1970*	*1979*	*1992*
AEU	3	16	17	13
Apex	—	3	5	—
ASTMS(MSF)	—	3	8	13
Cohse	—	—	3	6
EETPU	1	3	4	3
GMB	8	12	14	18
NCU	—	1	3	3
NUM	35	20	16	14
Nupe	—	6	7	12
NUR(RMT)	12	5	12	12
Sogat(GMPU)	—	—	—	5
Tass(MSF)	—	4	4	—
TGWU	17	19	21	38
TSSA	9	4	3	2
Ucatt	5	2	2	—
UCW	—	1	2	2
Usdaw	6	9	5	9
Others	25	8	8	2
Total	121	108	126	152
PLP	393	288	269	271

Source: Alan Travis, *The Guardian*, 13 August 1992.

Item D

Number of strikes and percentage of workforce registered unemployed 1978–87

	No. of Strikes	Registered Unemployed (%)
1978	2498	5.7
1979	2125	5.3
1980	1348	6.8
1981	1344	10.4
1982	1538	12.1
1983	1364	12.9
1984	1221	13.1
1985	903	13.5
1986	1074	11.7
1987	1016	10.7

Source: Adapted from R. Hyman: *What's Happening to the Unions*?.

I.

1. Examine Item A.
   - (i) Suggest some reasons why the largest union is likely to have more female members than male in the future.
   - (ii) Suggest some reasons why union membership has generally declined since 1979, although some (for example MSF) have attracted more members.
   - (iii) Account for the resilience of trade unions in the public services and for their lack of appeal in the private sector.

2. Examine Item B.
   - (i) Discuss the view that trade unions have wider and more varied functions than just seeking confrontation with employers and higher pay for their members.
   - (ii) Consider also the evidence in Item A and suggest why there has been a move towards the emergence of 'super unions'.
   - (iii) Suggest how such unions might affect the future role, image and policies of the TUC.

3. Examine Item C.
   - (i) Suggest why sponsorship of Labour MPs by trade unions reached an all-time high in 1992, at a time when membership was falling and the Labour Party remained in opposition.
   - (ii) Why might some Labour MPs oppose the continued sponsorship of MPs by unions?

4. Examine Item D.
   - (i) This suggests a link between the level of unemployment and the number of strikes. Discuss the arguments for and against this view.
   - (ii) Discuss some of the problems in interpreting such statistics; consider official and unofficial strikes; the length of stoppages; changing legislation; definitions of unemployment.

5. Using information from all the items, discuss the view that while there has been a decline in the number of strikes and in trade union membership, nevertheless unions retain important functions on behalf of their members as a countervailing power to that of employers.

II.

Read the following extract from a study of medical examinations in a hospital setting, and answer the questions which follow.

> 'Immersed in the medical world where close inspection of the patient's body constitutes a routine, the staff assume the responsibility for a credible performance. Doctors and nurses take part in medical examinations many times a day, while the patient is a fleeting visitor. The major definition to be sustained is "this is a medical situation", which calls for a matter-of-fact stance. The scene is credible precisely because both doctors and nurses act as if they have every right to do what they are doing: any hint of doubt from them would compromise the medical definition. Normally a person has rights over his or her own body, for example, rights to privacy. Therefore medical work requires the suspension of this normal framework of rights. A particular environment is created in which the medical staff are able to suspend the normal rules and to treat the patient like an object.
> The pervasiveness of the medical definition is expressed by indicators that the scene is enacted in a medical setting, for example, a hospital ward or examination room. The staff wear medical uniforms, don medical gloves, use medical instruments. The special language found in staff-patient contacts means that the situation becomes less embarrassing and more impersonal, for example, the staff refer to "the . . ." rather than "your . . ." when referring to a part of the body. Scientific-sounding medical terms facilitate communication, whilst substituting dictionary terms for everyday words adds formality. Yet the common avoidance of explicit terminology in doctor-patient contacts suggests that, despite all the precautions to ensure that the medical definition prevails, many patients remain somewhat embarrassed by the whole procedure. To avoid provoking this embarrassment, euphemisms and understood references are used when possible; for example, the doctor might ask, "When did you first feel pain in that area?"'

(a) Using illustrations from your studies of medical or other welfare professionals, explain what you understand by 'the staff assume the . . . performance' (lines 1–2). What other factors, in addition to dress and vocabulary, might form part of that performance?
(b) Select **one** other 'delicate' situation and briefly indicate how it is 'managed' by professional workers such as doctors or social workers.
(c) Evaluate the usefulness of the sociological perspective employed in the extract for analysing the relationship between professionals and their clients.

Source: JMB (June 1983).

Index of selected authors

Index